MW00564395

Kodály Today

Kodály Today

A Cognitive Approach to Elementary Music Education

Mícheál Houlahan and Philip Tacka

2008

OXFORD
UNIVERSITY PRESS

Oxford University Press, Inc., publishes works that further
Oxford University's objective of excellence
in research, scholarship, and education.

Oxford New York
Auckland Cape Town Dar es Salaam Hong Kong Karachi
Kuala Lumpur Madrid Melbourne Mexico City Nairobi
New Delhi Shanghai Taipei Toronto

With offices in
Argentina Austria Brazil Chile Czech Republic France Greece
Guatemala Hungary Italy Japan Poland Portugal Singapore
South Korea Switzerland Thailand Turkey Ukraine Vietnam

Published by Oxford University Press, Inc.
198 Madison Avenue, New York, New York 10016

www.oup.com

Library of Congress Cataloging-in-Publication Data
Houlahan, Mícheál.
Kodály today : a cognitive approach to elementary
music education / by Mícheál Houlahan and Philip Tacka.
p. cm.
Includes bibliographical references.
ISBN 978-0-19-531409-0
1. School music—Instruction and study. 2. Cognitive learning.
3. Kodály, Zoltán, 1882–1967. I. Tacka, Philip. II. Title.
MT1.H838 2007
372.87—dc22 2006100161

9 8 7 6 5

Printed in the United States of America
on acid-free paper

We are the music-makers,
And we are the dreamers of dreams,
Wandering by lone sea-breakers,
And sitting by desolate streams—
World-losers and world-forsakers,
On whom the pale moon gleams—
Yet we are the movers and shakers
Of the world forever, it seems.

Arthur O'Shaughnessy, "Ode"
(first stanza)

Acknowledgments

We would like to thank Mme. Kodály for her support of this project in allowing us to quote from the *Selected Writings* of Zoltán Kodály. We were both fortunate enough to study at the Franz Liszt Academy/Kodály Pedagogical Institute in Hungary and at the Kodály Center of America with world-renowned Kodály experts, many of whom were Kodály's pupils and colleagues, who shared their knowledge with us over many years. Among them were Erzsébet Hegyi, Ildiko Herboly-Kocsár, Lilla Gabor, Katalin Komlos, Katalin Forrai, Mihály Ittzés, Klára Kokas, Klára Nemes, Eva Vendrai, Helga Szabo, Laszlo Eösze, Peter Erdei, and Katalin Kiss. Special thanks is due Virginia Womack-Pohlmeier for her critical reading of the manuscript and her insightful suggestions regarding this approach to instruction and learning.

Kodály Today has profited from the many contributions of our teachers and students. We are especially grateful to Millersville University of Pennsylvania for their support of this project. The university's library assistance, technical, administrative, and financial support, and overall encouragement for this project have allowed us to bring this volume to completion.

Many individuals have provided us with invaluable advice and assistance in both scholarly and practical matters. We would like to thank Fine Arts Director Dr. John May of the Austin Independent School District and Fine Arts Director Gary Patterson of the Houston Independent School District, both of whom allowed us to work with their music instructors to field-test the ideas presented in this publication.

Special acknowledgment must be made to Patty Moreno, Director of the Kodály Certification Program at Texas State University, San Marcos, Texas, for her support and continued encouragement of this project. We would also like to thank Holly Kofod for her contributions regarding assessment. Thanks to Vivian Ferchill, Cecilia Pena, Kathy Hunt, Nancy Cavendish, Kelly Laws, Jane Pippart-Brown, and Lisa Roebuck for their considered reading and critical comments that helped us bring this book to completion. Special thanks is also due to Magdelena Fitzsimmons on the faculty of the American Kodály Institute for her thorough examination of *Kodály Today.*

Many of our students in Kodály Certification Programs at Texas State University, Belmont University in Nashville, Tennessee, The Eastman School of Music in Rochester, New York, have all helped us shape the approach instruction and learning that is presented herein. Our many years working together have not only contributed to the information we present but also have served as a continuing source of inspiration in working with the pedagogical processes we outline. In practical matters we would like to thank our students at

Millersville University for helping us with initial drafts. A special thanks is due Paul Gallello, Abigail Kozlowski, Rachel Dennison, Emily Murphy, and Nate Sheffer.

We would like to thank Alan Browning, Headmaster of the Blue Coat School, Birmingham, England, for his encouragement and support in allowing his staff and students to become involved in the development of this teaching approach. The high standard achieved by the students of the Blue Coat School is a testament to his commitment to music.

This book would not be as complete in terms of pedagogy and educational content were it not for the critical readings and comments from Blaithín Burns, Kodály instructor at the Blue Coat School and Birmingham Conservatory of Music, Birmingham, England. She provided invaluable assistance in the initial design of *Kodály Today* and field-tested many teaching strategies. Richard Schellhas deserves thanks for his personal patience and understanding as well as words of encouragement and advice throughout the writing of this manuscript.

Research for this publication was supported by a grant from Millersville University, the State System for Higher Education in Pennsylvania. We would like to express our gratitude to Dr. Sandra Mathias, Director of the Kodály Program at Capital University, for giving us permission to include songs from ¡Vamos a cantar! *230 Folk Songs of Spanish-Speaking People to Sing, Read, and Play* and *My Singing Bird,* vol. 2 of *150 American Folk Songs from the Anglo-American, African-American, English, Scottish and Irish Traditions,* published by Kodály Institute at Capital University, 2006. All songs with text in Spanish are reprinted from ¡Vamos a Cantar! with permission.

We wish to thank Suzanne Ryan, senior editor at Oxford University Press, for her encouragement and critical guidance. We thank Norm Hirschy, assistant editor at Oxford University Press, and Bob Milks, senior production editor, for their support in the production of this manuscript.

We hope that you'll find *Kodály Today* informative and useful, and if we can answer questions, please don't hesitate to contact us at michealhoulahan@aol.com and philiptacka@aol.com.

Contents

Kodály Today

Introduction

> I learned, amazed, how much there is for a Bard to know, outside and beyond his music, and I began to realize the power that lies in the harper's hands; power greater than a king's reaching beyond a man's own death-day, into the tomorrow of the world. Like all mysteries, one cannot speak of it, except to a fellow craftsman, for it has to do with hidden things, that must not be profaned. Like all mysteries, its core is the truth in man, and in his relationship to the world he knows, and the universe beyond it. At its deepest level it is concerned with the harmony, the measure, the rhythm out of which all things were created, and by which they must be governed, consciously or unconsciously. It is the life thread that holds us suspended safely above ultimate chaos, and the navel cord that joins life to eternity.[1]

"To teach music effectively, we must know our subject—music. We must embody and exemplify musicianship. This is how children develop musicianship themselves: through actions, transactions, and interactions with musically proficient teachers"[2] This is no small task. "Teachers with insufficient musicianship or educatorship are highly prone to philosophical and practical misunderstandings. Thus many school choral and instrumental programs squander the opportunity to educate students musically because the teachers involved are not concerned with authentic musical performing and artistic music listening, only with simplistic 'sound producing.'"[3]

Like the Bard from *The Pendragon,* music instructors must exemplify excellent musicianship in order to transmit to their students the "strict meticulous discipline" of music that will allow students control of their voices and the instruments they perform on so that "the truth can sing" through them "and touch the spirit of those who listen."[4]

Since its introduction to the United States in the early 1970s, the Kodály philosophy of music education, long associated with the transmission of excellent musicianship, has gained significant importance in undergraduate and graduate music methods courses as well as elementary, middle, and high school choral curriculums. In a Kodály music classroom children first are

> actively involved in a combination of music making, singing, creating rhythmic and vocal accompaniments to songs, and active listening. Second, the Kodály approach offers a rich array of tools and concepts for the development of musical literacy. Third, Kodály specialists have been at the forefront of the movement to include world folk music in the curriculum. Fourth, Kodály teaching techniques provide excellent ways of approaching what Elliott calls "musical problem solving" and "problem reduction" in music education. Fifth, children

> who study music in a Kodály-based program tend to develop lifelong skills and excellent musical ears.[5]

Kodály inspired music instruction has also had a significant impact on student behavior outside the music classroom. The broad effects of this type of teaching and learning have been documented by Dr. Martin F. Gardiner of the Center for the Study of Human Development at Brown University. He writes:

> The specific methods of arts training common to these studies is Kodály music training. The Kodály training is a methodology for building skills in individual and group singing that, along with specific musical skills, gives the children an opportunity to practice and build individual attitudes of attention, learning and sensitivity to the group, and capabilities for working together. It is possible to hypothesize that attitudes and behaviors towards learning in this arts training helped to build the more general improvements in classroom attitudes and behaviors that were documented by the teachers . . . and were in turn closely related to improvements in reading. Teacher reports support this viewpoint, as does recent data showing greater improvements in classroom behavior in those students receiving more extensive Kodály training. (*The Teaching Exchange,* January 1999, "Arts Training in Education")[6]

We have written this book as a basic introduction to the the Kodály vision of music education for experienced music instructors, inservice and pre-service teachers, and college methods professors who are looking for a way to enhance the musicianship of their students. Our future publications will address early childhood music education and teaching instrumental music. For additional information on teaching music fundamentals please consult Houlahan and Tacka, *From Sound to Symbol: Fundamentals of Music Theory* (New York: Oxford University Press, 2008).

The motivating force for writing this book was our work with teachers over the last decade. We conducted focus discussions and surveys to learn and understand the pedagogical needs and concerns of music specialists. These teachers repeatedly voiced their concerns about the lack of specificity concerning issues relating to the teaching of music according to the Kodály philosophy of music education. Of particular concern are issues dealing with:

- how to select repertoire for the music classroom from the aural/oral and written traditions,
- how to analyze repertoire from the aural/oral and written traditions,
- how to actively develop the skill of music listening,
- how to teach traditional notation in tandem with rhythmic and melodic solfège syllables,
- how to understand the different rhythm syllable systems in current use,
- how to teach compound meter,
- how to teach music to older beginners,
- how to design lesson plans that develop critical thinking skills,
- how to develop strategies for developing musical skills and keep track of these skills throughout the year,
- how to develop harmonic hearing in the elementary classroom,

- how to teach improvisation and composition,
- how to develop evaluation and assessment tools for use in the classroom.

This text expands upon the work we first present in our Sound Thinking Music Series and provides viable answers to the concerns and questions raised by music teachers working in the field. All of the ideas and lesson plans in the text have been field-tested over a period of six years with music teachers.

Through our experiences working with teachers in the field and our work in the area of music perception and cognition, we have developed and modified aspects of processes and procedures commonly associated with Kodály's philosophy for music education that are congruent with national and state standards. We may have strayed from what some teachers recognize as the Kodály concept of music education but we believe that the findings and procedures we present in this book are in keeping with the composer's philosophy. Kodály asserts: "It is the fate of science that each successive age produces new results and usually modifies or completely refutes the results obtained by the preceding age."[7] In his lecture *Ancient Traditions—Today's Musical Life,* Kodály said: "But this is part and parcel of the development of science. Science keeps on changing and fluctuating."[8]

Dr. Klára Kokas, a psychologist and graduate of the Franz Liszt Academy of Music in Budapest and a pupil of Kodály, has long been a proponent of adaptation and modification of the Kodály philosophy, Since the early 1970s the "musical compass" through which she researches and develops her own approach to teaching has been grounded by Kodály's philosophy for music education. In the following quote Kokas provides a rationale as to why the Kodály concept requires modification and adaptation.

> In Hungary, Kodály's principles were applied and developed within the traditional framework of centralized education. The central control exercised by the Ministry of Education, its lower representative organs, and the centralized form of assessment of teaching standards left little room for teacher initiative. Our personal visions were strongly circumscribed by the Marxist-Leninist philosophy and the aesthetics introduced by the establishment as a compulsory component at each level of education. Thus the frameworks in kindergartens—and even more so in school education—were strictly limited. In the given political set-up, Kodály's method had little scope for further refinement and development.[9]

We have developed this book with teachers. Over the past decade we have been engaged in a dialogue with music instructors who teach in title one schools, urban schools, private schools, and other public schools; with teachers who see their students three and four times a week and teachers who see their students three times a month; with teachers who have a strong background in teaching pedagogies and with beginning music instructors. Instead of continually forcing our pedagogical procedures on them we worked with them to address their needs and concerns both musical and practical.

The aim of this book is to provide elementary level music instructors with a practical guide for teaching a Kodály-based music curriculum. We hope that *Kodály Today* will enable music instructors to initiate their students into the many dimensions of musicianship that are common in the both the aural/oral and written music traditions. Some of these dimensions include performing, critical thinking, listening, improvising, composing, and becoming stewards of a cultural heritage that includes knowledge of aural/oral (folk music) and written musical traditions (classical music). Teaching procedures and lesson preparation examples are presented in considerable detail but need not be taken literally.

They should, instead, be used as a point of departure for each teacher's own creativity and personality. It is expected that teachers will apply these suggestions in a way that is responsive to the needs, backgrounds, and interests of their own students. The sample lesson plans and sample curriculums we provide are not meant to be comprehensive. We expect that music instructors will infuse these ideas with their own national and regional benchmarks for teaching. *Kodály Today* offers teachers a practical way to help children develop as performers, listeners, critical thinkers, composers and improvisers, and stewards of their cultural heritage. We appreciate that teachers must develop their own philosophy for teaching music, their own repertoire of songs reflecting the musical needs of their communities, the procedures, and the processes for teaching musical skills while considering such factors as the frequency of music instruction, the size of the class, the length of the class, and current music abilities of students.

Outline

Each chapter in *Kodály Today* begins with key questions that provide a context for issues discussed in every chapter. At the end of each chapter there are discussion questions as well as on-going assignments that allow the reader to practice and reflect upon the suggestions offered in the text. All chapters also include a bibliography.

Kodály Today is divided into eleven chapters. Chapter 1, "Constructing a Teaching Resource Portfolio," introduces some of the general considerations for developing a teaching portfolio for each grade. This portfolio includes a philosophy statement that guides teaching practices in the classroom, repertoire list, sequence for teaching music literacy, strategy plans for teaching concepts, lesson plans, activities for developing music skills, listening examples, and samples of evaluation and assessment forms. All components of this portfolio will be further discussed in subsequent chapters of this book.

Chapter 2, "Kodály's Philosophy of Music Education," provides a brief introduction to Kodály's philosophy of music education and allows teachers to understand how a curriculum can be developed using Kodály's educational philosophy. (Appendix 1 includes a sample curriculum for grades one through five.) This chapter includes a discussion of how the adoption of the Kodály's philosophy for music education affects the design of a music curriculum.

Chapter 3, "Children as Stewards of Their Cultural and Musical Heritage: Selecting Music Repertoire for the Classroom," deals with how to select and analyze a song repertoire. This chapter provides a rationale for the selection of music repertoire for teaching as well as addresses how the selection and analysis of musical repertoire affects lesson planning. (Appendix 2 includes an alphabetized list of songs.)

Chapter 4, "Children as Performers: Singing, Movement and Playing Instruments in the Elementary Music Classroom," addresses the various components of teaching performance skills in an elementary music class including singing, ensemble work, movement, and playing musical instruments. Included in this chapter is a discussion of how teaching performance skills, such as singing, movement, and playing instruments, affects the design of a lesson.

Chapter 5, "Children as Critical Thinkers and Problem Solvers: Developing Music Literacy Skills," discusses how to develop a sequence of rhythmic and melodic elements for teaching music literacy. Included in this chapter is a discussion of the different types of rhythmic syllable systems. The emphasis in this chapter is to demonstrate the importance of teaching traditional notation to students and how rhythmic and melodic syllables are successful tools to accomplish this outcome. This chapter addresses how teaching music literacy affects lesson planning. (Appendix 3 includes a list of suggested songs for teaching specific musical concepts.)

Chapter 6, "From Sound to Symbol: A New Learning Theory Model," presents our model of music learning and instruction. This model is based on current research in the field of music perception and cognition as well as standard techniques used by Kodály teachers in the classroom.

Chapter 7, "Developing Musicianship Skills," describes how various musical skills can be developed. (Appendix 4 includes monthly plans for grades one through five. These monthly plans also provide the musical skills to be developed in each grade.)

Chapter 8, "Teaching Strategies for Rhythmic and Melodic Musical Elements," presents teaching strategies for elementary rhythmic and melodic elements based on the model of learning presented in chapter 6.

Chapter 9, "Sequencing and Lesson Planning," continues to define the different types of lesson plan structures. We also show how the teaching strategies described in chapter 8 are transformed into lesson plans. Included in this chapter are sample lesson plans based on the suggested lesson plans.

Chapter 10, "Teaching Musicianship Skills to Older Beginners," describes how to implement a Kodály program for students who have not been exposed to techniques associated with the Kodály approach. Included is a discussion of vocal development and selection of repertoire for older students.

Chapter 11, "Evaluation and Assessment," describes how to assess and evaluate both student learning and the instructor's success to design and implement a lesson plan.

Outstanding Features

- *Kodály Today* is research based. Teaching techniques delineated in this text may already be known to educators familiar with Kodály-inspired teaching. However, we have combined these ideas with current research findings in the field of music perception and cognition to develop a model of music instruction and learning that offers teachers a map to follow for developing their students' musical understandings.
- *Kodály Today* is an instructor-centered and child-centered publication. The procedures and suggestions outlined in this volume have been shaped through numerous discussions with music teachers, observations, and the authors' research and experience teaching at all levels of education. Music instructors will be able to use the ideas and materials in this book as a springboard for developing music lessons that will allow children to grow as performers, critical thinkers, listeners, creative human beings, and stewards of their cultural heritage.
- This text provides a comprehensive approach to music teaching that positions music performance, movement, age-appropriate repertoire, instruments, music literacy skills, music creativity, and music listening as the basis for a music education.

- The building blocks of music are derived from repertoire from both the aural/oral tradition as well as from the classical music tradition.
- *Kodály Today* presents an approach to teaching music skills such as singing, movement, playing instruments, improvisation, composition, ensemble work, inner hearing, form and analysis, memory, listening, and harmonic hearing. We are interested in teaching musical concepts and elements that are common to all musical styles. While numerous works describing Kodály-based techniques and curriculums exist, few spell out in detail teaching procedures for presenting musical concepts and elements as well as ideas for developing musical skills.
- We delineate two processes: (1) the process for developing a curriculum based on the Kodály approach and (2) the process for teaching music according to Kodály's philosophy of music education. While several music books describe teaching techniques and provide sequenced materials for teaching repertoire, few offer detailed teaching procedures for presenting musical concepts according to the Kodály concept. *Kodály Today* presents a clear picture of how the teaching and learning processes go hand-in-hand during the music lesson.
- The book presents a learning theory model. This model builds upon the accepted process of teaching music elements: prepare, make conscious, reinforce, and assess. While we have adopted these phases of learning, each one of these phases is further broken down into stages that allow for the sequential teaching of music elements, development of musical skills, as well as the means for their assessment. This learning theory model builds upon current research in the field of music perception and cognition. It is a model that incorporates the learning practices associated with folk music tradition and classical music.
- Each chapter includes discussion questions and ongoing assignments that allow the reader to absorb the content of each chapter.
- Each chapter includes a general bibliography; many chapters also contain a specific bibliography, relating to the Kodály concept that is germane for that chapter.

Chapter 1

Constructing a Teaching Resource Portfolio

Key Question

What are the key components of a Teaching Resource Portfolio?

As well as outlining the key components of a teaching resource portfolio, this chapter will provide an outline of the entire book.

What Is a Teaching Resource Portfolio?

A resource portfolio contains practical information that an instructor will use for teaching music. The information contained in each section of this portfolio will be updated throughout your professional career. This process will allow you to organize your processes for teaching.

The key components of a teaching resource portfolio for each grade can include:

1. Statement of Teaching Philosophy and Reflective Practice
2. Curriculum Goals
3. Repertoire
4. Performance
5. Critical Thinking, Problem Solving, and Music Literacy Goals
6. Music Improvisation and Composition
7. Listening
8. Assessment

Table 1.1 Components of a teaching portfolio, by chapter

Components of a Teaching Portfolio	Related Chapter
Statement of teaching philosophy and reflective practice	Chapter 2
Curriculum goals	Appendix 1
Repertoire	Chapter 3 and Appendix 2
Performance	Chapter 4

continued

Table 1.1 *Continued*

Components of a Teaching Portfolio	Related Chapter
Critical thinking and music literacy goals	Chapter 5; Chapter 6; Chapter 7; Chapter 9
Music improvisation and composition	Chapter 7
Listening	Chapter 7
Assessment	Chapter 11
Class profiles	Chapter 11
Resources	Chapter 9

9. Class Profiles
10. Resources

Statement of Teaching Philosophy and Reflective Practice

The first component of your teaching resource portfolio is a statement concerning your philosophy of music education that will shape the design of your curriculum. This statement provides a rationale for the inclusion of music in the curriculum and should be linked to the school's mission, vision, and philosophy statement. The philosophy statement provides the instructor with a basis for developing realistic curriculum goals and lesson plans. In chapter 2 we provide a brief summary of Zoltán Kodály's philosophy of music education that may provide a model for developing your personal philosophy of music education.

Curriculum Goals

Curriculum goals provide instructors with a practical guide for creating a sequenced and well-structured musical education for their students. The curriculum should meet local, state, and national standards as well as reflect current research findings from the fields of music pedagogy and music perception and cognition. There are a number of factors that will affect the success of a music curriculum. These include the musicianship and the pedagogical background of the music instructor, the singing and musical abilities of students, the number of music lessons per week, and the length of each class period.

Once you have developed a philosophy statement it is easier to determine your curriculum goals. Appendix 1 includes a sample of curriculum goals appropriate for grades one through five. Curriculum goals are broad in nature and should incorporate the same language as your philosophy statement. For example, curriculum goals for teaching music may include:

1. Repertoire for developing singing, instrumental performance, and movement.
2. Performance goals for developing singing, ensemble singing, movement, and playing instruments.
3. Music literacy goals.

4. Creativity goals that include the development of improvisation and composition skills.
5. Listening goals.
6. Curricular connections to other disciplines.

Repertoire

In this section of your portfolio keep a copy of songs for developing singing, movement, and instrumental skills for each grade. In selecting repertoire you may want to ask yourself:

How many songs should be multicultural?
How many songs need to be included for specific holidays, seasonal songs, commemoration days, and patriotic celebrations?
Which songs should be taught by rote or by note?

Chapter 3 provides ideas concerning the selection of repertoire for each grade. Also included are procedures and guidelines for analyzing this repertoire from both a music theory and pedagogical perspective. Appendix 2 provides an alphabetical list of sample songs.

Performance

This section of your teaching portfolio includes strategies for developing singing, ensemble, and movement skills, as well as performing on instruments. Chapter 4 provides ideas for developing the singing voice, a movement sequence, as well as a sequence for introducing instruments to students. Specific strategies and ideas for presenting songs are included in this chapter.

Critical Thinking, Problem Solving, and Music Literacy

This component of your teaching portfolio includes a list of repertoire arranged by musical concept and elements that you will use for teaching music literacy skills that also promotes critical thinking and problem solving skills. The bulk of chapters 5, 6, 7, 8, and 9 provide information to assist you in developing your students' music literacy and critical thinking skills.

Appendix 3 includes a pedagogical list of rhythmic and melodic elements to be taught in each grade. Chapter 8 includes strategies for teaching musical concepts and elements. Lesson plans are examined in detail in chapter 9. Chapter 7 discusses techniques for the development of musical skills such as reading, writing, memory, inner hearing (audiation), form, and ensemble work.

Music Improvisation and Composition

The purpose of this section of the portfolio is to have a list of suitable strategies, activities, and worksheets for developing improvisation and composition skills appropriate for each grade. Chapter 7 presents techniques for developing improvisation and composition skills.

Listening

This component of the portfolio is for instructors to compile a list of listening repertoire and ideas for sequencing music listening activities for the classroom as well as appropriate worksheets. Chapter 7 discusses appropriate repertoire and music listening activities.

Assessment

The purpose of assessment is to improve instruction. Assessment is an essential component of teaching and learning. The instructor needs to determine how to assess musical growth throughout the year as well as design rubrics to measure students' musical development. In the teaching resource portfolio the instructor should include assessment activities and scoring rubrics for each grade. In chapter 11 we provide examples of assessment and scoring rubrics that may be adapted for any grade level.

Class Profiles

In this section create a record of both class and student progress for the year. During the first weeks of each academic year the instructor can conduct informal and formal assessments of student knowledge. This information can be used to design a class and individual student profile and can be updated as the year progresses. In chapter 11 we provide examples of student and class profiles.

Resources

This component of your teaching portfolio includes such things as sample lesson plans, internet resources, sources for purchasing instruments, books and recordings, as well as videos that reinforce other areas of the curriculum. Chapter 9 provides examples of different types of lesson plans.

› Discussion Questions

1. What components should be included in a teaching resource portfolio?
2. Review the national or state standards for music education in your state. How do these standards affect a music curriculum?
3. Interview a successful music instructor in your community and find out what his or her long-term and short-term plans for music instruction entail.
4. Identify web resources that could be useful for music instructors.

› Ongoing Assignment

Imagine that you have been hired by a school to teach music for grades one through five next September. Create a teaching resource portfolio for each grade. Get a binder for each grade and tab the binder according to the ten teaching portfolio components. This is an ongoing assignment and you will be adding to each grade's portfolio as you progress through each chapter in the book.

References

Choksy, Lois, Robert M. Abramson, Avon E. Gillespie, David Woods, and Frank York. *Teaching Music in the Twenty-first Century.* 2nd ed. Upper Saddle River, N.J.: Prentice-Hall, 2000.

Drake, Susan M. *Planning the Integrated Curriculum: The Call to Adventure.* Alexandria, Va.: Association for Supervision and Curriculum Development, 1993.

Chapter 2

Kodály's Philosophy of Music Education

"Legyen A Zene Mindenkié"
[Music Should Belong to Everyone]

Philosophy works to render the implicit explicit, with the ultimate intent of enriching both understanding and perception. Among its greatest allies is a persistent curiosity. Its enemies are the habitual, the stereotypical, the unexamined, the acritical, the "common sense" assumption or assertion. The philosophical mind critically challenges and explores received doctrine, renounces the security and comfort of dogma, exposes inconsistencies, weighs and evaluates alternatives. It explores, probes, and questions, taking very little for granted.

Wayne Bowman, "Philosophy, Criticism, and Music Education: Some Tentative Steps Down a Less Traveled Road"

Key Questions

What are the major tenets of the Kodály philosophy of music education?

How can the Kodály philosophy of music education provide a model for developing a personal philosophy of music education?

What are the multiple dimensions of musicianship training?

How do the multiple dimensions of musicianship training connect to the Kodály philosophy of music education? How can we develop a music curriculum based on the Kodály philosophy of music education?

How can we develop a lesson plan framework based on a music curriculum inspired by the Kodály philosophy of music education?

How is the Kodály philosophy of music education connected to the national content standards for music education?

What you teach and how you teach will be determined by your personal philosophy of music education. Understanding Zoltán Kodály's philosophy of music education can provide a useful model for developing your own personal philosophy of music education. Having a philosophy of music education allows you to understand your goals and purpose in the classroom. A philosophy of music education puts you in a better position for becoming an advocate for the inclusion of music in the school curriculum. The goal of this chapter is to provide a brief introduction to Kodály's philosophy of music education and to identify the components that need to be considered in the design of a successful music curriculum. Appendix 1 includes a sample curriculum for grades one through five. To provide a context for understanding Kodály's philosophy of music education we are providing a brief biographical outline of the composer.

Zoltán Kodály: A Biographical Outline

The Early Years: 1882–1905

Zoltán Kodály (1882–1967)[1] was a Hungarian composer, ethnomusicologist, and music educator, who along with Béla Bartók is recognized for creating a new style of Hungarian art music based on the folk music heritage of Hungary. Through his efforts in music education, Kodály sought to cultivate a far-reaching, musically literate Hungarian society. His philosophical and pedagogical contributions to the field of music education have become known as the Kodály concept or Kodály method of music education now in worldwide use.[2]

Kodály's early musical experiences and education prepared him for a career as an artist and a scholar. His father, an amateur violinist, and his mother, an amateur pianist and singer, filled the Kodály house with chamber music of the European masters. He studied language and literature at Eőtvős University and composition at the Ferenc Liszt National Academy of Music in Budapest, Hungary. He earned degrees in both composition and teaching in 1904 and 1905, respectively. In April 1906 he was awarded the Ph.D. for his thesis *A Magyar népdal strófaszerkezete* [The Stanzaic Structure of Hungarian Folk Song]. Kodály compiled research material from existing Hungarian folk music collections, music that he had gathered in Galánta, and Béla Vikár's phonograph cylinder recordings. The work reflects his interests and scholarship in the interdisciplinary aspects of music and language. After receiving his doctorate, Kodály settled in Buda and began an ambitious investigation of Hungarian folk tradition.

The Young Composer: 1905–1922

In 1906, Kodály took part in a study tour in Berlin and Paris and then began his teaching career as a music theory instructor at the Budapest Ferenc Liszt Academy of Music. At the same time, Kodály continued collecting folk songs, composing, and writing articles on all aspects of music and performance. His folk song collection grew to over three thousand songs. His compositions included piano, chamber, and choral works. Kodály's musical criticism appeared in literary journals and newspapers.

Association with Béla Bartók led to a joint concert of their works in 1910. Contradictory criticism of the concert was consistent with the style of commentary for the period. Kodály's use of folk tunes and unfamiliar harmonies earned him the title "deliberate heretic." He was accused of holding "both thought and melody in contempt." This derogatory view of Kodály was to change within the course of a decade.

The Creative Period: 1923–1939

The years 1923–1939 were Kodály's most prolific, both as a composer and an author. His most noted compositions of the period were written for the opera and chorus. Kodály wrote *Psalmus Hungaricus,* for choir and orchestra, to mark the 50th anniversary of the united city of Budapest. The period saw the premiere, first in Hungary then abroad, of the singspiel *Háry János, Dances of Galanta,* and the *Concerto.* Kodály made his international conducting debut in Amsterdam with the Concertgebouw Orchestra in 1927.

His scholarly works of the period included a number of articles in which Kodály sought to define the nature of Hungarian folk music. Kodály contributed a historical survey of Hungarian folk music to the *Zenei lexikon* [Dictionary of Music]. He then published his own work on the topic, entitled *Folk Music of Hungary.*

Kodály said that 1925 was the year in which his attention was directed toward the musical education of children. Beginning in 1927, Kodály's former students started the Youth Choral Movement in Hungary. The most famous of these were Jenő Ádám, Lajos Bárdos, György Kerényi, Zoltán Vásárhelyi, Endre Borus, and Adrienne Sztojanovits. The first choral collection, *Little Pieces for Children's Choir,* was published in 1928 and edited by György Kerényi. In 1929 Kodály realized that music education must be methodical and that only music materials of the highest quality should be included in the curriculum. In addition, he came to realize that the only form of music education accessible for every child is based on singing. In 1937 Kodály wrote the first volume of *Bicinia Hungarica,* in which he discusses the benefits of using relative solmization.[3] *The ABC of Singing* [*Énekes Á bécé*], a music textbook containing folk music materials and the first real effort to use relative solmization in Hungary, was compiled by György Kerényi and Benjamin Rajeczky in 1938 and published by Magyar Kórus, Budapest. Based on relative solmization, it contained about 300 folk songs, classical music, and fundamentals of music. A teacher's manual, *Éneklő iskola* [Singing School], was published two years later in 1940 by Irma Bors and György Gulyás.

The Educator: 1940–1967

In his later years, Kodály pursued with even greater zeal the improvement of musical education in Hungarian schools. He edited numerous songbooks tailored specifically for children and set forth principles for early musical education in works such as "Zene az ovodában" [Music in the Kindergarten]. In 1943–1944, Magyar Kórus published Kodály and Kerényi's two-volume school song collection *Iskolai énekgyüjtemény I–II* [Collected Songs for Schools]. This was a collection of 630 melodies, including Hungarian and European folk songs and canons arranged according to a methodological sequence. In 1943 Kodály's 333 reading exercises were published.[4] The *Szó-mi* I–VIII books were written with Jenő Ádám and published in 1944 and 1946. This was a selection of materials from the *Collected Songs for Schools* for grades one through eight. During 1944 a handbook to Kodály's School Song Collection and to the *Szó-mi* songbook by Kodály and Ádám was published by Jenő Ádám called *Módszeres Énektanítás a Relativ Solmizáció Alapján* [Methodical Music Teaching Based on Relative Solmization]. In these books Kodály began melodic training with the minor third interval. In 1945 and 1947 Kodály published *Pentatonic Music.*[5] In 1945 Kodály gave a lecture in Pécs on 19 November titled "Hungarian Musical

Education." He discussed the importance of basing Hungarian musical education on Hungarian folk music. The composer defended the notion of teaching Hungarian music as a prerequisite to the music of other nations. He also addressed the efficacy of teaching singing before teaching an instrument.[6]

In 1946, a specialized primary school was established in keeping with Kodály's principles. His article "100 éves terv" [A Hundred Year Plan] was published in *Énekszó*. The aim of Kodály's plan was to restore Hungarian musical culture by making reading and writing music a part of general education throughout the Hungarian school system. Kodály's plan can best be summarized with his own words: "The aim: Hungarian musical culture. The means: making the reading and writing of music general, through the schools. At the same time the awakening of a Hungarian public taste in music and continual progress towards what is better and more Hungarian. To make masterpieces of world music literature public property, to convey them to people of every kind and rank."[7] The Hungarian minister of education recognized his efforts and invested Kodály with the Grand Cross of the Order of the Republic in 1948. He was a member and then president of the Hungarian Academy of Sciences (1946–1949), where he established the folk music research group.

Kodály lobbied Hungarian leaders for better music education for children in the schools and in 1950 the first music primary school started in Kecskemét, led by Márta Nemesszeghy. In a preface to Erzsébet Szőnyi's *Musical Reading and Writing*,[8] Kodály provides a brief overview of music education focusing on the German model and commenting on the curriculum of the Paris Conservatory. He praises the *Musical Reading and Writing* text for providing an outline for a music education but cautions that it is the artistry of the teacher that will provide the musical example for the students, not books.[9] In the foreword to *Let Us Sing Correctly*[10] published in 1964, Kodály explains that proper intonation in singing matches the acoustic, not the tempered intervals and that the singing teacher or choral director should not depend on the piano for pitch. He examines the use of part singing and solfège for developing good intonation. Musical examples are presented and analyzed.

The 1964 Budapest Conference of the International Society for Music Education drew international attention to the musical phenomenon taking place in Hungarian music education; this was called "the Kodály Method."[11] Accordingly, Kodály was recognized as a prominent figure in twentieth-century music education.

Further accolades were bestowed upon Kodály in his final years; he was presented with three Kossuth prizes as well as honorary degrees from Oxford, Humboldt, and Toronto Universities. Kodály became a citizen of the world. He was invited to conduct in Great Britain, the Soviet Union, and the United States. He was selected to chair conferences held by the International Folk Music Council and the International Society for Music Education. He was an honorary president of the latter. As a final tribute from his own people, Kodály received the title of "Eminent Artist" from the Hungarian People's Republic.

A Brief Examination of Zoltán Kodály's Philosophy of Music Education

In order to understand Kodály's philosophy of music education, it is best to understand his philosophy of music through his musical compositions, writings, and speeches. Here we examine some of his most famous statements concerning the justification for the inclusion of music in the school curriculum and the importance of a well-trained music teacher, as well as his views on the essential components of a music education for students. The majority of these statements were originally written in Hungarian and translated into English. We have not attempted to correct grammatical errors or English translations. The quotes appear as they have originally been translated. While some statements are awkward, the essence of Kodály's thoughts is evident.

We have chosen quotes from Kodály's writings that provide insights into the following: (1) justifying music in the school curriculum; (2) the importance of excellent artist-teachers; and (3) the multiple dimensions of musicianship. These dimensions include performance, stewardship of culture, critical thinking, creativity, and listening.

Justifying Music in the School Curriculum

Kodály believed that music should belong to everyone and not just to a musical elite. "It is the right of every citizen to be taught the basic elements of music, to be handed the key with which he can enter the locked world of music. To open the ear and heart of the millions to serious music is a great thing."[12]

He believed that "with a few years' technical preparation children can achieve results measurable by the most exacting of absolute artistic standards."[13] He observed, "With music, one's whole future life is brightened. This is such a treasure in life that it helps us over many troubles and difficulties. Music is nourishment, a comforting elixir. Music multiplies all that is beautiful and of value in life."[14]

> Taken separately, too, the elements of music are precious instruments in education. Rhythm develops attention, concentration, determination and the ability to condition oneself. Melody opens up the world of emotions. Dynamic variation and tone colour sharpen our hearing. Singing, finally, is such a many-sided physical activity that its effect in physical education is immeasurable—if there is perhaps anyone to whom the education of the spirit does not matter. Its beneficial effect in health is well known; special books have been written on this.[15]

> With us it is scarcely every twentieth person who uses his speech and breathing organs correctly. This, too, should be learned during the singing lesson. The discipline of rhythm, the training of the throat and lungs set singing right beside gymnastics. Both of them, no less than food, are needed daily.[16]

> The curriculum and instructions (as we should term them) for British schools declare on the role of music in education: "By now the value of music in school life is so well recognized that it is superfluous to dwell at length upon it."[17]

> Our age of mechanization leads along a road ending with man himself as a machine; only the spirit of singing can save us from this fate.[18]

The Importance of Excellent Artist-Teachers

We believe that students must be taught music based on an apprenticeship model of instruction that closely mirrors a teaching model used by exceptional studio instructors.

Simply stated, students learn the craft of music from individuals who themselves are excellent musicians. "There is a need for better musicians, and only those will become good musicians who work at it every day. The better a musician is the easier it is for him to draw others into the happy, magic circle of music. Thus will he serve the great cause of helping music to belong to everyone."[19]

The following quotes verify Kodály's conviction that only excellent music instructors should be allowed to teach.

> It is more important who the singing master at Kisvárda is than who the director of the Opera House is, because a poor director will fail. [Often even a good one.] But a bad teacher may kill the love of music for thirty years in thirty classes of pupils.[20]

> Only excellent artist teachers will be able to:

> Teach music and singing at school in such a way that it is not a torture but a joy for the pupil; instill a thirst for finer music in him, a thirst which will last for a lifetime. Music must not be approached from its intellectual, rational side, nor should it be conveyed to the child as a system of algebraic symbols, or as the secret writing of a language with which he has no connection. The way should be paved for direct intuition. If the child is not filled at least once by the life-giving stream of music during the most susceptible period-between his sixth and sixteenth years—it will hardly be any use to him later on. Often a single experience will open the young soul to music for a whole lifetime. This experience cannot be left to chance, it is the duty of the school to provide it.[21]

Music instructors need to develop students' inherent musical abilities in the classroom through performance, creativity, listening, critical thinking, and musical literacy skills as well as enabling students to become stewards of their musical and cultural heritage. The goal of music instruction is to create a community of learners in the music classroom that experience and explore all of the various facets of music and begin to share this knowledge as a service to the community.

> But professional music education in music itself is still not sufficiently inspired by the idea that music-making is not an end in itself but that it must stand at the service of the whole people.[22]

> It is the bounden duty of the talented to cultivate their talent to the highest degree, to be of as much use as possible to their fellow men. For every person's worth is measured by how much he can help his fellow men and serve his country. Real art is one of the most powerful forces in the rise of mankind and he who renders it accessible to as many people as possible is a benefactor of humanity.[23]

The Multiple Dimensions of Musicianship

In addition to speaking about the value of music in the school curriculum, Kodály wrote about the multiple dimensions of musicianship training. These dimensions include performance, musical literacy and critical thinking skills, creativity skills, listening, as well as stewardship of musical and cultural heritage. Therefore it is clear that when developing children's musicianship skills we need to address the different facets of what it means to be a musical human being. If we are to develop children's self-knowledge, self-awareness, and emotions, we need to educate them to be:

1. Performers (we mean the act of making and sharing music)
2. Stewards of musical and cultural heritage
3. Critical thinkers
4. Creative human beings
5. Listeners

Children as Performers: Singing, Instruments, and Movement

Music performance is at the core of a music program. Through performance students engage in singing, movement, playing instruments, and conducting.

Singing

Kodály was convinced that singing is the most direct means to a musical education. Singing requires the rapid internalization of sound and provides immediate participation in the musical experience. Kodály's intent was to lead students to a deep appreciation of art music. Since the human voice is the most intimate of all instruments and the inner ear is more easily developed through this personal medium, the voice is the most logical starting point.

> If one were to attempt to express the essence of this education in one word, it could only be—singing. The most frequent word to be heard on Toscannini's lips during his orchestral rehearsals was "Cantare!" expressed in a thousand and one shades of meaning.[24]

> Fortunate indeed is the child who creates with his own voice the first association linking it with the picture of the notes. If he starts singing based on the concepts of instrumental techniques, then our endeavors to make the singing and aural concepts primary can hardly succeed. And if he does not sing at all, it will be nearly impossible for him to achieve free and intimate "singing" on any instrument. Even the most talented artist can never overcome the disadvantages of an education without singing.[25]

> There is a well-known saying of Bulows: He who cannot sing, be his voice good or bad, should not play the piano either. What did Bulow mean by this? He did not mean that every movement and part of a Beethoven sonata should be sung before it is played. But that nobody can play it well if he does not feel and know where the essence of the melody is, and if he cannot bring it to life with his voice whatever his voice may be like.[26]

> Most singing teachers and chorus masters believe in controlling the pitch of the voice by the piano. But singing depends on the acoustically correct "natural" intervals, and not on the tempered system. Even a perfectly tuned piano can never be a criterion of singing, not to speak of the ever "out-of-tune" pianos available at schools and rehearsal rooms. Yet how often have I found chorus masters attempting to restore the shaky intonation of their choirs with the help of a mistuned piano![27]

Instruments

Kodály believed that instrumental instruction should also incorporate the use of singing.

> Understand once and for all what this is all about: the psychological procedure of our whole music making is faulty—it must be inverted. So far it is the fingers that have run ahead, with the head and heart hobbling after them. The way for the true musician is the opposite: he starts with the head and the heart and from there directs the fingers, the larynx, or whatever instrument. It is because they do not go about it in this way that so many of our pianists play mechanically. When someone is twenty or thirty they announce that he has no talent. But perhaps if he had tried to make music with his voice when he was six years old, he might have come closer to the soul of the music and his piano playing might have been more musical as a result.[28]
>
> We should not allow anyone even to go near an instrument until he or she can read and sing correctly. It is our only hope that one day our musicians will be able also to "sing" on their instruments.[29]
>
> To teach a child an instrument without first giving him preparatory training and without developing singing, reading and dictating to the highest level along with the playing is to build upon sand.[30]
>
> I heard the finest singing in the world by the world's worst voice—Toscaninni, when at rehearsal he demonstrated a phrase in his blunt hoarse voice for his players and singers. And this is why they could sing so beautifully under his baton. His most frequent comment to the orchestra was "Cantare! Cantare!"[31]

Kodály did acknowledge the use of instruments to provide appropriate and tasteful song accompaniments in the classroom. "But it is an even greater 'pleasure and amusement' for children if they accompany themselves on their instruments. . . . The xylophone is not so bad either. I shall never forget the charming sight and sound in Nagyvárad in 1942 of forty children playing the xylophone simultaneously."[32] Kodály believed that students should perform simple melodies on instruments. "However, these pieces can be played on any other instrument or can be sung unaccompanied, wordlessly or with a text if a suitable one can be invented."[33]

Movement

The composer was convinced that movement through singing games and folk dancing is critical for the musical development of children.

> Children's singing games allow a more profound insight than anything else into the primeval age of folk music. Singing connected with movement and action is a much more ancient and, at the same time, more complex phenomenon than is a simple song. It offers much more hitherto untouched material to science for all kinds of investigation than any other branch of folk music, on which its thorough examination can also throw new light.[34]
>
> We must look forward to the time when all people in all lands are brought together through singing, and when there is a universal harmony.[35]

In order to develop children's musicianship skills as performers, we should include activities for developing children's singing, instrument playing, and movement skills. Movement activities may also include teaching simple conducting patterns.

Children as Stewards of Their Cultural Heritage: Music Repertoire

Although some music educators[36] believe that the music education of children is more important than the transmission of a musical and cultural heritage, Kodály believed otherwise.

> Not even the most excellent individual creation can be a substitute for traditions. To write a folksong is as much beyond the bounds of possibility as to write a proverb. Just as proverbs condense centuries of popular wisdom and observation, so, in the traditional songs, the emotions of centuries are immortalized in a form polished to perfection. No masterpiece can replace traditions.[37]

Kodály voiced concern that art be presented in such a way that it was not a torture, but a joy for the pupil, so that it would instill in the child a thirst for finer music and affect his or her level of taste in a way that would last for a lifetime.[38] When children gain knowledge of different musical repertoires beginning with music of their own community and expanding to include music of other communities as well as art music they are in a position to become stewards of their cultural legacy. Kodály believed that material suited to the physical, developmental, and psychological needs of the young could be best found in folk songs of their community. Kodály valued folk songs for their simplicity, beauty, and heritage, but he emphatically stressed the importance of using only authentic folk songs, linking them to folk music of other cultures, to the finest art songs, art music and recently composed music.

Through the use of folk songs and singing games in the school, the teacher can proceed with suitable material that is already part of the child's cultural experience. Ruth Crawford Seeger believed also that it is "one of the aims of education to induct the child into the realities of the culture in which he will live, may we not say that this traditional music and language and ideology, which has not only grown out of but has in turn influenced that culture—and is still influencing and being used by it—should occupy a familiar place in the child's daily life, even though it may not be current in the particular neighborhood in which he happens to be living."[39]

The connection between folk tradition, art music, and recently composed music is important in the music of each historical era. Therefore it becomes one of the goals of the music teacher to teach the best folk and composed music to children so that they can become the cultural stewards of this repertoire for their community.

It was Kodály's belief that the communication of inferior music inhibits the growth of maximum musical understanding. He maintained that the type of material used and the manner of presentation has a lasting effect on the development of a child's musical taste. As students' skills develop, folk songs of other cultures are gradually introduced along with art music of the great composers and recently composed music. "There are strictly speaking only two kinds of music: good and bad. . . . Bad foreign and bad native music are equally damaging, like the plague."[40]

> Bad taste spreads by leaps and bounds. In art this is not so innocent a thing as in, say, clothes. Someone who dresses in bad taste does not endanger his health, but bad taste in art is a veritable sickness of the soul. It seals the soul off from contact with masterpieces and from the life giving nourishment emanating from them without which the soul wastes away or becomes stunted, and the whole character of the man is branded with a peculiar mark.[41]

> The pure soul of the child must be considered sacred; what we implant there must stand every test, and if we plant anything bad, we poison his soul for life.[42]

The use of contrived or diluted music is not suitable for instruction.

> Let us stop the teachers' superstition according to which only some diluted art-substitute is suitable for teaching purposes. A child is the most susceptible and the most enthusiastic audience for pure art; for in every great artist the child is alive—and this is something felt by youth's congenial spirit. Conversely, only art of intrinsic value is suitable for children! Everything else is harmful. After all, food is more carefully chosen for an infant than for an adult. Musical nourishment which is rich in vitamins is essential for children.[43]

Quality music literature for each grade will expand students' knowledge of folk songs, art music, and recently composed music. Instructors will need to decide how many songs and from what cultural origins should be included in their curricula. From that point they can determine which materials may be taught through music reading, or through a rote approach to learning. Through their tradition of oral transmission, folk songs have long been considered ideal for developing ear-training and musical memory. This renders them well-suited to fostering musical literacy.

Children as Critical Thinkers and Problem Solvers: Music Literacy

Kodály believed that all students should become musically literate, that is, they should be able to read and write music with ease; comparable to the ease with which they read and write their own language. "I was always amazed how an intelligent adult was willing without the slightest protest to let himself be treated like a parrot. A choir which has even half an idea of reading will in a given period of time learn ten times as many works and its perspectives will become ten times as broad as one which repeats like a parrot by ear."[44]

Kodály inspired many musicians and teachers to work with folk materials and to analyze them from a musicological and pedagogical perspective. After careful analysis, a music curriculum and pedagogical sequence was established that introduced the most common intervals, rhythms, meters, and forms that are common in Hungarian music to students. This approach differed from the older subject-logic approach to music learning in which the material was taught in a manner that is logical in terms of content, but did not take into account how children learn. For example, rhythm was often taught beginning with the whole note, then dividing the whole into half notes, quarter notes, and so on. The Kodály concept advocates beginning the study of rhythm with the patterns most common to children's singing games and chants. Thus, patterns of quarter and eighth notes are taught in the context of music that the child has already experienced in many ways.

As Kodály's ideas were developed, Hungarian teachers began using teaching techniques that have sometimes been thought to constitute a "Kodály method." These techniques include the use of the moveable *do* system of solmization, the use of hand signs to indicate the notes of the scale, rhythmic syllables, and a form of musical shorthand derived from the solfège and rhythmic systems. These devices were adapted by Kodály's colleagues and found useful in teaching music to children. However, they did not originate with Kodály-based teaching.

The moveable *do* or tonic-solfa system can be traced to the eleventh century, when Guido d'Arezzo used it for musical instruction. An Englishman, John Curwen, developed the hand signs used to represent the notes of the scale in 1862. Hand signs provide physical and visual reinforcement of the musical sound. Musical shorthand, or stick notation, was developed in Hungary and is simply a rapid way of writing music without the use of the staff.

It is the use of these teaching techniques in combination with the folk song and art music in a child-centered curriculum where children develop their critical thinking skills through discovery learning that makes the Kodály concept of music education unique.

> For the roots of science and of art are the same. Each, in its own way, reflects the world. The basic conditions: sharp powers of observation, precise expression of the life observed, and raising it to a higher synthesis. And the foundation of scientific and artistic greatness is also the same: just man, vir Justus.[45]

> On the basis of what has been said, the characteristics of a good musician can be summarized as follows: a well trained ear, a well trained intelligence, a well trained heart, and a well trained hand. All four must develop together, in a constant equilibrium. As one lags behind or rushes ahead, there is something wrong.[46]

Children will develop critical thinking skills through the analysis of familiar music repertoires. Music tools such as rhythmic and solfège syllables should be used to aid in identifying typical rhythmic and melodic patterns, referred to as "building blocks," commonly found in this repertoire. A knowledge of the basic components of a music repertoire will enable students to develop their performance, listening, composition, and improvisation skills. For example, much like a jazz musician, when students understand the basic building of a particular repertoire of music, they can manipulate these building blocks to create other compositions.

Children as Creative Human Beings: Music Composition and Improvisation

Music improvisation, the art of composing extemporaneously, and composition, the art of formulating and writing music, are indispensable components of a music education. Kodály believed that students should possess a well-trained ear to engage in music composition. "How often has it happened that pupils studying composition without a trained ear write down something quite different from what they have imagined? . . . Here, too, we have seen often enough what a struggle the study of composition, and even of simple harmony, is for one who failed to learn the reading and writing of music early enough."[47]

Two types of improvisation and composition activities are used in the music classroom: one type where students improvise a rhythm or melody without thinking about the pitches or sounds being used and another type where students consciously use specific rhythmic or melodic elements. The instructor who teaches music inspired by the Kodály concept uses improvisation and composition in order that the students will develop the ability to understand the creative process in music as well as understand the stylistic elements of a piece of music. Students who are able to improvise and compose music based on typical forms, and melodic and rhythmic patterns commonly found in a particular style of music will develop a greater feeling and understanding for that style. Improvisation and composition skills should be closely correlated to the conscious and unconscious knowledge of rhythmic and melodic elements.

Children as Listeners

Music listening is an important component of the Kodály concept. No matter what the activity in the music classroom children are constantly taught how to listen when they perform, create, or while developing their critical thinking skills. Of course the music instructor also needs to provide students with specific listening activities that will enable them to form connections between the song repertoire they are singing and art music.

Kodály believed that there was a connection between folk music and art music. "For instance, Haydn, the best to begin with, has manifest connection with folksong, but even in many works of Mozart it is easy to recognize the sublimated Austrian folk songs. Beethoven's many themes are also folk-song like."[48]

Kodály believed that listening was of paramount importance for the music student.

> It is not enough to listen once, fleetingly, to great works; one has to prepare for them and to follow the notes through the pages before and after hearing them in order to implant them abidingly in one's mind.[49]

> It is the richness of both the musical experiences themselves and the memory of them that makes a good musician. Individual singing plus listening to music (by means of active and passive well-arranged experiences) develops the ear to such an extent that one understands music one has heard with as much clarity as though one were looking at a score; if necessary—and if time permits—one should be able to reproduce such a score. This, and certainly no less, is what we expect from the student of a language; and music is a manifestation of the human spirit similar to a language. Its great men have conveyed to mankind things unutterable in any other language. If we do not want such things to remain dead treasures, we must do our utmost to make the greatest possible number of people understand their secrets.[50]

Activities for developing students' listening skills should be included in the curriculum. These activities should be closely correlated to the conscious knowledge of rhythmic and melodic elements and used in practicing melodic or rhythmic elements. Listening activities should include songs to be sung or performed by the classroom teacher or other students in the music school as well as the performance of repertoire by professional musicians for students. Specific pieces of repertoire should be listed in the curriculum and should include music that reinforces elements and concepts taught.

Linking the Kodály Concept, the Multiple Dimensions of Musicianship, and the National Content Standards for Music Education

A music curriculum built on the Kodály concept of music education aligns with the national content standards for music education.[51] The following is a brief summation of how a curriculum built on the philosophy of Kodály is reflective of the national content standards. Each standard is cited along with a brief overview of how it relates to a Kodály curriculum.

Content Standard One: Singing, Alone and with Others, a Varied Repertoire of Music

Singing provides the foundation of all learning in the Kodály classroom. Through singing students are guided to discover and subsequently internalize the elements of music. Students learn a varied repertoire of multicultural music, classical music, and recently composed music through singing. The curriculum engages students in group and solo singing, call and response songs, melodic ostinati, rounds, canons, partner songs, and art music.

Content Standard Two: Performing on Instruments, Alone and with Others, a Varied Repertoire of Music

Kodály teachers use a variety of rhythm instruments as reinforcement of beat and rhythm concepts. Melody instruments such as barred instruments and step bells are used to perform borduns and ostinati and may be used to practice melodic concepts. Recorders, guitar, and auto harp may be introduced into classroom activities once students have reached a level of maturation that enables them to perform on the instruments. In keeping with the main tenets of the Kodály concept, students should first sing what is to be performed on instruments.

Content Standard Three: Improvising Melodies, Variations, and Accompaniments

Students use their knowledge of rhythmic and melodic elements as well as their stylistic knowledge of folk music as the basis for their improvisation activities and compositions in the classroom. Instructors engage students in a myriad of improvisation activities such as improvising rhythmic or melodic answers to questions, improvising within a given form as well as creating melodic and rhythmic ostinati. These activities also provide assessment of student understanding of musical elements and musical styles as well as their skill of performance.

Content Standard Four: Composing and Arranging Music within Specific Guidelines

Students in a Kodály classroom learn to audiate music (audiation, the skill of thinking music) before they write it down rather than using a computer or instruments to first create the sounds they write. Activities may include learning to create rhythmic and melodic ostinati to known music, learning to create melodies to a given text, learning to arrange a folk song for two voices, and learning to compose a new song within given compositional parameters.

Content Standard Five: Reading and Writing Music

Kodály-trained students learn to read and write music using stick or staff notation, solfège and rhythm syllables, and hand signs. Beginning reading and writing exercises and examples include simple pentatonic, pentachord, and hexachord melodies and progress to diatonic major, minor, and modal melodies as well as two- and three-part compositions.

Content Standard Six: Listening to, Analyzing, and Describing Music

Kodály-trained students are guided to listen, analyze, and describe music using their knowledge of music elements. Young students are taught how to listen for elements in a piece of music and how to describe these elements. Instructors may focus on analysis when they sight-sing additional pieces of music that include the same elements in listening examples. Both rhythmic and melodic dictation strategies include identifying the forms and compositional elements of musical examples.

Content Standard Seven: Evaluating Music and Music Performance

Because singing and performance is at the heart of the Kodály classroom, instructors and students continually evaluate their performance. Knowledge of musical elements improves the stylistic knowledge of the repertoire studied. The instructor may provide assessment rubrics for performance that can be used by students for evaluation.

Content Standard Eight: Understanding Relationships between Music, the Other Arts, and Disciplines outside the Arts

Kodály-inspired music education develops students' kinesthetic abilities as well as spatial, mathematic, and reading aptitudes in the music classroom; skills that are readily transferred to other areas of the curriculum.

Content Standard Nine: Understanding Music in Relation to History and Culture

Kodály-trained students study the folk music and art music of different cultures and eras. Children learn the text of folk songs in their original language; something that permits the music instructor as well as classroom teachers to discuss historical information and make connections to related disciplines and art forms. The study of art music includes history, an understanding of the various style periods common to other art forms: visual arts, architecture, and dance.

Building the Framework of a Curriculum Based on Kodály's Concept of Musicianship and the National Content Standards for Music Education

In appendix 1, we have included a sample curriculum for a music program for grades one through five. Each section of the curriculum will be discussed in greater detail in subsequent chapters. Of course we have only provided a shell of a music curriculum as the teaching demands placed upon music teachers are different from one school district to another. The goal of this curriculum is to provide a model for constructing your own curriculum. We have purposely not addressed every teaching situation in terms of curriculum and lesson plan design. Once you have an understanding of the Kodály philosophy and the approach to teaching you will be able to make the modifications to suit your particular teaching situation.

The following is a framework for a grade one music curriculum based on the philosophy of Zoltán Kodály. The specific musical skills need to be modified according to the frequency of instruction.

I. **Repertoire: Children as Stewards of their Cultural and Musical Heritage**
   Expand song repertoire to add to students' knowledge of children's songs and games, folk music of the children's culture, art music, and recently composed music.

II. **Performance: Children as Performers**
   Broaden performance skills to include:
   A. Singing
      1. Be familiar with a repertoire of thirty folk songs and singing games, classical music and recently composed music.
      2. Know by memory ten to fifteen songs and are able to sing these with solfège and rhythm syllables.
      3. Perform all songs with accurate intonation, clear diction, clear head tone, musical phrasing/breathing, appropriate dynamics, and tempi.

   B. Part Work
      1. Sing songs antiphonally.
      2. Practice intervals simultaneously with hand signs.
      3. Accompany a song with a rhythmic ostinato using quarter and eighth notes and quarter note rests.

4. Accompany a song with a melodic ostinato using *la, so,* or *mi.*
5. Sing simple rhythmic or melodic canons derived from familiar songs.
6. Perform two-part rhythmic exercises based on rhythmic motifs from known songs.

C. Movement
1. Perform acting-out games with chase element.
2. Perform winding games
3. Perform simple line games
4. Perform circle games
5. Improvise words and movement to known songs.

D. Instruments
1. Students demonstrate first grade melodic and rhythmic concepts on classroom instruments.
2. Students accompany classroom singing on classroom instruments.
3. Students conduct in duple meter.

III. Music Literacy: Children as Critical Thinkers and Problem Solvers

A. Rhythmic Elements
1. Know names and written symbols for quarter, eighth notes, and quarter note rest, accented beat, bar lines. Conduct in $\frac{2}{4}$ meter.
2. Perform ostinati using quarter and eighth notes consciously.
3. Perform two-part rhythmic exercises and canons.
4. Improvise short motives with quarter, eighth notes, and quarter note rest.
5. Recognize tunes from clapped rhythm patterns.
6. Identify a skipping song and marching song.

B. Melodic Elements
1. Be able to perform solfège and hand signs for child chant patterns (pentatonic bi chords and tri chords):
   so, mi, la and intervals formed by them
   (*so–mi mi–so so–la la–so mi–la la–mi*).
2. Learn to read melodic patterns that use the notes *so, mi, la* from rhythmic and staff notation.

C. Reading and Writing
1. Read or write well-known rhythmic or melodic patterns found in students' repertoire, from hand signs, traditional rhythmic notation, and staff notation.
2. Write rhythmic patterns from memory or when dictated by the teacher.
3. Write melodic patterns found in focus songs from memory or when dictated by the teacher using stick or staff notation.

D. Inner Hearing
1. Silently sing "inside" from the teacher's hand signs.
2. Silently sing known songs with melodic syllables.
3. Silently read either full or partial rhythms or melodies written in stick or staff notation.
4. Sing back short melodic or rhythmic motives from memory using text, rhythm syllables, or solfège syllables.

E. Form
1. Recognize same, similar, or different phrases in a song either aurally or through music reading.

2. Use letters to describe a form: AABA.
3. Use repeat signs correctly in reading and writing.

F. Musical Memory
1. Echo four- and eight-beat rhythm patterns clapped by the instructor.
2. Memorize short melodies through hand signs.
3. Memorize phrases of four or eight beats from known songs using stick or staff notation.
4. Echo rhythm patterns clapped by the teacher saying correct rhythm syllables.
5. Memorize rhythm patterns read from stick notation.

IV. Improvisation/Composition: Children as Creative Human Beings

A. Improvise rhythm patterns of four or eight beats using rhythm instruments.
B. Improvise rhythm patterns of four or eight beats by clapping and saying rhythm syllables.
C. Improvise short musical motives (*la–so–mi*) using hand signs, hand staff, or body signs.
D. Improvise pentatonic bi and tri chord (*so–mi–la*) melodies to simple four- to eight-beat rhythms using the voice or a barred instrument.
E. Improvise a new rhythm and melody to one measure or more of a well-known song.
F. Improvise question and answer motives using known rhythm or melodic patterns.

V. Listening: Children as Listeners

A. Expand listening repertoire and revisit kindergarten musical concepts.
1. Recognize musical features in classroom song repertoire, folk music, and masterworks.
2. Recognize rhythmic features in classroom song repertoire, folk music, and masterworks including quarter, eighth notes, and quarter note rest.
3. Develop awareness of expressive controls, that is, dynamics, tempo, timbre, and their distinctive characteristics in masterworks of various historical periods.
4. Recognize phrase forms (same/different) in classroom song repertoire, folk music, and masterworks.

Developing a Lesson Plan Framework Based on a Music Curriculum Inspired by Kodály's Philosophy of Music Education

At the end of each chapter we will provide you with information on developing specific lesson plans for teaching music. In this chapter we present a generic lesson plan format that reflects the key components of the Kodály philosophy of music education and the national content standards for music education. Throughout this book we will modify this basic design to incorporate and reflect knowledge acquired from each chapter.

The following is a general lesson plan design that can be modified to accommodate all learning objectives for developing children's skills as performers, critical thinkers, improvisers, composers, listeners, and stewards of their cultural and musical heritage. There are three main sections of a lesson plan: the introduction, core activities, and closure.

Table 2.1 Lesson Plan Structure

Focus	Activities, Procedures, and Assessments
Introduction	
Performance and demonstration of known musical concepts and elements.	Students demonstrate their prior knowledge of repertoire and musical elements through performance. This segment of the lesson includes vocal warm-up exercises
Core Activities	
Acquisition of repertoire	Teach a new song that expands students' repertoire and prepares for the learning of a music rhythmic or melodic concept or element
Performance and preparation of a new concept or element	Learning activities in which students are prepared to discover the attributes of a new musical concept or element through known songs
Movement development	Focus on the sequential development of age-appropriate movement skills through songs and folk games
Performance and musical skill development	Students reinforce their knowledge of previously taught musical concepts and elements working on the skill areas of form, memory, inner hearing, ensemble work, improvisation and composition, and listening through known songs
Closure	
Review and summation	Review and assessment of lesson content and the instructor may perform the next new song to be learned in a subsequent lesson

Explanation of the Framework of Lesson Plan

The following is an explanation of the lesson plan structure shown in table 2.1. Remember that there should be periods of concentration and relaxation throughout the lesson.

Lesson Section One: The Introduction

Performance and Demonstration of Known Repertoire and or Concepts or Elements

One goal of the introduction of the lesson is for children to develop beautiful singing. Another goal is for children to demonstrate their knowledge of music repertoire. In this section of the lesson the children are able to demonstrate through performance that they are stewards of their cultural heritage as well as performers. Another goal of this section of the lesson is for children to demonstrate known rhythmic or melodic musical elements through performance. This may include singing songs with rhythm or solfège syllables. In this portion of the lesson, we develop beautiful singing through breathing exercises and vocal warm-up exercises.

Lesson Section Two: Core Activities

The first period of concentration in the lesson involves the acquisition of repertoire and the performance of new concepts or elements.

Acquisition of Repertoire: Teach a New Song

Instructors present new repertoire to students for a variety of reasons. Sometimes they wish to teach a song to students to develop their singing ability, another time a song may be taught because they need to provide a musical context for teaching future musical concepts. When teaching a new song, try to link the new song to the activities in the lesson's introduction—either by using the same key, same rhythmic or melodic motifs, the same meter, the same character, or simply the same tempo.

Performance and Preparation of a New Concept or Element

During this section of the lesson, the instructor will be preparing and presenting concepts that are outlined in the music curriculum under the title of "Children as Critical Thinkers." Students develop their critical thinking skills by developing their knowledge of music literacy. It is through discovery-based learning that children develop their acquisition of music literacy skills.

This first period of concentration is followed by a period of relaxation.

Movement Development

During this section of the lesson, the teacher will be preparing and presenting movement concepts that are associated with specific games outlined in the music curriculum under the title of "Children as Performers." In this section of the lesson, the instructor develops students' movement skills based on game activities associated with song material. A sequence for age-appropriate movement skill development is provided in chapter 4.

This period of relaxation is followed by a second period of concentration.

Performance and Musical Skill Development

In this section the instructor will be practicing concepts outlined in the music curriculum under the title of "Children as Critical Thinkers." This is the section of the lesson that reinforces knowledge of known or previously taught musical elements while focusing on a particular music skill such as reading, writing, or improvisation and composition.

Lesson Section Three: Closure

This is a period of relaxation.

Performance and Lesson Review

Review the new song. Students may review known songs or play a game. The instructor may also perform the next new song to be learned in a subsequent lesson.

› Discussion Questions

1. Explain the value of a music education and the place of music in the school curriculum.
2. For you as a teacher, what may be the benefits of using a philosophy of music education to guide your instruction?
3. How would you describe the Kodály concept of music education?
4. Compare and contrast the Kodály concept of music education with other approaches to music teaching.
5. Collect four research articles that document the effects of music on cognitive development of students. Discuss your findings with your peers.
6. What are the characteristics of a well-trained music instructor?
7. What are the multiple dimensions of musicianship training?
8. How does Kodály's concept of musicianship training align with the national content standards for music education?
9. Check web sites for three school districts. Locate their philosophy statement and write a summary statement for each district.

› Ongoing Assignment

1. Write a statement of your personal philosophy of music education. How will your philosophy statement change for each grade level you teach?
2. Review the curriculum goals for grades one through five in appendix 1. Compare these curriculum goals with another music instructor. Add curriculum goals into section two of your portfolio folder for each grade.
3. Using the template of a lesson plan provided in this chapter, determine some teaching activities for each section of the lesson for grades one and three. You may use repertoire that is age appropriate.

References

Alperson, Philip. "What Should One Expect from a Philosophy of Music Education." *Journal of Aesthetic Education* 25/3 (Fall 1991): 215–229.

———. "Introduction: The Philosophy of Music," in *What is Music? An Introduction to the Philosophy of Music,* ed. Philip A. Alperson. New York: Haven Publications, 1987.

Choksy, Lois. *The Kodaly Method,* 2nd ed. Upper Saddle River, N.J.: Prentice-Hall, 1999.

Eisner, E. "Educating the Whole Person: Arts in the Curriculum." *Music Educators Journal* 73/2 (1987), 41–97.

Gardner, Howard. *Frames of Mind: The Theory of Multiple Intelligences.* New York: Basic Books, 1983.

Hanley, Betty, and Janet Montgomery. "Contemporary Curriculum Practices and Their Theoretical Bases," in *The New Handbook of Research on Music Teaching and Learning,* ed. Richard Colwell and Carol Richardson. New York: Oxford University Press, 2002.

Jorgensen, Estelle. *In Search of Music Education.* Urbana: University of Illinois Press, 1997.

———. "Philosophical Issues in Curriculum Method," in *The New Handbook of Research on Music Teaching and Learning,* ed. Richard Colwell and Carol Richardson. New York: Oxford University Press, 2002.

Kodály, Zoltán. *The Selected Writings of Zoltán Kodály,* ed. Ferenc Bónis, trans. Lili Halápy and Fred Macnicol. London: Boosey & Hawkes, 1974.

Music Educators National Conference. *What Every Young American Should Know and be Able to Do in the Arts: National Standards for Arts Education.* Reston, Va.: Music Educators National Conference, 1994.

Shehan Campbell, Patricia. *Songs in Their Heads: Music and Its Meaning in Children's Lives.* New York: Oxford University Press, 1998.

Small, Christopher. *Musicking.* Hanover, N.H.: Wesleyan University Press, 1998.

Wittgenstein, Ludwig. *Philosophical Investigations.* Oxford: Blackwell, 1953.

Chapter 3

Children as Stewards of Their Cultural and Musical Heritage

Selecting Music Repertoire for the Classroom

Children are not simply musical embryos waiting to become musical adults but have a musical culture of their own, with its own musical and social rules, and with functions such as integration of person and expression of ethnicity.

Bruno Nettl, in foreword to Patricia Shehan Campbell, *Songs in Their Heads: Music and Its Meaning in Children's Lives*

By giving status to children's own musical cultures in the formal music education environment, and by using their spontaneous music making as a springboard for adult-directed learning programs, we can provide contexts that offer children security and respect.

David J. Elliot, *Praxial Music Education*

It is through the indigenous musics of their cultures that children receive the stories of their people, those that ancestors pass down from generation to generation and others that are contemporary and reflect new customs. Folk music is the treasure trove of children's values, beliefs, cultures, knowledge, games and stores. The music of children's own cultures must be given respect and status in the classroom, indirectly giving children a sense of their own values and status. Receptivity toward the music of other cultures can be developed from this point of reference, thereby fostering cultural awareness, tolerance and respect.

David J. Elliot, *Praxial Music Education*

By building the multicultural musical experiences of the young, we are nurturing the familiar cultures of the children and facilitating their musical development within and across cultures. The musical experiences the children have now are those from which they create the music of their future.

David J. Elliot, *Praxial Music Education*

Key Questions

What songs should we select for teaching music?

What criteria do we use to select songs for teaching?

Why are pentatonic songs important to teach to students?

How can we construct a repertoire list of songs for each grade?

How do we analyze song repertoire for teaching?

What are some song resources for classroom use?

How can we modify our generic lessons plan structure to include a lesson plan for preparing and practicing musical concepts and elements?

How can we modify our generic lessons plan structure to include lessons for presenting the names of musical concepts and elements?

In chapter 2, we provided a brief survey of Kodály's philosophy of music education, explained how this philosophy can be used to build the basic framework for a music curriculum, and outlined a template for a basic lesson plan. A principal component of Kodály's philosophy is his insistence on selecting quality music repertoire for teaching. The purpose of this chapter is to provide information on how to select and analyze musical repertoire for teaching. Included in appendix 2 is an alphabetized list of songs suitable for grades one through five. The alphabetized list of songs can include the song title, date taught, tone set, and game. We are providing the song title and the date taught in our appendix. These songs have been primarily selected from five publications: Peter Erdei and Katalin Komlós, *150 American Folk Songs to Sing, Read and Play* (120 p.); Eleanor G. Locke, *Sail Away: 155 American Folk Songs to Sing, Read and Play* (164 p.); Ida Erdei, Faith Knowles, and Denise Bacon, *My Singing Bird* (164 p.); Faith Knowles, ed., *Vamos a Cantar 230 Folk Songs of Spanish-Speaking People to Sing, Read, and Play;* and Edward Bolkovac and Judith Johnson, *150 Rounds For Singing and Teaching.*

One of the hallmarks of success of the Hungarian system of music education has been the extensive folk song collections that Hungarian music educators could draw upon to create a music curriculum. Folk song research in Hungary was shaped by Kodály–Bartok techniques in folk music research. We have chosen these books because the editors of these collections have extensive experience collecting and analyzing folk music from primary sources as well as knowledge of the Kodály–Bartok techniques in folk music research. Generally, the editor of these collections has provided the sources for their collections and has not altered the original songs without providing a justification. Additionally, the repertoire in these collections have been melodically and rhythmically analyzed for pedagogical purposes.

Folk Music in the Classroom

As stated in the previous chapter, Kodály was convinced that a child's music education should begin with the folk music of his or her own culture. He believed that folk music is the "musical mother tongue" of all peoples in all nations; music instruction ought to begin with folk music[1] and children's singing games.

> Children's singing games allow a more profound insight than anything else into the primeval age of folk music. Singing connected with movement and action is a much more ancient and at the same time, more complex phenomenon than a simple song.[2]
>
> Each nation has a rich variety of folk songs, very suitable for teaching purposes. Selected gradually, they furnish the best material to introduce musical elements and make the children conscious of them. Singing first by ear, then writing, dictation, all methods combined make a surprisingly quick results. It is essential that the materials used should be musically attractive.[3]

Kodály believed that children should be taught folk music and that folk music should lead to the introduction of art music and composed music. The final purpose of all this must be to introduce pupils to the understanding and love of great classics of past, present and future."[4]

Once the connections to folk music are established, students may be guided to understand the association between folk music and classical music.

> For instance Haydn, the best to begin with, has manifest connection with folk song, but even in many works of Mozart it is easy to recognize the sublimated Austrian folk song. Beethoven's many themes are also folk-song like. And all the national schools originated already in 19th century are based on the foundations of their own folk music.[5]

Kodály on the Subject of Authenticity in Folk Music

The subject of authenticity arises in most discussions of folk music.

> That is a difficult question, I confess that even with us in Hungary, in the years around the turn of the century it was not at all clarified. Hungary was resounding with hundreds of popular songs known by everybody, regarded generally as folk songs. It is mostly this material which in foreign countries was regarded as Hungarian folk music. But closer research turned out that many of those songs were relatively very new, composed by still living or recently dead composers. Some decades of field-work were necessary to probe that there is another folk song the authors of which will never be found. And this is the layer of the old tradition and it has taken much time to understand the difference.[6]

Sometimes folk song texts are not appropriate for school use. There are instances when the instructor can and should modify folk song texts. Kodály notes, "The folksong entitles us to exchange the text for another one, if it is less suitable for one reason or other. Such an intervention is quite justified, even desirable, if we want to save a melody that has a poor text, by finding a good one for it."[7]

In 1966 Kodály spoke about some of the difficulties American music educators face when selecting repertoire for music programs. In an address at the International Society for Music Education Conference held at Interlochen, Michigan, Kodály states:

> Now, I know, for Americans it is a difficult question, what is American folk song? I have just read some redlections [*sic*, reflections] about it by Bernstein. Bernstein talking about the multifarious ancestry of Americans asks, what, is it that we have in common, what we could

> call our folk music? He points out that America is a very young country, has not had very much time to develop a folk music, and since the Americans are descendants of all nations on the earth, its folk music is probably the richest in the world. . . . I think, since America is such a very big country, uniform American music will hardly ever exist. If little Hungary produced as many Hungarian styles as there are composers that may apply all the more to America.[8]

In other words, teachers may begin developing a curriculum based on songs of the cultural heritage of their community. Ideally, the music specialist should explore and research to find the most authentic folk music for their music curriculum. The ultimate task for the music specialist is the selection of quality materials. It is up to the music specialist to research and find the most authentic folk songs belonging to the child's culture.

Selecting the best teaching material from the vast folk repertoire involves selecting songs that are suitable for specific age levels. The text as well as the music must be interesting and comprehensible to the students. In the best folk songs there is a unity between the rhythm and melody; word and musical accents fall together logically. The body of songs selected for classroom use must include not only songs that incorporate musical elements for teaching but also songs for pleasure, seasonal songs, and songs that provide students an opportunity for artistic expression.

Folk Music of Closely Related Cultures

Music teachers in the United States often include a selection of Anglo-American, African-American, Hispanic, Asian-American, and Hebrew materials. Music of England, Ireland, Scotland, Wales, France, and Germany may be introduced because of its close connection with Anglo-American folk music. If teachers are working with a predominantly Latino population, music of Mexico, South and Central America, and Spain may form the basis of their curriculum.

The Role of Pentatonic Music

Kodály-inspired teaching appears to place an emphasis on pentatonic music in the primary grades. It is important to consider Kodály's rationale for the inclusion of pentatonic music in the music curriculum.

> Nowadays it is no longer necessary to explain why it is better to start teaching music to small children through the pentatonic tunes: first, it is easier to sing in tune with out having to use semitones (half -steps), second, the musical thinking and the ability to sound the notes can develop better using tunes which employ leaps rather than stepwise tunes based on the diatonic scale often used by the teacher.[9]

Kodály's ethnographic research and musicological investigations made it possible for him to determine the connection between art music and folk music.

> Finally, pentatony is an introduction to world literature: it is the key to many foreign world literatures, from the ancient Gregorian chant, through China to Debussy.[10]

> Nobody wants to stop at pentatony. But indeed, the beginning must be made there; on the one hand, in this way the child's biogenetical development is natural and, on the other, this is what is demanded by rational pedagogical sequence. Only in this way are we able to create in the child an impression of it which will last for a lifetime.[11]

The pentatonic scale most accessible to young students uses the first, second, third, fifth, and sixth degrees of the major scale. These notes create a major second or a minor third from each other. When considering solfège syllables, a pentatonic scale uses the notes *do, re, mi, so,* and *la.*

Selecting Folk Music for Classroom Use

The aforementioned considerations provide guiding principles concerning the types of musical materials we select for classroom use.

1. Songs must be of the highest musical quality.
2. Songs must have a musical appeal.
3. The text of the song and the music should complement each other; the rhythmic accent and melodic inflection should match the structure of the language.
4. Songs should be developmentally appropriate; songs should be relevant for specific age groups.
5. Selected songs should reflect the cultural backgrounds of students in your classroom.
6. Some songs should be selected for their pedagogical function.

Performance of Folk Music

It is important that music teachers remember that the music notation of a folk song only provides us with some clues as to how the song should be performed. To perform a folk song as authentically as possible, it is important to try and hear a recording of the song by a musician who is familiar with the style of the music. In this way the music instructor will better understand how to provide an authentic performance for their students. If it is not possible to listen to a recording of the folk song, try and memorize the song from the notation and then try to sing it without recourse to the notation. Sometimes folk songs are written using the wrong time signature. For example, there are songs that are notated in simple meter but would be better notated in compound meter. By singing the song several times, you will begin to get the "feel" for the melody and rhythm of the folksong. It is important to concentrate on the words of the song and how they "fit" with the melody.[12]

Song Repertoire

Music materials are critical to the success of a music curriculum. Both the instructor and students should enjoy the songs, games, and activities. Selected repertoire should include:

- Songs for singing, movement, and playing on instruments
- Songs for listening
- Songs for pedagogical use

Songs for Performance: Singing, Movement, and Playing on Instruments

Music curricula may include songs with no specific pedagogical purpose other than the enjoyment of singing. These songs may have little merit in terms of musical elements or concepts; they are simply fun to sing. Such songs often provide opportunities for solo singing as well as improvisation. In some songs, the students will be able to sing all verses while in others it might be appropriate for students to sing selected verses. When considering song materials for primary grades, instructors may also select repertoire for children appropriate for listening as well as songs that can be performed on instruments.

Songs for classroom use should include the following:

1. Children's games

    Nursery rhymes and songs
    Jump-rope games
    Counting out rhymes
    Lullabies
    Acting out games
    Wind-up games
    Circle games
    Choosing games
    Chase games/double chase games
    Partner games
    Double circle
    Line games
    Double line games
    Square games
    Play parties
    Ballads
    Folk dances

2. Composed music
3. Recently composed music

Kodály believed that composers should dedicate a portion of their creative efforts to composing music for children. "Original works are to be written, compositions starting from the child's soul, from the child's voice in text, tune and colour alike."[13] Kodály himself wrote numerous song arrangements, piano compositions, and singing exercises for children and adults, many of which are based on Hungarian folk music.

> We have very few pentatonic folksongs of sufficiently limited compass and rhythm. For this reason smaller children need tunes written in the spirit of folksongs but without their diffi-

culties. In such pieces, by making them into games, we can prepare the ground for the genuine folksongs. With much the same object in view I wrote 333 Elementary Exercises, where most of the pieces can be used as tunes for marching and so on.[14]

Songs for Listening

Songs selected for listening activities function as an important part of the music curriculum. Songs used for listening in primary grades may be reintroduced in the upper elementary grades for teaching musical concepts. Although intended for listening, it may be appropriate to accompany some of these songs with simple rhythm instruments.

Songs for Pedagogical (Classroom) Use

This category of songs is included in the curriculum not just because they are beautiful examples of music; additionally they can be used to teach rhythmic or melodic elements. See Houlahan and Tacka, *Sound Thinking: Music for Sight-Singing and Ear Training,* vols. 1 and 2 (New York: Boosey & Hawkes).

Creating an Alphabetized Song Repertoire List for Each Grade

Based on the above criteria, we can compile a list of repertoire suitable for each grade, arrange the songs in alphabetical order, and perhaps include a rationale for selection of the song, tone set, and date taught. For example, we might have chosen a particular song not just because students will enjoy singing it but because it can also be used to reinforce a particular melodic or rhythmic concept or element. Include the source for the song and the type of game or movement activity associated with the song. This information may be organized in chart form as shown in table 3.1.

Table 3.1 Headings for an alphabetized song repertoire list

Song alphabetical listing	Date taught	Rationale	Game/movement	Source

The repertoire list should include songs that:

- Reflect the cultural diversity of the student population,
- Are appropriate for developing beautiful singing,
- Develop music literacy skills,
- Develop listening skills,
- Are suitable for creative activities such as improvisation and composition,
- Are appropriate for holidays and special events.

Appendix 2 includes a suggested repertoire of songs for each grade level.

Analyzing Song Repertoire

Analysis (the examination of a song's phrase structure, rhythmic and melodic content, and thematic elements) helps determine how a song may be used in a curriculum. Analysis enables us to see pedagogical implications within a body of song repertoire.

The following is a sample of a simplified analysis sheet that may be used for analyzing songs (figs. 3.1 and 3.2 and table 3.2). After analyzing your repertoire, you may construct a database or retrieval system using the information from the analysis of your songs to help you plan. The reader is encouraged to view the database of folk songs made available by the Kodály Program at Holy Names University in Oakland, California. (See http://www.kodaly.hnu.edu/).

Song Title: *Who's That Tapping at the Window?*

Origin: African-American

Comfortable Starting Pitch: F

Metronome Marking: 110

Figure 3.1 Staff notation for *Who's That Tapping at the Window*

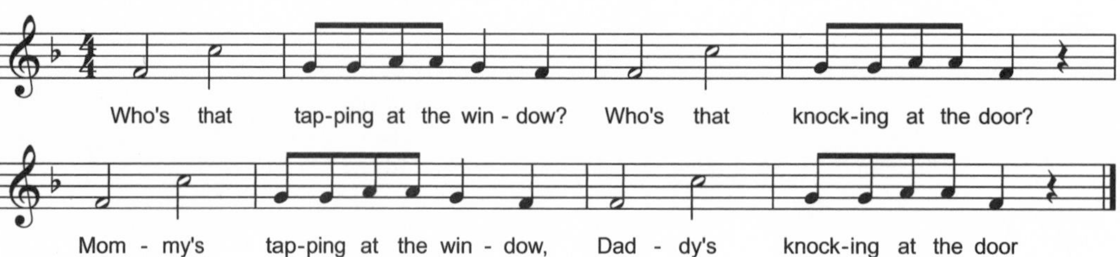

Figure 3.2 Stick notation for *Who's That Tapping at the Window*

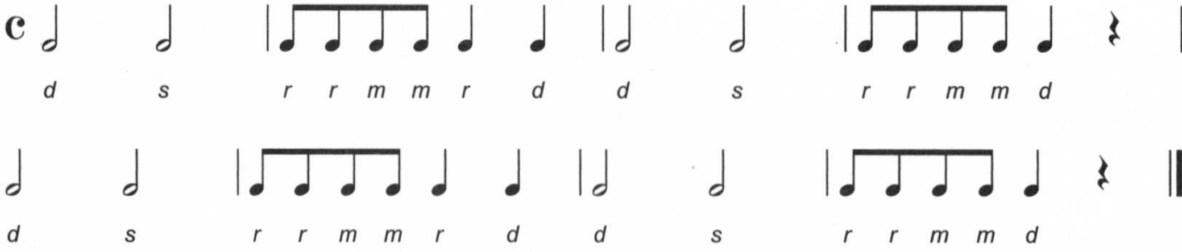

Table 3.2 Analysis sheet for songs

Analysis	**Pedagogical Use**
Tone set: ***do*** *re mi so*	Rationale: $\frac{4}{4}$ Meter *do–so* interval and *so–re* interval Half note preparation and practice
Rhythm: ♪, ♩, 𝄽𝅗𝅥	
Melodic form: A A	Connections to curriculum areas:
Game: Choosing game or voice identification 1. Have the children sit in a circle. 2. One child is selected to sit in the middle of the circle in a way that he or she cannot see who will be singing. 3. Everyone sings the first verse. 4. One child will answer back with, "I am tapping at the window. I am knocking at the door." 5. The child in the middle now needs to guess who was singing.	Text improvisation
Other:	Other: solo singing; playing a *do–so* ostinato on bells or xylophone.

Source: Peter Erdei et al., *150 American Folk Songs to Sing, Read and Play*. (New York: Boosey & Hawkes, 1985), 7.

Song Analysis Definitions

Name of the Song

Write the title of your song for inclusion in your retrieval system. It is usually best not to include articles such as "The" or "A" at the beginning of the title when you are putting this into your retrieval system for alphabetical purposes.

Origin

This category is for listing the ethnic origin of the song, geographic location, or any historical connections, for example, Hispanic folk song, Jamaican folk song, Civil War era, and so on.

Comfortable Starting Pitch (CSP)

Some song collections are written so that all songs in the collection end on the same pitch, G. Ethnomusicologists adopt this approach to notating songs so that it is easier to compare different variations of the same song. In this case, it is necessary to indicate the comfortable starting pitch to pitch the song in the best singing range for your students. If the song is written in a comfortable range for your students, then you do not need to indicate the comfortable starting pitch. Some ethnomusicologists don't use a key signature when notating songs. For example a song could be in the key of G major but since it does not include the seventh degree note then the key signature of F sharp is not included.

Metronome Marking

Indicate an appropriate metronome marking for performing the piece of music.

Staff Notation

Write the song on the page so that each phrase is on the next staff, so a four phrase song takes four lines. It is preferable to write the song phrase by phrase, as this allows you to see the structural similarities.

Stick Notation

Write the song in stick notation (traditional rhythmic notation without note heads on quarter and eighth notes; include the note heads for half and whole notes. For analysis purposes, it is sometimes easier to analyze songs written in stick notation. Clearly, it helps to see motives in solfège. Again, it is preferable to write the stick notation phrase by phrase.

Analysis and Pedagogical Use

You will notice that at the end of the analysis sheet for each song there are two sections: analysis and pedagogical (classroom) use. On our analysis sheet the following categories appear: tone set, rhythm, melodic form, game, rationale, connections to curriculum areas, other, and source.

Tone Set

This is sometimes referred to as pitch class set or scale. We use relative solfège syllables to indicate the notes of the tone set. Tone sets are written in ascending order. Write solfège syllables in lower case and italicized. When identifying notes below *do* use a subscript mark (*so,*), and notes above *ti* are marked with a superscript (*do'*). Underline or circle the final note to indicate the tonic of the song.

There are three different scale types: pentatonic, diatonic, and non-traditional used in folk song repertoire. We are only focusing on pentatonic and diatonic scale types.

Pentatonic Scales

The pentatonic scale is made of notes that emphasize intervals of a major second, perfect fourth, and minor third. In its simplest form, notes of the pentatonic system include *do–re–mi–so–la.* They can also be rearranged to fit a circle of fifths order: *do–so–re–la–mi.* Notes may appear in any octave.

Songs that contain all the notes of the pentatonic scale and end on *do* are called *do* pentatonic or major pentatonic. Songs that contain all the notes of the pentatonic scale and end on *la* are called *la* pentatonic or minor pentatonic. Accordingly, if a song ends on *re* it is called *re* pentatonic, and so on.

Figure 3.3 *Rocky Mountain* in *do* pentatonic scale

Figure 3.4 *Sioux Indian Lullabye* in *la* pentatonic scale

Naming Subset Scales of the Pentatonic Scale

In general, we use Latin prefixes to identify the number of different pitches in a melody or scale. Part one of the name is derived from the solfège syllable used to describe the final note of the song. Part two of the name uses Latin prefixes to identify the number of different pitches, for example, bi = two pitches, tri = three pitches, tetra = four pitches, penta = five pitches, hexa = six pitches. Ignore octave duplications when determining the number of pitches in the tone set.

Melodies that do contain fewer than the five pitches of the pentatonic may be considered subsets of the pentatonic scale. These melodies can be analyzed using three different methods. Method one is commonly used by Kodály teachers in the United States but Method two, while more complicated to apply, can be more effective for labeling different kinds of subsets of the pentatonic scale. Method three is a modification of Method two.

Method One

In this method,[15] we use the word *chord* to describe pitches that are adjacent; we use the word *tonic* to describe a skip between one note and another one. For example, a melody containing *mi–so* can be referred to as a bitonic scale or a child's chant. *See Saw* is an example of a bitonic melody.

Figure 3.5 *See Saw*—pentatonic bichord

A melody containing *do–re* can be described as a bichord scale or bichordal melody.

A melody containing *mi–so–la* can be described as a tritonic. The traditional children's chant *Lucy Locket* is an example of a tritonic melody or can be referred to as a child's chant.

Figure 3.6 *Lucy Locket*—pentatonic trichord

A melody containing *do–re–mi* is an example of a trichord. *Hot Cross Buns* is an example.

Figure 3.7 *Hot Cross Buns*—trichord

A melody containing *do–re–mi–so* can be described as a *do* tetratonic. *Dinah* is an example.

Figure 3.8 *Dinah—do* pentatonic tetrachord

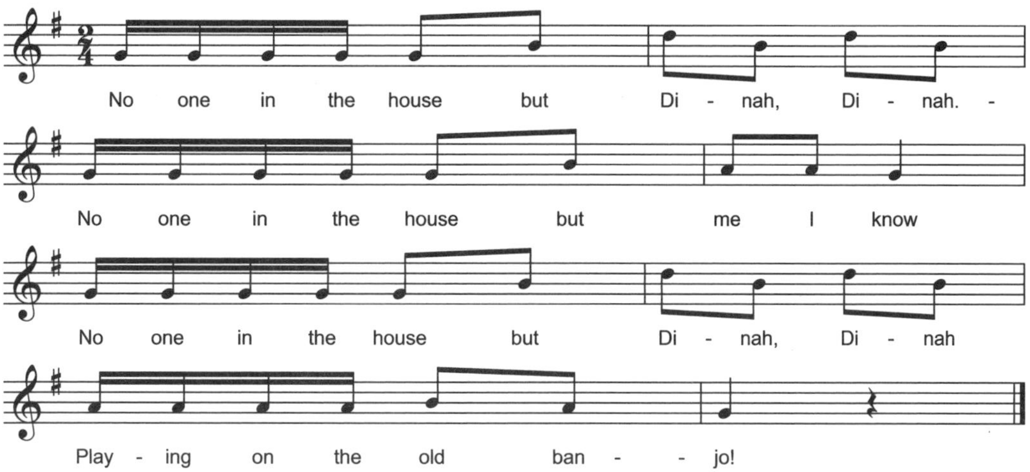

A melody containing *la,–do–re–mi* and ends on *la,* is a *la* tetratonic. *Skin and Bones* is an example.

Figure 3.9 *Skin and Bones—la* pentatonic tetrachord

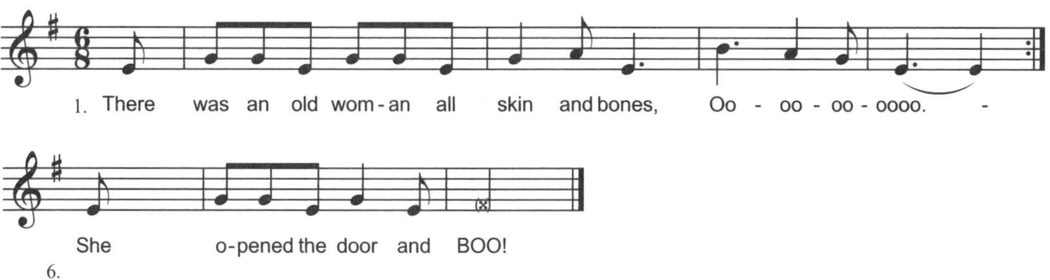

Method Two

Songs[16] containing *so–mi* and *la–so–mi* are commonly referred to as a child's chant. Songs that are composed of two notes that follow each other in the circle of fifths order of the pentatonic scale are called *bitonic.* Songs containing low *so,–do* are called *bitonic. La patita* and *A don chin chino* are examples of bitonic melodies.

Figure 3.10 *La patita—*

Figure 3.11 *A don chin chino—*

Songs that are composed of three notes that follow each other in the circle of fifths order of the pentatonic system are called *tritonic do–so–re; so,–do–re; Santo Domingo* is a *do* tritonic melody.

Figure 3.12 *Santo Domingo—do* tritonic plagal range

Note that the tone set for this melody is *so,–do–re* and *do* is the tonic note.

Songs that are composed of four notes that follow each other in the circle of fifths order of the pentatonic system are called tetratonic.

When the notes of a tone set do not follow the circle of fifths order, the following names may be used. In this case the lowest note in the tone set should be the tonal center of the folk song. Songs that are composed of two notes within the pentatonic system are called *pentatonic bichords. See Saw* is an example of a pentatonic bichord melody.

Figure 3.13 *See Saw—so–mi* pentatonic bichord

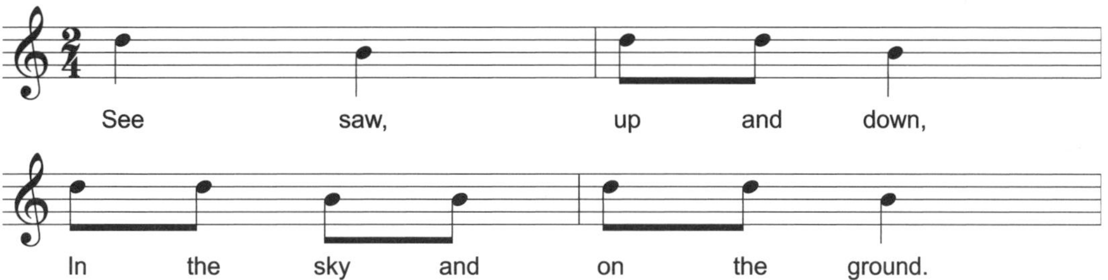

Songs that are composed of three notes within the pentatonic system are called pentatonic *trichords. Bounce High* is an example of a pentatonic trichord melody.

Figure 3.14 *Bounce High—la–so–mi* pentatonic trichord

Songs that are composed of four notes within the pentatonic system are called *pentatonic tetrachords. Dinah* is an example of a *do* pentatonic tetrachord.

Figure 3.15 *Dinah—do* pentatonic tetrachord

Skin and Bones is an example of a *la* pentatonic tetrachord.

Figure 3.16 *Skin and Bones—la* pentatonic tetrachord

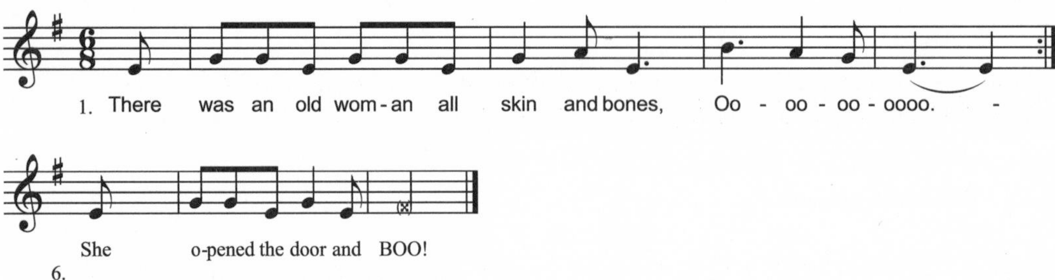

If songs having notes of the pentatonic scale do not fit the above criteria, then we can label them as *incomplete pentatonic scales. Lonesome Road* is an example of an incomplete *do* pentatonic scale.

Figure 3.17 *Lonesome Road*—incomplete *do* pentatonic scale

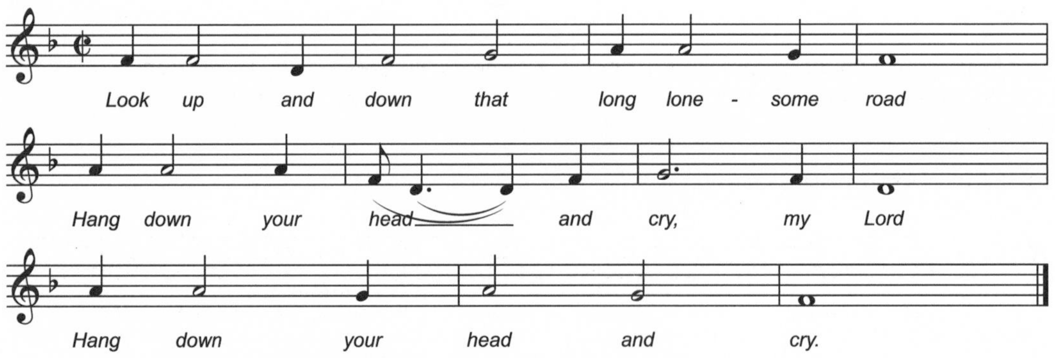

Method Three

In this method, we use the words *pentatonic* and *chord* to describe pitches. For example, a melody containing *mi–so* can be referred to as a pentatonic bichord or a child's chant. *See Saw* is an example of a pentatonic bichord. A melody containing *do–re* can be described as a bichordal melody. A melody containing *mi–so–la* can be described as a pentatonic trichord. The traditional children's chant *Lucy Locket* is an example of a pentatonic trichord melody or can be referred to as a child's chant.

A melody containing *do–re–mi* is an example of a trichord. *Hot Cross Buns* is an example.

A melody containing *do–re–mi–so* can be described as a *do pentatonic* tetrachord. *Dinah* is an example.

A melody containing *la,–do–re–mi* and ends on *la,* is a *la pentatonic* tetrachord. *Skin and Bones* is an example.

Diatonic Scales

Major Scale

The notes of a major diatonic scale include *do–re–mi–fa–so–la–ti–do'. Alleluia* is an example of a major diatonic scale melody.

Figure 3.18 *Alleluia*—major diatonic scale

Minor

The notes of a minor diatonic scale include *la,–ti,–do–re–mi–fa–so–la.* This is referred to as the *natural* minor scale. *Hushabye* is an example of a minor diatonic melody.

Figure 3.19 *Hushabye*—natural minor scale

If using the harmonic minor, then *so* is raised to *si;* if using melodic minor, then *fa* and *so* are raised to *fi–si* ascending and *fa–so* descending.

The following are subsets of the diatonic scale. When there are three adjacent notes within a diatonic scale, we call it a trichord. In a major scale *do re mi* is a *do* trichord; *la ti do'* is a *la* trichord. Four adjacent notes are labeled a tetrachord. In a major scale *do re mi fa* is a *do* tetrachord; *la ti do re* is a *la* tetrachord. Five adjacent notes are labeled a pentachord. In a major scale *do re mi fa so* is a *do* pentachord; *la ti do re mi* is a *la* pentachord. Six adjacent notes are a hexachord. In a major scale *do re mi fa so la* is a *do* hexachord; *la ti do re mi fa* is a *la* hexachord.

do trichord *do re mi*
do tetrachord *do re mi fa*
do pentachord *do re mi fa so*
do hexachord *do re mi fa so la*

la trichord *la ti do,*
la tetrachord *la ti do re*
la pentachord *la ti do re mi*
la hexachord *la ti do re mi fa*

Aunt Rhody is an example of a *do* pentachord.

Figure 3.20 *Aunt Rhody—do* pentachord

Twinkle, Twinkle Little Star is an example of a *do* hexachord.

Figure 3.21 *Twinkle, Twinkle Little Star—do* hexachord

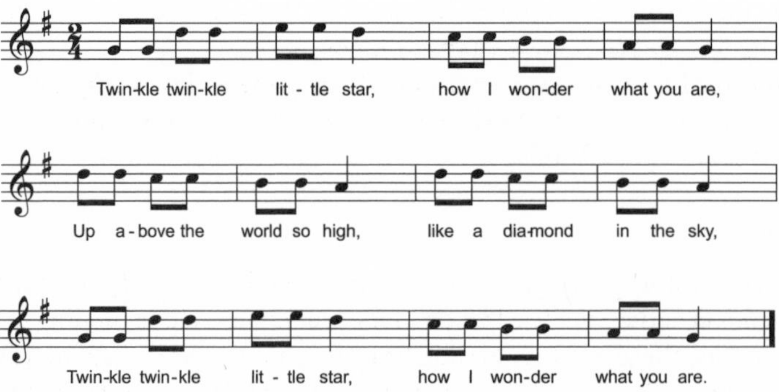

Modal Scales

Modal scales are composed of the tone sets *do re mi fa so la ti* but have different ending notes. The following chart indicates the connection between the ending note and the modal scale name.

Ending Note	*Modal Scale Name*
do	Ionian/Major
re	Dorian (also sung with *la* plus *fi*)
mi	Phrygian (also *la* and *ta*)
fa	Lydian (*do* plus *fi*)
so	Mixolydian (*do* plus *ta*)
la	Aeolian/Minor
ti	Locrian

The Difference between a Major Scale and the Ionian Mode

When a song ends on *do* and notes of the melody outline triads, we usually refer to the song as being related to the major scale. When a song ends on *do* and the melody moves in steps, we may refer to the melody as being related to the Ionian mode.

The Difference between a Minor Scale and the Aeolian Mode

When a song ends on *la,* and notes of the melody outline triads, we usually refer to the song as being related to the minor scale. When a song ends on *la,* and the melody moves in steps, we can refer to the song as being related to the Aeolian mode.

Modes and Their Comparative Scale Names

When we sing a Dorian, Ionian, Aeolian, Mixolydian, or Lydian modal scales from the same pitch, we can classify each mode as either major-like or minor-like. This classification is dependent on the interval between the root and the third of the mode.

For example, Mixolydian mode begins *so–la–ti.* The distance between *so* and *ti* is a major third. Because the Mixolydian mode has a major third between the root (*so*) and the third (*ti*) we designate Mixolydian mode as a major mode.

The Dorian mode begins *re–mi–fa.* The distance between *re* and *fa* is a minor third. Because the Dorian mode has a minor third between the root (*re*) and the third (*fa*), we designate Dorian mode as a minor mode.

Major Modal Scales

Ionian mode is clearly a major mode because it begins and ends on *do* and the half steps occur between *mi–fa* and *ti–do'.* The Lydian mode is another major sounding mode. There are two ways to use solfège syllables to sing the Lydian mode. The Lydian mode may be sung without altering solfège syllables when sung from *fa–fa.* Because the first three notes on the Lydian mode are major seconds, the Lydian mode may also be sung beginning on *do* and ending on *do'* if we raise the fourth degree a half step.

Figure 3.22 Lydian mode

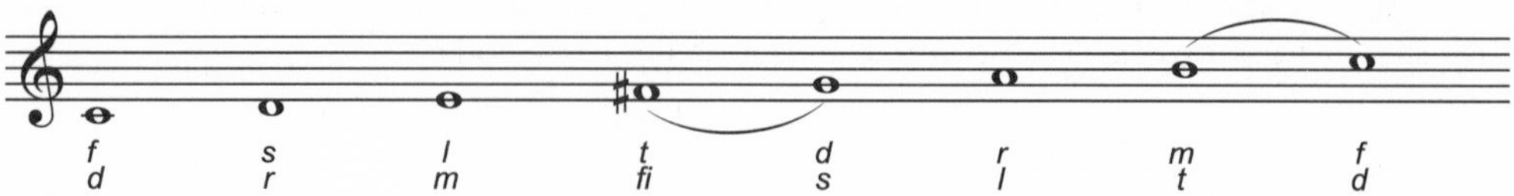

Mixolydian mode is another major sounding scale because the first six notes of the Mixolydian mode match the major scale structure; in Mixolydian mode the seventh degree is lowered. For that reason, the Mixolydian mode may be sung from *so–so* using solfège syllables or from *do–do* using the lowered seventh degree. *Old Joe Clark* is an example of a melody in the Mixolydian mode.

Figure 3.23 Mixolydian mode

Figure 3.24 *Old Joe Clark*

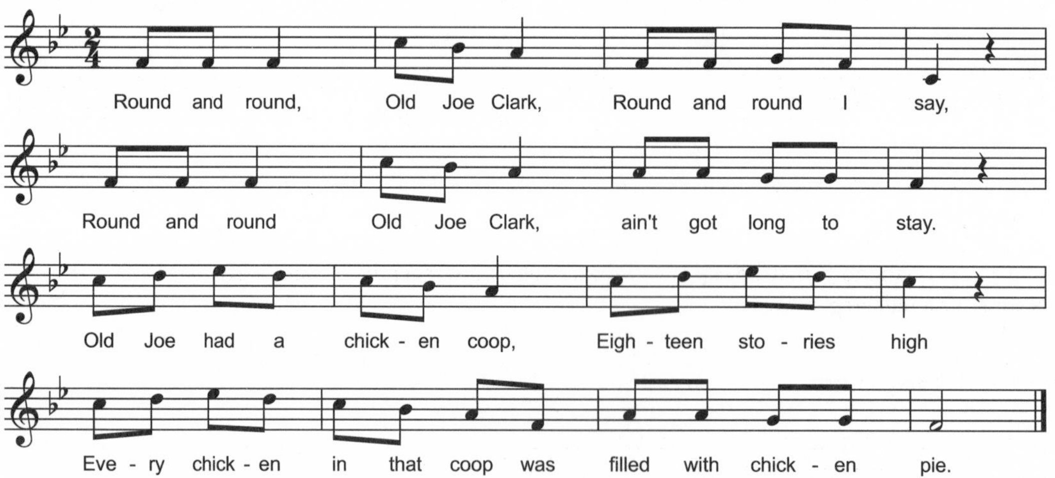

Minor Modal Scales

Aeolian mode is clearly a minor mode because it begins and ends on *la* and the half steps occur between *ti–do* and *mi–fa*. The Dorian mode is another minor sounding mode. There are two ways to use solfège syllables to sing the Dorian mode. The Dorian mode may be sung without altering solfège syllables when sung from *re–re*. Because the first three notes on the Dorian mode consist of a major second followed by a minor second, the Dorian mode may also be sung beginning on *la* and ending on *la* if we raise the sixth degree a half step. *Scarborough Fair* is an example of a Dorian mode melody.

Figure 3.25 Dorian mode

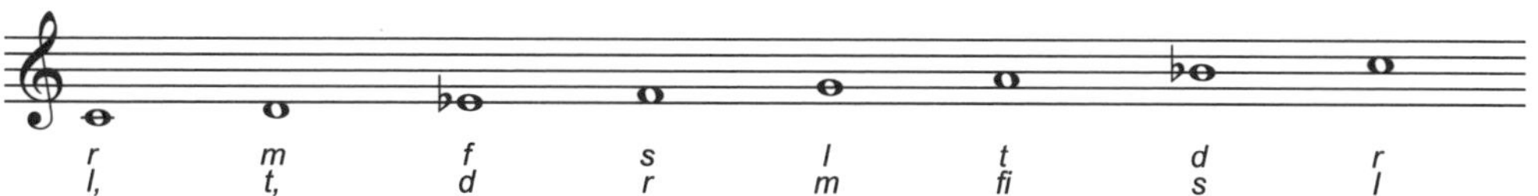

Figure 3.26 *Scarborough Fair*

Phrygian Mode

The Phrygian mode may be sung as a minor scale by lowering the second degree of the minor scale a half step.

Figure 3.27 Phrygian scale

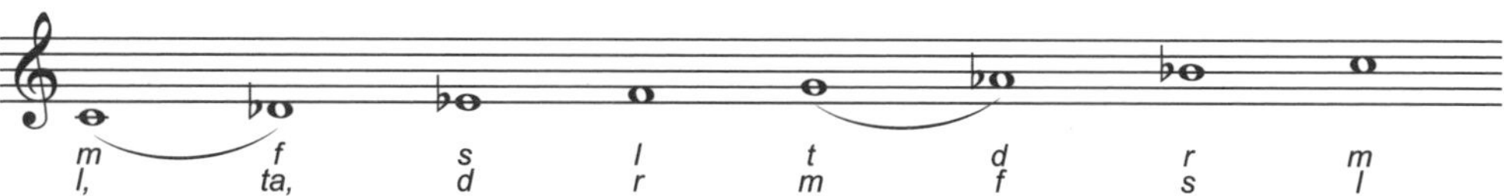

We can also have incomplete forms of the above scales as well.

Range of Notes

You may wish to indicate the range of the notes of a composition. The final note is indicated with 1. Notes above the final are written using Arabic numbers and notes below the final are written using Roman numerals. For the sake of simplicity and comparing variations of the same folk songs we use the diatonic scale system for describing the range of notes in the pentatonic system. For example, in a major pentatonic melody where the tone set is *do re mi so la* the range of the notes is 1–6 even though there are only five notes.

Rhythm

This section is for listing the specific note values and rests (such as quarter notes, half notes, and so on) from the smallest to largest note value. You may also include the meter of the song as well as whether the song has upbeats. Target rhythmic motives (usually found in four-beat patterns) may also be included in this category.

The rhythmic form of a song may be different from the melodic form. *Isorhythmic* refers to phrases having the same rhythm. *Heterorhythmic* refers to phrases of a song that are different.

Podia refer to the number of rhythmic stresses within a phrase. We use the terms *bipodic* to describe two stresses within a phrase; *tripodic* to describe three stresses within a phrase; or *tetrapodic* to describe four stresses within a phrase. When a song has the same number of stresses per phrase we can refer to this as *isopodic;* when a song has a different number of stresses in each phrase we refer to this as *heteropodic.* Normally the number of stresses in a phrase equates to the number of measures in a phrase.

Melodic Form

Indicate the form of phrases using letters. When a phrase is four beats in length, use capital letters. For phrases or motifs that are less than four beats, use lower case letters. Variants of phrases may be indicated with a subscript "v," for example, AAv. Use a superscript with a number to indicate sequences occurring in a folk song or songs containing transpositions of phrases: AA^5A^5vA. Some ethnomusicologists prefer to use lower case to identify musical phrases and upper case to identify large sections.

Game

Describe the type of game (circle, double circle, partner, double line, etc.). You might also describe the category of song, such as a holiday song or work song.

Analysis: Other

This will allow you to note anything interesting about the song. For example, does the song have a sequence or repeated phrase where a repeat sign might be used?

Rationale

This is where we indicate the pedagogical purpose for using the song. A song can be used for many reasons including singing, teaching a game, performing on an instrument, as the basis of an improvisation exercise, for noting a specific form, listening, or teaching a rhythmic or melodic element. When we teach a melodic or rhythmic element we use three phases of learning: preparation, presentation, and practice. During the preparation stage, we teach a variety of songs that include the rhythmic or melodic element to be taught. For teaching elementary music literacy skills, we isolate the new rhythmic or melodic element usually in a four-beat motif noting the placement of the new element within the four-beat motif. The most common occurrence of the new element on a particular beat is referred to as the target pattern. The song containing the target pattern is referred to as the focus song. Refer to appendix 3 for each musical element, song repertoire, a focus song, the target pattern, and additional patterns (related patterns) associated with the new element are listed.

Connections to Curriculum Areas

This category is useful for integrating music into additional areas of the school curriculum. Indicate connections to literacy or other subject areas, for example, "work songs" or "Civil War songs" may be linked to particular eras in a social studies curriculum.

Pedagogical Use: Other

Indicate whether the song is appropriate for movement or improvisation, form, and so on. Sometimes you might want to list a listening example that could be connected to this folk song. You may wish to note any melodic and rhythmic difficulties students could encounter in learning the song.

Source

Source refers to the resource where the song was found. Generally speaking, it is important to list whether the source is a primary or secondary source. It is also useful to include references to other variations of the folk song.

Developing a Lesson Plan Framework Based on Quality Musical Repertoire

As a result of the information presented in this chapter, the following points may be considered for inclusion into our lesson plan:

1. Selection of song materials that are age appropriate for singing
2. Selection of song materials that can be used for music literacy development
3. Selection of movement and game activities that are age appropriate
4. Selection of appropriate song materials for listening.

We have provided a selection of appropriate song materials in appendix 2.

Table 3.3 Lesson plan framework incorporating repertoire

Focus	Activities, Procedures, and Assessments
Introduction	
Performance and demonstration of known musical concepts and elements	Students demonstrate their prior knowledge of known repertoire and musical elements through performance of songs **selected from the alphabetized repertoire list**
Core Activities	
Acquisition of repertoire	**New song selected from the alphabetized repertoire list** that expands students' repertoire or prepares for the learning of a music rhythmic or melodic concept of element
Performance and preparation of a new concept or element	Learning activities in which a new musical concept or element is prepared through known songs **found in the alphabetized repertoire list**
Movement development	Focus on the sequential development of age-appropriate movement skills through songs and folks games **found in the games section of the alphabetized list of songs**
Performance and musical skill development	Students reinforce their knowledge of musical concepts and elements working on the skill areas of form, memory, inner hearing, ensemble work, improvisation and composition and listening through **known songs found in the alphabetized repertoire list**
Closure Review and summation	Review of lesson content and the instructor may perform the next new song to be learned in a subsequent lesson **found in the alphabetized repertoire list**

Using a Generic Lesson Plan Format to Design a Preparation/Practice Lesson

The generic plan can now be adopted and adapted for developing a lesson plan that prepares the teaching of a new concept or element as well as practices a familiar element. Generally speaking, we try to develop children's rhythmic and melodic abilities in one lesson. When we are preparing a rhythmic element in the first part of a lesson, we practice a melodic element in the second part of a lesson. If we are preparing a melodic element in the first part of a lesson, we practice a rhythmic element in the second part of a lesson.

During the performance and preparation section of a lesson, we enable students to discover the concept behind a new element. For example, if we want to teach the musical elements of quarter and eighth notes, students must be guided to understand the concept of one or two sounds on a beat.

During the performance and musical skill development section of the lesson the instructor reinforces and further develops students' understanding of previously learned musical elements through a variety of musical skills. (Of course, the skills area can also be practiced during any section of the lesson plan.) This section of the lesson plan may also include assessment activities to help the instructor identify students who may require extra help.

In this lesson we continue to develop singing abilities, teach new repertoire, and develop movement skills and listening skills of students. Each preparation/practice lesson has an instructional context (preparation) and a reinforcement (practice) context. During the preparation/practice lesson, we do not name the new concept or element but provide opportunities for music students to discover the attributes of the new concept or element being studied. This dual structure of the preparation/practice lesson provides students with the time to process their understandings of the new concept, while providing opportunities to further develop their musical skills with the previously learned musical element. This is crucial for building the positive self-esteem and enjoyment needed for learning to take place.

In the close of the lesson we can review the new song. Students may review known songs or play a game. The instructor may also perform the next new song to be learned in a subsequent lesson.

In the lesson plans provided in this chapter and subsequent chapters, we focus on the structure of the lesson plan. We emphasize the sections of the lessons that we modify and develop.

Table 3.4 Sample preparation/practice lesson plan

Focus	Activities, Procedures, and Assessments
Introduction	
Performance and demonstration of known musical concepts and elements	Students demonstrate their prior knowledge of repertoire and musical elements through performance of known songs selected from the alphabetized repertoire list
Core activities	
Acquisition of repertoire	**New song** selected from the alphabetized repertoire list that expands students' repertoire or prepares the future learning of a music rhythmic or melodic concept of element. **Instructional context: When we are preparing a rhythmic element, the new song should be selected to prepare the next melodic element. When we are preparing a melodic element, the new song should be selected to prepare the next rhythmic element.**
Performance and preparation of a new concept or element	Learning activities in which students are taught a new musical concept or element through known songs found in the alphabetized repertoire list. **When preparing a rhythmic element, the second part of the lesson practices a melodic element. When preparing a melodic element, the second part of the lesson practices a rhythmic element.**
Movement development	Known song or game found in the alphabetized repertoire list Focus on the sequential development of age-appropriate movement skills through songs and folks games

continued

Table 3.4 *Continued*

Focus	Activities, Procedures, and Assessments
Performance and musical skill development	Students reinforce their knowledge of musical concepts and elements working on the skill areas of form, memory, inner hearing, ensemble work, improvisation and composition and listening through known songs found in the alphabetized repertoire list. **When practicing a rhythmic element, the first part of the lesson prepares a melodic element. When practicing a melodic element the first part of the lesson prepares a rhythmic element.**
Closure	
Review and summation	Review of lesson content and the instructor may perform the next new song to be learned in a subsequent lesson found in the alphabetized repertoire list

Developing a Presentation Lesson Plan Framework Based on Quality Musical Repertoire

As a result of the information presented in this chapter, the following points may be considered for inclusion into our Presentation lesson plan:

1. Selection of song materials that are age appropriate for singing.
2. Selection of song materials that can be used for presenting concepts or elements.
3. Selection of movement and game activities that are age appropriate.
4. Selection of appropriate song materials for listening.

Using a Generic Lesson Plan Format to Design a Presentation Lesson

The generic plan can now be adopted and adapted for developing a presentation lesson plan that presents the name of the new concept or element. The introduction of the lesson and the teaching of the new song repertoire in core activities is exactly like the preparation lesson.

Instead of the performance and preparation section of a lesson, we now have the performance and presentation section where we label the new element with solfège or rhythm syllables and present the notation for the new element. After this section, we have the movement section which is similar to the preparation lesson. After the movement section, we now have another performance and presentation section where we label the new element with rhythm or solfège syllables in another song and show the notation for the new element. In the close of the lesson, we can review the new song. Students may then review known songs or play a game. The instructor may also perform a new song to be learned in a subsequent lesson.

In this lesson we continue to develop singing abilities, teach new repertoire, and develop movement skills and listening skills of students.

Table 3.5 Sample presentation lesson plan

Focus	**Activities, Procedures, and Assessments**
Introduction	
Performance and demonstration of known musical concepts and elements	Students demonstrate their prior knowledge of repertoire and musical elements including the new musical element to be presented through performance of songs selected from the alphabetized repertoire list
Core activities	
Acquisition of repertoire	**New song** selected from the alphabetized repertoire list that expands students' repertoire or prepares for the learning of a music rhythmic or melodic concept of element. Instructional context: When we are preparing a rhythmic element, the new song should be selected to prepare the next melodic element. When we are preparing a melodic element, the new song should be selected to prepare the next rhythmic element.
Performance and presentation/labeling of rhythm/solfège syllables or notation for the new element in the focus pattern	**Music instructor first labels the name of the new musical element with rhythm or solfège syllables and secondly presents the notation for the focus pattern**
Movement development	**Known song** or game found in the alphabetized repertoire list Focus on the sequential development of age-appropriate movement skills through songs and folks games
Performance and presentation/labeling of rhythm/solfège syllables or notation for the new element in the focus pattern	**Music instructor first labels the name of the new musical element with rhythm or solfège syllables and secondly presents the notation in a related pattern**
Closure	
Review and summation	Review of lesson content and the instructor may perform the next new song to be learned in a subsequent lesson found in the alphabetized repertoire list

Discussion Questions

1. How is an alphabetized repertoire list useful for teaching?
2. What kinds of repertoire should be included in an alphabetized repertoire list?
3. What criteria do we use for selecting repertoire for an elementary music curriculum?
4. Talk to a reading specialist or kindergarten or pre-kindergarten teacher and ask them to explain how they select books to read to their students. Make a list of all of their suggestions and try to draw a parallel between selecting books for use in the classroom and selecting musical repertoire.

5. What does an analysis of a folk song entail?
6. How important is it to think about the quality of the song material you use when teaching?
7. How can we further develop a lesson plan framework based on the selection of musical repertoire?
8. Discuss each section of a preparation/practice lesson plan.
9. Discuss each section of a presentation lesson plan.

› Ongoing Assignment

1. For your teaching portfolio sing through a selection of the songs in the alphabetized list of songs. Provide a sample analysis of several songs.
2. Interview a Kodály music teacher and ask him or her to share with you how he or she chooses song material for the classroom. Begin to compile your own lists of songs to include in your teaching portfolio based on the selection criteria outlined in this chapter.
3. Using the lesson plan formats provided in this chapter, create a lesson plan where you prepare a rhythmic element and practice a melodic element for grade one and grade three.

References

Anderson, William M., and Patricia Shehan Campbell, eds. *Multicultural Perspectives in Music Education.* Reston, Va.: Music Educators National Conference, 1996.

Choksy, Lois, and David Brummitt. *120 Singing Games and Dances for Elementary Schools.* Englewood Cliffs, N.J.: Prentice Hall, 1987.

Nettl, Bruno. *Folk and Traditional Music of the Western Continents.* 2nd ed. Englewood Cliffs, N.J.: Prentice Hall, 1991.

Nettl, Bruno, Charles Capwell, Philip V. Bohlman, Isabel K. F. Wong, and Thomas Turino. *Excursions in World Music.* 3rd ed. Englewood Cliffs, N.J.: Prentice Hall, 2000.

Shehan Campbell, Patricia, Sue Williamson, and Pierre Perron. *Songs from Singing Cultures.* Miami: Warner Bros. Publications, 1996.

Catalogues

The Whole Folkways Catalog (a catalog of historic folkways recordings). Smithsonian/Folkways, Center for Folklife Programs and Cultural Studies, 955 L'Enfant Plaza, Suite 2600, Smithsonian Institution, Washington, DC 20560; (202) 287-3262.

World Music Press (a catalog of world music resources). West Music, 1208 Fifth Street, P.O. Box 5521, Coralville, IA 52241.

Internet resource: *http://kodaly.hnu.edu/.* See the American Folk Song Collection.

Selected Folk Music Bibliography

Abrahams, Roger, and George Foss. *A Singer and Her Songs: Almeda Riddle's Book of Ballads.* Baton Rouge: Louisiana State University Press, 1970.

Ames, L. D. *Missouri Play Party. Journal of American Folklore.* Vol. 24, 1937.

Armitage, Theresa. *Our First Music.* Boston: C. C. Birchard, 1941.

Arnold, Byron. *Folksongs of Alabama.* Birmingham: University of Alabama Press, 1950.

Asch, Moses. *104 Folk Songs.* New York: Robbins Music Corp., 1964.

Baez, Joan. *The Joan Baez Songbook.* New York: Ryerson Music Publishers, 1964.

Beckwith, Martha W. *Folk Songs of Jamaica.* Vassar College: Folklore Publications, 1922.

Bierhorst, John. *A Cry from the Earth: Music of the North American Indians.* New York: Four Winds Press, 1979.

———. *Songs of the Chippewa.* New York: Farrar Strauss & Giroux, 1974.

Botkin, Benjamin A. *The American Play Party.* New York: Frederick Ungar, 1963; 1st ed. University of Nebraska Press, 1937.

Botsford, Florence H. *Songs of the Americas.* New York: G. Schimer, 1930.

Boyer, Walter E., et al. *Songs of the Mahatongo.* Lancaster: Pennsylvania Folklore Center, 1951.

Broadwood, Lucy E. *English Country Songs.* London: Boosey, 1893.

Bronson, B. H. *The Singing Tradition of Child's Popular Ballads.* Princeton: Princeton University Press, 1976.

Brown, Florence W., and Neva L Boyd. *Old English and American Games for School and Playground.* Chicago: Soul Brothers, 1915.

Brown, Frank C. *Collection of North American Folklore.* Durham, N.C.: Duke University Press, 1962.

———. *North Carolina Folklore.* Durham, N.C.: Duke University Press, 1962.

Burlin, Natalie C. *Negro Folk-Songs.* New York: Schirmer, 1918.

Burton, Thomas G., and Ambrose N. Manning. *East Tennessee State University Collection of Folklore: Folksongs.* Institute of Regional Studies, Monograph #4, East Tennessee State University Press: Johnson, TN, 1967.

Chappell, Louis W. *Folk Songs of Roanoke and the Albemafe.* Morganstown, W.Va.: Ballard Press, 1939.

Chase, Richard. *American Folk Tales and Songs.* New York: Dover, 1971.

Colcord, Joanna. *Roll and Go.* Indianapolis: Bobbs-Merril, 1924.

———. *Songs of American Sailormen.* New York: Oak Publications, 1964.

Coleman, Satis N. *Songs of American Folks.* New York: John Day, 1942.

Courlander, Harold. *Negro Folk Music USA.* New York: Columbia University Press, 1963.

———. *Negro Songs from Alabama.* New York: Oak Publications, 1963.

Cox, John Harrington. *Traditional Ballads, Mainly from West Virginia.* New York: National Service Bureau, 1939.

Creighton, Helen. *Songs and Ballads from Nova Scotia.* New York: Dover, 1972.

Dallin, Leon, and Lynn Dallin. *Heritage Songster.* Dubuque, Ia.: W. C. Brown, 1966.

Dykema, Peter. *Twice 55 Games with Music.* Boston: Birchard, 1924.

Eddy, Mary O. *Ballads and Songs from Ohio.* Hatboro, Penn.: Folklore Associates, 1964.

Erdei, Ida, Faith Knowles, and Denise Bacon. *My Singing Bird,* vol. 2 of *150 American Folk Songs from the Anglo-American, African-American, English, Scottish and Irish Traditions.* Columbus, Ohio: The Kodály Center of America, 2002.

Erdei, Peter, and Katalin Komlos. *150 American Folk Song for Children to Sing and Play.* New York: Boosey & Hawkes, 1974.

———. *150 American Folk Songs to Sing, Read and Play,* ed. Peter Erdei and the staff of the Kodály Musical Training Institute. Collected principally by Katalin Komlós. New York: Boosey & Hawkes, 1985.

Farnsworth, Charles H., and Sharp, Cecil F. *Folk-Songs, Chanteys and Singing Games.* New York: H. W. Gray, 1916.

Fenner, T. P. *Religious Folk Songs of the Negro.* Hampton, Va.: Hampton Institute Press, 1909.
Fife, Austin E., and S. Alta. *Cowboy and Western Songs.* New York: Clarkson N. Potter, 1969.
———. *The Songs of the Cowboys.* Thorp Collection. New York: Clarkson N. Potter, 1966.
Fowke, Edith. *Sally Go Round the Sun.* Garden City, N.Y.: Doubleday, 1969.
Fowke, Edith, and Cazden, Norman. *Lumbering Songs from the North Woods.* Austin: University of Texas Press, for the American Folklore Society, 1970.
Gillington, Alice E. *Old Surrey Singing Games.* London: J. Curwen & Sons, 1909.
Glass, Paul. *Songs and Stories of the North American Indians.* New York: Grosset and Dunlop, 1968.
Gomme, Alice B., and Sharp, Cecil J. *Children's Singing Games.* London: Novello, 1912.
———. *Traditional Games on England, Scotland, and Ireland,* 2 vols. New York: Dover, 1964. 1st ed. 1894–1898.
Gordon, Dorothy. *Sing It Yourself.* New York: E. P. Dutton, 1928.
Greenleaf, Elisabeth B., and Mansfield, Grace Yarrow. *Ballads and Songs of Newfoundland.* Cambridge, Mass.: Harvard University Press, 1933.
Greig, Duncan. *Folk Song Collection I.* Aberdeen, Scotland: Aberdeen University Press, 1981.
Harlow, Frederick Pease. *Chanteying Aboard American Ships.* Barre, Mass.: Barre Gazette, 1962.
Henry, Millinger E. *Still More Ballads and Folk-Songs from the Southern Highlands. Journal of American Folklore.* Vol. 45, 1932.
Hofman, Charles. *American Indians Sing.* New York: John B. Day, 1967.
Hopekirk, Helen. *Seventy Scottish Folk Songs.* Boston: Oliver Ditson, 1905.
Hudson, Florence. *Songs of the Americas.* New York: G. Schirmer, 1922.
Hugill, Stan. *Shanties and Sailor's Songs.* New York: Frederick A. Praeger, 1969.
Ives, Burl. *The Burl Ives Song Book.* New York: Ballantine Books, 1953.
Jackson, Bruce. *Wake up, Dead Man.* Cambridge, Mass.: Harvard University Press, 1972.
Jackson, George Pullen. *Spiritual Folksongs of Early America.* New York: Augustin, 1937.
Johnson, Guy B. *Folk Culture on St. Helena Island, South Carolina.* Hatboro, Penn.: Folklore Associates, 1968.
Johnson, James Weldon, and J. Rosamund. *The Books of Negro Spirituals.* New York: Viking Compass Book, 1969. 1st ed. Viking Press, 1925.
Jones, Bessie, and Bess Lomax Hawes. *Step it Down.* New York: Harper and Row, 1972.
Karpeles, M. *Folksongs from Newfoundland.* London: Faber and Faber, 1971.
Katz, Fred. *The Social Implications of Early Negro Music in the US.* New York: Arno Press, 1963.
Kennedy, Robert E. *Black Cameos.* New York: Albert & C. Boni, 1924.
Kenney, Maureen. *Circle Round the Zero.* St. Louis: Magnamusic-Baton, 1974.
Knowles, Faith, ed. ¡Vamos a Cantar! *230 Folk Songs of Spanish-Speaking People to Sing, Read, and Play.* Columbus, Ohio: Kodály Center of America, Capital University.
Kolb, Sylvia, and John Kolb. *A Treasury of Folk Song.* New York: Bantam Books, 1948.
Korson, George. *Pennsylvania Songs and Legends.* Philadelphia: University of Pennsylvania Press, 1949.
Kwami, Robert Mawuena. *African Songs for School and Community.* New York: Schott, 1998.
Landeck, Beatrice. *Songs to Grow On.* New York: Edward B. Marks Music Corporation, 1950.
Langstaff, John. *Hi-Ho the Rattlin' Bog.* New York: Harcourt Brace and World, 1969.
Langstaff, John, P. Swanson, and G. Emlen. *Celebrate the Spring: Celebrations for Schools and Communities.* Watertown, Mass.: Revels, 1999.
Larkin, Margaret. *The Singing Cowboy.* New York: Alfred F. Knopf, 1931.
Leisy, James. *The Folk Song Abecedary.* New York: Hawthorne Books, 1966.
Linscott, Eloise Hubbard. *Folk Songs of Old New England.* Hamden, Conn.: Archon Books, 1962.
Lloyd, A. L., et al. *Folk Songs of the Americas.* New York: Oak Publications (for UNESCO), 1966.
Locke, Eleanor G. *Sail Away: 155 American Folk Songs to Sing, Read and Play.* New York: Boosey & Hawkes, 1981.
Lomax, Alan. *The Folk Songs of North America.* New York: Doubleday, 1960.

Lomax, John, and Alan Lomax. *Our Singing Country.* New York: Macmillan, 1941.
Lomax, John, and Alan Lomax, with Charles Seeger and Ruth Crawford Seeger. *Folk Song USA.* New York: Signet New American Library, 1966.
Matteson, Maurice. *American Folksongs for Young Singers.* New York: G. Schirmer, 1947.
McIntosh, David. *Singing Games and Dances.* New York: Association Press, 1957.
———. *Folk Songs and Singing Games of the Illinois Ozarks.* Carbondale and Edwardsville: Southern Illinois University Press, 1974.
Mendoza, Vicente T. *Lirica Infantile de Mexico.* Mexico D. F.: El Colegio de Mexico, 1980.
Morse, Jim, et al. *Folk Songs of the Caribbean.* New York: Bantam Books, 1958.
Moses, Irene E. P. *Rhythmic Action, Plays and Dances.* Springfield, Mass.: Milton Bradley, 1915.
Newell, William Wells. *Songs and Games of American Children.* New York: Dover, 1963. 1st ed. 1882.
Niles, John Jacob. *Seven Kentucky Mountain Songs.* New York: G. Schirmer, 1929.
Okun, Milton. *Something to Sing About.* New York: Macmillan, 1958.
Owens, Bess A. *Songs of the Cunberlands. Journal of American Folklore.* Vol. 49, 1936.
Owens, William A. *Swing and Turn: Texas Play and Party Games.* Dallas: Tardy, 1936.
Pieteoforte, Alfred. *Songs of the Yokuts and Paiutes.* Healdsburg, Calif.: Naturegraph Publications, 1965.
Porter, Grace Cleveland. *Negro Folk Singing Games and Folk Games of the Habitants.* London: J. Curwin and Sons, 1914.
Randolph, Vance. *Ozark Folksongs.* Columbia: State Historical Society of Missouri, 1949.
Richardson, Ethel Park. *American Mountain Songs.* New York: Greenburg, 1927.
Ritchie, Jean. *Golden City.* Edinburgh: Oliver A. Boyd, 1965.
———. *Singing Family of the Cumberlands.* New York: Oxford University Press, 1955.
Rosenbaum, Art, Margo Newmark Rosenbaum, and Bela Foltin, Jr. *Folk Visions and Voices: Traditional Music and Song in North Georgia.* Athens, Georgia: University of Georgia Press, 1983.
Sandburg, Carl. *The American Songbag.* New York: Harcourt Brace & Co., 1927.
Scarborough, Dorothy. *On the Trail of Negro Folksongs.* Hatboro, Penn.: Folklore Association, Inc., 1963.
Seeger, Pete. *American Favorite Ballads.* New York: Oak Publications, 1961.
Seeger. Ruth Crawford. *American Folk Songs for Children.* Garden City, N.Y.: Doubleday, 1948.
———. *American Folk Songs for Christmas.* Garden City, N.Y.: Doubleday, 1953.
———. *Animal Folk Songs for Children.* Garden City, N.Y.: Doubleday, 1950.
Sharp, Cecil J. *Twelve Folksongs from the Appalachian Mountains.* London: Oxford University Press, 1945.
Sharp, Cecil J., and Maud Karpeles. *English Folk Songs from the Southern Appalachians.* London: Oxford University Press, 1932. Vols. 1 and 2.
Siegmeister, Ellie. *Work and Sing.* New York: William R. Scott, 1945.
"Song Out." *The Folk Song Magazine.*
Sturgis, Edith, and Robert Hughes. *Songs from the Hills of Vermont.* Boston: G. Schirmer, 1919.
Tobitt, Janet Evelyn. *A Book of Negro Songs.* Pleasantville, N.Y.: Copyright by J. E. Tobitt, 1950.
Trent-Johns, Altona. *Play Songs of the Deep South.* Washington, D.C.: Associated Publishers, 1945.
Trinka, J. *Bought Me a Cat and Other Folk Songs, Singing Games and Play Parties for Kids of All Ages.* With CD. Columbus, Ohio: Folk Music Work, 1988.
———. *John, the Rabbit and Other Folk Songs, Singing Games, and Play Parties for Kids of All Ages.* With CD. Columbus, Ohio: Folk Music Works, 1989.
———. *The Little Black Bull and Other Folk Songs, Singing Games, and Play Parties for Kids of All Ages.* With CD. Columbus, Ohio: Folk Music Works, 1996.
———. *My Little Rooster and Other Folk Songs, Singing Games, and Play Parties for Kids of All Ages.* With CD. Columbus, Ohio: Folk Music Works, 1987.
Walter, Lavinia Edna. *Old English Singing Games.* London: A & C Black, 1926.
Warner, Anne, and Frank Warner. *Collection of Traditional American Folksongs.* New York: Syracuse University Press, 1984.

The Weavers Songbook. New York: Harper & Brothers, 1960.
White, Newmann Ivey. *American Negro Folk Songs.* Hatboro, Penn.: Folklore Associates, 1965.
White, Newmann Ivey, with Jan Schinhan, music editor. *The Frank C. Brown Collection of North Carolina Folklore.* Durham, N.C.: Duke University Press, 1962.

Discography

1, 2, 3, and a Zing, Zing, Zing. Tony Schwartz, Folkways Records, FC 7003 A.
Afro-American Games and Blues Songs. Library of Congress, Recording Laboratory, AAFS L4.
American Favorite Ballads, Vol. I. Pete Seeger, Folkways Records.
American Folk Songs. The Seegers, Folkways Records, FA 2005.
American Folk Songs for Children. Mike and Peggy Seeger, Rounder Records, 8001, 8002, 8003.
American Folk Songs for Children. Pete Seeger, Folkways Records, FP 701.
American Folksongs for Children. Southern Folk Heritage Series, Atlantic, SD 1350.
American Play Parties. Pete Seeger, Folkways Records, 1959, FC 7604.
American Sea Songs and Chanties. Library of Congress, Recording Laboratory, AAFS L26.
Anglo-American Songs and Ballads. Library of Congress, Recording Laboratory, AAFS L12 and AAFS L14.
Animal Folk Songs for Children. Peggy Seeger, Scholastic Records, 1958, SC 7551.
Anthology of American Folk Music. Harry Smith, Folkway Records, 2951, 2952, 2953.
Asch Recordings. Compiled by Moses Asch and Charles E. Smith, Folkways Records, ACSH AA 3/4.
Birds, Beasts, and Bigger Fishes. Pete Seeger, Folkways Records.
Birds, Beasts, and Little Fishes. Pete Seeger, Folkways Records.
Brave Boys. Sandy Paton, Recorded Anthology of American Music, NWR 239.
Children's Jamaican Songs and Games. Folkways Records, FC 7250.
Children's Songs and Games, from the Southern Mountains. Sung by Jean Ritchie—Folkways Records, FC 7059.
The Cool of the Day. The Dusma Singers (Jean Ritchie), Greehays Recordings, 1991.
Cowboy Songs, Ballads and Cattle Calls from Texas. Compiled by John Lomax, Library of Congress, Recording Laboratory. AAFS L28.
A Cry from the Earth. John Bierhorst, Folkways Records, 7777.
Edna Ritchie of Viper Kentucky. Folk-Legacy Records, Inc., FSA-3; Sharon, CN.
Folk Music from Wisconsin. Library of Congress, Recording Laboratory, AAFS L9.
Folk Music USA. Folkways Records, FE 4530.
Folk Song and Minstrelsy. Vanguard Recordings, RL 7642.
Georgia Sea Island Songs. Alan Lomax, Recorded Anthology of American Music, NWR 278.
Instrumental Music of the Southern Appalachians. Diane Hamilton, Tradition Records, TLP 1007.
I've Got a Song. Sandy and Caroline Paton, Folk-Legacy Records, FSK 52.
Jean Ritchie Sings Children's Songs and Games. Folkways Records, FC 7054.
Latin American Children's Game Songs. Hanrietta Yurchenco, Folkways Records, FC 7851.
The Negro People in America. Heirloom Records, 1964.
Negro Work Songs and Calls. Library of Congress, Recording Laboratory, AAFS L8.
Old Mother Hippletoe. Kate Rinzler, Recorded Anthology of American Music, NWR 291.
Old Times & Hard Times. Hedy West, Folk-Legacy Records, 1967, FSA 32.
Play and Dance Songs and Tunes. Library of Congress, Recording Laboratory, AAFS L55.
Ring Games. Harold Courlander and Ruby Pickens Tartt, Folkways Records, FC 7004.
Ring Games, Line Games, and Play Party Songs of Alabama. Folkways Records, FC 7004.
So Early in the Morning. Diane Hamilton, Tradition Records, TLP 1034.
Songs and Ballads of the Anthracite Miners. Library of Congress, Recording Laboratory, AAFS L16.

Songs of Love, Luck, Animals, and Magic. Charlotte Heth, Recorded Anthology of American Music, NWR 297.
Songs of the Michigan Lumberjack. Library of Congress, Recording Laboratory, AAFS L56.
Songs Traditionally Sung in North Carolina. Folk-Legacy Records, FSA 53.
Sounds of the South. Alan Lomax, Atlantic Recording Corporation, Southern Folk Heritage.
Spanish-American Children's Songs. Jenny Wells Vincent, Cantemos Records.
Spiritual with Dock Reed and Vera Hall Ward. Folkways Records, FA 2038.
Step It Down. Bessie Jones, Rounder Records, 8004.
Versions and Variants of "Barbara Allen." Library of Congress, Recording Laboratory, AAFS L54.

Chapter 4

Children as Performers

Singing, Movement, and Playing Instruments in the Elementary Music Classroom

Key Questions

How do I develop students' singing voices?

What types of vocal warm-up exercises are appropriate for elementary age children?

What are the approaches to teaching a song?

How can I develop a sequence for teaching movement activities?

How can I integrate instruments into a music lesson?

How can I develop a lesson plan framework that includes techniques for developing a child's performance skills?

What are the differences between a preparation/practice lesson plan, a presentation lesson plan, and an initial practice lesson plan?

In the previous chapter, we discussed the criteria necessary for selecting songs for classroom use. The goal of this chapter is to present ideas for developing children's singing voices to perform this repertoire. (This chapter is an overview of how to teach singing and is not presented as a comprehensive approach to teaching singing. Please consult the additional references offered at the end of this chapter.) The chapter also includes a section on approaches to teaching a new song, as well as guidelines for developing students' performance and movement abilities. Also included is a discussion of how teaching performance skills, such as singing, movement, and playing instruments, affects the planning and design of a music lesson.

Singing

Children love to sing.[1] Listen to children as they are playing on a playground. When they are playing any type of game with other children, the game is often accompanied by a song or chant.

Every child has the ability to sing; the voice is the most accessible musical instrument. Regardless of social background, race, or musical ability, the voice is the one instrument that is available to all children. Singing has a significant impact on a child's intellectual development. Singing facilitates language development through the performance of beat and rhythm in music. Singing helps children learn and articulate the text of a song; it facilitates memory, as well as the development of vocabulary.

In the classroom we can encourage singing for enjoyment and at the same time promote correct intonation and a proper singing tone. The instructor's vocal example can significantly improve students' singing and the development of good vocal intonation. Young voices have less volume, less endurance, and naturally higher ranges than adult voices. The adult instructor must modify his or her voice to accommodate this. Male instructors should consider singing in a falsetto range until young students are able to match pitch.

A capella singing will allow children to hear their own voices and enjoy active music making. Kodály addressed the importance of *a capella* singing.

> Most singing teachers and chorus masters believe in controlling the pitch of the voice by the piano. But singing depends on the acoustically correct "natural" intervals, and not on the tempered system. Even a perfectly tuned piano can never be a criterion of singing, not to speak of the ever "out-of-tune" pianos available at schools and rehearsal rooms. Yet how often have I found chorus masters attempting to restore the shaky intonation of their choirs with the help of a mistuned piano![2]

When teaching music to children please consider the following vocal ranges. These ranges are only suggestions, but might help teachers select appropriate repertoire for their students. Table 4.1 provides a guide to children's vocal skills and ranges.

Table 4.1 Guide to children's vocal skills and ranges

Grade	Vocal Skills	Vocal Range
Pre-kindergarten	Perform child's chants and say nursery rhymes with voice inflection	
Kindergarten	Understands the concept of singing and speaking voice	Sing in tune from D–B (D above middle C). This range could be lower or higher for some children
Grade 1	Develop head voice. More control of pitch	
Grade 2	More control of head voice. Perform simple canons or melodic ostinati in tune	Sing in tune from C to high D
Grade 3	Greater expressive control of voice. Can sing simple canons and two part songs in tune	Can sing up to high Eb
Grade 4	More resonance in voice. Can begin to perform three-part songs	Can sing up to high E

Singing Posture

The following suggestions will help students find their correct posture for singing. The body needs to be balanced for students to project a beautiful singing tone.

1. Balance the head.

   To accomplish this, the face should look straight ahead. Try several exercises, such as moving the head up and down and sideways to relax the head and neck muscles.

2. Shoulders should be relaxed and rotated towards the back.
3. Hands should be relaxed at the sides.
4. Knees should be relaxed and very slightly bent.
5. Feet should be firmly placed on the ground and roughly about 10 to 12 inches apart.
6. If students are sitting when singing, they should be at the edge of their chairs.

Preparing Children to Sing

The following exercises are suggestions to help develop children's singing voices.

Body Warm-Up Exercises

Begin the class by allowing students to stretch and bend to relax their bodies. Eliminate tension by performing the following stretching exercises with your students:

Tip head from side to side and roll head up and down.
Rotate your shoulders in circles forward and backward.
Try to drop your jaw and say "mah, mah, mah" several times.

Breathing Exercises

Breathing exercises teach children to inhale and exhale correctly. Controlled exhaling is a useful exercise.

Show students how to sip through a straw correctly and expand their waist.
Show students how to release air using a "sss" sound.
Show students how to release air using a "sts" sound or using the words "ha."
Guide the student to yawn, as this opens up the back of the throat and relaxes the voice.
Sighing is a gentle way of using a higher voice than you usually speak with. Try sighing a few times, starting each sigh a little higher than the last.

Vocal Warm-Up Exercises and Vocalizations

Vocal warm-up exercises and vocalizations help develop beautiful singing. Encourage student to vocalize high and low sounds, as well as soft and loud sounds.

1. Songs that contain the "oo" sound are particularly good for developing in-tune singing.

Figure 4.1 *Cuckoo*

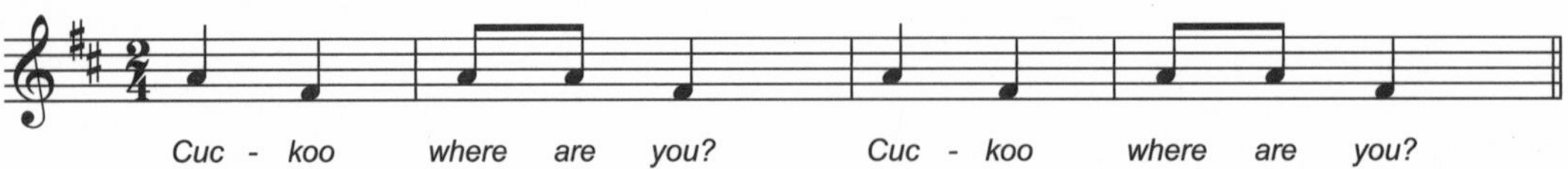

Consider adding a high pitch "toot" to the end of the traditional children's chant, *Engine Engine #9* as the students are marching while chanting.

Engine, engine number 9,
Going down Chicago line,
If the train should jump the track,
Would you want your money back?
Yes, no, maybe so,
Toot, toot, toot, toot.

Figure 4.2 *Engine Engine #9*

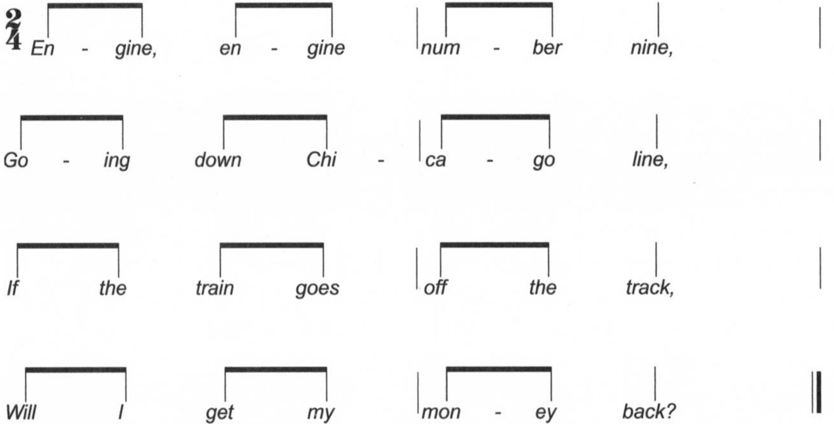

2. Many ordinary vocal sounds are actually excellent warm-up exercises. Sing known songs with neutral syllables such as "noo," "moo," "la," and so on.
3. Humming is a gentle (and quiet) way of using the singing voice. Humming a favorite song before singing it also provides students with an opportunity to focus on the song's melody.
4. Imitating a siren is something young students delight in. It also engages the voice in such a way that the extremes of one's vocal range can be explored without straining the voice. When imitating sirens, challenge the children to make soft and loud, high and low, long and short sirens, sirens that just go up, just come down, or do both.

5. Copying animal sounds, such as barking like a dog, roaring like a lion, or meowing like a cat also engages the extremes of a child's vocal range.
6. Sing a phrase of a pentatonic melody with the "nn" placement sound or the "noo" vowel sound.

Developing Singing Skills

Head Voice and Chest Voice

The technical difference between "head voice" and "chest voice" has to do with how vocal cords vibrate when singing. We use the terms "head" and "chest" to designate where vibrations are most strongly felt when singing. When singing in "head voice," the vibrations are felt behind your nose and your cheeks. When singing in "chest voice," vibrations are felt in your throat and chest. When children learn to sing, they normally sing in their chest voice and need help finding their head voice.

Finding Your Head Voice

There are a number of initial vocal exercises you can do to find your head voice:

1. Pretend that you are talking to a baby. Notice how your speaking voice is much higher in pitch. You may also pretend to talk like Mickey Mouse. For those students who know the character, this exercise often inspires them to change the focus of their voices quickly.
2. Pretend to be an owl and make a high-pitch "whoooo" sound. Repeat this several times; each time try to make the "whoooo" a little higher than the last.
3. Pretend to be a child on a playground, taunting another child: "Nyah-nyah-nyah-nyah-nyah."
4. Pretend you're falling off a cliff "aaaahhhhhhhhhhhhh."
5. Say "Cock-a-doodle-doo" or "Qui-quiri qui" (Spanish for "Cock-a-doodle-doo").

The head voice vibrates and radiates more in your head. The head voice is helpful for leading children in singing because they are still trying to make the distinction between singing and speaking. We are not saying that children should not sing at all in the chest voice; for instance, many songs in the African American tradition sound better in the chest voice. However, as music educators we need to make students aware of the different energy and aspects of head and chest voices. Often children have a tendency to shout rather than sing in an effort to sing loudly. Model appropriate singing for your students whether singing in head or chest voice.

Steps to Finding the Singing Voice

The following activities may be used to help children find their singing voice using their head and chest voice.

1. *Pitch exploration exercises* (these exercises can also be used as vocal warm-ups)

   Pitch exploration exercises allow students to activate the vocal muscles that are used when singing in the "head voice." When using these exercises, it is best to begin with descending and ascending sliding sounds. Begin these exercises as a class activity. Ask students to imitate the sliding sounds of a slide whistle with their voice. Once the class is comfortable with the exercises, encourage individual students to perform the exercises on their own. The following are examples of pitch exploration exercises.
   - When telling stories in class modulate your voice to include a high, medium, and low voice for characters in the story or high, low, and medium sounds for events in the story. Repeat the story and ask children to make the sounds.
   - As the instructor moves a flashlight beam projected on to the blackboard in a room, ask students to follow the contour of the moving beam of light.
   - Imitate the sound of a siren whistle with the voice.

2. *Awareness of different types of voices*

   Music instructors can help students discover the difference between their speaking voice and singing voice. Young children need to become aware of the different sounds their voices can produce. Guide students to discover that they have the following types of voices:

   Talking voice
   Whispering voice
   Loud voice
   Soft voice
   Singing voice
   Internal voice

3. *Voice modulation*

   Select songs and rhymes that can be used to develop a child's singing voice. As young children say chants, they may be guided to speak using a "baby bird voice" (high) or a "grandfather's voice" (low). Chanting using these different voice types will teach a young learner to explore their vocal ranges. Guide young students to perform the chant *Bee Bee Bumble Bee* using a high voice; then perform the chant using a low voice.

Figure 4.3 *Bee Bee Bumble Bee*

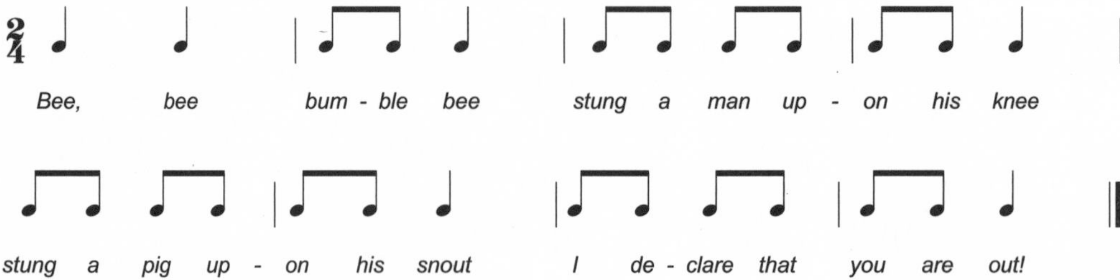

Perform *Engine Engine #9* using a "grandfather's voice" or a "baby's voice."

Figure 4.4 *Engine Engine #9*

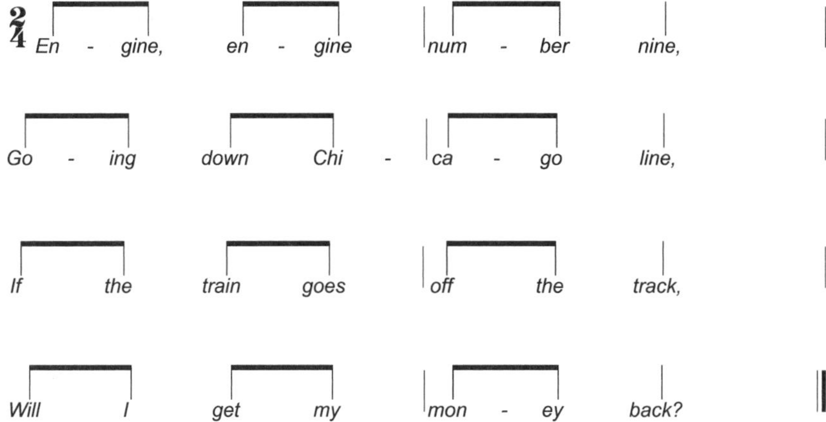

4. *Song with narrow range*

   Sing songs that use two or three pitches, such as *Bounce High Bounce Low.*

Figure 4.5 *Bounce High Bounce Low*

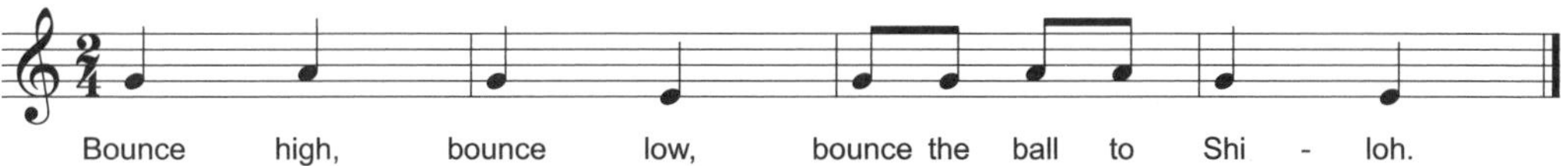

5. *Descending melodic patterns*

   Generally songs that begin with a descending melodic pattern are easier for young children to hear and sing; therefore this type of song provides a greater opportunity for the young learner to hear accurately and subsequently a better chance to sing in tune. Songs such as *Doggie Doggie* and *Lemonade* have simple descending melodic patterns.

Figure 4.6 *Lemonade*

continued

Figure 4.6 *Continued*

6. *Call and response singing*

Call and response songs are ideal for developing children's singing, as students simply sing a repeated melodic pattern. *Pizza Pizza* is an example of a call and response song.

Figure 4.7 *Pizza Pizza*

When teaching a call and response song, the following procedure may be used:

- Sing the call and response song for the children as a listening activity. Consider using two hand puppets to distinguish which part of the song is the call and which is the response.
- Sing the phrase and guide students to echo; use a pretend microphone to help young students understand the alternation.
- Have a group echo the instructor.
- Later, when the song is well learned have individual students echo the instructor.
- Ask individual students to take the role of the instructor; they can sing the call and the class can echo the response.

7. *Providing a model for singing*

The instructor must model the song correctly; sing with good intonation, clear pronunciation, and model the song's character. Begin each song on a comfortable starting pitch for your students. The majority of songs used in teaching are learned by listening to many repetitions sung by the instructor. Indicate the starting pitch of the song clearly; consider singing the first phrase of the song to clearly establish the starting pitch. The instructor should sing using an appropriate tempo for the song. If the tempo is too fast, then children could sing out of tune.

8. *Singing softly*

   Children should be encouraged to sing songs softly as a means for developing good intonation.

9. *Movement*

   Singing in combination with movement helps reinforce the concept of beat and, if song material is well-known, can help with vocal intonation.

10. *Individual singing*

    The instructor should allow students to sing on their own. This helps the young learner develop greater vocal independence. Some children can sing in tune with a group but do not sing in tune when singing on their own. One way to help a child having trouble singing on their own is to sit in front of the child and have the child observe the movement of your mouth. Allowing students to sing individually develops independence and provides the instructor with an opportunity to evaluate the progress of the class. Once children know a song well and can sing it fluently, the instructor should not sing with the class. Singing alone and in small groups will encourage vocal independence.

11. *Singing names to simple melodic motifs*

    Encourage young children to sing their names to short motifs based on patterns found in song material. When seated in a circle, the instructor may roll a ball or toss a bean bag to a child and ask them to sing their names.

12. *Recognizing different timbres*

    Guide the young learner to recognize different timbres—environmental sounds, as well as the sounds of instruments and voices.

13. *Piano accompaniments*

    Avoid using piano accompaniments when teaching a new song because young students need to hear the voice of the instructor, as well as their own voice. Playing an accompaniment to a new song may decrease students' ability to hear their own singing voices. The piano may be used for accompaniment once students have learned a new song or know a song from memory.

14. *Vowels and consonants*

    The correct pronunciation of vowels is critical for the development of good intonation. Practice singing vowels using the words "no," "nu," "naw," "ni," and "nah" on descending pentachord scales. Consonants help define the rhythmic character of singing. Vocalizations that include *n* and *m* consonants encourage good singing and proper pronunciation.

15. *Singing a greeting to students*

Begin the music class by greeting the students. The greeting may be sung by the instructor or use a puppet for younger children. The puppet then leads the class in singing a greeting "Good Morning Boys and Girls." Sing a greeting to each child individually by name or singing pairs of names with the student pair responding.

The teacher sings,

Figure 4.8 Teacher's greeting

and students respond,

Figure 4.9 Students' response

Sing using a beat motion like waving.

The teacher sings,

Figure 4.10 Teacher's greeting

and students respond,

Figure 4.11 Students' response

16. *Correcting Students*

The reason students do not sing in tune in many music classrooms is because teachers are afraid to tell students they are "out of tune." Gentle and specific simple corrections are completely acceptable. A simple, "a little higher" and then lavish praise when they perform the task correctly will not damage self-esteem. The entire class starts to listen and ask themselves whether they sing in tune.

Teaching Songs

Songs form the basis of all music instruction. The quality of music teaching is governed (1) by the choice of musical materials and (2) by the methods of presenting that material.

The Kodály concept of music education incorporates folk songs and art songs to encourage music appreciation, as well as develop music literacy skills. Folk songs are particularly appropriate for classroom use. In general, there are two methods for teaching songs, by rote or by note.

Teaching Songs by Note

This method of teaching songs can be used either to teach the whole song or sections or phrases of a song. When teaching songs by note, the teacher presents the notation of the song to the students and sequentially guides students to read the song from notation. The following procedure may be used for teaching songs by note:

- Make students aware of the meter of the song. The meter can be prepared by singing and conducting a known song that has the same meter of the new song.
- Practice each rhythmic pattern found in the song with the students. They can either echo clap or read these rhythm patterns from notation. Difficult rhythms abstracted from the song, can be practiced with suitable rhythmic ostinati that can include the subdivision of the beat.
- Make students aware of the key of the song. Students can sing another known song reading from the staff using the key of the song to be taught by rote.
- Practice melodic patterns found in the song with students. The teacher shows important melodic patterns abstracted from the song with handsigns and students read with solfege syllables, note names, and/or neutral syllables.
- Discuss the form of the song.
- Students think through the rhythm of the entire song.
- Students clap the rhythm of the song and say the rhythm syllables.
- Students think through (inner hear) the melody of the entire song. Students may conduct or use hand signs while thinking through the melody.
- Students sing the song with solfege and handsigns.
- Students sing the song with neutral syllables.
- Students sing the song with words.

Teachers should find the quickest and most fun way to teach the song. Be creative and make the song come to life! Don't get stuck doing the song the same way all the time.

Teaching Songs by Rote

When teaching songs by rote, the initial presentation of the song is made by the instructor. Remember that it might take several lessons to teach one song. The teacher serves as a model for the correct performance of the song. For this reason, music must be presented in an authentic or stylistically correct manner. For example, folk songs should be sung in a manner that brings out the character and mood of the song. Listening to recordings of folk singers performing folk song repertoire can provide a performance model.

The mood for the presentation of the song may be set through a story or another well-known song. It is important for the instructor to talk about the phrasing, mood, style, and form of the song. Students may quietly pat the beat the second time the instructor sings the new song. It is important for the children to determine the phrasing and form of a new song. Once the initial presentation is made, the following techniques may be used for teaching a song by rote.

Techniques for Teaching a Song by Rote

Questioning Techniques

Ask questions relating to specific musical elements or to the text of the song. Asking questions can (1) direct students' attention, (2) help strengthen their analytical skills, and (3) aid in remembering the song.

Guidelines for Asking Questions

Use the fewest words possible. By asking specific questions, the teacher gives the students listening tasks that help them focus their attention on a particular musical element. Start by asking questions pertaining to the end of the folksong. This will allow students to memorize the song more easily.

Sing the song for the students before asking each question. In this way the students will become familiar with the melody and text before they are asked to sing the song.

Figure 4.12 *Starlight, Starbright*

The instructor may sing the song and ask the following questions before allowing the students to sing.

1. "How many phrases do you hear?"
2. "What does the word 'may' mean?"
3. "Does the pitch for 'may' go up or down?"

Figure 4.13 *Rocky Mountain*

Figure 4.13 *Continued*

A questioning procedure for presenting the song *Rocky Mountain* might be as follows:

1. After performing the entire song several times, perform the first phrase.
2. Ask "How many times do the words 'Rocky Mountain' appear together?" (three times)
3. Ask "Does each 'Rocky Mountain' use the same pitches?" (no)
4. Ask "Which one is different?"
5. Ask "How is it different?"
6. Perform the phrase.

When students can sing the first half of the song, the teacher may ask questions about the second half of the song such as:

1. How many phrases did I sing?
2. Are the phrases exactly the same?
3. How are they different? (the first goes up, the second goes down)
4. Perform the entire song.

This type of questioning can be applied to most songs.

Phrase-by-Phrase Song Presentation

A phrase-by-phrase presentation is helpful when presenting longer and more complex songs by rote. This approach is more appropriate when working with older students. Younger students should hear the song repeated many times in its entirety. Reserve the use of phrase-by-phrase presentation of songs for upper grade students. The phrase-by-phrase presentation is exactly that, presenting each phrase of a song and having students repeat the phrase.

1. Sing the song in its entirety.
2. Focus on one phrase at a time. If a song is particularly difficult, the teacher may ask the students to perform it with a simple rhythmic activity, for example, keeping

the beat when listening. This keeps the students occupied and focused on the song while the teacher presents the entire song again.

The unique or salient features in the song will suggest the best means for presentation of the song. The song's text, rhythmic, and melodic elements will enable the instructor to make decisions as to the best teaching approach.

Presenting a Song Using Games and Movement

Performing motions or acting out a story line helps students memorize songs and rhymes. For example:

Figure 4.14 *Bee Bee Bumble Bee*

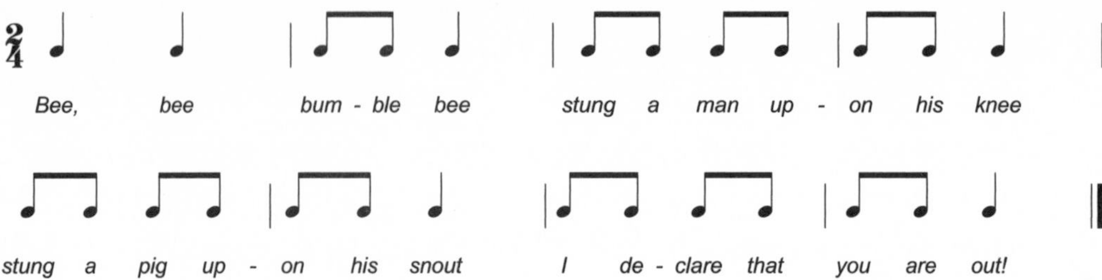

1. Phrase one: students flap their arms to the beat.
2. Phrase two: students point to their knee to the beat.
3. Phrase three: students point to their nose to the beat.
4. Phrase four: students point to other children in the circle to the beat.

For *Engine Engine #9,* the students move their arms, imitating the motion of the wheels of the engine, and march around the classroom while chanting:

Engine, engine number 9,
Going down Chicago line,
If the train should jump the track,
Would you want your money back?
Yes, no, maybe so,
Toot, toot, toot, toot.

Figure 4.15 *Hunt the Slipper* (also known as *Cobbler Cobbler*)

Figure 4.15 *Continued*

Students can pantomime hammering their shoes to the beat of the rhyme.

Movement activities help students learn and memorize songs quickly and easily. The teacher and students may create their own games and motions to accompany songs. For example, high and low or up and down motions may be used with the song *See Saw* to convey the concept of high and low. Later the simple motion of bending knees may be used to reflect the solfege syllables, *so–mi.* Motions that are initiated by the instructor or students may reflect the beat or recurring rhythmic patterns. Encourage students to use their imaginations and create motions to accompany songs.

Call and Response Songs

Songs containing repeated patterns can be practiced in call and response style. Initially, young children should sing only the response; the instructor sings the *call.* After many repetitions, students may sing either or both the *call* and the *response.*

Teach a Song Using Visuals

Pictures associated with the text of a song can be a combination of visuals that remind the students of the text coupled with visuals that remind students of form or melodic contour.

Teaching Songs Using Manipulatives

For example, when teaching *Old Mr. Rabbit* children can select a fruit or a vegetable to help them remember sequence of verses.

Teaching Songs Using Motions that Associate the Text with the Melody

For example, when teaching *Bobby Shaftoe,* the instructor may show a motion for each phrase of the song. This motion should emphasize the beat.

Assessing the Presentation of a Song

The following questions will help you assess and evaluate your teaching of songs to your students.

- Did I introduce song in an interesting manner?
- Have I memorized the song correctly?
- Did I determine the best method of presentation for introducing this song?
- Did I sing the song in a stylistically appropriate manner?

- Did I begin singing the song on a pitch that is appropriate for the students I am teaching?
- Did I engage my students with the eye contact and facial expressions as I performed the song?
- Did I use clear mouth movements?
- Did I stay in tune as I sang the song?
- Was the tempo appropriate for learning? Was my pronunciation clear? Could the text be easily understood?
- Did I conduct?
- Did I keep a steady beat and tempo as the children were singing phrase by phrase?
- Was the teaching pace appropriate for students to understand and learn the song?
- Did I correct students' mistakes and intonation problems?
- Was it fun for the students?
- Was it the most fun way and quick way to teach the students?

The Many Uses of a Folk Song

The same song may be sung many times throughout the year and even revisited in different grade levels. Selecting quality song materials allows the instructor to repeat the song many times without students becoming bored. Generally speaking, if the song is a quality song, students will enjoy performing it. The following are suggestions for using the same song for a variety of activities.

- Songs may be presented as listening activities.
- Songs may be learned for their formal structure (AABA, and so on).
- Perform songs with a repeated rhythmic pattern (ostinato).
- Sing the song with text and then with rhythm syllables.
- Sing the song with text and then with solfege syllables.
- Perform pentatonic songs in canon.
- Use the song to make particular rhythm or melodic elements known to the students.

Singing Games and Movement Activities

Singing games are a wonderful way to reinforce musical concepts and skills, as well as develop students' social, emotional, and kinesthetic skills and abilities. Singing games should be age appropriate; the game or movement activity should correspond to the students' developmental abilities. Movement and motions in the games should be simple for children to follow as they sing.

The role of the instructor is critical when presenting singing games and movement activities; the instructor must be able to sequence the presentation of movements and motions in a logical manner as well as perform the song at the same time. Large beat motions and moving to the beat is usually best presented before more complicated movements at specific points in the performance. The instructor may determine it best to present the song to the children before introducing the game, movements, or motions. There are situations when it is appropriate for students to learn the motions immediately as they sing the song. When presenting the song along with a game, it is important for students to listen (and not sing) as the instructor sings and focuses the learning on motions or movement activities.

Table 4.2 provides a sequence of movement activities appropriate for the young learner.

Table 4.2 Sequence of movement activities

	Grade				
	Pre-kindergarten	**Kindergarten**	**Grades 1/2**	**Grade 3**	**Grades 4/5**
Games/ movement	Free movement in place (sitting) Free movement in space Movement to a beat while sitting Movement to a beat while walking Standing in a circle Instructor plays with the child as a partner Movements with a partner Starting and stopping with music	Begins to develop greater control of small muscles Changing directions Acting-out games Wind up games Line games Circle games	Marching and skipping to the beat Choosing games Chasing games with a circle Develop the ability to clap the rhythm of a rhyme or melody	Can perform beat on a drum or triangle as well as clap the rhythm of an uncomplicated song in simple and compound meter Can perform hand-clapping games Can conduct in duple meter Can perform sustained bourdons on xylophone Chasing games Jumping games Line games Partner games Double circle games	Can perform beat on a drum or triangle, as well as clap the rhythm of more rhythmically complicated songs in simple and compound meter Can conduct in duple, triple, and quadruple meter Can perform simple ostinati on xylophones Students have developed muscle coordination for playing recorder, keyboard Can respond quickly and accurately through movement to tempo, rhythmic patterns, texture Double line games Square games Square dances

Sequential Progression for Teaching Games

The following is a suggested game sequence for teaching folk games.

Acting Out

Long Legged Sailor
Wishy Washy

Wind Up

Snail Snail

Circle

Circle Round the Zero
Old Mister Rabbit
Wishy Washy
Wallflowers
Down in the Valley

Choosing

Wishy Washy
Down in the Valley

Chase

Charlie Over the Ocean
Cut the Cake
Mouse Mousie

Partner

Quaker Quaker
Bow Wow Wow
Long Legged Sailor
Wishy Washy
Fed My Horse (starts out as a partner game)
Miss Mary Mack (starts out as a partner game)
Down in the Valley (2×2)

Double Circle (late 3rd grade)

Tideo
Dance Josey
Fed My Horse
Miss Mary Mack
Great Big House
Turn the Glasses Over–I've Been to Harlem

Double Line-Reel (4th grade)

Alabama Gal
Amassee
Billy Billy
Zudio
Over the River to Feed my Sheep
Paw Paw Patch
I Wonder Where Maria Has Gone?
Bow Belinda

Single Line

Twenty-four Robbers
Debka Hora
Hashivenu

Square Games

Weevily Wheat
Draw a Bucket
Four White Horses

Square Dances

Old Brass Wagon
Red River Valley
Knock the Cymbals (Texas Star)
Golden Ring Around the Susan Girl (Birdy in the Cage)
I's the By (Duck for the Oyster, Dive for the Clam)
Old Betty Larkin (Grapevine Twist)
O Susanna
Goin Down the Cairo (more difficult)

Acting Out Games (Kindergarten and First Grade)

Children may sing a song and act out motions suggested by the text. We believe that in kindergarten it is important for children to begin to find their own "internal beat" before they can imitate a beat given by the teacher. Students may create their own beat movement. For example, when singing *Rain Rain,* they may point to imaginary drops of rain on the window.

Figure 4.16 *Rain Rain*

Figure 4.17 *Hop Old Squirrel*

Students may sing and create their own movement in a space. Ask them to consider all the ways a squirrel can move; they can sing and hop, skip, walk, jump, or climb to the beat as they sing *Hop Old Squirrel.*

Figure 4.18 *Let Us Chase the Squirrel*

Students may create their own movement to a beat while listening to a "classical" composition. Consider using the following musical compositions.

"March" from *The Nutcracker Suite* by Pyotr Ilyich Tchaikovsky (1840–1893)
"Hornpipe" from *Water Music* by George Frideric Handel (1685–1759)
"Spring" from *The Four Seasons* by Antonio Vivaldi (1678–1741)

In acting out games, students will act out a motion without keeping a steady and even beat. Later with more experience they can do the motion and keep the beat.

Figure 4.19 *Hot Cross Buns*

Students copy the instructor's beat movement while singing known songs.

Students may perform specific beat movements suggested by the song. Students remain in one position, sitting or standing, and perform a motion to accompany a song. These beat motions often help illustrate the mood as well as text of a song. For example: hold a doll and rock it in your arms for the song *Bye Baby Bunting*.

Figure 4.20 *Bye Baby Bunting*

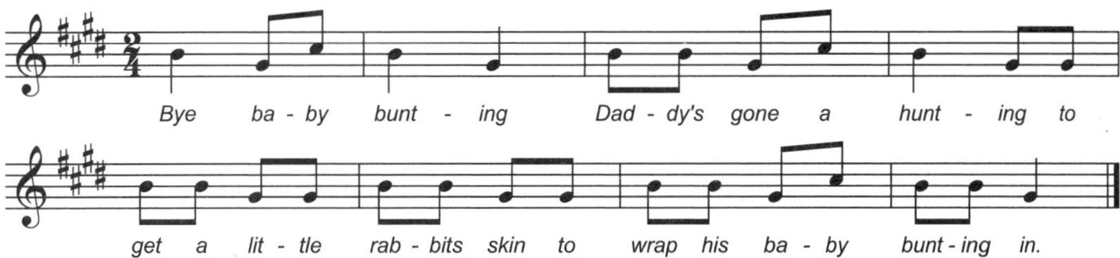

Guide students to make a cake while they sing *Hot Cross Buns.* Using motions that follow the beat, students can mix the batter, spoon the batter into the cake pan, or place the hot cross buns on a tray.

Wind Up Games (Kindergarten and First Grade)

The instructor leads the circle of students to sing and forms a circle that winds inward to form the shell of a snail.

Figure 4.21 *Snail Snail*

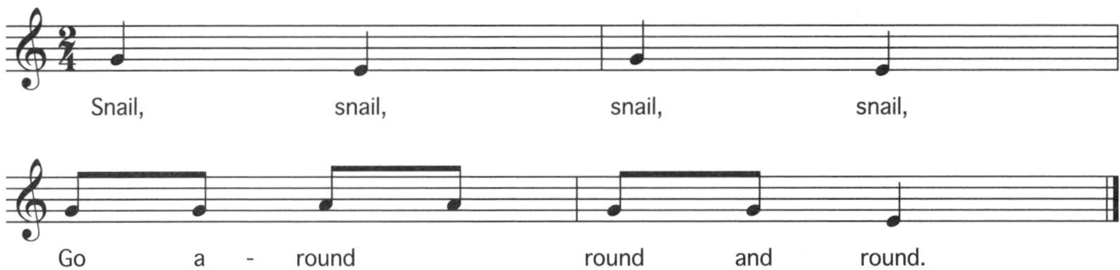

Line Games (Kindergarten and First Grade)

Students form a small line and move around the classroom. For example, students playing the game *Page's Train* sing the song and pretend they are an engine as they walk to the beat.

Circle Games (Kindergarten and First Grade)

Games may involve circles, such as *Wall Flowers* and *Ring around the Rosy.*

Figure 4.22 *Ring Around the Rosy*

Students join hands and walk in a circle and "fall down" at the end of a song.

Figure 4.23 *Bow Wow Wow*

1. Children form a circle and stand facing a partner.
2. "Bow wow wow" stamp your feet four times (right, left, right, left).
3. "Whose dog art thou?" Point four times to the beat as you speak the words.
4. "Little Tommy Tucker's Dog" partners join hands and circle in place.
5. "Bow wow wow" stamp your feet three times, then jump in the air and turn your back to your partner at which point you will see your new partner.

Figure 4.24 *Wall Flowers*

Figure 4.24 *Continued*

Students join hands and walk in a circle. One student stands in the center of the circle. In phrase three, the child in the center points to a friend during "Let's all go to Mary's house." (Substitute the child's name for Mary.) That student stays in the circle but turns around and faces the outside. The game continues until all students are facing out.

Another type of circle game involves moving around the circle with improvised motions like *Walk Daniel* or *Jim Along Josie.*

Figure 4.25 *Jim Along Josie*

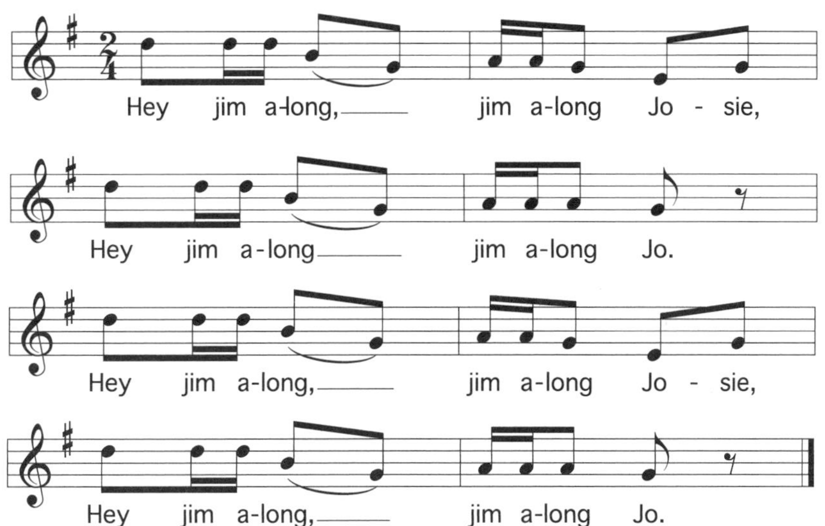

Students improvise actions while walking in a circle. For example: "skip Jim along" or "jump Jim along."

Choosing Games (First and Second Grade)

Figure 4.26 *Little Sally Water*

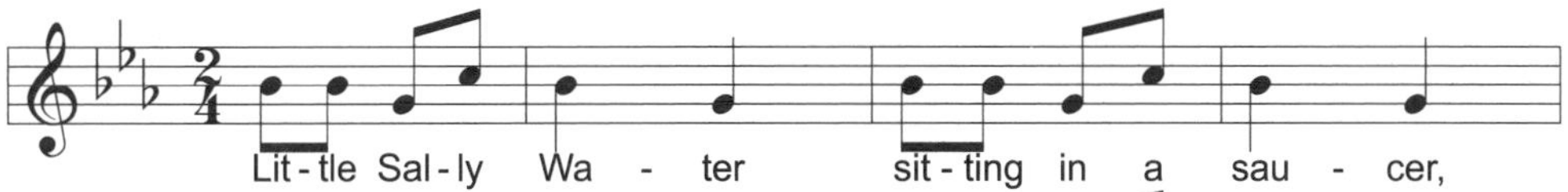

continued

Figure 4.26 *Continued*

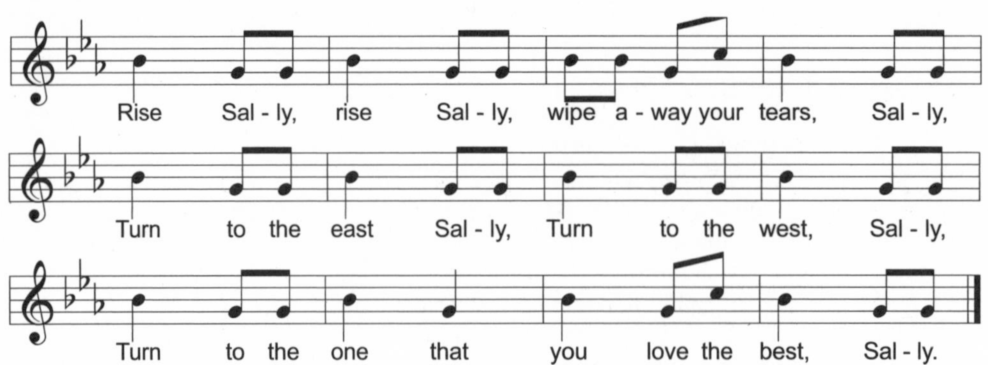

Little Sally Water is both an acting-out singing game and a choosing game. Sing *Little Sally Water* with students standing, holding hands, and walking in a circle. The student in the center of the circle performs the motions suggested in the text: *sit, rise, wipe your tears, turn to the east, turn to the west,* and *turn to the one that you love the best.* At the end of the game, a new child is chosen to take the position in the center of the circle.

Figure 4.27 *Here Comes a Bluebird*

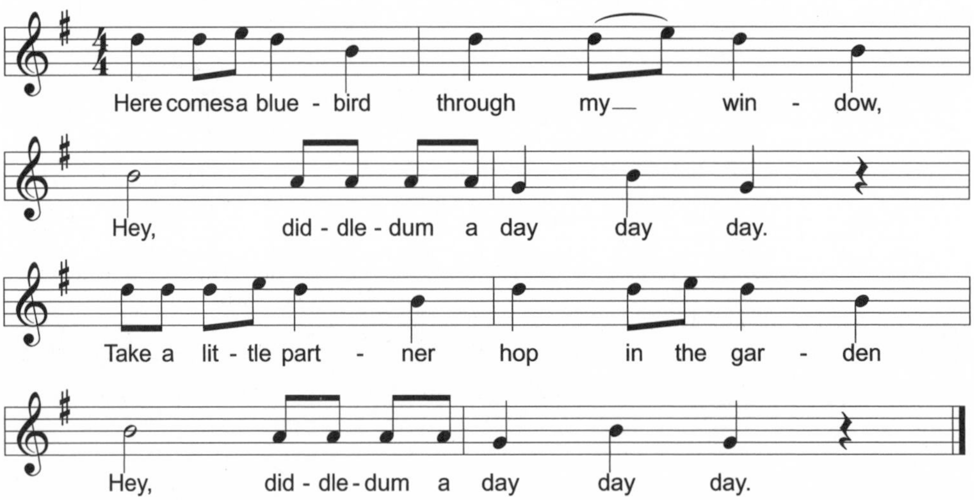

Students sing holding hands and walking in a circle. A child in the center chooses a child in the circle and they both *hop in the garden.* That child becomes the new "bluebird" and will subsequently choose another child.

Chase Games with and without a Stationary Circle (First and Second Grade)

Figure 4.28 *Charlie Over the Ocean*

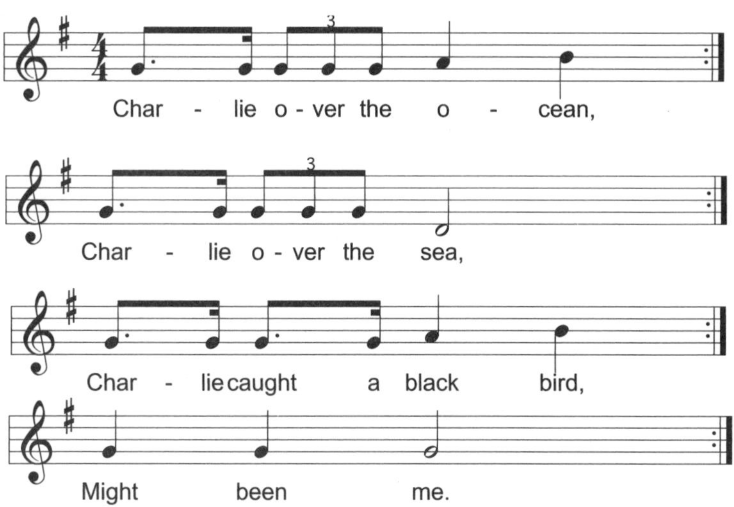

Figure 4.29 *A Tisket a Tasket*

We are Dancing in the Forest is an example of a Chase Game. Both *Charlie Over the Ocean* and *A Tisket a Tasket* are examples of a chase game with a stationary circle and can be played in the same manner. The students sit in a circle, sing the song, and keep the beat. A child walks around the outside of the circle successively tapping the beat on the head of each child in the circle. The person who is tapped at the end of the song chases the "tapper" around the circle. That child becomes the new "tapper."

Partner Games (Second and Third Grade)

Partner games are games in which two children act out or interact with each other performing a motion.

Figure 4.30 *Bow Wow Wow*

Line Games (Second and Third Grade)

Figure 4.31 *London Bridge*

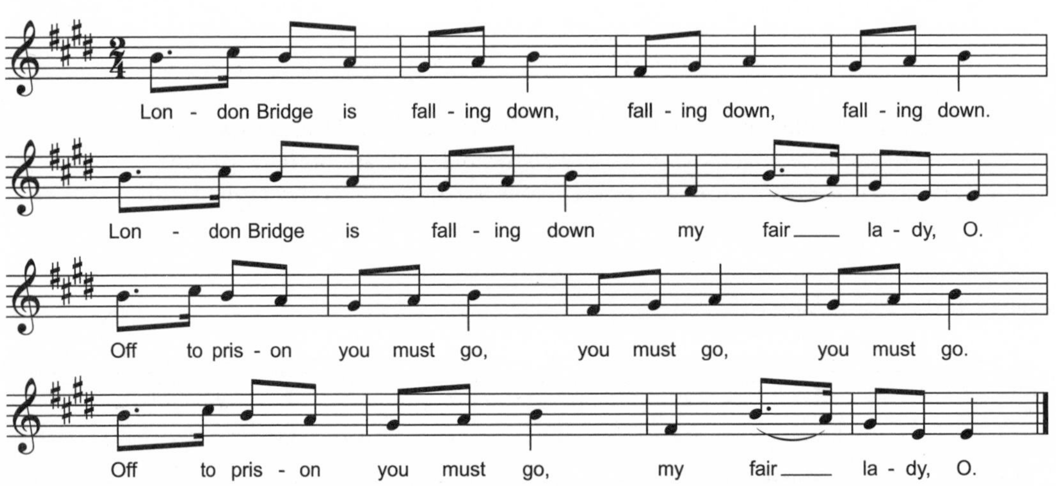

The most common way for students to play this game is that two players make an arch while the other players pass through in single file. On the word "lady," the arch is lowered to "catch" a player.

Double Circle Games (Third and Fourth Grade)

Students form two circles that interact together. An example of this game is *Great Big House in New Orleans.* More complicated forms of the double circle game involve changing partners during the game, such as *I've Been to Harlem.*

Figure 4.32 *Great Big House in New Orleans*

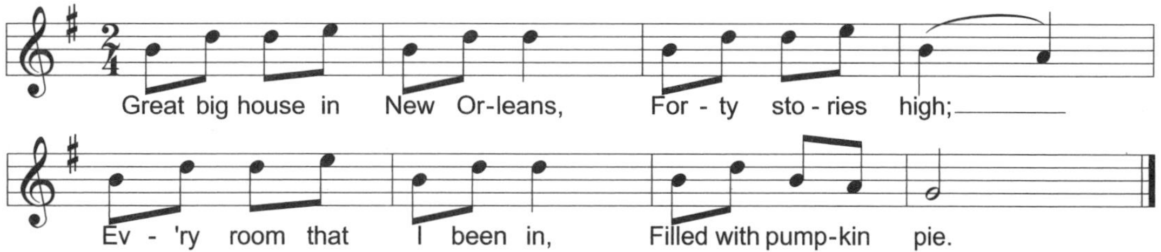

Dance formation: a single circle of partners, ladies on the right.

1. With a strutting step, and swinging arms, the circle sings and moves in a clockwise direction.
2. On "went down to the old mill stream," ladies take four small steps toward the center of the circle and join hands.
3. On "fetch a pail of water," the men move toward the center and reach both arms across between two ladies, and down toward the floor as if to pick up a pail of water.
4. Men join hands at the end of the "picking up" gesture and swing arms (on "put one arm") over the heads of the ladies making a circle behind their backs, at waist level.
5. On "the other round my daughter," the ladies raise their joined hands back over the men's heads, freeing the dancers, and on the fourth phrase "with the golden slippers," the men move over one position to be ready to start the next round with a new partner.

Figure 4.33 *I've Been to Harlem*

continued

Figure 4.33 *Continued*

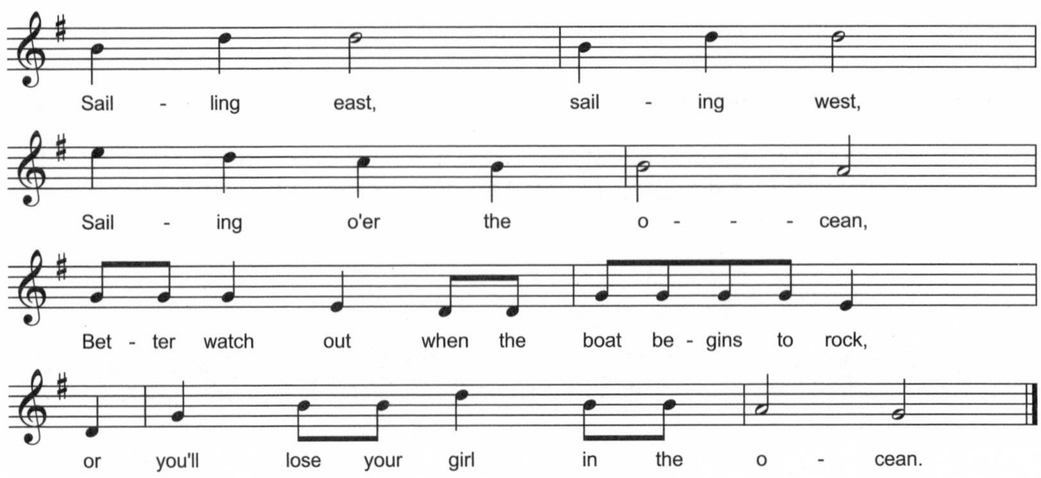

Children take partners, boys on girls' left, cross hands as in a skating position and walk around in a circle while singing the first part of this song. When they reach the word "over," partners "wring the dish rag," that is, raise their crossed hands while each child turns completely around without dropping his partner's hands. This movement is repeated twice. On "sailing east," hands are dropped and the boys make a circle inside the girls' circle. The boys move around in clockwise direction while the girls continue counterclockwise. At the end of the song, boys choose the girls they are nearest and the dance begins again.

Double Line Games (Fourth and Fifth Grade)

This category involves the "reel" type dancing. Sometimes these games are easier because the students can observe the lead couple. Examples of this include *Come Thru N'a Hurry.*

Figure 4.34 *Come Thru N'a Hurry*

Square Games (Fourth and Fifth Grade)

These include such games as *Four White Horses* and *Draw Me a Bucket of Water*

Square Dances (Fourth and Fifth Grade)

Movement activities can progress to more complicated dance forms, such as square dancing. *Old Brass Wagon* is an example of a square dance and can be performed with several verses and more complex dance formations.

Figure 4.35 *Old Brass Wagon*

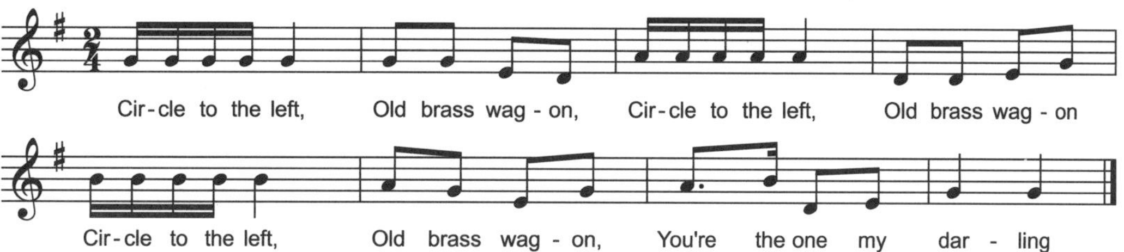

General Guidelines for Teaching Singing Games

Before introducing children to a new singing game, it may be a good idea to use the song as a listening activity at the close of a music lesson to introduce the song to the students.

Teach the song as a new song in a lesson. Phrases from the game song might be used to teach or reinforce known rhythmic or melodic elements.

Once the song is familiar to the students, the game may be taught. Of course, many games may be taught at the same time the song is introduced because the actions for the game are dictated by the text of the song. It is difficult to label a song as being purely one type of game song. Songs often encompass several different types of games. Tables 4.3 and 4.4 include games for kindergarten through grade three. Note that some songs have games that include components of different types of games. A special thanks is due Jane Pippart Brown for the following folk song classifications.

Table 4.3 Sample game list kindergarten and grade 1

	Acting Out	Windup	Circle	Choosing
All Around the Buttercup	X		X	X
Apple, Peach, Pear, Plum			X	X
A-Tisket, A-Tasket			X	X
Aunt Rhody				
Bee, Bee Bumblebee	X			
Bobby Shaftoe	X			
Bounce High, Bounce Low	X		X	
Bow Wow Wow	X		X	
Bye, Bye Baby	X			
Cobbler, Cobbler (Hunt the Slipper)	X			
Cocky Robin				
Daddy Shot a Bear	X		X	
Deedle, Deedle Dumpling	X			
Do, Do Pity My Case	X		X	X
Doggie, Doggie	X		X	X
Down Came a Lady			X	X
Ducks and Geese	X			X
Engine, Engine Number 9	X			X
Good Night, Sleep Tight				
Here Comes a Bluebird	X		X	X
Hush Baby	X			
Hush Little Minnie (The Mockingbird)	X			
Hush-a-Bye	X			
I Climbed Up the Apple Tree	X			
Johnny Works With One Hammer	X			
Johnny's It				X
Just from the Kitchen	X		X	X
Lazy Mary	X			
Lemonade	X			
Let's Hide the Pumpkin	X		X	X
Little Sally Water	X		X	X
London Bridge	X			X
Looby Loo	X		X	
Lucy Locket	X		X	X
Mary Had a Little Lamb				
Mister Rabbit	X			

Chase	Partner	Double Circle	Double Line (reel)	Single Line
X				
	X			
	X			
				X
				X
		X		
X				
				X
	X			X
			X	
	X			X
X				

continued

Table 4.3 *Continued*

	Acting Out	Windup	Circle	Choosing
Mother, Mother	X		X	X
Nanny Goat			X	X
Naughty Kitty Cat	X		X	X
No Robbers Out Today				X
Oliver Twist	X		X	X
On A Mountain			X	X
One, Two, Buckle My Shoe	X			
One, Two, Three, Four, Five	X			
Page's Train	X	X		
Pease Poridge Hot				X
Plainsies Clapsies	X		X	
Pumpkin, Pumpkin, Round the Fat	X		X	X
Quaker, Quaker	X		X	X
Queen, Queen Caroline				
Rain Rain				
Ring Around the Rosie	X		X	
Round and 'Round			X	X
Sally Go 'Round the Sun			X	X
Snail Snail		X		
Star Light, Star Bright				
Teddy Bear	X			
This Old Man	X			
Thread Follows the Needle	X		X	X
Twinkle, Twinkle Little Star				
Two Rubble Tum	X		X	X
Two, Four, Six, Eight				X
We Are Dancing in the Forest	X		X	X
Witch, Witch				X

Chase	Partner	Double Circle	Double Line (reel)	Single Line
X				
X				
X				X
	X			
	X			X
				X
	X			
X				
	X			X
		X		
				X
X				
X				
X				X
X				

Table 4.4 Sample games grade 2 and 3

	Acting Out	Windup	Circle	Choosing
Alabama Gal (Girl) (Come Thru 'Na Hurry) L3				
Amasee (not in collection)				
Billy, Billy L1				
Bow Bow Wow L1				
Closet Key (The)			X	X
Dance Josey (Chicken on the Fencepost)				
Deedle, Deedle Dumpling				X
Drunken Sailor (Bow Belinda L3)				
Draw a Bucket of Water L3				
Fed my Horse				
Fire in the Mountain				
Four White Horse (not in collection)				
Golden Ring				
Great Big House				
Head and Shoulders				
Hogs in the Cornfield				
How Many Miles to Babylon				
Hunt the Cows	X		X	
I Lost the Farmer's Dairy Key			X	X
Johnny Cuckoo	X			
Jolly Miller				X
King's Land				
Knock the Cymbals				
Let us Chase the Squirrel			X	
Long Legged Sailor				
No Robbers out Today				
Oh, Green Fields Roxy (not in collection)				
Old Brass Wagon				
Over the River				
Paw Paw Patch				
Pease Porridge Hot L1				
Pizza Pizza	X		X	X
Quaker, Quaker L1				
Rosie Darling Rosie				
Sailing on the Ocean				
Sammy Sacket				X
Tideo				
Turn the Glasses Over				
Twenty Four Robbers				
Two Rubble Tum	X			
Wallflowers			X	X
Weevily Wheat L3				

Chase	Partner	Double Circle	Double Line (reel)	Square	Square Dance: Set	Single Line
			X			
			X			
			X			
		X				
		X				
			X			
				X		
	X	X				
		X				
				X		
					X	
		X				
	X					
	X					
			X			
		X				
X						
					X	
	X					
	X					
X						
	X					
					X	
			X			
			X			
	X					
	X	X				
		X				
					X	
	X	X				
	X	X				
						X
				X		

Instruments

Kodály believed that music education should begin with singing but be enhanced by the introduction of musical instruments.

> An instrumental culture can never become a culture of the masses. . . . Why, is it only through tormenting the violin, through strumming on the piano that the path leads to the holy mountain of music? Indeed it often rather then leads away from it. . . . What is the violin or piano to you? You have an instrument in your throat, with a more beautiful tone than any violin in the world, if you will only use it. With this instrument you will come invigoratingly near to the greatest geniuses of music—if there is only somebody to lead you on![3]
>
> How valuable are "brilliant" pianists if they cannot sing simple folksongs without making errors? There must be a strenuous attempt to replace music that comes from the fingers and the mechanical playing of instruments with music from the soul and based on singing. We should not allow anyone even to go near an instrument until he or she can read and sing correctly. It is our only hope that one day our musicians will be able also to "sing" on their instruments.[4]

Table 4.5 provides a possible sequence for introducing instruments to children.

Table 4.5 Sequence for introducing instruments

Grade	Grade 1	Grades 2/3	Grades 4/5
Instruments	Tambourine Claves, Chime bars Finger cymbals/bongo Hand drums Mallet Triangle Rhythm stick Shakers	Finger cymbals bongo Hand drums Mallet Triangle Rhythm sticks Maracas Congo drum Tone bells Orff instruments Xylophones—for simple drones, bourdons, and ostinatos Recorder Autoharp Keyboard	Xylophone—for playing a moving drone, ostinato, and melodies two mallets striking Recorder—more extended range autoharp guitar—for playing chords Keyboard orchestral winds and brass Hand chimes Congo drums

Using Instruments in the Classroom

Before the beginning of each lesson, always have your instruments available so you do not have to spend time taking them out during the music lesson.

Remember to consider the size of the students and their motor skill ability when choosing instruments. Instruct children to hold the mallets with the main grip being the fore finger and the thumb with the rest of the fingers gently folded around the mallet. The mallet head should lightly bounce off the bar rather than land on the bar like a pancake. Before using instruments in the classroom as part of a lesson, encourage children to experiment with the sound of the instruments.

Incorporating Instruments into the Music Curriculum

1. *Beat*

   Use simple percussion instruments to keep the beat of a rhyme or folk song.

2. *Beat and rhythm*

   Use simple rhythmic instruments to perform the beat with a folk song and the rhythm to a folk song. Then use simple rhythmic instruments to perform the beat and rhythm of a folk song simultaneously.

3. *Rhythmic ostinati*

   Use simple rhythmic instruments to perform a rhythmic ostinato (a repeated rhythmic pattern) to a folk song. Then use simple rhythmic instruments to perform two simultaneous sounding ostinati to a folk song.

4. *Melodic ostinati*

   Use glockenspiels, xylophones, metallophones, and melody bells to perform a melodic ostinato to a folk song.

5. *Recorder*

   The music instructor can begin the teaching of recorder in the third or fourth grade. It is recommended that all students sing all music before it is performed on the recorder. This way the students will have internalized the sound and will play more musically because they can aim to imitate the sound of singing on their instruments.

Harmonic Instruments

Children learn to play harmonic instruments such as autoharps and guitars in the fourth and fifth grade. Use the following teaching progression when playing melodic, rhythmic, or harmonic instruments in the classroom.

1. Sing the music with rhythm syllables.
2. Sing the music with solfège syllables.
3. Sing the music with rhythm syllables while performing on a rhythmic instrument.
4. Inner hear the melody using rhythm syllables while performing the rhythm on an instrument.

5. Sing the melody with solfège syllables while performing on a melodic instruments such as an Orff instrument.
6. Inner hear the melody with solfège syllables while performing with an instrument.

Using a Generic Lesson Plan Format to Design a Preparation/Practice Lessons That Includes Singing Movement and Instrumental Activities

The generic plan can now be adopted and adapted for developing a lesson plan that prepares the teaching of a new concept or element as well as practices a familiar element. The introduction of the lesson can now include appropriate vocal warm up exercises as well as activities to develop the singing voice. During the core activities section of the lesson, the teacher can now teach a new song in the key that falls within the vocal range of the children. Likewise the teacher must choose the best techniques for teaching a new song.

Between the "Performance and Preparation" section of a lesson and the "Performance and Musical Skill Development" section of the lesson, the instructor can develop children's movement skills by teaching folk games that follow the game sequence outlined in this chapter. During the "Performance and Musical Skill Development" section of the lesson, the instructor may introduce instruments to reinforce previously learned concepts or elements. The class ends with a review of the new song and newly learned musical concepts. The instructor may conclude with a listening activity such as singing a new song that will be taught in a subsequent class.

Developing a Preparation/Practice Lesson Plan Framework That Includes Singing, Movement, and Instrumental Activities

In this chapter we have presented activities for developing a child's singing voice, movement skills, and instrumental skills, as well as how the instructor can present folk music appropriately. As a result of the information contained in this chapter, the following modifications to our preparation/practice lesson plan can include:

1. Developing a child's voice through singing exercises.
2. Establishing comfortable starting pitch (CSP) for each song.
3. Selecting appropriate techniques for teaching a new song by rote.
4. Selecting appropriate movement activities.
5. Selecting appropriate instrumental activities.

Table 4.6 Preparation/practice lesson plan

Focus	Activities, Procedures, and Assessments
Introduction Performance and demonstration of known musical concepts and elements	**Body warm-ups and breathing exercises** Students demonstrate their prior knowledge of repertoire and musical elements through performance of songs selected from the alphabetized repertoire list. **These songs may be accompanied by rhythmic or melodic instruments.**
Core activities	
Acquisition of repertoire	**Teach a new song by rote using an appropriate technique for teaching a new song by rote**
Performance and preparation of a new concept or element	Learning activities in which students are taught a new musical concept or element through known songs found in the alphabetized repertoire list
Movement development	Focus on the sequential development of age-appropriate movement skills through songs and folks games
Performance and musical skill development	Students reinforce their knowledge of musical concepts and elements working on the skill areas of reading and writing, form, memory, inner hearing, ensemble work, **instrumental work,** improvisation and composition and listening through known songs found in the alphabetized repertoire list
Closure	
Review and summation	Review of lesson content and the instructor may perform the next new song to be learned in a subsequent lesson found in the alphabetized repertoire list

Using a Generic Lesson Plan to Design a Presentation Lesson Plan Framework That Includes Singing, Movement, and Instrumental Activities

The generic plan can now be adapted for the presentation of a new concept or element and the practice of a familiar element.

Table 4.7 Presentation lesson plan

Focus	Activities, Procedures, and Assessments
Introduction Performance and demonstration of known musical concepts and elements	**Body warm-ups and breathing exercises** Students demonstrate their prior knowledge of repertoire and musical elements through performance of songs selected from the alphabetized repertoire list and may contain the new element. **These songs may be accompanied by rhythmic or melodic instruments.**

continued

Table 4.7 *Continued*

Focus	Activities, Procedures, and Assessments
Core Activities	
Acquisition of repertoire	**Teach a new song by rote using an appropriate technique for teaching a new song by rote**
Performance and **presentation** of a new concept or element in the target pattern	Instructor presents the name of the new musical element in the focus pattern of a known song
Movement development	**Known song or game** found in the alphabetized repertoire list: **CSP** Focus on the sequential development of age-appropriate movement skills through songs and folks games
Performance and **presentation** of a new concept or element in a related pattern	Instructor presents the name of the new musical element in related patterns found in known repertoire
Closure	
Review and summation	Review of lesson content and the instructor may perform the next new song to be learned in a subsequent lesson found in the alphabetized repertoire list

The introduction of the lesson can now include appropriate vocal warm up exercises as well as activities to develop the singing voice. During the core activities section of the lesson, the teacher can teach a new song in the key appropriate to the vocal range of the children. Likewise, the teacher must choose the best techniques for teaching a new song. The next section of the lesson plan includes the performance and presentation of the name of the new concept or element being prepared. In this lesson plan format, we suggest that the instructor "label the sound," that is, present the syllables for the new element or concept. Once the sound has been aurally labeled in the focus song, the instructor should guide the students to label the sound in similar patterns in other song material. The second stage of presentation is showing how to represent this new musical element using notation. After this section of the lesson the instructor will develop the children's movement ability by teaching folk games that follow the game sequence outlined in this chapter. This section is followed again by the performance and presentation of the name of the new concept of element being prepared. This provides another opportunity for the instructor to label the new element with syllables. The important activity is for the instructor and the students to engage in a singing dialogue incorporating the newly learned musical element in known song material. The presentation of notation occurs after the students are secure with the sound of the new element in their song repertoire. The class ends with a review of the new song and new concepts covered during the lesson. The teacher can also sing the next new song to be taught as a listening activity.

➤ Discussion Questions

1. What kinds of songs should we include in our repertoire list that will promote singing in tune?
2. Discuss the different types of vocal warm-up exercises that you can use in your music lessons.
3. Discuss the various techniques that you would use with your children to discover their head voice.
4. What kinds of instruments should you have in your music classroom?
5. Discuss how your music program can connect to the physical education curriculum?
6. Discuss the principal ways of teaching a song by rote to children.
7. What are some of the key questions you need to answer in order to evaluate your effectiveness in teaching a new song to your students?
8. What do we mean by the use of the word "performance" in the school curriculum?
9. How can we further develop a preparation/practice lesson plan framework that includes singing, movement, and instrumental activities?
10. How can we further develop a presentation lesson plan framework that includes singing, movement, and instrumental activities?

➤ Ongoing Assignment

1. Familiarize yourself with the performance outcomes for all the music curriculums for each grade.
2. Select a song from each grade you are going to teach next year and write a teaching strategy of how you are going to teach this song.
3. Select a game from each grade you are going to teach next year and write a teaching strategy for how you are going to present the game.
4. Using the lesson plan formats provided in this chapter, create a lesson plan where in the performance and preparation of a new element you prepare a rhythmic element, and in the performance and development of skills you practice a melodic element.
5. Using the lesson plan formats provided in this chapter, create a lesson plan where you present a melodic element and another where you present a rhythmic element.

References

Adzinyah, Abraham K., Dumisani Maraire, and Judith Cook Tucker. *Let Your Voice be Heard! Songs from Ghana and Zimbabwe.* Danbury, Conn.: World Music Press, 1997.

Ansdell, Gary. "Musical Companionship, Musical Community: Music Therapy and the Process and Value of Musical Communication," in *Musical Communication,* ed. Dorothy Miell, Raymond Macdonald, and David J. Hargreaves. New York: Oxford University Press. 2005.

Bachmann, Marie_Laure. *Dalcroze Today: An Education through and into Music,* trans. David Parlett. New York: Oxford University Press, 1993.

Burakoff, Gerald. *How to Play the Recorder.* Ft. Worth, Tex.: Sweet Pipes, 1997.

Choksy, Lois, and David Brummitt. *120 Singing Games and Dances for Elementary Schools.* N.J: Prentice-Hall; Englewood Press: 1987.

Cox, Heather, and Richard Garth. *Sing, Clap, and Play the Recorder,* Vol. 1–2. St. Louis: Magnamusic-Baton, 1985.

Davidson, Jane. "Bodily Communication in Musical Performance," in *Musical Communication,* ed. Dorothy Miell, Raymond Macdonald, and David J. Hargreaves. New York: Oxford University Press, 2005.

Findlay, Elsa. *Rhythm and Movement: Applications of Dalcroze Eurhythmics.* Evanston, Ill.: Summy-Birchard, 1999.

Green Gilbert, Anne. *Creative Dance for All Ages.* Reston, Va.: NDA/AAHPERD, 1992.

———. *Brain Dance* (video). Reston, Va.: NDA/AAHPERD, 2003.

———. *Brain Compatible Dance Education.* Reston, Va.: NDA/AAHPERD, 2004. A concept-based approach, in which the students learn the elements and principles of dance through a variety of learning processes (perceiving, understanding, doing, creating, and valuing) is the foundation for this book. Beginning with the basics of movement, Gilbert uses vocabulary and concepts simplified from Rudolph von Laban's work in movement analysis. Each chapter focuses on one of the elements of dance (and movement) and is presented in a basic lesson plan that is divided into 5 main sections progressing from (1) introduction and warm-up using the dance element, (2) exploring the element, (3) developing dance skills, (4) creating with the element explored, and (5) cooling down.

Kopiez, Reinhard. "Making Music and Making Sense through Music: Expressive Performance and Communication," in *MENC Handbook of Musical Cognition and Development,* ed. Richard Colwell. New York: Oxford University Press, 2006.

Marsh, Kathryn, and Susan Young. "Musical Play," in *The Child as Musician: A Handbook of Musical Development,* ed. Gary McPherson. New York: Oxford University Press, 2006.

McPherson, Gary E., and Jane W. Davidson. "Playing an Instrument," in *The Child as Musician: A Handbook of Musical Development,* ed. Gary McPherson. New York: Oxford University Press, 2006.

MENC, *What Every Young American Should Know and be Able to do in the Arts: National Standards for Arts Education.*

Phillips, Kenneth H. *Directing the Choral Music Program.* New York: Oxford University Press, 2004.

———. *Teaching Kids to Sing (with Supporting Materials).* New York: Schirmer Books, 1993.

Rao, Doreen. *Will Sing! Choral Music Experience for the Classroom Choir.* New York: Boosey and Hawkes, 1994.

Schmid, Will. *World Music Drumming: A Cross-Cultural Curriculum.* Milwaukee: Hal Leonard, 1998.

Schmidt, Oscar. *The Many Ways to Play Autoharp* Union, N.J.: Oscar Schmidt-International, 1966.

Shehan Campbell, Patricia. *Songs in their Heads.* New York: Oxford University Press, 1998.

Shehan Campbell, Patricia, and Bonnie C. Wade. "Performance as Enactive Listening," in *Teaching Music Globally: Experiencing Music, Expressing Culture and Thinking Musically: Experiencing Music, Expressing Culture.* New York: Oxford University Press, 2004.

Sloboda, John. "Talent and Skill Development: The Acquisition of Music Performance Expertise," in Sloboda, *Exploring the Musical Mind: Cognition, Emotion, Ability, Function.* New York: Oxford University Press, 2005

Thaut, Michael H. "Rhythm, Human Temporality and Brain Function," in *Musical Communication,* ed. Dorothy Miell, Raymond Macdonald, and David J. Hargreaves. New York: Oxford University Press, 2005.

Warner, Brigitte. *Orff-Schulwerk: Applications for the Classroom.* Englewood Cliffs, N.J.: Prentice Hall, 1997.

Weikart, Phyllis. Leading Movement & Music Educator, Founder of HighScope's *Education Through Movement—Building the Foundation* program. She is the author or co-author of 13 books about movement, music, and dance at all levels, and the producer of 8 videos and 15 CDs, including the *Rhythmically Moving* and *Changing Directions* recorded music series. Her wide-ranging experiences have led to the development of a teaching approach that ensures teachers' success with students of all ages. See web site: www.highscope.org.

Welch, Graham F. "Singing and Vocal Development," in *The Child as Musician: A Handbook of Musical Development,* ed. Gary McPherson. New York: Oxford University Press, 2006.

———. "Singing as Communication," in *Musical Communication,* ed. Dorothy Miell, Raymond Macdonald, and David J. Hargreaves. New York: Oxford University Press, 2005.

Chapter 5

Children as Critical Thinkers and Problem Solvers

Developing Music Literacy Skills

Among other things, we are still living in a musical culture that exists without writing. And yet it is indeed a real culture: one which includes instrumental music after the oral tradition—playing by ear. . . . But the time for a culture of handed-down oral tradition is over, and outside Hungary the world has long since entered into the era of a written culture. In our own country, there is no more urgent task than the hastening of this transition if we do not want to be left behind for good. Without literacy today there can no more be a musical culture than there can be a literary one. Thus the promotion of musical literacy is as pressing now as was the promotion of linguistic literacy between one and two hundred years ago.

Zoltán Kodály, "Preface to *Musical Reading and Writing*," in *The Selected Writings of Zoltán Kodály*

Part of the musicianship of many (but not all) musical practices worldwide is knowledge about notation and knowledge of how to decode and encode musical sound patterns in staff notation, graphic notation, hand signs, or rhythmic syllables. But "music literacy," or the ability to decode and encode a system of musical notation, is not equivalent to musicianship. It is only part of the formal and procedural dimensions of musicianship. Moreover, literacy should be taught and learned parenthetically and contextually—as a coding problem to be gradually reduced within the larger process of musical problem solving through active music making.

D. J. Elliot, *A New Philosophy of Music Education: Music Matters*

Key Questions

How do we develop a sequence for teaching rhythmic and melodic elements for elementary music students based on a song repertoire?

What teaching approaches can we use to teach rhythmic and melodic elements?

How do pedagogical tools affect our teaching of music literacy skills?

In the previous chapter we provided a survey of how we can develop children's performance skills in the classroom through singing, movement, and playing instruments. The goal of this chapter is to discover how to develop children's music literacy skills based upon the repertoire they are performing in the classroom. In other words, the common rhythmic and melodic elements (building blocks) within the repertoire become the basis for teaching music literacy.

Music teachers should simultaneously develop students' knowledge of repertoire, critical thinking, problem solving, and music literacy skills. When music lessons are taught twice each week, all of these skills can easily be developed in tandem. A challenge arises when music lessons are less frequent. For example, students that have music lessons once each week will not be advanced in their knowledge of rhythmic and melodic elements as students who have lessons twice each week. Games associated with the repertoire for teaching music literacy in a once a week setting are not sufficiently challenging for developing students' movement skills. Age appropriate games and activities often require more advanced repertoire.

Included in this chapter is a discussion of the different types of rhythmic syllable systems. The emphasis here is to demonstrate the importance of teaching traditional notation to students as a means of understanding the repertoire they are performing and how rhythmic and melodic syllables are successful tools to accomplish this outcome. The chapter addresses how teaching music literacy affects lesson planning. Appendix 3 includes suggested songs for teaching specific musical concepts and elements.

Teaching Tools

To accommodate the teaching of rhythmic and melodic elements, Hungarian music teachers gradually began adapting certain teaching tools that have sometimes been mistakenly thought to be the "Kodály method." These *tools* simply facilitate instruction and learning; they facilitate students' musical skill development, as well as their musicality. They include the use of the moveable *do* system of solmization; the use of hand signs to indicate the pitches of the scale; rhythmic syllables; musical shorthand derived from solfège and rhythmic syllables (stick notation). These teaching tools or techniques were adapted by Kodály's colleagues and consistently used in classroom teaching.

Solfège Syllables and Relative Solmization

> From the example of the Paris Conservatoire it will be seen that the time is approaching when it is acknowledged that, just as writing cannot be learned unless reading has been learned first, singing or playing an instrument cannot be mastered unless solfège has itself been mastered first.[1]

> Finally: relative solmization can be of great help and should not be dismissed. Successions of syllables are easier and more reliably memorized than letters; in addition, the syllables indicate at the same time the tonal function and, by memorizing the interval, we develop our sense of the tonal function.[2]

Kodály was convinced that students would gain greater command of their voices through systematic solfège instruction and that relative solmization was valuable for developing both ear training and sight-singing abilities. Relative solmization is used to describe an approach to teaching melodic elements beginning with so-mi. Moveable *do* is used to describe an approach to teaching melodic elements beginning with the complete major scale. The moveable *do* or tonic-solfa system can be traced to the eleventh century when Guido d'Arezzo used a form of it for musical instruction. This system was later adapted by Sarah Glover an English music teacher; her system was adopted by John Curwen. Relative solmization links sounds to tonal images in one's hearing and may be used with any tonal system; major, minor, modal, or pentatonic music.

Figure 5.1 shows the solfège syllables for the natural, raised, and lowered steps of the major scale. Solfège syllables are always written in lower case, italicized letters. The major scale tonic is *do* and *la* is the minor scale tonic.

Raised scale steps			*di*		*ri*	*			*fi*		*si*		*li*		*	
Natural scale steps		*d*		*r*		*m*		*f*		*s*		*l*		*t*		*d*
Lowered scale steps	*		*ra*		*ma*		*		*sa*		*lo*		*ta*			
* not used																

Figure 5.1 Solfege syllables for the natural, raised, and lowered steps of the major scale

The upper octave is indicated by a superscript prime placed on the syllable, for example, *do'*. The lower octave is indicated by a subscript prime on the syllable, for example, *so,*.

Letter Names

In the pedagogy associated with the Kodály concept students learn solfège syllables prior to letter names. When learning an instrument such as the recorder, students may use solfège syllables and learn letter names (absolute pitch names). Letter names become significant to students when they are applied to an instrument because a letter name has both an absolute position on the staff and an absolute fingering on the instrument. The German letter names are used for singing because they may be sung with one syllable and therefore singing with letter names will not compromise the rhythmic integrity of the musical example. For example, instead of singing F sharp (two syllables) students sing "fis." Letter names are always written with upper case. The German system of letter names is as follows.

German Letter Names

sharps	Ais	Bis	Cis	Dis	Eis	Fis	Gis
natural	A	B	C	D	E	F	G
flats	Ass	Bes	Ces	Des	Ees	Fes	Ges

Ais is pronounced as Ice and we can say Ace instead of Ass.

Hand Signs

The hand signs used to represent the notes of the scale were developed by the Englishman, John Curwen, in 1862. In order to position solfège syllables, the solfège syllable is given a specific hand sign. Hand signs physically and visually help orient students to intervallic relationships. They were adopted and adapted in Hungary. Hand signs help develop a student's ability to audiate. Hand signs should be made with the whole arm and should be spatially placed to give an indication of position in the scale.

Figure 5.2 Hand signs for the solfege syllables

Tone Steps

Tone steps can be used to show the steps of the scale. The *do* pentatonic scale is shown in figure 5.3.

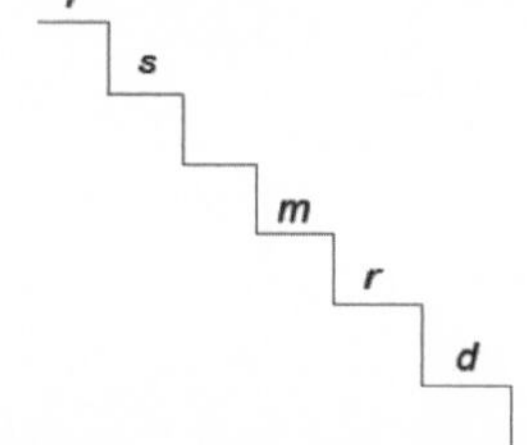

Figure 5.3 Tone steps for the *do* pentatonic scale

Once the tone steps are placed on the board, the instructor may point to the solfège syllables of a song; students sing the syllables. Tone steps help students visualize the steps, skips, and leaps in music.

Finger Staff

If you spread your fingers and hold your hand parallel to your body, your hand creates a representation of the music staff, the four fingers and thumb serving as the five lines of the staff. Use a finger from your other hand to point to the notes. This provides another means of helping students visualize notes on a staff.

Child's Piano or Xylophone

Position students in standing, kneeling, or sitting positions to represent a particular tone set. The tallest student may be the lowest sound if you are showing a barred instrument or piano string but this may be confusing for the children. A half step may be represented by positioning students so their shoulders touch.

Notes on the Staff

The music instructor writes the tone set on a staff and points to notes that create a new or familiar melody.

Rhythm Syllables

Rhythm syllables help the learner associate a "syllable" with the number of sounds they hear on particular beats. The French pedagogue Emil Chevé developed rhythm syllables in the nineteenth century. Hungarians adopted and adapted this system to suit the Hungarian language.

There are many rhythmic reading systems available. Figure 5.4 indicates two different rhythm syllable systems that can be used for reading rhythms. The first rhythm system is

Rhythmic Element Duple Meter	Ta ka di mi Rhythm Syllables	Kodály Rhythm Syllables
	ta	*ta*
	ta di	*ti ti*
	ta ah	*Ta ah*
	ta ah ah ah	*Ta ah ah ah*
	ta ka di mi	*ti ri ti ri*
	ta di mi	*ti ti ri*
	ta ka di	*ti ri ti*
	ta mi	*tim ri*
	ta ka	*ri tim*
	ta——di	*tie—ti*
	ta-di——di	*syn—co—pa*
3	*ta ki da*	*tri o la*
Compound Meter		
	ta ki da	*ti—ti ti*
	ta	*ta*
	ta da	*ta ti*
	ta ki	*ti ta*

Figure 5.4 Two rhythm syllable systems

the *ta ka di mi*[3] syllables; the second is the traditional Kodály rhythm syllables. We use the *ta ka di mi* system with slight modifications. Note that we use dashes in the ta ka di mi system to indicate that the rhythm occurs over two beats. These rhythm syllables are not related to the notation of music but rather to the number of sounds occurring on the beat.

Linking Common Rhythmic Elements to Rhythm Syllables

Rhythm syllables, now associated with the Kodály concept, have been adopted or adapted in many countries. A shortcoming of several rhythm syllable systems is that the syllables themselves do not enable the learner to distinguish where a particular note falls on a beat. Consider the rhythm system that uses *ta* for a quarter note and *ti ti* for two eighth notes. The rhythm syllable for the eighth note *ti* is used both in simple and compound meter. This system is used in common simple meter where the beat is equal to a quarter note or for compound meters where the beat is equivalent to a dotted quarter note. While the Kodály rhythm syllables have been effective in elementary school teaching, they have not been widely adopted by middle school teachers, high school teachers, or college instructors. Finding a system of rhythm syllables that can be used by music specialists at all levels of instruction that can be correlated with counting using numbers is necessary for consistency. The *ta ka di mi* system of rhythm pedagogy provides this link. We have adopted this system with very slight alterations.

The *ta ka di mi* system emphasizes "location within a beat." The following is a simple illustration. Any attack on the beat is called *ta;* an attack on the second half of the beat is called *di.* In figures 5.5 and 5.6, there are two examples of the song *Rocky Mountain;* one written in $\frac{2}{4}$ and the other written in $\frac{2}{2}$. Both versions of *Rocky Mountain* can be sung with the same rhythm syllables. Therefore, the rhythm syllables do not become associated with note values but with the concept behind the note values. For example, one sound on a beat will always be *ta* and two sounds on a beat will always be *ta di* in simple meter regardless of the value of the beat.

Figure 5.5 Rocky Mountain in $\frac{2}{4}$

Figure 5.5 *Continued*

Figure 5.6 Rocky Mountain in $\frac{2}{2}$

Example of Rhythm Syllables

The following melody can be sung with rhythm syllables. Note that the same syllables can be used if the piece were written in $\frac{2}{2}$ or $\frac{2}{8}$. This concept is particularly important for children studying instruments.

Figure 5.7 *Paw Paw Patch*

Using the *ta ka di mi* system for reading *Paw Paw Patch*

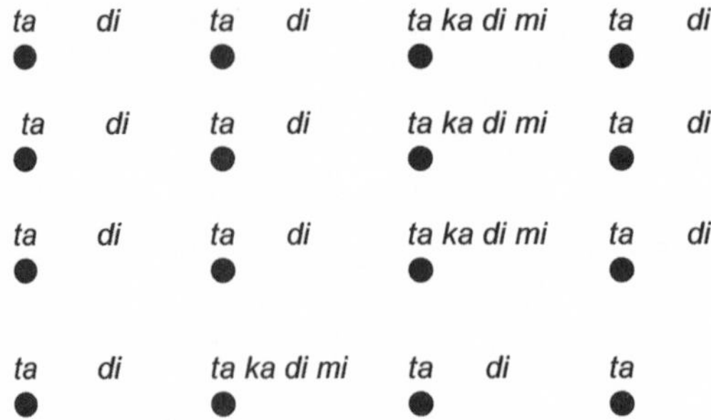

Figure 5.8 *Paw Paw Patch* using the *ta-ka-di-mi* system for reading

The *ta ka di mi* system easily transfers to using a number system for counting. Because *ta* is the unit of beat, *ta* relates to the number used as a beat. Remember, rhythm syllables are most often used to aurally access sound. When students encounter the rhythm pattern ♩ ♩ ♫ ♩ it is far easier to recognize it as *ta ta ta di ta* than it is to recognize it as 1—2—3-&—4. We are convinced that the *ta ka di mi* system is much closer to counting with numbers than traditional Kodály rhythm syllables and that the *ta ka di mi* rhythm syllables are more flexible than other rhythm syllable systems.

Rhythm Notation and Stick Notation

A musical shorthand or stick notation was developed in Hungary and is simply a rapid way of writing music without using staff notation. The most frequently used rhythm name system with the corresponding stick notation is shown in the chart in figure 5.9. Rhythms are written without their note heads (except for the half notes and whole notes); solfège syllables may be written below these notes.

Figure 5.9 Traditional rhythmic notation

Figure 5.10 Stick notation

A Rhythmic and Melodic Sequence for Developing Music Literacy Skills

A primary goal of music education is to guide students in their love of the art of music and music making. This love and respect for the art form normally grows when students discover the many meanings of the repertoire they sing. Performance with understanding is one of the goals of teaching music. We are convinced that understanding comes from the ability to listen, sing, memorize, describe, and analyze what you hear and perform. This implies that learning takes place in the context of performance and listening; the ability to describe and analyze the performance is facilitated by knowledge of the elements of music. When presented musically, logically, and sequentially, students gain understanding that leads to appreciation.

Teaching music begins with collecting and selecting a body of musical repertoire appropriate to the age and experience of the student population. The parameters and suggestions for song material have been outlined in chapter 4. Once repertoire and materials are selected, they need to be analyzed to determine song type, frequency of rhythmic and melodic patterns, tone sets, scale and tonality, among additional classifications as outlined in chapter 3.

The rhythmic and melodic sequences set out in tables 5.1 and 5.2 provide a suggested outline of musical elements that may be presented based on the song materials found in this book (see chapter 3 for a list of sources we suggest for song repertoire). This sequence may change depending on the repertoire you use with your own students. Our progression of rhythmic and melodic elements is based generally on the frequency of musical elements as they usually appear in typical four-beat patterns in the repertoire selected for this book. We can determine the rhythmic and melodic sequence from the frequency of occurrence in the repertoire. Select the most common four-beat pattern for teaching a new musical element. Once we have determined the frequency of recurring patterns, a rhythmic and melodic sequence becomes clear. We approach the teaching of music literacy skills through discovery-based learning activities—a sound to symbol orientation. In other words, children understand the concept behind the sounds before a symbol is presented. Traditional approaches to teaching music literacy begin with the symbol associated with the sound of music—a symbol to sound approach. For example, "this is a whole note, it gets four beats; this is a half note, it gets two beats."

Table 5.1 A teaching sequence for beginning rhythmic elements

Teaching quarter and eighth notes
Quarter note rest
Meter $\frac{2}{4}$
Half note and half note rest
Tie
Teaching sixteenth notes
Meter $\frac{4}{4}$
Whole note and whole note rest

continued

Table 5.1 *Continued*

Teaching sixteenth note combinations made up of one eighth note or two sixteenth notes or two sixteenth note and one eighth note

Internal upbeats

External upbeats

Syncopation

Dotted quarter note followed by an eighth note

$\frac{3}{4}$ meter

Dotted eight followed by sixteenth note

Sixteenth note followed by a dotted eighth note

Eighth note followed by a dotted quarter note

Eighth note rest

$\frac{6}{8}$ meter with even division

$\frac{6}{8}$ meter with uneven divisions

Triplet

Duplet

$\frac{2}{2}$ meter

Ties across the barline

Changing meter

Asymmetric meter $\frac{7}{8}$

Asymmetric meter $\frac{5}{4}$

Note: Prior to teaching any rhythmic elements, the concept of beat must be taught in the kindergarten classroom and reviewed in grade one.

Table 5.2 A teaching sequence for beginning melodic elements

1. Introducing notes of the pentatonic scale *so–mi* *la–so–mi* *la–so–mi–do* *la–so–mi–re–do* 2. Introducing notes of the extended pentatonic scale low *la,* low *so,* high *do'*	3. The diatonic scales Notes of the major pentachord scale Notes of the major hexachord scale Notes of the minor pentachord scale Notes of the minor hexachord scale Notes of the major scale Notes of the natural minor scale Notes of the harmonic minor scale Notes of the melodic minor scale Modal scales Dorian mode Mixolydian mode

Note: Prior to teaching any melodic elements, speaking voice and singing voice and the concept of high and low must be taught in the kindergarten classroom and reviewed in grade one.

The Relationship between Musical Concepts and Elements

We are interested in teaching three aspects of each musical element: (1) the *concept* behind the element, (2) the *solfège* or *rhythm syllables* of the new element that can be used for aural identification and reading purposes, and (3) the *traditional notation* used to represent the sound of the syllable. Once students sing a song that contains the new element, the instructor can isolate the phrase or motif containing this element. Through questioning, the instructor enables students to discover the concept behind the element. For example, when considering rhythmic elements such as quarter and eighth notes, the underlying concept is the number of sounds occurring on the beat. Once students understand the concept, the teacher can present the traditional notation. Table 5.3 provides an initial list of rhythmic and melodic elements and the concept associated with each element.

Table 5.3 A teaching sequence for beginning rhythmic elements: Concepts associated with rhythmic elements

Element	Concept	Rhythm Solfège	Related Elements, Music Theory
Quarter and eighth notes	1 and 2 sounds on a beat	*ta* and *ta di*	
Quarter note rest	a beat with no sound		
Meter $\frac{2}{4}$	Pattern of strong and weak beats		Time signature Barlines, measures Double bar lines
Half note	1 sound that lasts for 2 beats	*ta-ah*	
Half note rest	2 beats with no sound		Rhythms can be written in $\frac{2}{4}$ and $\frac{2}{2}$. Students may rewrite melodies containing one, two, or no sound on the beat. In $\frac{2}{2}$ meter, one sound on the beat is a half note, two sounds on the beat is two quarter notes, and no sound on the beat is a half note rest.
Tie	A curved line that connects two notes together		
Sixteenth notes	4 even sounds within 1 beat	*ta ka di mi*	Rhythms can be written in $\frac{2}{8}$ meter (introduction of the single eighth note)
Single eighth note and eighth note rest			Rhythms can be written in $\frac{2}{8}$ meter (single eighth note)
Meter c	A group of 4 beats; 1 strong and 3 weak beats within a measure		Rhythm can be written in c, $\frac{4}{2}$, and $\frac{4}{8}$ meter

continued

Table 5.3 *Continued*

Element	Concept	Rhythm Solfège	Related Elements, Music Theory
Whole note Whole note rest	1 sound that lasts 4 beats = 4 beats with no sound		Songs written in **C** may be written in $\frac{4}{2}$
Sixteenth note combinations made up of one eighth note or two sixteenth notes or two sixteenth notes and one eighth note	3 sounds on a beat that are not even; the first sound is longer than the last two sounds, long sound followed by two short sounds	*Ta di mi*	
	3 uneven sounds on a beat; the last sound is held longer than the first two sounds, two short sounds followed by a long sound	*ta ka di*	
Internal upbeats	Internal phrases begin with unstressed beats		
External upbeats	External phrase begin with unstressed beats		
Syncopation	3 uneven sounds over 2 beats, one short, one long and one short	*Ta di di*	
Dotted quarter followed by eighth note	2 uneven sounds over 2 beats where the first sound lasts a beat and a half	*Ta———di*	Dot placed after a note
$\frac{3}{4}$ meter	A pattern of 1 strong and 2 weak beats within a measure		
Dotted eight followed by sixteenth note	2 uneven sounds on 1 beat; the first sound is three times longer than the second	*Ta mi*	Dot placed after a note
Sixteenth note followed by a dotted eighth	2 uneven sounds on 1 beat; the first sound is shorter than the second	*Ta ka*	
Eighth note followed by a dotted quarter note	2 uneven sounds over 2 beats where the first sound lasts half a beat and the second sound lasts a beat and a half	*Ta di———*	
$\frac{6}{8}$ meter three eighth notes quarter note followed by eighth note; dotted quarter note; eighth note followed by a quarter note	1 sound on the beat; 3 even sounds on the beat; 2 sounds on the beat, 2 long followed by 1 short; 2 sounds on the beat, 1 short followed by 1 long	*Ta* *Ta ki da* *Ta da* *Ta ki*	

Table 5.3 *Continued*

Element	**Concept**	**Rhythm Solfège**	**Related Elements, Music Theory**
$\frac{6}{8}$ meter with uneven divisions dotted eighth note followed by sixteenth note and eighth note		*Ta di da*	
Triplet	3 sounds on 1 beat in simple meter	*Ta ki da*	
Duplet	2 sounds on 1 beat in compound meter	*Ta di*	
Changing meter			
Asymmetric meter			

Table 5.4 A teaching sequence for beginning melodic elements: Concepts associated with melodic elements

Element/Solfege	**Concept**	**Related Elements, Music Theory**
Introduction to the pentatonic scale		
so-mi	Two pitches one higher one lower a skip apart (minor third)	Bichord of the pentatonic scale
la	A note a step (major second) above *so*	Trichord of the pentatonic scale
do	A skip (major third) down from *mi*	Tetrachord of the pentatonic scale
re	A note between *do* and *mi.* A step above *do* (major second), a step below *mi* (major second)	Major pentatonic scale
low *la,*	*la,* is a note a (minor third) skip down from *do*	Major extended pentatonic scales Minor pentatonic scale
low *so,*	*so,* is a note a (perfect fourth) skip down from *do;* or a step (major second) from *la,*	Major extended pentatonic scale Minor extended pentatonic scale
high *do'*	*do'* a note, a skip (minor third) above *la*	Major extended pentatonic scale
	A composition that uses the notes *do re mi so la* where the final note is *re*	*re* pentatonic
	A composition that uses the notes *do re me so la* where the final note is *so*	*so* pentatonic

continued

Table 5.4 *Continued*

Element/Solfege	Concept	Related Elements, Music Theory
Introduction to the diatonic scale		
fa	*fa* a note between *mi* and *so;* a step down from *so* (major second); a step up from *mi* (minor second)	Major pentachord scale Intervals: Minor 2 Major 2 Major 3 Perfect 4 Perfect 5 Flat Major hexachord scale
ti, (low t)	*ti,* a note a step (major second) above *la,* and a step (minor second) below *do*	Minor pentachord sharp Intervals: Diminished 5 Minor hexahcord scales Intervals: Minor sixth
ti	A note a step above low *la* and a step below high *do*	
do re mi fa so la ti do'		Major scale Intervals Major sixth Major seventh
la ti do re mi fa so la		Minor scale Minor sixth Minor seventh
si *la ti do re mi fa si la*	*si* is a note a half step below *l*	Harmonic minor scale Intervals: Augmented second
fi *la ti do re mi fi si la* *so fa mi re do ti la*	*fi* is a note a whole step above *m*	Melodic minor scale
Modes		
re mi fa so la ti do re Or *la ti do re mi fi so la*		Dorian mode
so la ti do re mi fa so Or *do re mi fa so la ta do*		Mixolydian mode
mi fa so la ti do re mi Or *la ta do re mi fa so la*		Phrygian mode
fa so la ti do re mi fa Or *do re mi fi so la ti do*		Lydian mode

The Preparation, Presentation, and Practice of Musical Elements for Grades One through Five

Most teachers would agree that there are three phases of instruction and learning for teaching: preparation, presentation, and practice. In chapters 3 and 4 we have already looked at the different lesson plan formats that accommodate the teaching of music literacy in this manner.

The teaching of musical concepts depends on several factors: the age of the students, their physical and emotional maturity, and the frequency of their music instruction. Older students and those with prior musical experience generally tend to require less preparation for rhythmic elements but need more practice with melody. If the music instructor is fortunate enough to see the students several times a week, the lessons may include more variety and practice. Students who have music lessons once or twice a week require more review, thus fewer elements will be covered during each school year. Melodic elements and concepts should not be taught until the majority of students can sing in tune!

To assist instructors interested in teaching music literacy, we have created a preparation/practice teaching progression for rhythmic and melodic elements. There are between five and seven new rhythmic and melodic elements suggested for each grade. The musical elements are presented in charts like the one in table 5.5. The upper left portion of each chart indicates the new element and concepts being prepared. For each new element being prepared, we provide the name of a focus song that features this new element. For the preparation, presentation, and practice of this new element, it is important that the instructor teach approximately five songs in which the new element appears. The lower left portion of each chart indicates the element and concepts being practiced, as well as indicating any theoretical terms that can be addressed in combination with this element. In a preparation/practice lesson, the upper portion of the lesson is taught during the preparation of the new element. The lower portion is taught during the development of music skills segment of the lesson. The right portion of the chart provides the information that is presented during the presentation lesson.

Table 5.5 Basic form of a preparation, practice, and presentation teaching progression for rhythmic and melodic elements

<table>
<tr><td>Prepare
Here we list the element being prepared</td><td>Concept: Here we define the concept of the musical element being prepared

Focus song: Here we list the focus song used to teach the concept</td><td rowspan="2">Present
This portion of the chart provides the information that is presented during the presentation lesson and includes: rhythm or melodic syllables, traditional notation associated with the presentation of the new musical element, music theory, including theoretical terms that need to be presented</td></tr>
<tr><td>Practice
Here we list the element being practiced</td><td>Practice known musical elements

Here we practice different patterns associated with known musical elements. Additional information relating to this musical element is included in the practice portion of the lesson</td></tr>
</table>

Preparation, Practice, and Presentation Charts

The charts in tables 5.6a–5.6e are samples of how rhythmic and melodic concepts and elements can be prepared, presented, and practiced for grades one through five. This is only an example of a possible sequence that has been based upon the repertoire suggested for this book; there are many more possible teaching sequences.[4] What is unique about the following sequence is the fact that we have paired a rhythmic and melodic element together so that in a music lesson the music instructor will always be working on both a melodic and a rhythmic element.

Table 5.6a Preparation, practice, and presentation teaching progression for rhythmic and melodic elements: **Grade One**

Prepare High and low	**Concept:** Singing voice and tuneful singing; voice inflection; voice recognition; pointing to melodic contours. **Focus song:** *so–mi* and *mi–so–la* songs	**Present** Pitch Melodic contour
Practice Beat	Practice beat using stepping songs $\frac{2}{4}$ meter Skipping songs $\frac{6}{8}$ meter	

Prepare ♩ ♫	**Concept:** One and two sounds on a beat **Focus song:** *Rain Rain* (1st phrase)	**Present** **Syllables:** Rhythm syllables: *ta* and *ta di* **Traditional notation:** Quarter and paired eighth notes ♩ ♫ **Music theory:** Note head, stem, beam, stick and traditional notation
Practice Tuneful Singing	Responsorial singing Phrase Same and different	

Prepare *so–mi*	**Concept:** Two pitches a skip apart **Focus song:** *Rain Rain* (1st phrase) and *See Saw*	**Present** **Syllables:** Solfège syllables: *so* and *mi* **Traditional notation:** *so* and *mi* with traditional rhythmic notation *so* and *mi* on different staff placements **Music theory:** Staff, lines, spaces, skip; two-note Child's Chant
Practice ♩ ♫	Practice quarter and eighth note patterns in different 4-beat rhythm patterns extracted from the students' repertoire	

Table 5.6a *Continued*

Prepare 𝄽	**Concept:** A beat with no sound **Focus song:** *Hot Cross Buns*	**Traditional notation:** 𝄽 **Music theory:** Quarter note rest
Practice *so-mi*	Reading and writing in C, F, and G *do* positions	

Prepare *la*	**Concept:** *A* pitch that is a step higher than *so* **Focus song:** *Bounce High Bounce Low*	**Present** **Syllables:** Solfège syllable: *la* **Traditional notation:** *la* as related to *so* on different staff placements **Music theory:** Step
Practice 𝄽		

Prepare $\frac{2}{4}$ Meter	**Concept:** Pattern of strong and weak beats **Focus song:** *Bounce High Bounce Low*	**Traditional notation:** $\frac{2}{4}$ **Music theory:** Bar lines, measure, double bar lines, repeat sign, time signature, strong and weak beats
Practice *la*	Reading and writing *mi–so–la* patterns *so–la–so–mi* and *so-so–la-la–so–mi* in C, F, and G *do* positions	

Prepare $\frac{6}{8}$ meter	**Concept:** Skipping songs and they also have 2 beats per measure **Focus Song:** *Jack and Jill*	No element is being presented.
Practice *la*	Reading and writing *mi–so–la* patterns *so–mi-la–so–mi* in C, F and G *do* positions	

Table 5.6b Preparation, practice, and presentation teaching progression for rhythmic and melodic elements: **Grade Two**

Prepare *do*	**Concept:** A pitch that is a skip lower than *mi* **Focus song:** *Bow Wow Wow* (3rd phrase)	**Present** **Syllables:** Solfège syllables: *do* **Traditional notation:** *do* on different staff placements **Music theory:** Staff, lines, spaces, skip, incomplete pentatonic scale
Practice $\frac{2}{4}$		

Prepare half note	**Concept:** One sound that lasts for two beats **Focus song:** *Here Comes a Bluebird*	**Present** **Syllables:** Rhythm syllables: *ta*----ah **Traditional notation:** Half note **Music theory:** Half note and half note rest
Practice *do*	Reading and writing in C, F, and G *do* positions	

continued

Table 5.6b *Continued*

Prepare *re*	**Concept:** A pitch between *mi* and *do* **Focus song:** *Hot Cross Buns*	**Present** **Syllable:** Solfège syllables: *re* **Traditional notation:** *r* on different staff placements **Music theory**: Staff, lines, steps, major pentatonic scale
Practice half note		

Prepare $\frac{6}{8}$	**Concept:** The subdivision of the beat in skipping songs is in three **Focus song:** *Here We Go Round the Mulberry Bush*	There is no presentation of $\frac{6}{8}$ at this time, it occurs in a later grade.
Practice *re*	Reading and writing r in C, F, and G *do* positions–d r m and m r d	

Prepare ***do pentatonic scale***	**Concept***:* Scale that is made up of steps and skips **Focus songs:** *Rocky Mountain; Dance Josey* (4th phrase)	**Present** **Syllables:** Solfège syllables: *do–re–mi–so–la* **Traditional notation:** *do–re–mi–so–la written* on different staff placements **Music theory:** Major pentatonic scale
Practice $\frac{6}{8}$	Identifying the subdivision of the beat in $\frac{6}{8}$ and in $\frac{2}{4}$ meter songs.	

Prepare ♬♬	**Concept:** Four sounds on a beat **Focus song:** *Paw Paw Patch*	**Present** **Syllables:** Rhythm syllables: *ta ka di mi* **Traditional notation:** Sixteenth notes ♬♬ **Music theory**: Sixteenth notes
Practice ***do pentatonic scale***		

Prepare $\frac{4}{4}$ meter using *d* pentatonic melodies	**Concept:** A pattern of 4 beats; 1 strong and 3 weak beats within a measure **Focus song:** *Knock the Cymbals*	**Present** **Syllables:** None **Traditional notation:** $\frac{4}{4}$ **Music theory:** Time signature, meter, whole note, and whole rest
Practice ♬♬		

Table 5.6c Preparation, practice, and presentation teaching progression for rhythmic and melodic elements: **Grade Three**

Prepare	**Concept:** Three uneven sounds on a beat; the first sound is longer than the last two sounds **Focus songs:** *Fed My Horse; Mama Buy Me a Chiney Doll*	**Present** **Syllables:** Rhythm syllables: ta di mi **Traditional notation:** **Music theory:** Eighth note followed by two sixteenth notes
Practice *do pentatonic*		

Prepare *la,* (low *la*)	**Concept:** A note that is a skip lower than *do* **Focus song:** *Phoebe in Her Petticoat*	**Present** **Syllables:** Solfège Syllable: *(la,)* **Traditional notation:** *la* on different staff placements **Music theory:** A skip below *do;* *la* pentatonic scale
Practice		

Prepare	**Concept:** Three uneven sounds on a beat; the last sound is held longer than the first 2 sounds. **Focus songs:** *Hogs in the Cornfield; Do, Do Pity My Case*	**Present** **Syllables:** Rhythm syllables: *ta ka di* **Traditional notation:** 2 sixteenth notes followed by an eighth note **Music theory:** Two sixteenth notes followed by an eighth note
Practice *la,*		

Prepare *so,*	**Concept:** A note that is a step lower than *low l* **Focus song:** *Dance Josey* (phrase 2)	**Present** **Syllables:** Solfège syllables: low *so* (*so,*) **Traditional notation:** *so,* on different staff placements
Practice		

Prepare internal upbeat	**Concept:** A phrase that begins before the strong beat (split 8th note) **Focus song:** *Old Mr. Rabbit*	**Traditional notation:** Single eighth note **Music theory:** Single eighth note as an internal upbeat
Practice *so,*		

continued

Table 5.6c *Continued*

Prepare high *do'*	**Concept:** A note that is a skip higher than *l* **Focus song:** *Hogs in the Cornfield* (phrase 2)	**Present** **Syllables:** Solfège syllables: *do'* **Traditional notation:** *d'* on different staff placements
Practice internal upbeat		

Prepare external upbeats	**Concept:** Phrases beginning with unstressed upbeats **Focus songs:** Quarter note external upbeat: *I'll Sell My Hat* Two eighth notes as an external upbeat: *Band of Angels* Single eighth note: *The Jolly Miller*	**Traditional notation:** Quarter and paired eighth notes and single eighth note **Music theory:** External upbeat
Practice *do'*		

Prepare $\frac{6}{8}$	**Concept:** Skipping songs; identifying 1,2 and 3 sounds on a beat **Focus song:** *Row Row Your Boat*	**Present** There is no presentation for $\frac{6}{8}$ at this time.
Practice *do' extended pentatonic scale*		

Table 5.6d Preparation, practice, and presentation teaching progression for rhythmic and melodic elements: **Grade Four**

Prepare syncopation ♪ ♩ ♪	**Concept:** Three uneven sounds (short–long–short) occurring over 2 beats **Focus song:** *Canoe Song*	**Present** **Syllables:** Rhythm syllables: *ta di———di* **Traditional notation:** Eighth note followed by a quarter note followed by an eighth note ♪ ♩ ♪ **Music theory:** Syncopation
Practice high *d'*		

Prepare *la, pentatonic*	**Concept:** *l,* Pentatonic scale **Focus song:** *Land of the Silver Birch*	**Present** **Syllables:** Solfège syllables: *la,–do–re–mi–so–la* **Traditional notation:** *l,* pentatonic scale in different staff placements
Practice ♪ ♩ ♪		

Table 5.6d *Continued*

Prepare ♩. ♪	**Concept:** Two uneven sounds over 2 beats where the first sound lasts a beat and a half **Focus song:** *Liza Jane* (phrases 3 and 4)	**Present** **Syllables:** Rhythm syllables: *ta——di* **Traditional notation:** Dotted quarter note followed by an eighth note ♩. ♪ **Music theory:** Dotted note
Practice *la*, pentatonic		

Prepare *fa*	**Concept:** A note between *m* and *s*—the new pitch *fa* is closer to *m* **Focus song:** *Hungarian Canon*	**Present** **Syllables:** Solfège syllables: *fa* **Traditional notation:** *f* on different staff placements **Music theory:** Major pentachord and hexachord scale; half step, B♭; major and minor seconds; perfect fourth and fifth and major sixth
Practice ♩. ♪		

Prepare $\frac{3}{4}$	**Concept:** Three beat meter, a pattern of one strong and two weak beats within a measure **Focus song:** *Oh How Lovely Is the Evening*	**Traditional notation:** $\frac{3}{4}$ time signature **Music theory:** Time signature
Practice *fa*	Reading *d* pentachord melodies in F major. *fa* = *B flat* when *do* = F	

Prepare $\frac{6}{8}$	**Concept:** $\frac{6}{8}$ meter; uneven divisions of sounds on a beat **Focus song:** *Early to Bed*	**Present** There is no presentation of $\frac{6}{8}$ meter at this time
Practice *fa*	Melody *fa = B flat when do = F*	

Table 5.6e Preparation, practice, and presentation teaching progression for rhythmic and melodic elements: **Grade Five**

Prepare *ti*, (low t)	**Concept:** A pitch between *d* and *low l*; a note that is a half step below *d* and a whole step above *low l* **Focus song:** *Birch Tree*	**Present** **Syllables:** Solfège syllable: *ti*, (low t) **Traditional notation:** *t*, on different staff placements **Music theory:** *la*, pentachord scale; major and minor third; perfect fourth and fifth and Minor sixth; diminished fifth
Practice $\frac{3}{4}$		

continued

Table 5.6e *Continued*

Prepare ♪.♬ ♬♪.	**Concept:** Two uneven sounds on 1 beat; the first sound is longer than the second; 2 uneven sounds on 1 beat; the first sound is short and the second sound is long **Focus song:** *Donkey Riding*	**Present** **Syllables:** Rhythm syllables: *ta mi* and *ta ka* **Traditional notation:** Dotted eighth followed by a sixteenth note–*ta mi;* the reverse a sixteenth note followed by a dotted eighth note–*ta ka* ♪.♬ ♬♪. **Music theory:** dotted eighth note
Practice *ti,* (low *ti*)	practice *la,* hexachord *F sharp* in the key of e minor and reading major and minor melodies	

Prepare high *ti'*	**Concept:** *Major scale*—a series of eight pitches with half steps between the third and fourth pitches and the seventh and eighth pitches and whole steps between all others **Focus song:** *Alleluia*	**Present** **Syllables:** Solfège syllables: *ti* **Traditional notation:** *ti* on different staff placements **Music theory**: Major scale; major seventh
Practice ♪.♬ ♬♪.		

Prepare ♪ ♩.	**Concept:** Two uneven sounds over 2 beats where the first sound lasts half a beat and the second sound lasts a beat and a half **Focus song:** *Charlotte Town*	**Present** **Syllables:** Rhythm syllables: *ta ka----------* **Traditional notation:** Eighth note followed by a dotted quarter ♪ ♩.
Practice *ti*	C sharp and the key of D major	

Prepare Minor scale	**Concept:** *Minor scale*—a series of eight pitches with half steps between the second and third pitches and the fifth and sixth pitches and whole steps between all others **Focus song:** *Alleluia (in minor)*	**Present** **Syllables:** Solfège syllables: *la,–ti,–do–re–mi–fa–so–la* **Traditional notation**
Practice ♪ ♩.		

Table 5.6e *Continued*

Prepare $\frac{6}{8}$ ♪♪♪ ♩ ♪ ♩.	**Concept:** Compound meter 3 even sounds on a beat, 1 even sound on a beat, 2 uneven sounds on a beat where the first sound is twice as long as the second sound **Focus song:** *Row, Row, Row Your Boat*	**Present** **Syllables:** Rhythm syllables: *ta, ta ki da, ta da* **Traditional notation:** 3 eighth notes; dotted quarter note; quarter note; single eighth note ♪♪♪ ♩ ♪ ♩. **Music theory:** $\frac{6}{8}$ time signature
Practice minor scale		

Prepare *fi*	**Concept:** Sound that is a half step above *fa;* raised 6th of a natural minor scale **Focus song:** *Scarborough Fair*	**Present** **Syllables:** Solfège syllables: *fi* **Traditional notation:** *fi* on different staff placements **Music theory:** Dorian mode
Practice rhythm patterns in compound meter ♪♪♪ ♩ ♪ ♩.		

Prepare uneven subdivisions of beats ♪. ♬ ♪ in $\frac{6}{8}$ meter	**Concept:** Uneven divisions of the beat in compound meter **Focus song:** *Early To Bed*	**Present** **Syllables:** Rhythm syllables: *ta di da* **Traditional notation:** Dotted eighth note followed by a sixteenth note followed by an eighth note ♪. ♬ ♪ **Music theory:** Uneven divisions of the beat in compound meter
Practice *fi* and Dorian mode		

Prepare *si*	**Concept:** A pitch a half step below *la;* raised 7 of a harmonic minor scale **Focus song:** *Ah, Poor Bird*	**Present** **Syllables:** Solfège syllables: *la,–ti,–do–re–mi–fa–si–la* **Traditional notation** **Music Theory:** Harmonic minor scale; augmented second
Practice uneven subdivisions of beats ♪. ♬ ♪ in compound meter		

continued

Table 5.6e *Continued*

Prepare rhythmic patterns in compound meter	**Concept:** Subdivision of the beat in compound meter **Focus songs:** *Morning Is Come; Come Let's Dance*	**Present** **Syllables:** Rhythm syllables: *ta va ki da; ta ki di da ma* **Traditional notation:**
Practice *si* and harmonic minor scale		

Prepare melodic minor scale	**Concept:** A natural minor scale with a raised sixth and seventh degrees and descends in natural minor **Focus Song:** *Who Can Sail*	**Present** **Syllables:** Solfège syllables: *la,–ti,–do–re–mi–fi–si–la–so–fa–mi–re–do–ti,–la,*
Practice rhythmic patterns in compound meter		

Prepare triplet	**Concept:** Three even sounds on a beat in simple meter **Focus Song:** *Every Night When the Sun Goes Down*	**Present** **Music theory:** Rhythm syllables: *ta ki da,*
Practice melodic minor scale		

Prepare *ta*	**Concept:** A note that is a half-step lower than the seventh degree of a major scale **Focus Song:** *Old Joe Clark*	**Present** **Syllables:** Solfège syllables: *do–re–mi–fa–so–la–ta–do'*
Practice		

Repertoire List Arranged by Element and Fundamental Patterns

Included in appendix 3 is the repertoire list for each grade arranged by element as it appears in the above sequence of combined melodic and rhythmic elements. The focus song containing the key pattern is suggested for the preparation, presentation, and practice of that element. Each element is further broken into additional related patterns that may be used in the initial practice lesson and practice lesson.

Developing a Preparation/Practice Lesson and a Presentation Lesson Plan Framework That Includes Music Literacy Activities

The goal of this section is to incorporate information for developing musical literacy into the preparation/practice and presentation lesson plan formats. Our lesson plan formats may now include:

- Singing and performing known songs with rhythmic and solfège syllables.
- Specific melodic and rhythmic concepts selected according to the sequence of musical elements for each grade.
- Introducing the rhythm syllables, traditional names, and traditional notation (during the presentation lesson for a rhythmic element).
- Introducing the solfège syllables, hand signs, and tone steps (during the presentation lesson for a melodic element).

The Preparation/Practice Lesson

In a preparation/practice lesson, we prepare a specific new concept and practice a familiar element based on the music literacy sequence chart for each grade. During this lesson, we continue to develop singing abilities, teach new repertoire, develop movement skills, and listening skills of students. To write this lesson plan we need:

- curriculum goals to determine objectives (see appendix 1)
- alphabetized list of songs to determine new song to be taught (see appendix 2)
- preparation, practice, and presentation chart to determine what elements to prepare and practice (found in this chapter)
- pedagogical use of songs to determine songs for the preparation and practice of each new musical element (see appendix 3)

Table 5.7 presents a sample preparation/practice lesson plan for preparing sixteenth notes and practicing *do* pentatonic melodies. This is just a sketch and we are not attempting to create smooth transitions between one section of the lesson and another at this time; we will focus on musical transitions in later chapters.

Table 5.7 Developing a preparation/practice lesson plan framework: Preparation of sixteenth notes and the practice of *re*

Focus	Activities, Procedures, and Assessments
Introduction	
Performance and demonstration of known musical concepts and elements	Vocal warm-up exercises Develop singing skills through beautiful singing, vocal warm-ups, and breathing exercises Sing with text and play the game *Here Comes a Bluebird* Sing with rhythm syllables Sing with text (while instructor plays in canon on the recorder)
Core activities	
Acquisition of repertoire	**Teach *Down Came a Lady* in preparation for teaching $\frac{4}{4}$ meter**
Performance and preparation of new concept	**Teacher provides students with a series of discovery learning activities that will develop their knowledge of four sounds on a beat (sixteenth notes) through known songs such as *Paw Paw Patch***
Movement development	Known song: *Tideo* Focus on the sequential development of age-appropriate movement skills
Performance and musical skill development	**Students reinforce their knowledge of *re* working on the skill areas selected from the following: reading and writing, form, and memory through known songs such as *Frosty Weather***
Closure Review and summation	Listening activity Teacher sings the next new song to be learned by students as a listening activity

Table 5.8 Developing a lesson plan framework for the presentation of sixteenth notes

Focus	Activities, Procedures, and Assessments
Introduction	
Performance and demonstration of known musical concepts and elements	Develop singing skills through beautiful singing, vocal warm-ups, and breathing exercises Students demonstrate their prior knowledge: Sing *Rocky Mountain* with text Sing rhythm syllables Sing with solfège syllables Sing in Canon

Table 5.8 *Continued*

Focus	**Activities, Procedures, and Assessments**
Core activities	
Acquisition of repertoire	Teach *Ida Red* using an appropriate method of presentation selected from the repertoire list for the grade
Performance and presentation of the syllable of the new element in the target pattern	**Present rhythm syllables for four sounds on a beat and sing the target pattern with rhythm syllables using *Paw Paw Patch***
And traditional notation	Present the traditional notation for the song and read with rhythm syllables
Movement development	Focus on the sequential development of age-appropriate movement skills using the song *Tideo*
Performance and presentation of the syllable of the new element in a related pattern	**Present rhythm syllables for four sounds on a beat and sing the related pattern with rhythm syllables using the song *Dinah*** Present the notation for the song and read with rhythm syllables
Closure	
Review and summation	Listening activity Teacher sings *Knock the Cymbals* as a listening activity

Discussion Questions

1. How can teaching tools aid students' abilities to read and write music?
2. How does the choice of song repertoire affect the teaching sequence of rhythmic and melodic concepts and elements?
3. Discuss the difference between a concept and an element.
4. Explain the organization of the preparation, presentation, and practice charts found in this chapter.
5. Explain the organization of the pedagogical list of songs provided for each grade.
6. How can teaching tools help with teaching elements in a classroom?
7. We should not destroy the enjoyment of singing in the classroom by using folk songs and games to develop music literacy skills. Actually spending time teaching music literacy skills is not relevant to today's music students. Music theory concepts should be taught through abstract exercises and worksheets where students learn how to write and practice different scales, intervals, and learn traditional notation. Discuss.

➤ Ongoing Assignment

1. Design a preparation/practice lesson plan for a first grade class. What resources provided in this text did you use to develop your lesson plan?
2. Design a preparation/practice lesson plan for a third grade class. What resources provided in this text did you use to develop your lesson plan?
3. Choose a concept to prepare and an element to practice for a third grade class. Create a preparation/practice lesson plan and a presentation lesson plan. You will need the curriculum goals (appendix 1), alphabetized list (appendix 2), and repertoire list arranged by concepts (appendix 3).

References

Bamberger, Jeanne. "How the Conventions of Music Notation Shape Musical Perception and Performance," in *Musical Communication,* ed. Dorothy Miell, Raymond Macdonald, and David J. Hargreaves. New York: Oxford University Press, 2005.

Barrett, Margaret. "Representation, Cognition and Musical Communication: Invented Notation in Children's Musical Communication," in *Musical Communication,* ed. Dorothy Miell, Raymond Macdonald, and David J. Hargreaves. New York: Oxford University Press, 2005.

Campbell, Patricia Shehan. *Lessons from the World.* New York: Schirmer Books, 1991.

Choksy, Lois, Robert M. Abramson, Avon E. Gillespie, David Woods, and Frank York. *Teaching Music in the Twenty-first Century.* 2nd ed. Upper Saddle River, N.J.: Prentice-Hall, 2000.

Cohen, Annabel J. "Musical Cognition: Defining Constraints on Musical Communication," in *Musical Communication,* ed. Dorothy Miell, Raymond Macdonald, and David J. Hargreaves. New York: Oxford University Press, 2005.

Colwell, Richard, and Carol Richardson, eds. *The New Handbook of Research on Music Teaching and Learning.* A Project of the Music Educators National Conference. New York: Oxford University Press, 2002.

Frazee, Jane. *Discovering Orff: A Curriculum for Music Teachers.* New York: Schott, 1997.

Juslin, Patrik N. "From Mimesis to Catharsis: Expression, Perception and Induction of Emotion in Music," in *Musical Communication,* ed. Dorothy Miell, Raymond Macdonald, and David J. Hargreaves. New York: Oxford University Press, 2005.

MENC. *What Every Young American Should Know and be Able to Do in the Arts: National Standards for Arts Education.* Reston, Va.: Music Educators National Conference, 1994.

Mills, Janet, and Gary E. McPherson. "Musical Literacy," in *The Child as Musician: A Handbook of Musical Development,* ed. Gary McPherson. New York: Oxford University Press, 2006.

Sloboda, John. "Cognitive Processes," in *Exploring the Musical Mind: Cognition, Emotion, Ability, Function* New York: Oxford University Press, 2005.

Stauffer, Sandra Lee. *Strategies for Teaching K–4 General Music.* Reston, Va.: Music Educators National Conference, 1989.

Chapter 6

From Sound to Symbol

A New Learning Theory Model

The intuitive experience and enjoyment of music should come first, such that the latter acquisition of formal musical skills occurs inductively, that is, as an integral growth of the child's experience. A good deal of traditional music education has worked deductively: the formal rules have been taught in the abstract, for example, through verbal description or written notation, rather than in the practical context of making the sounds themselves.

David J. Hargreaves, *The Developmental Psychology of Music*

Key Questions

What do we mean by the preparation, presentation, and practice of a musical element?

What are the learning stages of the cognitive phase of instruction?

What are the learning stages of the associative phase of instruction?

What is the difference between a target pattern and a related pattern?

What are the learning stages of the assimilative phase of instruction?

How does this learning theory model affect the construction of a lesson plan?

How does this learning theory model affect the construction of a preparation/practice lesson plan?

How does this learning theory model affect the construction of a presentation lesson plan?

How can we design an initial practice lesson once we have presented a concept?

In the previous chapters, we describe the components of a teaching portfolio and music curriculum for the elementary school, Kodály's philosophy, repertoire aspects of performance, sequential curricular planning, and basic lesson planning. In chapter 5 we discuss a sequence for rhythmic and melodic musical elements. In this chapter we present a model of how basic music literacy skills can be systematically developed through a sound to symbol orientation to teaching.

For decades music educators have proclaimed the importance of "sound before symbol" but no one has provided a methodology that makes this all-important dictum possible. The focus of this chapter is to make the process of teaching from sound to symbol accessible to all who believe in the veracity of this statement.

A major concern, voiced by the music teachers we worked with, was addressing how to get students to think about sound. The ultimate challenge became how to get students to think about sound and then describe what they heard. We believe that the learning theory model we present in this chapter is an important step in guiding students to understand music as a sound event. We have delineated a process of instruction that draws on the students' musical experience and guides them to undestand music from the point of their perception of sound. In this way we are unique. We delineate a process of instruction—a model of learning and instruction—that draws on the students' musical experience and guides them to understand music from their perception of sound.

Introduction

A common thread in the psychological literature concerning the teaching of music literacy is the "sound before symbol" principle that is adopted in music education circles and is of paramount importance for teaching music literacy. This idea stemmed from the work of the Swiss educator Heinrich Pestalozzi (1746–1827).[1] His work shaped the efforts of such great American music educators as Lowell Mason, as well as the current teaching methodologies adopted for use by American music teachers. "The earliest methods used in public school music instruction thus were based on the logic of 'sound before sight' and 'practice before theory;' listening and singing experiences led to an understanding of notation and theory."[2]

Jerome Bruner's work has enhanced our understanding of the "sound before symbol" principle. Bruner's theory of instruction proposes that learning may be accomplished using three teaching and learning strategies: (1) enactive, (2) iconic, and (3) symbolic. For example, when students are learning how to read a new melodic pattern they can (1) trace the melodic contour of the new melodic pattern with their arm as they sing the words of the melody or hum the contour (Strategy 1: enactive); (2) point to icons that represent the melodic contour (Strategy 2: iconic); or (3) read the traditional notation for this melodic contour on the staff (Strategy 3: symbolic).[3] However, this theory of instruction is at its most complex when students move from the iconic stage to the symbolic stage. While a student's theoretical understanding may be enhanced through this approach we have no way to document whether students are developing their auditory imagery—their ability to create the sound of the new element mentally without singing or playing. Edwin Gordon's theory of music learning[4] also attempts to expand our understanding of the sound before sight principle.

A New Learning Theory Model

The learning theory model proposed in this chapter provides a cohesive model for linking the sound of music to the symbol. Additionally, it allows us to examine the learning processes associated with the acquisition of basic music literacy skills. This systematic model of learning permits students to develop the ability to read and write music[5] as a consequence of music instruction that is perceptually based. Constructivist and cognitive theories,[6] as well as the work of Kodály scholars,[7] were used as a foundation for this research. Building upon the work of Kodály scholars, we have developed a model of instruction and learning that identifies and classifies cognitive scaffolding activities used to facilitate the development of music literacy in the music classroom through a sound to symbol approach to teaching.[8] Music performance and critical thinking strategies become critical teaching techniques associated with this model of learning. **Students become active learners not simply learning about the musical concept but additionally learning about the process of their own learning through music performance.**[9]

This learning theory model provides teachers with a path that enables students to gain musical knowledge, understanding, comprehension, and mastery of the basic building blocks[10] of music fundamentals. (In chapter 5, we provide a melodic and rhythmic learning sequence appropriate for grades one through five.) Additionally students develop musical skills such as reading, writing, improvisation, and composition. (Chapter 7 provides a detailed explanation of musical skill development.) Our model for learning and teaching is divided into three phases of learning: **cognitive phase, associative phase,** and **assimilative phase.**

- In the cognitive phase, students experience and perceive the new concept and element in a target pattern through kinesthetic, aural, and visual activities always within the context of performance and the enjoyment of music.
- In the associative phase, students connect their kinesthetic, aural, and visual understanding of the target pattern and related patterns to solfège or rhythm syllables and staff placement.
- In the assimilative phase, students continue to develop their musicianship skills incorporating the newly learned musical element.

Table 6.1 A model for music learning and teaching

Phase One: The Cognitive Phase
Preparation

Stage 1: Developing Kinesthetic Awareness. Constructing Kinesthetic Understanding through Performance and Movement

Students listen to the instructor sing the new song.
Students perform the new song with movement.
Rationale: To match patterns of experience to patterns of music.

Stage 2: Developing Aural Awareness. Constructing Aural Understanding by Responding to Questions

Students aurally analyze the characteristics of the new musical element with the help of the instructor.
Students describe the characteristics of the new element.
Rationale: To verbalize what they perceive.

Stage 3: Developing Visual Awareness. Constructing a Visual Representation of the Aural Understanding

Students create a visual representation based on their aural understanding.
Rationale: To visually represent what they have heard and verbalized.

↓

continued

Table 6.1 *Continued*

Phase Two: The Associative Phase
Presentation

Stage 1: Associate the sound of the new element with solfège or rhythmic syllables in the target pattern and related patterns
Stage 2: Associate traditional notation with the sound of the new musical element in the target pattern or related patterns. Students read this notation using rhythm syllables, numbers, solfège syllables, letter names, and/or scale degree numbers.

↓

Phase Three: Assimilative Phase
Practice and Assessment

Stage 1: Students aurally and visually recognize the new element in familiar and new songs
Stage 2: Students practice the new element in conjunction with previously learned musical elements and musical skills.
Stage 3: The instructor assesses students' understanding of the new musical element.

Cognitive Phase: Preparation

In this phase students learn song material that contains the primary rhythmic and melodic patterns that will be used for teaching reading and writing. Research reveals that students do not initially perceive music as isolated events (note-to-note events) but as patterns according to recognized Gestalt principles for perceptual organization.[11] Initially the instructor presents song material containing the core structural melodic and rhythmic patterns that can later be extracted. Once presented, each pattern[12] will provide the musical scaffolding for more advanced melodic and rhythmic patterns and concepts. In this manner students are always comparing the characteristics of unknown musical patterns and structures to known musical patterns and structures. This provides students with the opportunity to assimilate, accommodate, and construct music knowledge within familiar stylistic frameworks.

In our model, the cognitive phase of learning is divided into three stages:

Stage 1: Developing Kinesthetic Awareness
Stage 2: Developing Aural Awareness
Stage 3: Developing Visual Awareness

Stage I: Developing Kinesthetic Awareness

In the kinesthetic stage, students are taught a selection of core song materials by rote containing the new element[13] typically found within a four-beat pattern. The song material is taught in a stylistically correct manner, and the instructor models a kinesthetic motion that focuses the students' attention on the new element. Movement activities[14] help guide students to hear the new element in the target phrase. The goal is for students to sing while performing a motion that emphasizes the new musical element on their own. At the same time, the instructor should address musicality components such as phrasing, dynamics, and general issues related to musicality, for students to gain a broader perspective of musical literacy skills.

Movement, rote learning, and the development of musical memory form a foundation for the promotion of musical literacy.[15] Students must be able to sing some of their repertoire fluently and independently before moving on to the aural awareness stage. Cutietta and Booth's research suggests that "the repeated act of performing a piece of music, without the aid of written notation or language-based instruction can lead to substantive changes in an individual's internal representation of that melody's primary features."[16] Peretz has noted that pitch contour is the first aspect of melody that is stored upon hearing a new melody and contour extraction is "a preliminary and indispensable step to the precise encoding of intervals."[17] This also has a positive effect on short-term musical memory.[18]

Examples of Kinesthetic Activities for Rhythm

1. Students conduct to feel the meter.
2. Students perform the song while clapping the rhythm.
3. Students learn to sing songs by rote and perform a kinesthetic motion that highlights the new rhythmic element. For example, students may clap the rhythm of the phrase containing the target pattern and keep the beat on their knees for the other phrases of a song.
4. Students perform the song while pointing to pictures or icons showing the number of sounds per beat. Initially these students are following the motions of the instructor. We believe that this procedure is a kinesthetic activity for the student; students are performing a kinesthetic activity by pointing to icons, and no explanation is made as to what these symbols represent. Students perform the new rhythmic pattern with the basic beat. The class may be divided into two groups. One group performs the rhythm pattern and the other performs the beat. This activity may be practiced in different combinations. We suggest the following order of performance: teacher/class, class/teacher, divided class, and two individuals. The most advanced activity for this concept is for individual students to sing the song while walking the beat and clapping the rhythm.
5. Students inner hear (sing the song silently in their head) the four-beat phrase of the song containing the new element while clapping the rhythm.

Examples of Kinesthetic Activities for Melody

1. Students perform the song and point to a representation that outlines the melodic contour.
2. Students use simple body signs, for example, touch shoulders for *high* and waist for *low* sounds.
3. Students perform the song and demonstrate the direction of the melodic line with arm motions. These motions should be natural and musical.

Stage 2: Developing Aural Awareness

The goal of the aural awareness stage is for students to aurally recognize and describe the characteristics or attributes of the new rhythmic or melodic concept. Bartholomew observes that to teach the sounds of music before the signs helps students become more responsive to music as well as the connections and relationships in the music.[19] Petzold's study concludes that aural perception should precede visual perception and that one must be able to hear music in order to develop skills in music reading.[20] Hewson's work suggests that aural experiences prior to encountering notation facilitates the development of sight-singing skills.[21] Results of Gromko and Poorman's recent research support findings that there is a strong connection between what a child aurally perceives and their ability to represent this information using their own personal representations of music.[22]

To develop students' aural awareness, the instructor asks questions that guide students to describe the position and attributes of the new musical element. For rhythmic elements, the goal is for students to be able to identify the number of sounds within a beat. For example, if we are teaching sixteenth notes, students must be able to perceive and identify four sounds on a beat. For melodic elements, the goal is for students to aurally describe and compare the new melodic element to previously known elements. For example, if students know the pentachord scale (*do–re–mi–fa–so*) and we want to teach the new note *la,* students must describe the new sound (*la*) as being higher than *so.* (We do not label this new sound until the associative phase.) In the aural awareness stage, students will sing hexachord songs with solfège but replace singing the *a* solfège syllable with the word "high." *Twinkle, twinkle little star* would be sung *do–do–so–so–high high–so*). The "new" information gained in the aural awareness stage is now embedded in the students' memory through the kinesthetic experience and further encoded through the students' verbalization of the aural and kinesthetic experiences.

Examples of Aural Awareness Questions for Rhythm

- Sample Questions for Rhythmic Elements that Occur on One Beat
  Perform the target pattern and ask:
  1. How many beats did we perform?
  2. On which beat did you hear *the new sound?*[23]
  3. How many *sounds* did you perform on that beat?
  4. How would you describe these sounds? (For example, two short sounds, or a long sound followed by two short sounds, etc.)
- Sample Questions for Rhythms that Last Longer than One Beat
  1. Is there a place in our target pattern where a sound lasts longer than one beat?
  2. On which beat does it begin?
  3. For how many beats do we hold the sound?
  4. How would you describe these sounds?
- Sample Questions for Uneven Rhythm Patterns Lasting Longer than a Beat
  1. Is there a place in the target pattern where the rhythm is uneven?
  2. On which beats do you perform the uneven pattern?
  3. How many sounds do you perform on *those beats?*
  4. Describe the placement of sounds on *those beats?*
  5. How would you describe these sounds?

Examples of Aural Awareness Questions for Melody

1. How many beats did we perform?
2. On what words or syllables or beats does *the new melodic pitch* occur?
3. Is *the new pitch* higher than or lower than all of the pitches we know?

Stage 3: Developing Visual Awareness

In the visual awareness stage, we confront students with the problem of creating a visual representation of the target pattern. Drawing on knowledge gained through the kinesthetic awareness and the aural awareness stages, students construct their own visual representation of the target pattern. This may be accomplished by providing students with unifix cubes. (Plastic manipulative blocks commonly used in elementary math classes.) For example, if students are asked to show a representation of the number of sounds on a beat, students can use four unifix cubes attached together to show one sound on a beat, two groups of two unifix cubes attached to show two sounds on a beat, and four individual unifix cubes to show four sounds on a beat. If students are asked to show a representation of melodic contour, then each individual unifix cube can represent a pitch. Allowing children to construct their own representation of music is a form of problem solving that allows the music instructor to gauge a students understanding of a music concept and permits students to continue to understand their knowledge of a concept.[24]

By connecting the aural awareness stage to the visual stage, the student is allowed time to make the connection between what they hear and how to represent it. Bamberger argues, "if the reader of the symbols (teacher/researcher or child) has failed to do the work of constructing the elements, properties, and relations inherent in the framework through which these symbols gain meaning, neither a teacher/researcher reading a child's invented symbol system nor a child reading the privileged symbol systems taught in school can make of the phenomena described by the symbols the particular sense the symbols-makers intend."[25] This approach to teaching is similar to the radical constructivism philosophy. Knowledge and understanding is constructed as a result of students being presented with a series of learning encounters that de-stablize their current understanding of a concept; equilibration is restored through student/student, student/teacher interaction and subsequent student reflection.[26] For example, when asking students to construct a representation of a target rhythm pattern, some students will create a representation that focuses on the duration of the sounds. Other students will focus on the placement of the sound (point of attack) within the beat. Both representations are valid; we believe that students must understand both before any labeling can take place. For melodic elements, some students choose to show the melodic contour of a target melodic pattern as described in "Visual Awareness Activities for Melody." Other students choose to create a visual representation, focusing on the "height of the notes." In order for students to understand both of these representations, the teacher leads the students to trace the height of each block vertically that represents a musical pitch and place this graph horizontally on a flat surface. Students come to an understanding that both representations actually represent the same concept.

Visual awareness activities are tangible indications of how students understand new concepts. Once students have completed a visual representation of the target pattern, it is critically important that the instructor asks students to sing the target pattern and point to what they have drawn. The instructor may ask (using language appropriate to children):

- What were the significant factors that contributed to your representation of the target pattern?
- What information does your representation capture?
- Identify known rhythmic and melodic patterns in the target pattern.

How a student represents a target pattern provides the instructor with an opportunity to observe a student's musical development. If a student cannot represent a target pattern at the visual awareness stage, more work in both the kinesthetic and aural awareness stage is required. Initially some students may not be able to represent the target phrase accurately but when asked to point to their representation, their pointing may be correct. The instructor may need to help the students to find a way to help students how to represent their action in a visual representation. Other times students are able to provide a representation that seems perfectly logical to them but the instructor may need to work with students to help them create a superior representation of the concept.

Visual Awareness Activities for Rhythm

- Students are asked to create a visual representation of the target pattern containing the new rhythmic element. We suggest using unifix cubes; this provides a challenge and an opportunity for students to use a three-dimensional object to represent a rhythmic or melodic pattern. We suggest using pencil and paper with older students; however, they may not use traditional musical notation. It is not unusual for the students' representation to be similar to the representation used in the kinesthetic stage.
- Students create a visual representation for the specific rhythmic pattern. Students should be encouraged to identify all known rhythmic elements in their representation.
- Students may write the text of a song over the beats in the target pattern.
- Students may write the solfège syllables over each beat to indicate the number of sounds over the beats for a phrase.

Visual Awareness Activities for Melody

- Students create the melodic contour of the target pattern with unifix cubes.
- Students write the text of the song spatially to show the melodic contour.
- Students write the solfège syllables of the target pattern spatially using a question mark to indicate the placement of new melodic element.
- More advanced students use horizontal lines to indicate the duration and contour of each note of the melody. This is sometimes referred to as *piano roll notation.*[27] Students may also identify all known elements in their representation.

The three stages of learning in the cognitive phase offer a valuable path to musical understanding and the development of critical thinking skills. The cognitive phase provides students with the opportunity of understanding the characteristics of the new element from a kinesthetic, aural, and visual perspective. This phase allows students' time to re-envision and re-conceptualize their intuitive knowledge and provides the instructor with a foundation for presenting traditional notation.[28]

We believe that the instructor must address the kinesthetic, the aural, and the visual awareness stages of learning in this order. (This model of learning will also help the different types of learners—kinesthetic, aural, visual, and mixed—in your classroom.) Some Kodály instructors believe that the kinesthetic, aural, and visual stages of learning can be addressed in random order. We disagree. For example, we believe that during the aural stage of learning, no visual aids should be used to help students describe the characteristics of the new element. The instructor should ask questions without referring to a visual representation. It is vitally important that students think about what they have heard without the help of a visual aid. After describing what they have heard, students ought to be given time to draw their own representation of the musical phase containing the new element. A student's visual representation offers clues as to how they perceive the new musical element. It also provides the instructor with information for the kinds of questions and activities that could aid students who need help. Without this assessment opportunity, we lose the chance to understand the student's current perception of the new element.

Associative Phase: Presentation

Once students can visually represent the target pattern using their own notation, we proceed to the associative phase. The associative phase is broken into two stages.

Stage 1: Associate the Sound with Rhythm or Solfège Syllables

The instructor guides students to review the critical aural attributes of the target pattern. We label the sound of the target pattern with either rhythm or solfège syllables (and the corresponding hand sign[29]). For solfège syllables, introduce the hand sign for the new note. During this stage we also practice related patterns that contain the new element. Studies by Colley, Palmer, and Shehan have concluded that the use of musical tools such as solfège and rhythmic syllables and hand signs are effective pedagogical devices.[30] The use of musical tools allows students to explore their musical knowledge beyond their starting point that makes possible new achievements and understanding.[31]

Stage 2: Associate Traditional Notation with the Sound

Once the students aurally identify the new element in the target pattern with syllables, the instructor associates traditional notation with the sound of the target pattern. The instructor can then present the notation for other related patterns. The associative phrase of instruction ensures that students are not introduced to music theory before they can hear what they see and see what they hear.[32]

In this model of teaching and learning, students are taught conceptual information based on their perceptual understandings attained through musical performance. The new musical element is constructed and written and subsequently read with solfège or rhythm syllables. In this manner the writing of music "not only provides the readiness for attaining higher levels of learning but also reinforces the ability to read music."[33]

Assimilative Phase: Practice and Assessment

In the assimilative phase, students begin to reinforce and integrate knowledge of the new musical element in a variety of four-beat patterns and in conjunction with musical skills.

The instructor guides students to understand how new musical knowledge relates to previously learned knowledge within the context of familiar and new musical repertoire. The same processes for teaching a new element in the cognitive phase may be repeated in this phase but the name for the new element must be used. It is critical for students to continue to work on aural and visual fluency. The assimilative phase is broken into two stages.

Stage 1: Students aurally and visually recognize the new element in familiar and new songs.
Stage 2: Students practice the new element in conjunction with previously learned musical elements and musical skills.
Stage 3: The instructor assesses students' understanding of the new musical element.

All patterns associated with the new element are practiced over an extended period of time with rhythm syllables in conjunction with curriculum goals and musical skills or enriching activities. These musical skills include:

- Development of rhythmic and melodic elements and concepts
- Writing
- Counting with numbers
- Solfège syllables
- Letter names and scale degree numbers
- Reading
- Sight-singing
- Development of musical memory
- Development of audiation skills
- Dictation and ear-training
- Ensemble singing
- Form and analysis
- Listening
- Instrumental experience
- Developing harmonic hearing
- Music theory vocabulary

Throughout this stage of learning the newly learned musical elements are identified while additional musical concepts are prepared. As the new element is identified, named, and practiced in the students' repertoire of songs, the instructor guides students to recognize familiar musical elements that are "re-presented" within the context of each new element. Thus evaluation is "built-in" the process of instruction and is ongoing in each type of lesson.

Regardless of age, students need a consistent approach to instruction and learning if we are to teach them basic musical elements and concepts that will develop music literacy. Using a perceptual orientation first promotes the development of aural acuity; students are guided to verbally discuss what they hear and then reflect their observations using their own notation. Once the instructor is assured that students can hear and represent the new element, labeling can take place. Our learning theory model provides a perceptual orientation to teaching and learning that allows for the integration of aural observations prior to focusing on notation and traditional representations of musical knowledge.

In our learning theory model, (1) students develop their musicianship skills through the study of music repertoire that is familiar to them; (2) musicianship skills are developed through aural/oral and written repertoires; (3) students are engaged in a learning process that is associated with the aural/oral traditions (jazz and popular musicians) and notated traditions (classical musicians); (4) students engage in collaborative learning; (5) individualized instruction enables students to develop musical skill preferences such as performance, improvisation, or composition; (6) knowledge of repertoire, musical performance through singing, movement and playing instruments, listening, creativity, and critical thinking skills are integrated.[34]

In summary "the various features of a tune which at first remained unnoticed become liberated from the meld, and this process needs to occur over and over again in different ways: at each stage new entities, new features are made to come into existence, requiring in turn the mental construction of new relations and new coordinating schemata. And as features and relations become accessible for manipulation and scrutiny and are coordinated in new ways, the coordination's form the basis for the construction of stable general structures in terms of which particular, unique instances can be described, compared, and understood."[35] Therefore, one role of the instructor in the learning of symbolic notation becomes clearer: to deconstruct the musical material into melodic and rhythmic schemes so that they become reconstructed into cognitive schemes by the student in order that this information becomes operational for them through the learning process.

A Comparison of the Houlahan/Tacka Model of Learning with Current Teaching Approaches Adopted by Kodály Instructors

Most Kodály instructors adopt a model of teaching musical elements based on four steps:

1. Prepare
2. Make conscious, or presentation
3. Reinforce or practice
4. Assessment

For the basis of comparison, we use the Choksy model of learning associated with the Kodály concept. This model represents the one most closely followed by Hungarian and American Kodály instructors.[36] The Choksy model of learning emphasizes the importance of experiencing the song material before any notation takes place during the preparation phase.

> They do not, at this time, see the notation for these songs. They engage in whatever musical activities suit the nature of each song; they may sing them softer or louder and determine appropriate dynamics; they may sing them faster and slower and determine appropriate

> tempo; they may step the beat, clap an ostinato, perform the song rhythms that are known, and they may diagram the form. They may play the game if there is one. In other words they may engage in all the activities that require only a singing knowledge of the songs.[37]

While we agree with this approach to teaching we also believe that the preparation phrase of instruction requires more sequenced activities in combination with the performance of music repertoire. During the preparation phase of learning, we provide students with a series of activities that allow them to develop their kinesthetic awareness, aural awareness, and finally visually awareness of the new concept or element. Emphasis on the preparation phase allows students the time to understand because it accommodates three modes of learning. This phase of learning is actually an equalizer for special education students who might be kinesthetic, aural, or visual learners. The preparation phase also strengthens weaknesses. It provides an opportunity for visual learners to become more aural, for kinesthetic learners to become more visual, and so on. We believe that students must work sequentially through these stages and they cannot be mixed up. Students are provided an opportunity to develop their aural awareness skills and draw upon their perceptual skills in order to begin to construct their own understanding of the new concept. Instructors can then assess students' aural awareness skills by asking students to create a visual representation of the melody using a form of pre-notation. If a student can correctly create a representation of the melody while using his or her auditory imagery, then they are in a better position to understand how sounds can be labeled with solfège syllables and traditional notation. It is our contention that if the students cannot aurally describe, without any visual aid, such things as the shape of the melodic contour, the number of pitches contained in the contour, the starting pitch, the final pitch, and sing the pitch collection from the lowest note to the highest note, their aural awareness skills will not develop in tandem with their visual skills. These activities promote audiation and permit the instructor to assess student comprehension.

This work has led us to consider the following. Pointing to an iconic representation of the melodic contour is an effective teaching strategy in the beginning stages of developing students' kinesthetic understanding of a new melodic pattern. However, if the student does not create his or her own visual representation of a melodic contour derived solely from knowledge gained in the aural awareness stage, the presentation of notation (whether it be solfège syllables, note names, numbers, or a staff representation of the melodic contour) can create additional complications for teaching students music literacy skills. For example if asked to create a representation of a rhythm pattern, some students might want to represent the durations while others might want to show the point of attack on the beat for each element. Before any labeling takes place students must understand why the two types of representations are correct.

Strategy 3 (symbolic) of Bruner's instructional theory gains meaning only after students have made two important connections: the successful aural analysis of the primary characteristics of the new element and an illustration of their aural understanding in a visual representation using pre-notational graphs. Gromko contends that this kind of activity can "prompt the classification, organization, and connections that enable the child to transform the concrete experience into one that can be represented in icons or symbols."[38] Presenting students with visuals (Bruner's strategy 2, iconic) and subsequently moving to the symbolic stage (Bruner's strategy 3) without developing students' aural awareness, shortchanges students' perceptual understanding and may significantly compromise the parallel development of aural imagery skills.

During the presentation phase of learning, Choksy suggests the following. "Selecting one song in which the new learning is prominent, the teacher will ask adroit questions to lead the children to discover the new element. . . . When the questions have been accurately answered the teacher names and shows notation for the new rhythm or gives the solfa and hand sign for the new note, and shows its notation on staff."[39] In other words, the symbol and the sound are presented together. Choksy does not use traditional note names but rather uses syllables to aurally represent the sound and visually label the sound. At a later stage, students learn the traditional note names. In our model of instruction and learning, we always associate the sound of music with the rhythm or solfège syllable. We do not use visual representations to do this. For example, when we are teaching quarter and eighth notes, students must be able to (1) tap the beat, (2) clap the rhythm, (3) perform beat and rhythm, and (4) aurally identify how many sounds occur on each beat. The music instructor labels the new element with rhythm syllables without the use of any visuals. Once students can aurally identify the new element in the focus pattern with rhythm syllables, we then show how sounds can be represented using traditional notation and how students may use syllables to decode this notation. This is not difficult for young students and will ultimately allow them to make sense of what they experience musically in instrumental lessons or as members of a choir.

Developing a Lesson Plan Framework Based on the Learning Theory Proposed in This Chapter

The goal of this section is to incorporate information for developing musical literacy into the preparation/practice, presentation, and practice lesson plan formats. After a presentation lesson plan, we believe that this should be followed by an initial practice lesson plan that basically reviews that presentation lesson with familiar material. Our lesson plan formats may now include:

- Presenting three different preparation stages (kinesthetic, aural, and visual) before the presentation of a musical element. Each stage has its own sequential procedures.
- In the presentation lesson plan, we are dividing the presentation of the new element into two stages. Stage 1 is the aural presentation of the new rhythmic syllables using the target pattern and related patterns. Stage 2 is the visual presentation of the target pattern using traditional notation.

The Preparation/Practice Lesson

The following lesson is the same lesson presented in chapter 5, but it is now modified to reflect the new information in this chapter. In this lesson format we are putting all preparation activities (kinesthetic, aural, and visual) into the performance and preparation of new concept segment of the lesson plan. This is the sketch of a lesson plan; we are not attempting to create smooth transitions between one section of the lesson and another.

Table 6.2 Developing a preparation/practice lesson plan framework: Preparation of sixteenth notes and the practice of *re*

Focus	Activities, Procedures, and Assessments
Introduction	
Performance and demonstration of known musical concepts and elements	Develop singing skills through beautiful singing, vocal warm-ups, and breathing exercises Sing with text and play the game *Here Comes a Bluebird* Sing with rhythm syllables Sing with text (while instructor plays in canon on the recorder)
Core activities	
Acquisition of repertoire	Teach *Down Came a Lady* in preparation for teaching $\frac{4}{4}$ meter
Performance and preparation of new element	**Teacher provides students with a series of discovery learning activities that will develop their knowledge of four sounds on a beat (sixteenth notes) through known songs** **Kinesthetic awareness stage:** **a) Sing *Paw Paw Patch* and keep the beat** **b) Sing and clap the rhythm** **c) Sing and point to a representation of phrase one** — — — — — — — — — — **d) Sing *Paw Paw Patch*, walk the beat, and clap the rhythm** **Aural awareness stage:** **a) Review Kinesthetic** **b) T & S sing phrase one and keep the beat** **c) T: "Andy, how many beats did we keep?" four** **d) T: "Andy, which beat has the most sounds?" beat three** **e) T: "How many sounds are on beat 3?" four sounds** **f) T: "If beat three has four sounds, how many sounds are on the other beats?" two sounds** **Visual awareness stage:** **a) Review the kinesthetic and aural awareness activities** **b) Students create a visual based on their aural awareness. Students need to determine how many beats are in the phrase and the number of sounds on each beat. Use manipulatives (cut outs, magnets, unifix cubes, etc)** **c) Students sing and point to their representation** **d) Instructor may ask questions concerning their representation** **e) "Identify any rhythmic and melodic elements you recognize"**
Movement development	Focus on the sequential development of age-appropriate movement skills in the game *Tideo*
Performance and musical skill development	**Students reinforce their knowledge of *re* working on the skill areas selected from the following: reading and writing, form, and memory through known songs such as *Frosty Weather***

Table 6.2 *Continued*

Focus	Activities, Procedures, and Assessments
Closure	
Review and summation	Review new song, *Down Came a Lady* Teacher sings the next new song, *Ida Red,* as a listening activity in preparation for *d* pentatonic and eighth and two sixteenth note rhythm patterns. See pedagogical lists of songs in appendix 3, grade 3

Developing a Lesson Plan Framework for the Presentation of Sixteenth Notes

The following lesson framework is the same lesson presented in the chapter 5, but it is now modified to reflect the new information in this chapter. In the presentation lesson plan, we are dividing the presentation of the new element into two stages. Stage 1 is the aural presentation of the new rhythmic syllables using the target pattern and related patterns; stage 2 is the visual presentation of the target pattern and related patterns using traditional notation. We believe that for the initial musical concept and elements the presentation of a new musical element should be divided into two presentation lessons. Presentation lesson one focuses on the aural presentation. Presentation lesson two focuses on the notation. During the performance and initial practice section of the lesson, the instructor uses the target pattern in another known song and practices the musical skills, reading, and writing. The target pattern contained in the focus song used in the presentation can be found in the pedagogical list of songs in appendix 3.

Table 6.3 Presentation 1: Developing a lesson plan framework for the presentation of rhythm syllables sixteenth notes

Focus	Activities, Procedures, and Assessments
Introduction	
Performance and demonstration of known musical concepts and elements	Develop singing skills through beautiful singing, vocal warm-ups, and breathing exercises Students demonstrate their prior knowledge by singing *Rocky Mountain* Sing with text Sing rhythm syllables Sing with solfège syllables Sing in canon
Core activities	
Acquisition of repertoire	Teach *Ida Red* using an appropriate method of presentation selected from the repertoire list for the grade
Performance and presentation of the rhythm syllables for the new element in the focus pattern	**Stage one aural presentation** Briefly review the kinesthetic, aural, and visual awareness activities using *Paw Paw Patch* **Present the name of the new element** **a) T: "When we hear four sounds on a beat we call it "ta ka di mi"** **b) T & S sing whole song with rhythm syllables and clap the rhythm** **c) Individual students sing the target phrase with rhythm syllables**

continued

Table 6.3 *Continued*

Focus	**Activities, Procedures, and Assessments**
Movement development	**Focus on the sequential development of age-appropriate movement skills using the song *Tideo***
Performance and presentation of the rhythm syllable for the new element in a related pattern	**Students aurally identify the rhythm syllables for the four phrases of the song *Dinah***
Closure	
Review and summation	Review new song *Ida Red* Listening activity Teacher sings the next new song, *Knock the Cymbals,* in preparation for learning *do* pentatonic

Table 6.4 Presentation 2: Developing a lesson plan framework for the presentation of notation for sixteenth notes

Focus	**Activities, Procedures, and Assessments**
Introduction	
Performance and demonstration of known musical concepts and elements	Develop singing skills through beautiful singing, vocal warm-ups, and breathing exercises Students demonstrate their prior knowledge of *Rocky Mountain* Sing with text Sing rhythm syllables Sing with solfège syllables Sing in canon
Core activities	
Acquisition of repertoire	Teach *Knock the Cymbals* using an appropriate method of presentation selected from the repertoire list for the grade
Performance and presentation of the notation for the new element in the target pattern	Briefly review the kinesthetic, aural, and visual awareness activities using *Paw Paw Patch* **Stage two visual presentation** Review stage one aural presentation a) **We can use four sixteenth notes to represent four sounds on a beat. A sixteenth note has a note head and a stem and two flags. Four sixteenth notes have a double beam.** b) **Our first phrase of *Paw Paw Patch* looks like this:** ♫ ♫ ♬ ♫ ♥ ♥ ♥ ♥ c) **We can read this rhythm pattern using our rhythm syllables** d) **T sings rhythm syllables while pointing to the heartbeats, S echo sing using rhythm syllables while pointing to the heartbeats** e) **Stick notation is an easy way to write rhythmic notation. Stick notation is traditional notation without the note heads for quarter and eighth notes. Our first phrase of *Paw Paw Patch* looks like this in stick notation:** ⊓ ⊓ ⊓⊓ ⊓

Table 6.4 *Continued*

Focus	Activities, Procedures, and Assessments
Movement development	**Focus on the sequential development of age-appropriate movement skills using *Tideo***
Performance and presentation of the notation for the new element in the related pattern	**Transform the rhythm of *Great Big House* into the rhythm of *Dinah* Students sing with solfège and hand signs Students read *Dinah* from staff notation**
Closure	
Review and summation	Review new song *Knock the Cymbals* Listening activity Teacher sings the next new song, *Fed My Horse,* to be taught as a listening activity in preparation for learning eighth note followed by two sixteenth notes

Initial Practice Lesson for Sixteenth Notes

The initial practice lesson follows the presentation lesson. In the initial practice lesson, we review the presentation of the new element in the target pattern as well as practice the new element in other basic patterns using different repertoire and continue to build students' musical skills. Some of the activities in this lesson can be expanded upon as we move into the next unit for preparing a new element and we continue to do more concentrated practice of the recently presented element.

Table 6.5 Initial practice lesson for sixteenth notes

Focus	Activities, Procedures, and Assessments
Introduction	
Performance and demonstration of known musical elements	Develop singing skills through beautiful singing, vocal warm-ups, and breathing exercises Students demonstrate their prior knowledge of *Rocky Mountain* Sing with text Sing in canon Sing with rhythm syllables Sing in unison
Core activities	
Acquisition of repertoire	Teach *Dance Josey* using an appropriate method of presentation selected from the repertoire list for the grade
Performance and re-presentation of new element	• **Review the aural awareness stage questions using *Paw Paw Patch.* Use the rhythm syllables to identify the new element.** • **Review the visual awareness activities and associate traditional notation with the visual representation. Read with rhythm syllables.** • **Identify another song that includes the target pattern motif or a closely related pattern. Review the aural awareness and visual awareness activities as above.**

continued

Table 6.5 *Continued*

Focus	Activities, Procedures, and Assessments
Movement development	Focus on the sequential development of age-appropriate movement skills using *Tideo*
Performance and musical skill development	**Transform the target pattern into other four-beat patterns found in the student's song material. For example transform *Paw Paw Patch* into *Cumberland Gap* and work on other skill areas such as reading writing improvisation/composition and listening.**
Closure	
Review and summation	Review new song *Dance Josey* Listening activity Teacher sings the next new song, *Johnny Cuckoo*, in preparation for the next musical element—eighth notes and two sixteenth notes

Discussion Questions

1. What are the three phases of learning a new music element?
2. How are the phases of learning broken into stages?
3. What is the purpose of the kinesthetic stage?
4. What is the purpose of the aural awareness stage?
5. What is the purpose of the visual awareness stage?
6. What are the stages in the associative phase?
7. What is the assimilative phase?
8. The model of learning in this chapter promotes dictation skills and sight-reading skills. Discuss.
9. Compare and contrast the model of learning presented in this chapter with the Choksy model of learning.
10. The model of learning presented in this chapter is too cumbersome for instructors to follow. It is much more effective to present information in a theoretical manner and then use this information to practice music skills of reading and writing. Discuss.
11. Students must be able to write before they can read music. Discuss.
12. Describe the initial practice lesson.

Ongoing Assignment

1. You have been asked to present a talk on the Houlahan/Tacka Learning Theory Model for Developing Music Literacy. Develop a power point presentation for your presentation. Be able to explain how this model of learning might be useful for classroom, instrumental, and choral instruction.

2. Choose a concept to prepare and an element to practice for a first grade class. Create a preparation/practice lesson, a presentation lesson, and practice lesson. In chapter eight you will find detailed procedures for teaching specific rhythmic and melodic concepts and elements.
3. Choose a concept to prepare and an element to practice for a third grade class. Create a preparation/practice lesson, a presentation lesson, and a practice lesson.

References

Anderson, William M., and Patricia Shehan Campbell, eds. *Multicultural Perspectives in Music Education.* 2nd ed. Reston, Va.: Music Educators National Conference, 1996.

Bamberger, Jeanne. "What Develops in Musical Development?" in *The Child as Musician: A Handbook of Musical Development,* ed. Gary McPherson. New York: Oxford University Press, 2006.

Barbe, Walter B., and Raymond S. Swassing. *Teaching through Modality Strengths Concepts and Practices.* Columbus, Ohio: Laner Bloser, 1979.

Barkóczi, Ilona, and Csaba Pléh. *The Effect of Kodály's Musical Training on the Psychological Development of Elementary School Children.* Kecskemét: Zoltán Kodály Pedagogical Institute, 1982.

Barrett, Margaret. "Graphic Notation in Music Education." Christchurch, New Zealand, University of Canterbury, 1990.

———. "Music Education and the Natural Learning Model." *International Journal of Music Education* 20 (1992): 27–34.

———. "Children's Aesthetic Decision-Making: An Analysis of Children's Musical Discourse as Composers." *International Journal of Music Education* 28 (1996): 37–61.

Colwell, Richard, and Carol Richardson, eds. "Section D: Perception and Cognition," in *Handbook of Research on Music Teaching and Learning.* New York: Schirmer Books, 2002.

Duffy, Thomas M., and David H. Jonasson. *Constructivism and the Technology of Instruction.* Hillsdale, N.J.: Lawrence Erlbaum, 1992.

Feierabend, John. "Integrating Music Learning Theory into the Kodály Curriculum," in *Readings in Music Learning Theory,* ed. Darrell Walters and Cynthia Taggart Crump. Chicago: G.I.A, 1989.

———. "Kodály and Gordon: Same and Different." *Bulletin of the International Kodály Society* 17/1 (Spring 1992): 41–50.

Flohr, John, S. C. Woodward, and L. Suthers. "Rhythm Performance in Early Childhood." Cape Town, International Society for Music Education, 1998, 1998.

Gagne, Robert M. *The Conditions of Learning.* New York: Holt, Rinehart & Winston, 1995.

Gardner, Howard. *Frames of Mind: A Theory of Multiple Intelligences.* New York: Basic Books, 1993.

Gordon, Edwin E. *Learning Sequences in Music: Skill, Content, and Patterns.* Chicago: G.I.A. Publications, 2003.

———. *The Psychology of Music Teaching.* Englewood Cliffs, N.J.: Prentice-Hall, 1971.

Hargreaves, David J. *The Developmental Psychology of Music.* Cambridge: Cambridge University Press, 1986.

Hallam, Susan. "Musicality," in *The Child as Musician: A Handbook of Musical Development,* ed. Gary McPherson. New York: Oxford University Press, 2006.

Hetland, Lois. "Learning to Make Music Enhances Spatial Reasoning." *Journal of Aesthetic Education* 34/3–4 (2000): 179–238.

Hodges, Don A. "The Musical Brain," in *The Child as Musician: A Handbook of Musical Development,* ed. Gary McPherson. New York: Oxford University Press, 2006.

Parncutt, Richard. "Prenatal Development," in *The Child as Musician: A Handbook of Musical Development,* ed. Gary McPherson. New York: Oxford University Press, 2006.

Peery, J. Craig, Irene Weiss Peery, and Thomas W. Draper, eds. *Music and Child Development.* New York: Springer-Verlag, 1987.

Reimer, Bennett. "Music as Cognitive: A New Horizon for Musical Education." *Kodály Envoy* 6/3 (Spring 1980): 16–17.

Serafine, Mary Louise. *Music as Cognition.* New York: Columbia University, 1988.

Sinor, Jean. "Musical Development of Children and Kodály Pedagogy." *Kodály Envoy* 6/3 (Spring 1980): 6–10.

Trehub, Sandra E. "Infants as Musical Connoisseurs," in *The Child as Musician: A Handbook of Musical Development,* ed. Gary McPherson. New York: Oxford University Press, 2006.

Vygotsky, Lev. *Mind in Society: The Development of Higher Psychological Process.* Cambridge, Mass.: Harvard University Press, 1980.

Chapter 7

Developing Musicianship Skills

Key Questions

What do we mean by musical skill development?

How are musical skills integrated into lesson plans?

What is a monthly plan?

How can monthly be used as a reference for developing lesson plans?

In previous chapters we have presented lesson plan frameworks for three types of lessons: preparation/practice lessons, presentation lessons, and practice lessons. Musical elements are continually practiced in combination with specific musical skills (referred to as *skill areas*). The goal of this chapter is to provide instructors with ideas concerning the practice of known elements in the preparation/practice lesson plan format as well as in the practice lesson plan format. Practicing music skills in the music classroom should be (1) appropriate to student abilities, (2) varied, and (3) motivating.

Although the development of musical skills occurs throughout the teaching process, we suggest specific strategies for developing and practicing specific musical skills. We suggest that music lessons include the concentrated practice of known rhythmic and melodic concepts using specific musical skills. A brief list of specific musical skills is given in the next section. These skills are discussed in detail in the subsequent sections of this chapter.

Musical Skills

This chapter describes how various musical skills can be developed. Appendix 4 includes monthly plans for grades one through five and provides an outline of the musical skills to be developed in each grade. All of these plans are derived from the curriculum guide provided for each grade in appendix 1. The monthly plans are only a sketch of what can be accomplished in the music classroom based on teaching music twice a week. We suggest that the instructor should determine what's feasible for their own teaching situation. Your curriculum goals need to be adjusted according to the frequency of your teaching. The goal of the monthly plans is to provide music teachers with a basis for the design of their own music curriculum. For example, we have not included specific composition activities as the improvisation activities should provide the instructor with ideas for creating composition activities.

We have labeled the monthly plans in terms of grades but teachers should consider them as levels of achievement. For example, a music instructor that teaches once a week music lessons to a third grade class may only cover concepts and skills in the grade two monthly plans. Flexibility is built into these plans. Please note that some monthly plans review and revise previously taught concepts. For example the grade five monthly plans begin with a review of the grade four monthly plans. Generally speaking we prepare a rhythmic concept and practice a melodic concept or prepare a melodic concept and practice a rhythmic concept. We introduce aspects of compound meter over the course of several grade levels. As a result, the teaching sequence of rhythmic and melodic elements may be interrupted if the instructor chooses to teach compound meter.

Musical Skill Areas

The following are brief definitions of music skills that can be incorporated into the music lesson.

Singing

This is the skill where students are able to use their singing voices using correct breathing, posture, range, expression, and intonation. Students must also develop the ability to aurally and visually recognize as well as perform different styles of music repertoire alone or in a vocal ensemble.

Music Reading

This is the skill where students must be able to translate the symbol of music into the sound of music and produce it with their voices and on an instrument. Music reading can include reading known melodies. Sight-singing refers to reading unknown vocal music and sight-reading refers to reading unknown music for instrumental music. Both known and new songs and phrases of songs may be practiced as reading examples. Music reading is practiced once students have learned a new musical element. Remember that if we want to select a particular music example for melodic reading we can always simplify a folksong that has a complex rhythmic structure and provide a structural reduction of the piece of music for reading. It is important for teachers to be able to create their own music reading exercises based on the repertoire students are singing in the classroom.

Writing

This is the skill where students must be able to translate the sound of music into a music symbol using pre-notation skills, traditional rhythmic notation, or staff notation. We suggest three modes of writing. The first approach to writing is to allow students to use manipulatives; this is particularly effective with young learners. Manipulatives can include popsicle sticks for writing rhythmic stick notation, disc magnets on a magnetic board for showing the melodic contour, unifix cubes for constructing rhythms or melodic contours, felt staves and felt discs, and individual erasable lap boards. The second is to have students write at the board; this is usually accomplished by having a student complete the phrase of a song written on the board. Some instructors use individual dry erase boards for this purpose. The third approach is allowing students to use a paper and pencil or a computer program such as Note Pad.

Improvisation

Within the context of the Kodály philosophy, improvisation is connected to the practice of known musical elements. But this does not mean that students cannot create their own improvisations using other patterns and elements. Improvisation permits students to spontaneously create rhythms, melodies, movements, new forms as well as new texts to a melody. Students may improvise a musical answer to the instructor's musical question. For example, if the instructor claps a question rhythm saying rhythm syllables, the student may clap and say a different rhythm in response. This same technique may be achieved melodically using solfège syllables. Of course students should also be encouraged to improvise without having to name rhythmic or melodic elements they are using.

Composition

Within the context of the Kodály philosophy, composition permits students to create rhythms and melodies in a written form. All improvisation activities can be extended by changing them into composition activities.

Part-work and Harmonic Hearing

This is the skill where students develop their abilities to perform two or more activities at the same time. This includes singing while performing the beat or singing and clapping the rhythm. An example is having students sing a song as they walk the beat and perform the rhythm; three modes of performance occurring at the same time. These are preliminary skills and necessary for the subsequent performance of works in several parts and the development of harmonic thinking. This also includes the ability of students to aurally and visually identify basic chord progressions related to different styles of music.

Memory

Music memory is a critical skill for the development of all musical skills. Teachers need to be cognizant of the fact that nearly all their teaching helps develop both aural and visual memory.

Inner Hearing

This is the ability to hear a melody inside one's head without any acoustical stimulation. Inner hearing is also known as "audiation."

Form

This refers to the phrase structure of a piece of music. Students need to be able to determine both rhythmic form and melodic form of a piece of music both aurally and visually. Determining form begins with the ability to identify same, different, and similar phrases. The ability to identify form significantly affects the development of musical memory.

Listening

This is the ability to aurally understand and visually analyze a piece of music. Several types of listening skills are developed in the music class. Live classroom performances and recorded musical examples are included in this skill area.

Conducting

The ability to keep the beat of a piece of music using standard conducting gestures.
The following skills are not included in the monthly plans but are discussed in curriculum plans because they are embedded in other skill areas.

Movement Development

This is the ability of students to be able to express space, time, and force through their bodies.

Instrumental Development

This includes the ability to recognize music instruments both visually and aurally as well as play simple rhythmic and melodic instruments in the elementary classroom.

Terminology

This is the ability to use standard musical terms and symbols to read and write music.

The following sections of this chapter include many suggestions for developing musical skills. In appendix 4, we have included skeleton monthy plans for each grade level to serve as a guide for accomplishing curriculum goals. As well as including repertoire for teaching and listing the musical elements to be prepared, practiced, and presented, these plans also include activities for developing the different musical skill areas. Depending on the grade you are teaching, you will be preparing, presenting, and practicing approximately five or six concepts each year. You need to review your academic calendar for each grade and make a tentative guess as to when you will be teaching each concept. Remember that you must figure out how many music lessons you are teaching in a year, make allowances for the first few weeks of the year for review of concepts taught during the preceding year, figure out how much time you need to devote to your end of term performances. At a minimum you can assume that it will take you about five lessons to teach each musical element.

The monthly plans are based upon:

1. Curriculum goals for each year
2. Alphabetized list of songs

3. Pedagogical list of songs
4. Preparation, presentation, practice sequence charts
5. Musical skills presented in this chapter

Reading Monthly Plans

The following is a guide as to how to read the monthly plans for each year that have been set out in appendix 4. Please follow the chart from left to right as we explain each of the title headings.

Month

This section provides the instructor with a guide as to when to teach repertoire and when to prepare, present practice particular concepts and elements.

Songs

These are songs that can be used for singing, preparing, presenting, and practicing musical concepts and elements as well as developing students' movement abilities.

Prepare, Present, Practice

The plans include the concept/element to be prepared while simultaneously practicing a known element. The presentation lists the element along with the syllables to be presented.

Musicianship Development

These are examples of skill areas that include reading, writing, improvising, part work (sometimes referred to as ensemble work), memory, inner hearing, form, listening, and error detection that can be practiced during the preparation/practice, presentation, and practice lesson plan.

Practicing Rhythm and Melody through Reading, Writing, and Memory Exercises

> **Key Questions**

How can I address the prerequisite skills that accompany musical reading and writing?

How do we practice rhythmic and melodic elements?

How do we develop our students writing, reading, and memory skills?

If reading is an important component to a music curriculum, what reading activities can be used to practice musical elements?

What types of writing activities can young learners perform?

What additional learning skills are involved when a student reads or writes music?

Musical reading and writing are skills that can reinforce comprehensive musicianship. These two skills may be practiced during each music lesson in a manner that does not detract from the enjoyment of making music. Although the terms "reading" and "sight-singing" are interchangeable, we make the following distinction. We use the term "reading" when students read known song material; "sight-singing" refers to students reading unfamiliar musical material. Similarly, we use the term "writing" when referring to writing known musical patterns; "dictation" refers to writing unknown musical patterns.

We identify specific activities that can be used to practice rhythm and melody once students have knowledge of a few concepts and elements. Musical reading and writing are fundamental skills that can be built upon. For example, a reading exercise can be formulated into an improvisation or musical form activity. The musical form activity may subsequently evolve into a memory exercise that can be performed in canon; the canon performance could ultimately progress to a listening activity.

The following exercises can be modified and adapted to any level of instruction. Once you gain the practical experience of working through some of our suggestions, you will undoubtedly begin to develop more interesting and varied activities by turning them into inner hearing, memory, and part-singing activities.

Twenty-Four Ways to Practice Rhythm

1. Speak or sing the rhythm patterns of well-known songs while tapping the beat.
2. Put the rhythm of a song on the board and allow students to figure out the correct placement of the heartbeats.
3. Speak/sing the rhythm of a pattern or song while conducting.
4. Echo patterns with rhythm syllables.
5. Sing a known or unknown phrase of a song with words and have the students sing back the phrase with rhythm syllables.
6. Sing a known or unknown song on a neutral syllable (*loo*) and have the students sing back with rhythm syllables.
7. Sing a known or unknown song with solfège and have the students sing back with rhythm syllables.
8. Play a melody on an instrument and have the children sing back with rhythm syllables.
9. Play a game where *ta* is placed on the child's head and *ta di* is placed on their shoulders. The students tap their head and shoulders as they sing a song. Perform this activity slowly. Of course, this can be practiced with other rhythmic combinations.
10. Match song titles to written rhythms. List the titles of four songs on the board. Write a phrase from each of the four songs in stick notation. Students match the rhythm to the title of the song.
11. Sing or clap the rhythm of well-known songs reading from stick or staff notation. Inner hearing may be used with this exercise.
12. Ask students to figure out the rhythm of an unknown song taught by rote.

13. Identify the meter and rhythm patterns clapped or sung by another person.
14. Read a rhythm from the board and simultaneously clap it in canon.
15. Error detection. The instructor or a student writes a sixteen-beat rhythm pattern then claps a slightly different pattern. Another student must identify the phrases and the beats where the changes occur.
16. Clap a four-beat phrase, sixteen-beat rhythm pattern while singing a known song of the same length.
17. Improvise rhythm patterns. First, select a meter and length for the improvisation. For example, a simple task could be to improvise four, four-beat phrases. The form can be AABA. Select four students. Each student will perform a phrase. The first student (A) improvises a four-beat pattern. The second student (A) has to remember the pattern and perform it. The third student (B) improvises a different pattern. The fourth student (A) must remember the A pattern and perform it. This exercise can be performed with different forms and longer length phrases.
18. Improvise rhythm patterns in specified meters. The instructor must specify the phrase length and form (for example, AABA).
19. Perform a rhythmic canon. We suggest the following procedure:
    a. Students say the rhythm syllables while clapping the rhythm.
    b. Instruct students to think the rhythm syllables and clap the rhythm.
    c. Divide the class and have them perform the rhythm in canon.
    d. Two individual students perform the canon.
    e. Challenge individual students to perform the rhythmic canon alone by saying the rhythm syllables but clapping the rhythm in canon at the same time.
20. Transform the rhythm of one song into the rhythm of another. Write the rhythm of a known song on the board but clap a slightly different pattern than the one written. Ask students to identify the phrase and beats that need to be changed to match what was clapped. The instructor continues to do this until the rhythm has been transformed into the rhythm of another known song. Once identified, students may sing the transformed song with rhythm syllables.
21. Write a rhythm pattern on the board. After discussing the form, the students may memorize the beat pattern and write it from memory.
22. Write a known song on the board with a measure or several missing measures. Students write in the missing measures.
23. Rhythm Telegraph: The instructor claps a four-beat rhythm pattern to a student in a circle who then passes this pattern on to other students. The last student may write this pattern on the board.
24. Flashcard Activities
    a. Read several flashcards using four beat-patterns written in traditional notation in succession.
    b. Place the cards on the ledge of the chalkboard and perform them in order. Change the order of the cards. Have individual students read different patterns by changing the order of the cards. Gradually arrange the order of the cards to move from one song to another in a lesson. A card may be removed and an individual student may improvise a rhythm to replace the missing pattern. By extending the number of phrases involved in this activity, different forms may be practiced.

c. Have a student draw a rhythm card from a box. Another student may tell her how to perform the rhythm (clapping, jumping, tapping, stamping, blinking, nodding, and so on). The class may echo the rhythm.
d. Read a series of rhythm flashcards in succession; have the class read them in succession; or have students read them backwards.
e. Ask students to rearrange a series of flash cards to create a known song.
f. Students memorize four-, eight-, twelve-, or sixteen-beat patterns from flashcards and sing back with rhythm syllables or write the memorized patterns using stick notation.

Eighteen Ways to Practice Melody

1. Children's Piano. Each child becomes a musical pitch and takes a place in order from high to low so that the instructor can play the piano by pointing to each child to sing the pitch. Arranging students in order of pitch is also a way to practice singing intervals.
2. Sing known melodies or phrases with solfège syllables and hand signs.
3. Sing with solfège syllables and conduct.
4. Sing a known song with solfège syllables and hand signs reading stick or staff notation.
5. Sing a known song or phrase with solfège syllables and/or letter names and hand signs and have the students echo.
6. Sing a known song with text and have the students echo with hand signs and solfège syllables and/or letter names.
7. Show a melody with hand signs or finger staff and have the students sing with hand signs and solfège syllables and/or letter names.
8. Hum a known song or phrase and have the students echo back with hand signs and solfège syllables or letter names.
9. Point to a melody on the staff or tone ladder and have the students sing with hand signs and solfège syllables or letter names.
10. Sing a phrase with rhythm syllables and have the students echo sing the phrase with solfège syllables or letter names.
11. Play a melody on recorder and have the students sing with solfège syllables and/or letter names.
12. Show a pattern with hand signs or point to a tone chart or tone ladder. Ask an individual student to sing the pattern.
13. Sing a melody or play a melody on the piano and have the students sing in canon with solfège syllables, letter names, or rhythm syllables.
14. Perform a three-part canon in the following manner. The instructor plays a melody on piano, group one sings in canon after two measures, and group two sings in canon with group one.
15. Students read a music example with solfège syllables; at a given signal from the instructor, students switch to singing with absolute letter names.
16. Divide class into two groups; each group reads a pentatonic melody of the same phrase structure and phrase length simultaneously.
17. Play a melody on piano and have the students play it back immediately.
18. Sing a melody in retrograde.

Activities for Developing Reading Skills

Reading a piece of music necessitates that students know all the rhythmic and melodic elements contained in the reading example. The instructor may decide to focus on a given phrase that contains melodic or rhythmic elements the students already know. Prepare the reading activity by directing students attention to the meter and tonality, as well as rhythmic and interval difficulties. The following activities can be used during the preparation or practice of a new music element.

Reading Known Melodic Patterns

Once target patterns from song material have been learned, practice reading and writing these patterns and related patterns. For example, after teaching the pentatonic tri-chord *la–so–mi* we need to consider ways to practice the *mi–la* interval. The *mi–la* interval usually occurs on the second beat within a four-beat song phrase. Students may be guided to read the *mi–la* pattern if the instructor manipulates known *mi–so* and *so–la* melodic patterns. The following is a suggestion for easily getting students to read and perform the *mi–la* interval.

Teaching the *mi–la* interval is common to a number of children's chants, yet making students conscious of this melodic turn requires some careful but logical preparation. Students should be able to sing several or all of the following songs in their entirety and know the solfège syllables *so–mi* and *la*. Please note that what is presented below is only a portion of a lesson plan.

1. Students read the following pattern silently while showing hand signs then sing aloud. Ask individual students to sing and show hand signs.

   Figure 7.1 *La* 1

2. The instructor changes the pattern. "I'm going to see if I can trick you." The students read the following pattern silently while showing hand signs then sing aloud. Ask individual students to sing and show hand signs.

   Figure 7.2 *La* 2

3. The instructor changes the pattern. "I'm going to see if I can trick you again." The students read the following pattern silently while showing hand signs then sing aloud. Ask individual students to sing and show hand signs.

   Figure 7.3 *La* 3

   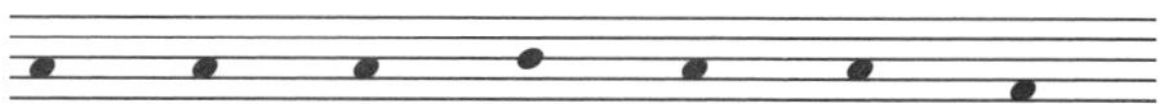

4. The instructor changes the pattern. "I'm going to see if I can trick you again." The students read the following pattern silently while showing hand signs then sing aloud. Ask individual students to sing and show hand signs.

Figure 7.4 *La* 4

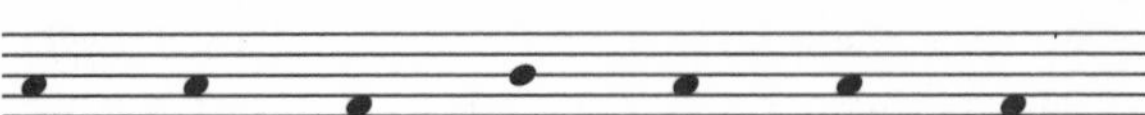

5. The instructor says, "That reminds me of a song we know." (You have a choice of many songs). Once the song is identified, the students sing the song with solfège syllables.

The *mi–la* pattern occurs in the second phrase of: *Rain Rain* and *Doggie Doggie.* The *mi–la* pattern occurs throughout the following songs: *Doggie Doggie, Little Sally Water, Bye Baby Bunting, No Robbers Out Today, Ring Around the Rosie, Johnny's It, Nanny Goat,* and *Fudge Fudge.*

Reading the Rhythm of a Known Song

Figure 7.5 *Let Us Chase the Squirrel*

1. The instructor taps the beat as the students read the rhythm of the complete song or the rhythm of a specific phrase using inner hearing or aloud while tapping the beat.
2. The instructor taps the beat:
   a. as the students read phrases 1 and 3 and the instructor reads phrases 2 and 4 in succession.
   b. as the instructor reads phrases 1 and 3 and the students read phrases 2 and 4 in succession.

By guiding students to read using this procedure, you teach them to become aware of the form and structure of the song.

Reading the Melody of a Song from Rhythmic Notation

Figure 7.6 *Bounce High, Bounce Low*

1. The instructor points to the notation, keeping the beat while the students read the rhythm syllables and clap the rhythm.
2. The students locate the highest and lowest notes.
3. The instructor provides the starting pitch and may have the students sing the tone set.
4. The students show the hand signs and use their inner hearing while the instructor points to keep the beat. The instructor may hum an occasional note to help the students.
5. The students perform the exercise aloud singing with solfège syllables.
6. The students perform the exercise aloud singing on a neutral syllable.

Reading a Known Melody from Staff Notation

The instructor should prepare both melodic and the rhythmic patterns to help students read a new song from staff notation. For example, if students are to read the song *Let Us Chase the Squirrel,* the instructor can use familiar songs to prepare the intervals and the tone set of the new song. The steps outlined above may be used when reading from staff notation. For example, the tone set of *Bye, Bye Baby* prepares the *so–mi–re–do* tone set of *Let Us Chase the Squirrel.*

Figure 7.7 *Let Us Chase the Squirrel*

Changing a Reading Activity into a Sight-Singing Activity

We suggest the following procedure:

1. Put a known song on the board using traditional notation and solfège syllables written under the notation.
2. Clap and say the rhythm syllables.
3. Sing with solfège syllables and hand signs.
4. Transform the song. Change one beat at a time; have the students identify where the change occurred.
5. Then sight-sing the new melody.
   a. Ask: How many beats are in each measure?
   b. Have the students read the rhythm.
   c. Compare and contrast measures 3, 5, 6, 7.
   d. Ask the students to sing the exercise in their heads and show hand signs.
   e. Sing the entire exercise. Challenge the students to strive for accuracy.
6. Transform the sight-singing example into a canon.

General Considerations for Sight-Singing Melodies

1. Kinesthetic Activities that Prepare Sight-Singing

   Prepare students to read a musical example by performing physical activities such as echo clapping the rhythms of the example, tracing the melodic contour of the melody, or singing melodic motives from the sight-singing example with hand signs.

2. Reading from the Board

   Begin sight-singing by guiding students to read from the board or from a chart. The instructor should point to the beats (not to each note) and ask students to sing or read in their heads (inner hear). After students have read through the example silently, they may sing it aloud. Once students can read from the board, they can read from a worksheet.

3. Begin with Short Phrases

   Beginning reading exercises should use short musical phrases. Read a complete phrase; do not stop on each beat. Reading examples or exercises should be slightly easier than the rhythmic and melodic elements being studied.

4. Read Known Melodies and Phrases First

   Practice reading musical examples that are familiar to students. You can always transform the known melody into an unknown melody.

5. Allow Students to be Independent

   Avoid guiding the students too much by always tapping the rhythm or the beat for every sight-singing example. Work to develop independent readers who can read without your help.

6. The Performance

   Students need to realize that although they are sight-singing (something that is usually challenging), they must attempt to make their performance musical. Before each sight-singing exercise, the instructor should practice basic rhythmic and melodic patterns from the exercise with the students while the students follow the staff notation. Difficult rhythms can be practiced with an appropriate rhythmic ostinato or with the subdivision of the beat. Sing these preparatory exercises in the same key as the reading example. Exercises should be sung in solfège, letter names, and neutral syllables.

The following procedure may be used for sight-singing new material:

1. Make the students aware of the meter and key. Chose an appropriate tempo.
2. Discuss the form of the exercise. Look for repeated patterns.
3. The students should then think through the entire rhythm silently saying the rhythm syllables and then clap the rhythm and perform the rhythm with rhythm syllables.
4. The students should then think through the entire melody with solfège and handsigns. The students may use hand signs while thinking through the melody.
5. The students sing the exercise with solfège, neutral syallalbes, and conducting.

Sight-singing exercises may be memorized and notated. Students should continually practice reading melodic patterns with or without a specific rhythm. The instructor should devise a variety of ways to practice a reading exercise, for example, reading the melody backwards, reading a unison melody while clapping a rhythmic ostinato, or singing a melody in canon at the fifth with only the first voice given.

Reading and Inner Hearing (Audiation)

Inner hearing can be practiced in several ways. The following are specific inner hearing activities that can be used in the classroom. We suggest you connect inner hearing to as many activities as possible. The first example is perhaps the most consistently practiced form of inner hearing used by many music instructors.

1. Prior to reading a musical example, allow a student to sing through the example silently (inner hear) while performing a beat.
2. The students sing a song aloud and at a signal from the instructor, they inner hear a phrase or portion of a phrase. For younger students use a puppet or symbol as a signal for them to inner hear or to sing aloud.
3. Recognize a song from hearing the instructor clap its rhythm.
4. Recognize a song from stick or staff notation on the board without hearing it performed aloud.
5. Recognize a song from the instructor's hand signs.
6. Recognize a song from the instructor pointing to solfège syllables on the steps.

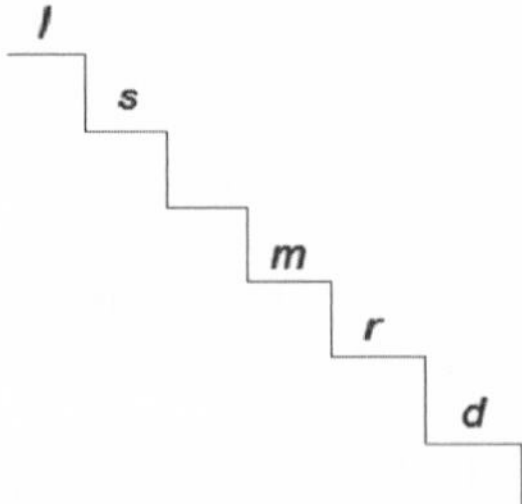

Figure 7.8 Solfege syllables on the step

Activities for Developing Writing Skills

The ability to discern individual pitches, vocally reproduce them, and echo rhythm patterns are prerequisites for writing music accurately. Writing a melody involves the skills of memory and inner hearing. Students need to know and understand the rhythmic and melodic content of piece of music they are trying to write. Dictation is a skill and can therefore be broken down into incremental steps. Writing beats, echoing activities, and determining solfège syllables are pre-dictation skills.

Using Manipulatives for Writing

Manipulatives such as felt disks placed on a felt staff or popsicle sticks for writing rhythms make the initial stages of music writing more imaginative for students. The students determine the melodic contour for a particular phrase; this pattern may be taken from a song or an exercise. Students can then create a visual for this pattern using disks.

An alternative would be:

1. The instructor writes the pattern with disks then plays or sings using a neutral syllable.
2. The instructor then changes one beat of the pattern: *so–so–so so–mi.*
3. The students sing the new pattern.
4. Students create their own patterns by manipulating the disks.

Writing Beats

Ask students to mark the beats on their desks moving from left to right as the instructor sings and marks beats on the board. The beats should be marked according to the number of phrases in the song and the number of beats per phrase. For example, *Rocky Mountain* has four phrases of eight beats. A beat chart for *Rocky Mountain* is shown in figure 7.9.

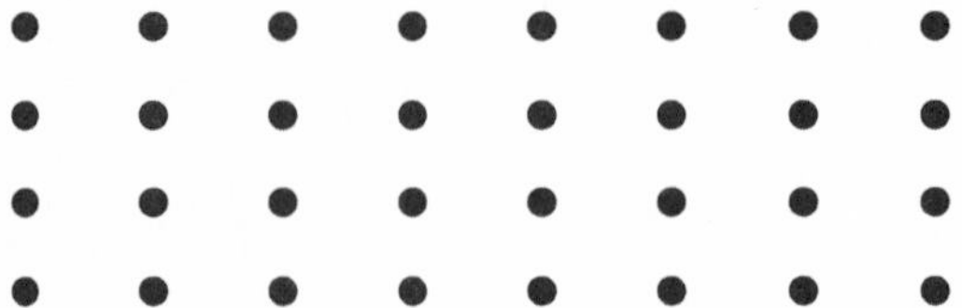

Figure 7.9 A beat chart for *Rocky Mountain*

Ask a student to come to the board and point to a beat chart while the class and instructor sing a song or have the students create such a chart as they sing the song.

Translating the Rhythm Syllables of a Song Into Notation

Choose a song or rhyme and challenge the students to figure out the rhythm solfège syllables. This activity can be performed at any level of instruction. For example:

Engine, Engine #9

1. Chant with words.
2. Chant with rhythm syllables.
3. The instructor or another student writes the rhythm in stick notation after the students say the rhythm syllables).

See, Saw (first phrase): "See, saw up and down"

1. Sing with words.
2. Sing with rhythm syllables.
3. The instructor or another student writes the stick notation of the rhythm.

Translating the Solfège Syllables of a Melody Into Notation

The instructor sings a melodic motif on a neutral syllable and the students echo.

1. The students echo sing and clap the rhythm.
2. The students echo sing with rhythm syllables.
3. Guide the students to determine the solfège syllables.
   a. "What is the solfège syllable for the last pitch?"
   b. "What is the solfège syllable for the first pitch?"
   c. Students sing with solfège syllables and handsigns.
4. The instructor or another student writes the rhythm pattern with solfège syllables beneath the rhythm notation.
5. The instructor or another student writes the melody on the staff. This must be done with careful preparation of the placement of the notes on the staff.

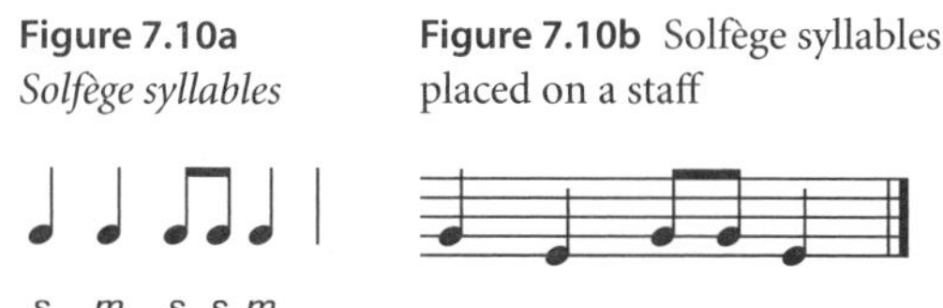

Figure 7.10a *Solfège syllables*

Figure 7.10b Solfège syllables placed on a staff

Writing Known Rhythmic Patterns

1. Play or sing the rhythm pattern.
2. The students sing the phrase and tap the beat.

3. The students sing the phrase and clap the rhythm.
4. The students sing the phrase with rhythm syllables.
5. The students memorize the musical example.
6. The students sing and write the phrase using stick notation.

Writing a Known Melodic Pattern

1. The instructor plays or sings the music to be written.
2. The students memorize the musical example.
3. The students sing it back first with rhythm syllables, then with solfège syllables both as a class and individually.
4. Practice the example on the hand staff.
5. Simultaneously sing and write the melodic phrase on the staff.

Dictation of Musical Examples

The ability to take musical notation is linked to the development of musical memory, inner hearing, as well as reading and writing skills. Memory is essential for dictation. As indicated above, initial writing activities should be based on patterns that have been memorized by the students. As students' memory develops, the instructor can formulate longer examples for practicing dictation. We are convinced that students should perform the melody before notating it in order that the instructor may be certain students are hearing it accurately. We also believe that the material for dictation should be familiar to students. Dictation examples that are derived from repertoire being studied help assure familiarity.

A Six-Step Procedure for Rhythmic Dictation

1. The instructor plays a melody on the piano while the students establish the meter and the number of bars.
2. The instructor plays and the students conduct.
3. The students conduct and sing the melody using rhythm syllables.
4. The students write the rhythm.
5. One student writes the rhythm on the board.
6. The instructor plays once more while the students sing and follow their score.

A Fifteen-Step Procedure for Melodic Dictation

1. The instructor prepares the key of the dictation with hand signs and staff notation.
2. The instructor shows typical melodic patterns extracted from the melody used for dictation and the students sing in solfège and letter names. At the beginning stages of formal dictation, the instructor may also give the student a score with bar lines and selected notes or rhythms filled in to help the students' memory.
3. The instructor plays the melody on the piano or on another instrument.
4. The students determine the meter.
5. The students sing the extract and keep the beat.
6. The students sing the extract and conduct.

7. The students sing the extract and clap the rhythm.
8. The students sing the extract with rhythm syllables and conduct.
9. The students determine the final note and the beginning note as well as some or all of the following, as appropriate: scale or mode, melodic cadences, melodic contour, patterns, and meter.
10. The students sing the melody with solfège names and hand signs.
11. The students sing the melody using hand signs and absolute letter names.
12. The students sing the melody from memory.
13. The students write the melody.
14. One student writes the melody on the board.
15. The students sing the melody from their score. This melody may be used to practice other skills such as transposing it into other keys or practicing the intervals in the melody.

Activities for Developing Musical Memory

Musical memory plays an important role in accurate singing. The ability to recall a pattern or a musical phrase is critical for musical reading and writing.
There are three ways to memorize a music example:

1. Memorizing by ear
2. Memorizing from hand signs
3. Memorizing from staff notation

Memorizing by Ear

Memorizing by ear is more difficult than memorizing from notation as it involves no visual aids. Melodies used for memorizing by ear should be simpler than those used with notation. The following procedures may be used for both rhythmic and melodic memorization. The instructor should sing the musical example and ask students to identify or perform the following in sequence. Be certain to sing the musical example prior to asking students to determine each point.

1. The students identify the meter.
2. The students sing the example with rhythm syllables.
3. The students identify the solfège for the ending and starting pitches.
4. The students sing the example and conduct.
5. The students sing the example with solfège and hand signs.
6. The students sing the example with absolute pitch names and hand signs.
7. The students write the exercise or play it back on the piano. Later, the example may be transposed.
8. The instructor may also play a melody and ask the students to sing it back in canon on "loo" or on solfège syllables while memorizing the example. At a more advanced level, students may sing back the canon at a different interval.

Memorizing from Hand Signs

Hand signs help students to learn and understand melodic contours. A sequence of hand signs evokes the memory of melodic patterns.

1. Show typical melodic patterns and ask the students to sing patterns back. Start with short patterns such as *so–la–so–mi* or *mi–fa–mi–re–mi.*
2. When the melodic patterns are mastered, progress to singing four-bar and eight-beat melodies.
3. Select a pentatonic melody and show it with hand signs. Challenge students to sing the melody in canon immediately using solfège syllables or absolute letter names. Extend this activity by asking students to write the melody from memory.
4. The instructor may also give the starting pitch and ask students to sing a melody with absolute letter names while showing hand signs.

Memorizing from Staff Notation

1. The students look at a score and memorize a phrase of the musical example by silently singing in their head using hand signs.
2. If some phrases of the musical example are known and others unknown, the students may sing the known phrases and the instructor may sing the unknown phrases. Students listen and learn the unfamiliar phrases.
3. Students may write the melody on staff paper. At a more advanced level, the students can write the example in another key using a different clef.
4. Have students look at a new piece of music that uses the musical elements they know. Ask students to memorize the example without singing it aloud or playing it.

Memorizing Two-Part Musical Examples

When students have gained experience in unison memory work, they can begin to memorize two-part extracts. Accompaniments may be drawn from a rhythmic pattern, a rhythmic or melodic ostinato, chord roots, a contrapuntal melodic line, or typical cadential idioms in modal or harmonic music. Memory work may also include three- and four-part work.

1. Sing the selected extracts in two parts.
2. Memorize one part silently using rhythm and solfège syllables.
3. Sing the memorized part out loud while conducting.
4. Practice the other part following steps 1 through 3.
5. Sing both parts in a group and then as solos, using both solfège syllables and note names.
6. Write both parts of the musical example.
7. Sing one part and play the other on the piano, or sing one part and show the second part with hand signs.

➤ Discussion Questions

1. What do we mean when we say that rhythmic and melodic elements need to be practiced?
2. How can we connect skill areas such as the development of musical memory and inner hearing to the teaching of musical reading and writing? Provide specific examples.
3. The most successful way for students to read and write music is through constant practice using lots of drills. Several computer programs could be incorporated into the music lesson so students develop their reading and writing ability. Discuss.
4. What is the difference between reading and sight-singing?
5. What is the difference between writing and dictation?

➤ Ongoing Assignment

1. When we present an element to students in a focus pattern, it is important that we practice additional patterns containing the element on a different beat or surrounded by known elements. Choose an element that you are going to teach next year from your first, third, and fifth grade classes. List the steps that you would use to practice a variation of this pattern through reading and writing activities.
2. How can you extend the above reading and writing activities to develop inner hearing, memory, sight-singing, and dictation activities?
3. Describe how you would teach a new piece of music to your students through sight-singing.

References for Practicing Rhythm and Melody through Reading, Writing, and Memory Exercises

Houlahan, Mícheál, and Philip Tacka. *Sound Thinking: Music for Sight-Singing and Ear Training.* 2 vols. New York: Boosey & Hawkes, 1991.

Children as Creative Human Beings: Practicing Form, Improvisation, and Composition

➤ Key Questions

1. What is musical form?
2. How do we develop the concept of form in the elementary classroom?
3. What is the difference between improvisation and composition?

4. What do we mean by kinesthetic, aural, and visual improvisation activities?
5. What types of rhythmic and melodic improvisation activities can be used with all grade levels?

Activities for Developing a Sense of Musical Form

Teaching the structure of a song (form) begins early in a child's musical education. As students learn to clap the rhythm of songs and sing in tune with correct breathing and dynamics, they are already learning significant aspects of musical form such as phrasing and dynamics. Teaching form begins in the early childhood classroom with the understanding of same, different, and similar. These simple concepts lead to understanding binary and ternary forms; a prerequisite for understanding larger sonata and symphonic forms.

Activities That Emphasize Structure and Form

An understanding of musical form is closely linked to the development of musical memory, reading, writing, improvisation, composition, and inner hearing skills. The following are activities that lead students to recognize the structure of songs. Any of these activities can be further expanded into composition and improvisation activities.

1. Same and Different. Students are guided to discover:
   a. The number of phrases in a song.
   b. The number of beats in each phrase.
   c. Whether phrases are the same or different.
2. Use letters to identify same and different phrases in simple songs. For young students the teacher may call an A phrase *Apple* and a B phrase *Banana.* Phrases that are nearly the same are referred to as *variants.*
3. Repetition and Repeat Sign. The use of repeat signs may be explained as a kind of music shorthand.
4. First and Second Endings. First and second endings are simply another way to use the repeat sign and emphasize form. The use of first and second endings may be explained as a kind of musical shorthand. Consider the song *Great Big House in New Orleans.*

Figure 7.11 *Great Big House in New Orleans*

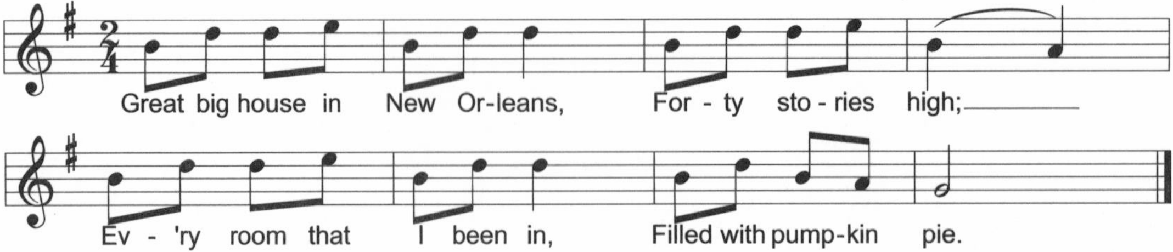

Great Big House in New Orleans may be written as in figure 7.12:

Figure 7.12 Another way to write *Great Big House in New Orleans*

5. Question and Answer Forms. Question and answer forms can be similar (easiest) and in AAv form or different, AB form.
6. Students should be guided to aurally and visually recognize simple song forms such as AABA, ABAC, and ABAB. Understanding form is valuable in helping students develop their musical memory. For example, *Great Big House in New Orleans* is in ABAC form. This form is clearly audible when performed with a breath every two measures.
7. Period Structure. There are many excellent examples of folk songs with period structure. When exploring period structure use songs that have the structure AAv, or AB, where the final of A ends on the dominant note and the final of the Av phrase ends on the tonic note. Consider the song *Love Somebody. Love Somebody* is written in the key of E. The final note of the first line is a B and is the dominant note in the key of E. The final note of the second line is an E, the tonic note in the key of E.

Figure 7.13 *Love Somebody*

Love Somebody is a simple musical example in which we can see the relationship between harmony and form. To demonstrate the form of *Love Somebody,* divide the class into two groups. One group sings the first half of the song and the second group may sing the second half. Allow students to aurally compare the melodic material in each part of the period; consider

1. the number of measures in each part,
2. the opening and closing notes of each phrase, and
3. the relationship between the two phrases (one is open and one is closed or one is finished and one is unfinished).

This song may be taught again when students are older. Guide students to compare the ending notes of each phrase. The first period ends on the note *so.* At the end of the first period, the students could sing the dominant chord *so–ti–re.* The second period ends on the note *do.* At the end of the second period, the students could sing the tonic chord *do–mi–so.*

Teaching Songs with Period Structure

1. The students sing the song in solfège syllables and conduct.
2. The students sing the song with letter names.
3. The students sing the song and identify the form of the song.
4. The instructor sings the song and the students identify the harmonic functions and chord tones.
5. Divide the class into two groups. One group sings the melody while the second group sings the harmonic functions or chord roots.
6. Discuss the period form of the song. Determine the form, opening and closing notes of each phrase, and the relationship between each phrase.
7. The students sing the song and carefully listen to the aspects of the music discussed above.
8. After learning the song, the students could improvise a new answer phrase to the first part of the period. This exercise may become more demanding if the students have to improvise a phrase not related to the material of the first phrase.

The following are classical music forms. Consider presenting the following forms as listening activities or as performances by students who study instruments privately.

1. Binary form: J. S. Bach, Partita No. 1 in B flat major, BWV 825 or J. S. Bach, Minuet in G from the Anna Magdalena Notebook
2. Ternary Form: Chopin, Mazurka in C major Op 33. No. 3; J. S. Bach, Musette from the Anna Magdalena Notebook
3. Rondo Form: ABACABA—Haydn, String Quartet in C major, Op 33, No. 2. Beethoven, last movement of Piano Sonata in G, Op. 14, No. 2
4. Theme and Variation: Vaughn Williams, Variation on Greensleeves
5. Sonata Allegro Form: Mozart Sonatas
6. Fugue: Tonal Answer and Real Answer. J. S. Bach, the Fugue from the Toccata and Fugue in D minor for Organ
7. Concerto: Mozart, Horn Concerto No. 4 in E flat, K. 495, rondo movement
8. Symphony: Haydn, Symphony No. 104 in D major, First Movement

Activities for Developing Improvisation and Composition

Improvisation, the art of composing extemporaneously, and composition, the art of formulating and writing music, are both integral components of the Kodály approach to teaching. Improvisation and composition extend and develop student creativity and musicianship. Improvisation can take many forms. Often young students invent words and melodies quite naturally. Substituting words in a song and choosing motions to accompany a song are early forms of improvisation.

The instructor must set the parameters for improvisation so simply and so clearly that everyone can perform the task. Another basic rule for improvisation games is that the students must keep the beat going. The improvisation game should not be stopped. The activity proceeds until everyone has had a turn. At the same time the instructor can observe and assess which students might need additional help with a particular concept.

Making up movements to accompany songs and changing the words to a song will encourage young students' spontaneity and creativity. The classroom atmosphere for such activities should be free and game-like so students can make an error without becoming embarrassed. In a game-like setting, students may be encouraged to have fun while putting their musical skills into practice immediately and instinctively.

Students with an understanding of typical rhythmic and melodic patterns in songs are well equipped to improvise and compose music based on the musical concepts. Rhythmic and melodic elements as well as form may be practiced through improvisation activities. Instructors should consider the students' age and assess the class's level of understanding to determine appropriate improvisation activities. If possible, some type of improvisation activity should accompany each musical element learned.

The following activities can be turned into composition exercises by writing down the improvisations.

Activities for Improvising Rhythm

Activities that involve improvising rhythmic elements are usually the first to be incorporated into music lessons. The following are kinesthetic, aural, and visual activities that aid in practicing rhythm and developing improvisation skills.

Kinesthetic Activities for Improvising Rhythms

Begin with simple activities. Movements to accompany songs, changing the words to a song, echo clapping, and echo singing should be used with young students to encourage spontaneity and creativity. The classroom atmosphere for these activities should be informal and game-like so students can make an error without becoming self-conscious.

1. Improvise a motion to a song suggested by the text. In the song *Hunt the Slipper,* the students can perform motions related to the text of the song such as performing the tapping motion of hammer to the beat. When singing *Hot Cross Buns,* the students can perform motions related to baking such as a stirring motion or a scooping motion.
2. Improvise a motion to the beat. In the song *That's a Mighty Pretty Motion,* a student may select a motion for the class to imitate such as clapping, jumping, patting, tapping, and so on.
3. Improvise a motion for the rhythmic form of a folk song. For example, the students may sing *Hot Cross Buns* while walking in a circle; they walk clockwise for the A phrases and counter-clockwise for the B phrase.
4. Perform a body canon using finger snaps or hand claps in a four-beat pattern. One student leads and the class follows.

5. Young students can pretend to accompany a song with a musical instrument. For example, they may perform a strumming motion that imitates playing a guitar or imitate playing a drum.
6. Improvise a two-beat rhythmic ostinato using body motions such as clapping hands for beat one and patting knees for beat two.
7. Improvise a rhythmic ostinato using Orff instruments.

Aural Activities for Improvising Rhythms

1. Improvise an Answer to a Four-Beat Rhythmic Question.
   a. The instructor establishes the beat.
   b. The instructor claps and says a rhythm and a student responds with a different rhythm.
   c. Initially the instructor may clap a pattern and ask the students to change one of the beats. As the students become more proficient, the instructor can ask students to name the rhythmic pattern clapped, change the length of the phrase, and the tempo. This activity leads to performing rhythmic conversations.

   Improvise a rhythmic ostinato to a song. A student can compose a rhythmic ostinato to a song. Initially these should be with simple two-beat ostinatio.
2. Question and Answer.
   a. The instructor claps a four-beat rhythmic question to the student and he or she must respond by clapping back a four-beat answer.
   b. The students may do this exercise without naming any of the rhythms. Later, the students can clap their answer and say rhythm syllables. Question and answer conversations can continue as a chain around the class.
3. First and Second Endings.
   a. After working with question and answer rhythms, the instructor may move to songs having first and second endings. The instructor or student performs the rhythm through the first ending, and another student performs the repeat of the rhythm but improvises a second ending. This type of activity involves memory development along with the improvisation.
4. Creating a New Rhythmic Composition Based on a Form Given by the Instructor.
   a. The instructor provides students with an A phrase (question) that is four beats long and asks students to improvise a B phrase (answer). This may be turned into a larger improvisation exercise using the form ABAC.
   b. The instructor may specify a longer composition, an AABA composition.
   c. This could be performed as a group activity or could be performed by an individual student. This exercise should be based on song material the class is studying.
5. Chain Improvisation Game. This is a game where students sit in a circle and improvise a four-beat rhythmic phrase. Once the beat is established and the game begins around the class, the momentum established by the beat should not be interrupted because of a hesitation or an error. The improvisation continues until each successive student has had a turn. An important aspect of this type of activity is that it teaches the students to make quick decisions. In many cases these decisions

are intuitive, which indicates that the musical elements in question have been completely internalized.

a. Child one performs a four-beat pattern.
b. Another student performs the pattern and adds another four-beat pattern. The next child repeats the patterns and adds his or her own four-beat pattern.
c. The game continues until someone makes a mistake.

A simplified version of the chain improvisation game is:

a. Child one performs a four-beat pattern.
b. Another student performs the last two beats of the first pattern and adds another two beats. The next child repeats the last two beats from the previous pattern and adds his or her own two beats.
c. The game continues until someone makes a mistake.

Aural Form. Four volunteers are each given a letter of the form AABA. Two will improvise the first A and B, the others will repeat. They will do four beats each; the instructor may provide the tempo.

Visual Activities for Improvising Rhythm

1. Improvising a New Ending or a New Measure.
   a. Put an easy rhythm on the board and erase one measure. Have a student perform the rhythm and improvise the rhythm of the missing measure.
   b. The instructor writes the rhythm of that song on the board but erases the last two measures.
   c. Individual students may clap the rhythm while saying the rhythm syllables and improvise the final two measures.
2. Fill-in Improvisation.
   a. Place a series of four flash cards on the board.
   b. Three of the flash cards have a rhythm written on them; the third card is blank.
   c. Ask student to clap flash cards one, two, and four while an individual student improvises a four-beat rhythm pattern for flash card three. (When beginning this activity, consider putting four beats on the third card and ask them to change only one beat.)
3. Improvising Form.
   a. Once students can identify quarter and eighth notes, the instructor can move on to improvisation activities that deal with form.
   b. The instructor writes two rhythm phrases on the board. Students clap the rhythm.
   c. The instructor names the phrases A and B.
   d. Erase the B phrase.
   e. Ask how many beats are in the A phrase.
   f. Ask how many beats should be in the B phrase.
   g. Ask individual students to improvise a new B line and write it.
   h. If the letter names A and B seem to be too abstract for the students, use pictures of fruits such as apples and bananas instead of letters.
   i. After this exercise use a similar procedure to work with ABAB form.

Activities for Improvising Melody

Kinesthetic Activities for Improvising Melodies

Have the students demonstrate the melodic contour of a melody through improvised motions and words. For the song *Snail Snail* improvise motions for the snail. Substitute the word *cat* or *squirrel* for snail and improvise appropriate motions.

Aural Activities for Improvising Melodies

1. Improvising Text. Students may improvise words with simple melodies. For example, the instructor may sing a question to the student using the notes *so–mi,* and the student improvises an answer using the same notes.

Figure 7.14 *How Are You Today*

2. Substitute Text. Consider the song *Teddy Bear.* Ask the students to substitute words for *Teddy Bear* like *Buzzing Bee* or *Kitty Cat.*
3. Question and Answer.
   a. The instructor establishes the beat. The instructor sings a four-beat melody, and the students respond with a different four-beat melody.
   b. The instructor may sing a pattern and ask the students to change one beat. (This can also be done visually and may be easier for some students.)
   c. As students become more proficient, the instructor lengthens the phrase and/or changes the tempo. This leads to the performance of melodic conversations. Question and answer conversations can continue as a chain around the class.
4. First and Second Endings.
   a. After working with question and answer melodies, the instructor may move to songs with first and second endings. The instructor defines the difference.
   b. The instructor or student performs the melody through the first ending, and another student performs the repeat of the rhythm but improvises a second ending.
   c. This type of activity develops musical memory as well as the ability to improvise.
5. Improvise Melodic Ostinato to Accompany Songs. The instructor asks students to improvise a melodic ostinato to a known pentatonic melody. It is important for the instructor to limit the number of solfège syllalbles that students will improvise with. For example students might begin to improvise using *la–so–mi* before moving to the notes of the pentatonic scale.
6. A Chain Improvisation Game.
   a. Child one performs a four-beat melodic pattern made up of quarter notes. Another student performs this pattern but changes one beat.

   b. Child one performs a four-beat melodic pattern. Another student performs this pattern and adds another four-beat pattern. The next student child repeats the new patterns and adds his or her own. The game is played until someone makes a mistake.
7. The students improvise a melody using the retrograde of a given pattern: *do–mi–so–la* in retrograde is *la–so–mi–do.* These particular solfège patterns are found in the song *Rocky Mountain.*
8. When presented with a melody, the students improvise a sequence based on this melody. The instructor may set the parameters. For example, ask the student to sing the pattern a step up or a step down. The instructor could sing the first measure of the following example and the student could sing the second measure.

Figure 7.15 Singing a pattern by stepping up

Visual Activities for Improvising Melodies

1. Fill-in a Four-Beat Pattern.
   a. Improvising with *so* and *mi.* The instructor writes four quarter notes on the board and puts solfège syllables under beats one, three, and four. The student has the choice of filling in beat two with a *so* or a *mi.*
   b. A student may sing the melody but improvise in the blank measure. The instructor may provide the rhythm. It is best to begin with a very simple rhythm before moving on to more complex ones. The instructor may write a simple melody on the board but leave one measure blank. Have a student sing the melody but improvise the blank measure. The rhythm for this measure may be improvised by the student or specified by the instructor.
   c. Students may arrange cards with rhythms and melodies to create a new song.
2. Improvising a Melody to a Given Rhythmic Pattern. Have a student improvise a rhythm to a given line of solfège syllables. For example: *so–la–so–mi* may be performed as *so–lala–so–mi* or *so–la–soso–mi.*
3. Place a series of four flash cards on the board.
   a. Three of the flash cards have a rhythm and solfège syllables written on them while the fourth one has only a rhythm written on the card.
   b. Ask a student to sing the flash cards with hand signs and improvise a new melody for the flash card with only the rhythm written on it.
4. Students may improvise a melody to a given scale.
5. Improvisation with Form. Improvise using the form of a composition. *Hot Cross Buns* is in AABA form. A student may sing the A sections of this song but improvise the B section.
6. Flash Cards. Cards with rhythmic and melodic patterns may be arranged by the students to create a new song.
7. Improvise a Melodic Ostinato to a Given Melody.
   a. Sing a song with a rhythmic ostinato.
   b. Each student may improvise a new ostinato for the folk song. Ask several students to perform their ostinato together while singing the song.
8. Improvise a Question and Answer.
   a. Read and perform the rhythm of the song.
   b. Ask: How many measures are there in the question?

c. How many measures are there in the answer?
d. Can the question end on *do?* (no)
e. Improvise questions and answers singing with hand signs.

Additional Improvisation Activities

1. Improvise percussion instrument accompaniments to songs using a two-beat or four-beat ostinato.
2. Improvise short melodic motives with hand signs.
3. Improvise melodies to simple given rhythms.
4. Improvise to complete missing melodic phrases in a melody.
5. Improvise rhythms in a chain around the classroom.
6. Improvise rhythms to the form of a simple folk song.
7. Improvise rhythmic accompaniments to familiar songs.
8. Improvise short melodies for poems and rhymes with known musical elements.
9. Improvise melodies using known melodic syllables in the form of the simplest songs. For example, ABA, AAAB, ABAB, and so on.
10. Improvise to complete a missing section of a song, following a given form.
11. Improvise using two-part hand signs.
12. Improvise short rhythmic canons.
13. Improvise several phrases of music to given forms.
14. Improvise a melodic chain.
15. Change simple major melodies to minor.
16. Improvise a song in a specified meter and scale.
17. Given a rhythmic or melodic skeleton, the students add more complex rhythms and melodic phrases without changing the length of the phrase.

All of these rhythmic, melodic, and form activities may be extended and varied taking into account the level and abilities of the students. Ostinati, both rhythmic and melodic, may be created and incorporated into the performance of many simple and complex folk songs. Possibilities are limitless when the music class is conducted in an atmosphere of creativity and spontaneity.

› Discussion Questions

1. Describe the difference between an improvisation and composition exercise.
2. How can you develop student's kinesthetic, aural, and visual improvisation abilities in the classroom?
3. Students should be allowed to compose music freely in the classroom using their own ideas and forms of expression. Activities based on the suggestions of this chapter are only another form of reading and writing and do not help students creative skills. Discuss.

➤ Ongoing Assignment

1. Review the goals for form and improvisation/composition in the curriculum for each grade.
2. Choose an element that you are going to teach next year from your first, third, and fifth grade classes. List the steps that you would use to practice this element through form, improvisation, and composition.
3. How can you extend the above improvisation and composition activities to develop inner hearing, memory, sight-singing, and dictation activities?

References for Children as Creative Human Beings: Practicing Form, Improvisation, and Composition

Improvisation

Alperson, Philip A. "On Musical Improvisation." *Journal of Aesthetics and Art Criticism* 43/1 (Fall 1984): 17–29.

Burnard, Pamela. "The Individual and Social Worlds of Children's Musical Creativity," in *The Child as Musician: A Handbook of Musical Development,* ed. Gary McPherson. New York: Oxford University Press, 2006.

Pressing, Jeff. "Improvisation: Methods and Models," in *Generative Processes in Music: The Psychology of Performance, Improvisation and Composition,* ed. John Sloboda. Oxford: Clarendon Press, 1987.

Composition

Barrett, Margaret. "Children's Aesthetic Decision Marking: An Analysis of Children's Musical Discourse as Composers." *International Journal of Music Education* 28 (1996): 37–62.

Bramhall, David. *Composing in the Classroom.* New York: Boosey & Hawkes, 1989.

Campbell, L. *Sketching at the Keyboard.* London: Stainer & Bell, 1985.

Chatterley, A. *The Music Club Book of Improvisation Projects.* London: Stainer & Bell, 1978.

Cropley, A. K. "Fostering Creativity in the Classroom: General Principles," in *Handbook of Creativity Research,* ed. M. A. Runco. Cresskill, N.J.: Hampton Press, 1997.

Csikszentmihaly, M. "Society, Culture and Person: A System View of Creativity," in *The Nature of Creativity,* ed. R. J. Sternbertg. New York: Cambridge University Press, 1988.

Dadson, P., and D. McGlashan. *The from Scratch Rhythm Workbook.* Portsmouth, N.H.: Heinemann, 1995.

Flohr, J. "Young Children's Improvisations: Emerging Creative Thought." *The Creative Child and Adult Quarterly* 10/2 (1985): 79–85.

Hamann, Donald L., ed. *Creativity in the Music Classroom: The Best of MEJ.* Reston, Va.: Music Educators National Conference, 1992.

Harris, Ruth, and Elizabeth Hawksley. *Composing in the Classroom.* Cambridge: Cambridge University Press, 1990.

Herboly-Kocsár, Ildikó. *Teaching of Polyphony, Harmony and Form in Elementary School,* ed. Lilla Gábor, trans. Alexander Farkas. Kecskemét: Zoltán Kodály Pedagogical Institute, 1984.

Houlahan, Mícheál, and Philip Tacka. *Sound Thinking: Music for Sight-Singing and Ear Training.* Vol. 2. New York: Boosey & Hawkes, 1991.

Kratus, J. "The Use of Melodic and Rhythmic Motives in the Original Songs of Children Ages 5 to 13." *Contributions to Music Education* 12 (1985): 1–8.

Laczó, Z. "Psychological Investigation of Improvisation Abilities in the Lower and Higher Classes of the Elementary School." *Bulletin of the Council for Research in Music Education* 66 and 67 (1981): 39–45.

McNicol, R. *Sound Inventions: 32 Creative Music Projects for the Junior Classroom.* Oxford: Oxford University Press, 1992.

Mead, Virginia Hoge. *Dalcroze Eurhythmics in Today's Classroom.* New York: Schott, 1994. See also: *Music Educators Journal.* September 1993; January 1995; November 1996; November 1997; November 1999.

Sloboda, John, ed. *Improvisation and Composition.* New York: Oxford University Press, 2001.

Smith, B., and W. Smith. "Uncovering Cognitive Process in Music Composition: Educational and Computational Approaches," in *Music Education: An Artificial Intelligence Approach,* ed. M. Smith, A. Smaill, and G. Wiggins. New York: Springer-Verlag, 1994.

Szabó, Helga. *Énekes improvizácio az iskolában* [*Vocal Improvisation in the Elementary School*]. In Hungarian. Vols. 1–5. Budapest: Zenemýkiadó, 1977.

———. *Vocal Improvisation in the School IV: Canon, Imitation and Fugue,* trans. Judit Pokoly. Kecskemét: Zoltán Kodály Pedagogical Institute, 1984. This volume traces the development of canon, imitation, and fugue. Numerous musical examples, largely drawn from the fifteenth to eighteenth centuries, are included.

Tillman, June, and Keith Swanwick. "Towards a Model of Development of Children's Musical Creativity." *Canadian Music Educator* 30/2 (1989: 169–174.

Upitis, Rena. *"Can I Play You My Song?" The Compositions and Invented Notations of Children.* Portsmouth, N.H.: Heinemann, 1992.

Webster, Peter. "Creativity as Creative Thinking." *Music Educators Journal* 76/9 (1990): 22–28.

Wiggins, Jackie. *Composition in the Classroom: A Tool for Teaching.* Reston, Va.: Music Educators National Conference, 1990.

———. "Children's Strategies for Solving Compositional Problems with Peers." *Journal of Research in Music Education* 42/3 (1994): 232–252.

Winner, Ellen, Lyle Davidson, and Larry Scripp. *Arts Propel: A Handbook for Music.* Cambridge, Mass.: Harvard Project Zero and Educational Testing Service, 1992.

Winters, G., and J. Northfield, *Starter Composing Packet.* Essex, England: Longman Group, 1992.

Part-Work and the Development of Harmonic Hearing

› Key Questions

What is Part-Work?

How do we develop part-singing in the classroom?

What is harmonic hearing?

How can we help students to develop their ability to find an accompaniment to a melody based on the roots of the primary chords?

How do we introduce chords to children?

> Many choir leaders think that singing folksongs in unison is not choral singing, and that it is not worthy work for a choir leader. This is a great mistake because to sing a folksong in unison is a big artistic task and it is but rarely that we hear a perfect performance in this field. Here I do not have in mind stuffing it with subtle nuances and rendering it more interesting by sophisticated dynamics and tempi. No. Often it is the simplest performance of a song that causes the greatest difficulty, because there is a tendency, more or less conscious, to try to make the performance interesting and this tendency is to be subdued, to be dampened down. Most of our folksongs are of a monumental character, the singers are to be guided toward simple and grandiose singing. This is by no means a trifling matter and the choir leader who succeeds in achieving it has good reason to be content.[1]

> Most singing instructors and chorus masters believe in controlling the pitch of the voices by the piano. But singing depends on the acoustically correct "natural" intervals, and not on the tempered system. Even a perfectly tuned piano can never be a criterion of singing, not to speak of the ever "out-of-tune" pianos available at schools and rehearsal rooms. Yet how often have I found chorus masters attempting to restore the shaky intonation of their choirs with the help of a mistuned piano! And how often does a teacher, lost amid the waves of the piano accompaniment, not even notice that the pitch of his singing class has gone wrong. . . . The advantages of singing in two parts can hardly be overestimated, but unfortunately it is often left until far too late. It assists aural development in every way, even in unison singing. In fact, those who always sing in unison never learn to sing in correct pitch. Correct unison singing can, paradoxically, be learned only by singing in two parts: the voices adjust and balance each other.[2]

Activities for Developing Part-Singing

Preparing students for two or three-part singing should take place from the early stages of a student's musical education. The following strategies will provide a foundation to approach two-part singing with confidence. All of these activities provide the instructor with a means to prepare and practice the musical elements at many levels of sophistication and difficulty. By incorporating these activities into the music class the instructor enlivens the vocal music program while developing in the students a precise and critical awareness of musical elements and performance practice. The following sequence or activities provides an ease and order to enable students to perform part music. Perform each musical activity as follows.

1. Instructor and class.
2. Class and instructor.
3. Divide the class into two groups; each performing their own part. Switch.
4. Two small ensembles; each performing their own part.
5. Two students; each performing their own part.

Preparatory Activities for Developing Part-Singing

1. Sing a song while marching, skipping, or walking to the beat. In this activity the students must concentrate on two different tasks at the same time.

2. Call and response singing. Although students only perform one phrase of music, they must be able to sing both phrases using inner hearing (audiation) if they are going to be able to sing rhythmically and musically. Call and response singing may be applied to folk songs (you may also think of call and response singing as responsorial singing).
3. Perform or point to a visual of the beat of a song while singing.
   a. Students sing while patting the beat or performing the beat on a percussion instrument.
   b. Students sing while pointing to a visual of a beat.
4. Sing a song while performing the rhythm. Students sing while clapping the rhythm or performing the rhythm on a percussion instrument.
5. Students sing while performing both the beat and the rhythm of the song.
   a. Two students may perform a simple folk song, one performs the beat the other performs the rhythm; use different timbres beat and rhythm.
   b. The instructor may write the rhythm of a known song on the board and place the beat below the rhythmic notation. Two students can go to the board and perform the song with one student pointing to the beat and the other pointing to the rhythm.
6. Rhythmic and melodic ostinati.
   a. The students sing the melody while the instructor claps a rhythmic ostinato.
   b. The students and the instructor exchange parts.
   c. Divide the students into two groups, one group sings and the other performs the ostinato. Switch tasks.
   d. Two students perform the work.
   e. One student sings while performing the second part on the piano.
7. The students perform known repertoire with simple melodic descants.
8. The students perform partner songs. For example, half of the class may perform the song *Liza Jane* while the other half of the class performs *Rocky Mountain.*
9. The students sing one song while clapping the rhythm of another. For example, the students may sing *Rocky Mountain* while reading and clapping the rhythm of *Tideo.* This activity requires that the two songs have the same number of beats per phrase. Students perform the rhythm of known songs in canon.
10. Rhythm canons. A rhythm canon is a canon that is performed saying rhythm syllables. Rhythm syllables are spoken without pitch. Although the rhythm of many folk songs can work well when performed in canon, the best songs to begin with are those that have a rest at the end of each phrase. A good example is *Bow Wow Wow.* Rhythm Canons may be performed aurally or visually.

Performing an Aural Rhythm Canon

Aural rhythm canons are performed without the aid of notation. If a motion is attached to a phrase, the exercise is simple to perform. For example, say *Ali Baba Forty Thieves* while tapping four beats. Tap the beats on different parts of your body and have students imitate. Once students are proficient at this activity perform it in canon after two beats. The instructor could also perform a rhythm and have students clap it back after two or four beats. Echo clapping is a preliminary preparation for aural canon work.

Procedure for Performing Aural Rhythm Canons

1. The instructor says the rhythm syllables and taps the rhythm using a drum or wood block; the students clap and say the rhythm syllables beginning after two beats.
2. The instructor taps without saying rhythm syllables; the students clap and say the rhythm syllables beginning after two beats.
3. The instructor claps the rhythm of an entire song without stopping and the students perform it in canon beginning after two beats. The students may say the rhythm syllables.

Performing a Visual Rhythm Canon

The first step to performing a rhythm canon is to have students read rhythm flash cards. To support memorization, the instructor should keep a steady pulse but show the card quickly and move on to the next card while the students are still performing the rhythm of the first card. In other words, give the students a brief look at each card in succession. The speed of this process may be increased so that the students are always saying something different from what they are seeing.

The following is a procedure for introducing a visual rhythm canon using the rhythm of a known song or rhyme.

Figure 7.16 *Bow, Wow, Wow*

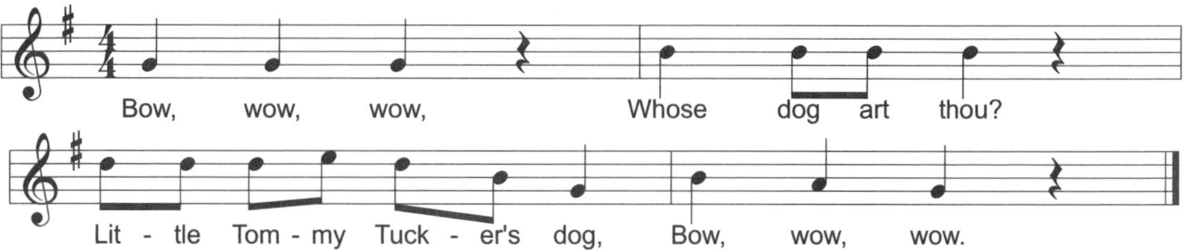

1. Perform the song with actions and words.
2. The instructor and students may perform *Bow, Wow, Wow* in canon after two beats.
3. Sing the song with rhythm syllables.
4. Say rhythm syllables while clapping the rhythm.
5. Think the rhythm syllables and clap the rhythm.
6. The students think and clap the rhythm while the instructor taps it in canon (use a different timbre).
7. The instructor writes the canonic part below the notation of the song. Ask: Where should we begin writing the second part? What should be written in the empty measures?
8. Students perform the canon.

11. Singing pentatonic melodies as canons. Carefully select pentatonic songs that may be performed as canons. The canon should begin on the same pitch that the first part is singing. The following songs meet this criteria:

Down Came a Lady	The second part begins after four beats.
I See the Moon	The second part begins after two or four beats.
Bow, Wow, Wow	The second part begins after two beats.

The same activities that prepare and practice part work may also be used to practice sight-reading. For example, the student may sing a simple song while pointing to the rhythm of that song in canon. This activity may be difficult for some young students but is an excellent activity for developing independence and dual thinking.

a. The instructor and students sing a song together.
b. Perform the same song again. Allow the class to start; the instructor sings the song starting several beats after the class.
c. Perform the same song; the class sings after the instructor, entering on a conducting cue.
d. After this step, the instructor may divide the class into two groups to perform the canon.
e. Two students perform the canon.

12. Hand sign singing.
    a. The students read the hand signs of the instructor.
    b. Focus their attention on both the melodic contour of the melody and the intervals of the exercise.
    c. Divide the class into two groups. One group sustains a note while the other sings several notes against the sustained note.
    d. Performing from the instructor's hand signs. Begin both groups on the same pitch with both hands. Show compatible pitch relationships with both hands. Move each part scale-wise in thirds.
    e. Start both groups on different pitches and sing to a cadence.
    f. Divide the class into three groups. One group sustains a pitch while the other groups perform a melody from the instructor's hand signs.
13. Simple melodic canons. Simple melodic canons may be introduced using the same procedures used for introducing rhythm canons. For a melodic canon, students can sing with solfège syllables or sing with letter names if they are advanced. The following is a procedure for introducing a melodic canon:
    a. Instructor sings canon and students determine the meter, rhythm syllables and form.
    b. The instructor says the rhythm syllables and taps the rhythm using a drum or wood block; the students clap and say the rhythm syllables beginning after two beats.
    c. The instructor taps without saying rhythm syllables; the students clap and say the rhythm syllables beginning after two beats.
    d. The instructor claps the rhythm of an entire song without stopping and the students perform it in canon beginning after two beats. The students may say the rhythm syllables.

e. The instructor sings the canon on a neutral syllable without stopping and the students perform it in canon beginning after two beats with "loo."
f. The instructor sings the canon on a neutral syllable without stopping and the students perform it in canon beginning after two beats with solfège syllables.
g. The students sing a known melody and clap in canon after two beats.
h. The students sing a known melody and show the hand signs in canon after two beats.
i. The students sing a known melody and play in canon on the piano after two beats.

14. Partner songs. Partner songs are songs that can be performed together. The following songs work well in combination:

    Dinah and *Bounce High*
    Bow, Wow, Wow and *I See the Moon*
    Land of the Silver Birch and *Who Killed Cock Robin*
    Liza Jane and *Come Through in a Hurry*
    Liza Jane, Come Through in a Hurry, All around the Brickyard, Dinah

15. Singing simple pentatonic folk songs in three parts. In this activity the class is divided into two groups and performs the pentatonic folk song as a two-part canon. When the students can perform the two parts with ease, the instructor may sing in canon with the students creating a third part.
16. Singing folk songs in thirds and sixths.

Figure 7.17 *Vamos a Belen*

17. Three-part singing.
    a. Sing a melody with two complimentary melodic ostinati.
    b. Sing a canon in two parts and add a melodic ostinato.
    c. Sing sustained roots of chords to a two-part piece of music.
18. Learning two-part song arrangements:
    a. Teaching the harmony part to a known song: Students should already be able to sing songs with rhythmic and melodic ostinati as well as sing songs in canon before learning simple two-part songs. If you are teaching a two-part arrangement of a folk song, the folk song should be familiar to students.

    The following is a teaching procedure for working with a two-part song arrangement where students already know the folk song used in the arrangement. The harmony part may be either aurally (rote) or visually (note).

1. The instructor sings the top part and plays the lower part on the piano. The instructor may also play a recording for the students.
2. The instructor sings the lower part and plays the top part on the piano.
3. Ask students questions based on the performance of the song.
4. How many phrases are there in this arrangement?
5. Did the two parts begin and end each phrase together?
6. Did both parts have the same text?
7. How would you describe the tune of the harmony line?
8. Did both parts begin and end on the same pitch?
9. The instructor sings the harmony line phrase by phrase and the students repeat. This can be done with rhythm or solfège syllables or on a neutral syllable if the students have not learned all the solfège or rhythm syllables. This is easiest when done with text.
10. The instructor may hum or perform the melody on the piano for each phrase as the students learn the harmony line phrase by phrase.
11. The students and instructor sing the harmony line while the instructor plays the melody line on the piano.
12. The students sing the harmony line while the instructor sings the melody line. Switch parts.
13. Divide the class into two groups. Group A sings the harmony and Group B sings the melody. Switch parts.

b. Teaching a new two-part song: Students should already be able to sing and perform songs with rhythmic and melodic ostinati, perform in canon, and perform simple two-part folk song arrangements prior to learning a two-part song that is not familiar. The following is a process for teaching the two-part song aurally. The procedure may also be adapted to teach the song using notation.
   1. The instructor performs the new two-part song by singing one part and playing the other on the piano or by singing and having a student sing the second part or play a recorded performance.
   2. Ask students questions based on the performance of the song. Perform the song again and then ask students for their response to the questions.
   3. How many different parts are there in this arrangement?
   4. What did you notice about the form of the piece?
   5. How many phrases are there in this arrangement?
   6. Did the two parts begin and end each phrase together?
   7. Did both parts have the same text?
   8. Did both parts begin and end on the same pitch?
   9. Which is the harmony line?
   10. How would you describe the tune of the harmony line?
   11. The instructor sings one part and plays the second part on the piano phrase by phrase and the students repeat from memory.
   12. The students and instructor sing the first part while the instructor plays the second part on the piano.
   13. The instructor sings the second part and plays the first part on the piano phrase by phrase and the students repeat from memory. The instructor

can hum or play the first part as the students are singing the second part phrase by phrase.

14. The students and instructor sing the second part while the instructor plays the first part on the piano. The students sing the second part while the instructor plays the first part on the piano.
15. The students sing the second part while the instructor sings the first part. Switch parts.
16. The instructor divides the class into two groups. Group A sings the top part and Group B sings the second. Switch parts.

19. Singing pentatonic major, minor, and modal scales in canon
    a. Sing different pentatonic scales in canon. These scales can be sung in two to five parts. Figure 7.18 illustrates a pentatonic scale beginning on *do* and performed in four parts.

Figure 7.18 Pentatonic scale beginning on *do* and performed in four parts

    b. Sing pentatonic scales in ascending and descending succession from the same starting pitch. Begin on a selected pitch, for example, D. Sing the pentatonic scale up from that pitch, change the top pitch to the new scale as directed by the = sign and follow the arrows.

d'	=	*r'*		*m'*	=	*s*		*l*	=	*d*
		d'		*r'*				*s*		
l				*d'*		*m*				*l*
s		*l*				*r*		*m*		*s*
		s		*l*		*d*		*r*		
m				*s*		,		*d*		*m*
r		*m*				*l,*		,		*r*
d		*r*	=	*m*		*s,*	=	*l,*		***d***
↑										

Ascending ↑ Descending ↓ Same Pitch =

Figure 7.19 Pentatonic scales in ascending and descending succession

Sing major and minor scales using solfège syllables or letter names in canon; begin after two notes. Perform the scales in three-part canon.

c. Singing major and minor scales from the same starting note. Using solfège syllables, sing the major scale beginning on *do* and starting on the pitch D; then sing the minor scale beginning on *la,* beginning on the same starting pitch. In this way, the students perform the major scale followed by its parallel minor scale.
d. Perform modal scales in canon.
e. Perform modal scales ascending and descending from the same starting pitch.
f. Sing pentatonic scales from the same starting pitch in canon. For example, see (b) above. Divide the class into two groups. One part begins the exercise and the second part follows after two beats.
g. Divide the class into three parts; give each part a note of the major triad to sing. Ask all groups to call this note *mi.* Instruct the groups to sing *Hot Cross Buns* with solfège syllables. The students will be singing the simple song in three parts in parallel major chords. This exercise may be repeated using a minor triad.

Music Literature for Children's Choir

The songs selected from *150 American Folk Songs* may be easily adapted for children's choirs. The teaching suggestions have been described in greater detail earlier in this chapter.

Table 7.1 Selected songs from *150 American Folk Songs*

Song	Performance Suggestions
All Night, All Day	Perform this song as a partner song with *Swing Low, Sweet Chariot*
Band of Angels	The students may extend the song by singing the numbers backwards
Blow Boys Blow	Audience participation
Cape Cod Girls	Divide the class into two groups and perform as a call and response song
Cock Robin	Accompany the song with a *la* drone and have soloists sing the verses
Cradle Hymn	Expressive singing
Dance Josey	Perform in canon after two beats
Deaf Woman's Courtship	Dramatization: the boys begin singing loudly but get softer and softer; the girls begin singing softly and get louder. The instructor should explain that in this song the word "smoking" refers to smoking meat and the word "carding" means combing and cleaning wool.
Father Grumble	Use soloists and a dramatization
Grey Goose	Expressive singing
Hold My Mule	Perform in canon after two beats
I'm Goin' Home on a Cloud	Expressive singing
Liza Jane	Solo and chorus. The song may be performed in canon at two or four beats
Mary Had a Baby	Perform as a canon after four beats

Table 7.1 *Continued*

Song	**Performance Suggestions**
Mister Frog Went a Courtin'	This song tells a story; different soloists may be used
Mister Rabbit	Use two soloists and perform the song as a call and response. It may also be performed in canon after four beats
Most Done Ling'ring Here	Sing in call and response style; the call may be given by different soloists
Old Bald Eagle	Divide the class up into two groups and perform as a call and response song
Old Joe Clark	Expressive singing
Old Sow	Two students may sing solos: one sings the first phrase, the second sings the second phrase, and the group sings phrases three and four
Paw Paw Patch	Expressive singing; perform play party dance
Riddle Song	Use a soloist for the second verse
Riding in a Buggy	1. Use soloists for each verse 2. Perform the verse and chorus simultaneously
Sailing O'er the Ocean	Divide the chorus and have each half alternate every two measures
Sailor's Alphabet	Use one soloist for each letter of the alphabet
Sweet William	Expressive singing
Turn the Glasses Over	Divide the chorus and have each half alternate every four measures

The songs selected from *Sail Away: 155 American Folk Songs* may be easily adapted for children's choirs. The teaching suggestions have been described in greater detail earlier in this chapter.

Table 7.2 Selected songs from *Sail Away: 155 American Folk Songs*

Song	**Performance Suggestions**
Amasee	Call and response
Birds Courtin' Song	Two groups, alternate singing verse by verse
Bob-A-Needle	Call and response
Boney	Solo and chorus
Chicka-hanka	Alternate singing between two groups
Didn't My Lord Deliver Daniel	Solo and chorus
Down in the Valley	Group 1 sings the song and Group 2 sings the harmonic chord roots
Go Tell it on the Mountain	Two groups for verse and refrain
Great Big House in New Orleans	Two-part canon after the second measure
Hammer Ring	Two groups for call and response
Jack, Can I ride?	Two soloists plus choir
Just from the Kitchen	Solo and chorus

continued

Table 7.2 *Continued*

Song	Performance Suggestions
La Bella Hortelana	Part work and rhythmic accompaniments
Lemonade	Dialogue song between two groups
Lucy Locket	Two-part canon after the second measure
Pizza Pizza	Call and response
Santy Anna	Solo and chorus
Ser Come el Aire Libre	Sing in two parts
Skin and Bones	Call and response and dramatization
Snail, Snail	Two-part canon after the second measure
Stew Ball II	Call and Response
Witch Witch	Use the first two bars as a melodic ostinato

The compositions and arrangements are identified with the Boosey & Hawkes order numbers.

Table 7.3 Unison and octavos for choirs arranged according to melodic range

Scale or Range	Title	Composer/Arranger	Number
la pentachord	*Before Rain*	Betty Bertaux	OC 3B6 192
do hexachord	*Coulter's Candy*	Betty Bertaux	OCUB6502
	Mrs. Jenny Wren	Arthur Baynon	OCUB6117
Natural minor scale	*I Give My Love an Apple*	Betty Bertaux	OC3B6370
	Hashivenu	Doreen Rao	OC3B6430
	Who Killed Cock Robin	Betty Bertaux	OCFB6240
Major scale	*Cock-a-Doodle-Do*	Betty Bertaux	OC2B6480
	Sing Alleluia Allelu	Mary Goetze	6126
	Shenandoah	Mary Goetze	6257
	Kookaburra	Mary Goetze	6255
	A Zig-A-Z	Mary Goetze	6276
	Give Way, Jordan	Mary Goetze	6183
	Pick a Bale of Cotton	Betty Bertaux	OCFB6191
	I Had Little Nut Tree	Betty Bertaux	OC2B6498
	The Holly and the Ivy	Betty Bertaux	OC3B6369
	Jubilate Deo	Michael Praetorius Doreen Rao	OCUB6450
	Musica Dei Domus Optimi	de Lassus Doreen Rao	OC4B6449

Table 7.3 *Continued*

Scale or Range	Title	Composer/Arranger	Number
	How Brightly Shines the Morning Star	Bach Doreen Rao	OCUB6418
	Nachlied	Betty Bertaux	OC3B6472
	To Music	Schubert Doreen Rao	OCUB6366
	May Day Carol	Betty Bertaux	OC3B6358
Harmonic minor scale	*Clear the Line*	Mary Goetze	6186
	Abbe Stadler	Betty Bertaux	OC3B6368
Altered notes	*The Shenandoah Blues*	Doreen Rao	OC2B6455
	Warm-Up	Leonard Bernstein	OC4B6354
	Where 'Er You Walk	Doreen Rao	OCUB6510
	Drunken Sailor	Betty Bertaux	OC5B6236
	Lullay, Lullow	Betty Bertaux	OC2B6371

The Development of Harmonic Hearing

Moveable *do* solfège is a means of leading students to develop harmonic hearing and subsequently part-writing skills. The Kodály approach to teaching harmony is based on the aural experience. Art songs as well as many folk songs may be used to teach concepts associated with harmony. The study of harmonic hearing and part writing may be introduced to students as more extensive examples of art music are incorporated into the students' repertoire. In studying harmony, students learn how chords are constructed; how they are connected; and how they relate to rhythm, melody, and texture. The following skills should be considered fundamental to developing harmonic hearing and thinking.

1. Sing intervals from hand signs or isolate intervals in songs and perform them with hand signs.
2. Sing the major and minor scale in thirds; sing the major and minor scale in fourths.
3. Identifying harmonic intervals.
   a. The instructor plays two pitches.
   b. The students echo the pitches on a neutral syllable from the lowest to the highest.
   c. The students identify the interval with solfège syllables and then name the interval.
4. The students hum a given pitch; the instructor hums a different pitch. The students identify the pitch hummed by the instructor.
5. The instructor plays two pitches on the piano establishing a tonality.
   a. The students identify the two pitches with solfège syllables and the interval.
   b. Continue the exercise using a series of intervals within one key.

6. The students aurally and visually recognize melodic patterns and typical diatonic scale patterns based on major and minor scales.
7. The students should be familiar with question and answer form and opened and closed phrases. The following songs provide clear examples of question and answer form.

    Grandma Grunts
    Rocky Mountain
    The Three Rogues

8. Given a series of pitches, students must aurally locate which pitch sounds like the tonic note.
9. Ask students to sing a familiar song. At a given signal from the instructor, students immediately sing the tonic note.
10. Follow the above procedure but use a canon. Ask the students to sing a familiar canon in parts. At a given signal from the instructor, students must sing the tonic note.
11. Students transpose a piece of music written in major to the parallel minor key and vice versa. Begin by transposing a *do* pentachord melody to a *la* pentachord melody. Moveable *do* and *la*-based minor enables students to analyze and compare the musical example as it places a melody into its tonal and functional position.
    a. The students sing the D major scale in solfège syllables.
    b. The students sing the d minor scale in solfège syllables.
    c. The instructor writes the solfège for both scales side by side as the students sing.
    d. The students locate and circle the half-step intervals.
    e. The students "realize" that the song will change because the half-step intervals are in different places.
    f. The students can sing *Row, Row Your Boat* or *Are You Sleeping* in major while pointing to the tone ladder.
    g. The students then point to *Row, Row Your Boat* or *Are You Sleeping* in minor while pointing to the tone ladder.

Tonic, Subdominant, and Dominant Chord Functions

An understanding of functional harmony occurs when the students understand the harmonic functions or chord function class. A chord function class contains chords that share the same harmonic function. In tonal music there are three function classes:

Tonic function
Subdominant function
Dominant function

Pentatonic and diatonic melodies provide a good basis for the development of functional and harmonic thinking. For *do*-centered and *la*-centered pentatonic songs, accompany the song by having a group of students sustain the tonal center while the class performs the song. This pitch is the chord root note of the tonic triad.

Figure 7.20 *Old Mister Rabbit—do* pentatonic

Figure 7.21 *Cock Robin—la* pentatonic

These songs may also be accompanied by a drone made up of *do–so* or *do–mi–so* (major tonic triad) for *do* pentatonic material and *la–mi* or *la–do–mi* (minor tonic triad) for *la* pentatonic material.

Accompanying Melodies with Tonic and Dominant Chords Roots

As students add the solfège syllables *fa* and *ti* to their melodic vocabulary, they begin to discover the need for a note other than *do* in major and *la* in minor melodies, for their accompaniments. While students are singing known pentachord, hexachord, and diatonic melodies, the instructor should quietly hum the functional notes (chord roots) *do* and *so* for *do*-centered pieces.

Figure 7.22 *Laugh, Ha, Ha*

Hum *la* and *mi* for *la*-centered pieces.

When the students are familiar with these accompanying pitches, the instructor guides the students to discover the solfège syllables of the new accompanying notes and introduces the terms: tonic function and dominant function.

Figure 7.23 *Ah, Poor Bird*

Accompanying Melodies with Tonic, Dominant, and Subdominant Chords Roots

The subdominant chord root may be introduced once the students have had sufficient practice with tonic and dominant chord roots. The procedures outlined for the presentation and practice of the tonic and dominant chord roots are the same for the subdominant chord roots. While the students sing melodies that contain clear tonic, subdominant, and dominant function triads, the instructor may hum or play the appropriate chord root on the piano. In this way, the students are led to discover the subdominant chord root in major is *fa* and the subdominant chord root in minor is *re.* The following melodies help focus the students' attention on the subdominant chord root.

Figure 7.24 *White Sand and Gray Sand*

Practice Suggestions

1. The students sing familiar songs while the instructor sings or plays the functional notes or chord roots, as an accompaniment.
2. The students sing familiar songs while showing with hand signs where the functional note or chord root in the melody changes.
3. Individual students sing familiar songs while showing with hand signs of the functional note or playing the functional notes on the piano.
4. The students identify the tonic, subdominant, and dominant functions of unknown melodies sung or played by the instructor.
5. The students transpose melodies into their parallel major or minor key and sing them with the corresponding functions.
6. The students should be presented with sight-reading materials that include both a melody and an accompaniment built on the tonic, subdominant, and dominant functions. These materials can also be used for dictation, memory work, and analyzing the harmonic basis of the melodies.
7. The students relate harmonic functions to their knowledge of form.

Practicing Harmonic Functions

Students should practice the following material with Roman numerals: I, IV, V, I and names of the scale degrees:

I	IV	V	I
Tonic	Subdominant	Dominant	Tonic

1. The students sing familiar songs while the instructor sings or plays the functional notes/chord roots as accompaniment. The students determine the names of the notes.

2. The students sing known and unknown songs while playing the accompaniment on the piano or showing the hand sign.

Figure 7.25 *Ah, Poor Bird*

3. The students transpose melodies into parallel keys.
4. Dictations should include two-part material to memorize and write. The Scherzo in figure 7.26 is an example.

Figure 7.26 Scherzo

Focusing Students' Attention on the Bass Lines

Students must develop the ability to hear music in several parts. This is a prerequisite skill for the understanding of harmonic functions and harmonic progressions. The instructor should practice exercises that focus the students' attention to the lower part of a composition.

Discovering Bass Lines

The instructor plays a two-part melody on the piano; the students listen and show the melodic contour of the lowest voice with arm motions.

1. The students discover the direction of the bass line.
2. The students discover the rhythm of the bass line.
3. The students sing the bass line with solfège syllables.
4. The students sing both parts.

Figure 7.27 W. A. Mozart, Cadences

Figure 7.27 *Continued*

Suggested Teaching Procedure

1. The instructor sings the upper voice and plays the lower voice on the piano.
2. The instructor plays both melodies on the piano while the students show the melodic contour of the lowest part.
3. The students write the melody and trace the melodic contour of the bass part. More advanced students may be encouraged to add the rhythm and melody to the bass part.
4. The instructor plays short two-part cadential examples on the piano. The students sing back the bass line with solfège syllables. These examples should include the tonic, subdominant, and the dominant notes in the lower voice.
5. The students listen to examples using more than one note in the lower part. They must be able to differentiate single or simultaneously sounded notes in the accompaniment.

Triads and Their Respective Functions

After students are thoroughly familiar with the tonic, subdominant, and dominant functions, they can be introduced to the concept of triads. Canons in major and minor keys with clearly defined triads at the cadence provide appropriate literature for initial experiences in hearing and analyzing harmony. Initially, the music material should be restricted to primary triads. Looking at both the melodic lines and harmonic aspects of music is essential for the students' understanding of harmonic concepts. The students should memorize canons and discover the harmonic functions implied by the different voices sounding together. The instructor may then draw the students' attention to individual melodic lines or melodic lines that are sounded together to create triads. These triads should be abstracted from the music material and sung by the class.

For example, sing the following major tonality canon in four parts and accompany each line with tonic or dominant notes.

- The fourth line of this canon uses the tonic and dominant notes.
- The notes that are circled are referred to as triads when they are performed together. Triads are composed of three notes: the root of the triad, the third of the triad, and the fifth of the triad. The root of the triad is the note on which the triad is based, so that in the root position the third of the triad is a note positioned a third above the root, and the fifth is a note positioned a fifth above the root.

Figure 7.28 Canon in G Major

- Sing the canon again and pause on the circled triads. Listen for each note of the triad as it is being sung.

The instructor should explain the meaning of root, third, and fifth of a triad, and how a triad is classified as either major or minor. Show how the tonic, subdominant, and dominant notes, and the triads built on them, define a key.

Sing the following minor tonality canon in four parts and accompany each line with tonic or dominant notes.

Figure 7.29 Canon in g minor

Using the same techniques for the preparation and practice of the tonic, subdominant, and dominant triads the instructor may introduce augmented and diminished triads. Explain the idea of primary and secondary triads. The triads built on the II, III, VI, and VII degrees can be shown to be related to one of the primary triads and have the same function. The II and VI belong to the subdominant class and III and V to the dominant. Chord VI can also belong to the tonic class.

Introducing Triad Inversions

Once the students have an understanding of root position primary triads, the instructor may introduce the concept of the inversion of triads. Introducing triad inversions does not involve a great deal of explanation if the students' understand the character and tonality of the triad. First inversion triads have the third in the bass; second inversion triads have the fifth in the bass. Examples from the musical literature should be used to introduce the concept of inversion of triads. It is best to concentrate on isolating triad inversions melodically and then harmonically. The same procedures outlined at the beginning of this chapter should be used.

The introduction of triad inversions should also include practice of the following.

1. The tonic, subdominant, and dominant triads in root position, first inversions, and second inversions in a triad sequence such as:

   I-IV-V-I, I6-IV6-V6-I6/4-V-I

2. Discuss the intervals included in these triads. For example, major triad, first inversion:

   mi—so—do'
   mi—so minor third
   mi—do' minor sixth
   so—do' perfect fourth

   Explain how the arrangement of intervals relates to their numerical intervals: I, I6, I6/4
3. To add interest to the harmonic accompaniments students may now be introduced to the concept that:

   mi can substitute for *do* and *ti* can substitute for *so* for tonic and dominant functions respectively in a major key
   do can substitute for *la* and *so* can substitute for *mi* for tonic and dominant functions respectively in a minor key.

4. The instructor may explore the effect of singing progressions in three parts using root position and inversions. Lead students to discover that singing certain chords in inversion will be much easier than singing them in root position. Once the students understand inversions, three-part chordal progressions may be used as accompaniments to the students' songs and as choral warm-up exercises.

Introducing Typical Harmonic Progressions

Once the students are familiar with the concepts of harmonic functions including chord roots and triads, the instructor can introduce chord patterns based on the tonic, subdominant, and dominant notes. Most chords used in tonal music of the common practice period can be grouped into the function classes of tonic, subdominant, and dominant. These will be abbreviated to T, S, and D. The basic harmonic progression in the common practice period is the movement from T-D-T or T-S-D-T. Most chord patterns can be analyzed as an extension of this basic chord sequence. (It should be noted that some chords have a prolonging function rather than a structural function). While these harmonic progressions are often colored by altered tones, the basic structure of the progressions remains the same.

The class should sing each of these progressions in four parts. Each voice part should show the bass note with hand signs while singing. These progressions should also be practiced with letter names. More advanced music students should memorize the pattern in all positions and be able to sing one voice with solfège syllables while playing the other three on the piano. The pattern should be practiced in several keys. The following example shows the I-V-I voice-leading pattern in its simplest form that is with each of the upper voices moving the shortest distance possible between chords. There are other voice-leading patterns, and the rules that govern these progressions and should be discovered or pointed out to the students before they begin to write exercises and do key board work. In this way the students will have a more meaningful grasp of written analysis and keyboard performance. The instructor should continually reinforce the harmonic concepts through sight-singing, melodic, and dictation skills.

Table 7.4 Solfège chart for I–V–I progression in major

do	*ti,*	*do*	*mi*	*re*	*mi*	*so*	*so*	*so*
so	*so*	*so*	*do*	*ti*	*do*	*mi*	*re*	*mi*
mi	*re*	*mi*	*so*	*so*	*so*	*do*	*ti*	*do*
do	*so*	*do*	*do*	*so*	*do*	*do*	*so*	*do*
I	V	I	I	V	I	I	V	I

Table 7.5 Solfège chart for I–V–I progression in minor

la	*si*	*la*	*do*	*ti*	*do*	*mi*	*mi*	*mi*
mi	*mi*	*mi*	*la*	*si*	*la*	*do*	*ti*	*do*
do	*ti*	*do*	*mi*	*mi*	*mi*	*la*	*si*	*la*
la	*mi*	*la*	*la*	*mi*	*la*	*la*	*mi*	*la*
I	V	I	I	V	I	I	V	I

The subdominant triad functions as part of the full cadence in the common practice period. In root position, the subdominant has the root doubled to strengthen the subdominant function of the chord. Voice-leading in closed position follows the same principles as the progression from tonic to dominant: the common tone is kept and the upper parts move by step.

Table 7.6 Solgége chart for I–IV–V–I progression in major (octave, third, and fifth in the top voice)

do	*do*	*ti*	*do*	*mi*	*fa*	*re*	*mi*	*so*	*la*	*so*	*so*
so	*la*	*so*	*so*	*do*	*do*	*ti*	*do*	*mi*	*fa*	*re*	*mi*
mi	*fa*	*re*	*mi*	*so*	*la*	*so*	*so*	*do*	*do*	*ti*	*do*
do	*fa,*	*so,*	*do*	*do*	*fa,*	*so,*	*do*	*do*	*fa,*	*so,*	*do*
I	IV	V	I	I	IV	V	I	I	IV	V	I

Table 7.7 Solfège chart for I–IV–V–I progression in minor (octave, third, and fifth in the top voice)

la	*la*	*si*	*la*	*do*	*re*	*ti*	*do*	*mi*	*fa*	*mi*	*mi*
mi	*fa*	*mi*	*mi*	*la*	*la*	*si*	*la*	*do*	*re*	*ti*	*do*
do	*re*	*ti*	*do*	*mi*	*fa*	*mi*	*mi*	*la*	*ti*	*si*	*la*
la	*re,*	*mi,*	*la*	*la*	*re,*	*mi,*	*la*	*la*	*re,*	*mi,*	*la*
I	IV	V(#)	I	I	IV	V(#)	I	I	IV	V(#)	I

If a minor third is added to a dominant triad, the new chord is called a dominant seventh.

The dominant seventh chord contains a diminished fifth interval that must be resolved correctly. In a major key, the *fa* resolves to *mi* and the *ti* resolves to *do.* In a minor key the *re* resolves to *do* and the *si* resolves to *la.* Seventh chords in root position can be written with the root in the bass and the third, fifth, and seventh in the upper parts. The dominant seventh can replace the dominant triad in any of the previous chord progressions. The students should always sing the notes of resolution following the dominant seventh chord.

Table 7.8 The V7 chord

Major	Minor
fa	*re*
re	*ti*
ti	*si*
so	*mi*

Modulation

As a more detailed study of the music of Haydn, Mozart, and Beethoven continues, the students will need to be introduced to the concept of modulation. Modulation is the process of moving from one key or tonal center to another. Modulation and chromaticism are related. It can be difficult to discern whether a modulation has taken place or a momentary tonal deviation has occurred if a harmonic background has not been supplied. If a modulation has been effected by the chromaticism, then the placement of *do* will have to be changed to read the modulating passage. If the melody is supported by subdominant, dominant, and tonic functions in the new key, then a modulation has occurred.

Before students begin to read modulating material, the following pedagogical steps should be covered.

1. Use hand signs to modulate from one pattern to another. The instructor shows a pattern with one hand and by changing the hand sign on a given note continues in a new key. The pivot note has two functions, one in the original key and the other in the new key.
   For example:

   right hand *do—re—mi—fi—so* (*so* becomes *do*)
   left hand *do—ti,— do—re—mi* (*mi* becomes *re*)
   right hand *re—do—ta,*

   Students should be fluent in transposing memorized unison and simple two-part melodies into various keys. The instructor may want to concentrate on having the students transpose a melody into related keys before discussing the concept of modulation. As the students become more familiar with reading and writing compositions in different keys, they should begin to compare and contrast different tone sets.

   Scale of C
   Solfège syllables *do re mi fa so la ti do'*
   absolute letter names C D E F G A B C

   Scale of G
   Solfège syllables *do re mi fa so la ti do'*
   absolute letter names G A B C D E F# G

2. The students should practice modulation exercise from the instructor's hand signs without using altered notes.

   For example, the instructor shows with the right hand *do—re—mi—fa—la—so.* The last note, *so* is shown as *do* with the left hand. In this way the students will already be practicing a modulation to the dominant key. Absolute letter names may also be used. After the students have gained sufficient practice, altered notes may be used. The introduction of the altered note *si* implies a modulation to the relative minor key, *fi* implies a modulation to the dominant key, *ta* which becomes *fa* in the new key, implies a modulation to the subdominant.

   As the students gain greater proficiency with the types of exercises described above, the instructor should begin to include more alterations, shortening the length of the phrases to two or three measures.
3. Once the students have mastered the above procedures, the instructor can explain to the students the different types of modulations and the need to change the placement of the *do* or *la* within a phrase. The technique of changing the placement of the *do* or *la* is based on the same rules used for pivot chord modulation; as discussed below. For example, *fi* in old key will become *ti* in the new key and *ta* in the old key will become *fa* in the new key. Students must be made aware of the need for changing the solfège syllables if there is an actual modulation.

Discussion Questions

1. What do we mean by the term "harmonic thinking"?
2. How are harmonic thinking and part-singing connected?
3. Discuss the sequential development of harmonic hearing.
4. Discuss the sequential development of part- singing.
5. How would you introduce the concept of triads to students?
6. It is more important for children to enjoy singing music together in an ensemble. Time spent learning how to read individual voice parts takes away from students' enjoyment of the music. When working with an elementary choir, an instructor can produce a CD of all of the individual voice parts. Students can learn their parts on their own by rote. Discuss.

Ongoing Assignment

- Choose a musical element that you are going to teach next year from your first, third, and fifth grade classes. Review the teaching strategies for these elements. Look carefully at the practice suggestions for your elements. Extend the reading and writing activities further by developing them into activities that are closely linked to the skills of part-singing and harmonic hearing.
- Choose a diatonic folk song and develop a teaching strategy for teaching students how to create an accompaniment based on the chord roots of the primary triads.

References for Part-Work and the Development of Harmonic Hearing

Bacon, Denise. *46 Two-Part American Folk Songs for Elementary Grades.* Wellesley, Mass.: Kodály Center of America, 1973.

———. *50 Easy Two-Part Exercises: First Steps in A Cappella Part Singing Using Sol-fa and Staff Notation.* 3rd ed. Clifton, N.J.: European American Music Corporation, 1980. Originally published as *50 Easy Two-Part Pentatonic Exercises,* published by European-American Music Corporation, 1977. Contains exercises written in both solfège and staff notation.

———. *185 Unison Pentatonic Exercises: First Steps in Sight-Singing Using Sol-fa and Staff Notation According to the Kodály Concept.* West Newton: Kodály Center of America, 1978.

Bartle, Jean Ashworth. *Sound Advice: Becoming a Better Children's Choir Conductor.* New York: Oxford University Press, 2003.

Darázs, Árpád. "Comprehensive Sight Singing and Ear Training, Part I." *Choral Journal* 4/6 (June–July 1964): 18–21. Part II. *Choral Journal* 5/1 (August–September 1964): 14–17. Presents a sequenced approach to teaching sight-singing and ear training based on the Kodály concept.

———. "The Kodály Method for Choral Training." *American Choral Review* 8/3 (March 1966): 8–13. Cites Kodály's significant contribution as the creator of a unique choral method that utilizes hand signs and relative solmization and emphasizes early training in musical literacy. Also found in *The Council for Research in Music Education Bulletin* 8 (Fall 1966): 59.

———. "Developing Musicianship in Choral Rehearsals." *Kodály Envoy* 5/1 (July 1978): 7–9. Discusses and provides examples of the activities that should be included in the choral rehearsal such as rhythm exercises, hand signs, solfège exercises, reading standard notation, listening activities, musical memory, inner hearing, voice warm-up, and improvisation.

Herboly-Kocsár, Ildikó. *Teaching of Polyphony, Harmony and Form in Elementary School,* trans. Alexander Farkas, revised by Lilla Gábor. Kecskemét: Zoltán Kodály Pedagogical Institute, 1984.

McRae, Shirley W. *Directing the Children's Choir.* New York: Schirmer Books, 1991.

Phillips, Kenneth H. *Directing the Choral Music Program.* New York: Oxford University Press, 2003.

Pohjola, Erkki. "The Tapiola Sound and Kodály." *Kodály Envoy* 20/1 (Fall 1993): 30–37.

Tacka, Philip, and Mícheál Houlahan. "Developing Harmonic Hearing." *Kodály Envoy* 19/3 (Winter 1993): 10–13.

———. "An Aural Approach to Harmonic Analysis." *Kodály Envoy* 19/4 (Spring 1993): 11–19.

Tacka, Philip, and Susan Taylor-Howell, eds. *Sourwood Mountain: 28 North American and English Songs Arranged for Two Voices.* Whitewater: Organization of American Kodály Educators, 1986.

Taylor-Howell, Susan, ed. *The Owl Sings.* Whitewater: Organization of American Kodály Educators, 1986.

Children as Listeners: Integrating Listening into a Music Lesson

> Only a few of them listened to the beautiful performance of Schubert's Quartet in A Minor, though with its richness of feelings this work is of outstanding value in cultivating the heart. For such works it is worth going on long pilgrimages. And yet it was played here on the premises—and they did not listen.[3]

> Individual singing plus listening to music (by means of active and passive well-arranged experiences) develops the ear to such an extent that one understands music one has heard with as much clarity as though one were looking at a score; if necessary—and if time permits—one should be able to reproduce such a score.[4]

› Key Questions

How can we develop students' listening skills based on folk song repertoire?

How can we reinforce musical elements through listening experiences?

How do we prepare students to listen to more extended examples of art music?

In the opinion of Kodály, a primary goal of a music education is "to make the masterpieces of world literature public property, to convey them to people of every kind and rank."[5] Accordingly, incorporating fine examples of music literature into music lessons is something all music instructors ought to consider. A primary goal of teaching should be to use singing as a means of opening the world of music literature to students. "The final purpose of all this must be to introduce pupils to the understanding and love of great classics of past, present and future."[6]

Depending on the ability of the child, the instructor needs to find ways to encourage active music listening in the music classroom.

> It is not enough to listen once, fleetingly, to great works; one has to prepare for them and to follow the notes through the pages both before and after hearing them in order to implant them abidingly in one's mind. Personal participation is worth more than anything else.[7]

The goal of this chapter is to provide instructors with examples of music listening activities that they may incorporate into their own teaching. The idea is to understand the various principles of teaching music literature and to inspire the instructor to collect examples and repertoire for their own teaching situations. Teachers may elect to devote a complete lesson plan to teaching listening or to incorporate listening into a preparation/practice lesson or an initial practice lesson.

What Listening Repertoire Should Be Included in a Music Curriculum?

Because most music instructors have only a few lessons a week with their students, the selection of music is important. The following are some guidelines to use when selecting music literature for the classroom:

1. Select music of the well-known composers.
2. Music must be of the highest quality.
3. Music must have a musical appeal for the students.
4. Music should be developmentally appropriate; relevant to specific age groups.
5. Knowledge of music literacy should be correlated with examples used for music listening.
6. Music should be selected from different style periods.
7. Try to include different genres of music in your music curriculum.
8. Consider using examples that highlight different solo instruments as well as a variety of small and large ensembles. Learning the instruments of the orchestra should be built into the music curriculum.

A Teaching Strategy for Music Listening

The same care and attention used for selecting song repertoire for the classroom must also be used when selecting music listening examples. Once the selections are made for music listening, then the question we need to address is: How do I prepare the students to listen to this piece of music with understanding? The same process used in teaching new musical elements and concepts (the cognitive, associative, and assimilative phases of learning) can be used for presenting a listening example.

The following guidelines can be used for developing a teaching strategy for listening to a piece of music.

Teacher Preparation Activities for Music Listening

1. Choose a piece of music that you and your students will enjoy.
2. Listen to the piece of music many times without and with a score.
3. Analyze the piece of music. Identify the following:
   - Character of the music
   - Dynamic changes
   - Form
   - Thematic material
   - Key changes
   - Harmonic structure
   - Meter, metric changes, rhythmic patterns, ostinati, tempo changes
   - Compositional devices
   - Instrumentation
   - Texture
   - Programmatic elements
4. Decide which themes the children may sing. Students do not have to read every theme they are listening to. Children can also memorize a theme by rote and sing it on a neutral syllable. Sometimes the key of the listening example will need to be transposed in order for the children to be able to perform it.
5. Review the children's knowledge of performance repertoire and try to find connections between this repertoire and the piece of music you are going to use for listening. It is important for students to compare and contrast different styles of music.
6. Decide what concepts and elements you want to teach.
7. Decide on what you want to teach the students about this piece of music during the year or if you are going to return to this composition in a future grade.
8. Beginning listening experiences should be short. Young students do not necessarily need to hear an entire movement.

Presentation Activities for Listening

1. Decide on how many times you are going to play the music example and what students are going to be actively engaged in as they listen repeatedly to the piece of music.
2. There should be a different focus for each repeated listening. Music instructors can also design listening maps for students as well as worksheets that will help students organize their knowledge of the listening example. Another useful teaching strategy is for the instructor to create a simplified score for singing.

Follow-Up Activities

Determine follow-up activities. For example, if students have listened to the Andante from Symphony No. 94 by Joseph Haydn, then they could be asked to write another variation on the theme.

Figure 7.30 Franz Joseph Haydn, Andante from Symphony No. 94

Listening to one piece of music could logically lead to listening to another piece of music. For example, in the Spring section of Haydn's oratorio *The Seasons,* the theme from the Andante of Symphony No. 94 is sung. Robert Schumann's *Exercises Etudes in the Form of Free Variations on Theme of Beethoven* can be played for students once they have listened to the Andante from Beethoven's Symphony No. 7.

From Folk Music to Art Music

There has been an emphasis, perhaps even an overemphasis on the role of the folk song in the Kodály concept. Much has been said about the rationale for basing a curriculum on folk songs. Kodály was convinced that folk songs were the ideal vehicle for leading the student to an appreciation and an understanding of the works of the great composers. He believed that children should be taught folk music and that folk music ought to lead to the introduction of art music and composed music.

> For instance Haydn, the best to begin with, has manifest connection with folk song, but even in many works of Mozart it is easy to recognize the sublimated Austrian folk song. Beethoven's many themes are also folk-song like. And all the national schools originated already in 19th century are based on the foundations of their own folk music.[8]

If instructors are aware of the possibilities inherent in folk song materials, they can skillfully guide students to an understanding of art music. The instructor should consider the intellectual capacity and interests of their students and determine the many types of music students will enjoy.

Music instructors should consider using art music examples containing melodic and rhythmic fragments that may be isolated for easy recognition. Such works may be orchestral, or they may be works that can be performed by the students. The musical examples contained in the Julliard Repertoire Project provide music from all eras within the student's vocal capabilities. The students' attention should be focused on the musical example they are listening to and not simply on the life of the composer or historical facts surrounding the composition of the work. While historical facts and stories may be interesting to some older students, young students need to be more actively engaged in listening and performing.

Ideally, it is best to introduce students to a live performance of a song or instrumental composition at the earliest stages of musical learning. Folk and ethnic instruments may be used to accompany songs for listening as well as songs for singing and performance. The instructor or older students who perform on instruments may provide the initial listening experiences for students. Later, students who are studying instruments can demonstrate them for the rest of the class. Consider the following activities.

1. The instructor sings folk songs for students at the close of music lessons. These songs may be taught to students in a subsequent lesson.
2. The instructor plays known folk songs on a musical instrument such as a recorder or dulcimer for students.
3. Older students may perform a folk song. Students with more secure musical execution can perform materials in several parts or in canon.
4. Students listen to the actual composition that includes the folk song.

Table 7.9 Examples of folk songs connected to music

Composer	Composition	Related Song for Classroom Performance
Barber Samuel	Excursion No. 3	Streets of Laredo
Beethoven Ludwig	Symphony No. 9 Movement 4	Ode to Joy
Bizet Georges	L'Arlesienne Suite No. 1	March of the Three Kings
Calliet Lucian	Theme and Variations on 'Pop Goes the Weasel'	Pop Goes the Weasel
Copland Aaron	Appalachian Spring	Simple Gifts
Copland Aaron	A Lincoln Portrait	Springfield Mountain
Copland Aaron	Billy the Kid	The Old Chisholm Trail
Gould Morton	American Salute	When Johnny Comes Marching Home
Ives Charles	Fourth of July Symphony	America
Ives Charles	Symphony No. 2	Camptown Races, Columbia the Gem of the Ocean, Turkey in the Straw
Ives Charles	Variations on 'America'	America
Mahler Gustav	Symphony No. 1 'The Titan' Movement 2	Frere Jacques (in minor)
Harl McDonald	Children's Symphony Movement One	London Bridge, Baa Baa Black sheep,
Harl McDonald	Children's Symphony Movement Three	The Farmer in the Dell, Jingle Bells
Mozart Wolfgang	Twelve Variations on 'Ah vous dirai je maman'	Twiinkle, twinkle Little Star
Schubert Franz	The Trout Quintet	The Trout

Table 7.9 *Continued*

Composer	Composition	Related Song for Classroom Performance
Schumann William	New England Triptych	Chester, When Jesus Wept
Sibelius Jean	Finlandia	Finlandia
Tchaikovsky Peter	Little Russian Symphony	The Crane
Vaughn-Williams Ralph	Fantasia on Greensleeves	Greensleeves

From Folk Music to Art Music: Introducing Short Listening Excerpts Based on Musical Elements

The following are procedures for incorporating listening activities into music lessons.

The instructor sings a theme from a musical example to the students. The students memorize the theme by singing the melody on a neutral syllable. The instructor may then play the piece of music for the students and have the students raise their hands when they hear the theme.

The instructor sings a theme to the students and repeats it over several classes of instruction. The students memorize the theme and figure out the known melodic or rhythmic elements in the theme. The instructor may then play the piece of music for the students. As reading and writing skills develop, the instructor will be able to use art music themes for memory work, sight-reading, dictation, and writing.

The table 7.10 contains a brief list of suggested listening examples that may be used to augment and enliven the teaching of musical elements. Additional examples have already been integrated throughout the text for specific musical elements.

Table 7.10 Musical elements

Concept	Composer	Musical Composition
Slow–Fast	Corelli	Concerto Grosso in F Major, Op. 6, Introduction and Movement 1
	Wagner	Overture to the Flying Dutchman
Loud–Soft	Beethoven	Symphony No. 7, First movement (note the sudden contrasts in dynamics); Egmont Overture
High–Low	Banchieri	Counterpoint to the Animals
Natural pulse in duple meter	Joplin	Rags

continued

Table 7.10 *Continued*

Concept	Composer	Musical Composition
Natural pulse in triple meter	Bach	Brandenburg Concerto No. 2 in F major
Call and response	Gabrielli	Brass Choir Compositions
Rhythmic ostinato	Beethoven	Symphony No. 7, Movement 2
Pentatonic themes	Mozart	Clarinet Quintet First Movement *so—mi—re—do*
	Grieg	Peer Gynt Suite, Morning *so—mi—re—do—re—mi—so—mi—re—do*
	Bach	D major Suite, Gigue *so—do—mi—re*
	Handel	Water Music, Suite No. 2 Alla Hornpipe *so—do—re—mi—do* sequential themes *re—mi—do—re—so—re—mi—do—re—so—re etc.*
	Mozart	Symphony No. 1 *do—mi—so so so so—so so so so—mi—do*
	Dvorak	Symphony No. 5 'New World', Second Movement *mi—so—so—mi—re—do—re—mi—so—mi—re* *mi—so—so—mi—re—do—re—mi—re—do—do*
Diatonic themes	Copland	Appalachian Spring Simple Gifts in Theme and Variation form
	Mahler	Symphony No. 1, Movement 2 Frere Jacques in minor
	Tchaikovsky	Symphony No. 4, Movement 4 The Birch Tree

From Folk Music to Art Music: A Sample Listening Activity

The following example demonstrates how the music instructor can move from a folk song to a listening activity. The listening activity pairs the Russian folk song *The Crane* with the principle theme from the final movement of Tchaikovsky's Symphony No. 2.

1. Students learn the Russian folk song *The Crane* with solfège and rhythm syllables.

Figure 7.31 *The Crane*

2. Students sing *The Crane* with piano accompaniment.

Figure 7.32 *The Crane* with piano accomplishment

continued

Figure 7.32 *Continued*

3. Students read Theme A from the symphony and discover where it deviates from the folk song.

Figure 7.33 *The Crane* Theme A

4. Students listen to a complete recording of the movement.

In the next example, the listening activity is based on Tchaikovsky's Finale of Symphony No. 4 and the Russian folk song *The Birch Tree.* The B theme of the symphonic movement, written in Sonata Rondo form, is based on *The Birch Tree.*

Figure 7.34 *The Birch Tree*

1. The students should be able to sing the song with text, solfège, and rhythm syllables.
2. The students should be able to perform the song in canon.
3. The instructor should sing the B theme for students so that they can aurally identify how Tchaikovsky changed the original folk song in his symphony.

Figure 7.35 Theme B

4. Students should read the B theme. Students compare the B theme to *The Birch Tree.* Children will discover that the composer switches the time signature from $\frac{2}{4}$ to $\frac{4}{4}$ and adds an extra two beats of rest per phrase.
5. Students should sing the B theme in canon.

The following listening activity is based on *L'Arlésienne Suite: Farandole. Allegro vivo e deciso* by Georges Bizet.[9]

Preparation Activity

1. The following are the main themes:

Figure 7.36a Theme A

Figure 7.36b Theme B

2. The following is a listening map for *Farandole. Allegro vivo e deciso*

Table 7.11 Listening map for *Farandole. Allegro vivo e deciso*

Form	Explanation
A	The A section is in a minor tonality. Simple presentation of theme. Two-part canon
B	The B section is in a major tonality
A'	A' is in minor.
B'	B' is in minor.
A"	A" is in minor with more thematic development.
B"	B" is in minor with thematic development.
C	C combines parts A and B in a major tonality.
Coda	The coda uses a portion of the B theme in a major tonality.

3. The following are some of the concepts we want to teach based on the listening example:

   - Practicing dotted eighth and sixteenth note patterns
   - Practicing dotted quarter and eighth note patterns
   - Canonic imitation
   - Variation
   - Themes played as partner songs
   - Transforming melodies from major to parallel minor and vice versa
   - Accompanying a major and minor melody with chord roots

4. The following folk songs may be used to reinforce rhythmic and melodic concepts:

   Big Fat Biscuit
   Dotted eighth note and sixteenth note patterns
   Shady Grove
   Dotted eighth note and sixteenth note patterns
   Liza Jane
   Partner song with *Tideo*
   Dotted quarter and eighth note patterns
   Tideo
   Partner song with *Liza Jane*
   Hey, Ho, Nobody Home
   Minor tonality canon

Are You Sleeping

Are You Sleeping can be used to demonstrate how we accompany a song with tonic and dominant chord roots. This song may also be transposed into the parallel minor and accompanied with chord roots *la* and *mi.*

5. Develop a listening chart as a guide for your listening. You can now create a simplified listening chart for your students based on your listening chart. Music instructors can also design listening maps for students as well as worksheets that will help students organize their knowledge of the listening example. Another useful teaching strategy is for the instructor to create a simplified score for singing

Table 7.12 A listening chart

Form	Description	Theme Instrument(s)	Accompaniment	Mode
A	Theme A	Full orchestra	None	Minor
	Two-part Canon	Woodwinds, horns, strings	None	Minor
	Transition	None	Tambourine	None
B	Theme B	Flute and clarinet	Strings and tambourine	Major
	Theme B	Flute and clarinet	Bassoon, horn, sweeping strings, and tambourine	Major
	Theme B	Flute, clarinet, and 1 oboe	Bassoon, horn, strings, and tambourine	Major
	Theme B	Flute, clarinet, and 2 oboes	Bassoon, horn, sweeping strings, and tambourine	Major
	Theme B	Flute, clarinet, oboes, bassoons, and strings	Horns, trumpets, trombones, timpani, tambourine, and double bass	Major
A'	Theme A	Oboes, clarinets, bassoons, horns, and strings	None	Minor
B'	Theme B	1 Flute, then 2 Flutes	Strings and tambourine	Minor
A"	Theme A development	Oboes, clarinets, bassoons, horns, and strings	None	Minor
B"	Theme B development	1 Flute, then 2 Flutes, then 1 oboe	Strings, tambourine, clarinets, horn	Minor
	Theme B development	Flutes, oboes, 1 clarinet, and violins	All other instruments	Minor
	Transition from minor to major	Flutes, oboes, clarinets, and violins	All other instruments except tambourine	Minor to Major
C	Both A and B themes as partner song	Flutes, oboes, clarinets, and high strings on B theme; 2 horns, 2 trumpets, and 1 trombone on A theme (in major mode)	All other instruments	Major

continued

Table 7.12 *Continued*

Form	Description	Theme Instrument(s)	Accompaniment	Mode
	Both A and B themes as partner song	Flutes, oboes, clarinets, and high strings on B theme; 2 horns, 2 trumpets, and 1 trombone on A theme (in major mode)	All other instruments	Major
coda	Portion of B theme is used	Flutes, oboes, clarinets, violins, violas, and cellos	All other instruments	Major

6. Decide on how many times you are going to play the music example and what the students are going to be actively engaged in as they listen repeatedly to the piece of music. There should be a different focus for each repeated listening.

Table 7.13 Following a piece of music through several lessons

1st listening	In previous lessons students have memorized Theme A and B singing on a neutral syllable. The instructor and the students review singing Theme A and Theme B. The students listen to the piece of music	**6th listening**	The students sing *Are You Sleeping* in solfege The students determine the tonic and dominant chord root tones Half sing song and half sing chord roots Listen to the orchestral work
2nd listening	Sing *Shady Grove,* perform the rhythm saying rhythm syllables Sing *Liza Jane,* perform the rhythm saying rhythm syllables Prepare and sight sing Theme A with solfege syllables Listen and count the number of times Theme A occurs	**7th listening**	Read Theme B Determine tonic and dominant chord roots for Theme B Combine both parts Listen and count the number of times Theme B occurs
3rd listening	Review Theme A with rhythm and solfege syllables Students write rhythm of Theme A from memory Listen and tap rhythm of Theme A when it occurs	**8th listening**	Prepare and sing Theme B, transform Theme B into the parallel minor key Rewrite Theme B in minor tonality by adding accidentals Listen and count how many major statements of B, and how many minor statements of B are in the piece
4th listening	Sing *Hey, Ho, Nobody Home* Identify as minor Sing again in 2-part canon The students read Theme A in unison; and sing in 2-part canon Listen	**9th listening**	Sight sing Theme A in minor Sight sing Theme B in minor The students listen and count when each theme occurs in each tonality

Table 7.13 *Continued*

5th listening	The students read Theme A and then prepare and sight sing Theme A extension The students sing *Are You Sleeping* and transform to parallel minor The students sing 8 measures of Theme A and transform into parallel major The students listen and count how many times Theme A occurs in a major tonality	**10th listening**	The students sing *Liza Jane* and *Tideo* as partner songs. The students sight sing Theme A in major; sing Theme B in major; sing both themes as a partner song The students sing combined themes with I-V harmony in three groups of students. See Score Listen to form map

Figure 7.37 is a score that can be used to perform the work in three parts. This section is the "C" portion of the work.

Figure 7.37 Three parts

7. Create worksheets for selected listening lessons. Selected examples follow.

L'Arlésienne Suite:
Farandole. Allegro vivo e deciso
Georges Bizet

Worksheet 1

1. Read the A section with solfège syllables. (Hint: it is a minor modality!)

Figure 7.38 Section A

2. What are the characteristic rhythmic elements in this theme?
3. How many times do you hear this theme? Keep track!

L'Arlésienne Suite:
Farandole. Allegro vivo e deciso
Georges Bizet

Worksheet 2

1. Sing the A section in canon after two beats.

Figure 7.39 Section A

2. Which instruments do you hear playing this canon?

L'Arlésienne Suite:
Farandole. Allegro vivo e deciso
Georges Bizet

Worksheet 3

1. Sing the B section with solfège syllables.

Figure 7.40 Section B

2. How many times do you hear this entire section? Keep track!
3. Identify the tonic and dominant chord roots that accompany this melody.
4. Design follow-up activities for your listening lesson.

A good follow-up piece of music to listen to after this example is the Funeral March, *Feirlich Und Gemess,* from Symphony No. 1 in D by Gustav Mahler (1860–1911). In this example the familiar folk song *Are You Sleeping* appears in a variation in the minor key. This theme is accompanied by a melodic ostinato based on the tonic and dominant chord root tones.

Figure 7.41 Funeral March

› Discussion Questions

1. What do we mean by the term "listening"?
2. How is the skill of listening connected to the development of music literacy?
3. How is the skill of music literacy connected to the development of listening?
4. It is more important for students to enjoy listening to music and avoid time spent learning how to read or write themes from the listening example. Discuss
5. Young students should be able to identify selected musical compositions, memorize facts about the life of the composer, and be able to identify specific themes and orchestral instruments. Discuss.

➤ Ongoing Assignment

Choose a piece of classical (art) music to present to your third grade students next year. Analyze the piece of music, decide what elements you can teach the students based on their knowledge of music, find songs from their repertoire list that will prepare elements found in the art music example. Develop a set of listening exposures and work sheets for the art music example. Include a listening chart that the students can follow. Describe how you can return to this piece of music in another grade with another set of listening exposures that match the students' knowledge of music literacy.

References for Children as Listeners: Integrating Listening into a Music Lesson

Choksy, Lois. *The Kodály Method II: Folksong to Masterwork.* Englewood Cliffs, N.J.: Prentice Hall, 1999.

Espeland, Magne. "Music in Use: Responsive Music Listening in the Primary School." *British Journal of Music Education* 4/3 (1987): 283–297.

Haack, P. "The Acquisition of Music Listening Skills," in *Handbook of Research on Music Teaching and Learning,* ed. D. Colwell. New York: Schirmer Books, 1992.

Heidsiek, Ralph G. "Folk Quotations in the Concert Repertoire." *Music Educators Journal* 56/1 (September 1969): 51.

Herboly-Kocsár, Ildikó. "The Place, Role and Importance of Art Music in School." *Bulletin of the International Kodály Society* 18/1 (Spring 1993): 41–44.

Kerchner, J. L. "Creative Music Listening." *General Music Today* (Fall 1996): 28–30.

Montgomery, Amanda. "Listening in the Elementary Grades: Current Research from a Canadian Perspective." *Bulletin of the International Kodály Society* 18/1 (Spring 1993): 54–61.

Rappaport, Jonathan C. *New Pathways to Art Music Listening: A Kodály Approach Appropriate for All Age Levels.* Marlborough: Pro Canto Press, 1983.

Rodriquez, C. X., and P. R. Webster. "Development of Children's Verbal Interpretive Responses to Music Listening." *Bulletin of the Council for Research in Music Education* 134 (Fall 1997): 9–30.

Shehan-Campbell, Patricia. "Beyond Cultural Boundaries: Listening as Learning Style." *Bulletin of the International Kodály Society* 19/1 (Spring 1994): 49–60.

———, and Bonnie C. Wade. "Learning through Engaged Listening," in Shehan-Campbell and Wade, *Teaching Music Globally* New York: Oxford University Press, 2004.

Thompson, William Forde, and E. Glenn Schellenberg. "Listening to Music," in *MENC Handbook of Musical Cognition and Development,* ed. Richard Colwell. New York: Oxford University Press, 2006.

Building a Lesson Plan Framework That Incorporates Musical Skill Development

➤ Key Questions

What are the primary skill areas?

How can we accommodate musical skill areas into the preparation/practice lesson plan format?

How can we accommodate musical skill areas into the presentation lesson plan format?

How can we accommodate musical skill areas into the initial practice lesson plan format?

Key skill areas include reading, writing, and improvisation. We can use these three skill areas as a means of developing all other skill areas. Activities must be developmentally appropriate. The monthly plans provide specific ideas related to specific concepts and elements. These skills can become the basic building blocks for other musical skills such as improvisation, composition, memory, part-singing, and listening. In the preceding sections we showed how reading, writing, and improvisation/composition activities can be expanded to include the development of additional musical skills.

For example, when students are asked to read a new song or the theme from an art music example, the following skill areas may be developed in conjunction with reading.

- The students can identify the form of the example
- The students memorize the example after sight-singing the melody
- The students can inner hear sections of the melody
- The students can notate motifs from the melody sung by the instructor in stick or staff notation
- The students can compose a variant of the sight-reading example
- The students may improvise an ostinato to accompany the musical example
- The students can play the ostinato on rhythm instruments
- The students may listen to a recording of a listening example

When the students are asked to complete a writing activity, many skill areas can be developed. For example, the instructor may write a well-known song on the board but ask the students to complete two measures. The following skill areas may be developed in conjunction with writing:

- The students can identify the form of the example
- The students can inner hear sections of the melody
- The students can notate motifs from the melody sung by the instructor in stick or staff notation
- The students compose a variant of the sight-reading example
- The students may create an ostinato to accompany the musical example
- The students may compose an alternative ending to the song
- The students may perform their variation on a melodic instrument

When students are asked to *improvise,* additional skill areas are developed. For example, the instructor may write a well-known song on the board but ask students to improvise two measures.

- The students write the newly improvised measures
- The students can identify the form of the example. Once a student completes the two measures, students can compare and contrast the variation to the original (include a discussion of form)

The following skills areas may be developed in conjunction with improvisation:

- The instructor can select one example improvised by a class member and the students memorize the newly improvised melody
- The students can inner hear sections of the melody
- The students can notate motifs from the melody sung by the instructor in stick or staff notation
- The students compose a variant of the sight-reading example
- The students may create an ostinato to accompany the newly composed melody

Developing a Lesson Plan Framework Based on Musical Skill Development

In previous sections of this chapter we have provided specific information for developing musical skills that may be incorporated into the preparation/practice, presentation, and practice lesson plan formats. The goal of this section is to provide examples of how musical skills may be incorporated into the different lesson plan formats. We have provided:

1. Twenty-four ways to practice rhythmic elements and eighteen ways to practice melodic elements.
2. A sequential approach for reading a known rhythm or melody from staff notation as well as sight-reading unknown rhythms and melodies.
3. Examples of written activities for writing known melodies and procedures for dictation of unknown rhythms and melodies.
4. Strategies for developing memorizing by ear, from hand signs, and from staff notation. Also included in this section are strategies for memorizing two-part musical examples.
5. Classroom activities that emphasize structure and form and how these activities are closely linked to memory, reading, writing, inner hearing, improvisation, and composition. Many kinesthetic, aural, and visual activities for rhythmic and melodic improvisation are included.
6. Examples of how to develop the students' part-singing. Included is a discussion of how to teach a two-part musical example. Closely related to the development of part-singing is the development of harmonic hearing.
7. Appendix 4 has monthly plans that help the instructor to develop musical skills sequentially by providing a list of activities related to the musical element being practiced.

The Preparation/Practice Lesson

The following lesson is the same lesson presented in the chapter 6, but it is now modified to reflect how musical skill development can be implemented into lesson plans. It is our intention that these ideas will generate additional ideas that will enliven the lesson. The specific skill area is in bold.

Table 7.14 Developing a preparation/practice lesson plan framework: Preparation of sixteenth notes and the practice of *re*

Focus	Activities, Procedures, and Assessments
Introduction	
Performance and demonstration of known musical concepts and elements	Develop singing skills through beautiful singing, vocal warm-ups, and breathing exercises Sing with text and play the game *Here Comes a Bluebird* **Ensemble work.** Sing and perform a two-beat ostinato **Reading.** Students read melodic motifs from the song shown from the instructors hand signs Sing with rhythm syllables **Ensemble Singing.** Sing song in canon after two beats
Core activities	
Acquisition of repertoire	Teach *Down Came a Lady*, in preparation for teaching $\frac{4}{4}$ meter **Form.** Students identify the form of the melody **Memorization.** Students memorize the song
Performance and preparation of new element	Teacher provides students with a series of discovery learning activities that will develop their knowledge of four sounds on a beat (sixteenth notes) through known songs Kinesthetic awareness stage: **Ensemble or part work. All of the following activities develop the ability to do more than one skill at the same time** a) Sing *Paw Paw Patch* and keep the beat b) Sing and clap the rhythm c) Sing and point to a representation of phrase one, — — — — – – – – — — d) Sing *Paw Paw Patch*, walk the beat, and clap the rhythm Aural awareness stage: a) Review Kinesthetic b) Teacher & Student sing phrase one and keep the beat c) Teacher: "Andy, how many beats did we keep?" four d) Teacher: "Andy, which beat has the most sounds?" beat three e) Teacher: "How many sounds are on beat 3?" four sounds f) Teacher: "If beat three has four sounds, how many sounds are on the other beats?" two sounds Visual awareness stage: a) Review the kinesthetic and aural awareness activities b) Students create a visual based on their aural awareness. Students need to determine how many beats are in the phrase and the number of sounds on each beat. Use manipulatives. (cut outs, magnets, unifix cubes, etc). c) Students sing and point to their representation d) Instructor may ask questions concerning their representation e) "Identify any rhythmic and melodic elements you recognize."

continued

Table 7.14 *Continued*

Focus	Activities, Procedures, and Assessments
Movement development	Focus on the sequential development of age-appropriate movement skills using *Tideo*
Performance and practice of known element	Students reinforce their knowledge of *re* working on the skill areas selected from the following: reading and writing, form, and memory through known songs such as *Frosty Weather* **Memory: Aural/Oral Dictation.** Instructor hums motifs from *Frosty Weather.* Students sing back with solfège syllables and hand signs **Writing.** Students write a section of the melody in stick or staff notation **Sight Singing.** Students sight sing a variation of *Frosty Weather* composed by the instructor **Ensemble singing.** Students sing *Frosty Weather* in canon after two beats **Improvisation.** Students improvise a new A phrase **Inner Hearing.** Students sing *Frosty Weather* with solfège syllables and hand signs but inner hear *r*
Closure	
Review and summation	Review new song *Down Came A Lady* Listening activity Teacher sings the next new song *Knock the Cymbals* to be learned by students as a listening activity

Developing a Lesson Plan Framework for the Presentation of Sixteenth Notes

The following lesson is the same lesson presented in the chapter 6, but it is now modified to reflect how musical skill development can be implemented into lesson plans. It is our intention that these ideas will generate additional ideas that will enliven the lesson. The specific skill area is in bold.

Table 7.15 Developing a lesson plan framework for the presentation of sixteenth notes

Focus	Activities, Procedures, and Assessments
Introduction	
Performance and demonstration of known musical concepts and elements	Develop singing skills through beautiful singing, vocal warm-ups breathing exercises Students demonstrate their prior knowledge of *Rocky Mountain* Sing with text Sing rhythm syllables Sing with solfège syllables **Ensemble work. Students sing in Canon after two beats; Students create an ostinato** **Reading. Students read from staff notation and sing rhythm or solfège syllables**

Table 7.15 *Continued*

Focus	**Activities, Procedures, and Assessments**
Core activities	
Acquisition of repertoire	Teach *Ida Red*, using an appropriate method of presentation selected from the repertoire list for the grade **Form. Students identify the form of the song** **Memory work. Students memorize the solfège syllables of *Ida Red***
Performance and presentation of new concept or element in the focus pattern	**Review stage one aural presentation using *Paw Paw Patch*** a) Teacher: "When we hear four sounds on a beat we call it "ta-ka-di-mi'" b) Teacher & Student sing whole song with rhythm syllables and clap the rhythm c) Individual students sing the target phrase with rhythm syllables **Stage two visual presentation (reading and writing)** a) We can use four sixteenth notes to represent four sounds on a beat. A sixteenth note has a note head and a stem and two flags. Four sixteenth notes have a double beam. b) Our first phrase of Paw Paw Patch looks like this: ♥ ♥ ♥ ♥ c) We can read this rhythm pattern using our rhythm syllables d) Teacher sings rhythm syllables while pointing to the heartbeats, Student echo sing using rhythm syllables while pointing to the heartbeats. e) Stick notation is an easy way to write rhythmic notation. Stick notation is traditional notation without the note heads for quarter and eighth notes. Our first phrase of Paw Paw Patch looks like this in stick notation:
Movement development	Focus on the sequential development of age-appropriate movement skills using *Tideo*
Performance and practice of new element in related patterns	**Reading and Writing** **Transform the rhythm of *Great Big House* into the rhythm of *Dinah.*** **Students sing with solfège and hand signs** **Students read *Dinah* from staff notation.**
Closure	
Review and summation	Review *Ida Red* **Listening activity:** **Teacher sings the next new song *Knock the Cymbals* to be learned by students as a listening activity**

The Initial Practice Lesson for Sixteenth Notes

The practice lesson follows the presentation lesson. In the initial practice lesson, we review the presentation of the new element in the target pattern as well as practice the new element in other basic patterns using different repertoire.

Table 7.16

Focus	Activities, Procedures, and Assessments
Introduction	
Performance and demonstration of known musical concepts and elements	Develop singing skills through beautiful singing, vocal warm-ups breathing exercises. Students demonstrate their prior knowledge using *Rocky Mountain* Sing with text Sing rhythm syllables Sing with solfège syllables **Ensemble work.** Students sing in canon after two beats; students create an ostinato **Reading.** Students read from staff notation and sing rhythm or solfège syllables
Core activities Acquisition of repertoire	Teach *Ida Red*, using an appropriate method of presentation selected from the repertoire list for the grade **Form.** Students identify the form of the song **Memory work.** Students memorize the solfège syllables of *Ida Red*
Performance and re-presentation of new element	**(Reading and writing)** • Review the aural awareness stage questions using *Paw Paw Patch.* Use the rhythm syllables to identify the new element. • Review the visual awareness activities and associate traditional notation with the visual representation. Read with rhythm syllables. • Identify another song that includes the target pattern motif or a closely related pattern. Review the aural awareness and visual awareness activities as above.
Movement development	Focus on the sequential development of age-appropriate movement skills using *Tideo*
Performance and practice of new element in related patterns	**Reading** **Read *Paw Paw Patch* with rhythm syllables** **Transform *Paw Paw Patch* into *Cumberland Gap*** **Select from the following reading, writing, improvisation/composition, and listening skills:** • **Echo sing rhythm syllables to phrases from *Cumberland Gap*** • **Writing** **Error recognition activity. Change the rhythm of *Dinah* into *Old Brass Wagon*. The instructor writes the rhythm of *Dinah* on the board but claps the rhythm of *Old Brass Wagon*. The students identify where the discrepancies occur and write the correction.** **Write rhythmic patterns from memory or when dictated by the instructor** • **Improvisation** **Improvise rhythm patterns of 4 or 8 beats either by clapping, using rhythm instruments, or clapping and saying rhythm syllables** **Improvise a new rhythm using sixteenth notes in one measure or more of a well-known song** **Improvise question and answer motives using known rhythm or melodic patterns**

Table 7.16 *Continued*

Focus	Activities, Procedures, and Assessments
	Improvise rhythms in a chain around the classroom **Improvise rhythm patterns to specific forms for example** ***A A A B*** **A B A B** **A Av B Bv** **A B A C** • ***Listening*** **Read the rhythm of some the following examples and then lisen to a recording:** **"Solfegetto" for piano by C. P. E Bach** **"Prelude in C Minor" from Book 1 of the *Well-Tempered Clavier*, by J. S. Bach**
Closure	
Review and summation	Review *Ida Red* Listening activity. Teacher sings the next new song to be learned by students as a listening activity

Discussion Questions

1. How are the skill areas of reading, writing, and improvisation related to all other skill areas?
2. How can the various musical skills be incorporated into the preparation/practice, presentation, and practice lesson plan formats? Provide specific examples

Ongoing Assignment

1. Design a preparation/practice, presentation, and initial practice lesson plan for a first grade class. Discuss how you have incorporated specific musical skills into your lesson plan.
2. Design a preparation/practice, presentation, and initial practice lesson plan for a third grade class. Discuss the how you have incorporated specific musical skills into your lesson plan.

Chapter 8

Teaching Strategies for Rhythmic and Melodic Musical Elements

Key Questions

What is the difference between a perceptual and conceptual orientation to teaching music?

What do we mean by a sound to symbol or symbol to sound orientation to teaching?

What is a teaching strategy?

What are the components of a teaching strategy?

What is the connection between a teaching strategy and the model of learning proposed in chapter 6?

Developing a Teaching Strategy for Teaching Music Elements

Lively exchanges on the pedagogical challenges and complexities associated with teaching music literacy frequently occur at national and international forums. Critical assessment of various teaching methods is often obfuscated by emotional arguments defending a solfège system, teaching tools, and techniques associated with a particular methodology. With the publication of the *Music Educators Journal* article, "An Alternative Orientation to Developing Music Literacy Skills in a Transient Society"[1] and the subsequent responses found in the Readers' Comments, Exception Taken by Jonathan Rappaport, and Author's Response[2] signals an opportunity for music educators to explore anew how the confluence of methodology and pedagogical tools affect the practice of teaching sight-singing and musicianship skills. These two articles reflect the enormous challenges that music teachers struggle with in the teaching of musical reading and writing: "the goal of simultaneously developing perceptual and conceptual understanding of musical events."[3] "The distinction between perceptual and conceptual understandings lies in the fact that the former entails the processing of external sounds or auditory images; the latter comprises the apprehension of concepts."[4] Another way to describe these two approaches to teaching is that a conceptual orientation to teaching music literacy is associated with a symbol to sound approach while a perceptual orientation to teaching is associated with a sound to symbol approach. Teachers generally emphasize one type of understanding over another in their teaching.

Lyle Davidson, Larry Scripp, and Patricia Welsh (1988) first brought forward this dichotomy arguing that pedagogy used to teach music theory can affect students' ability to represent and internalize their understanding of musical knowledge and notation.[5] The adoption of particular solfège and rhythm systems may not be sufficient to support musical understanding. Teaching a particular solfège system through a methodology that is not responsive to cognition research may be a significant factor contributing to the difficulty music students have in acquiring sight-singing and aural skills. The purpose of this chapter is to clarify what a sound to symbol approach to teaching music fundamentals entails.

This chapter presents teaching strategies for rhythmic and melodic elements based on the model of learning presented in chapter 6. Teaching strategies provide a narrative as to how to prepare, present, and practice the basic building blocks associated with the music repertoire children are studying using a sound to symbol orientation to teaching music. The teaching strategies are formulaic in structure; ultimately teachers will infuse these strategies with their own creativity to accommodate the changing settings of teaching situations. A critical component of the teaching strategies is the questions associated with the cognitive, associative, and assimilative phases of learning. The questions provide the metacognitive scaffolding that allows students to understand both the process and product of teaching. In this way we are unique. We delineate a process of instruction—a model of learning and instruction—that draws on the students' musical experience and guides them to understand music from the point of their perception of sound. We have included teaching strategies for the most important concepts. For more advanced concepts please consult *From Sound to Symbol: Fundamentals of Music Theory* (Oxford University Press, 2008). You will note that in the pedagogical list of songs and the monthly plans (both located in the appendix) additional concepts and elements are included.

Understanding the Components of a Teaching Strategy

The following template provides an example of the key components that need to be included within each teaching strategy. We have included sample teaching strategies for all grade levels.

Element	Concept	Syllables	Theory	Focus song	Additional songs

The following are the different components of the teaching strategy.

Cognitive Phase: Preparation

1. Activities for developing kinesthetic awareness
2. Activities for developing aural awareness
3. Activities for developing visual awareness

Associative Phase: Presentation

1. Label the sound
2. Present the notation

Assimilative Phrase: Practice

1. Initial practice activities
2. Practice activities:
   - Reading
   - Writing
   - Improvisation
   - Listening
   - Sight-reading materials

We suggest a minimum of five lessons to cover each teaching strategy for each musical element. Within the series of five lessons, it is important to assess activities covered in the previous lesson. For example, before developing aural awareness we suggest the instructor assess several of the kinesthetic activities from the previous lesson as all procedures and materials build on the experience and knowledge gained in the preceding lesson.

In developing kinesthetic awareness, the instructor should model the motions for beat, rhythm, and melodic contours for the students; in response, students are guided to imitate motions that will help them understand the musical concept or element being prepared for subsequent presentation. In the subsequent lessons, students may perform these movements, patterns, and contours independently. You will note that we have used a heartbeat icon as a representation for beat. Some instructors prefer using beat bars or a dot to represent the beat. The form of beat representation is at the discretion of the instructor.

In order to simplify the teaching process, we have determined one "focus" or "target" song through which the new musical element may be taught to students. Once the concept behind the new musical element is understood, it may be transferred to song repertoire that has related phrases and melodic contours. Consider focusing on teaching the first four beats of *Rain, Rain Go Away.* The goal might be teaching quarter and eighth notes, that is, the concept of one and two sounds on a beat. The students learn that in a pattern of four beats, beat three has two sounds and beats one, two, and four have one sound. During the practice lesson, the students can be guided to discover the relative position of one and two sounds on a beat; in other words, one or two sounds can occur on any beat.

The following teaching strategies provide a sequence of teaching activities that guide the students' understanding of specific musical concepts and elements. We have suggested some of the most important techniques for preparing, presenting, and practicing musical elements. The instructor may add any of the following suggestions to these teaching strategies during the cognitive phase of instruction.

Examples of Kinesthetic Activities for Rhythm

1. The students conduct to feel the meter.
2. The students perform the song while clapping the rhythm.
3. The students learn to sing songs by rote and perform a kinesthetic motion that highlights the new rhythmic element. For example, the students may clap the rhythm of the phrase containing the target pattern and keep the beat on their knees for the other phrases of a song.
4. The students perform the song while pointing to pictures or icons showing the number of sounds per beat. We believe that this procedure is a kinesthetic activity for the student; no explanation is made as to what these symbols represent.

Instructors may want the students to point to imaginary symbols without any reference to the icons.

5. The students perform the new rhythmic pattern with the basic beat. The class may be divided into two groups. One group performs the rhythm pattern and the other performs the beat. This activity may be practiced in different combinations. We suggest the following order of performance: teacher/class, class/teacher, divided class, and two individuals. The most advanced activity for this concept is for individual students to sing the song while walking the beat and clapping the rhythm.
6. Students inner hear (sing the song silently in their head) the four-beat phrase of the song containing the new element while clapping the rhythm or students inner hear the new element.

Examples of Kinesthetic Activities for Melody

1. The students perform the song and demonstrate the direction of the melodic line with arm motions. These motions should be natural and accompany the text and tempo of the song.
2. The students use simple body signs, for example, touch shoulders for *high* and waist for *low* sounds.
3. The students perform the song and point to a representation that outlines the melodic contour.
4. The students bend their knees on the lowest pitch.

Examples of Aural Awareness Questions for Rhythm

Sample Questions for Rhythmic Elements That Occur on One Beat

Perform the target pattern and ask:

1. How many beats did we perform?
2. On which beat did you hear *the new sound?* (The *new sound* may also refer to something specific, for example, the number of sounds on specific beats. The instructor might ask, "On which beat did you sing four sounds?")
3. How many *sounds* did you perform on that beat?
4. How would you describe these sounds? (e.g., two short sounds or a long sound followed by two short sounds, and so on).

Sample Questions for Rhythms That Last Longer than One Beat

1. How many beats did we tap?
2. Is there a place in our target pattern where a sound lasts longer than one beat?
3. On which beat does it begin?
4. For how many beats do we hold the sound?
5. How would you describe these sounds?

Questions for Uneven Rhythm Patterns Lasting Longer than a Beat

1. How many beats did we tap?
2. Is there a place in the target pattern where the rhythm is uneven?
3. On which beats do you perform the uneven pattern?
4. How many sounds do you perform on *those beats?*

5. Describe the placement of sounds on *those beats?*
6. How would you describe these sounds?

Examples of Aural Awareness Questions for Melody

1. How many beats did we perform?
2. On what words or syllables or beats does *the new melodic pitch* occur?
3. Is *the new melodic pitch* higher than or lower than all of the pitches we know?

We begin the teaching strategies with first grade concepts. In this text we assume that students have knowledge of beat, fast and slow, high and low, loud and soft, same and different, short and long, rhythm, and understand the words sound, pitch, and contour. These concepts are associated with kindergarten. We have suggested songs for each concept. The instructor should choose the most appropriate song for their students. Please note during the aural awareness stage we provide a sample teacher student script. We believe that calling on individual students to answer the question focuses the attention of the entire class. We use the name "Andy" to initiate each question. We do not mean to imply that we call on the same student all the time, but simply name a student then ask the question in a simple and direct manner. We also suggest checking the student's answer by saying to the class "Let's check." Check the student's answer by singing the phrase and keeping the beat and determining whether the response was correct.

Grade One Teaching Strategies

In grade one, we suggest teaching the following seven concepts. The order of concepts alternates between rhythmic and melodic concepts.

1. Teaching strategy for beat
2. Teaching strategy for melodic contour
3. Teaching strategy for quarter and eighth notes
4. Teaching strategy for a two-note child's chant *so—mi*
5. Teaching strategy for rest
6. Teaching strategy for a three-note child's chant *la—so—mi*
7. Teaching strategy for two-beat meter

Teaching Strategy for Beat

Table 8.1 Teaching strategy for beat

Element	Concept	Syllables	Theory	Focus Song	Additional Songs
	A level of pulsation used when we listen to music; inner energy			*Snail Snail*	*Bounce High* *Closet Key* *Good Night Sleep Tight* *Hunt the Slipper,* *Starlight Star Bright*

Cognitive Phase: Preparation

Stage One: Developing Kinesthetic Awareness

Try not to use the word "beat" until the presentation phase.

1. Sing *Snail Snail* and perform the beat. Perform the "beat" by patting knees, touching the heart, tapping the head, and so on. (We suggest that the beat not be clapped.) Children should learn to feel the even pulsation of songs and rhymes and express the pulsation through walking and other movements.
2. Demonstrate pulsation using motions while performing songs and chants such as:
   a. *Engine Engine # 9:* The students demonstrate the motion of wheels turning.
   b. *Bee Bee Bumble Bee:* The students demonstrate the motion of a bee's wings by flapping their arms.
   c. *Hunt the Slipper:* The students use a hammering motion to demonstrate the beat.
3. Sing and point to a representation of beat. You may also use four snails or four balls.

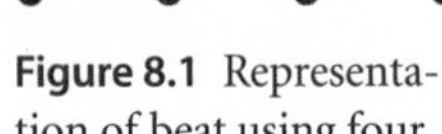

Figure 8.1 Representation of beat using four balls

4. If the students require assistance try (1) tapping the beat on their shoulders, (2) tapping the beat on their desks in front of them, or (3) taking their hands and moving them to the beat.
5. The understanding of beat may best be demonstrated by the ability to speed up or slow down when the tempo changes. This concept is closely related to tempo.

Stage Two: Developing Aural Awareness

Assess kinesthetic awareness by allowing the class to perform several of the above activities independently. The target phrase for aural awareness is the first phrase of *Snail Snail.* The teacher and the students sing phrase one of *Snail Snail* on "loo" and keep the beat on their knees or on a desk before asking each question.

Determine the number of beats in the phrase.

Teacher: "Andy, how many taps do we hear when we point to the snails on our desks?
Student: "Four."

Perform the same activity with different songs. Sing the first four or eight beats of a song on a neutral syllable and keep the beat. Ask individual students how many beats they kept. Change the tempo.

Stage Three: Developing Visual Awareness

Assess kinesthetic and aural awareness by allowing the class to perform several of the the kinesthetic and aural awareness activities.

1. The instructor hums the target phrase and asks the students to create a visual representation of the target phrase. The students may use manipulatives.

   Teacher: "How many snails do you need?" or "How many balls or blocks do you need?"

2. The students share their representations with each other.
3. The instructor invites one student to the board to share his or her representation with the class. If necessary, corrections to the representation can be made by reviewing the aural awareness questions.
4. The students sing the first phrase of *Snail Snail* with a neutral syllable and point to their representation.

Associative Phase: Presentation

Assess the kinesthetic, aural awareness, and visual awareness activities with the phrase one of *Snail Snail* and/or *Rain, Rain.*

Stage One: Label the Sound

Teacher: "When we tap on our knees we are keeping a *beat* or keeping the *heartbeat.*" "Sing and keep the beat of *Snail Snail.*"

Stage Two: Present the Notation

1. We can represent the beat using a heartbeat.
2. There are four heartbeats in the first phrase of *Snail Snail;* there are four heartbeats in phrase two of *Snail Snail.*

Figure 8.2 Heartbeats in *Snail Snail*

3. We can read this pattern of beats by pointing as we sing.

Assimilative Phase: Practice

Stage One: Initial Practice

1. Review the aural presentation.
2. Review the visual presentation and associate the heartbeat as a representation of pulsation or beat.

Stage Two: Practice

Reading

Practice the focus song and additional songs with the students by pointing to a beat chart and singing known songs. Begin with four-beat phrases and expand to eight and sixteen beats. Consider using the following songs: *Bounce High Bounce Low* and *Starlight Star Bright.*

Writing

The students may place visuals on the board representing the beat. Use any appropriate song in their repertoire.

Improvisation

1. Play an inner hearing game. For example, ask the students to respond to the mouth of a puppet. When the mouth is open, sing aloud and keep the beat, when the mouth is closed sing inside your head and keep the beat silently.
2. Improvise a motion that will demonstrate the beat of a known or unknown song in a fast or slow tempo.

Listening

"March" from *The Nutcracker Suite* by Pyotr IlyichTchaikovsky
"Hornpipe" from *Water Music* by George Frideric Handel
"Spring" from *The Four Seasons* by Antonio Vivaldi
"The Ball" from *Children's Games* by George Bizet
"This Old Man" from the album *Being a Bear*, from *Jazz for the Whole Family*, by Dan Barrett and Rebecca Kilgore, Arbors, 2000

Students may tap the beat while listening.

Assessment

Students point to a beat chart and sing *Bounce High Bounce Low.*

Teaching Strategy for Melodic Contour

Table 8.2 Teaching strategy for melodic contour

Element	Concept	Syllables	Theory	Focus Song	Additional Songs
Melodic contour	Demonstrating the shape of a melody		Melodic contour or shape, pitches	*Snail Snail*	*Doggie, Doggie; Rain, Rain; Cobbler Cobbler, Snail, Snail*

Cognitive Phase: Preparation

Stage One: Developing Kinesthetic Awareness

• • • •

Figure 8.3 Melodic contour of *Snail Snail*

1. The students sing and point to a representation of the melodic contour of *Snail Snail.*
   The contours may be icons or pictures associated with songs. These representations should be four beats in length. Consider using the first four beats of *Bounce High,* as well as the first four beats of *Hot Cross Buns.*

2. Sing *Snail Snail* and point to the melodic contour with high and low arm motions.
3. Sing *Bounce High* and/or *Hot Cross Buns and* point to the melodic contour with high and low arm motions.

Stage Two: Developing Aural Awareness

Assess kinesthetic awareness by allowing the class to perform several of the above activities independently. The target phrase for aural awareness is the first phrase of *Snail Snail.* The instructor may also sing the first phrase of *Bounce High* and/or *Hot Cross Buns.* The instructor sings the first phrase of one of the above songs on "loo" but does not show the contour. The task is for the students to individually show the shape of the melody in the air while singing and pointing to imaginary icons. Determine whether a student can sing back the phrase and show the correct contour. The instructor sings the first phrase of a song without showing the melodic contour.

Teacher: "Andy, sing the first phrase of *Snail Snail* and pretend to point to the snails." Or for *Bounce High,* "Sing that phrase and pretend to point to the balls as you sing." For *Hot Cross Buns,* "Sing the first phrase and pretend to point to the buns."

Stage Three: Developing Visual Awareness

Assess kinesthetic and aural awareness by allowing the class to perform several of the kinesthetic and aural awareness activities.

1. The instructor hums the target phrase and asks the students to create a visual representation of the melody of the target phrase. The students may use manipulatives. The instructor may say, "Show me a picture of the song."
2. Students share their representations with each other.
3. The instructor invites one student to the board to share his or her representation with the class. If necessary, corrections to the representation can be made by reviewing the aural awareness questions.
4. The students sing the first phrase of *Snail Snail* with a neutral syllable and point to their representation.

Associative Phase: Presentation

Assess the kinesthetic, aural awareness, and visual awareness activities with phrase one of *Snail Snail.*

Stage One: Label the Sound

Teacher: "When we point to the snails, we're pointing to the *shape* of the melody; the shape is the melodic contour, the snail icons are individual pitches. When we place the pitches together, they create a melodic contour."

Stage Two: Present the Notation

We can show our pitches using dots. Our first phrase of *Snail Snail* would look like the one shown in fig. 8.4.

●   ●
  ●   ●

Figure 8.4 First phrase of *Snail Snail*

Assimilative Phase: Practice

Stage One: Initial Practice

1. Review the aural presentation.
2. Review the visual presentation.
3. Transform the target pattern into other four-beat melodic patterns found in the student's song material.

Stage Two: Practice

Reading

Practice reading melodic contours with the students using flash cards; the melodic contour on the flash cards should be derived from well-known songs.

Writing

The instructor may sing patterns from well-known songs and students place manipulatives showing the melodic contour.

Improvisation/Composition

The instructor gives the students several icons to arrange. The students arrange the icons and sing their pattern. Initially this should be limited to two pitches: *so* and *mi*. More extensive exercises in reading, writing, and improvisation are included when students have more knowledge of musical concepts.

Assessment

Students point to the melodic contour of known repertoire and sing.

Teaching Strategy for Quarter and Eighth Notes

Table 8.3 Teaching strategy for quarter and eighth notes

Element	Concept	Syllables	Theory	Focus Song	Additional Songs
Quarter and eighth notes	One and two sounds on a beat	*ta, ta di*	Stems and note heads ♩ ♫	*Rain, Rain*	*Bee, Bee Bumble Bee; Queen, Queen Caroline; See Saw; Snail, Snail; Hunt the Slipper; Doggie, Doggie*

Cognitive Phase: Preparation

Stage One: Developing Kinesthetic Awareness

1. Sing *Rain, Rain* and perform the beat. Perform the "beat" by patting knees or touching the heart. (We suggest that the beat not be clapped.)

2. Sing *Rain, Rain* and clap the rhythm. Teacher: "Put the words in your hands" or "Clap the way the way the words go."
3. Sing and point:
   a. Sing and point to a representation of beat and rhythm.
   b. Sing the target phrase and point to the beat.
   c. Sing the target phrase and point to the rhythm.

● ● ●● ● ●● ●● ●● ●

Figure 8.5 Representation of beat and rhythm

4. Walk the beat, clap the rhythm, while singing the song.
5. Have two small groups of students and/or two individual students perform the beat and rhythm using two different percussion instruments.

Stage Two: Developing Aural Awareness

Assess kinesthetic awareness by allowing the class to perform several of the above activities independently. The target phrase for aural awareness is the first phrase of *Rain, Rain.* The teacher and student sing phrase one on "loo" and keep the beat before asking each question.

Determine the number of beats in the phrase.

Teacher: "Andy, how many beats did we tap?"
Student: "Four."

Determine which beats had more than one sound.

Teacher: "Andy, on which beat did we hear more than one sound?"
Student: "Beat three."
Teacher: "Andy, how many sounds were on beat three?"
Student: "Two sounds."

Determine the number of sounds on the other beats in the phrase.

Teacher: "Andy, if there are two sounds on beat three, how many sounds are on the other beats?"
Student: "One sound."
Teacher: "Sing phrase one with the text while keeping the beat and inner hear the beat with two sounds on it."

The instructor may repeat the same process with phrase two.

Stage Three: Developing Visual Awareness

Assess kinesthetic and aural awareness by allowing the class to perform several of the kinesthetic and aural awareness activities.

1. The instructor hums the target phrase and asks the students to create a visual representation of the target phrase. The students may use manipulatives. For example students can use unifix cubes to show the long long short short long pattern. We suggest using four unifix cubes to represent the long sound and two unifix cubes attached together to represent the short sounds.

   Teacher: "Pick up what you need to re-create what you heard" or "Draw what you heard." The teacher assesses the students' level of understanding.

2. The students share their representations with each other.
3. The instructor invites one student to the board to share their representation with the class. If necessary, corrections to the representation can be made by reviewing the aural awareness questions.
4. The students sing the first phrase of *Rain Rain* with a neutral syllable and point to their representation.

Associative Phase: Presentation

Assess the kinesthetic, aural awareness, and visual awareness activities with phrase one of *Rain, Rain.*

Stage One: Label the Sound

1. Teacher: "When we hear one sound on a beat we call it '*ta,*' when we hear two sounds on a beat we can call it '*tadi*'." *Ta's* and *ta-di's* are called rhythm syllables.
2. The teacher sings "Rain, Rain go away," with rhythm syllables and the students echo sing "*ta ta ta di ta.*"
3. The teacher sings phrase with "loo" and the students echo sing with rhythm syllables.
4. Repeat step three with related songs.

Stage Two: Present the Notation

1. We can represent one and two sounds on a beat using traditional notation. We can use a quarter note to represent one sound on a beat. A quarter note has a note head and a stem.
2. We can use two eighth notes to represent two sounds on a beat. Two eighth notes have two note heads, two stems, and a beam.
3. Our first phrase of *Rain Rain* looks like this:

   Figure 8.6 First phrase of *Rain Rain*

4. We can read this rhythm pattern using rhythm syllables.
5. The teacher sings rhythm syllables while pointing to the heartbeats; the students echo sing using rhythm syllables while pointing to the heartbeats.

6. Stick notation is an easy way to write rhythmic notation. Stick notation is traditional notation without the note heads for quarter and eighth notes. Our first phrase of *Rain Rain* looks like this in stick notation:

Figure 8.7 First phrase of *Rain Rain* in stick notation

| | ⊓ |

7. Sing *Rain, Rain* with rhythm syllables. Individual students sing and point to the target phrase (the A phrase) on the board as the class sings the song with rhythm syllables.

Assimilative Phase: Practice

Stage One: Initial Practice

1. Review the aural presentation and connect the sound to rhythm syllables.
2. Review the visual presentation and associate standard notation with the visual.
3. Transform the target pattern into basic four-beat patterns found in the student's song material.

Stage Two: Practice

Reading

Practice rhythm patterns derived from the focus song and additional songs with the students using flash cards.

- Name the Song

  Teacher claps the rhythm of a song. The student recognizes the song from hearing the rhythm.

- Matching and Inner Hearing

  Match the name of the song with a rhythm written on the board.

Flashcard activities may be used with both stick and staff notation.

1. Read the cards in succession.
2. Place the cards on the ledge of the chalkboard and perform them in order. Change the order of the cards to have the students read different patterns or change the order to move from one song to the next in a lesson. A card may be removed and an individual student may improvise a rhythm to replace the missing pattern. By extending the number of phrases involved in this activity, different forms may be practiced.
3. Have a student draw a rhythm card from a box. A classmate may tell him or her how to perform the rhythm (clapping, jumping, tapping, stamping, blinking, nodding, and so on). The class may echo the rhythm.
4. Perform on an instrument.

Writing

Snail Snail and *Rain Rain:*

1. The students sing *Snail, Snail* with text and write the rhythm on the board.
2. The students sing *Rain, Rain* with text, then sing again, clapping the text to compare it with the rhythm written on the board.
3. The instructor points to the rhythm to help the students determine if both songs have the same rhythm.
4. The students then sing *Rain, Rain* with words. The teacher points to the rhythm and asks whether or not it fits the song.

Improvisation

1. Write the rhythm of a phrase of a known song on the board. Ask the students to improvise a new rhythm for the second beat of a four-beat pattern.
2. Write the rhythm of a phrase of a known song on the board. Ask the students to improvise a new rhythm for the second phrase.
3. Improvise a new rhythm to one measure or more of a well-known song.
4. Use *Rain, Rain; Bee, Bee; Hunt the Slipper; Doggie, Doggie* (the first two phrases); *Engine Engine #9; Snail Snail; We Are Dancing in the Forest.*
5. Write the rhythm of a familiar eight-beat song on the board and leave the last two measures blank. Invite individual students to clap the rhythm while saying the rhythm syllables and improvise the final two measures.
6. Write sixteen beats on the board in four phrases leaving the last phrase blank. Ask a student to improvise the final four beats. Write the improvised phrase on the board. This type of activity combines improvisation, reading, and writing.
7. Question and answer rhythmic conversations can continue as a chain around the class. (The instructor claps a rhythmic question and individual students clap an answer).

Listening

"Allegretto" from Symphony No. 94, "The Surprise Symphony" by Joseph Haydn (fig. 8.8)

Figure 8.8 "Allegretto" from Symphony No. 94 by Haydn

"Bobby Shaftoe" from *Watching the White Wheat: Folksongs of the British Isles*, The King's Singers, EMI, 2003
"Pillow Dance" from *For Children* Vol. 1, No. 4, by Belá Bartók
"In the Hall of the Mountain King" from the *Peer Gynt Suite* No. 1 by Edvard Greig
For Children Vol. 2, No. 13, by Belá Bartók
Three Rondos on Folk Tunes No. 1 by Belá Bartók

Prepare the listening activity by having students recognize four-beat patterns found in known songs such as *Bobby Shaftoe, Bounce High,* and *All Around the Buttercup.*

Assessment

Students clap the rhythm of *Bobby Shaftoe.*
Students clap and say the rhythm syllables for the following songs *Bounce High Bounce Low.*

Sight-Singing

Houlahan, Mícheál, and Philip Tacka. *Sound Thinking: Music for Sight-Singing and Ear Training.* New York: Boosey & Hawkes, 1991. Vol. 1, p. 17.

Teaching Strategy for a Two-Note Child's Chant

Table 8.4 Teaching strategy for a two-note child's chant

Element	Concept	Syllables	Theory	Focus Song	Additional Songs
Bichord of the pentatonic scale	Two pitches, one higher one lower, a skip apart	*s–m*	Music staff, lines and spaces note head on staff	*Snail Snail*	*Doggie, Doggie; Rain, Rain; Cobbler Cobbler, Snail, Snail*

Cognitive Phase: Preparation

Stage One: Developing Kinesthetic Awareness

1. Sing *Snail Snail* and show the melodic contour with high and low arm movements or pointing to the shoulder for high and waist for low (body signs).
2. The students sing and point to a representation of the melodic contour of *Snail Snail.*
3. The students sing *Snail Snail* with rhythm syllables while showing the melodic contour.

Figure 8.9 Melodic contour of *Snail Snail*

Stage Two: Developing Aural Awareness

Assess kinesthetic awareness by allowing the class to perform several of the above activities independently. The target phrase for aural awareness is the first phrase of *Snail Snail.* The teacher and students sing phrase one on "loo" and keep the beat before asking each question.

Determine the number of beats in the phrase.

Teacher: "Andy, how many beats did we tap?"
Student: "Four."

Determine the number of different pitches. (It might be easier to only sing the first two beats of *Snail Snail.*)

Teacher: "Andy, how many different pitches did we sing?"
Student: "Two."

Determine whether the students can describe the pitches.

Teacher: "Andy, describe the pitches."
Student: "The first is high and the second is low."
Teacher: "Andy, I'll sing the words, you echo with high and low."
Teacher: "Snail Snail Snail Snail"
Student: "High low high low"

Stage Three: Developing Visual Awareness

Assess kinesthetic and aural awareness by allowing the class to perform several of the kinesthetic and aural awareness activities.

1. The instructor hums the target phrase and asks students to create a visual representation of the melody of the target phrase. The students may use manipulatives.

   Teacher: "Pick up what you need to re-create what you heard" or "Draw what you heard." The teacher assesses the students' level of understanding.
2. The students share their representations with each other.
3. The instructor invites one student to the board to share their representation with the class. If necessary, corrections to the representation can be made by reviewing the aural awareness questions.
4. Students sing the first phrase of *Snail Snail* with "high, low" and point to their representation.
5. Identify the rhythm of this phrase.

Associative Phase: Presentation

Assess the kinesthetic, aural awareness, and visual awareness activities with phrase one of *Snail Snail.*

Stage One: Label the Sound

1. Teacher: "We can label pitches with solfège syllables. We call the high sound *so* and the low sound *mi.*" Show the hand signs spatially using the whole arm.
2. Sing "*so mi so mi*" with hand signs. (The first phrase of *Snail Snail.*)

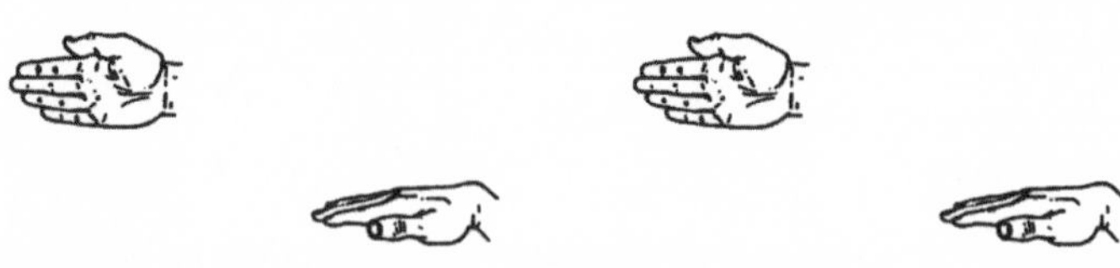

Figure 8.10 First phrase of *Snail Snail* with hand signs

3. The teacher sings "*so mi so mi*" with hand signs to individual students who echo the pattern.
4. The teacher sings "Snail Snail Snail Snail"; the students echo "*so mi so mi.*"

Stage Two: Present the Notation

- Introduce the "musical steps."

  Teacher: "*so–mi* looks like this on our musical steps. From *so* to *mi* is a skip." The instructor may hum *so–fa–mi* to prove that the distance between *so* and *mi* is a skip. Teacher: "We can write our phrase in traditional notation and put our solfège syllables under the notation." The instructor may direct students to write the stick notation and add the solfège syllables.

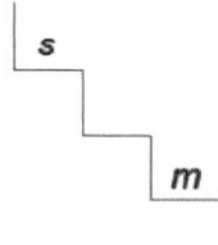

Figure 8.11 Music step for *so–mi*

Figure 8.12 Stick notation and solfege syllables

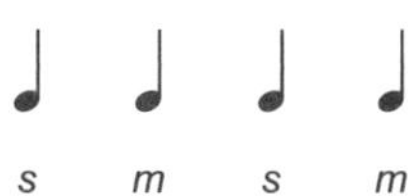

- Introduce the music staff

  One issue with music reading is the staff lines. When reading music on the staff, the instructor must make students aware of (1) five lines and four spaces; (2) counting the lines and spaces from the bottom to the top; and (3) notes in a space and notes on a line.

Figure 8.13 *So–mi* on the music staff

- Rule of placement (This is where the instructor presents the position of solfège notes on the staff.)

  The instructor may write the above pattern with note heads on the staff. If *so* is on a space, *mi* is on the next space down. If *so* is on a line, *mi* is on the next line down.

Sing *Snail Snail* with solfège syllables. Have individual students sing and point to the target phrase (the A phrase) on the board as the class sings the song with solfège syllables and hand signs.

Sing *Snail Snail* with rhythm syllables while showing hand signs. (This activity may be difficult for some students at first, but it is an accessible and valuable activity).

Assimilative Phase: Practice

Stage One: Initial Practice

1. Review the aural presentation and connect the sound to solfège syllables.
2. Review the visual presentation and associate staff notation with the visual.

3. Repeat the above activities using another known song.
4. Transform the target pattern into related four-beat melodic patterns found in the student's song material.
   Transform:

   Phrase 1 of *See Saw* into phrase 1 of *Rain, Rain*
   Phrase 2 of *See Saw* into phrase 1 of *Doggie Doggie*
   Phrase 1 of *Doggie Doggie* into phrase 1 of *Cobbler Cobbler*

Stage Two: Practice

Reading

1. Practice melodic patterns with the students using flash cards derived from the focus and additional songs.
2. Perform the above activity on a barred instrument.
3. Read *so–mi* ostinati and perform them as an accompaniment on barred instruments.
4. The students sing the first phrase of the following songs, following the instructor's hand signs: *Rain, Rain, Hunt the Slipper, Doggie Doggie, Snail Snail, This Old Man, Apple Tree, Teddy Bear.*
5. Read four-beat *so–mi* patterns and play on a xylophone or bells.
6. Read *Pala palita* and play it on an instrument.

Figure 8.14 *Pala palita*

Writing

1. The students write the first four beats of *Snail Snail* using traditional notation and solfège syllables and then on the staff.

Figure 8.15 Traditional notation and solfège syllables

2. The students write four beats of a known song on a staff using discs on a staff board.
3. Label notes written on the staff with solfège syllables.
4. Add stems to notes written on the staff (stem rule).
5. The instructor sings *Snail Snail* changing beat three from one to two sounds. The students identify the change and write it on the board. The students identify the song as *See Saw* or *Rain Rain.*

6. The instructor sings the above pattern and changes beat one from one to two sounds. The pattern is now *so so–mi—so so–mi.* The students identify the change and write it on the board. The students identify the song as *Teddy Bear.*
7. The instructor sings the above pattern and changes beat two from one to two sounds. The pattern is now *so–so–mi–mi–so–so–mi.* The students identify the change and write it on the board. The students identify the song as *Doggie Doggie.*
8. Write four-beat *so–mi* patterns and play on a xylophone or bells.
9. Write *so–mi* patterns in F, C, and G *do* positions on the staff.

s
m

Figure 8.16

Improvisation

1. Improvise four-beat *so–mi* motives using hand signs or on the xylophone or bells.
2. Improvise *so–mi* melodies to simple four- and eight-beat rhythms vocally or using a barred instrument.
3. Improvise question and answer motives using known rhythms and *so–mi* melodic patterns.
4. Improvise new words to a known song that uses *so–mi* such as *This Old Man.*

Listening

"Allegro" from "Toy Symphony" by Joseph Haydn

Assessment

Students use hand signs and sing the solfège syllables for the first phrase of *Snail, Snail* or *Rain, Rain.*

Sight-Singing

Houlahan, Mícheál, and Philip Tacka. *Sound Thinking: Music for Sight-Singing and Ear Training.* New York: Boosey & Hawkes, 1991. Vol. 1, pp. 24 and 26.

Teaching Strategy for Rest

Table 8.5 Teaching strategy for rest

Element	Concept	Syllables	Theory	Focus Song	Additional Songs
Quarter rest	A beat with no sound		𝄽 or a "Z"	*Hot Cross Buns*	*Bow Wow Wow, All Around the Buttercup; Pease Porridge Hot; Rocky Mountain; Down Came a Lady*

Cognitive Phase: Preparation

Stage One: Developing Kinesthetic Awareness

1. Sing *Hot Cross Buns* and keep the beat.
2. Sing *Hot Cross Buns* and perform the rhythm, "put the words in your hands."
3. Sing and point to a representation of the rhythm (for the heartbeats with no representation, ask students to put that beat on their shoulders).

Figure 8.17 Representation of the rhythm

4. Divide the class into two groups. Group A performs the beat while Group B performs the rhythm.
5. Clap the rhythm, walk the beat, while singing the song.

Stage Two: Developing Aural Awareness

Assess the students' kinesthetic awareness by allowing the class to perform several of the above activities independently. The teacher sings phrase one on "loo" while performing the beat before asking each question.

Determine the number of beats in the phrase.

Teacher: "Andy, how many beats did we keep?"
Student: "Four."

Determine which beat has no sound.

Teacher: "Andy, what can you tell me about beat four?" or "Andy, which beat has no sound?"
Student: "Beat four."

Determine the number of sounds on the other beats.

Teacher: "Andy, how many sounds are on the other beats?"
Student: "One."

Stage Three: Developing Visual Awareness

Assess kinesthetic and aural awareness by allowing the class to perform several of the kinesthetic and aural awareness activities.

1. The instructor hums the target phrase and asks students to create a visual representation of the target phrase. Students may use manipulatives.

   Teacher: "Pick up what you need to re-create what you heard" or "Draw what you heard." The teacher assesses students' level of understanding.

2. The students share their representations with each other.
3. The instructor invites one student to the board to share his or her representation with the class. If necessary, corrections to the representation can be made by reviewing the aural awareness questions.
4. The students sing the first phrase of *Hot Cross Buns* with a neutral syllable and point to their representation.
5. Identify known rhythmic elements.

Associative Phase: Presentation

Briefly review the kinesthetic, aural, and visual awareness activities.

Stage One: Label the Sound

1. Teacher: "We call a beat with no sound on it a *rest.*"
2. Immediately sing *Hot Cross Buns;* you may say "shh" every time you encounter a rest.
3. Sing *Hot Cross Buns* and perform the rhythm, put the "rest" on your shoulders.

Stage Two: Present the Notation

Illustrate the traditional notation: quarter notes and quarter rest. Our first phrase of *Hot Cross Buns* is shown in figure 8.18.

When writing in stick notation, use a "z" for the quarter rest.

Figure 8.18 First phrase of *Hot Cross Buns*

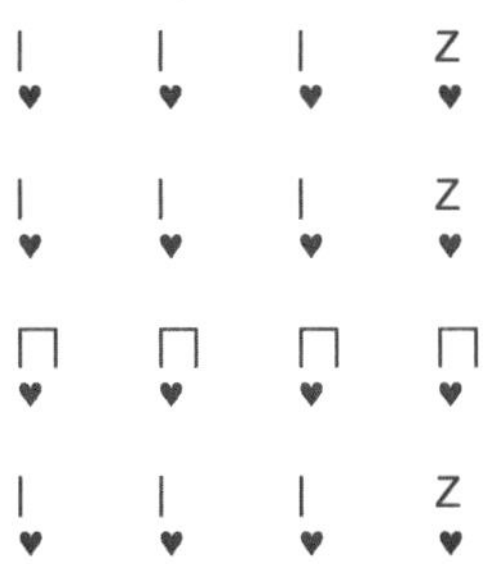

Figure 8.19 Use a "z" for the quarter rest

Assimilative Phase: Practice

Stage One: Initial Practice

1. Review the aural presentation and connect the sound to rhythm syllables.
2. Review the visual presentation and associate standard notation with the visual.

3. Transform the target pattern into basic four-beat patterns found in the student's song material.

Stage Two: Practice

Reading

1. Transform the rhythm of one song into another. For example, change the rhythm of *Hot Cross Buns* into *Bow Wow Wow.*
2. The instructor writes the rhythm of *Hot Cross Buns* on the board and the students clap the rhythm and sing the song with rhythm syllables.
3. The instructor writes the rhythm of *Bow Wow Wow* next to the *Hot Cross Buns;* the students clap the rhythm of *Bow Wow Wow* and sing the song with rhythm syllables.
4. The students identify that phrases one and four of both songs are the same.
5. The instructor asks, "Which beat is different in phrase two?"
6. The instructor asks, "Which beat is different in phrase three?"
7. Read selected phrases and play them on an instrument.
8. Read *Quién es esa gente?* and play it on an instrument.

Figure 8.20 *Quién es esa gente*

Writing

1. Place heartbeats over the rhythm of a known song.
2. In the early stages of writing, the teacher may provide a worksheet with rhythm patterns written with dashes that the students may trace.
3. The students sing *All Around the Buttercup* with text and write the rhythm on the board.
4. The students sing *Cut the Cake* with text, then sing again, clapping the text to compare it with the rhythm written on the board.
5. The students change the rhythm of *All Around the Buttercup* into the rhythm of *Cut the Cake.*
6. Dictation. Write a four- or eight-beat rhythm pattern dictated by the teacher.

Improvisation

1. Improvise a new rhythm to one measure or more of a well-known song.

   Use *Hot Cross Buns, All Around the Buttercup, Teddy Bear, Bow Wow Wow, Pease Porridge Hot, Here Comes a Bluebird, Down Came a Lady,* or *Rocky Mountain.* Complete the song using quarter notes, two eighth notes, and/or a rest.

2. Improvise using the form of a known composition. For example, *Hot Cross Buns* is in AABA form. Students could be guided to clap the A phrase but improvise a rhythm for the B phrase.

Listening

"Allegretto" from Symphony No. 7 in A, Op. 92 by Ludwig van Beethoven
"Children's Song" from *For Children* Vol. 1, No. 2, by Belá Bartók
"In the Hall of the Mountain King" Movement 4 from the *Peer Gynt Suite* No. 1, Op. 46, by Edvard Greig
"Allegretto" Movement 2 from Symphony No. 7 in A, Op. 92, by Ludwig van Beethoven

Figure 8.21 Rhythmic theme of the movement

Assessment

Students clap and say the rhythm syllables for Hot Cross Buns.
Students write the rhythm of Hot Cross Buns.

Sight-Singing

Houlahan, Mícheál, and Philip Tacka. *Sound Thinking: Music for Sight-Singing and Ear Training.* New York: Boosey & Hawkes, 1991. Vol. 1, pp. 18 and 19.

Teaching Strategy for a Three-Note Child's Chant

Table 8.6 Teaching strategy for a three-note child's chant

Element	Concept	Syllables	Theory	Focus Song	Additional Songs
Trichord of the pentatonic scale	Three pitches; a skip between one of the pitches	*la–so–mi*	Staff	*Bounce High Bounce Low* Or *Snail Snail*	*Snail Snail, Bobby Shaftoe, Lucy Locket, We Are Dancing in the Forest*

Cognitive Phase: Preparation

Stage One: Developing Kinesthetic Awareness

1. Sing *Bounce High* and point to a representation of the melodic contour.
2. Sing *Bounce High* and show the melodic contour with arm or body motions.

Figure 8.22 Melodic contour of *Bounce High*

3. Sing *Bounce High* with rhythm syllables while showing the melodic contour.

Stage Two: Developing Aural Awareness

Assess kinesthetic awareness by allowing the class to perform several of the above activities independently. The target phrase for aural awareness is the first phrase of *Bounce High*. The teacher and the students sing phrase one on "loo" and keep the beat before asking each question. We often say "so-mi" names instead of solfège syllables with younger students.

Determine the number of beats in the phrase.

Teacher: "Andy, how many beats did we tap?"
Student: "Four."

Determine what is known in the phrase.

Teacher: "Andy, what so-mi names do we use for the last two beats of the phrase?
Student: "*So-mi.*"
Teacher: "What hand signs do we use for these sounds? (*so* and *mi*)." Sing with hand signs.
Teacher: "What is the so-mi name for the first pitch of the phrase?"
Student: "*So.*"

Determine whether the student can describe the sound on beat two.

Teacher: "Andy, what can you tell me about the pitch on beat two?"
Student: "It's high."
Teacher: "I'll sing the text and you sing the so-mi names with hand signs."

The teacher models:	Bounce	high	bounce	low
The student echoes:	*so*	*high*	*so*	*mi*

Sing phrase one of *Bounce High* but inner hear the beat with the highest sound.

Teacher: "Andy, is our new pitch a step or a skip higher than *so?*"
Student: "A step."

If students have trouble with this, the teacher could sing *so—(ti-on a neutral sound)—so—mi* to determine whether they can hear the difference between a step and a skip.

Repeat the above for phrase two.

Stage Three: Developing Visual Awareness

Assess kinesthetic and aural awareness by allowing the class to perform several of the kinesthetic and aural awareness activities.

1. The instructor hums the target phrase and asks students to create a visual representation of the melody of the target phrase. Students may use manipulatives.

   Teacher: "Pick up what you need to re-create what you heard" or "Draw what you heard." The teacher assesses the students' level of understanding.

2. The students share their representations with each other.

3. The instructor invites one student to the board to share his or her representation with the class. If necessary, corrections to the representation can be made by reviewing the aural awareness questions.
4. Students sing the first phrase of *Bounce High* with a neutral syllable and point to their representation.
5. Identify known rhythmic elements.

Associative Phase: Presentation

Assess the kinesthetic, aural awareness, and visual awareness activities with phrase one of *Bounce High.*

Stage One: Label the Sound

Teacher: "We call our high sound on beat two *la.*" Show the hand sign.

The teacher sings "*so—la—so—mi*" with hand signs (the first phrase of *Bounce High*) to individual students who echo the pattern.

Figure 8.23
Hand sign for *la*

The teacher sings: "*Bounce High Bounce Low.*"
The students echo: "*so—la—so—mi.*"

Stage Two: Present the Notation

Show the position of la on the musical steps, in stick notation, and staff notation.

Teacher: "*La* looks like this on our steps."

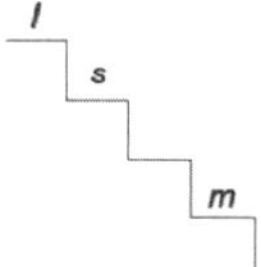

Figure 8.24
la, so, and *mi* on the steps

Teacher: "We can write our phrase using rhythm notation and put our solfège syllables under it."

Figure 8.25
Solfege syllables with stick notation

Figure 8.26
Notes on the music staff

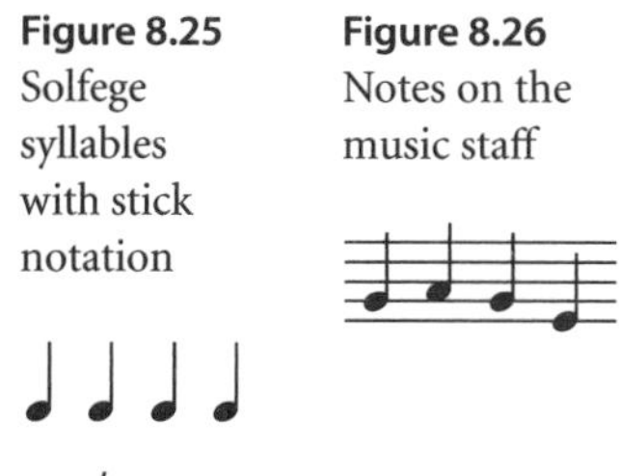

The rule of placement: "If *so* is on a line, *la* is in the space above and *mi* is on the next line down from *so*. If *so* is in a space, *la* is on the line above and *mi* is in the space below *so*."

Working from the above presentation phase, move to another song having the same pattern.

Assimilative Phase: Practice

Stage One: Initial Practice

- Review the aural presentation and connect the sound to rhythm syllables.
- Review the visual presentation and associate standard notation with the visual.
- Transform the target pattern into basic four-beat patterns found in the student's song material. The instructor may sing the following phrases:

  so *la* *so* *mi* *Bounce high bounce low*

  The students echo sing solfège syllables and use hand signs.

Stage Two: Practice

Reading

1. Using any of the above songs and melodic patterns, read well-known melodic patterns from hand signs, traditional notation, or staff notation. The above patterns illustrate the fact that the melodic contour of all phrases is related. *La* occurs on beat two.
2. Read a new song from staff notation.
3. Play a new song or known patterns on a barred instrument.
4. Practice part singing. The teacher may use the right hand and left hand to show two different *so—mi—la* patterns. Group A sings from the teacher's right hand and group B sings from the teacher's left hand.
5. Name the song. The teacher claps the rhythm of a song. The student recognizes the song from hearing the rhythm.
6. Matching and inner hearing. Match the name of the song with a rhythm written on the board. Read phrases from the instructor's silent hand signs. The students may sing back aloud with solfège syllables and hand signs.
7. Read a *la—so—mi* song from hand signs.
8. Perform a *la—so—mi* song on a xylophone or tone bells.
9. Read *A la ronda ronda* and play it on an instrument.

Figure 8.27 *A la ronda ronda*

Writing

1. Write the first eight beats of the song *We Are Dancing in the Forest* in staff notation.
2. After the students write and sing the two phrases with solfège syllables and hand signs, the instructor should sing it changing beat seven to one sound instead of two. The students identify the change on beat seven. Students then sing the song with the change. Students recognize that the melody has now become *Lucy Locket.*
3. Add rhythm to melody notes written on a staff.
4. Have students read the rhythm of *Lucy Locket,* change the rhythm one beat at a time to *We are Dancing in the Forest* and/or *Bobby Shaftoe.*
5. Write four beat *la—so—mi* patterns and play on the xylophone; use the pattern to accompany known songs.
6. Aurally identify the *mi—la* interval in target phrases of *Little Sally Water,* write them on the staff and play them on the xylophone.

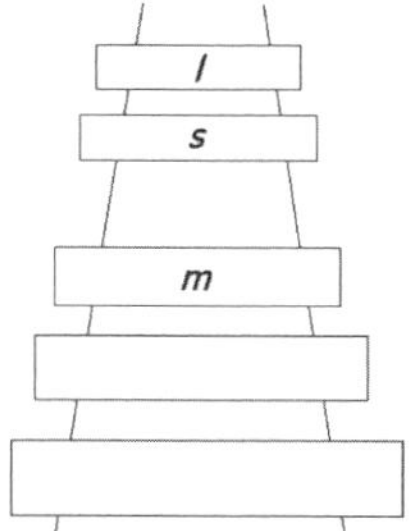

Figure 8.28 Target phrases of *Little Sally Water* on the xylophone

Improvisation

1. Improvise short musical motives (*la—so—mi*) using hand signs, hand staff, or body signs.
2. Improvise *so—mi—la* melodies to simple four- to eight-beat rhythms using the voice or a barred instrument.
3. Improvise a new rhythm and melody to one measure or more of a well-known song.
4. Improvise question and answer motives using known rhythm and melodic patterns.
5. Create an ostinato on a barred instrument using *la—so* and *mi.*

Sight-Singing

Houlahan, Mícheál, and Philip Tacka. *Sound Thinking: Music for Sight-Singing and Ear Training.* New York: Boosey & Hawkes, 1991. Vol. 1, pp. 28–32.

Assessment

Students sing focus songs with solfège syllables and handsigns.
Students write the notation for the target pattern using stick notation and solfège syllables or on the staff.

Teaching Strategy for $\frac{2}{4}$ Meter

Table 8.7 Teaching strategy for $\frac{2}{4}$ meter

Element	Concept	Syllables	Theory	Focus Song	Additional Songs
$\frac{2}{4}$	The organization of strong and weak beats		Accent; bar lines, measures; double bar-line, time signature	*Bounce High*	*Hunt the Slipper; Bye Baby Bunting; Little Sally Water*

Cognitive Phase: Preparation

Stage One: Developing Kinesthetic Awareness

Teacher: "Let's sing *Bounce High* and pretend to push your little brother on a swing."

1. The teacher and the students sing the first four beats with the following motions: pat, shoulders, pat, shoulders (pat knees and touch shoulders).
2. The students point to a representation of strong and weak *beats* (not rhythm).

● ○ ● ○ ● ○ ● ○

Figure 8.29 Strong and weak beats

3. Sing *Bounce High* with rhythm syllables with the following motions: pat, shoulders, pat, shoulders.

Stage Two: Developing Aural Awareness

Assess kinesthetic awareness by allowing the class to perform several of the above activities independently. The teacher and students sing the first four beats of *Bounce High* and keep the beat before asking each question.
Determine the number of beats in the phrase.

Teacher: "Andy, how many beats did we tap?"
Student: "Four."

Determine whether students feel the stress in the strong beats.

Teacher: "Andy, do all of the beats feel the same?"
Student: "Some beats are stronger."

Determine which beats are strong and which are weak.

Teacher: "Andy, which beats are stronger?"
Student: "Beats one and three."
Teacher: "If beats one and three are strong, beats two and four are ______."
Student: "Weak."
Teacher: "Let's sing and show our strong and weak beats."
Teacher: "Let's sing and inner hear the weak beats."

The teacher and students sing the first four beats with the following motions: pat, shoulders, pat, shoulders.

Stage Three: Developing Visual Awareness

Assess kinesthetic and aural awareness by allowing the class to perform several of the kinesthetic and aural awareness activities.

1. The instructor hums the target phrase and asks the students to create a visual representation of the target phrase. The students may use manipulatives.

Teacher: "Pick up what you need to re-create the strong and weak beats you heard" or "Draw what you heard." The students could show four or eight beats using unifix cubes. The strong and weak beats might be distinguished using colors. The teacher assesses the students' level of understanding.
2. The students share their representations with each other.
3. The instructor invites one student to the board to share his or her representation with the class. If necessary, corrections to the representation can be made by reviewing the aural awareness questions.
4. The students sing the first phrase of *Bounce High* with a neutral syllable and point to their representation.
5. The students sing all of *Bounce High* with rhythm syllables while pointing to their representation of strong and weak beats.

Associative Phase: Presentation

Assess the kinesthetic, aural awareness, and visual awareness activities with phrase one of *Bounce High.*

Stage One: Label the Sound

In music we call the strong beats accents. We can show the strong beats by conducting.

Sing *Bounce High* and conduct.

Figure 8.30 Show the strong beats by conducting

Stage Two: Present the Notation

Teacher: "We can show strong beats in two ways, using an accent or writing barlines."

Teacher: "In music, we call '>' 'accent' "

Teacher: "Instead of drawing accents, musicians use another method. We put a line before each strong beat. This is called a bar line." (*Accent defines bar line.*)

Teacher: "At the end we draw a double bar line."

Teacher: "Andy, how many beats are between the bar lines?"

Student: "Two beats."

Teacher: "Musicians call the distance between bar lines a 'measure.' "

Teacher: "Musicians show the number of beats in each measure by erasing the first bar line and writing a 'time signature.' When there are two beats in a measure, and each beat is a quarter note in length then the time signature is $\frac{2}{4}$."

Initially, the teacher might want to write a 2 over a heartbeat, then a 2 over a quarter note and finally $\frac{2}{4}$. This step can take many lessons to present.

Figure 8.31 $\frac{2}{4}$ meter

Assimilative Phase: Practice

Stage One: Initial Practice

1. Review the aural presentation and connect the sound to rhythm syllables.
2. Review the visual presentation and associate standard notation with the visual.
3. Using staff notation, transform *Bounce High* into *Rain Rain.*

Stage Two: Practice

Reading

1. Read the following songs with time signatures and bar lines: *Rain, Rain, See Saw, Snail Snail, Lucy Locket.* A subsequent activity is to number the measures and instruct the students to perform the rhythm in a specified order.
2. Read *Doggie Doggie* from traditional rhythmic notation written without barlines on the board. Select individual students to sing while the other students put strong beats on their imaginary tambourines or play on real instruments (for example, louder instrumentation on the first beat and softer instrument on the second beat).
3. After reading *Doggie Doggie* on the board:

   Teacher: "Andy, circle the strong beats."
   Teacher: "Andy, please put in the barlines for us."

4. Read selected patterns and play them on an instrument.

Writing

1. The teacher and students sing *Rain Rain* on "loo."

   Teacher: "Andy, come and place 8 heart beats on the board as we sing."

   The teacher and students sing *Rain Rain* on "loo."

   Teacher: "Andy, which beats are strong beats? How can we show strong and weak beats?"

   Write an ">" over the strong beats, after writing heartbeats on the board for *Rain Rain.*

2. *Lucy Locket*

   The teacher dictates the rhythm of *Lucy Locket.* The students write the rhythm on the board one phrase at a time and add bar lines and time signature. A student determines the solfège syllables and writes it beneath the rhythm. We may write the aforementioned songs in staff notation with bar lines. At this stage in their writing on the staff, the students may practice writing in relative positions.

Improvisation

1. Improvise a melody to a four- or eight-beat rhythm pattern. The students must conduct a two pattern as they are improvising.
2. The instructor asks the students to improvise a four-beat rhythm using *ta, ta-di,* and Z in between each phrase of *Pease Porridge Hot.* After each student claps and says rhythm names, the class echoes four beats later after singing the next part of song.
3. The class claps the A phrase; an individual student claps the B phrase, and the class claps this phrase two times. The students write the rhythm of the B phrase on the board using bar lines and the time signature.

Listening

"Allegro Assai" from Brandenburg Concerto No. 2 by Johann Sebastian Bach
"Finale" from Symphony No. 4 by Pyotr Ilyich Tchaikovsky

Sight-Singing

Houlahan, Mícheál, and Philip Tacka. *Sound Thinking: Music for Sight-Singing and Ear Training.* New York: Boosey & Hawkes, 1991. Vol. 1, p. 17.

Assessment

The teacher dictates the rhythm of known melody. The students write the rhythm on their paper one phrase at a time and then add bar lines and the time signature.

Focus Songs for Grade One

Focus Song for Quarter and Eighth Notes

Figure 8.32 *Rain Rain*

Focus Song for a Two-Note Child's Chant *so—mi*

Figure 8.33 *Snail Snail*

Focus Song for Rest

Figure 8.34 *Hot Cross Buns*

Focus Song for a Three-Note Child's Chant *la—so—mi*
Focus Song for Two-Beat Meter

Figure 8.35 *Bounce High Bounce Low*

Grade Two Teaching Strategies

In second grade we deal with six musical concepts. When teaching them, we alternate between rhythmic concepts and melodic concepts.

1. Teaching strategy for introducing the tonic note of the major pentatonic scale *do*
2. Teaching strategy for half note
3. Teaching strategy for introducing the second degree of the major pentatonic scale *re*
4. Teaching strategy for introducing the sixteenth notes
5. Teaching strategy for the major pentatonic scale
6. Teaching strategy for four-beat meter

Teaching Strategy for Introducing the Tonic Note of the Major Pentatonic Scale *do*

Table 8.8 Teaching strategy for introducing the tonic note of the major pentatonic scale *do*

Element	Concept	Syllables	Theory	Focus Song	Additional Songs
The tonic note of the major pentatonic scale	A pitch a skip lower than *mi;* Five steps lower than *so* and six steps lower than *l*	*do*	Tonic note	*Bow Wow Wow*	*Wall Flowers; Button You Must Wander; Dinah; Rocky Mountain; Knock the Cymbals*

Cognitive Phase: Preparation

Stage One: Developing Kinesthetic Awareness

1. Sing *Bow Wow Wow* and show the melodic contour with arm or body motions.
2. Sing *Bow Wow Wow* and point to a representation of the melodic contour of phrase 3 of *Little Tommy Tucker's Dog.*

Figure 8.36 Melodic contour of phrase 3 of *Little Tommy Tucker's Dog*

3. Sing *Bow Wow Wow* with rhythm syllables while showing the melodic contour.

Stage Two: Developing Aural Awareness

Review kinesthetic awareness. The teacher and students sing phrase three on "loo" while keeping the beat before each question.

Determine the number of beats in the phrase.

Teacher: "Andy, How many beats did we tap?"
Student: "Four."

Determine which beat has the new musical element and determine the characteristics of the new musical element on that beat.

Teacher: "Andy, what can you tell me about the pitch on beat four?"
Student: "It's low."

Determine known musical elements within the phrase.

Teacher: "Andy, let's sing the sounds on beats 1–3 with 'loo' and call the new pitch 'low.'"

The teacher sings *so—mi* (beat three) on "loo."

Teacher: "Andy, what solfège syllables can we use for these two pitches?"
Student: "*so—mi.*"
Teacher: "Let's sing the last two beats with *so—mi*—low."
Teacher: "Andy, what hand signs can we use at the beginning of the phrase?"
Student: "*so so—so la.*"
Teacher: "Let's sing with solfège and hand signs for beats one to three and for beat four let's sing 'low' and point down."
Teacher: "Let's sing the phrase and inner hear the lowest sound."

Stage Three: Developing Visual Awareness

Assess kinesthetic and aural awareness by allowing the class to perform several of the kinesthetic and aural awareness activities.

1. The instructor hums the target and asks students to create a visual representation of the melody of the target phrase. The students may use manipulatives.

   Teacher: "Pick up what you need to re-create what you heard" or "Draw what you heard." The teacher assesses the students' level of understanding.
2. The students share their representations with each other.
3. The instructor invites one student to the board to share his or her representation with the class. If necessary, corrections to the representation can be made by reviewing the aural awareness questions.
4. The students sing the third phrase of *Bow Wow Wow* with a neutral syllable and point to their representation.
5. Determine and write the rhythm for *Bow Wow Wow;* add barlines and a time signature.

Associative Phase: Presentation

Briefly review kinesthetic, aural, and visual awareness.

Stage One: Label the Sound

Figure 8.37 Hand sign for *do*

1. Teacher: "We call the low sound *do.*" Present the hand sign.
2. The class and individual students sing phrase 3 of *Bow Wow Wow* with solfège syllables and hand signs.
3. The teacher sings the words of phrase 3 of *Bow Wow Wow* and students echo sing using solfège syllables and hand signs.
4. The teacher echo sings with at least eight individuals.

Stage Two: Present the Notation

Place *do* on the steps.

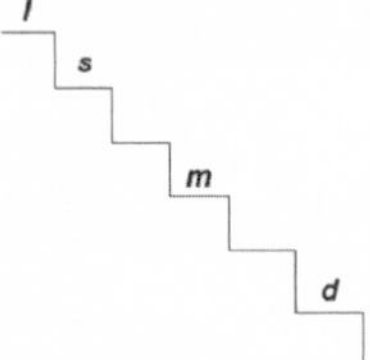

Figure 8.38 *do* on the steps

Write traditional rhythm notation with solfège syllables on the board.

Figure 8.39 Traditional rhythm notation with solfège syllables

Write the staff notation on the board; the student adds *do.* Everyone points and sings.

Figure 8.40 Staff notation

Assimilative Phase: Practice

Stage One: Initial Practice

1. Review the aural awareness stage and connect the sound to rhythm syllables of the focus pattern (this may include other known songs). Where is the lowest note? What do we call this note?
2. Review the visual awareness activities and associate standard notation with the visual (this may include other known songs). Draw me a picture of the focus phrase. Can you write in all of the known notes including our new note *do?*
3. Transform the target pattern into four-beat patterns found in the student's song material.

Stage Two: Practice

Reading

1. Read *Bow Wow Wow* from stick then staff notation.
2. Change several measures of the song so that it becomes a reading exercise.
3. Read and play selected target phrases on the xylophone or tone bells.

Writing

1. Write all of *Bow Wow Wow* in stick notation with solfège syllables.
2. Write *Bow Wow Wow* in staff notation.
3. Write well-known melodic patterns from hand signs using stick or staff notation.
4. Once the above patterns are written, play them on the xylophone or bells.
5. Consider writing phrases from *Knock the Cymbals, King's Land,* or *Rocky Mountain.*

6. Aurally identify *do* in a *so—do* pattern. Write it on the staff.
7. Aurally identify *do* in a *so—mi—do* pattern and write it on the staff.

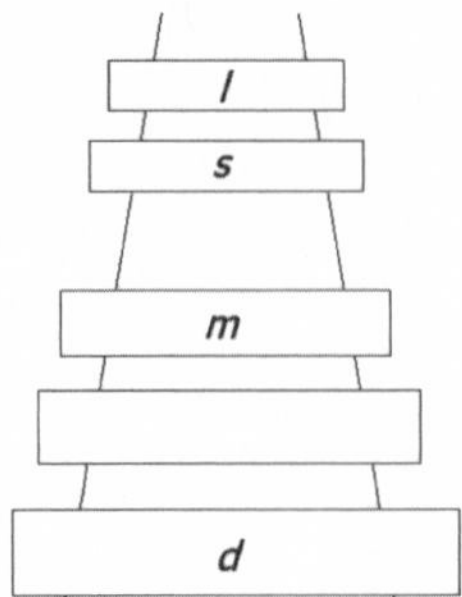

Figure 8.41 Well-known melodic patterns on the xylophone

Improvisation

1. Improvise: the teacher sings a question phrase; the students sing an answer phrase that ends on *do.*
2. Improvise short musical motives (*la–so—mi–do*) using hand signs, hand staff, or body signs.
3. Improvise *la–so—mi–do* melodies to simple four- to eight-beat rhythms using the voice or a barred instrument.
4. Improvise a new melody to one measure or more of a well-known song.

Listening

"Allegro" from Symphony No. 1 by Wolfgang Amadeus Mozart

Figure 8.42 "Allegro" from Symphony No. 1 by Mozart

Sight-Singing Materials

Houlahan, Mícheál, and Philip Tacka. *Sound Thinking: Music for Sight-Singing and Ear Training.* New York: Boosey & Hawkes, 1991. Vol. 1, p. 51, nos. 6–7.

Assessment

The students sing the third phrase of *Bow Wow Wow* with solfège syllables and hand signs.

Teaching Strategy for Half Note

Table 8.9 Teaching strategy for half note

Element	Concept	Syllables	Theory	Focus Song	Additional Songs
Half note	A note that lasts for two beats	ta ah	Tie	*Here Comes a Bluebird*	*Are You Sleeping*

Cognitive Phase: Preparation

Stage One: Developing Kinesthetic Awareness

1. Sing *Here Comes a Bluebird* and keep the beat.
2. Sing *Here Comes a Bluebird* and clap the rhythm.
3. Sing and point to a representation of phrases two and four.

______________ ___ ___ ___ ___ _______ ________ ______

Figure 8.43 Representation of phrases two and four

4. Divide the class into two groups; Group A performs the beat, Group B performs the rhythm. Reverse.
5. Sing *Here Comes a Bluebird,* walk the beat, and clap the rhythm.

Stage Two: Developing Aural Awareness

Review kinesthetic awareness. The teacher and students sing phrase two on "loo," while performing the beat before each question.

Determine the number of beats in phrase two.

Teacher: "Andy, how many beats did we keep?"
Student: "Eight!"
Teacher: "Andy, which beat has no sound?"
Student: "The last one—eight."

Determine which beat has the new musical element.

Teacher: "Andy, where did we sing the longest sound?"
Student: "At the beginning."
Teacher: "Andy, for how many beats did we sing the long sound?"
Student: "Two beats."
Teacher: "Andy, on which beats did we sing the long sound?"
Student: "One and two."

The teacher and students sing phrase two on "loo" and keep the beat.

Teacher: "Lets sing and clap the whole phrase with rhythm syllables and say *long* for beats one and two."

*long*______ *ta di* *ta di* *ta* *ta* *ta*
♥ ♥ ♥ ♥ ♥ ♥ ♥

Stage Three: Developing Visual Awareness

Assess kinesthetic and aural awareness by allowing the class to perform several of the kinesthetic and aural awareness activities.

1. The instructor hums the target phrase and asks students to create a visual representation of the target phrase. Students may use manipulatives.

   Teacher: "Pick up what you need to re-create what you heard" or "Draw what you heard." The teacher assesses the students' level of understanding.

2. The students share their representations with each other.
3. The instructor invites one student to the board to share his or her representation with the class. If necessary, corrections to the representation can be made by reviewing the aural awareness questions.
4. The students sing the second phrase of *Here Comes a Bluebird* with a neutral syllable and point to their representation.

Associative Phase: Presentation

Stage One: Label the Sound

1. Quickly review kinesthetic, aural, and visual stage.
2. Teacher: "When we hear one sound lasting for two beats, we call it 'ta-ah.'"
3. The teacher sings the target phrase with "loo" and individual students echo sing with rhythm syllables.
4. Repeat the above step with related patterns from known songs.

Stage Two: Present the Notation

1. We can use a half note to represent a sound that lasts for two beats. A half note has a note head and a stem.
2. Our second phrase of *Here Comes a Bluebird* is shown in figure 8.44. We can read it using our rhythm syllables.

Figure 8.44 Second phrase of *Here Comes a Bluebird*

3. When we write the target phrase, we can write using rhythm notation or stick notation.

Figure 8.45 Stick notation

4. We can read this rhythm pattern using our rhythm syllables.
5. The teacher sings rhythm syllables while pointing to the heartbeats; the students echo sing using rhythm syllables while pointing to the heartbeats.

Assimilative Phase: Practice

Stage One: Initial Practice

1. Review the aural awareness stage and connect the sound to rhythm syllables of the focus pattern (this may include other known songs).
2. Review the visual awareness activities and associate standard notation with the visual (this may include other known songs).
3. Transform the target pattern into four-beat patterns found in the student's song material.

Stage Two: Practice

Reading

1. Change one song to another. The students read and clap the rhythm of the second phrase of *Here Comes a Bluebird* (written on the board). The teacher changes one beat at a time on the board and the students clap each change until the eight-beat rhythm is changed to the first eight beats of *Who's That Tapping at the Window?* The students clap and say the rhythm and identify the song. Sing with words and rhythm syllables.
2. Read in traditional notation. Have the rhythm of *Are You Sleeping* on the board in traditional notation and have the students point and sing with rhythm syllables.
3. Read in canon. With rhythm to *Are You Sleeping* on the board, the students sing the song from memory and read and clap the rhythm two measures behind their singing.
4. Match song titles to a matching rhythm. List the titles of four songs on the board. The students match rhythms in rhythm notation to the song titles. Use the following songs:

   Here Comes a Bluebird
   Knock the Cymbals
   Are You Sleeping
   Who's That Tapping at the Window

   Sing and conduct all of the above.

Writing

1. Echo singing: the teacher sings the first phrase of *Are You Sleeping* and the students sing the phrase back to the teacher using rhythm syllables. The students write each rhythm on the board.
2. Write the rhythm. The students identify *Knock the Cymbals* from the teacher's clapping and write the rhythm for each phrase. The teacher invites one student to write the last phrase on the board.

3. Sing *Who's That Tapping* on "loo" and the teacher claps the rhythm while the students pat the beat. Select four individual students to echo sing an eight-beat phrase from the song with rhythm names. Direct each of those students to write their phrases on the board.
4. Write melodies using a tie instead of a half note.
5. Dictation: the students write the rhythm of a known listening example through dictation. The students will review "In the Hall of the Mountain King" from *Peer Gynt* by Edvard Grieg and write the following rhythm using this procedure:
   a. Play or sing the music to be written for dictation.
   b. The students sing the phrase and tap the beat.
   c. The students sing the phrase and clap the rhythm.
   d. The students sing the phrase with rhythm syllables.
   e. The students memorize the musical example.
   f. The students simultaneously sing and write the phrase using stick notation.

Improvisation

1. Improvise a new rhythm to the B section (phrase 2) of *Here Comes a Bluebird.* The teacher sings *Here Comes a Bluebird* on "loo" while clapping the rhythm. The teacher guides the students to sing phrases 1 and 3 with rhythm syllables while clapping the rhythm. Individual students clap an eight-beat rhythm pattern for phrase 2 and 4 using at least one half note.
2. The class reads rhythm flashcards. Individual students clap flashcards, creating a new rhythm if they are presented with a blank card.
3. Flashcard improvisation: the teacher puts four flashcards on the board. The students are asked to choose one and clap it as an answer to the teacher's question. Eventually, the teacher takes away flashcards and the students improvise an original answer.
4. Question and Answer: the teacher asks the students to improvise an "answer" rhythm. After the teacher claps a four-beat "question" rhythm using a half note, individual students improvise an answer rhythm. Initially encourage students to change only one beat. The class should clap back the improvised rhythm immediately.
5. Question and Answer: the teacher uses the first eight beats of *Who's That Tapping at the Window?* as a rhythmic question and the students clap back a rhythmic answer. Their answer must contain at least one half note.

Listening

Violin Concerto in D Movement 1 by Ludwig van Beethoven, from *Beethoven and Mendelssohn Violin Concertos,* performed by Camerata Salzburg with Joshua Bell and conducted by Sir Roger Norrington, Sony BMG Music Entertainment, 2002

"Death of Ase" Movement 6 from *Peer Gynt Suite* No. 1, Op. 46, by Edvard Greig

Three Rondos on Folk Tunes No. 1 by Belá Bartók

Sight-Singing Materials

Houlahan, Míchéal, and Philip Tacka. *Sound Thinking: Music for Sight-Singing and Ear Training.* New York: Boosey & Hawkes, 1991. Vol. 1, pp. 33–56.

Assessment

Read focus song with rhythm syllables.
Write focus song using stick notation.

Teaching Strategy for Introducing the Second Degree of the Pentatonic Scale

Table 8.10 Teaching strategy for introducing the second degree of the pentatonic scale

Element	Concept	Syllables	Theory	Focus Song	Additional Songs
The second degree of the pentatonic scale	A pitch between *mi* and *do*	*re*	Pentatonic trichord *m–r–d*	*Hot Cross Buns*	*Bow Wow Wow; All Around the Buttercup; Rocky Mountain; Ida Red; Button You Must Wander*

Cognitive Phase: Preparation

Stage One: Developing Kinesthetic Awareness

1. Sing Hot Cross Buns and show the melodic contour with arm and body signs.
2. Play a kinesthetic game that sets the students up to show the melodic contour with their bodies. Using the following motions allows students to show high, medium, and low as they are playing a hand clapping game.
   a. "Hot"—clap partner's hands
   b. "Cross"—clap your own hands
   c. "Buns"—Pat
3. Point to a visual representation of the whole song.

Figure 8.46 Visual representation of *Hot Cross Buns*

4. Sing *Hot Cross Buns* with rhythm syllables while showing the melodic contour.

Stage Two: Developing Aural Awareness

Review kinesthetic awareness. Sing the target phrase before asking each question. The teacher and students sing phrase one of *Hot Cross Buns on* "loo."

Teacher: "Andy, how many beats did we keep?"
Student: "Four."

The teacher and students sing on "loo" and check.

Teacher: "Andy, which beat had the highest pitch?"
Student: "Beat one."
Teacher: "Andy, which beat had the lowest pitch?"
Student: "Beat three."
Teacher: "Andy, if beat one has the high pitch and beat three has the low pitch, how would you describe the sound on beat two?"
Student: "It's in the middle."
Teacher: "Andy, do our three pitches move up or down?"
Student: "Down."
Teacher: "Andy, do our three pitches move in steps or skips?"
Student: "Steps."
Teacher: "Let's sing this phrase on 'loo' and hide the pitch on beat two."

Stage Three: Developing Visual Awareness

Assess kinesthetic and aural awareness by allowing the class to perform several of the kinesthetic and aural awareness activities.

1. The instructor hums the target phrase and asks the students to create a visual representation of the target phrase. The students may use manipulatives.

   Teacher: "Pick up what you need to re-create what you heard" or "Draw what you heard." The teacher assesses the students' level of understanding.

2. The students share their representations with each other.
3. The instructor invites one student to the board to share his or her representation with the class. If necessary, corrections to the representation can be made by reviewing the aural awareness questions.
4. The students sing the first phrase of *Hot Cross Buns* with a neutral syllable and point to their representation.
5. Determine the rhythm and perform the song with the melodic contour and rhythm syllables.

Associative Phase: Presentation

Stage One: Label the Sound

Figure 8.47 Hand sign for *re*

1. Briefly review kinesthetic, aural, and visual awareness.
2. Teacher: "We call these three pitches that move in steps *mi—re—do.* Our new note between *mi* and *do* is called *re.*" Show the hand signs.
3. Sing "*mi re do*" with hand signs.
4. The teacher sings phrase one of *Hot Cross Buns* with solfège syllables and hand signs and the students echo.

Perform the above activity with at least eight individual students.

Stage Two: Present the Notation

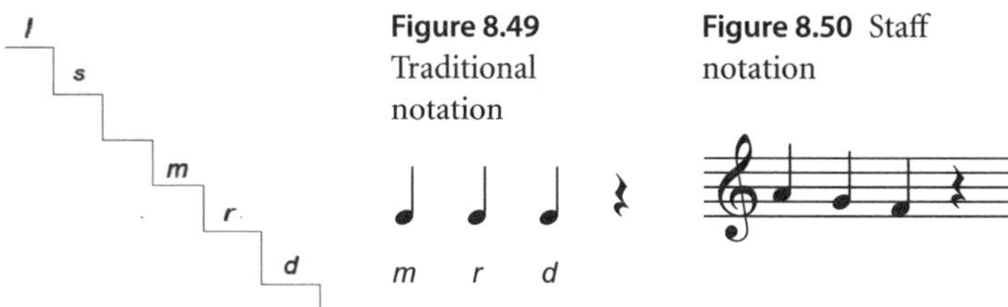

Figure 8.49 Traditional notation

Figure 8.50 Staff notation

Figure 8.48 Steps are used to name new solfege syllables

Assimilative Phase: Practice

Stage One: Initial Practice

1. Review the aural awareness stage and connect the sound to rhythm syllables of the focus pattern (this may include other known songs).
2. Review the visual awareness activities and associate standard notation with the visual (this may include other known songs).
3. Transform the target pattern into four-beat patterns found in the student's song material.

Stage Two: Practice

Reading

1. Practice reading *mi—re—do* and *do—re—mi* for a few lessons working in staff notation. Consider using four-beat patterns from *All Around the Buttercup, Rocky Mountain,* and *Tideo.*
2. Write motives of *Rocky Mountain, Hot Cross Buns,* and *Mama Buy Me a Chiney Doll* on the board. The students must decide which pattern fits which song.
3. Put the solfège steps on the board. The instructor points to various notes and the students sing with hand signs. This activity is a preparation for sight reading.
4. Read *Frog in the Meadow* from staff notation and identify the song.
5. Read *Closet Key* with staff notation using first and second endings.
6. Aurally and visually identify *re* in *mi—re—do, so—mi—re—do,* and *la—so—mi—re—do* patterns.
7. Aurally identify *re* in *so—re* and *re—so* patterns and read the intervals in staff notation.
8. Read *Matarile* and play it on an instrument.

Figure 8.51 *Matarile*

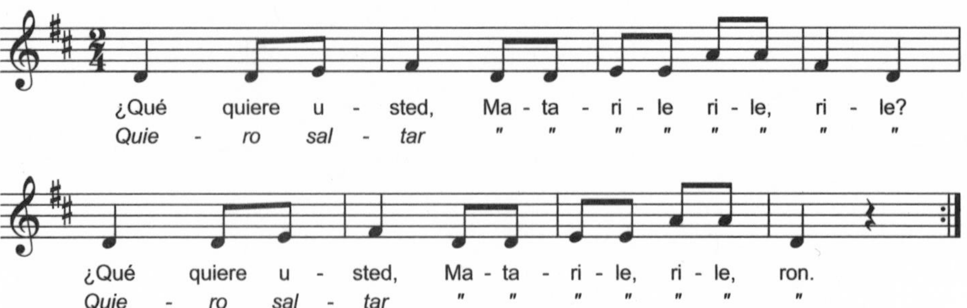

Writing

1. The students sing *All Around the Buttercup* with text and write the rhythm and solfège syllables on the board.
2. The students sing *Rocky Mountain* with text; students write the fourth phrase with staff notation. Different staff position may be incorporated into the writing activity.
3. Play four-beat patterns on the xylophone or bells.

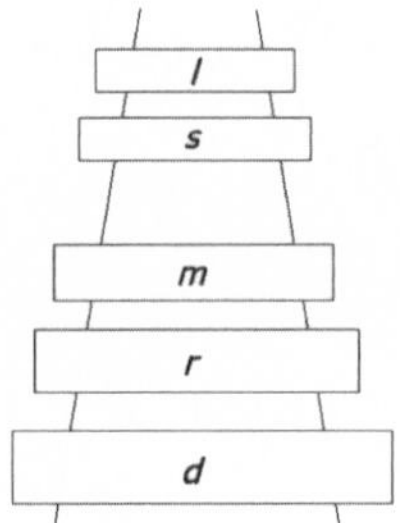

Figure 8.52 Four-beat pattern on the xylophone

Improvisation

1. Put a twelve-beat rhythm on the board and ask a student to improvise an additional four beats. Write the improvised phrase on the board. This type of activity combines improvisation, reading, and writing.
2. Question and answer rhythmic conversations can continue as a chain around the class using *mi—re—do; so—mi—re—do* and *la—so—mi—re—do.*

Listening

mi–re–do listening examples

"Hot Cross Buns" from *Six Songs on Mother Goose* by Donald Draganski, sung by Anita Rieder on Albany Records. This composition uses the text of "Hot Cross Buns" but uses a completely different melody from the traditional one.

"Carillon" from *L' Arlésienne Suite* No. 1 by Georges Bizet

la–so–mi–re–do listening example
"Who's That Tapping at the Door?" from the album *American Folks Songs for Children* sung by Mike and Peggy Seeger

Sight-Singing Materials

Houlahan, Mícheál, and Philip Tacka. *Sound Thinking: Music for Sight-Singing and Ear Training.* New York: Boosey & Hawkes, 1991. Vol. 1, pp. 33–56.

Teaching Strategy for the Trichord *mi—re—do* as One Motif

This strategy is used for when you want to teach *mi-re-do* as one unit. It is basically the same as teaching *re* with some slight modifications.

Table 8.11 Teaching strategy for the trichord *mi–re–do*

Element	Concept	Syllables	Theory	Focus Song	Additional Songs
Trichord *mi–re–do*	Three pitches that move by step	*mi–re–do*	Pentatonic trichord *mi–re–do*	*Hot Cross Buns*	*Bow Wow Wow; All Around the Buttercup; Rocky Mountain; Ida Red; Button You Must Wander*

Cognitive Phase: Preparation

Stage One: Developing Kinesthetic Awareness

This is the same as stage one for teaching *re.*

Figure 8.53 Visual representation of *Hot Cross Buns*

Stage Two: Developing Aural Awareness

Sing the target phrase, (phrase one of *Hot Cross Buns*) before asking each question. Review kinesthetic awareness activities. The teacher and the students sing phrase one of *Hot Cross Buns* on "loo."

Teacher: "Andy, how many beats did we keep?"
Student: "Four."

The teacher and the students sing phrase one of *Hot Cross Buns* on "loo."

Teacher: "Andy, how many different pitches did we sing?"
Student: "Three."
Teacher: "Andy, describe the three pitches."
Student: "They move down."
Teacher: "Andy, do our three pitches move in steps or skips?"
Student: "Steps."

Stage Three: Developing Visual Awareness

Same as stage three for teaching *re.*

Associative Phase: Presentation

Stage One: Label the Sound

1. Quickly review kinesthetic, aural, and visual awareness.
2. Teacher: "We call these three pitches that move in steps *mi—re—do.* Show the hand signs.
3. Sing "*mi—re—do*" with hand signs.
4. The teacher sings phrase one of *Hot Cross Buns* with solfège syllables and hand signs and the students echo.

Perform the above activity with at least eight individual students.

Stage Two: Present the Notation

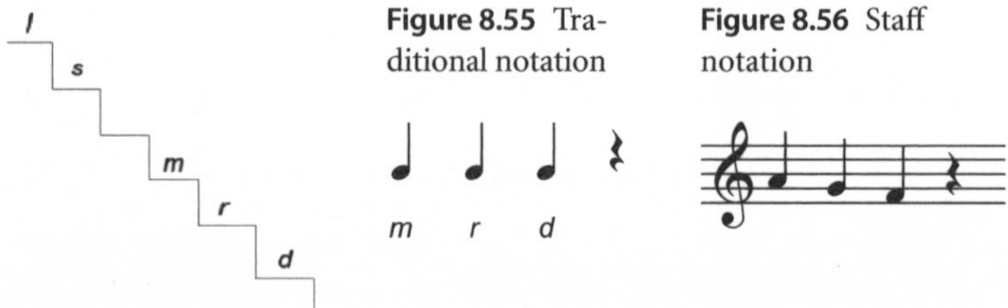

Figure 8.54 Steps are used to name new solfege syllables

Figure 8.55 Traditional notation

Figure 8.56 Staff notation

Assimilative Phase: Practice

Same as for teaching *re.*

Teaching Strategy for Sixteenth Notes

Table 8.12 Teaching strategy for sixteenth notes

Element	Concept	Syllables	Theory	Focus Song	Additional Songs
Four sixteenth notes	Four sounds on a beat	*ta ka di mi*		*Paw Paw Patch*	*Dinah, Dance Josey; Old Brass Wagon, Tideo; Kookaburra*

Cognitive Phase: Preparation

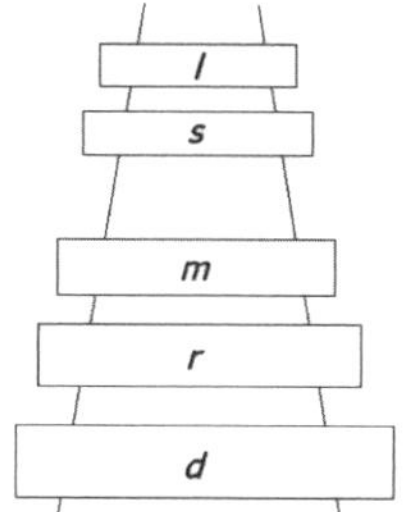

Figure 8.57

Stage One: Developing Kinesthetic Awareness

1. Sing *Paw Paw Patch* and keep the beat.
2. Sing and clap the rhythm.
3. Sing and point to a representation of phrase 1.

Figure 8.58 Representation of phrase 1

4. Sing *Paw Paw Patch,* walk the beat, and clap the rhythm.
5. Two students perform beat and rhythm on rhythm instruments.

Stage Two: Developing Aural Awareness

Review kinesthetic awareness. The teacher and students sing phrase one and keep the beat before asking each question. Sing the target phrase on "loo."

Teacher: "Andy, how many beats did we keep?"
Student: "Four."
Teacher: "Andy, which beat has the most sounds?"
Student: "Beat three."
Teacher: "How many sounds are on beat 3?"
Student: "Four sounds."
Teacher: "If beat three has four sounds, how many sounds are on each of the other beats?"
Student: "Two sounds."
Teacher: "Sing the phrase with rhythm syllables, keep the beat but sing our four sounds on beat three with *loo.*"

Stage Three: Developing Visual Awareness

Assess kinesthetic and aural awareness by allowing the class to perform several of the kinesthetic and aural awareness activities.

1. The instructor sings the target phrase with a neutral syllable and asks the students to create a visual representation of the target phrase. The students may use manipulatives.

   Teacher: "Pick up what you need to re-create what you heard" or "Draw what you heard." The teacher assesses the students' level of understanding.

2. The students share their representations with each other.
3. The instructor invites one student to the board to share his or her representation with the class. If necessary, corrections to the representation can be made by reviewing the aural awareness questions.
4. The students sing the first phrase of *Paw Paw Patch* with a neutral syllable and point to their representation.

Associative Phase: Presentation

Stage One: Label the Sound

1. Briefly review the kinesthetic, aural, and visual awareness activities.
2. Teacher: "When we hear four sounds on a beat we call it 'ta ka di mi.'"
3. The teacher and students sing the whole song with rhythm syllables and clap the rhythm.
4. The teacher echo sings individual phrases with at least eight individual students.

Stage Two: Present the Notation

1. We can use four sixteenth notes to represent four sounds on a beat. A sixteenth note has a note head, a stem and two flags. Four sixteenth notes have a double beam.
2. Our first phrase of *Paw Paw Patch* is shown in figure 8.59.

Figure 8.59 First phrase of *Paw Paw Patch*

3. We can read this rhythm pattern using our rhythm syllables.
4. The teacher sings rhythm syllables while pointing to the heartbeats. The students echo sing using rhythm syllables while pointing to the heartbeats.
5. Stick notation is an easy way to write rhythms. Our first phrase of *Paw Paw Patch* is shown in figure 8.60.

Figure 8.60 Stick notation for first phrase of *Paw Paw Patch*

Assimilative Phase: Practice

Stage One: Initial Practice

1. Review the aural awareness stage and connect the sound to rhythm syllables of the focus pattern (this may include other known songs).
2. Review the visual awareness activities and associate standard notation with the visual (this may include other known songs).
3. Transform the target pattern into related four-beat patterns found in the student's song material.

Stage Two: Practice

Reading

1. Echo sing on rhythm syllables and write using traditional rhythm notation.
   a. *Tideo,* phrases 4 and 6
   b. *Old Brass Wagon,* phrases 1–3
   c. *Dance Josey,* phrases 1–3
   d. *Are You Sleeping,* phrase 3
2. Read the above phrases and perform them on instruments.
3. Match the name of the song with a rhythm written on the board.
4. Perform a rhythmic composition that uses sixteenth notes in canon.

Writing

Practice error recognition. Change the rhythm from one song into another song. The instructor may put a sixteen-beat pattern on the board but claps a different pattern. The students identify where the discrepancies occur and write the correction.

Write rhythmic patterns from memory or when dictated by the teacher.

Improvisation

1. Improvise rhythm patterns of four- or eight-beats either by clapping, using rhythm instruments, or clapping and saying rhythm syllables.
2. Improvise question and answer motives using known rhythm or melodic patterns.
3. Improvise rhythms in a chain around the classroom.
4. Improvise rhythm patterns to specific forms for example.

   AAAB
   ABAB
   AAvBBv (Av stands for a variation of A can also be shown with A1)
   ABAC

Listening

"Solfègetto" for piano by Carl Philip Emanuel Bach
"Solfèggetto" by Carl Philip Emannuel Bach sung by The Swingle Singers from the album *Anyone for Mozart, Bach, Handel, Vivaldi?* Philips recording
"Solfèggetto" by Carl Philip Emannuel Bach, performed by Vernizzi Jazz Quartet and Corrado Giuffredi, Arts Crossing, 2006

"Prelude in C Minor" from Book 1 of the *Well-Tempered Clavier* by Johann Sebastian Bach

"Andante" (Variation 3) from Symphony No. 94 by Joseph Haydn

Figure 8.61 Rhythm of variation 3

Rondo "Alla Turca" for piano by Wolfgang Amadeus Mozart

Figure 8.62 Rhythm of theme 1, Rondo "Alla Turca" by W. A. Mozart

Figure 8.63 Rhythm of theme 1, Rondo "Alla Turca" by W. A. Mozart, part 2

"The Paw Paw Patch" from *Folksongs and Bluegrass for Children*, performed by Phil Rosenthal, Rounderkids, 2000

Sight-Singing Materials

Houlahan, Mícheál, and Philip Tacka. *Sound Thinking: Music for Sight-Singing and Ear Training.* New York: Boosey & Hawkes, 1991. Vol. 1, pp. 57–70.

Assessment

Read the rhythm of Paw Paw Patch with rhythm syllables. Read Dinah with Rhythm syllables and solfège syllables.

Teaching Strategy for a Major Pentatonic Scale

Table 8.13 Teaching strategy for a major pentatonic scale

Element	Concept	Syllables	Theory	Focus Song	Additional Songs
Major pentatonic scale	Five pitches *do-re-mi-so-la* with a skip between *mi* and *so*. Ends on *do*	*do pentatonic scale*	Scale	*Rocky Mountain*	*Cut the Cake; Knock the Cymbals; Button You Must Wander*

Cognitive Phase: Preparation

Stage One: Developing Kinesthetic Awareness

1. Sing the fourth phrase of *Rocky Mountain* and point to a representation of the melodic contour at the board.
2. Sing *Rocky Mountain* and show the melodic contour of the fourth phrase.

Figure 8.64 Melodic contour of phrase 4 of *Rocky Mountain*

3. Sing *Rocky Mountain* with rhythm syllables while showing the melodic contour.

Stage Two: Developing Aural Awareness

Review the kinesthetic awareness activities with the focus song *Rocky Mountain.* Sing the last phrase while keeping the beat before asking each question. Determine the lowest and highest notes.

Teacher: "Andy, sing the lowest note of the phrase."
Student: "*do*"
Teacher: "Andy, sing the highest note of the phrase."
Student: "*la*"

Determine the solfège syllables from the lowest to the highest pitch.

Teacher: "Andy, on which beats do we sing the lowest pitch *do?*"
Student: "Beat one and seven."

The teacher sings the last four beats on "loo."

Teacher: "Andy, sing that with solfège syllables and hand signs."
Student: "*mi—mi—re—re—do.*"

The teacher sings the five different pitches in the song on "loo" *do–re–mi–so–la.*

> Teacher: "Andy, sing those five pitches with solfège and hand signs from the lowest to the highest pitch."
> Student: "*do–re–mi–so–la.*"

The teacher and students sing the five pitches with solfège syllables and hand signs. The teacher invites several students to echo the pattern with solfège syllables and hand signs.

Stage Three: Developing Visual Awareness

Assess kinesthetic and aural awareness by allowing the class to perform several of the kinesthetic and aural awareness activities.

1. The instructor sings the target phrase with a neutral syllable and asks the students to create a visual representation of the melody of the target phrase. Students may use manipulatives.

   Teacher: "Pick up what you need to re-create what you heard" or "Draw what you heard." The teacher assesses the students' level of understanding.
2. The students share their representations with each other.
3. The instructor invites one student to the board to share his or her representation with the class. If necessary, corrections to the representation can be made by reviewing the aural awareness questions.
4. The students sing the fourth phrase of *Rocky Mountain* with a neutral syllable and point to their representation.
5. The students identify the rhythm of phrase four.
6. The students identify the solfège syllables used in this phrase.

Associative Phase: Presentation

Stage One: Label the Sound

1. Review the kinesthetic, aural awareness, and visual awareness activities with the focus song *Rocky Mountain.*
2. The teacher and students sing the five pitches of phrase four of *Rocky Mountain* and label as the notes of the *do* pentatonic scale. This can also be termed a "major pentatonic scale" because it has five different pitches with a skip between *mi* and *so,* and "*major* pentatonic" because the lowest note is *do* and the piece of music ends on *do.* We can refer to this note as the tonic note of the major pentatonic scale.
3. The teacher sings the major pentatonic scale from low to high. The students echo.
4. The teacher sings the major pentatonic scale from high to low. The students echo.

Stage Two: Present the Notation

Present the pattern for the *do* pentatonic scale on the tone ladder or musical steps. The major pentatonic scale on the steps is shown in figure 8.65. Identify all steps and skips.

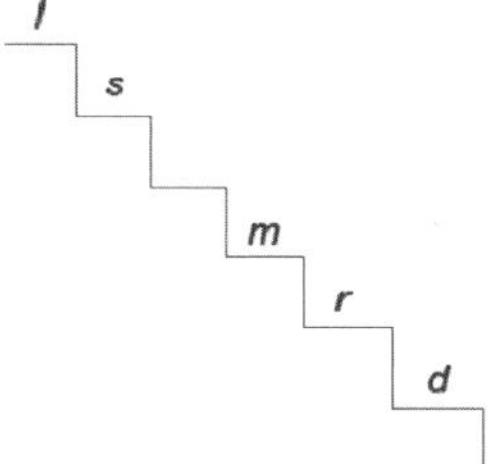

Figure 8.65 Major pentatonic scale on the steps

Present the pattern for the *do* pentatonic scale on the staff and identify the steps and skips (depending on student level, identify steps as seconds and skips as thirds).

Figure 8.66 Major pentatonic scale on the staff

The major pentatonic scale may be practiced in other keys.

Assimilative Phase: Practice

Stage One: Initial Practice

1. Review the aural awareness stage and connect the sound to rhythm syllables of the focus pattern (this may include other known songs).
2. Review the visual awareness activities and associate standard notation with the visual (this may include other known songs).
3. Transform the target pattern into related four-beat patterns found in the student's song material.

Stage Two: Practice

Reading

1. Read *Rocky Mountain* in stick notation and staff notation. Read the range of notes from lowest to highest.
2. Read *Knock the Cymbals* with first and second endings and identify the range of notes from lowest to highest.
3. Read and play the range of all known pentatonic songs on the xylophone or bells.
4. Divide the class into two parts; the instructor shows different hand signs from the right and left hand; the students read.

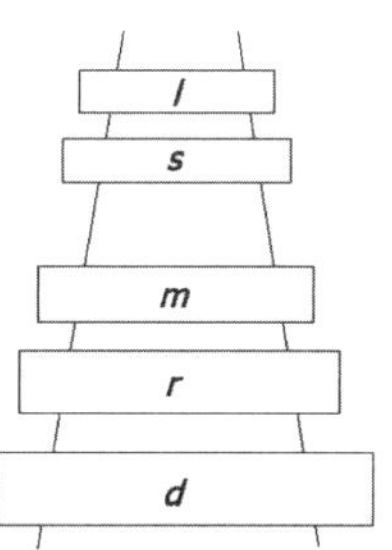

Figure 8.67 Pentatonic range on the xylophone

Writing

1. Write *Rocky Mountain* in stick notation and staff notation. Write the range of notes from lowest to highest and highest to lowest.
2. Read and/or write well-known melodic patterns from hand signs, stick notation, or staff notation. Write the letter names of the notes on the staff.
3. Use examples from the repertoire to read, write, and improvise: *Rocky Mountain, Great Big House, Wall Flowers, Mama Buy Me a Chiney Doll.*
4. Write melodic patterns found in song repertoire from memory or when dictated by the teacher using stick or staff notation.
5. Expand reading and writing of melodic patterns from four to eight to sixteen beats.
6. Sight-sing melodic phrases and songs with solfège syllables.
7. Aurally identify solfège syllables from known motifs and write them in staff notation.

Improvisation

1. The teacher sings a question phrase in solfège syllables using the *do* pentatonic scale, the students echo an answer phrase in solfège syllables.
2. Improvise short musical motives (*la—so—mi—re—do*) using hand signs, hand staff, or body signs.
3. Improvise *la—so—mi—re—do* melodies to simple four- to eight-beat rhythms using the voice or a barred instrument.
4. Improvise a new melody to one measure or more of a well-known song.
5. Create a melodic ostinato as an accompaniment to known songs.

Teaching Absolute Letter Names

After five notes of the major pentatonic scale (*do, re, mi, so, la*) are introduced, the teacher should begin to teach absolute letter names. Before reaching this point, the students should be able to transpose solfège syllables to the keys of C, F, and G *do* positions. The preparation period for teaching absolute letter names requires considerable concentration on the part of the students. The students must understand the idea of transposing. For example, students should be able to modulate through the use of hand signs. This is accomplished as follows:

1. The teacher leads the students as they sing in solfège syllables and shows hand signs with the right hand.
2. At an arbitrary point in the singing, the teacher stops on a particular solfège syllable and changes that hand sign to another hand sign with the left hand. From this point the teacher leads the singing in another key (transposition).

For example:

C = *do* right hand *do re mi so la so mi re do re mi so la*

G = *do* left hand *do re mi so la so mi do*

This type of activity needs quite a bit of practice. The teacher should use familiar melodic turns and patterns that may be taken from song material that is being used in the classroom.

The instructor can introduce the keyboard and show how the notes are labeled. The recorder, xylophone, or bells may also be used.

Working in different "*do*" positions must precede the conscious learning of absolute letter names. This is accomplished through singing, modulating, and writing. Just before the presentation of letter names, the teacher must concentrate on one "*do*" area. It is best to present at least three notes at a time. The teacher should work in the key of G.

1. Sing *Hot Cross Buns* in G = *do.*
2. Write the tone set on the board for *do–re–mi.*
3. Introduce the treble clef and the note G.
4. Introduce A from the tuning fork.
5. Introduce the note B and identify the notes as G A B.
6. Sing *Hot Cross Buns* with hand signs and letter names in the key of G.
7. Transpose to the key of F and then the key of C using solfège syllables and letter names.
8. Students should be taught how to play the notes C D E, F G A, and G AB on the keyboard and how all of these notes can be sung with the same solfège.

The following sequence may be used when teaching the recorder.

1. G A B = *do–re–mi*
2. A G E = *la–so–mi*
3. F G A = *do–re–mi*
4. G A B D = *do–re–mi–so*
5. F G A C = *do–re–mi–so*
6. G A B D E = *do–re–mi–so–la*
7. F G A C D = *do–re–mi–so–la*

Ultimately, the range of playing should be from middle C to E' (10th).

The use of these ten notes is enough to secure all the pentatonic scales in the keys of C, F, and G.

Listening

"Largo" from Symphony No. 9 by Antonin Dvorak; "Going Home" sung by Kathleen Battle in her recording *So Many Stars* is based on this theme.

"Mexican Dance" from the *Billy the Kid Suite* by Aaron Copland uses the folk tune "Good Bye Old Paint." This is a pentatonic melody.

Mikrokosmos Vol. 3, No. 78, by Belá Bartók

Sight-Singing Materials

Houlahan, Mícheál, and Philip Tacka. *Sound Thinking: Music for Sight-Singing and Ear Training.* New York: Boosey & Hawkes, 1991. Vol. 1, pp. 33–56.

Assessment

Students sing the last phrase of *Rocky Mountain* with solfège syllables and letter names from the staff when do = F, do = G and do = C.

Teaching Strategy for Four-Beat Meter

Table 8.14 Teaching strategy for four-beat meter

Element	Concept	Syllables	Theory	Focus Song	Additional Songs
$\frac{4}{4}$ time signature	A pattern of four beats, one strong and three weak beats within a measure		Bar lines; measures; double bar lines; time signature	*Are You Sleeping*	*Knock the Cymbals; Button You Must Wander*

Cognitive Phase: Preparation

Stage One: Developing Kinesthetic Awareness

1. Sing *Are You Sleeping* and keep the beat.
2. Sing *Are You Sleeping.* Clap the rhythm syllables
3. Sing *Are You Sleeping* with an ostinato *clap pat pat pat.*
4. The students point to a representation of strong and weak beats in phrase one.

● ○ ○ ○ ● ○ ○ ○

Figure 8.68 Strong and weak beats in phrase one

Stage Two: Developing Aural Awareness

Review kinesthetic awareness activities. The teacher and students sing phrase one and keep the beat.

Teacher: "Andy, how many beats did we keep?"
Student: "Eight."
Teacher: "Andy, Do all the beats feel the same?"
Student: "Some are stronger."
Teacher: "Andy, which beats are stronger?"
Student: "One and five."
Teacher: "If beats one and five are strong, all the other beats are ____."
Student: "Weak."
Teacher: "Let's sing and show with our motions our strong and weak beats."

Stage Three: Developing Visual Awareness

Assess kinesthetic and aural awareness by allowing the class to perform several of the kinesthetic and aural awareness activities.

1. The instructor sings the target phrase with a neutral syllable and asks students to create a visual representation of the melody of the target phrase. Students may use manipulatives.

   Teacher: "Pick up what you need to re-create what you heard" or "Draw what you heard." The teacher assesses the students' level of understanding.

2. The students share their representations with each other.
3. The instructor invites one student to the board to share his or her representation with the class. If necessary, corrections to the representation can be made by reviewing the aural awareness questions.
4. The students sing the first phrase of *Are You Sleeping* with a neutral syllable and point to their representation.
5. Identify the rhythm syllables.
6. Identify the solfège syllables for phrase one.

Associative Phase: Presentation

Briefly review the kinesthetic, aural, and visual awareness activities.

Stage One: Label the Sound

In music, we call the strong beats accents. We can show accents by conducting. Sing *Are You Sleeping* and conduct.

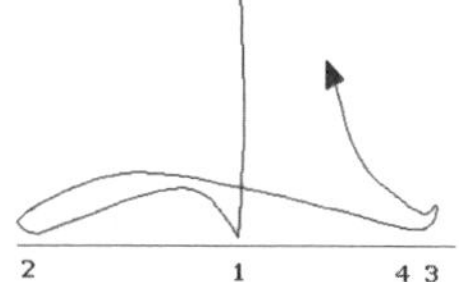

Figure 8.69 Conduct *Are You Sleeping*

Stage Two: Present the Notation

Teacher: "Just as we do in $\frac{2}{4}$ time, we put a bar line before each strong beat."
Teacher: "At the end we draw a double bar line."
Teacher: "Andy, how many beats are between the bar lines?"
Student: "Four beats."
Teacher: "Erase the first bar line and put in a $\frac{4}{4}$; this is called a time signature."
Teacher: "At the beginning, we write the number of beats in each 'measure'. A measure is the distance between 2 bar lines."

Figure 8.70 Rhythmic pattern in $\frac{4}{4}$ meter (**C** is another way of writing a $\frac{4}{4}$ time signature)

Teacher: "At the end we draw a double bar line."
The students add bar lines to the visual on the board.
Teacher: "When we had two beats in each measure, what number did we put at the beginning?"
Student: "Two."

Teacher: "How many beats do we have in each measure now?"
Student: "Four."
Teacher: "There are four beats in each measure. So, we put the number 4 in the time signature. The first beat in each measure is strong, and beats 2, 3, and 4 in each measure are weak."

Assimilative Phase: Practice

Stage One: Initial Practice

1. Review the aural awareness stage and connect the sound to rhythm syllables of the focus pattern (this may include other known songs).
2. Review the visual awareness activities and associate standard notation with the visual (this may include other known songs).
3. Transform the rhythm of *Are You Sleeping* into *Knock the Cymbals.*

Stage Two: Practice

Reading

1. Read *Knock the Cymbals* from stick notation without barlines on the board. Select individual students to sing while the other students put strong beats on their imaginary tambourines or play on real instruments (for example, louder instrumentation on the first beat and softer instrumentation on beats two, three, and four).
2. Read *Duerme pronto* and play it on an instrument.

Figure 8.71 *Duerme pronto*

Writing

1. After reading the rhythm of *Are You Sleeping* on the board:

   Teacher: "Andy, circle the strong beats."
   Teacher: "Andy please put in the barlines."

2. After reading the rhythm of *Button You Must Wander* on the board:

   Teacher: "Andy, circle the strong beats."
   Teacher: "Andy, please draw in the barlines."

3. The teacher claps a four-beat rhythm and students place magnets on the board to show each beat.

4. The students put the rhythm on the board one phrase at a time, and then add bar lines.
5. The teacher changes the rhythm from *Button You Must Wander* two beats at a time until the entire song is changed to *Are You Sleeping.* The students should perform the new rhythm with rhythm syllables after each change.
6. After a rhythmic improvisation exercise:

   Teacher: "Andy, come and write your rhythm of the first phrase on the board."

7. Complete the missing measures of a known song such as *Button You Must Wander* or *Are You Sleeping.*
8. Formulate a worksheet where students have to add stems to notes and barlines to complete a selected song.
9. Write *Duerme pronto* from memory.

Improvisation

1. Chant rhythm syllables and clap the rhythm of *Knock the Cymbals.* Improvise a new rhythm to the form of this song.

Listening

"March" from *The Love for Three Oranges* by Sergei Prokofiev
"Tortoises" from *The Carnival of the Animals* by Camille Saint-Saëns

Sight-Reading

Houlahan, Mícheál, and Philip Tacka. *Sound Thinking: Music for Sight-Singing and Ear Training.* New York: Boosey & Hawkes, 1991. Vol. 1. Select examples in 4/4 meter.

Assesment

Sing *Are you Sleeping* and conduct.

Focus Songs for Grade Two

Focus Song for Introducing the Tonic Note of the Major Pentatonic Scale *do*

Figure 8.72 *Bow Wow Wow*

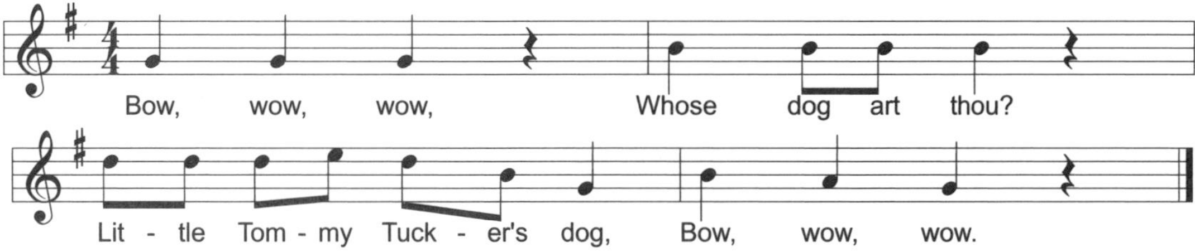

Focus Song for Half Note

Figure 8.73 *Here Comes a Bluebird*

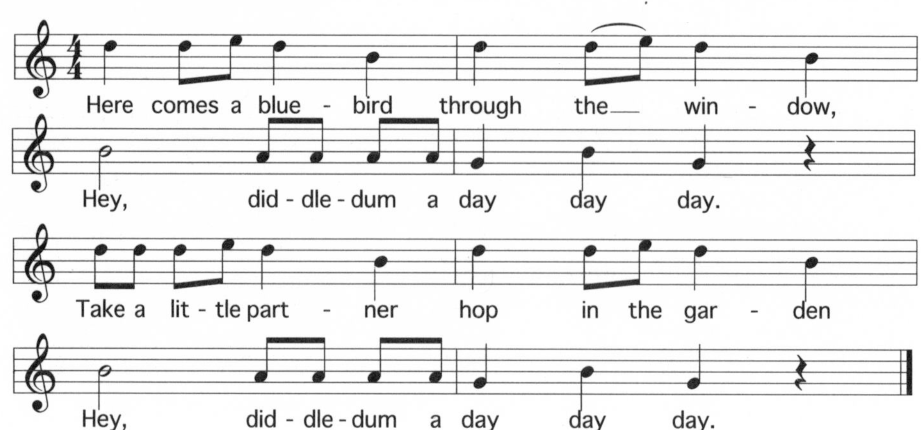

Focus Song for Introducing the Second Degree of the Major Pentatonic Scale *re*

Figure 8.74 *Hot Cross Buns*

Focus Song for Introducing the Sixteenth Notes

Figure 8.75 *Paw Paw Patch*

Focus Song for the Major Pentatonic Scale

Figure 8.76 *Rocky Mountain*

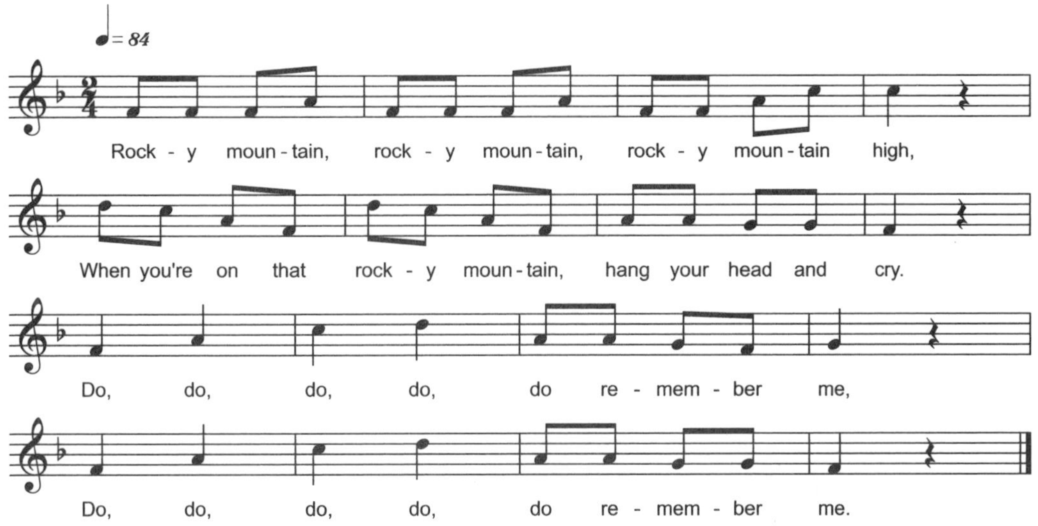

Focus Song for Four-Beat Meter

Figure 8.77 *Are You Sleeping*

Grade Three Teaching Strategies

In third grade we deal with seven musical concepts. We alternate between rhythmic concepts and melodic concepts throughout the year.

1. Teaching strategy for an eighth note followed by two sixteenth notes
2. Teaching strategy for *low la* (*la,*)
3. Teaching strategy for two sixteenth notes followed by an eighth note
4. Teaching strategy for *low so* (*so,*)
5. Teaching strategy for internal upbeat
6. Teaching strategy for *high do* (*do'*)
7. Teaching strategy for external upbeat

Teaching Strategy for an Eighth Note Followed by Two Sixteenth Notes

Table 8.15 Teaching strategy for an eighth note followed by two sixteenth notes

Element	Concept	Syllables	Theory	Focus Song	Additional Songs
An eighth note followed by two sixteenth notes	Three sounds on a beat. Not evenly distributed; the first sound being longer than the last two sounds	*ta di mi*	Sixteenth note subdivisions of the beat	*Fed My Horse*	*Ida Red; Mama Buy Me a Chiney Doll; How Many Miles to Babylon*

Cognitive Phase: Preparation

Stage One: Developing Kinesthetic Awareness

1. Sing *Fed My Horse* and pat the beat for the target phrase.
2. Sing *Fed My Horse* and clap the rhythm for the target phrase.
3. Sing *Fed My Horse* and point to a representation of the rhythm on the board (fig. 8.78).

—— ——   ——— —— —— ——— ———   ————

Figure 8.78 Representation of the rhythm of *Fed My Horse*

4. Sing *Fed My Horse.* Step the beat and clap the rhythm.
5. Have two students perform the song on rhythm instruments. One performs the beat and one performs the rhythm.

Stage Two: Developing Aural Awareness

Assess the kinesthetic activities with the focus song. The teacher and students sing the target phrase using a neutral syllable while keeping the beat before asking each question.

Determine the number of beats in the phrase.

Teacher: "Andy, how many beats did we tap?"
Student: "Four."

Determine the number of sounds on each beat.

Teacher: "Andy, which beat had one sound?"
Student: "Beat four."
Teacher: "Andy, which beats have two sounds?"
Student: "Beats one and three."
Teacher: "Andy, how many sounds did we sing on beat two?"
Student: "Three sounds."
Teacher: "Describe these sounds with long and short."
Student: "The first sound was long and the last two sounds were two short."

Sing the first two phrases of *Fed My Horse* as follows:

ta di *long short short* *ta di* *ta*

Stage Three: Developing Visual Awareness

Assess kinesthetic and aural awareness by allowing the class to perform several of the kinesthetic and aural awareness activities.

1. The instructor hums the target phrase and asks the students to create a visual representation of the target phrase. The students may use manipulatives.

   Teacher: "Pick up what you need to re-create what you heard" or "Draw what you heard." The teacher assesses the students' level of understanding.
2. The students share their representations with each other.
3. The instructor invites one student to the board to share his or her representation with the class. If necessary, corrections to the representation can be made by reviewing the aural awareness questions.
4. The students sing the first phrase of *Fed My Horse* with a neutral syllable and point to their representation.
5. The students determine the solfège syllables for the first four phrases of *Fed My Horse.*

Associative Phase: Presentation

Assess the kinesthetic and aural awareness and visual awareness activities with the focus song *Fed My Horse.*

Stage One: Label the Sound

1. Teacher: "We call three sounds on a beat where the first is long and the second and third are short *ta di-mi.*"
2. The teacher sings the target phrase of *Fed My Horse* with rhythm syllables. The students echo with rhythm syllables while clapping the rhythm.

ta di *ta di mi* *ta di* *ta*

3. The teacher sings the target phrase of *Fed My Horse* with text. The students echo with rhythm syllables while clapping the rhythm.
4. The teacher echo sings with at least eight individual students.

Stage Two: Present the Notation

We can use an eighth note followed by two sixteenth notes to represent three sounds unevenly spaced on a beat.

1. Our first phrase of *Fed My Horse* in traditional rhythm notation is shown in figure 8.79.

Figure 8.79 First phrase of *Fed My Horse* in traditional rhythm notation

2. Our first phrase of *Fed My Horse* in stick notation is shown in figure 8.80.

Figure 8.80 First phrase of *Fed My Horse* in stick notation

3. We can read this rhythm pattern using rhythm syllables.

Assimilative Phase: Practice

Stage One: Initial Practice

1. Review the aural awareness stage and connect the sound to rhythm syllables of the focus pattern (this may include other known songs).
2. Review the visual awareness activities (students create a visual using a pencil and paper to create a presentation) and associate standard notation with the visual (this may include other known songs).
3. Transform the target pattern into four-beat patterns found in the student's song material.

Stage Two: Practice

Reading

1. Read phrases one and two of *Fed My Horse* in traditional rhythm notation.
2. Perform this rhythm on rhythm instruments or barred instruments.
3. Read the rhythm of *San Serafín del monte* with rhythm syllables and play the rhythm on an instrument.

Figure 8.81 *San Serafín del monte*

Writing

1. Write phrases one and two of *Fed My Horse* in stick notation.
2. Write phrase one of *Ida Red* and perform it on rhythm instruments.

Improvisation

The teacher claps a question phrase using rhythm syllables. The students clap an answer phrase using rhythm syllables. Use songs *Ida Red* (phrase 1), *Mama Buy Me a Chiney Doll,* and *Sailing O'er the Ocean.*

Listening

"Russian Dance" from the *Nutcracker Suite*, Op. 71a, by Peter Illyich Tchaikovsky
Rosamunde ballet music by Franz Schubert

Figure 8.82 *Rosamunde* rhythmic themes

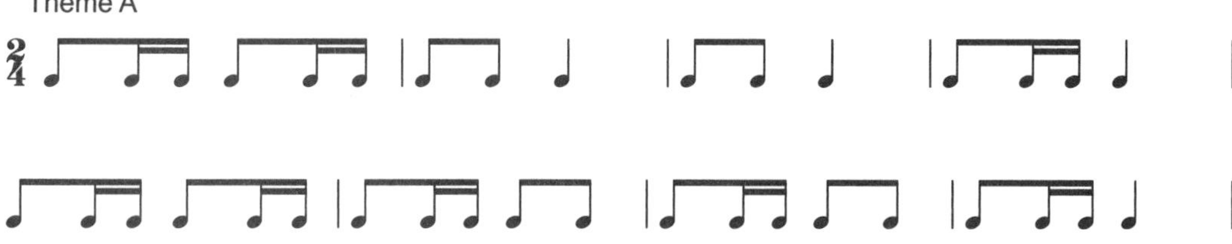

continued

Figure 8.82 *Continued*

Sight-Singing Materials

Houlahan, Mícheál, and Philip Tacka. *Sound Thinking: Music for Sight-Singing and Ear Training.* New York: Boosey & Hawkes, 1991. Vol. 1, pp. 57–70.

Assessment

Reading the focus song, *Fed My Horse* with rhythm syllables.

Teaching Strategy for low *la,*

Table 8.16 Teaching strategy for *la,*

Element	Concept	Syllables	Theory	Focus Song	Additional Songs
low *la*	A pitch a skip lower than *do*	la,	*la,* may function as a tonic note; extended pentatonic scale	*Phoebe in Her Petticoat*	*Jim Along Josie; Old Mr. Rabbit, Poor Little Kitty Cat*

Cognitive Phase: Preparation

Stage One: Developing Kinesthetic Awareness

1. Sing *Phoebe in Her Petticoat* and show the melodic contour for the target phrase, phrase one.
2. Sing *Phoebe in Her Petticoat* and point to a representation of the melodic contour at the board.

Figure 8.83 Representation of the melodic contour of *Phoebe in Her Petticoat*

3. Sing *Phoebe in Her Petticoat* with rhythm syllables while showing the melodic contour.

Stage Two: Developing Aural Awareness

Review the kinesthetic activities with the focus song *Phoebe in Her Petticoat.* Sing while keeping the beat before asking each question.

Determine the number of beats.

Teacher: "Andy, how many beats did we tap?"
Student: "Four."

Determine which beat has the lowest pitch.

Teacher: "Andy, which beat had the lowest pitch?"
Student: "Beat four."

or

Teacher: "Andy, what can you tell me about the pitch on beat four?"
Student: "It's low".
Teacher: "Let's sing the phrase on 'loo' but sing 'low' for the lowest note."

Determine the solfège of known elements and sing "low" for the new note.

Teacher: "Let's sing the first four pitches."
The teacher sings the first four pitches on "loo." The students echo.
Teacher: "Andy, sing that with solfège syllables and hand signs."
Student: "*mi—re—do—do.*"

The teacher sings the first phrase on "loo"; the students echo in solfège and hand signs (*mi—re—do—do—re—do—low*). The students should point down with their hands when they sing the "low" note.

Teacher: "Andy, is our new sound a step or a skip from *do?*"
Student: "A skip."

Stage Three: Developing Visual Awareness

Assess kinesthetic and aural awareness by allowing the class to perform several of the kinesthetic and aural awareness activities.

1. The instructor hums the target phrase and asks the students to create a visual representation of the target phrase. The students may use manipulatives.

   Teacher: "Pick up what you need to re-create what you heard" or "Draw what you heard." The teacher assesses the students' level of understanding.

2. The students share their representations with each other.

3. The instructor invites one student to the board to share his or her representation with the class. If necessary, corrections to the representation can be made by reviewing the aural awareness questions.
4. Students sing the first phrase of *Phoebe in Her Petticoat* with a neutral syllable and point to their representation.
5. Identify the rhythm for the first phrase of *Phoebe in Her Petticoat.*

Associative Phase: Presentation

Review the kinesthetic, aural awareness and visual awareness activities with the focus song *Phoebe in her Petticoat.*

Stage One: Label the Sound

Figure 8.84 Hand sign for *la,*

1. Teacher: "When we hear a pitch a skip below *do,* we call it *low la.*" The instructor shows the hand sign.
2. The teacher sings phrase one of *Phoebe in her Petticoat* with solfège syllables and students echo sing (*mi—re—do—do—re—do—la,*).
3. The teacher echo sings with at least eight individual students.

Stage Two: Present the Notation

Present the position of *la,* on the steps.

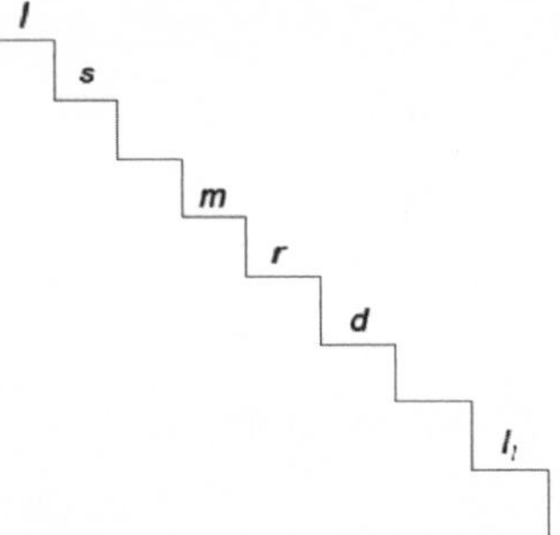

Figure 8.85 The position of *la,* on the steps

Present the target phrase of *Phoebe in Her Petticoat* in stick notation. Identify *do—la,* as being a skip of a third.

Figure 8.86 Target phrase of *Phoebe in her Petticoat* in stick notation

Present the target phrase of *Phoebe in her Petticoat* in staff notation and present the rule of placement.

Figure 8.87 Target phrase of *Phoebe in her Petticoat* in staff notation

Assimilative Phase: Practice

Stage One: Initial Practice

1. Review the aural presentation and connect the sound to rhythm syllables.
2. Review the visual presentation and associate standard notation with the visual.
3. Transform the target pattern into basic four-beat patterns found in the student's song material.

Stage Two: Practice

Reading

1. Read *Phoebe in Her Petticoat* in stick notation and staff notation.
2. Change several measures of the song *Phoebe in Her Petticoat* so that it becomes a reading exercise.
3. Read *Who Killed Cock Robin* from stick or staff notation.

Writing

1. Write *Jim Along Josie* in stick notation and staff notation.
2. Write *Phoebe in Her Petticoat* in stick and staff notation.
3. Have students play the first phrase of *Phoebe in Her Petticoat* from staff notation.
4. Once the patterns from the songs are written, have the students perform them on a xylophone.

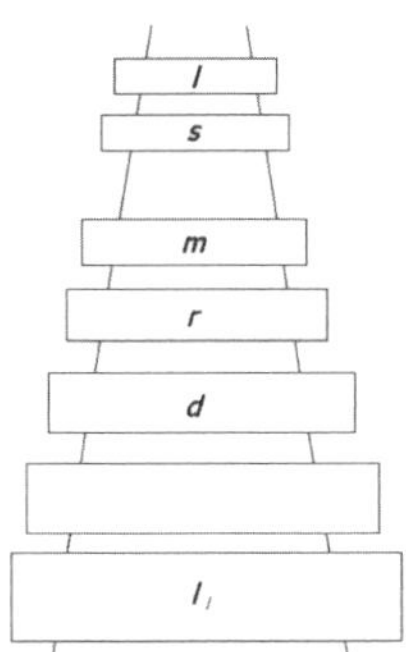

Figure 8.88 Pattern from *Jim Along Josie* and *Phoebe in Her Petticoat* on the xylophone

Improvisation

1. The teacher sings a question phrase in solfège syllables using the *la* pentatonic scale. The students echo an answer phrase in solfège syllables.
2. Improvise short musical motives (*la—so—mi—re—do—la,*) using hand signs, hand staff, or body signs.
3. Improvise *la—so—mi—re—do—la,* melodies to simple four- to eight-beat rhythms using the voice or a barred instrument.
4. Improvise a new melody to one measure or more of a well-known song.
5. Create a melodic ostinato as an accompaniment to known songs.

Listening

Mikrokosmos, Vol. 5, No. 127, by Belá Bartók
Mikrokosmos, Vol. 3, No. 78, by Belá Bartók
"An Evening in the Village" from *Hungarian Sketches* by Belá Bartók
"Pentatonic Tune" from *For Children* Vol. 1, No. 29, by Belá Bartók
"Wayfaring Stranger," recording by Anonymous 4 on the album *Gloryland*
"Nuages" from *Nocturnes* by Claude Debussy

Sight-Singing Materials

Houlahan, Mícheál, and Philip Tacka. *Sound Thinking: Music for Sight-Singing and Ear Training.* New York: Boosey & Hawkes, 1991. Vol. 1, pp. 71–76.

Asssessment

Sing the focus song, *Phoebe in Her Petticoat* with solfège syllables and handsigns. Write *Phoebe in Her Petticoat* on the staff where do is F, C or G.

Teaching Strategy for Two Sixteenth Notes Followed by an Eighth Note

Table 8.17 Teaching strategy for two sixteenth notes followed by an eighth note

Element	Concept	Syllables	Theory	Focus Song	Additional Songs
Two sixteenth notes followed by an eighth note	Three sounds on a beat. Not evenly distributed; the first two sounds being shorter than the last sound	*ta ka di*		*Hogs in the Cornfield* phrase two	*Over the River; (Charlie); Hop Old Squirrel; Jim Along Josie, Skipping Rope Song, Sailing O'er the Ocean*

Cognitive Phase: Preparation

Stage One: Developing Kinesthetic Awareness

1. Sing phrase two of *Hogs in the Cornfield* and pat the beat.
2. Sing phrase two of *Hogs in the Cornfield* and clap the rhythm.
3. Sing phrase two of *Hogs in the Cornfield* and point to a representation of the rhythm.

—— —— —— —— ———— ——— —— —— —— ——

Figure 8.89 Representation of phrase two of *Hogs in the Cornfield*

4. Sing phrase two of *Hogs in the Cornfield* while stepping the beat and clapping the rhythm.
5. Split the class into two groups. Group one pats the beat for phrase two and group two claps the rhythm. Switch.
6. Sing *Hogs in the Cornfield.* Step the beat and clap the text.

Stage Two: Developing Aural Awareness

Review the kinesthetic activities with the focus song. Sing phrase two of *Hogs in the Cornfield* using a neutral syllable while keeping the beat before asking each question.

Determine the number of beats in the phrase.

Teacher: "Andy, how many beats did we keep?"
Student: "Four."

Determine the number of sounds on each beat.

Teacher: "Andy, which beats had two sounds?"
Student: "Beats one and four."
Teacher: "Andy, how many sounds did we sing on beat three?"
Student: "Three sounds."
Teacher: "Andy, describe these sounds using the words long and short."
Student: "Long short short."
Teacher: "Andy, what rhythm syllables would we use?"
Student: "*ta di-mi.*"

Determine the number of sounds on the target beat.

Teacher: "Andy, how many sounds did we sing on beat two?"
Student: "Three sounds."
Teacher: "Andy, describe these sounds with the words long and short?"
Student: "Short short long."

Sing the phrase as follows:

ta di *short short long* *ta di mi* *ta di*

Stage Three: Developing Visual Awareness

Assess kinesthetic and aural awareness by allowing the class to perform several of the kinesthetic and aural awareness activities.

1. The instructor hums the target phrase with a neutral syllable and asks the students to create a visual representation of the target phrase. The students may use manipulatives.

   Teacher: "Pick up what you need to re-create what you heard" or "Draw what you heard." The teacher assesses the students' level of understanding.

2. The students share their representations with each other.
3. The instructor invites one student to the board to share his or her representation with the class. If necessary, corrections to the representation can be made by reviewing the aural awareness questions.
4. The students sing the first phrase of *Hogs in the Cornfield* with a neutral syllable and point to their representation.

Associative Phase: Presentation

Briefly review kinesthetic, aural, and visual awareness.

Stage One: Label the Sound

Teacher: "When we hear three sounds on a beat where the first two sounds are short and the third sound is long we call it *ta ka di.*"

The teacher sings the target phrase of *Hogs in the Cornfield* on "loo." The students echo with rhythm syllables while clapping the rhythm.

Stage Two: Present the Notation

We can use two sixteenth notes followed by an eighth note to represent three sounds on the beat; two short and one long. We can read this pattern using our rhythm syllables.

Figure 8.90 Pattern using rhythm syllables

We can write this pattern using stick notation.

Figure 8.91 Pattern using stick notation

Assimilative Phase: Practice

Stage One: Initial Practice

1. Review the aural presentation and connect the sound to rhythm syllables.
2. Review the visual presentation and associate the standard notation with the visual.
3. Transform the target pattern into basic four-beat patterns found in the student's song material.

Stage Two: Practice

Reading

Read phrases one and two of *Hogs in the Cornfield* in traditional rhythm notation. Read *Hop Old Squirrel* in traditional rhythm notation. Change the rhythm of *Hop Old Squirrel* into *Hogs in the Cornfield.* Have two students perform the beat and rhythm of *Hogs in the Cornfield, Hop Old Squirrel,* or *Over the River (Charlie).*

Writing

Write the text of *Hogs in the Cornfield.* Have the students write the correct rhythm notation above the text. Write phrases one and two of *Hogs in the Cornfield* in stick notation. Write the rhythm of *Ida Red* and perform it on rhythm instruments.

Improvisation

The teacher claps a question phrase in rhythm names. The students clap an answer phrase in rhythm names. Use the following songs for improvisation with this concept: *Ida Red* (phrase 2), *Jim Along Josie* (entire song), or *Early in the Morning* (entire song).

Sight-Singing Materials

Houlahan, Mícheál, and Philip Tacka. *Sound Thinking: Music for Sight-Singing and Ear Training.* New York: Boosey & Hawkes, 1991. Vol. 1, pp. 57–70.

Assessment

Sing *Hogs in the Cornfield* with rhythm syllables.

Teaching Strategy for *so,*

Table 8.18 Teaching strategy for *so,*

Element	Concept	Syllables	Theory	Focus Song	Additional Songs
Low *so*	A pitch a step lower than *la,*	Low *so* (*so,*)		*Dance Josey target phrase two*	*Sailing O'er the Ocean; Turn the Glasses Over; Old MacDonald; Walk Along John*

Cognitive Phase: Preparation

Stage One: Developing Kinesthetic Awareness

1. Sing phrase two of *Dance Josey* and point to a representation of the melodic contour at the board.
2. Sing phrase two of *Dance Josey* and show the melodic contour.

Figure 8.92 Melodic contour of phrase two of *Dance Josey*

3. Sing *Dance Josey* with rhythm syllables while showing the melodic contour of phrase two.

Stage Two: Developing Aural Awareness

Review the kinesthetic activities with the focus song *Dance Josey.* Sing while keeping the beat before asking each question. Determine the solfège for phrase 1 (*do-do-do-do-do-do—mi—re—mi—so*).

Determine the number of beats.

Teacher: "Andy, how many beats did we tap?"
Student: "Four."

Determine which beat has the lowest pitches.

Teacher: "Andy, which beat had the lowest pitches?"
Student: "Beat four."
Teacher: "Let's sing the phrase on 'loo.'"

Determine the number of different pitches on beat four.

Teacher: "Andy, how many different pitches did we sing on beat four?"
Student: "Two."

Determine the solfège of known elements and sing "low" for the new note.

Teacher: "Andy, since this phrase starts like phrase one, sing it with solfège and hand signs but sing 'low' for the last note.
Student: "*do-do-do-do-do-do-do—re—do—la,—low.*"
Teacher: "Andy, is our new sound a step or a skip lower than *la?*"
Student:" Step lower than *low la.*"

Stage Three: Developing Visual Awareness

Assess kinesthetic and aural awareness by allowing the class to perform several of the kinesthetic and aural awareness activities.

1. The instructor hums the target phrase and asks the students to create a visual representation of the melody of the target phrase. The students may use manipulatives.

   Teacher: "Pick up what you need to re-create what you heard" or "Draw what you heard." The teacher assesses the students' level of understanding.
2. The students share their representations with each other.
3. The instructor invites one student to the board to share his or her representation with the class. If necessary, corrections to the representation can be made by reviewing the aural awareness questions.
4. The students sing the first phrase of *Dance Josey* with a neutral syllable and point to their representation.
5. Determine the solfège syllables for phrases one, three, and four of *Dance Josey.*

Associative Phase: Presentation

Stage One: Label the Sound

Review the kinesthetic and aural awareness and visual awareness activities with the focus song *Dance Josey.* We call the pitch that is a step lower than *low la low so.* The teacher shows the hand sign, same as *so,* but lower in comparison to *low la.* The students immediately echo sing phrase two of *Dance Josey* with solfge syllables and hand signs.
The teacher sings phrase two of *Dance Josey* with text. The students echo with solfège and hand signs.

Figure 8.93 Hand sign for *so,*

Stage Two: Present the Notation

Present the position of *so,* on the musical steps.

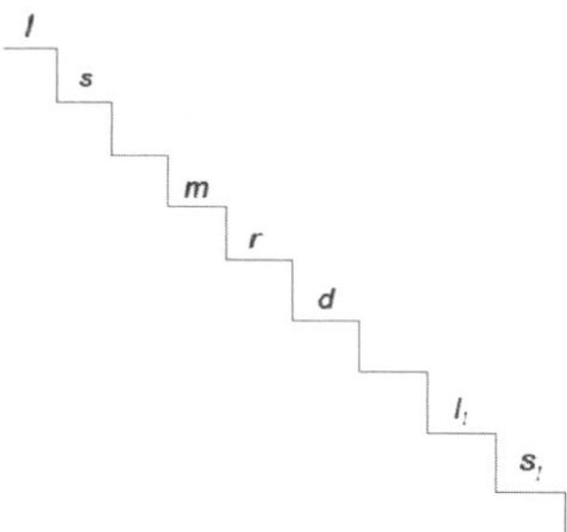

Figure 8.94 Position of *so,* on the steps

Present the target phrase of *Dance Josey* in traditional rhythm notation.

Figure 8.95 Target phrase of *Dance Josey* in traditional rhythm notation

Present the target phrase of *Dance Josey* in staff notation and present the rule of placement.

Figure 8.96 Target phrase of *Dance Josey* in staff notation

Assimilative Phase: Practice

Stage One: Initial Practice

1. Review the aural presentation and connect the sound to solfège syllables.
2. Review the visual presentation and associate the standard notation with the visual.
3. Transform the target pattern into basic four-beat patterns found in the student's song material.
4. Identify patterns ending on *do* or *la,* or *so,*.

Stage Two: Practice

Reading

1. Read *Dance Josey* in stick notation and staff notation.
2. Use the solfège steps. The instructor points to the notes of *Turn the Glasses Over* and the students sing with solfège and hand signs.
3. Read *Over the River to Charlie* from traditional rhythm notation with solfège syllables.
4. Read the following patterns *so,-la,-do; do–la,-so,; so,-do; so,-re; so,-mi.*

Writing

1. Write *Dance Josey* in stick notation and staff notation.
2. Provide the students with the staff notation of *Dance Josey* and/or *Over the River to Charlie* and have the students circle all steps and put a box around all skips in the melody.

After writing phrase two of *Dance Josey* in staff notation, have the students play the phrase on the xylophone or bells.

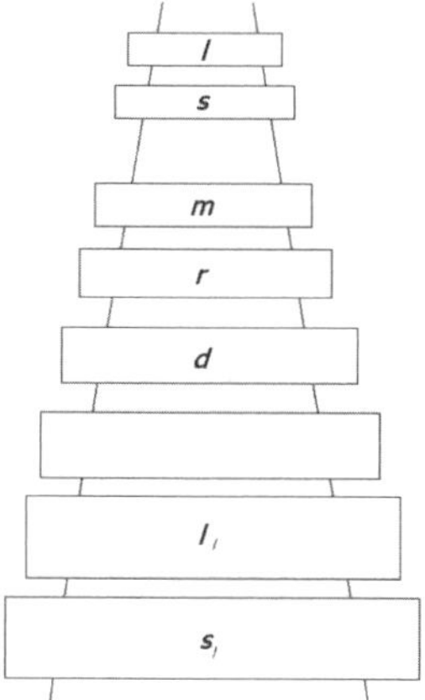

Figure 8.97 Phrase two of *Dance Josey,* xylophone

3. Write *Sailing O'er the Ocean* in stick and staff notation.
4. Aurally identify *so,* in *so,-la,-do* and *do–la,-so,* motifs. Write these patterns in stick or staff notation.
5. Sing a melodic ostinato to accompany a pentatonic song. After learning the ostinato, write it in stick or staff notation. Consider figure 8.98.

Figure 8.98 Sample melodic ostinato

Improvisation

1. The teacher sings a question phrase in solfège syllables. The students echo an answer phrase in solfège syllables.
2. Examples to read and write and use for improvisation activities include: *Dance Josey* (entire song), *Turn the Glasses Over* (entire song), *Sailing O'er the Ocean* (entire song), *Old Mac Donald* (entire song).
3. Improvise patterns using *so, - la, - do* and *do–la, - so,* patterns.
4. Improvise questions and answers using *la–so–mi–re–do–la, - so,*.

Listening

"Promenade" from *Pictures at an Exhibition* by Modest Moussorgsky

Sight-Singing Materials

Houlahan, Mícheál, and Philip Tacka. *Sound Thinking: Music for Sight-Singing and Ear Training.* New York: Boosey & Hawkes, 1991. Vol. 1, pp. 77–86.

Assessment

Sing *Dance Josey* with solfège and handsigns.
Read *Dance Josey* from notation.

Teaching Strategy for Internal Upbeats

Table 8.19 Teaching strategy for internal upbeats

Element	Concept	Syllables	Theory	Focus Song	Additional Songs
Single eighth note	A sound that occurs before a strong beat	Dependant on where the sound falls in relation to the beat	Internal upbeat or pick up	*Old Mr. Rabbit*	*Down Came a Lady; Bye Baby Bunting; Do, Do Pity My Case*

Cognitive Phase: Preparation

Stage One: Developing Kinesthetic Awareness

1. Sing *Old Mister Rabbit* and draw the phrases in the air.
2. Sing *Old Mister Rabbit* and pat the beat.
3. Sing *Old Mister Rabbit* and clap the ostinato "clap, pat, pat, pat."
4. Sing *Old Mister Rabbit* and point to the beat of the four phrases as shown in figure 8.99.

Figure 8.99 Beat of *Old Mister Rabbit*

5. Sing *Old Mister Rabbit* and point to a representation of the phrases and rhythm on the board. It is important that the students sing each phrase clearly.

Figure 8.100 Representation of phrases and rhythm of *Old Mister Rabbit*

Stage Two: Developing Aural Awareness

Review the kinesthetic activities with the focus song. Sing and pat the beat before asking each question. Determine the downbeat of each phrase.

Teacher: "Andy, on which word do we clap our hands in phrase one?"
Student: "Old."
Teacher: "Andy, on which word do we clap our hands in phrase two?"
Student: "Got."
Teacher: "Andy, on which word do we clap our hands in phrase three?"
Student: "Jumping."
Teacher: "Andy, on which word do we clap our hands on phrase four?"
Student: "Eating."
Teacher: "Andy, what's the first word in phrase two?
Student: "You've."
Teacher: "Andy, what's the first word in phrase three?"
Student: "Of."
Teacher: "Andy, what's the first word in phrase four?"
Student: "And."
Teacher: "Andy, do these words fall on the strong part of the beat or the weak part of the beat?"
Student: "Weak beats."

Stage Three: Developing Visual Awareness

Assess kinesthetic and aural awareness by allowing the class to perform several of the kinesthetic and aural awareness activities.

The instructor asks the students to create a visual representation showing where the phrases begin and end in the song.

1. The students share their representations with each other.
2. The instructor invites one student to the board to share his or her representation with the class. If necessary, corrections to the representation can be made by reviewing the aural awareness questions.
3. The students sing the first phrase of *Old Mr. Rabbit* with a neutral syllable and point to their representation.

♥	♥	♥	♥
Old	Mister	Rab-	bit
♥	♥	♥	♥
got			
♥	♥	♥	♥
jumping			
♥	♥	♥	♥
eating			

Figure 8.101 *Old Mister Rabbit*

Teacher: "Where should we write the word 'you've,' 'of,' and 'and'?" The point is to let the students discover this.

Figure 8.102 *Old Mister Rabbit*

Associative Phase: Presentation

Review the kinesthetic and aural awareness and visual awareness activities with the focus song *Old Mister Rabbit.*

Stage One: Label the Sound

1. Teacher: "A lead-in note that precedes the strong beat of a phrase is called an upbeat or a pick up. Because the upbeat occurs within the piece of music and not at the beginning, we call it an internal upbeat."
2. The teacher sings *Old Mr. Rabbit* with rhythm syllables and the students echo sing with rhythm syllables and conducts.
3. The teacher echo sings with at least eight individual students.

	ta ♥	*ta-di* ♥	*ta* ♥	*ta-* ♥
di	*ta-di* ♥	*ta-di* ♥	*ta* ♥	*ta-* ♥
di	*ta-di* ♥	*ta-di* ♥	*ta* ♥	*ta-* ♥
di	*ta-di* ♥	*ta-di* ♥	*ta-di* ♥	*rest* ♥

Figure 8.103 *Old Mister Rabbit* in rhythm syllables

Stage Two: Present the Notation

Teacher: "When we split the beamed eighth notes, it looks like this (separate eighth notes with flags) and sometimes we take a breath between beats. We can call the single eighth note an *upbeat* or a *pick up note.*"

Write the rhythm syllables and the traditional notation. Read with rhythm syllables.

Figure 8.104 Rhythm syllables and traditional notation

Assimilative Phase: Practice

Stage One: Initial Practice

1. Review the aural presentation and connect the sound to rhythm syllables.
2. Review the visual presentation and associate the standard notation with the visual.
3. Transform the rhythm of *Old Mr. Rabbit* into *Down Came a Lady.* Guide the students to discover that there is an upbeat to the final phrase.

Stage Two: Practice

Reading

1. Read traditional notation. Have the rhythm of *Old Mister Rabbit* on the board in traditional rhythm notation; the students point and read with rhythm syllables.
2. Change one song to another: read rhythmic notation of *Old Mister Rabbit* and *Do Do Pity My Case* in stick notation, with the internal upbeat.

Writing

Students write *Down Came a Lady* in stick notation and in four phrases; they must write the final phrase with the internal upbeat (i.e., place a single eighth note at the beginning of the final phrase).

Improvisation

1. Begin by having the students chant and clap the rhythm of any well-known song. Write these rhythms on the board and ask them to create internal up beats.
2. Guide the students to improvise the final phrase of a known song with the stipulation that the final phrase begins with an upbeat. For example, a student could perform the rhythm of *Rocky Mountain* or *Great Big House in New Orleans,* but at the final phrase, he or she must improvise a new phrase that begins with an upbeat.

Sight-Singing Materials

Houlahan, Mícheál, and Philip Tacka. *Sound Thinking: Music for Sight-Singing and Ear Training.* New York: Boosey & Hawkes, 1991. Vol. 1, pp. 87–109.

Teaching Strategy for High *do'*

Table 8.20 Teaching strategy for *do'*

Element	Concept	Syllables	Theory	Focus Song	Additional Songs
High *do*	A pitch a skip higher than *la*	*do'*	Octave; extended pentatonic scale	*Hogs in the Cornfield* target phrase 2	*Liza Jane; I've Lost the Farmer's Dairy Key; Riding in a Buggy; Tideo*

Cognitive Phase: Preparation

Stage One: Developing Kinesthetic Awareness

1. Sing *Hogs in the Cornfield* and show the melodic contour for the target phrase, phrase two.
2. Sing *Hogs in the Cornfield* and point to a representation of the melodic contour at the board.

Figure 8.105 Melodic contour of *Hogs in the Cornfield*

3. Sing *Hogs in the Cornfield* with rhythm syllables while showing the melodic contour.

Stage Two: Developing Aural Awareness

Review the kinesthetic activities with the focus song *Hogs in the Cornfield.* Sing phrase two on "loo" while keeping the beat before asking each question.

Determine the number of beats.

Teacher: "Andy, how many beats did we keep?"
Student: "Four."

Determine which beat has the lowest pitch and highest pitch.

Teacher: "Andy, which beat has the highest pitch?"
Student: "Beat one."
Teacher: "Andy, which beat has the lowest pitch?"
Student: "Beat four."

Determine the solfège syllable of the final pitch

Teacher: "Andy, what is the solfège syllable of the final pitch?"
Student: "*do.*"

Determine the solfège syllables for beats three and four.

Teacher: "Class, let's sing the pitches on beats three and four."
Teacher: "Andy, sing that in solfège."
Student: "*mi—re-re—do—do.*"

Determine the solfège syllables for beats one and two.

Teacher: "Let's sing the first three pitches."
Teacher: "Andy, how would you describe the first pitch?"
Student: "High"
Teacher: "Andy, sing 'high' for the first note and sing the rest in solfège."
Student: "*High—la-so—so—so.*"
Teacher: "Andy, sing the whole phrase with hand signs."
Student: "*High—la-so—so—so—mi—re-re-do—do.*"

Stage Three: Developing Visual Awareness

Assess kinesthetic and aural awareness by allowing the class to perform several of the kinesthetic and aural awareness activities.

1. The instructor hums the target phrase and asks the students to create a visual representation of the melody of the target phrase. The students may use manipulatives.

   Teacher: "Pick up what you need to re-create what you heard" or "Draw what you heard." The teacher assesses the students' level of understanding.

2. Students share their representations with each other.
3. The instructor invites one student to the board to share his or her representation with the class. If necessary, corrections to the representation can be made by reviewing the aural awareness questions.
4. The students sing the second phrase of *Hogs in the Cornfield* with a neutral syllable and point to their representation.
5. Determine the rhythm of the song and sing it with rhythm syllables.

Associative Phase: Presentation

Stage One: Label the Sound

Review the kinesthetic and aural awareness and visual awareness activities with the focus song *Hogs in the Cornfield.*

1. Teacher: "When we hear a sound a skip above *la* we call it *high do.*" The instructor shows the hand sign.

Figure 8.106 Hand sign for *do'*

2. The teacher sings phrase two of "*Hogs in the Cornfield,*" with solfège syllables and the students echo sing (*do'–la–so–so–so–mi–re–re–do–do*).
3. The teacher echo sings with at least eight individual students.

Stage Two: Present the Notation

Present the position of high *do* on the musical steps. Identify the interval *la–do'* as a skip of a third.

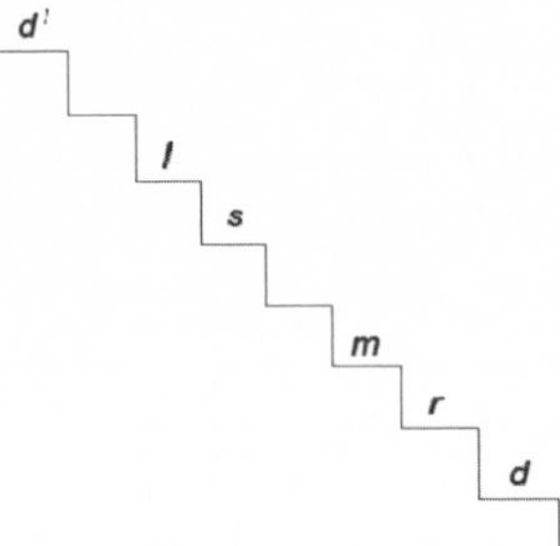

Figure 8.107 Position of *do'* on the steps

Present the target phrase of *Hogs in the Cornfield* using rhythmic notation with solfège letters.

Figure 8.108 Target phrase of *Hogs in the Cornfield* in stick notation

Present the target phrase of *Hogs in the Cornfield* in staff notation and explain the rule of placement.

Figure 8.109 Target phrase of *Hogs in the Cornfield* in staff notation

Assimilative Phase: Practice

Stage One: Initial Practice

1. Review the aural presentation and connect the sound to solfège syllables.
2. Review the visual presentation and associate the standard notation with the visual.
3. Transform the target pattern into basic four-beat patterns found in the last phrase of *The Farmer's Dairy Key.*

Stage Two: Practice

Reading

1. Read *Hogs in the Cornfield* in stick notation and staff notation.
2. Read *The Farmer's Dairy Key* in stick notation and staff notation.
3. Read and play the two phrases of *Hogs in the Cornfield* on the xylophone or tone bells.

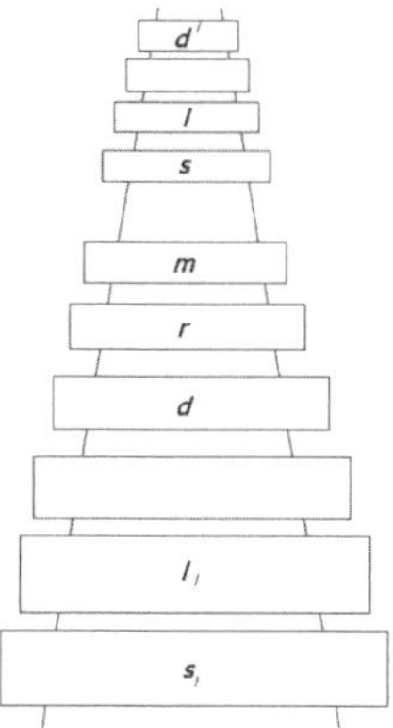

Figure 8.110 *Hogs in the Cornfield* on the xylophone

Writing

1. Write either the last phrase of *Hogs in the Cornfield* or the last phrase of *The Farmer's Dairy Key* in stick notation and/or staff notation.

Improvisation

1. The teacher sings a question phrase in solfège syllables. The students echo an answer phrase in solfège syllables. At first, do this with *Hogs in the Cornfield* and *The Farmer's Dairy Key.*
2. Gradually change the question phrase to a different phrase. The students may still echo the last phrase of *Hogs in the Cornfield* or *The Farmer's Dairy Key.*
3. Once the students are comfortable echoing an answer phrase beginning on *do'* ask them to improvise a different phrase that begins on *do'* or uses *do'.*

Listening

"The Empress of Pagodas" from *Mother Goose Suite* by Maurice Ravel

Sight-Reading Materials

Houlahan, Mícheál, and Philip Tacka. *Sound Thinking: Music for Sight-Singing and Ear Training.* New York: Boosey & Hawkes, 1991. Vol. 2, pp. 15–24.

Teaching Strategy for External Upbeats

Table 8.21 Teaching strategy for external upbeats

Element	Concept	Syllables	Theory	Focus Song	Additional Songs
An eighth note external upbeat	A sound that precedes the strong beat at the beginning of a composition	Dependent on where the external upbeat falls in relation to the beat		*The Jolly Miller*	*Above A Plain, Shoes of John, Band of Angels*

Cognitive Phase: Preparation

Stage One: Developing Kinesthetic Awareness

1. Sing *The Jolly Miller* and pat the beat.
2. Sing *The Jolly Miller* and clap the rhythm.
3. The students perform the beat by clapping the first beat of each phrase and patting the subsequent seven beats.

Figure 8.111 How to perform the beat for each phrase of *The Jolly Miller*

4. Sing *The Jolly Miller* and point to a representation of the phrases on the board.

Figure 8.112 Representation of phrases in *The Jolly Miller*

Stage Two: Developing Aural Awareness

Review the kinesthetic activities with the focus song. Sing before asking each question.

Teacher: "Andy, on what word does the first phrase begin?"
Student: "There."
Let's sing and clap . . . .

Teacher: "Andy, when do we clap the first beat of the phrase?"
Student: "When we sing 'was,' after we sing 'There.'"
Teacher: "Andy, does the word "There" fall on the strong part of the beat or the weak part of the beat?"
Student: "Weak beats."

Stage Three: Developing Visual Awareness

Assess kinesthetic and aural awareness by allowing the class to perform several of the kinesthetic and aural awareness activities. The instructor asks the students to create a visual representation showing the phrases of the focus melody. The teacher assesses the students' level of understanding.

1. The students share their representations with each other.
2. The instructor invites one student to the board to share his or her representation with the class. If necessary, corrections to the representation can be made by reviewing the aural awareness questions.
3. The students sing *The Jolly Miller* with a neutral syllable and point to their representation.

♥ ♥ ♥ ♥ ♥ ♥ ♥ ♥

There was a jol-ly mil-ler and he lived by him-self. (When the)

Figure 8.113 The beat and text underlay of the phrase in *The Jolly Miller*

Associative Phase: Presentation

Stage One: Label the Sound

Teacher: "A lead-in note that precedes the strong beat of a phrase is called an upbeat or a pick up. Because the upbeat/pick up occurs at the beginning the piece of music, we call it an external upbeat."

The teacher sings *The Jolly Miller* with rhythm syllables and the students echo sing with rhythm syllables. The teacher echo sings with at least eight individual students.

Stage Two: Present the Notation

Teacher: "Because *The Jolly Miller* begins with an upbeat, we can use a single eighth note at the beginning of the song."

Figure 8.114 *The Jolly Miller*

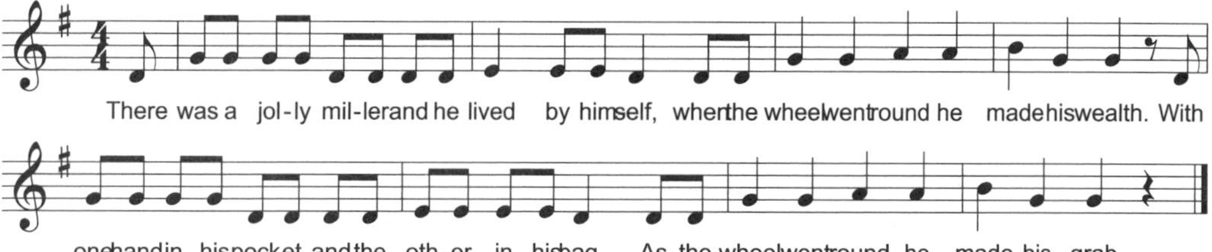

Assimilative Phase: Practice

Stage One: Initial Practice

1. Review the aural presentation and connect the sound to solfège syllables.
2. Review the visual presentation and associate the standard notation with the visual.
3. Transform the rhythm of the first phrase of *The Jolly Miller* into the first phrase of *The Shoes of John.*

Stage Two: Practice

Reading

1. Read *The Jolly Miller* in rhythmic notation, with the upbeats beginning each phrase.
2. Read *The Shoes of John* in rhythmic notation, with the upbeats beginning each phrase.
3. Read *Above the Plain* in rhythmic notation, with the upbeats beginning each phrase.

Writing

Write *The Jolly Miller* in stick notation, with the upbeats beginning each phrase. Do the same for *Above the Plain, Angel Band,* and *The Shoes of John.*

Improvisation

1. Begin with the rhythm of a song the students know well. For example, consider *Dance Josey* and *Sailing O'er the Ocean.* Guide the students to improvise the beginning phrase of the songs with the stipulation that the first phrase begins with an upbeat. For example, a student could perform the rhythm of *Dance Josey* or *Sailing O'er the Ocean* or any well-known song but he or she would have to start the rhythm of the song with an upbeat. The upbeat can be either a single quarter note, two eighth notes, or an eighth note.

Listening

Appalachian Spring by Aaron Copland. Section A of the *Shaker Hymn* begins with an upbeat.
"Bandinerie" from Suite No. 2 in b minor by Johann Sebastian Bach

Figure 8.115 "Bandinerie" from Suite No. 2 b minor by J. S. Bach

Figure 8.115 *Continued*

"Badinerie" from *Suite Dreams: The Music of Johann Sebastian Bach for Flute and Jazz Orchestra*, performed by I-Chee Lee/Union Square Group
"Sleepers Wake" Cantata No. 140 by Johann Sebastian Bach

Figure 8.116 "Sleepers Wake" Cantata No. 140 by J. S. Bach

Sight-Singing Materials

Houlahan, Mícheál, and Philip Tacka. *Sound Thinking: Music for Sight-Singing and Ear Training.* New York: Boosey & Hawkes, 1991. Vol. 1, pp. 87–109.

Focus Songs for Grade Three

Focus Song for an Eighth Note followed by Two Sixteenth Notes

Figure 8.117 *Fed My Horse* (only phrase one)

Focus Song for *low la*

Figure 8.118 *Phoebe in Her Petticoat*

Focus Song for Two Sixteenth Notes Followed by an Eighth Note

Figure 8.119 *Hogs in the Cornfield*

Focus Song for *low so*

Figure 8.120 *Dance Josey* (only phrase two)

Focus Song for Internal Upbeat

Figure 8.121 *Old Mister Rabbit*

Figure 8.121 *Continued*

Focus Song for *high do*

Figure 8.122 *Hogs in the Cornfield* (only phrase two)

Focus Song for External Upbeat

Figure 8.123 *The Jolly Miller*

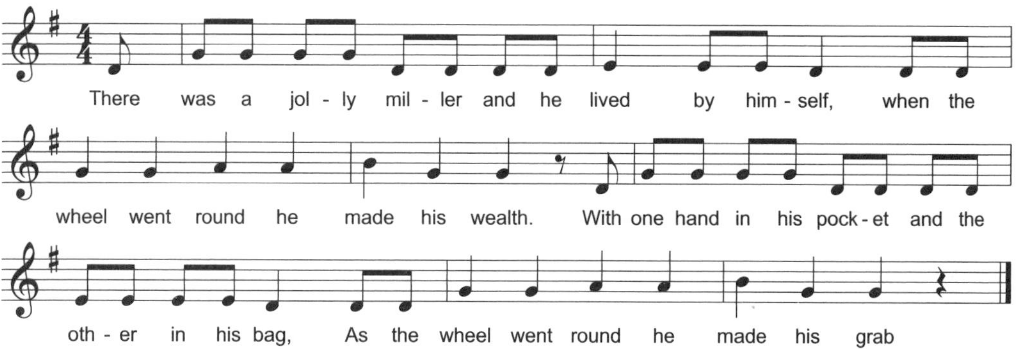

Grade Four Teaching Strategies

In fourth grade, we deal with seven musical concepts.

1. Teaching strategy for syncopation
2. Teaching strategy for *la* pentatonic scale
3. Teaching strategy for dotted quarter followed by an eighth note
4. Teaching strategy for *fa*
5. Teaching strategy for triple meter
6. Teaching strategy for low *ti* (*la* pentachord and *la* hexachord)
7. Teaching strategy for Dotted eighth note followed by a sixteenth note

Teaching Strategy for Syncopation

Table 8.22 Teaching strategy for syncopation

Element	Concept	Syllables	Theory	Focus Song	Additional Songs
Eighth notes followed by a quarter note and eighth note	Three sounds unevenly distributed over two beats	*ta di---di*	Syncopation	*Canoe Song*	*Liza Jane, Riding in a Buggy, Land of the Silver Birch, Alabama Gal, Weevily Wheat; My Good Old Man*

Cognitive Phase: Preparation

Stage One: Developing Kinesthetic Awareness

The kinesthetic procedure may be guided with non-verbal communication. The instructor guides students to:

1. Sing *Canoe Song* and perform the beat for the target phrase.
2. Sing *Canoe Song* and clap the rhythm for the target phrase.
3. Sing *Canoe Song* and point to a representation of the target phrase on the board but perform the beat for the other phrases.

Figure 8.124 Representation of the target phrase of *Canoe Song*

4. Sing the *Canoe Song.* The teacher performs the beat; the students perform the rhythm. Switch.
5. Divide the class into two groups; one performs the beat and the other the rhythm while singing. Switch.
6. Sing *Canoe Song* while stepping the beat and clapping the text.
7. Sing *Canoe Song* and conduct.

Stage Two: Developing Aural Awareness

Review the kinesthetic activities with the focus song. The teacher sings the target phrase, phrase 1, using a neutral syllable while performing the beat before asking each question.

Determine the number of beats in the phrase.

Teacher: "Andy, how many beats did you tap?"
Student: "Four."
Teacher: "Let's check."

Determine the number of sounds on each beat.

Teacher: "Andy, which beat has one sound?"
Student: "Beat four."
Teacher: "Let's check."
Teacher: "Andy, how many sounds did you hear on beat three?"
Student: "Two sounds."
Teacher: "Let's check."
Teacher: "Andy, how many sounds did you hear on beats one and two?"
Student: "Three sounds."
Teacher: "Andy, describe these three sounds."
Student: "Short, long, short."
Teacher: "Let's sing the phrase with '*short–long–short*' and our rhythm syllables for beats three and four and keep the beat and conduct the beat."
Student: "*Short–long–short–ta-di ta.*"

Stage Three: Developing Visual Awareness

Assess kinesthetic and aural awareness by allowing the class to perform several of the kinesthetic and aural awareness activities.

1. The instructor hums the target phrase and asks the students to create a visual representation of the target phrase. The students may use manipulatives.

   Teacher: "Pick up what you need to re-create what you heard" or "Draw what you heard." The teacher assesses the students' level of understanding.

2. The students share their representations with each other.
3. The instructor invites one student to the board to share his or her representation with the class. If necessary, corrections to the representation can be made by reviewing the aural awareness questions.
4. The students sing the first phrase of *Canoe Song* with a neutral syllable and point to their representation.
5. Once the students have represented the rhythm pattern they should place heartbeats under the rhythm to show the placement of the beat.
6. The students may identify the solfège of the target phrase (*mi mi re do la, la,*).

Associative Phase: Presentation

Assess the kinesthetic, aural awareness and visual awareness activities with the phrase one of the *Canoe Song.*

Stage One: Label the Sound

1. Teacher: "When we hear three uneven sounds over two beats where the first is short, the second is long, and the third is short we can label these sounds with our rhythm syllables *ta di————di.*"
2. The teacher sings the target phrase of *Canoe Song* with rhythm syllables *ta di—— di ta di ta.* The students echo sing with rhythm syllables while clapping the rhythm.

3. Individual students echo the rhythm syllables. Perform this activity with the rhythm of the entire song.
4. The teacher sings a phrase of *Canoe Song* with text. The students echo but use rhythm syllables while clapping the rhythm.
5. The teacher sings a phrase of *Canoe Song* with text. The students echo but use rhythm syllables while conducting.
6. The students sing *Canoe Song* with rhythm syllables and conduct.

Stage Two: Present the Notation

Teacher: "We can represent three sounds over two beats using the traditional notation."

Figure 8.125 Three sounds over two beats using traditional notation

The target pattern is shown in figure 8.127.

Figure 8.126 Target pattern in traditional notation

"We can read our target pattern using rhythm syllables."
"When we write our target pattern, we can use stick notation."

Figure 8.127 Target pattern in stick notation

"Sing the *Canoe Song* with rhythm syllables." Individual students sing and point to the target phrase (the A phrase) on the board as the class sings the song with rhythm syllables. Explain the concept of syncopation to students.

Assimilative Phase: Practice

Stage One: Initial Practice

Review the aural presentation of *ta di———di* in the *Canoe Song*. Review the visual presentation.

Stage Two: Practice

Transform the target phrase of *Canoe Song* into similar four-beat phrase(s) of a known song with the *ta di———di* rhythm pattern. Consider the following songs:

Come Thru 'Na Hurry
Shoo My Love
Liza Jane
Hill and Gully Rider
Riding in the Buggy
Weevily Wheat

The ostinato in figure 8.128 may be sung or played with *Come Thru 'Na Hurry, Shoo My Love, Liza Jane, Riding in a Buggy,* and *Weevily Wheat.*

Figure 8.128 Melodic ostinato

The ostinato in figure 8.129 may be sung or played with any of the above songs.

Figure 8.129 Melodic ostinato

Reading

1. Transform *Canoe Song* into *Alabama Gal.*
2. Read *Alabama Gal* in traditional rhythmic notation with rhythm syllables.
3. Read the rhythm to *Somebody's Knockin' at Your Door.* Teach the song after the students have read the rhythm.

Writing

1. Write *Shoo My Love* in stick notation.
2. Add heartbeats below the stick notation.

Improvisation

1. The teacher claps a question phrase and chants rhythm syllables. The students clap an answer phrase and chant rhythm syllables using the new rhythms.
2. The instructor writes the following songs in stick notation but leaves out four beats. The students improvise four-beat rhythms that use syncopated rhythms.
3. These songs contain syncopation: *Riding in the Buggy, Shoo My Love, Liza Jane, Alabama Gal, Come Thru 'Na Hurry, Hill and Gully Rider, Weevily Wheat.*

Listening

"Three Rondos" Movement 3 by Belá Bartók
Mikrokosmos Vol. 5, No. 122, by Belá Bartók
"Jamaican Rumba" by Arthur Benjamin from James Galway, *Dances for Flute*
"The Red Poppy," Op. 70, from *The Russian Sailors' Dance* by Reinhold Glière

Sight-Singing Materials

Houlahan, Mícheál, and Philip Tacka. *Sound Thinking: Music for Sight-Singing and Ear Training.* New York: Boosey & Hawkes, 1991. Vol. 1, pp. 87–109.

Teaching Strategy for *la* Pentatonic Scale

Table 8.23 Teaching strategy for *la* pentatonic scale

Element	Concept	Syllables	Theory	Focus Song	Additional Songs
A scale ending on low *la*	Five pitches *l, d r m s* with a skip between *la,* and *do* and a skip between *mi* and *so.* Ends on *la,*	*la pentatonic scale*	Scale	*Land of the Silver Birch*	*Canoe Song*

Cognitive Phase: Preparation

Stage One: Developing Kinesthetic Awareness

1. Sing *Land of the Silver Birch* and point to a representation of the melodic contour of the third phrase.
2. Sing *Land of the Silver Birch* and show the melodic contour of each phrase.

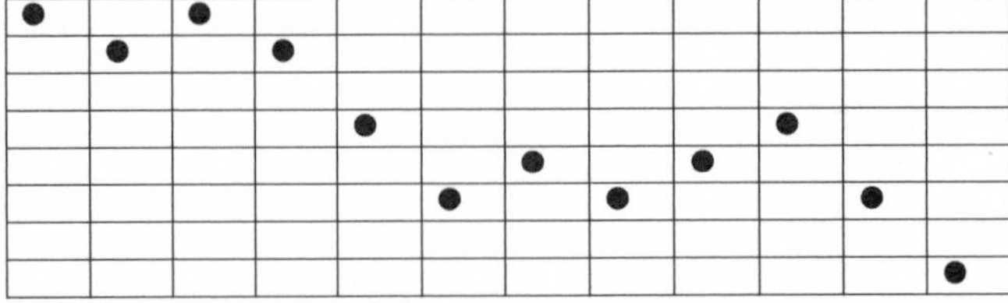

Figure 8.130 Melodic contour of phrase three of *Land of the Silver Birch*

3. Sing *Land of the Silver Birch* with rhythm syllables while showing the melodic contour.

Stage Two: Developing Aural Awareness

Review the kinesthetic activities with the focus song *Land of the Silver.* Sing on a neutral syllable while keeping the beat before asking each question. Determine the lowest and highest notes.

Teacher: "Andy, sing the lowest note of the phrase."
Student: "*la.*"
Teacher: "Andy, sing the highest note of the phrases."
Student: "*la.*"

Determine the solfège syllables from the lowest to the highest note.

Teacher: "Andy, what solfège syllable do we use for the lowest note?"
Student: "*Low la.*"
Teacher: "Andy, if the first pitch is *la* what is the next pitch?"
Student: "*So.*"

The teacher collects all the pitches in the same manner (*la-so-mi-re-do-la,*). Students sing this collection of pitches from highest note to lowest note and from lowest to highest. Next the students sing the entire song with solfège syllables and show hand signs.

Stage Three: Developing Visual Awareness

Assess kinesthetic and aural awareness by allowing the class to perform several of the kinesthetic and aural awareness activities.

1. The instructor hums the target phrase and asks the students to create a visual representation of the melody of the target phrase. The students may use manipulatives.

   Teacher: "Pick up what you need to re-create what you heard" or "Draw what you heard." The teacher assesses the students' level of understanding.
2. The students share their representations with each other.
3. The instructor invites one student to the board to share his or her representation with the class. If necessary, corrections to the representation can be made by reviewing the aural awareness questions.
4. The students sing the third phrase of *Land of the Silver Birch* with a neutral syllable and point to their representation.
5. Sing the third phrase of *Land of the Silver Birch* with rhythm syllables.

Associative Phase: Presentation

Stage One: Label the Sound

Review the kinesthetic and aural awareness and visual awareness activities with the focus song *Land of the Silver Birch.*

1. The teacher and students sing the five pitches of the "*la pentatonic* scale," from low to high. The teacher specifically names it a "*la* pentatonic scale," pentatonic because it has five different pitches with a skip between *la,* and *do* and "*la* pentatonic" because the piece of music ends on *low la.*
2. The teacher sings the *la* pentatonic scale from low to high. The students echo with hand signs.
3. The teacher sings the *la* pentatonic scale from high to low. The students echo with hand signs.
4. The students sing the whole song with hand signs.

Stage Two: Present the Notation

1. Present the pattern for the *la* pentatonic scale on the steps, stick notation, and staff.
2. Present the *la* pentatonic scale in staff notation and present the rule of placement.

Figure 8.131 *La* pentatonic scale in staff notation

Assimilative Phase: Practice

Stage One: Initial Practice

1. Review the aural awareness stage and connect the sound to solfège syllables.
2. Review the visual awareness activities and associate the standard notation with the visual.
3. Transform the target pattern in *Land of the Silver Birch* into other related patterns

Stage Two: Practice

Reading

1. Read all of *Land of the Silver Birch* in traditional rhythm notation with solfège syllables.
2. Read *Land of the Silver Birch* in staff notation.

Writing

1. Write *Land of the Silver Birch* in traditional notation and solfège syllables.
2. Write in staff notation.
3. Play phrases from *Land of the Silver Birch* on the xylophone or tone bells.

Improvisation

1. The students sing the first four beats of song on "loo" from traditional notation and solfège syllables and there are four-beat lines next to it. The teacher improvises for the last four beats on "loo."

2. The students read the first four beats again, but a student improvises on "loo"for the last four beats.
3. The students read first four beats with solfège syllables, and the teacher improvises with solfège syllables.
4. The students read first four beats with solfège syllables, and a student improvises with solfège syllables.
5. Repeat with individual students doing both parts.

Sight-Singing Materials

Houlahan, Mícheál, and Philip Tacka. *Sound Thinking: Music for Sight-Singing and Ear Training.* New York: Boosey & Hawkes, 1991. Vol. 1, pp. 71–76.

Teaching Strategy for *so* Pentatonic Scale

The *so* pentatonic teaching strategy is provided for those music instructors who want to teach *so* pentatonic.

Table 8.24 Teaching strategy for *so* pentatonic scale

Element	Concept	Syllables	Theory	Focus Song	Additional Songs
A scale ending on low *so*	Scale	*so,-la,-do-re-mi-so*		*Over the River to Charlie*	*Ridin' of a Goat*

Cognitive Phase: Preparation

Stage One: Developing Kinesthetic Awareness

1. Sing the third and fourth phrase of *Over the River to Charlie* and point to a representation of the melodic contour at the board.
2. Sing *Over the River to Charlie* and show the melodic contour of the third and fourth phrase.

Figure 8.132 Melodic contour of phrases three and four of *Over the River to Charlie*

3. Sing *Over the River to Charlie* with rhythm syllables and show the melodic contour.

Stage Two: Developing Aural Awareness

Review the kinesthetic activities with the focus song *Over the River to Charlie.* Sing while keeping the beat before asking each question. Determine the lowest and highest notes.

Teacher: "Andy, sing the lowest note of the phrases."
Student: "*so,*."
Teacher: "Andy, sing the highest note of the phrases."
Student: "*mi.*"

Determine the solfège syllables from the lowest to the highest note.

Teacher: "Andy, what solfège syllable do we use for the lowest note?"
Answer: "*Low so.*"
Teacher: "Andy, if the first pitch is *so* what is the next pitch?"
Answer: "*Low la.*"

The teacher collects all the pitches in the same manner (*so,-la,-do–re–mi*). Sing the entire song on solfège and show hand signs.

Stage Three: Developing Visual Awareness

Assess kinesthetic and aural awareness by allowing the class to perform several of the kinesthetic and aural awareness activities.

1. The instructor hums the target phrase and asks the students to create a visual representation of the melody of the target phrase. The students may use manipulatives.

   Teacher: "Pick up what you need to re-create what you heard" or "Draw what you heard." The teacher assesses the students' level of understanding.
2. The students share their representations with each other.
3. The instructor invites one student to the board to share his or her representation with the class. If necessary, corrections to the representation can be made by re-viewing the aural awareness questions.
4. The students sing the fourth phrase of *Over the River to Charlie* with a neutral syllable and point to their representation.
5. Sing the fourth phrase of *Over the River to Charlie* with rhythm syllables.

Associative Phase: Presentation

Stage One: Label the Sound

Review the kinesthetic, aural awareness and visual awareness activities with the focus song *Over the River to Charlie.*

1. The teacher and student sing the five pitches of the "*so pentatonic* scale" from low to high. The teacher specifically names it as a "*so* pentatonic scale," pentatonic because it has five different pitches with a skip between *la,* and *do* and "*so* pentatonic" because the lowest note is *so* and the piece of music ends on *low so.*
2. The teacher sings the *so* pentatonic scale from low to high; the students echo.
3. The teacher sings the *so* pentatonic scale from high to low; the students echo.

Stage Two: Present the Notation

1. Present the pattern for the *so* pentatonic scale.
2. Identify the steps and skips of the *so* pentatonic scale

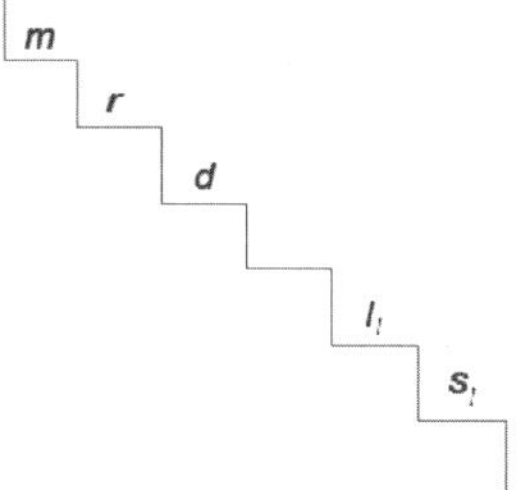

Figure 8.133 Steps and skips of *so* pentatonic scale

3. Present the *so* pentatonic scale in staff notation and present the rule of placement.

Figure 8.134 *So* pentatonic scale in staff notation

4. Present the rhythmic notation for the second phrase of *Over the River to Charlie.* Allow students to write in the solfège syllables beneath the stick notation.

Figure 8.135 Phrase two of *Over the River to Charlie* in stick notation

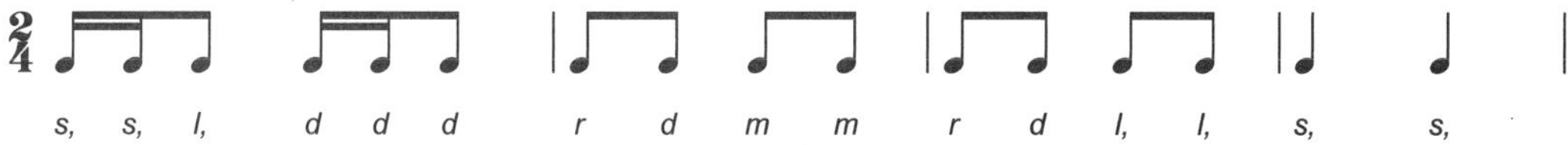

5. Present the second phrase of *Over the River to Charlie* in staff notation.

Figure 8.136 Phrase two of *Over the River to Charlie* in staff notation

Assimilative Phase: Practice

Stage One: Initial Practice

1. Review the aural awareness stage and connect the sound to solfège syllables.
2. Review the visual awareness activities and associate the standard notation with the visual.
3. Transform the target pattern in *Over the River to Charlie* to the beginning of the song *Riding of a Goat.*

Stage Two: Practice

Reading

1. Read all of *Over the River to Charlie* in traditional rhythm notation with solfège syllables.
2. Read *Over the River to Charlie* in staff notation.
3. Read phrases of *Over the River to Charlie* and *Riding of a Goat* in stick or staff notation and play them on the xylophone or tone bells.

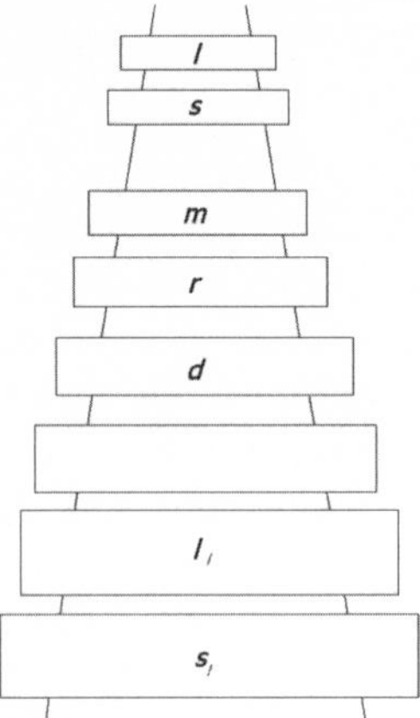

Figure 8.137 Phrases of *Over the River to Charlie* and *Riding of a Goat* on xylophone

Writing

1. Write *Over the River to Charlie* and/or *Riding of a Goat* in traditional notation and solfège syllables.
2. Write *Over the River to Charlie* and/or *Riding of a Goat* in staff notation.

Improvisation

1. The students sing the first four beats of the song on "loo" from traditional notation and solfège syllables. There are four-beat lines next to it. The teacher improvises for the last four beats on "loo."
2. The students read the first four beats again, but one student improvises on "loo" for the last four beats.
3. The students read the first four beats with solfège syllables and the teacher improvises with solfège syllables.
4. The students read the first four beats with solfège syllables and one student improvises with solfège syllables.
5. Repeat with individual students doing both parts.

Listening

"Promenade" from *Pictures at an Exhibition* by Modest Moussorgsky
"Hornpipe" from *Water Music* by George Frideric Handel (Theme A)
24 *Canons for the Black Keys No. 1* by Zoltán Kodály. Listen to a performance played by the music instructor.
Volume 2, No. 21 from *For Children* by Belá Bartók

Sight-Singing Materials

Houlahan, Mícheál, and Philip Tacka. *Sound Thinking: Music for Sight-Singing and Ear Training.* New York: Boosey & Hawkes, 1991. Vol. 1, pp. 71–76.

Teaching Strategy for a Dotted Quarter Note Followed by an Eighth Note

Table 8.25 Teaching strategy for a dotted quarter note followed by an eighth note

Element	Concept	Syllables	Theory	Focus Song	Additional Songs
Dotted quarter note followed by an eighth note	Two sounds distributed over two beats, the second sound occurring after the second beat	*ta——di*	Rule for a dot after a note	*Liza Jane*	*John Kanaka; Sweet William, Chairs to Mend; Long Road of Iron; Viva la Musica; Above the Plain*

Cognitive Phase: Preparation

Stage One: Developing Kinesthetic Awareness

1. Sing *Liza Jane* and pat the beat for the target phrase four.
2. Sing *Liza Jane* and clap the rhythm for the target phrase four.
3. Sing *Liza Jane* and point to a representation of the rhythm on the board.

Figure 8.138 Representation of the rhythm of phrase four of *Liza Jane*

4. Sing *Liza Jane* while performing the following ostinato.

Figure 8.139 Ostinato to *Liza Jane*

Stage Two: Developing Aural Awareness

Review the kinesthetic activities with the focus song. Sing the target phrase using a neutral syllable while keeping the beat before asking each question.

Determine the number of beats in the first half of phrase four.

Teacher: "Andy, how many beats did we keep?"
Student: "Four."

Determine the number of sounds on each beat.

Teacher: "Andy, which beats have one sound on them?"
Student: "Beats three and four."
Teacher: "Andy, how many sounds did we sing on beats one and two?"
Student: "Two sounds."
Teacher: "Andy, describe the two sounds on beats one and two."
Student: "The first is long, the second is short."
Teacher: "Andy, where do we sing the first sound?"
Student: "On beat one."
Teacher: "Andy, where do we sing the second sound?"
Student: "After beat two."

Stage Three: Developing Visual Awareness

Assess kinesthetic and aural awareness by allowing the class to perform several of the kinesthetic and aural awareness activities.

1. The instructor hums the target phrase with a neutral syllable and asks the students to create a visual representation of the target phrase. The students may use manipulatives.

   Teacher: "Pick up what you need to re-create what you heard" or "Draw what you heard." The teacher assesses the students' level of understanding.

2. The students share their representations with each other.
3. The instructor invites one student to the board to share his or her representation with the class. If necessary, corrections to the representation can be made by reviewing the aural awareness questions.
4. The students sing the fourth phrase of *Liza Jane* with a neutral syllable and point to their representation.
5. Identify the solfège syllables for the fourth phrase of *Liza Jane* and sing the entire song with solfège syllables.

Associative Phase: Presentation

Review the kinesthetic, aural awareness, and visual awareness activities with the focus song *Liza Jane.*

Stage One: Label the Sound

1. Teacher: "We call two uneven sounds over two beats where the first is long and the second is short *ta-di*."
2. The teacher sings the target phrase of *Liza Jane* with rhythm syllables.
3. The students echo with rhythm syllables and conduct

Figure 8.140 Target phrase of *Liza Jane* with rhythm syllables

4. The students sing the last two phrases with rhythm syllables; half of the class sings rhythm syllables and claps the rhythm while the other half sings the rhythm syllables and performs the beat. Switch.

Stage Two: Present the Notation

Present the symbol for *ta-di* on the board in stick notation and then traditional notation. The students immediately clap and echo sing the target phrase of *Liza Jane* using rhythm names.

Figure 8.141 Target phrase of *Liza Jane* in rhythm names

Assimilative Phase: Practice

Stage One: Initial Practice

1. Review the aural awareness stage and connect the sound to rhythm syllables.
2. Review the visual awareness activities and associate the standard notation with the visual.
3. Transform the target pattern into basic four-beat patterns found in the student's song material. Transform the rhythm of phrase four of *Liza Jane* into phrase two of *John Kanaka*.

Stage Two: Practice

Reading

1. Read *Liza Jane* in traditional rhythm notation.
2. Read *John Kanaka* in traditional rhythm notation.
3. Read phrases of *John Kanaka, Liza Jane,* or *Canoe Song* on the xylophone or tone bells.

Writing

1. Write *Liza Jane* in stick notation.
2. Write *John Kanaka* in stick notation.
3. Play phrases from both songs on the xylophone or tone bells.

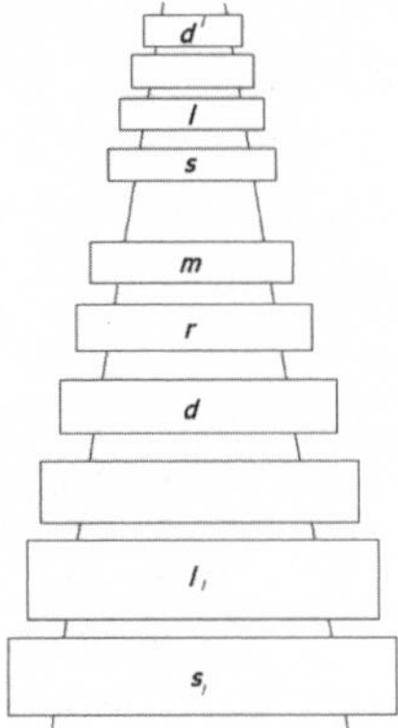

Figure 8.142 Phrases from *Liza Jane* and *John Kanaka* on xylophone

Improvisation

1. The teacher claps a question phrase in rhythm names. The students clap an answer phrase using the new rhythm pattern but names all rhythms.
2. Improvise the rhythm of the last four beats of any phrase in the following songs: *Above the Plain, Dona Dona Dona, Drill Ye Tarriers, Hushabye, John Kanaka, Long Road of Iron, Viva La Musica.*

Listening

"Play Song" from *44 Duets,* No. 9 by Belá Bartók

"The Birch Tree," sung by Slavyanka, Grey Smoke records, 1991. This theme is used by Peter Tchaikovsky in Symphony No. 4 in F minor, Op. 36, Movement 4 *Allegro con fuoco.*

"Variations on a Shaker Theme" from *Appalachian Spring* Movement 7 by Aaron Copland

"Finlandia" by Jean Sibelius. The Indigo Girls have a version of the hymn tune on their recording *Rarities.*

Figure 8.143 Section B of the Shaker Hymn *Simple Gifts*

Sight-Singing Materials

Houlahan, Mícheál, and Philip Tacka. *Sound Thinking: Music for Sight-Singing and Ear Training.* New York: Boosey & Hawkes, 1991. Vol. 1, pp. 71–76.

Assessment

Students sing *Liza Jane* with rhythm syllables while keeping the beat.

Teaching Strategy for *fa*

Table 8.26 Teaching strategy for *fa*

Element	Concept	Syllables	Theory	Focus Song	Additional Songs
fa	A pitch a whole step below *so* and a half step above *mi*	*fa*	B flat; pentachord; hexachord	*Hungarian Canon* phrase two	*Hungarian Canon Aunt Rhody; Alabama Gal; Chairs to Mend; On A Mountain; Redbirds and Blackbirds; Down to the Baker's Shop*

Cognitive Phase: Preparation

Stage One: Developing Kinesthetic Awareness

1. Sing *Hungarian Canon* and point to a representation of the melodic contour of phrase two at the board.

Figure 8.144 Melodic contour of phrase two of *Hungarian Canon*

2. Sing *Hungarian Canon* and show the melodic contour for phrase two.
3. Sing *Hungarian Canon* with rhythm syllables while clapping the melodic contour.

Stage Two: Developing Aural Awareness

Review the kinesthetic activities with the focus song *Hungarian Canon.* Sing while keeping the beat before asking each question.

Determine the number of beats in phrase two of *Hungarian Canon.*

Teacher: "Andy, how many beats did we tap?"
Student: "Four."

Determine the direction of the melody line.

Teacher: "Andy, what is the direction of the melodic line?"
Student: "Up."

Determine the number of different pitches in the phrase.

Teacher: "Andy, how many different pitches do we sing in phrase two?"
Student: "Five."
Teacher: "Andy, do these pitches move in steps or skips?"
Student: "Steps."

Determine whether the distance between each of the five steps is the same or different.

Teacher: "Andy, are all the steps the same distance apart?"
Student: "No, step 3–4 is a smaller step."

Stage Three: Developing Visual Awareness

Assess kinesthetic and aural awareness by allowing the class to perform several of the kinesthetic and aural awareness activities.

1. The instructor hums the target phrase and asks the students to create a visual representation of the melody of the target phrase. The students may use manipulatives.

   Teacher: "Pick up what you need to re-create what you heard" or "Draw what you heard." The teacher assesses the students' level of understanding.
2. The students share their representations with each other.
3. The instructor invites one student to the board to share his or her representation with the class. If necessary, corrections to the representation can be made by reviewing the aural awareness questions.
4. Students sing the second phrase of *Hungarian Canon* with a neutral syllable and point to their representation.
5. Sing the phrase with rhythm syllables. Identify the "small step" interval.

Associative Phase: Presentation

Review the kinesthetic, aural awareness and visual awareness activities with the focus song *Hungarian Canon.*

Stage One: Label the Sound

Figure 8.145 Hand sign for *fa*

1. Teacher: "When we hear a sound between *mi* and *so* we call it *fa*." The instructor shows the hand sign.
2. The teacher sings phrase two of "*Hungarian Canon*," with solfège syllables and the students echo sing (*do–re–mi–fa–so–so*).
3. The teacher echo sings with at least eight individual students.

Stage Two: Present the Notation

1. Present the position of *fa* on the steps.
2. Identify the steps between the notes of the phrase as large or small steps.

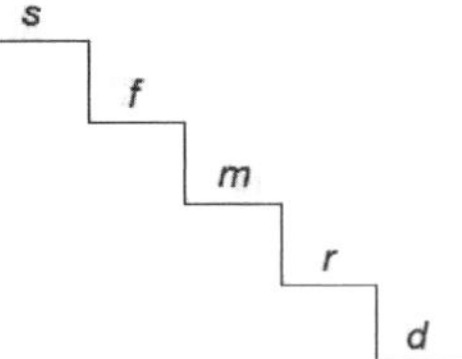

Figure 8.146 *Fa* on the steps

3. Present the target phrase of *Hungarian Canon* in traditional notation with solfège syllables *do re mi fa so so.*

Figure 8.147 Target phrase of *Hungarian Canon* in traditional notation

4. Present the target phrase of *Hungarian Canon* in staff notation and present the rule of placement in C = *do.*

Figure 8.148 Target phrase of *Hungarian Canon* in staff notation (C = *do*)

5. Present the target phrase of *Hungarian Canon* in staff notation and present the rule of placement in G = *do.*

Figure 8.149 Target phrase of Hungarian Canon in staff notation (G = *do*)

When we write the pitches of *Hungarian Canon* in ascending order, we discover that there are five adjacent pitches. We can label these pitches with solfège syllables *do–re–mi–fa–so,* and numbers 1–2–3–4–5, respectively. The final note of the composition is *do,* so we can refer to this as the tonic note. We refer to this collection of notes as a *do,* or major, pentachord scale. The *do* pentachord scale is *do–re–mi–fa–so.*

Table 8.27 Major pentachord scale

Solfège Syllable	Degree Number
so	5
fa	4
mi	3
re	2
do	1

Table 8.28 Major pentachord scale with scale degree number

Whole Steps Major 2	Half Steps Minor 2
d–r	m–f
r–m	
f–s	

Use your hand to demonstrate the whole step/half step relationships between the notes.

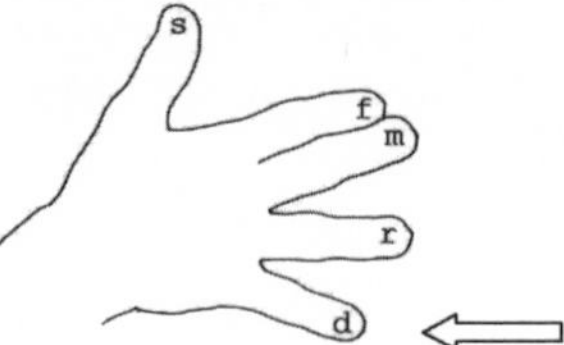

Figure 8.150 Hand demonstration of whole step/half step relationships

Assimilative Phase: Practice

Stage One: Initial Practice

1. Review the aural awareness stage and connect the sound to solfège syllables.
2. Review the visual awareness activities and associate standard notation with the visual.
3. Reverse the target pattern into the last four-beat patterns found in the song *Redbirds and Blackbirds.*
4. Identify intervals. Major second and minor second.

Stage Two: Practice

Reading

1. Read *Hungarian Canon* in traditional rhythm notation.
2. Read the *Hungarian Canon* in staff notation.
3. Read *This Old Man* in traditional rhythm notation or staff notation.
4. Read *Aunt Rhody* in traditional rhythm notation or staff notation.
5. Read *Aunt Rhody* and *Hungarian Canon* in stick or staff notation and play them on the xylophone or tone bells.
6. Read *Entre las matas* and play it on an instrument.

Figure 8.151 *Entre las matas*

Writing

1. Write *Hungarian Canon* and *Redbirds and Blackbirds* in stick notation and staff notation.
2. Mark the half steps and add appropriate accidentals depending on the key you are writing in.
3. Write a *do* pentachord scale on the staff. Mark the half step and appropriate accidentals.
4. Write a *do* hexachord scale on the staff. Mark the half step and appropriate accidentals.
5. Play the *Hungarian Canon* on the xylophone or bells.

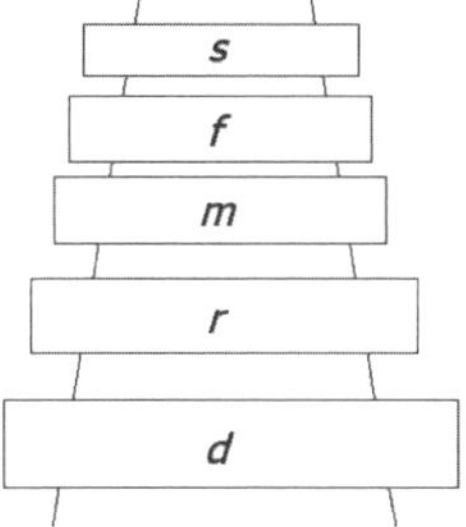

Figure 8.152 *Hungarian Canon* on xylophone

6. Write pentachord and hexachord scales in the following key areas: C, F, G, D, and B flat. This needs to be accomplished over many weeks of practice.

Improvisation

The teacher sings a question phrase using solfège syllables and the new note *fa.* The students echo an answer phrase incorporating *fa* into their phrase. The question phrase could move in an ascending direction while the answer phrase may move in a descending direction.

Introducing♭—the Flat Sign

Before the flat is taught, the students should be secure with different pentachord positions. In teaching the flat, use the visual tools such as piano and xylophone keys, or steps drawn on the board to replicate the exact intervals in the aural exercises. The students may require help to recognize the letter names of the notes on the piano or xylophones.

1. The students should work with songs having the range of a pentachord and aurally identify the large and small seconds in the song.
2. Give the students the opportunity to play these songs on xylophones or other instruments that show the whole and half steps clearly.
3. The students should play these songs while singing them with letter names. The teacher should work toward getting letter names as secure as solfège syllables. Use both C- and G- *do* positions because these positions do not have any accidentals. The hexachord may then be practiced with numbers (1, 2, 3, 4, 5, 6) in the following manner:
   a. Ask the students to sing a *do*-pentachord scale beginning on G. Reinforce the concept that the distance between *mi* and *fa* is a half step. The students will note the closeness of b and c in the G-*do* position.
   b. Ask the students to sing a *do*-pentachord scale beginning on F. Have the students discover that the note B must be moved closer to the note A. Play or sing the notes A–B and ask the students to determine if the distance is a half or a whole step.
   c. The students must discover the need to lower the sound. The teacher should demonstrate this on the piano by using the black note to lower the sound.
   d. Name the lowered sound, B-flat.
   e. Draw a flat sign: ♭.
   f. Write it on the staff.

Figure 8.153 B flat on the staff

Explain that the sign is placed before the note. Name this new note "bes" to use in singing with absolute letter names.

Key signatures should not be used at first. Add the flat signs in front of each pitch for several lessons. Later put the flat at the beginning and explain the purpose of key signatures. The following activities should now be practiced:

1. Read songs with hand signs and letter names.
2. The teacher shows melodic phrases using hand signs and the students sing these phrases using letter names.
3. The students echo sing using letter names sung by the teacher using solfège syllables.
4. The students memorize a melodic pattern aurally using solfège syllables and notate it from memory using F = *do* position.

Listening

Major pentachord examples:
Mikrokosmos, Vol. 1, Nos. 1, 2, 6, 17, 26; Vol. 3, Nos. 74 and 86, by Belá Bartók
"March Making Song" from *44 Duets for Two Violins* No. 1 by Belá Bartók
"Pillow Dance" from *For Children* Vol. 1, No. 4, by Belá Bartók
Vol. 2, No. 1, from *For Children* by Belá Bartók
"Round Dance I" from *For Children* Vol. 2, No. 6, by Belá Bartók
"The Five Fingers Eight Very Easy Melodies on Five Notes" by Igor Stravinksy

Major hexachord examples:
"Ah! vous dirai-je maman" Variations *on Twinkle Twinkle Little Star* K.265 by Wolfgang Amadeus Mozart
"Variations on a Nursery Song" Op. 25 by Ernö Dohnányi (1877–1960)
"Maypole Dance" No. 2 from *44 Duets for Two Violins* by Belá Bartók
"Children at Play" For Children Vol. 1, No. 1, by Belá Bartók
For Children Vol. 2, Nos. 2 and 3, by Belá Bartók

Sight Singing

Houlahan, Mícheál, and Philip Tacka. *Sound Thinking: Music for Sight-Singing and Ear Training.* New York: Boosey & Hawkes, 1991. Vol. 2, pp. 25–44.

Triple Meter

Table 8.29 Three-beat meter

Element	Concept	Syllables	Theory	Focus Song	Additional Songs
$\frac{3}{4}$ meter	The organization of one strong and two weak beats		Bar lines, measures; double barline, time signature	*Oh How Lovely Is the Evening*	*Around the Green Gravel; Rise Up Oh Flame; Sweet Betsy from Pike; Goodbye Old Paint*

Cognitive Phase: Preparation

Stage One: Developing Kinesthetic Awareness

1. The students sing *Oh How Lovely is the Evening* with a *pat clap clap* ostinato at a slow tempo. If this song is performed with a fast tempo it will sound as if written in compound meter. The instructor can also choose shorter songs that have up-beats.

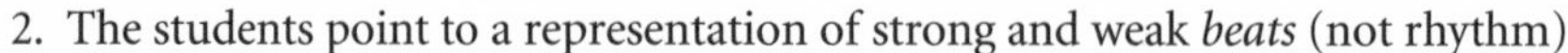

2. The students point to a representation of strong and weak *beats* (not rhythm)

Figure 8.154 *Oh How Lovely Is the Evening*

3. Clap the rhythm, walk the beat, while singing the song.

● ○ ○ ● ○ ○ ● ○ ○ ● ○ ○ ● ○ ○ ● ○ ○

Figure 8.155 Representation of strong and weak beats

Stage Two: Developing Aural Awareness

Review kinesthetic activities. Remember the teacher and students sing the phrase before every question.

Teacher: "Andy, do all of the beats feel the same?"
Student: "No, some beats are stronger and some are weaker."

Determine the strong and weak beats.

Teacher: "Andy, Can you describe the pattern of strong and weak beats?"
Student: "Strong weak weak."
Teacher: "Let's sing and show our strong and weak beats using a pat clap clap ostinato."

The teacher and students sing the song with the above ostinato.

Stage Three: Developing Visual Awareness

Assess kinesthetic and aural awareness by allowing the class to perform several of the kinesthetic and aural awareness activities.

1. The instructor hums the target phrase and asks the students to create a visual representation of the target phrase. The students may use manipulatives.

   Teacher: "Pick up what you need to re-create what you heard" or "Draw what you heard." The teacher assesses the students' level of understanding.

2. The students share their representations with each other.
3. The instructor invites one student to the board to share his or her representation with the class. If necessary, corrections to the representation can be made by reviewing the aural awareness questions.
4. The students sing the first phrase of *Oh How Lovely Is the Evening* with a neutral syllable and point to their representation.

Associative Phase: Presentation

Stage One: Label the Sound

1. Review kinesthetic, aural, and visual awareness.
2. Teacher: "When we have a pattern of three pulsations with the first being strong and the next two being weak we have a pattern of three beats per measure. This is referred to as triple meter. Each measure is divided into three beats."
3. Teacher shows the conducting motion for triple meter.

Stage Two: Present the Notation

The teacher can write *Oh How Lovely Is the Evening* as shown in figures 8.156 and 8.157.

Figure 8.156 *Oh How Lovely Is the Evening*

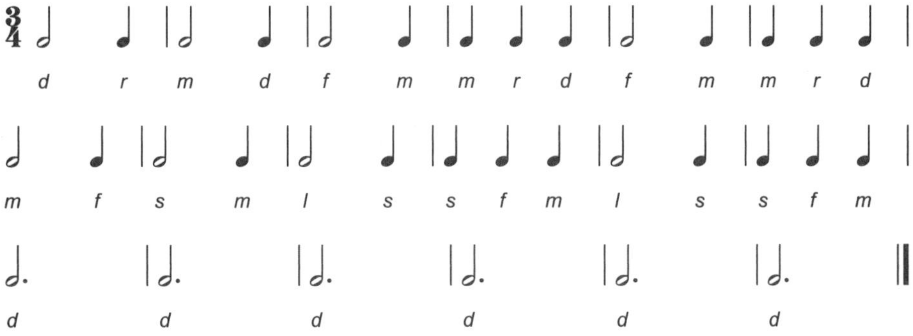

Figure 8.157 *Oh How Lovely Is the Evening*—Staff In G

Assimilative Phase: Practice

Stage One: Initial Practice

1. Review the aural awareness stage and connect the sound to rhythm syllables.
2. Review the visual awareness activities and associate standard notation with the visual.

3. Transform the target pattern into basic patterns found in the student's song material.

Stage Two: Practice

Reading

1. Read *Oh How Lovely Is the Evening* and *Rise Up Oh Flame* in traditional rhythmic notation with solfège syllables written beneath the rhythm notation.
2. Read *Oh How Lovely Is the Evening* and *Rise Up Oh Flame* in staff notation.
3. Read *Good Bye Old Paint* in traditional rhythmic notation with solfège syllables written beneath the rhythm notation.

Writing

Write *Oh How Lovely Is the Evening* and *Rise Up Oh Flame* in traditional rhythmic notation with solfège syllables written beneath the rhythm notation and/or staff notation.

Improvisation

Begin with the rhythm of a song the students know well. For example, consider *Oh How Lovely Is the Evening.* Guide the students to improvise a different rhythm to the second phrase and/or third phrase. They may keep the same basic pattern of solfège syllables, but the rhythm should be changed.

Listening

Minuet in G by Johann Sebastian Bach

Sight -Singing Materials

Houlahan, Mícheál, and Philip Tacka. *Sound Thinking: Music for Sight-Singing and Ear Training.* New York: Boosey & Hawkes, 1991. Vol. 1, pp. 16–19.

Teaching Strategy for *low ti* (*la* pentachord and *la* hexachord)

Table 8.30 Teaching strategy for *ti,*

Element	Concept	Syllables	Theory	Focus Song	Additional Songs
ti, the second degree of the minor pentachord and hexachord scale	A pitch a half step below *do*	*Low ti*	Minor pentachord and minor hexachord; (in major, leading tone)	*The Birch Tree*	*When I First Came to this Land; The Three Rogues; The Birch Tree*

Cognitive Phase: Preparation

Stage One: Developing Kinesthetic Awareness

1. Sing *Birch Tree* and show the melodic contour for phrase one.
2. Sing *Birch Tree* and point to a representation of the melodic contour at the board.

Figure 8.158 Melodic contour for phrase one of *Birch Tree*

3. Sing *Birch Tree* with rhythm syllables while showing the melodic contour.

Stage Two: Developing Aural Awareness

Review the kinesthetic activities with the focus song *Birch Tree.* Sing while keeping the beat before asking each question. Sometimes the teacher will sing the first phrase of *Birch Tree* on "loo" and sometimes he or she will sing the minor pentachord scale (*mi–re–do–ti, -la,*) on "loo" to help students answer the following questions:

Determine the number of beats.

Teacher: "Andy, how many beats did we keep?"
Student: "Six."

Determine the direction of the melody line.

Teacher: "Andy, in which direction do these pitches move?"
Student: "Down."

Determine the number of different pitches in the phrase.

Teacher: "Andy, how many different pitches did we sing?"
Student: "Five."
Teacher: "Andy, sing the pitches from highest to lowest using loo."
Student: [Andy sings the pitches on "loo."]

Determine the lowest and highest pitches

Teacher: "Andy, what's the name of the lowest pitch in solfège syllables?" Student: "*Low la.*"
Teacher: "Andy, if *low la* is the name of the lowest pitch, what is the solfège syllable for the highest pitch?"
Student: "*mi.*"

Determine the solfège syllable for the beginning and ending pitch of the phrase.

Teacher: "Andy, describe the five pitches with solfège syllables." [Remind Andy about the notes we know and the placement of the new sound; ask him to sing the new sound on "loo."]
Student: "*mi–re–do–'loo'–low la.*"
Teacher: "Andy, how would you describe our new sound in relation to *la?*"
Student: "Higher."
Teacher: "Andy, how would you describe our new sound in relation to *do?*"
Student: "Lower."

Stage Three: Developing Visual Awareness

Assess kinesthetic and aural awareness by allowing the class to perform several of the kinesthetic and aural awareness activities.

1. The instructor hums the target phrase and asks the students to create a visual representation of the melody of the target phrase. The students may use manipulatives.

   Teacher: "Pick up what you need to re-create what you heard" or "Draw what you heard." The teacher assesses the students' level of understanding.

2. The students share their representations with each other.
3. The instructor invites one student to the board to share his or her representation with the class. If necessary, corrections to the representation can be made by re-viewing the aural awareness questions.
4. The students sing the first phrase of the *Birch Tree* with a neutral syllable and point to their representation. Circle the half-step interval.
5. Sing the phrase with rhythm syllables.

Associative Phase: Presentation

Review the kinesthetic and aural awareness and visual awareness activities with the focus song *Birch Tree.*

Stage One: Label the Sound

Figure 8.159 Hand sign for *ti*

1. The teacher names the new note "*low ti.*" The teacher shows the students the hand sign.
2. The students immediately echo sing phrase one of *Birch Tree* with solfège and hand signs (*mi–mi–mi–mi–re–do–do–ti,-la,*).
3. The teacher echo sings with at least eight individual students.

Stage Two: Present the Notation

1. Present the position of *la,* (*low la*) on the steps. Discuss the large and small steps. Identify them as major and minor seconds and whole steps and half steps.

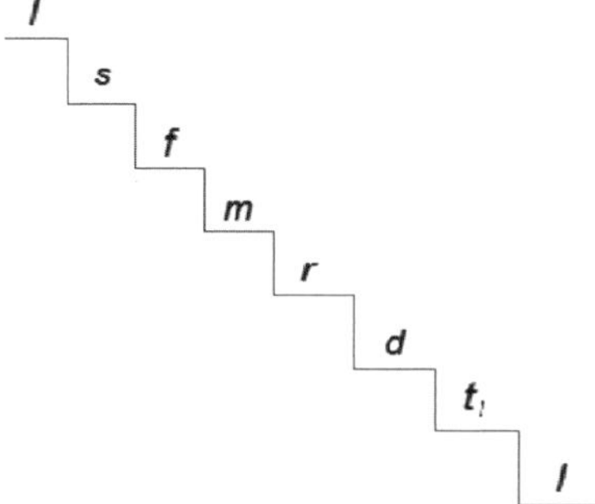

Figure 8.160 Position of *la* on the steps

2. Present the target phrase of *Birch Tree* in traditional rhythm notation with solfège syllables.

Figure 8.161 Target phrase of *Birch Tree* in traditional rhythm notation

3. Write the target phrase of *The Birch Tree* in stick notation.

Figure 8.162 Target phrase of *Birch Tree* in stick notation

4. Present the target phrase of *The Birch Tree* in staff notation and present the rule of placement.

Figure 8.163 Target phrase of *Birch Tree* in staff notation

When we write the pitches of *The Birch Tree* in descending order, we discover that, just as in the major pentachord, there are five adjacent pitches. We can label these pitches with solfège syllables *mi–re–do–ti,–la,* and numbers 5–4–3–2–1, respectively. The final note of the composition is *low la;* we can refer to this as the tonic note. We refer to this collection of notes as a *la* or minor pentachord scale.

Table 8.31 Minor pentachord scale

Solfege Syllable	Corresponding Number
mi	5
re	4
do	3
ti,	2
la,	1

Intervallic Distance between the Notes of the Minor Pentachord Scale

Note the intervals between *low la-low ti, do-re, re-mi* are a whole step. The distance between *low ti-do* is a half step. We can refer to whole steps as major seconds (M2) and half steps as minor seconds (m2).

Table 8.32 Major and minor second intervals of the minor pentachord scale

Whole Steps Major 2	**Half Steps Minor 2**
l,–t,	*t,–d*
d–r	
r–m	

Use your hand to demonstrate the whole step/half step relationships between the notes.

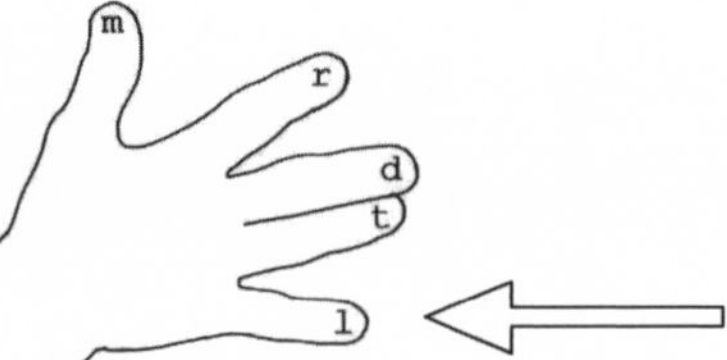

Figure 8.164 Hand demonstration of whole step/half step relationships

Assimilative Phase: Practice

Stage One: Initial Practice

1. Review the aural awareness stage and connect the sound to rhythm syllables.
2. Review the visual awareness activities and associate standard notation with the visual.
3. Transform the target pattern by starting with the notes *la, - ti, - do–re–mi* and read the beginning of the song *Rise Up O Flame.*
4. Identify major and minor second intervals.
5. Read and perform parallel and relative position pentachord and hexachord scales.

Stage Two: Practice

Reading

1. Read *The Birch Tree* and *Rise Up O Flame* in stick notation and staff notation.
2. Create a reading exercise using the notes of the minor pentachord scale.

3. Read *Las horas* and play it on an instrument.

Figure 8.165 *Las horas*

4. Play *The Birch Tree* on the xylophone or bells.

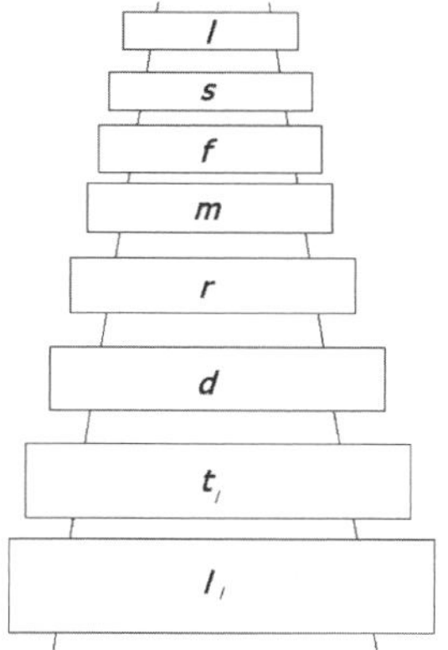

Figure 8.166 *The Birch Tree* on the xylophone

Writing

1. Write *The Birch Tree* and *Rise Up Oh Flame* in stick notation and include solfège syllables.
2. Write phrase one of *Ida Red* and perform it on rhythm instruments.

Improvisation

The teacher sings a question phrase in solfège syllables. The students echo an answer phrase in solfège syllables. The initial question phrases should be in the range of a minor pentachord and ascend; the answer phrase should descend. Guide students to improvise a different second phrase for *Birch Tree.*

Introducing the Sharp Sign (♯)

The same steps that were outlined for the flat may be used to introduce the sharp sign.

1. Students sing the *la* pentachord scale beginning on a D.
2. The instructor writes the *la* pentachord scale on the board and marks the half steps.
3. The instructor associates the letter names for a D minor or pentachord with the solfège syllables.
4. The instructor sings the scale with letter names while students show the hand signs.
5. Repeat steps 1–3 for *la* pentachord scale that begins on E.
6. Students aurally discover the *la-ti* interval is a whole step and that E to F is too small and must be raised by a half step.
7. The instructor introduces F♯.

At this stage in the conceptual sequence, the introduction of the sharp sign is simply a formality. Remember that absolute letter names should be sung by the students when a clef sign is used at the beginning of the line of music. Sing in the key in which the piece is written. Work with songs using the diatonic scale. Some of these songs should be sung and played by students on the xylophone or other instruments that have the whole and half steps clearly visible.

The following activities should now be practiced with *la* pentachord and hexachord songs before practicing letter names in major and minor scales.

1. Read songs with hand signs and letter names.
2. The teacher shows melodic phrases using hand signs and the students sing these phrases using letter names.
3. The students echo sing using letter names sung by the teacher using solfège names.
4. The students memorize a melodic pattern aurally using solfège names and notate it from memory using F = *la,* E = *la,* D = *la,* and G = *la,* position.

Listening

Minor pentachord examples:
For Children Vol. 1, No. 3, by Belá Bartók
"Study for the Left Hand" from *For Children* Vol. 1 by Belá Bartók
"Round Dance" from *For Children* Vol. 1. by Belá Bartók

Minor hexachord examples:
Dance from *For Children* Vol. 2, No. 8, by Belá Bartók

Sight Reading Materials

Houlahan, Mícheál, and Philip Tacka. *Sound Thinking: Music for Sight-Singing and Ear Training.* New York: Boosey & Hawkes, 1991. Vol. 2, pp. 45–56.

Teaching Strategy for a Dotted Eighth Note Followed by a Sixteenth Note

Table 8.33 Teaching strategy for a dotted eighth note followed by a sixteenth note

Element	Concept	Syllables	Theory	Focus Song	Additional Songs
Dotted eighth note followed by a sixteenth note	Two sounds on one beat, the first being long and the second being short	*ta mi*	Subdivision of the beat into sixteenth notes	*Donkey Riding*	*Sail Away Ladies; Charlotte Town, Circle Round the Zero; Yankee Doodle; Shady Grove*

Cognitive Phase: Preparation

Stage One: Developing Kinesthetic Awareness

1. Sing *Donkey Riding* and pat the beat for the target phrase one.
2. Sing *Donkey Riding* and clap the rhythm for the target phrase one.
3. Sing *Donkey Riding* and point to a representation of the rhythm on the board.

—— - —— —— —— —— —— —— —— —— —— —— —— —— ——

Figure 8.167 Representation of the rhythm of *Donkey Riding*

4. Sing *Donkey Riding* performing the ostinato in figure 8.170.

Figure 8.168 Ostinato

Stage Two: Developing Aural Awareness

Sing the target phrase using a neutral syllable while keeping the beat before asking each question. Review the kinesthetic activities with the focus song.

Determine the number of beats in each phrase.

Teacher: "Andy, how many beats did we keep in phrase one?"
Student: "Eight."

Determine the number of sounds on each beat for the first four beats.

Teacher: "Andy, which beats have one sound on them?"
Student: "Beat four and beat eight."
Teacher: "Andy, how many sounds did we sing on beat one?"
Student: "Two sounds."

Teacher: "Andy, how many sounds did we sing on beats two and three?
Student: "Two sounds."
Teacher: "Andy, describe the two sounds on beat one."
Student: "The first is long, the second is short."
Teacher: "Sing this phrase with long and short for beat one and rhythm syllables for all other beats.

Stage Three: Developing Visual Awareness

Assess kinesthetic and aural awareness by allowing the class to perform several of the kinesthetic and aural awareness activities.

1. The instructor hums the target phrase and asks the students to create a visual representation of the target phrase. Students may use manipulatives.

   Teacher: "Pick up what you need to re-create what you heard" or "Draw what you heard." The teacher assesses the students' level of understanding.

2. The students share their representations with each other.
3. The instructor invites one student to the board to share his or her representation with the class. If necessary, corrections to the representation can be made by reviewing the aural awareness questions.
4. The students sing the first phrase of *Donkey Riding* with a neutral syllable and point to their representation.
5. Determine the solfège syllables for the target phrase.

Associative Phase: Presentation

Review the kinesthetic, aural awareness, and visual awareness activities with the focus song *Donkey Riding.*

Stage One: Label the Sound

1. Teacher: "We call two uneven sounds on one beat where the first is long and the second is short *ta mi.*"
2. The teacher sings phrase one of *Donkey Riding* with rhythm syllables.

   ta mi ta di ta di ta ta di ta di ta di ta

   Figure 8.169 Phrase one of *Donkey Riding* with rhythm syllables

3. The students echo with rhythm syllables while clapping the rhythm.

Stage Two: Present the Notation

Present the symbol for *ta-mi* on the board in traditional rhythm notation. The students immediately clap and echo sing the target phrase of *Donkey Riding* in rhythm names.

1. Present the target phrase of *Donkey Riding* in stick notation.

Figure 8.170 Target phrase of *Donkey Riding* in stick notation

2. Present the target phrase of *Donkey Riding* in staff notation.

Figure 8.171 Target phrase of *Donkey Riding* in staff notation

Assimilative Phase: Practice

Stage One: Initial Practice

1. Review the aural awareness stage and connect the sound to rhythm syllables.
2. Review the visual awareness activities and associate standard notation with the visual.
3. Transform the target pattern into basic four-beat patterns found in the student's song material. Transform the rhythm of phrase three and four of *Donkey Riding* into phrase three and four of *Charlotte Town.*

Stage Two: Practice

Reading

1. Read *Donkey Riding* in traditional rhythm notation.
2. Read *Charlotte Town* in traditional rhythm notation.

Writing

1. Write *Donkey Riding* in stick notation and include the solfège syllables.
2. Write *Charlotte Town* in stick notation and include the solfège syllables.

Improvisation

The teacher claps a question phrase in rhythm names. The students clap an answer phrase in rhythm names. Improvise the rhythm of the last four beats of any phrase in the following songs: *Sail Away Ladies, Charlotte Town, Circle Round the Zero,* and *Yankee Doodle.*

Listening

"London Bridge Is Falling Down," performed by Count Basie in *The Complete Decca Recordings of Count Basie*
"London Bridge" in *Most Lost Treasures of Ted Heath* Vol. 1–2
"Hommage a Robert Schumann" in *Mikrokosmos* Vol. 3, No. 80, by Belá Bartók
Andante from Symphony No. 94 by Joseph Haydn
"Feierlich und gemessen" from Symphony No. 1 by Gustav Mahler
Largo from Symphony No. 9 by Antonin Dvorak; "Going Home," sung by Kathleen Battle in her recording *So Many Stars*, is based on this theme

Figure 8.172 Andante from Symphony No. 94 by Joseph Haydn (1732–1809)

Sight-Singing Materials

Houlahan, Mícheál, and Philip Tacka. *Sound Thinking: Music for Sight-Singing and Ear Training.* New York: Boosey & Hawkes, 1991. Vol. 1, pp. 62–64.

Focus Songs for Grade Four

Focus Song for Syncopation

Figure 8.173 *Canoe Song*

Focus Song for *so* Pentatonic Scale

Figure 8.174 *Over the River to Charlie* (only the last two phrases)

Focus Song for Dotted Quarter Followed by an Eighth Note

Figure 8.175 *Liza Jane*

Focus Song for *fa*

Figure 8.176 *Hungarian Canon*

Focus Song for Triple Meter

Figure 8.177 *Oh How Lovely Is the Evening*

Focus Song for *low ti*

Figure 8.178 *The Birch Tree*

Focus Song for Dotted Eighth Note Followed by a Sixteenth Note

Figure 8.179 *Donkey Riding*

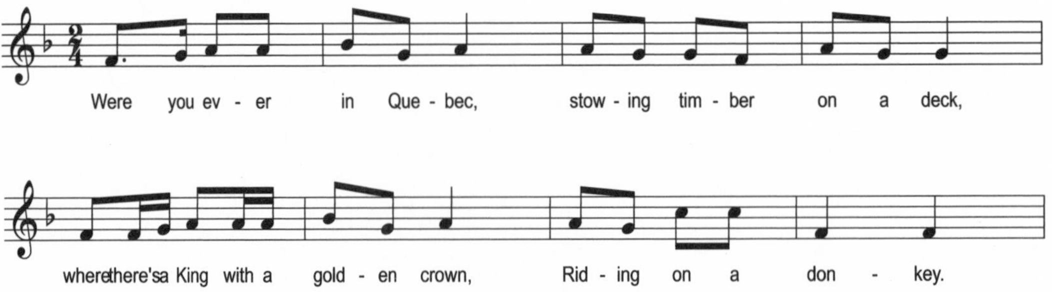

Figure 8.179 *Continued*

Grade Five Teaching Strategies

In fifth grade, we deal with seven musical concepts.

1. Teaching strategy for high *ti* (major scale)
2. Teaching strategy for an eighth note followed by a dotted quarter note
3. Teaching strategy for natural minor scale
4. Teaching strategy for *si* (harmonic minor)
5. Teaching strategy for compound meter (patterns in $\frac{6}{8}$ meter)
6. Teaching strategy for *fi* (Dorian mode)
7. Teaching strategy for *ta* Mixolydian mode)

Teaching Strategy for high *ti* (Major Scale)

Table 8.34 Teaching strategy for a major scale

Element	Concept	Syllables	Theory	Focus Song	Additional Songs
High ti	A series of seven pitches with half steps between the third and fourth degrees and the seventh and eighth degrees.	*ti*	Major diatonic scale	*Alleluia*	*Handsome Butcher, Roman Soldiers, Ship the Never Returned; Kookaburra, Joy to the World, Johnny Has Gone for a Soldier; Viva la Musica*

Cognitive Phase: Preparation

Stage One: Developing Kinesthetic Awareness

1. Sing the second phrase and point to a representation of the melodic contour at the board.

Figure 8.180 Melodic contour of phrase two of *Alleluia*

2. Sing *Alleluia* and show the melodic contour of the second phrase.
3. Sing phrase two of *Alleluia* with rhythm syllables while showing the melodic contour.

Stage Two: Developing Aural Awareness

Review the kinesthetic activities with the focus song *Alleluia* Sing on "loo" while keeping the beat before asking each question.

Determine the number of beats per phrase and the general direction of the melody.

Teacher: "Andy, how many beats are in the second phrase?"
Student: "Eight."
Teacher: "Andy, what is the general direction of the melodic contour?"
Student: "It goes up."

Determine the lowest and highest notes.

Teacher: "Andy, sing the lowest note of the phrase."
Student: Student sings *do* on "loo."
Teacher: "Andy, which beat has the lowest pitch?"
Student:" Beat one."
Teacher: "Andy, which solfège syllable can we use for that pitch?"
Student: "*do.*"
Teacher: "Andy, sing the highest note of the phrase."
Student: Student sings high *do* on "loo."
Teacher: "Andy, which beat(s) has the highest pitch?"
Student: "Six and eight."
Teacher: "Andy, sing all the pitches from the lowest to the highest."
Student: Andy hums all pitches from lowest to highest.
Teacher: "Andy, how many different pitches did we sing?"
Student: Student sings *do-re-mi-fa-so-la-ti-do'* on "loo."

Determine the minor second intervals. Collect all the pitches from lowest to highest.

Teacher: "Andy, if the first pitch is *do,* what is the next pitch?"
Student: "*re.*"

The teacher collects all the pitches in the same manner (*do–re–mi–fa–so–la–ti do'*). Sing the entire phrase on solfège and show hand signs.

Stage Three: Developing Visual Awareness

Assess kinesthetic and aural awareness by allowing the class to perform several of the kinesthetic and aural awareness activities.

1. The instructor hums the target phrase and asks the students to create a visual representation of the melody of the target phrase. The students may use manipulatives.

   Teacher: "Pick up what you need to re-create what you heard" or "Draw what you heard." The teacher assesses the students' level of understanding.
2. The students share their representations with each other.
3. The instructor invites one student to the board to share his or her representation with the class. If necessary, corrections to the representation can be made by reviewing the aural awareness questions.
4. The students sing the second phrase of *Alleluia* with a neutral syllable and point to their representation.
5. Sing the phrase with rhythm syllables.

Associative Phase: Presentation

Review the kinesthetic and aural awareness and visual awareness activities with the focus song *Alleluia.*

Stage One: Label the Sound

1. The teacher and student sing the eight pitches of the "*major* scale" from low to high with solfège syllables. The teacher specifically names it a "major diatonic scale."
2. The teacher hums the major diatonic scale from low to high. The students echo with solfège syllables and handsigns.
3. The teacher hums the major diatonic scale from high to low. The students echo with solfège syllables and handsigns.

Stage Two: Present the Notation

1. Present the pattern for the major diatonic scale and note the position of the half-step intervals.

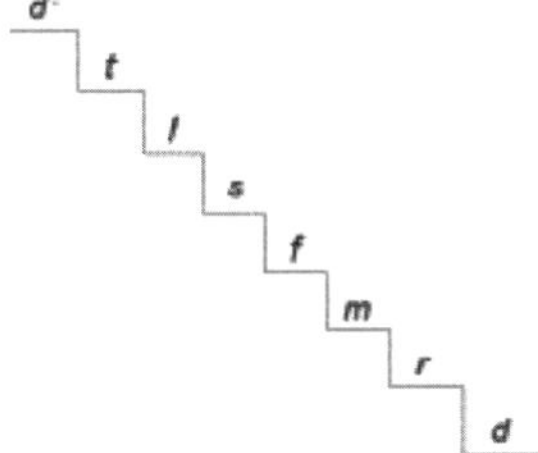

Figure 8.181 Solfège steps

Figure 8.182 C major scale

When we write the pitches of *Alleluia* in ascending order, we discover that there are seven adjacent pitches. We can label these pitches with solfège syllables, *do–re–mi- fa-so-la-ti-do',* and numbers, 1–2–3–4 - 5–6-7-1, respectively. This scale is called the major scale. Mark the half steps between *mi-fa and ti-do.*

Table 8.35 Labeling pitches with solfège syllables

Solfège Syllables	**Corresponding Number**
do'	*1*
ti	*7*
la	*6*
so	*5*
fa	*4*
mi	*3*
re	*2*
do	*1*

Intervallic Distance between the Notes of the Major Scale

Note the intervals between *do–re, re–mi, fa–so, so–la, la–ti* are whole steps. The distance between *ti,-do* and *mi-fa* is a half step. We can refer to whole steps as major seconds (M2) and half steps as minor seconds (m2).

Assimilative Phase: Practice

Stage One: Initial Practice

Review the aural and visual presentation of the *major diatonic scale* in *Alleluia.* Read both phrases of *Alleluia* in two different key areas.

Stage Two: Practice

Reading

1. Read *Alleluia* in stick notation and staff notation.
2. Using the structural notes (the notes that occur on each beat) of *Kookaburra* as a start, construct a reading exercise. Gradually add pitches to each beat until the entire song is constructed.

3. Read the following songs: *Handsome Butcher, Roman Soldiers, Kookaburra,* and *Joy to the World* and play patterns on the xylophone or tone bells.
4. Play the second phrase of *Alleluia* on the xylophone or tone bells.

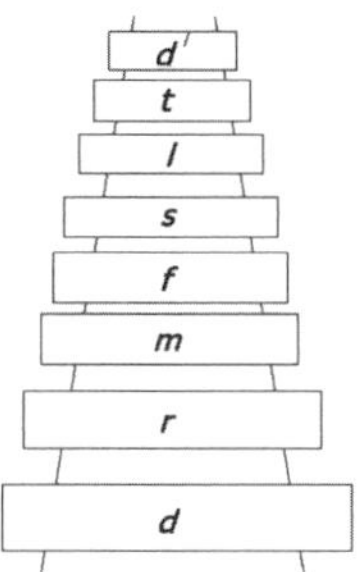

Figure 8.183 Second phrase of *Alleluia* on xylophone

Writing

1. Write *Alleluia* in stick notation and staff notation. When writing in staff notation use at least two different key areas.
2. Write patterns from the following songs: *Handsome Butcher, Roman Soldiers, Kookaburra,* and *Joy to the World.*

Improvisation

1. The instructor or another student may sing a descending major scale with a specific rhythm. A student improvises an ascending major scale with the same or a different rhythm.

Figure 8.184 Instructor sings a descending major scale with a specific rhythm

Figure 8.185 Student improvises an ascending major scale

2. The teacher sings a question phrase in solfège syllables using the notes of the major scale. The students echo an answer phrase in solfège syllables.

Listening

For Children, Vol. 1, No. 11, by Belá Bartók
"All Through the Night," recorded by the Mormon Tabernacle Choir; also on the recording *A Nancy Wilson Christmas*, sung by Nancy Wilson
"Ce fut en May," Trouvere Song
"In Dulce Jubilo," recorded by the King's College Choir of Cambridge, conducted by Simon Preston and David Wilcox
"Variations on a Theme by Haydn" Op. 56a by Johannes Brahms
"The Holly and the Ivy," sung by Anonymous 4 from their recording *Wolcum Yule*
"Rigadoon" by Henry Purcell, from the recording *Purcell: Works for Harpsichord*, played by John Gibbons
Minuet in G from *The Notebook of Ana Magdalena* by Johann Sebastian Bach
"Jupiter" from *The Planets* Op. 32 by Gustav Holst
"*Tallis Canon*" from the album *Into the Light* by Harry Christophers, Karori Muraji, and The Sixteen

Teaching Strategy for an Eighth Note Followed by a Dotted Quarter Note

Table 8.36 Teaching strategy for an eighth note followed by a dotted quarter note

Element	Concept	Syllables	Theory	Focus Song	Additional Songs
Eighth note followed by a dotted quarter note	Two sounds distributed over two beats where both sounds occur on beat one	*ta di --------*		*Charlotte Town*	*All Night, All Day; The Erie Canal; Billy Boy; Great Big Dog; Walk Along John; Go Down Moses*

Cognitive Phase: Preparation

Stage One: Developing Kinesthetic Awareness

1. Sing *Charlotte Town* and pat the beat for the target phrase one.
2. Sing *Charlotte Town* and clap the rhythm for the target phrase one.
3. Sing *Charlotte Town* and point to a representation of the rhythm on the board.

—— —— —— —— ————— —————

Figure 8.186 Representation of the rhythm of target phrase one of *Charlotte Town*

4. Sing *Charlotte Town* while performing the following ostinato.

Figure 8.187 Ostinato to *Charlotte Town*

Stage Two: Developing Aural Awareness

Review the kinesthetic activities with the focus song. Sing the target phrase using a neutral syllable while keeping the beat before asking each question.

Determine the number of beats in phrase one.

Teacher: "Andy, how many beats did we keep?"
Student: "Eight."

Determine the number of sounds on each beat.

Teacher: "Andy, are there any beats that have one sound on them?"
Student: "Two and four."
Teacher: "Andy, which beats have two sounds?"
Student: "One, three, five, and seven."
Teacher: "Andy, what is different about the two sounds we sing on beats five and seven? Listen." [The teacher sings on "loo" (the second sound is longer).]

Sing the phrase with rhythm syllables and short long.

ta di ta ta di ta Short long--------------- Short long---------------

Figure 8.188 Target phrase with rhythm syllables and short long

Stage Three: Developing Visual Awareness

Assess kinesthetic and aural awareness by allowing the class to perform several of the kinesthetic and aural awareness activities.

1. The instructor hums the target phrase and asks the students to create a visual representation of the target phrase. The students may use manipulatives.

   Teacher: "Pick up what you need to re-create what you heard" or "Draw what you heard." The teacher assesses the students' level of understanding.

2. The students share their representations with each other.
3. The instructor invites one student to the board to share his or her representation with the class. If necessary, corrections to the representation can be made by reviewing the aural awareness questions.
4. The students sing the first phrase of *Charlotte Town* with a neutral syllable and point to their representation.
5. Determine the solfège syllables for the first phrase of *Charlotte Town.*

Associative Phase: Presentation

Review the kinesthetic, aural awareness, and visual awareness activities with the focus song *Charlotte Town.*

Stage One: Label the Sound

1. Teacher: "We call two uneven sounds over two beats where the first is short and the second is long *ta di.*"
2. The teacher sings the target phrase of *Charlotte Town* with rhythm syllables.
3. The students echo with rhythm syllables while clapping the rhythm or performing the beat.

Figure 8.189 Performing the beat to *Charlotte Town*

Stage Two: Present the Notation

Present the symbols for *ta di* on the board in traditional notation and then stick notation. The students immediately clap and echo sing the target phrase of *Charlotte Town* in rhythm names.

Teacher: "We can write this rhythm using an eighth note followed by a dotted quarter note."

Figure 8.190 *Charlotte Town* in traditional notation

Teacher: "We can also write this phrase using stick notation and solfège syllables."

Figure 8.191 *Charlotte Town* in stick notation

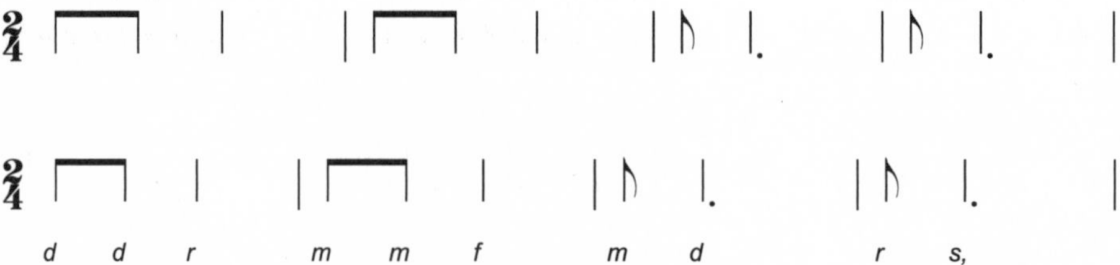

Assimilative Phase: Practice

Stage One: Initial Practice

1. Review the aural awareness stage and connect the sound to rhythm syllables.
2. Review the visual awareness activities and associate standard notation with the visual.

3. Transform the target pattern into basic four-beat patterns found in the student's song material. Transform the rhythm of phrase one of *Charlotte Town* into phrase two of *All Night, All Day.*

Stage Two: Practice

Reading

1. Read *Charlotte Town* in stick notation.
2. Read *All Night, All Day* in stick notation.

Writing

1. Write *Charlotte Town* in stick notation.
2. Write *All Night, All Day* in stick notation.

Improvisation

The teacher claps a question phrase using rhythm syllables. The students clap an answer phrase using rhythm syllables. Improvise the rhythm of the last four beats of any phrase in the following songs: *Above the Plain, Dona Dona Dona, Drill Ye Tarriers, Hushabye, John Kanaka, King Kong Kitchie, Long Road of Iron,* and *Viva La Musica.*

Sight-Singing Materials

Houlahan, Mícheál, and Philip Tacka. *Sound Thinking: Music for Sight-Singing and Ear Training.* New York: Boosey & Hawkes, 1991. Vol. 1, pp. 71–76.

Listening

"An Evening in the Village" from *Hungarian Sketches* Theme No. 2 by Belá Bartók
Mikrokosmos Vol. 3, No. 95, by Belá Bartók

Figure 8.192 Theme 2 of *An Evening in the Village*

Teaching Strategy for Natural Minor Scale

Table 8.37 Teaching strategy for natural minor scale

Element	Concept	Syllables	Theory	Focus Song	Additional Songs
	Natural minor scale; a series of seven pitches with a half-step between the 2-3, 5-6 scale degrees	la,–ti,–do–re–mi–fa–so–la	Scale structure of minor scale	*Alleluia* in Minor	*Ghost of Tom* *Dona, Dona, Dona* *Drill Ye Tarriers* *To Work Upon the Railway* *Sweet William Hashivenu (w/solfège syllables)* *Come to the Land* *Tumbalalaika*

Cognitive Phase: Preparation

Stage One: Developing Kinesthetic Awareness

1. Sing *Alleluia in Minor* and point to a representation of the melodic contour at the board for the last two phrases.

Figure 8.193 Melodic contour of *Alleluia in Minor*

2. Sing *Alleluia in Minor* and show the melodic contour of the whole song.
3. Sing *Alleluia in Minor* with rhythm syllables and show the melodic contour.

Stage Two: Developing Aural Awareness

Sing while keeping the beat before asking each question. Review the kinesthetic activities with the focus song *Alleluia in Minor.*

Determine the lowest and highest notes.

Teacher: "Andy, sing the lowest note of the song."
Student: "*la,.*"
Teacher: "Andy, sing the highest note of the song."
Student: "*la.*"

Determine the solfège syllables from the lowest to the highest note.

Teacher: "Andy, what solfège syllable do we use for the lowest note?"
Student: "*Low la.*"
Teacher: "Andy, if the first pitch is *low la,* what is the next pitch?"
Student: "*Low ti.*"

The teacher collects all the pitches in the same manner (*la, ti, do re mi fa so la*). The students sing the entire song with solfège and hand signs.

Stage Three: Developing Visual Awareness

Assess kinesthetic and aural awareness by allowing the class to perform several of the kinesthetic and aural awareness activities.

1. The instructor hums the target phrase and asks the students to create a visual representation of the melody of the target phrase. The students may use manipulatives.

   Teacher: "Pick up what you need to re-create what you heard" or "Draw what you heard." The teacher assesses the students' level of understanding.
2. The students share their representations with each other.
3. The instructor invites one student to the board to share his or her representation with the class. If necessary, corrections to the representation can be made by reviewing the aural awareness questions.
4. The students sing the *Alleluia in Minor* with a neutral syllable and point to their representation.
5. Determine the solfège syllables for *Alleluia in Minor.*

Associative Phase: Presentation

Review the kinesthetic and aural awareness and visual awareness activities with the focus song *Alleluia in Minor.*

Stage One: Label the Sound

1. The teacher and students sing the seven pitches of the *natural minor scale* from low to high with solfège syllables and handsigns.
2. The teacher specifically names it a "natural minor scale" because it has seven pitches from *la,* to *la* with half steps between *mi/fa* and *ti,/do.*
3. The teacher hums the natural minor scale from low to high. The students echo with solfège and handsigns.
4. The teacher hums the natural minor scale from high to low. The students echo with solfège and handsigns.

Stage Two: Present the Notation

1. Present the notes for the natural minor scale on the staff.
2. Mark the half step intervals between *fa* and *mi,* and *do* and *low ti.*

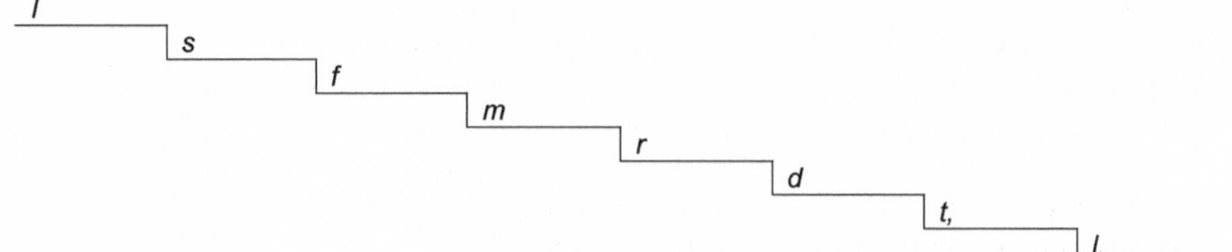

Figure 8.194 Solfège steps

3. Present the natural minor scale in staff notation and present the rule of placement.
4. Present *Alleluia in Minor* in stick notation.
5. Present *Alleluia in Minor* in staff notation.

Assimilative Phase: Practice

Stage One: Initial Practice

1. Review the aural awareness stage and connect the sound to solfège syllables.
2. Review the visual awareness activities and associate standard notation with the visual.
3. Transform the target pattern into basic eight-beat patterns found in the student's song material.

Stage Two: Practice

Reading

1. Read *Alleluia in Minor* in stick notation and staff notation.
2. Read from stick or staff notation any of the following songs: *Hashivenu, Ghost of Tom, Dona, Dona, Dona, Sweet William, Come to the Land,* or *Tumbalalaika.*

Writing

1. Write *Alleluia in Minor* in stick notation and staff notation.
2. Write in stick or staff notation any of the following songs: *Hashivenu, Ghost of Tom, Dona, Dona, Dona, Sweet William, Come to the Land,* or *Tumbalalaika.*

Improvisation

The teacher sings a question phrase in solfège syllables using the natural minor scale. The students echo an answer phrase in solfège syllables.

Listening

"Sweet William," similar version sung by Alasdair Roberts on the recording *No Earthly Man*
"Shalom Chaverim," sung by the Weavers on the recording *The Album at Carnegie Hall*, Vanguard Records, 1988
"When Jesus Wept" by William Billings

"Dona Dona" on the album *From Jewish Life*, Signum Classics, performed by John Lenehan and Paul Marleyn; also on the album *Amulet*, sung by Nikitov, Chamsa Records, 2004
"Hushabye" by Mike and Peggy Seeger on *Album for Children*; also found on the album *So Many Stars*, as "The Little Horses," sung by Kathleen Battle
Theme from "Psalmus Hungaricus" by Zoltán Kodály
Theme from the "Peacock Variations" by Zoltán Kodály

Sight-Singing Materials

Houlahan, Mícheál, and Philip Tacka. *Sound Thinking: Music for Sight-Singing and Ear Training.* New York: Boosey & Hawkes, 1991. Vol. 2, pp. 84–85.

Teaching Strategy for *si* (harmonic minor)

Table 8.38 Teaching strategy for *si*

Element	Concept	Syllables	Theory	Focus Song	Additional Songs
si	*si* is a minor second below *l*	*si*	Scale structure	*Ah, Poor Bird*	*Go Down, Moses* *Vine and Fig Tree*

Cognitive Phase: Preparation

Stage One: Developing Kinesthetic Awareness

1. Sing *Ah, Poor Bird* and point to a representation of the melodic contour at the board.
2. Sing *Ah, Poor Bird* and show the melodic contour of the whole song.

Figure 8.195 Melodic contour of *Ah, Poor Bird*

3. Sing *Ah, Poor Bird* with rhythm syllables and showing the melodic contour.

Stage Two: Developing Aural Awareness

Review the kinesthetic activities with the focus song *Ah, Poor Bird.* Sing while keeping the beat before asking each question.

Determine the lowest and highest notes.

Teacher: "Andy, sing the lowest note of the song."
Student: "*la,.*"
Teacher: "Andy, sing the highest note of the song."
Student: "*la.*"

Determine the solfège syllables for the third phrase.

Teacher: "Andy, what solfège syllable begins phrase three?"
Student: "*mi.*"
Teacher: "Andy, what is the highest solfège syllable in phrase three?"
Student: "*la.*"

The teacher collects all the pitches in the same manner, humming on unknown element *si* (*mi la la hum la mi mi re*). Note: make sure the scale includes *la-si-la* rather than a leap to *si.*

Stage Three: Developing Visual Awareness

Assess kinesthetic and aural awareness by allowing the class to perform several of the kinesthetic and aural awareness activities.

1. The instructor hums the target phrase with a neutral syllable and asks the students to create a visual representation of the melody of the target phrase. The students may use manipulatives.

   Teacher: "Pick up what you need to re-create what you heard" or "Draw what you heard." The teacher assesses the students' level of understanding.

2. The students share their representations with each other.
3. The instructor invites one student to the board to share his or her representation with the class. If necessary, corrections to the representation can be made by reviewing the aural awareness questions.
4. Circle all half steps.
5. The students sing *Ah Poor Bird* with a neutral syllable and point to their representation.
6. Sing *Ah Poor Bird* with rhythm syllables.

Associative Phase: Presentation

Review the kinesthetic and aural awareness and visual awareness activities with the focus song *Ah, Poor Bird.*

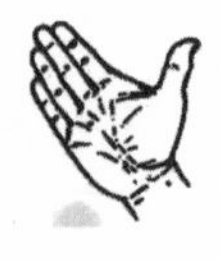
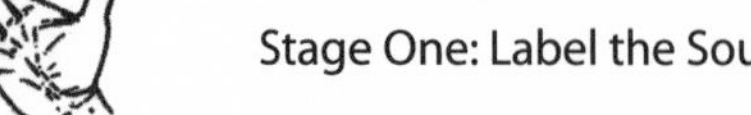

Figure 8.196 Hand sign for *si*

Stage One: Label the Sound

The teacher specifically names the leading tone as *si,* since it leads to *la,* and names the new minor scale as harmonic minor, because it contains the leading tone *si* instead of *so.*

The teacher shows the students the hand sign for *si* and the students copy. (This hand sign is most often showed with fingers slightly spread.)

The teacher sings the complete harmonic minor scale from low to high. The students echo with solfège and handsigns. The teacher sings the complete harmonic minor scale from high to low. The students echo with solfège and handsigns.

Stage Two: Present the Notation

1. Present the pattern for the harmonic minor scale.

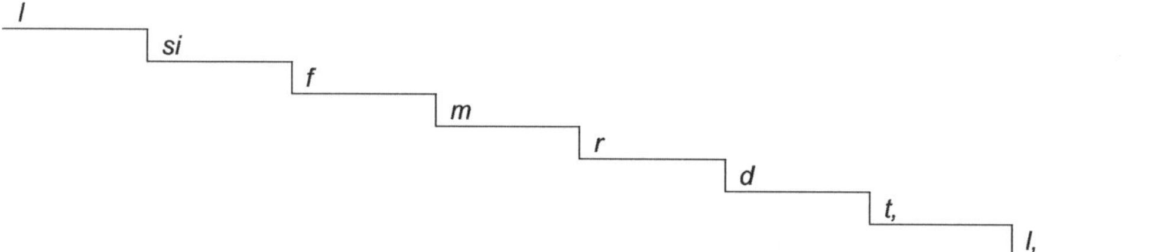

Figure 8.197 Pattern for the harmonic minor scale

2. Present the harmonic minor scale in staff notation and present the rule of placement.

Figure 8.198 Harmonic minor scale in staff notation

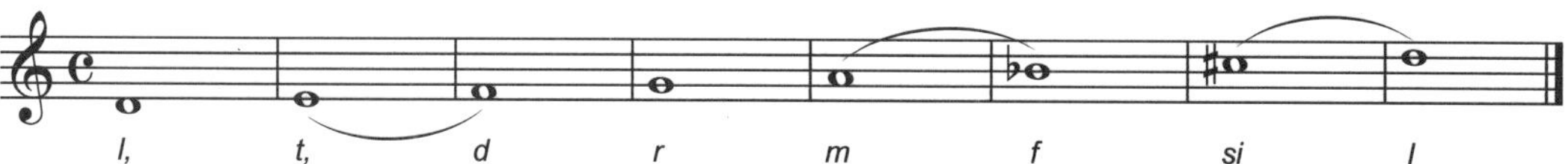

3. Present *Ah, Poor Bird* in stick notation.

Figure 8.199 *Ah, Poor Bird* in stick notation

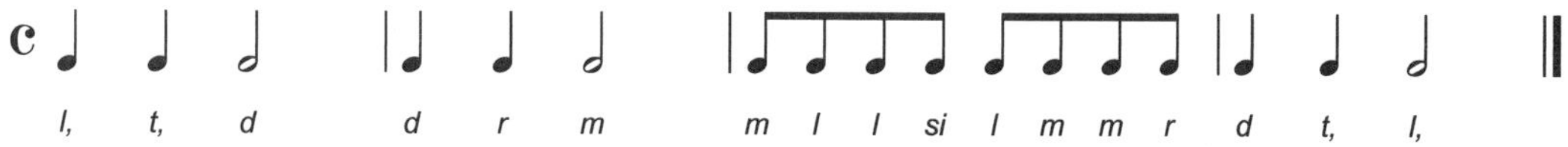

4. Present *Ah, Poor Bird* in staff notation.

Figure 8.200 *Ah, Poor Bird* in staff notation

Assimilative Phase: Practice

Stage One: Initial Practice

1. Review the aural awareness stage and connect the sound to solfège syllables.
2. Review the visual awareness activities and associate standard notation with the visual.

3. Transform the target pattern into a harmonic minor scale and perform the scale in canon.
4. Review the aural and visual presentation of *harmonic minor scale.*
5. Example to read and write and use for improvisation activities from repertoire: *Go Down Moses* and *Vine and Fig Tree*

Stage Two: Practice

Reading

1. Read *Ah, Poor Bird* in rhythm notation with solfège syllables notation and staff notation.
2. Read *Go Down Moses* and/or *Vine and Fig Tree* in rhythm notation with solfège syllables or staff notation.

Writing

1. Write *Ah, Poor Bird* in rhythm notation with solfège syllables notation and staff notation.
2. Write *Go Down Moses* and/or *Vine and Fig Tree* in rhythm notation with solfège syllables or staff notation.

Improvisation

The teacher sings a question phrase in solfège syllables using the harmonic minor scale. The students echo an answer phrase in solfège syllables.

Sight-Singing Materials

Houlahan, Mícheál, and Philip Tacka. *Sound Thinking: Music for Sight-Singing and Ear Training.* New York: Boosey & Hawkes, 1991. Vol. 2, pp. 80–82.

Listening

"Ah Poor Bird" from Mark Gilston's album *American Roots*, 2007
"Rose Rose" from the album *Bosed Psaltery Psongsters*
Little Fugue in G minor by Johann Sebastian Bach
Sonata No. 9 in E major Movement 2 by Ludwig van Beethoven
"Joshua Fit the Battle of Jericho," recorded by Chris Barber's Jazz Band, 1957
Passacaglia in C minor, BWV 582, by Johann Sebastian Bach
"The Wild Rider" from *Album for the Young* by Robert Schumann
"Sun Rise Sun Set" from the musical *Fiddler on the Roof*, music by Jerry Bock, lyrics by Sheldon Harnick

Teaching Strategy for Compound Meter $\frac{6}{8}$ Time Signature

Table 8.39 Teaching strategy for compound meter $\frac{6}{8}$ time signature

Element	Concept	Syllables	Theory	Focus Song	Additional Songs
♩. ♪♪♪ ♩ ♪ ♪♩	Two pulsations per measure; each pulsation having three micro pulsations	*ta* *ta ki da* *ta da* *ta ki*	Major diatonic scale	*Row, Row, Row Your Boat*	*Oh How Lovely Is the Evening*

Cognitive Phase: Preparation

Stage One: Developing Kinesthetic Awareness

1. Sing *Row, Row, Row Your Boat* and pat the beat for the entire song.
2. Determine the macro and micro beats (beat subdivision).
3. Sing *Row, Row, Row Your Boat* and clap the rhythm for the entire song.
4. Sing *Row, Row, Row Your Boat* and point to a representation of the rhythm on the board.

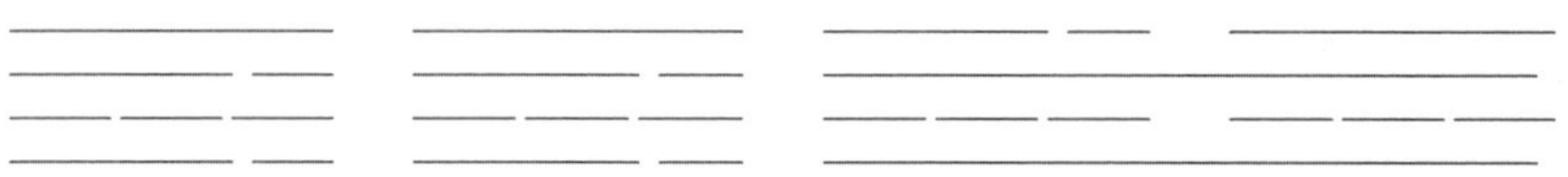

Figure 8.201 Representation of the rhythm of *Row, Row, Row Your Boat*

5. Divide the class into two groups. Group one pats the beat for the target phrase and group two clap the rhythm. Switch.
6. Sing *Row, Row, Row Your Boat.* Step the beat and clap the rhythm.

Stage Two: Developing Aural Awareness

Review the kinesthetic activities with the focus song. Sing the target phrase while keeping the beat before asking each question.

Determine the number of beats in the phrase.

Teacher: "Andy, how many beats did we keep?"
Student: "Four."

Questions for target phrase 3.

Teacher: "Andy, how many sounds did we sing on each beat?"
Student: "Three sounds."
Teacher: "Andy, describe these sounds."
Student: "They are even."

Questions for target phrase 2.

Teacher: "Andy, how many beats did we keep in phrase two?"
Student: "Four."
Teacher: "Andy, was there a pitch that lasted two beats?"
Student: "Yes, on beats three and four."
Teacher: "Andy, how many sounds did we sing on beat one?"
Student: "Two sounds."
Teacher: "Andy, describe these sounds."
Student: "Long, short."
Teacher: "Andy, how many sounds did we sing on beat two?"
Student: "Two sounds."
Teacher: "Andy, describe these sounds."
Student: "Long, short."

Determine that phrase four has the same rhythm as phrase two.
Questions for target phrase one.

Teacher: "Andy, how many beats did we keep in phrase one?"
Student: "Four."
Teacher: "Andy, how many sounds were on beats one and two?"
Student: "One sound."
Teacher: "Andy, how many sounds did we sing on beat four?"
Student: "One sound."
Teacher: "Andy, how many sounds did we sing on beat three?"
Student: "Two sounds."
Teacher: "Andy, describe these sounds."
Student: "Long, short."

Stage Three: Developing Visual Awareness

Assess kinesthetic and aural awareness by allowing the class to perform several of the kinesthetic and aural awareness activities.

1. The instructor hums the target phrase and asks the students to create a visual representation of the target phrase. The students may use manipulatives.

   Teacher: "Pick up what you need to re-create what you heard" or "Draw what you heard." The teacher assesses the students' level of understanding.

2. The students share their representations with each other.
3. The instructor invites one student to the board to share his or her representation with the class. If necessary, corrections to the representation can be made by reviewing the aural awareness questions.
4. Students sing *Row Row Row Your Boat* with a neutral syllable and point to their representation.
5. Figure out the solfège syllables for the phrase.

Associative Phase: Presentation

Assess the kinesthetic, aural awareness, and visual awareness activities with the phrase one of *Row Row Row Your Boat.*

Stage One: Label the Sound

1. In compound meter, we call one sound on a beat *ta.*
2. When we hear three sounds that are evenly distributed over one beat, we call it *ta ki da.*
3. When we hear two sounds on a beat, one long followed by a short sound, we call it *ta da.*
4. Sing *Row, Row, Row Your Boat* with rhythm syllables while tapping the beat.
5. Sing *Row, Row, Row Your Boat* with rhythm syllables while conducting the beat.

Figure 8.202 *Row, Row, Row Your Boat* with rhythm syllables

Stage Two: Present the Notation

Dotted Quarter Note

In compound meter, the macro beat is a dotted quarter note.

Three Eighth Notes

Three even sounds that occur on one beat, where the beat is equal to a dotted quarter note, are called three eighth notes.

Figure 8.203 Dotted quarter note in $\frac{6}{8}$

Dotted Half Note

One sound on two beats, where the beat is equal to a dotted quarter note, is called a dotted half note.

Figure 8.204 Dotted half note in $\frac{6}{8}$

Quarter Note Followed by an Eighth Note

Two sounds on a beat, where the first sound is twice as long as the second sound, are called a quarter note followed by an eighth note.

Figure 8.205 Quarter note followed by an eighth note in $\frac{6}{8}$

Eighth Note Followed by a Quarter Note

Two sounds on a beat, where the first sound is short and the second sound is long, are represented as an eighth note followed by a quarter note.

Figure 8.206 Eighth note followed by a quarter note in $\frac{6}{8}$

Assimilative Phase: Practice

Stage One: Initial Practice

Review the aural presentation of *ta ki da* in *Row, Row, Row Your Boat.* Review the visual presentation of dotted quarter notes, three eighth notes, a dotted half note, and a quarter note followed by an eighth note in $\frac{6}{8}$ meter.

Stage Two: Practice

Reading

1. Transform the rhythm of *Row, Row, Row Your Boat* into *Oh, How Lovely Is the Evening.*

2. Read *Row, Row, Row Your Boat* in traditional rhythmic notation with rhythm syllables.
3. Read the rhythm notation of *Oh, How Lovely Is the Evening.*

Writing

1. Write *Row, Row, Row Your Boat* in stick notation.
2. Add heartbeats below the stick notation.

Improvisation

The teacher claps a question phrase and chants rhythm syllables. The students clap an answer phrase and chant rhythm syllables. The instructor writes a song in stick notation but leaves out four beats. The students improvise four-beat rhythms that use syncopated rhythms.

Listening

Jesu Joy of Man's Desiring from Cantata No. 147 by Johann Sebastian Bach
Movement 3, Violin Concerto by Ludwig van Beethoven
Horn Concerto No. 4 in E flat major, K. 495, Movement III, Rondo by Wolfgang Amadeus Mozart
"When Johnny comes Marching Home" from *Songs of the Civil War*, played by the United States Military Academy Band

Sight-Singing Materials

Houlahan, Mícheál, and Philip Tacka. *Sound Thinking: Music for Sight-Singing and Ear Training.* New York: Boosey & Hawkes, 1991. Vol. 2, pp. 15–24, 45–56, 105–120.

Teaching Strategy for *fi* (Dorian mode)

Table 8.40 Teaching strategy for *fi*

Element	Concept	Syllables	Theory	Focus Song	Additional Songs
fi	Dorian mode and melodic minor scale	*fi*	Scale structure	*Drunken Sailor*	

Cognitive Phase: Preparation

Stage One: Developing Kinesthetic Awareness

1. Sing the fourth phrase and point to a representation of the melodic contour at the board.

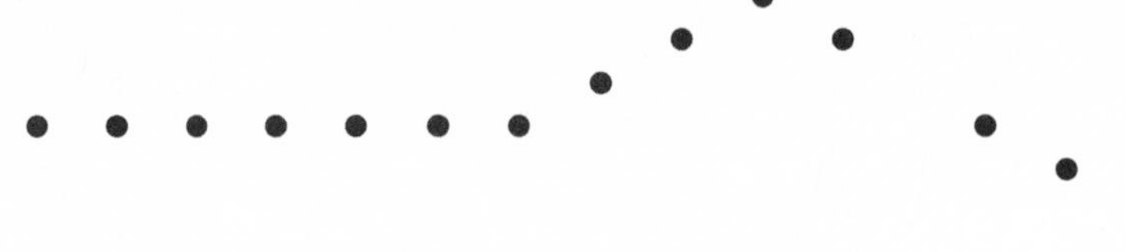

Figure 8.207 Melodic contour of phrase four of *Drunken Sailor*

2. Sing the fourth phrase of *Drunken Sailor* and show the melodic contour.
3. Sing the fourth phrase of *Drunken Sailor* with rhythm syllables and show the melodic contour.

Stage Two: Developing Aural Awareness

Review the kinesthetic activities with the focus song *Drunken Sailor.* Sing while keeping the beat before asking each question.

Teacher: "Andy, how many beats are in phrase four?"
Student: "Eight."

Determine the lowest and highest notes.

Teacher: "Andy, sing the lowest note of the phrase on "loo."
Student: Andy sings low *la.*
Teacher: "Andy, on which beat do you hear the lowest note of that phrase?"
Student: "Seven and eight."
Teacher: "Andy, tell me the solfège syllable for the last two beats."
Student: "Low *la,.*"
Teacher: "Andy, sing the highest note of the phrase."
Student: "*la.*"
Teacher: "Andy, on which beat do you hear the highest pitch?"
Student: "Second half of fourth beat."
Teacher: "Andy, tell me the solfège syllable for that pitch."
Student: "*la.*"

Determine the solfège syllables for the first four beats of the target phrase.

Teacher: "Andy, what solfège syllable begins the phrase?"
Student: "*mi.*"
Teacher: "Andy, if the first pitch is *mi,* how many times do we sing that pitch at the beginning of the phrase?"
Student: "Seven times."

The teacher sings the first four beats on "loo."

Teacher: "Andy, describe the direction of the pitches."
Student: "Stepwise and ascending." [The student will most likely say that the pitches are *mi fa so la.*]

The teacher sings *mi fa so la* and then hums *mi fi so la* and asks the students to describe the difference. The teacher asks the students to name the pitches if they move stepwise ascending from *mi* to *la*. The students recognize that the second pitch is higher than the *fa* that the instructor originally sang. The students should verbalize that the phrase begins on *mi* but the second pitch is not *fa* but rather a whole step higher than *mi*.

Stage Three: Developing Visual Awareness

Assess kinesthetic and aural awareness by allowing the class to perform several of the kinesthetic and aural awareness activities.

1. The instructor hums the target phrase and asks the students to create a visual representation of the melody of the target phrase. The students may use manipulatives.

   Teacher: "Pick up what you need to re-create what you heard" or "Draw what you heard." The teacher assesses the students' level of understanding.
2. The students share their representations with each other.
3. The instructor invites one student to the board to share his or her representation with the class. If necessary, corrections to the representation can be made by reviewing the aural awareness questions.
4. The students sing the fourth phrase of *Drunken Sailor* with a neutral syllable and point to their representation.
5. Sing the fourth phrase of *Drunken Sailor* with rhythm syllables.

Associative Phase: Presentation

Assess the kinesthetic, aural awareness, and visual awareness activities with the phrase one of the *Drunken Sailor.*

Stage One: Label the Sound

1. The teacher and students collect the eight pitches of the Dorian mode from low to high.
2. The teacher names new syllable in sequence "*fi*" and shows the hand sign.
3. The teacher specifically names the sequence "Dorian mode."
4. The teacher sings the Dorian mode from low to high and back with solfège syllables and hand signals. The students echo.
5. Eight students sing the Dorian mode with hand signs and solfège syllables.

Figure 8.208 Hand sign for *fi*

Stage Two: Present the Notation

Present the pattern for the Dorian mode. The Dorian mode is a minor sounding mode. There are two ways to use solfège syllables to sing the Dorian mode. The Dorian mode may be sung without altering solfège syllables when sung from *re* to *re*. Because the first three notes on the Dorian mode consist of a major second followed by a minor second, the Dorian mode may also be sung beginning on *la* and ending on *la* if we raise the sixth degree a half step.

Figure 8.209 Dorian Mode

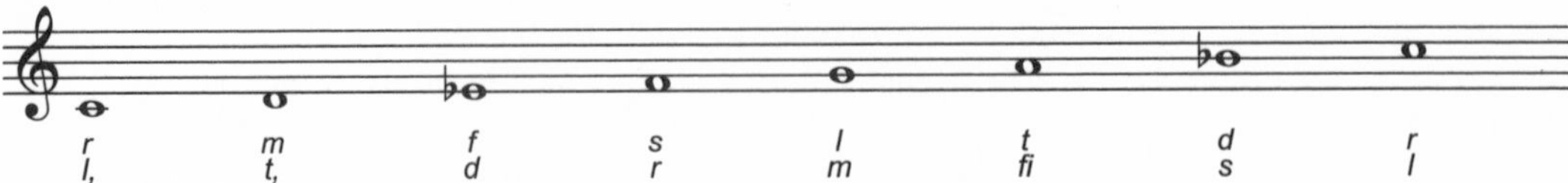

Assimilative Phase: Practice

Stage One: Initial Practice

Intervallic Distance between the Notes of the Dorian Mode

Note the intervals between *la,-ti, do-re re-mi mi-fi so-la* are whole steps. The distance between *ti,-do* and *fi-so* is a half step. We can refer to whole steps as major seconds (M2) and half steps as minor seconds (m2).

Stage Two: Practice

Reading

Read *Drunken Sailor* in rhythm notation with solfège syllables and staff notation. Students should also be taught to read the Dorian mode using re as the tonic note.

Writing

Write *Drunken Sailor* in rhythm notation with solfège syllables and staff notation.

Improvisation

The instructor or another student may sing a descending Dorian scale with a specific rhythm. A student improvises an ascending Dorian scale with the same or a different rhythm.

Students create a different ending to Dorian folk songs.

Listening

Mikrokosmos Vol. 1, Nos. 31 and 32, and Vol. 2, No. 65, by Belá Bartók
"Round Dance II" from *For Children* Vol. 2, No. 9, by Belá Bartók

Teaching Strategy for *ta* (Mixolydian mode)

Table 8.41 Teaching strategy for *ta*

Element	Concept	Syllables	Theory	Focus Song	Additional Songs
ta	Mixolydian mode	*ta*	Mixolydian scale structure	*Old Joe Clark*	

Cognitive Phase: Preparation

Stage One: Developing Kinesthetic Awareness

1. Sing the last phrase of *Old Joe Clark* and point to a representation of the melodic contour at the board.

Figure 8.210 Melodic contour of last phrase of *Old Joe Clark*

2. Sing the last phrase of *Old Joe Clark* and clap the melodic contour.
3. Sing the last phrase with rhythm syllables while clapping the melodic contour.

Stage Two: Developing Aural Awareness

Review the kinesthetic activities with the focus song *Old Joe Clark.* Sing while keeping the beat before asking each question.

Teacher: "Andy, how many beats are in the last phrase?"
Student: "Eight."
Teacher: "Andy, what is the general direction of the melodic contour?"
Student: "Up and then down."

Determine the final and beginning pitch of the target phrase.

Teacher: "Andy, sing the lowest note of the phrase." (The student sings on "loo"–*do.*)
Teacher: "Andy, what is the beginning pitch of the phrase?"
Student: "*so.*"

Determine the solfège syllables for the first three pitches.

Teacher: "Andy, if we start on *so,* what would the next pitch be?"
Student: "*la.*"
Teacher: "Andy, if the next pitch is *la,* what would the next pitch be?" [The student will most likely say *ti.*]

The teacher sings the beginning of the last phrase using "real *ti*" (*so la ti* instead of *so la ta*).

Teacher: "Andy, is that how our song goes?"
Student: "No."
Teacher: "Is that third note higher or lower than *ti?*"
Student: "Lower."

The teacher sings the first three pitches using *so, la,* and humming *ta.* The students should verbalize that the third pitch of the phrase is a half step above *la* rather than a whole step above *la.*

Stage Three: Developing Visual Awareness

Assess kinesthetic and aural awareness by allowing the class to perform several of the kinesthetic and aural awareness activities.

1. The instructor hums the target phrase and asks the students to create a visual representation of the melody of the target phrase. The students may use manipulatives.

   Teacher: "Pick up what you need to re-create what you heard" or "Draw what you heard." The teacher assesses the students' level of understanding.
2. The students share their representations with each other.
3. The instructor invites one student to the board to share his or her representation with the class. If necessary, corrections to the representation can be made by reviewing the aural awareness questions.
4. The students sing the last phrase of *Old Joe Clark* with a neutral syllable and point to their representation.
5. The students sing the last phrase of *Old Joe Clark* with rhythm syllables.

Associative Phase: Presentation

Assess the kinesthetic, aural awareness, and visual awareness activities with the last phrase of *Old Joe Clark.*

Stage One: Label the Sound

Figure 8.211 Hand sign for *ta*

1. The teacher and student sing the tone set that makes the Mixolydian mode (*do–re–mi–fa–so–la–ta–do'*) and show the hand sign.
2. The teacher specifically names it a "Mixolydian scale." Collect pitches starting *do* and altering *ti* to *ta.*
3. Teacher: "We have a note that is between *la* and *ti.* We call it *ta.*"
4. The teacher sings Mixolydian mode from low to high students will echo sing with solfège syllables and hand signs.

Stage Two: Present the Notation

1. Present the scale on G using solfège and using hands signs as we sing from the staff.
2. The teacher draws tone steps on the board and a student comes to the board and writes solfège on the steps.
3. The teacher has a student come to the board and write stick notation and solfège beneath the notation.

Figure 8.212 C Mixolydian scale

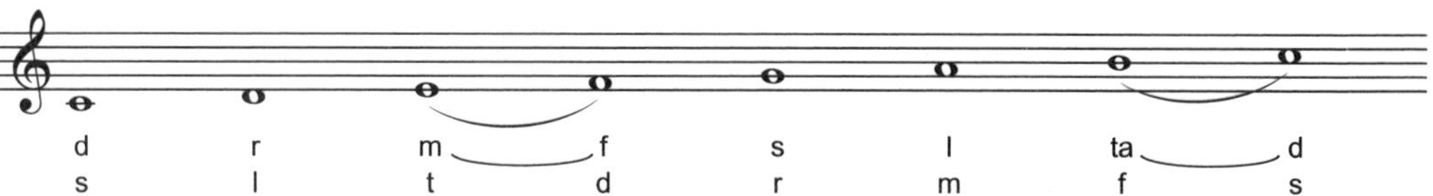

We can read the Mixolydian scale using two different tone sets.

Intervallic Distance between the Notes of the Mixolydian Mode

Note the interval between *ta–do'* is a whole step. The half steps of *mi-fa* and *ti-do* remain in the same relationship. We can refer to whole steps as major seconds (M2; *ta* and *do'*) and half steps as minor seconds (m2; *ti-do'*).

Assimilative Phase: Practice

Stage One: Initial Practice

Review the aural and visual presentation of Mixolydian mode in *Old Joe Clark.*

Stage Two: Practice

Reading

Read *Old Joe Clark* in rhythm notation with solfège syllables notation and staff notation. Students need to be taught how to read Mixolydian melodies beginning on *so.*

Writing

Write *Old Joe Clark* in rhythm notation with solfège syllables notation and staff notation.

Improvisation

The instructor or another student may sing a descending Mixolydian scale with a specific rhythm. A student improvises an ascending Mixolydian scale with the same or a different rhythm.

Students create different ending to folk songs in Mixolydian mode.

Listening

"Old Joe Clark" from the album *Bluegrass Mandolin Extravanganza*
Mikrokosmos Vol. 2, Nos. 40 and 48, by Belá Bartók

Focus Songs for Grade Five

Focus Song for Major Scale

Figure 8.213 Alleluia

Focus Song for an Eighth Note Followed by a Dotted Quarter Note

Figure 8.214 *Charlotte Town*

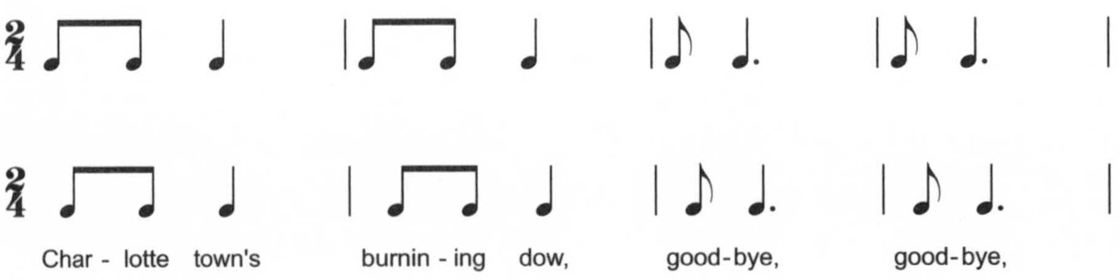

Focus Song for Natural Minor Scale

Figure 8.215 *Alleluia* in Major

Figure 8.216 *Alleluia* in Minor

Focus Song for *si*

Figure 8.217 *Ah, Poor Bird*

Focus Song for Compound Meter (patterns in $\frac{6}{8}$ meter)

Figure 8.218 *Row, Row, Row Your Boat*

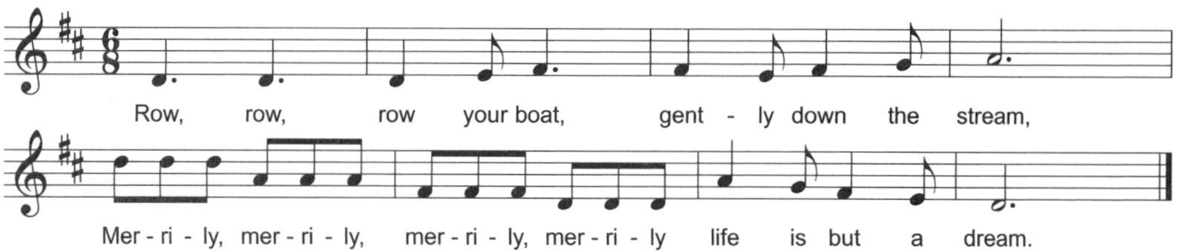

Focus Song for *fi*

Figure 8.219 *Drunken Sailor*

continued

Figure 8.219 *Continued*

Focus Song for *ta*

Figure 8.220 *Old Joe Clark*

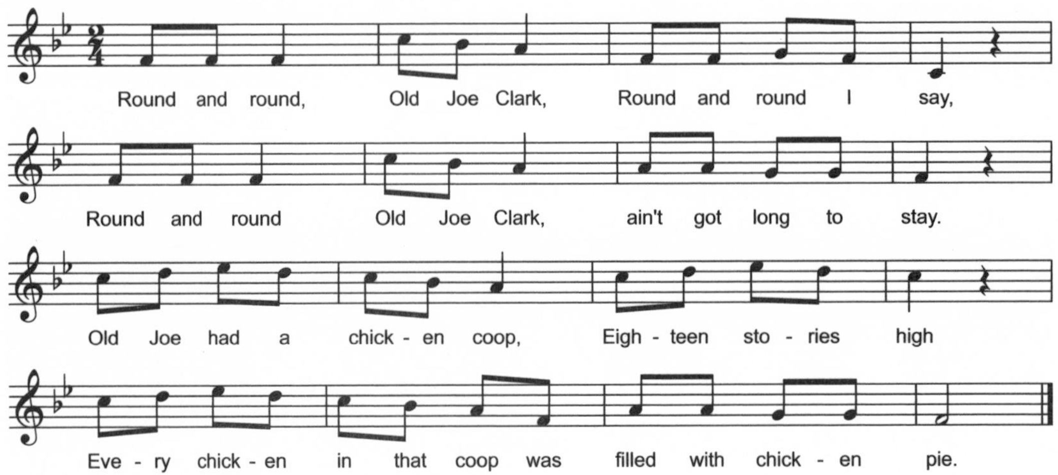

➤ Discussion Questions

1. How do we construct a teaching strategy for each element based on the model of learning presented in chapter 6?
2. Teaching strategies promotes dictation skills and sight-reading skills. Discuss.
3. Discuss the role of questioning in developing meta-cognition skills.
4. Discuss the in-built assessment opportunities when using the teaching strategy.
5. How does the implementation of the teaching strategy promote independent learning in the classroom?

6. The teaching strategies presented in this chapter are too cumbersome for instructors to follow. It is much more effective to present information in a theoretical manner and then use this information to practice music skills of reading and writing. Discuss.

➤ Ongoing Assignment

1. Develop teaching strategy plans based on the model provided in this chapter for your teaching portfolio. Demonstrate how you have infused your teaching strategy with your own creative ideas.

Suggested Readings

Choksy, Lois. *The Kodály Method Comprehensive Music Education.* 3rd ed. Upper Saddle River, N.J.: Prentice Hall, 1999.

Eisen, Ann, and Lamar Robertson. *An American Methodology.* Lake Charles, La.: Sneaky Snake Publications, 1997.

Houlahan, Mícheál, and Philip Tacka. *Sound Thinking: Developing Musical Literacy.* 2 vols. New York: Boosey & Hawkes, 1995.

Chapter 9

Sequencing and Lesson Planning

Every lesson should be built in such a way that at its end the child should feel his strength increased rather than any sense of tiredness; moreover he should look forward to the next.

Zoltán Kodály, Preface to the Volume "Musical Reading and Writing by Erzsébet Szönyi," in *The Selected Writings.*

Key Questions

How does a philosophy of music education influence individual music lessons?

What are the key components of a lesson plan?

What is the connection between the music lesson plan, curriculum goals, monthly plans, and teaching strategies?

What are the lesson plans associated with the cognitive phase of instruction?

What is the lesson plan associated with the associative phase of instruction?

What is the lesson plan associated with the assimilative phase of instruction?

How can we musically transition between the different sections of a lesson?

How do we evaluate a lesson plan?

How many lessons does it take to teach a specific musical concept or element?

Why do we define musical concepts prior to teaching specific musical elements?

Are there activities or procedures that can be consistent in every music lesson?

What can constitute new learning in every music lesson?

What activities can be used to practice known musical concepts and elements?

How can practice activities be varied so that they are interesting rather than repetitive exercises or drills?

How can we define music elements in terms of how a child experiences music?

How can a music instructor come to an understanding of how a young learner thinks?

How can a music instructor guide a student's perceptual understanding of a sound event?

What modes of learning and understanding are most common to young learners?

What modes of learning are necessary for students to come to an understanding of a particular musical concept?

In the second part of this book we have presented a model for teaching the building blocks of commonly associated with children's games and folk music as well as presenting various strategies for teaching specific elements. At the end of each chapter we have provided you with a sample of the different kinds of lesson plan structures to use. The goal of this chapter is to review the different types of lesson plans as well as link them to written objectives built upon the curriculum goals for each grade.

Introduction

A primary goal of this chapter is to provide teachers with the technique for developing and executing lesson plans. We are also concerned with developing a child's cognitive "thinking" skills that leads to a deeper understanding and appreciation of music through performing, critical thinking, music literacy, listening, as well as composing and improvising.

Components of a Lesson Plan: Overview

Lesson Objectives

Instructors ought to formulate behavioral objectives for teaching. Behavioral objectives are directly linked to activities that the students will perform in the course of their lessons. The objectives should be stated specifically; each objective needs a focus. Each objective should refer to a specific song or phrase within a song. In a series of music lessons, there should be objectives for performance through singing, movement, playing on instruments, conducting, developing critical thinking skills through music literacy, listening, and improvisation/composition.

The following are samples of general objectives that the instructor can modify when writing lesson plans. Remember, the more specifically these objectives are stated, the easier it is for teachers to devise questions that will ensure the students' participation in the learning process and the development of cognitive skills.

The students will:

- Tunefully sing songs that will be used to focus the students' attention on the new element while performing the beat internally and or externally
- Aurally identify the beat on which the new rhythmic or melodic sound occurs during preparation and presentation phases

- Create a visual representation of the target phrase containing the new element
- Write melodic motifs of unknown songs using stick or staff notation
- Identify a known song by hearing melodic patterns from the song
- Sing selected songs indicating strong and weak beats
- Sing selected songs and clap the rhythm
- Identify a known song from hearing the rhythm of the song
- Sing selected songs using rhythm syllables
- Read known songs from stick and staff notation
- Read new songs from stick and staff notation
- Read known songs using rhythm syllables
- Read new unfamiliar songs using rhythm syllables
- Write rhythmic motifs of known songs using stick or staff notation
- Improvise and create music with the new musical element

Connecting the Lesson Plan to Objectives, Curriculum Goals, Monthly Plans, and Teaching Strategies

We suggest a minimum of five lessons are required in order to prepare and make conscious any musical element. The objectives for each of these types of lessons are derived from activities suggested in the teaching strategies (chapter 8). Although the lessons will differ across the three phases of learning, all preparation lessons, regardless of the element being prepared, will be similar in structure. The same is true for all presentation and practice lessons. This text provides suggested teaching activities for the five different lessons for each element. These lessons are set out in table 9.1.

Table 9.1 Five lessons for each element

Learning Phase	Lesson Plan
The Cognitive Phase of Learning	The Kinesthetic Preparation Lesson The Aural Awareness Preparation Lesson The Visual Awareness Preparation Lesson
The Associative Phase of Learning	Presentation Lesson
The Assimilative Phrase of Learning	Practice Lesson

Of course, additional practice of the new element takes place during the next preparation/practice lessons.

Lesson Plans for the Cognitive Phase of Instruction and Learning

The goal of the cognitive phase of instruction and learning is to prepare students to recognize patterns encountered in their song materials. At the same time, the instructor simultaneously develops their vocal production and musicianship skills. The cognitive phase of instruction addresses three modes of learning:

- Developing kinesthetic awareness
- Developing aural awareness
- Developing visual awareness

The cognitive phase of instruction and learning cannot be rushed; time invested will help prevent confusion.

The Preparation/Practice Lesson

In preparation/practice lessons, we develop singing abilities, instrumental skills, teach new repertoire, and develop movement skills. The primary goal of preparation/practice lessons is to prepare a new concept and practice known musical elements. Each preparation lesson has an instructional context (preparation) and a re-enforcement (practice) context. This dual structure of the preparation lesson provides the students with the time to process their kinesthetic, aural, and visual understandings of the new concept, while providing opportunities to further develop their musical skills with the previously learned musical elements. In chapter 7 we defined the three primary skill areas as reading, writing, and improvisation and showed how they were related to all other musical skills. These three skills become the focal points for the practice segment of the preparation/practice lessons.

There are three types of preparation/practice lessons:

1. Lesson plan for *developing kinesthetic awareness* of a new melodic or rhythmic concept and concentrated practice of known melodic or rhythmic elements through reading
2. Lesson plan for *developing aural awareness* of a new melodic or rhythmic concept and concentrated practice of known melodic or rhythmic elements through writing
3. Lesson plan for *developing visual awareness* of a new melodic or rhythmic concept and concentrated practice of known melodic or rhythmic elements through improvisation and composition

Lesson Plan for *Developing Kinesthetic Awareness* of a New Melodic or Rhythmic Concept and Practice of Known Melodic or Rhythmic Element through Reading

During a kinesthetic preparation/practice lesson, the instructor reviews several songs containing the new element in a variety of patterns to students in a stylistically correct manner. At the same time the teacher models a kinesthetic motion that focuses the students' attention on the new element. This provides the students with time to respond to and interact with the musical structures. Movement such as clapping hands or tapping or pointing to visuals enhances students' understanding of elements. Initially the teacher should guide students through these activities until they can sing and perform independently.

During the practice part of the lesson, the instructor reinforces and further develops the students' understanding the preceding musical element through a concentrated reading activity. The practice section of the lesson should also include assessment activities to help the teacher identify the students who require extra help.

Sample Lesson Objectives for Developing Kinesthetic Awareness of a New Rhythmic or Melodic Concept and Practice of Known Rhythmic or Melody Concept through Reading

The following are sample objectives for the kinesthetic preparation/practice lesson plan. All of the following objectives need to be modified by relating them to specific songs and phrases.

Lesson Objectives

1. Performance of Known Musical Concepts and Elements
   a. The students will review known repertoire through singing, playing on instruments, movement, and conducting during the introductory part of the lesson.
   b. The students will review known rhythmic or melodic elements as well as music skills through singing during the introductory part of the lesson. For example, if the instructor is preparing a rhythmic element, then all known rhythmic elements will be reviewed in the introduction of the lesson.
2. Acquisition of Repertoire: Learning a new song and/or game to prepare the next element. Students will learn the text of a new song and identify the form.
3. Performance and Preparation of New Element: Kinesthetic preparation of a new rhythmic or melodic concept. The students will demonstrate their understanding of a new rhythmic or melodic concept kinesthetically by:
   - singing and keeping a beat
   - singing and clapping the rhythm
   - singing and pointing to a representation of new rhythmic or melodic concept in the target phrase
   - singing and performing beat and rhythm simultaneously, or for melodic concepts, clapping the melodic contour while singing rhythm syllables
4. Movement Development: The students will practice the movement skill of . . . while playing . . .
5. Performance and Musical Skill Development: Practice of known element. The students will practice reading the preceding rhythmic or melodic elements.
6. Listening: The instructor will provide a listening experience by singing or playing a song.

Table 9.2 Framework of a kinesthetic awareness lesson plan

Focus	Activities, Procedures, and Assessments
Introduction	
Performance and demonstration of known musical concepts and elements.	Develop singing skills through beautiful singing, vocal warm-ups breathing exercises Review of known rhythmic or melodic elements

continued

Table 9.2 *Continued*

Focus	Activities, Procedures, and Assessments
Core activities	
Acquisition of repertoire Performance and preparation of new element	Teacher provides students with a series of discovery learning activities that will develop their knowledge of four sounds on a beat (sixteenth notes) through known songs Developing kinesthetic awareness: a) Sing *Paw Paw Patch* and keep the beat b) Sing and clap the rhythm c) Sing and point to a representation of phrase one, — — — — — — — — — — — d) Sing *Paw Paw Patch,* walk the beat, and clap the rhythm
Movement development	
Performance and development of musical skills	Students read *Frosty Weather* from stick or staff notation
Closure	
Review and summation	

Lesson Plan for *Developing Aural Awareness* of a New Melodic or Rhythmic Concept and Practice of Known Melodic or Rhythmic Elements through Writing

During the aural preparation stage, the students construct an aural understanding of the new musical concept. Students aurally identify and describe the new musical concept and distinguish it from familiar ones. The aural preparation is dependent upon information students have gained in the kinesthetic lesson. Questions need to be formulated that focus students on the phrase structure of the song and move to the phrase that will be used for describing the new musical concept.

The practice activities in an aural preparation lesson focus on writing. The practice section of the lesson should also include assessment activities to help the instructor identify students who require extra help in learning a particular concept.

Sample Lesson Objectives for Developing Aural Awareness of a New Rhythmic or Melodic Concept and Practice of Known Rhythmic or Melodic Concept through Writing

The following are sample objectives for the aural preparation/practice lesson plan. All of the following objectives need to be modified by relating them to specific songs and phrases.

Lesson Objectives

1. Performance of Known Material
   a. The students will review known repertoire through singing, playing on instruments, movement, and conducting during the introductory part of the lesson.
   b. The students will review known rhythmic or melodic elements as well as music skills through singing during the introductory part of the lesson.
2. Acquisition of Repertoire: Learning a new song or game to prepare the next element. Students will learn the text of a new song and identify the form.
3. Performance and Preparation: Aural preparation of new rhythmic or melodic concept:
   a. Assess students' understanding of known rhythmic or melodic elements through singing during the introductory part of the lesson.
   b. The students will demonstrate their aural understanding of new rhythmic or melodic concept by:
      - independently singing and keeping a beat
      - independently singing and clapping the rhythm
      - independently singing and pointing to a representation of new rhythmic or melodic concept in the target phrase
      - independently singing and performing beat and rhythm simultaneously, or for melodic concepts, clapping the melodic contour while singing rhythm syllables
      - verbally describing the characteristics of the new concept
4. Movement Development. The students will practice the movement skill of . . . while playing . . .
5. Performance and Musical Skill Development: Practice of known element. The students will practice writing using stick and staff notation of known rhythmic and melodic elements.
6. Listening. The instructor will provide a listening experience by singing or playing a song.

Table 9.3 Framework for developing aural awareness lesson plan

Focus	Activities, Procedures, and Assessments
Introduction	
Performance and demonstration of known musical concepts and elements	Develop singing skills through beautiful singing, vocal warm-ups breathing exercises Review of known rhythmic or melodic elements
Core activities	
Acquisition of repertoire	

continued

Table 9.3 *Continued*

Focus	Activities, Procedures, and Assessments
Performance and preparation of new element	Aural awareness stage Known song: *Paw Paw Patch* a) Review Kinesthetic b) Teacher & Student sing phrase one and keep the beat c) Teacher: "Andy, how many beats did we keep?" four d) Teacher: "Andy, which beat has the most sounds?" beat three e) Teacher: "How many sounds are on beat 3?" four sounds f) Teacher: "If beat three has four sounds, how many sounds are on the other beats?" two sounds
Movement development	
Performance and development of musical skills	Students write the final phrase of *Great Big House* from memory using stick notation and solfège syllables
Closure Review and summation	

Lesson Plan for *Developing Visual Awareness* of a New Melodic or Rhythmic Concept and Practice of Known Melodic or Rhythmic Elements through Improvisation and Composition

In the visual stage, students are asked to create a visual representation of the new concept. This representation should be based upon information learned from the kinesthetic and aural stages as well as from their intuitive knowledge. In this manner perception leads to conceptual information and ultimately musical understanding. By connecting the aural stage to the visual stage, the student is allowed time to make the connection between what they hear and how to represent it. Practice activities in a visual lesson focus on improvisation/composition. The practice section of the lesson should also include assessment activities to help the teacher identify students who require extra help in learning a particular concept.

Sample Lesson Objectives for Developing Visual Awareness of a New Rhythmic or Melodic Concept and Practice of Known Rhythmic or Melodic Concept through Improvisation and Composition

The following are sample objectives for the visual preparation/practice lesson plan. All of the following objectives need to be modified by relating them to specific songs and phrases.

Lesson Objectives

1. Performance and Demonstration of Known Musical Elements
   a. The students will review known repertoire through singing, playing on instruments, movement, and conducting during the introductory part of the lesson.

   b. The students will review known rhythmic or melodic elements as well as music skills through singing during the introductory part of the lesson.
2. Acquisition of Repertoire: Learning a new song and/or game to prepare the next element. Students will learn the text of a new song and identify the form.
3. Performance and Preparation: Visual preparation of new rhythmic or melodic concept:
   a. Assess the students' understanding of known rhythmic or melodic elements through singing during the introductory part of the lesson.
   b. The students will demonstrate their visual understanding of a new rhythmic or melodic concept by:
      - independently singing and keeping a beat
      - independently singing and clapping the rhythm
      - independently singing and pointing to a representation of new rhythmic or melodic concept in the target phrase
      - independently singing and performing beat and rhythm simultaneously, or for melodic concepts, clapping the melodic contour while singing rhythm syllables
      - verbally describe the characteristics of the new concept
      - creating a visual representation of the target phrase
4. Movement Development. The students will practice the movement skill of . . . while playing . . .
5. Performance and Musical Skill Development: Practice of known element. The students will practice known rhythmic and melodic elements through improvisation and composition.
6. Listening. The instructor will provide a listening experience by singing or playing a song.

Table 9.4 Developing visual awareness lesson plan

Focus	**Activities, Procedures, and Assessments**
Introduction	
Performance and demonstration of known musical concepts and elements	Develop singing skills through beautiful singing, vocal warm-ups breathing exercises Review of known melodic or rhythmic elements
Core activities	
Acquisition of repertoire	
Performance and preparation of new element	a) Review the kinesthetic and aural awareness activities using *Paw Paw Patch.* b) Students create a visual based on their aural awareness. Students need to determine how many beats are in the phrase and the number of sounds on each beat. Use manipulatives. (magnets, unifix cubes, etc). c) Students sing and point to their representation.

continued

Table 9.4 *Continued*

Focus	Activities, Procedures, and Assessments
	d) Instructor may ask questions concerning their representation. e) "Identify any rhythmic and melodic elements you recognize."
Movement development	
Performance and musical skill development	Students compose a new ending to *Frosty Weather* using the note *re*
Closure	

Lesson Plans for the Associative Phase of Instruction and Learning

There are two presentation lessons in the associative phase. The goal of the first presentation lesson is to label the new sound with rhythm or solfège syllables. The goal of the second presentation lesson is to present the notation for the new element. The following are sample objectives for the first presentation lesson plan. All of the following objectives need to be modified by relating them to specific songs and phrases.

Lesson Objectives for Presentation Lesson Plan One

1. Performance and Demonstration of Known Musical Concepts and Elements
   a. The students will review known repertoire through singing, playing on instruments, movement, and conducting during the introductory part of the lesson.
   b. The students will review known rhythmic or melodic elements as well as music skills through singing during the introductory part of the lesson.
2. Acquisition of Repertoire: Learning a new song and/or game to prepare the next element. Students will learn the text of a new song and identify the form.
3. Performance and Presentation of Rhythmic or Melodic Syllable for New Musical Concept
   a. Assess the students' understanding of the new element kinesthetically by . . .
   b. Review their aural awareness of the new element in phrase . . . of song . . .
   c. Create a visual representation of the new musical element in the target phrase:
      i. The teacher will present the solfège/rhythm syllables . . . aurally and (show the hand signs for the **target pattern** in the song . . .). The students will sing the target phrase with solfège/rhythm syllables and hand signs. Perform this activity with eight individual students.
      ii. The teacher will present the solfège/rhythm syllables . . . aurally and (show the hand signs for the **related pattern** in the focus song . . .). The students will sing the target phrase with solfège/rhythm syllables and hand signs. Perform this activity with eight individual students.
4. Movement Development. The students will practice the movement skill of . . . while playing . . .

5. Listening. The instructor will provide a listening experience by singing or playing a song.

Table 9.5 Framework for presentation lesson plan one

Focus	Activities, Procedures, and Assessments
Introduction	
Performance and demonstration of known musical concepts and elements	Develop singing skills through beautiful singing, vocal warm-ups breathing exercises
Core activities Acquisition of repertoire	
Performance and presentation the syllables for the new element in the target pattern	Stage one aural presentation a) Teacher: "When we hear four sounds on a beat we call it "ta—ka—di—mi" b) Teacher & Student sing whole song with rhythm syllables and clap the rhythm c) Individual students sing the target phrase with rhythm syllables
Movement development	
Performance and presentation the syllables for the new element in related patterns	Transform the rhythm of *Great Big House* into the rhythm of *Dinah* Students sing with solfège and hand signs Students read *Dinah* from staff notation
Closure	

The following are sample objectives for the second presentation lesson plan. All of the following objectives need to be modified by relating them to specific songs and phrases.

Lesson Objectives for Presentation Lesson Plan Two

1. Performance and Demonstration of Known Musical Concepts and Elements
   a. The students will review known repertoire through singing, playing on instruments, movement, and conducting during the introductory part of the lesson.
   b. The students will review known rhythmic or melodic elements as well as music skills through singing during the introductory part of the lesson.
2. Acquisition of Repertoire: Learning a new song and/or game to prepare the next element. Students will learn the text of a new song and identify the form.
3. Performance and Presentation of Rhythmic or Melodic Syllable for New Musical Concept
   a. The teacher will review the presentation of the solfège/rhythm syllables . . . aurally and (show the hand signs for the target pattern in the song . . .). The

students will sing the target phrase with solfège/rhythm syllables and hand signs. Perform this activity with eight individual students.

b. The instructor will present the rhythmic or melodic notation using the tone steps, stick notation, and staff notation.

4. Movement Development. The students will practice the movement skill of . . . while playing . . .
5. Listening. The instructor will provide a listening experience by singing or playing a song.

Table 9.6 Framework for presentation lesson plan two

Focus	Activities, Procedures, and Assessments
Introduction	
Performance and demonstration of known musical concepts and elements.	Develop singing skills through beautiful singing, vocal warm-ups breathing exercises
Core activities Acquisition of repertoire	
Performance and presentation of the notation for the new element in the target phrase	Review aural presentation Stage two visual presentation a) We can use four sixteenth notes to represent four sounds on a beat. A sixteenth note has a note head and a stem and two flags. Four sixteenth notes have a double beam. b) Our first phrase of *Paw Paw Patch* looks like this: ♥ ♥ ♥ ♥ c) We can read this rhythm pattern using our rhythm syllables d) Teacher sings rhythm syllables while pointing to the heartbeats, Student echo sing using rhythm syllables while pointing to the heartbeats. e) Stick notation is an easy way to write rhythmic notation. Stick notation is traditional notation without the note heads for quarter and eighth notes. Our first phrase of *Paw Paw Patch* looks like this in stick notation:
Movement development	
Performance and presentation of the notation for the new element in related patterns	Transform the rhythm of *Great Big House* into the rhythm of *Dinah* Students sing with solfège and hand signs Students read *Dinah* from staff notation
Closure	

Lesson Plan for the Assimilative Phase of Presentation of Harmony

In the initial practice lesson, the song repertoire and patterns from the presentation phase may be used again to reinforce the new musical concept or element. Entire songs may be used for reinforcement, but attention must first be directed to the phrase or phrases that contain the new element. The students should be given many opportunities to aurally identify the new musical element in known song material.

Lesson Objectives for the Initial Practice of a New Rhythmic or Melodic Concept

The following are sample objectives for the initial practice lesson plan. All of the following objectives need to be modified by relating them to specific songs and phrases.

Initial Practice Lesson Objectives

1. Performance of Known Material
   a. The students will review known repertoire through singing, playing on instruments, movement, and conducting during the introductory part of the lesson.
   b. The students will review known rhythmic or melodic elements as well as music skills through singing during the introductory part of the lesson.
2. Acquisition of Repertoire: Learning a new song and/or game to prepare the next element. The students will learn the text of a new song and identify the form.
3. Performance and Review of Presentation of the New Musical Element
   a. The teacher will review the aural presentation the new musical element.
   b. The teacher will review the visual presentation the new musical element.
   c. The teacher will present the written notation for the new element.
4. Movement Development. The students will practice the movement skill of . . . while playing . . .
5. Performance and Practice of New Element
   a. The students will aurally and visually identify the element in a different four- or eight-beat configurations in known songs.
   b. The Teacher will present the notation for these patterns.
6. Listening: The instructor will provide a listening experience by singing or playing a song.

Briefly review the presentation of the new musical element and practice the new musical element in target patterns and supplementary patterns related to song material containing phrases that are similar to the target phrase. This may involve practicing the new element and working on several musical skill areas.

Table 9.7 Framework for practice lesson

Focus	Activities, Procedures, and Assessments
Introduction	Develop singing skills through beautiful singing, vocal warm-ups breathing exercises
Core activities	
Acquisition of repertoire	

continued

Table 9.7 *Continued*

Focus	Activities, Procedures, and Assessments
Performance and review of presentation of new element	• Review the rhythm syllables to identify the new element in *Paw Paw Patch.* • Review the traditional notation. Read with rhythm syllables. • Identify another song that includes the target pattern motif or a closely related pattern. Review the aural awareness and visual awareness activities as above.
Movement development	
Performance and practice of new element	Transform the target pattern into other four-beat patterns found in the student's song material. For example, transform *Paw Paw Patch* into *Cumberland Gap* and work on other skill areas such as reading writing improvisation/composition and listening.
Closure	

Moving from One Segment of a Lesson to Another Using Transitions

Transitions are the cement that holds the different segments of a lesson together. The following are examples of some of the different types of transitions that can be used during a lesson. The best transitions are musical transitions. If you are transitioning into a segment of a lesson where the focus is on rhythm have a rhythmic focus or if you are moving into a melodic segment of the lesson have a melodic focus.

Story Line Connection

Connecting lessons using a story line may be used in the early childhood classroom. The instructor builds a story around all of the song material used during the lesson. Each song introduced in the lesson is woven into the story line connection.

Using Specific Directions

1. Giving students directions without any verbal language. For example, students may be singing a known folk song and the teacher indicates to the students that they form a circle to play the game.
2. Giving students directions using the melody of a song they are about to sing.

Unconscious Rhythmic or Melodic Connections

1. Sing several songs in the same tonality.
2. Sing several songs with the same time signature and tempo.
3. Sing several songs that have the same form.
4. Sing several songs having the same character or mood.
5. Try conducting a song and ask the students to keep conducting while you sing the next song in the lesson.

Conscious Rhythmic Connections

1. Sing several songs with the same time signature.
2. Sing several songs having the same character or mood.
3. Sing songs that share the same tempo.
4. Sing songs that share rhythmic motifs: *Canoe Song* and *Liza Jane.*
5. Rhythmic reduction of one song can be used as accompaniment to another song.
6. A preceding rhythmic motif may become an ostinato for another song.
7. Transform the rhythm of one song into another song.
8. Sing several songs that have the same form.
9. Use a preceding rhythmic motif to become a rhythmic ostinato for another song.

Conscious Melodic Connections

1. Sing several songs in the same tonality. Preparation for this is done by pointing to the tone or staff ladder.
2. The teacher connects two songs together by using the same melodic motive, for example:
   a. *Bow, Wow, Wow* and *Hot Cross Buns* share the *mi—re—do* motif
   b. *Tideo* and *Great Big House* share the *mi-so—so-la—mi-so—so* motif
3. The music instructor can make use of structural reductions of folk songs to move from one song to another. To make a structural reduction, write the notes that occur on the strong beats of each phrase. Do not include any passing notes or repeated notes. For example, the structural reduction of *Lucy Locket* is the same as the first line of *Bounce High, Bounce Low.*
4. Structural reduction of one song can partner with other songs: *Liza Jane* and *Ridin' In a Buggy.*
5. Transform the melodic motif of one song into a motif of another song.
6. Use a preceding melodic motif to become a melodic ostinato for another song.

Table 9.8 Lesson plan demonstrating melodic connections between the different segments of a lesson

Focus	**Activities, Procedures, and Assessments** **Practice Lesson Plan to Focus on the Notes so–mi and la**
Introduction	Develop singing skills through beautiful singing, vocal warm-ups breathing exercises Known song: *Rocky Mountain* CSP D Students demonstrate their prior knowledge using the song *Rocky Mountain* Sing in unison Sing with rhythm syllables Sing in canon
Core activities	
Acquisition of repertoire	Teach *Tideo* using an appropriate method of presentation. Focus the students attention to the melody of the first phrase *m–s–s–l–m–s–s*

continued

Table 9.8 *Continued*

Focus	Activities, Procedures, and Assessments Practice Lesson Plan to Focus on the Notes so–mi and la
Performance and review of new element	Known song: *Lucy Locket* CSP A (same key as *Tideo*) • Students recognize Great Big House in New Orleans from the instructors hand signs using the notes *la so mi* Sing the entire song with text Write the melody on the board as follows: *la* *so so* *so so* *mi* *mi* Transition to the second phrase of *Snail Snail:* Change the melody of *Great Big House* by changing the second *m* into a *l* and read the phrase backwards. Using this transition, students will recognize the melody as phrase of *Snail Snail.* Play the game *Snail Snail* and have students sing it with solfège syllables
Movement activity	Instructor hums phrase two of *Snail Snail* and asks students if it reminds them of another song (*We Are Dancing In the Forest*) Instructor hums *We Are Dancing in the Forest* students recognize and sing with hand signs and solfège syllables. Teachers read the song from staff notation. Students improvises alternate ending to song.
Performance and review of new element	
Closure	The instructor plays another folk song based on the *m–s–l* tone set for students (recorder: *Little Sally Water*)

Evaluating a Lesson

1. All learning should stem from the enjoyment of singing songs, chanting rhymes, and playing games. The goals of a music lesson should be singing, playing instruments, listening, and the enjoyment of music. Musical concepts and elements are taught to enhance the enjoyment of music.
2. Reading and writing should be done during each lesson. If students can read or write even a small motive from a song, they develop a deeper understanding and appreciation of the song. There should be opportunities for constant reinforcement of musical elements and concepts.
3. A good lesson plan must provide clear answers to the following questions:
   a. Was the lesson presented in a musical manner?
   b. What were the primary and secondary goals of the lesson?
   c. How were the goals of the lesson achieved?
   d. How many songs and games were used in the lesson? What activities used in conjunction with the song material led students to an understanding of the

goals of the lesson? Was there an emphasis on singing and making music? Was there a sufficient variety of songs used in the lesson?

e. Were the goals of the lesson achieved?
f. Was new material prepared and presented in the lesson? What exercises were used in the lesson? Did the musical exercises planned for the lesson help the students achieve the goals?
g. Was there a logical sequence and pacing in the lesson?
h. Was the culmination of the lesson clear?
i. Were there periods of relaxation and concentration in the lesson?
j. What musical skills were developed in the lesson?
k. Were the students active collectively and individually during the lesson?
l. Did the lesson plan provide a means to assess student progress?
m. Was the lesson enjoyable for the students?
n. Did the lesson begin and end with singing?

Teaching Evaluation

1. Did I select the most appropriate repertoire to teach the new element?
2. Did I select the correct musical element to teach?
3. Did one song lead to another using an appropriate transition?
4. Did the students have the prerequisite skills to understand the new element?
5. Were my teaching objectives specific?
6. Were my teaching strategies for teaching each objective specific? Did I review what the students already knew and did I reinforce new information?
7. Could students independently demonstrate their new understanding?
8. When working with the rhythmic or melodic elements of a song did we sing the song as a performance one more time to ensure the musicality of the lesson?

General Points for Planning Your Lesson

1. Goals for each lesson should come from the outcomes listed in the concept plans but singing in tune should always be a primary goal of each lesson.
2. Always select the best song material for each class and make sure that you enjoy this material. You should have about three to five songs in a 30-minute lesson. Memorize all of the song material. Remember that there should be a variety of moods and tempi reflected in the repertoire chosen.
3. Remember that every new song you teach should be introduced appropriately.
4. When you are teaching a new element using a particular song, does the new element appear surrounded by well-known patterns?
5. Work with both a rhythmic and melodic element in each lesson. Remember that when you extract a pattern or motif from a song always sing the song again to give students the experience of enjoying the performance of the song.
6. Have you picked the right songs for the preparation, presentation, and practice of a particular element?
7. Remember that there should be a focus to each section of the lesson that can be assessed by you informally and formally.
8. Know your materials. Be able to analyze the materials for each lesson both from an analytical, performance perspective and a pedagogical one.

9. Try to find variety in the song material that you have chosen for the lesson.
10. One activity should also prepare the next activity.
11. Remember to include periods of relaxation and concentration. Does your lesson plan have a climax? Pacing of a lesson is critical.
12. Provide the students with plenty of individual experiences in the classroom. It is important to work from the group activities to individual activities.

Discussion Questions

1. How can we use this learning theory to develop lesson plans in order to teach our students?
2. How are lesson objectives related to each segment of the lesson?
3. Discuss the different kinds of transitions in a lesson and provide a concrete example of each one.
4. Teaching is meant to be fun. Will these lesson plan structures help teachers sleep better at night?

Ongoing Assignment

1. Choose a concept to prepare and an element to practice for a first grade class. Write the objectives for each type of lesson. Please include titles of songs you will be using.
2. Choose a concept to prepare and an element to practice for a third grade class. Write the objectives for each type of lesson. Please include titles of songs you will be using.
3. Review several lesson plans that you have designed. Please try to indicate how you will move smoothly from one activity to another.

References

Boshkoff, Ruth. "Lesson Planning the Kodály Way." *Music Educators Journal* 79/2 (October 1991): 30–34.

Kodály, Zoltán. "Children's Choirs," in *The Selected Writings,* 121–22.

Regelski, Thomas A. "On 'Methodolatry' and Music Teaching as 'Critical' and Reflective Praxis." *Philosophy of Music Education Review* 10/2 (2002): 102–124.

Zemke, Lorna, Sr. "How to Get Started with Lesson Planning." *Keeping Up with Kodály Concepts in Music Education* 1/1 (November–December 1974): 3–8.

Chapter 10

Teaching Musicianship Skills to Older Beginners

Anyone who studies carefully these one hundred lessons cannot stray from the path to good musicianship. Nor should he despair at not having completed them by the age of twelve; he can still win laurels. Even an adult musician will experience renewed discovery through studying these lessons, which may indeed overcome many small shortcomings in his proficiency.

Zoltán Kodály, Preface to the volume "Musical Reading and Writing by Erzsébet Szönyi," in *The Selected Writings.*

Key Questions

How do we select songs for teaching older beginners?

How do we teach songs to older beginners?

How does the sequence for teaching rhythmic and melodic elements to older beginners differ from that of the beginning student?

What types of lesson plans do we use to teach older beginners?

For a comprehensive approach to teaching music fundamentals to older beginners please see Houlahan and Tacka, *From Sound to Symbol: Fundamentals of Music Theory* (New York: Oxford University Press, 2008). This work includes a text, instructor's manual, CD of recorded musical examples, and an extensive technology component.

In previous chapters we have tried to describe how to provide music students with a music education beginning in grade one and moving sequentially through the various elementary grades. Occasionally teachers face the challenge of teaching students in grades two through five who have never had a music education inspired by the Kodály concept. Therefore, the students lack performance skills in singing knowledge of music literacy. The goal of the music instructor when teaching older beginners is to provide students with an accelerated music program in order to allow them to catch up with their peers who have received a sequential music education.

When developing curriculum goals for the older beginner, the instructor may have to modify curriculum expectations several times during the course of instruction. For example, a fourth grade class that has never had sequential music literacy training will not be able to cover the same topics as a fourth grade class that has had sequential music training. The song repertoire should remain appropriate to the fourth grade students, but the concepts and musical elements may need to include such rudimentary concepts as one and two sounds on a beat and simple melodic concepts. The first goal of the music instructor is therefore to assess the knowledge of the students and design a curriculum plan for that class.

Selecting Song Repertoire for Older Beginners

The selection of music materials is critical for the success of teaching older beginners. Song materials are chosen for a variety of purposes including developing students':

- Knowledge of repertoire
- Vocal skills
- Music literacy skills
- Movement skills through the selection of singing games
- Basic instrumental skills
- Creative skills
- Listening skills

Criteria for the selection of song material:

- Songs must be of the highest musical quality
- Songs must have an aesthetic and musical appeal
- Songs should be developmentally appropriate for the students
- Songs should be selected to reflect the cultural make-up of the classroom
- Songs should also be chosen for teaching specific musical concepts

Repertoire for Older Beginners

Based on the above criteria, we can develop a repertoire list for the older beginner. The repertoire list should include the rationale for selection of the song, the source for the song, and the type game. The sequence of elements should be determined by their frequency of appearance in the song repertoire. Elements can be isolated from phrases or motives of songs. Simple folk songs may be used without the text to teach rhythmic and melodic concepts.

Table 10.1 Repertoire list for the older beginner

Alphabetical Listing	Rationale	Source	Game

Vocal Warm-Up Exercises

Vocalizations and humming are valuable exercises for developing beautiful singing. The students should vocalize high and low sounds, as well as soft and loud sounds, to develop the full range of their voice. Songs sung using the "*oo*" sound are particularly good for developing intonation. Vocal exercises should be a part of the introduction for each music lesson. Sample vocal exercises are shown in table 10.2.

Table 10.2 Sample vocal exercises

Yawning	This opens up the back of the throat, and relaxes the voice
Sighing	This is a gentle way of using a higher voice than you usually speak with. Try sighing a few times, starting each sigh a half step higher than the last. Use an open vowel sound.
Humming	This is a gentle (and quiet) way of using the singing voice. Humming a favorite song before singing it also gives children an opportunity to practice the song's melody without being distracted by the text.
Descending scale pattern	Sing songs that begin with a descending vocal scale pattern using a neutral syllables; this enables accurate intonation as well as develops the "head voice"
Slide whistle	Students imitate the sliding sounds of a slide whistle to develop their head voice
Flashlight beam	Students vocally follow a flashlight beam projected on a wall or board; students follow the contour of the moving beam of light
Sirens and roller coasters	Students vocally imitate the sound of a siren and roller coaster
Call and response songs	Repeating simple melodic patterns helps develop students' intonation; the repetition of simple melodic patterns helps to secure the placement of each pitch

Teaching Songs to Older Beginners

A Seven-Point Song Teaching Procedure

1. Show the students the musical score.
2. Sing the song for the students using your head voice and do not overuse vibrato.
3. Sing the song and ask the students to follow the score. Focus the students' attention on the text or on the melodic contour.
4. Ask questions relating to the text or specific musical elements. This strengthens listening and analytical skills, as well as the students' ability to memorize. Aural skill and analysis may be developed simultaneously with older beginners.
5. Questions must be specific. Sing the song or phrase of the song before asking each question. This enables the students to hear the song several times before they sing and will give them a better grasp of melodic contours and rhythmic complexities.
6. Have the students repeat selected phrases. This focuses attention on a difficult interval or rhythmic pattern. Melodic and rhythmic discrimination abilities are developed and practiced through singing.
7. Challenge older beginners to concentrate. Ask the students to perform a rhythmic or a melodic ostinato while the instructor sings the song.

Getting Started

Initially the instructor may sing songs in the class, and the students should have a pencil and paper ready for drawing the phrase marks and heartbeats of each song. This simple task provides the instructor with an opportunity to sing the song many times before asking the students to sing the song on their own. When the instructor is singing a new song, students must be listening and doing one of the following activities: (1) tapping the beat, (2) drawing the phrases of the song in the air, or (3) conducting the meter. The instructor may ask the students to draw the phrases and mark the beats on paper during the first performances of the song. This keeps the students on task while they are listening to the song. These procedures engage students in doing two things at the same time: listening and writing.

Teach the concepts of phrase and phrase mark, beat, meter, and form to the students as soon as possible.

Singing should be developed before melodic elements are introduced. Therefore, rhythmic elements may be introduced while working on the students' vocal skills. In general, the presentation of rhythmic elements is similar to that used when teaching younger students. However, the presentation of melodic elements is different. Because of the frequency of the *mi-re-do* motif in older students' song repertoire the *mi-re-do* pattern can be the first pattern introduced to students rather than the *so-mi* pattern. Several songs are suggested in the following sequence of rhythmic and melodic elements. Simple songs make learning concepts more comprehensible.

Sample Curriculum

The following is a sample rhythmic and melodic teaching sequence appropriate for the older beginner. The same teaching strategies (see chapter 9) used with younger students may be followed when working with older beginners. It is important to remember that if necessary, the teacher must spend more time developing the students' singing voices before the introduction of any melodic concepts or elements.

Table 10.3 Concepts associated with rhythmic elements

Rhythm/Theory	Corresponding Concept	Rhythm Syllables	Songs
Beat			*Rocky Mountain* *Zudio* *Tideo* *Sailing on the Ocean*
Simple duple, triple, and quadruple meter			
Form			
Dynamics			
Rhythm			*Tideo* *Great Big House*
Quarter and eighth notes and rests ♩ ♫ 𝄽 𝄾	1 & 2 even sounds on a beat	*ta, ta di*	*Are You Sleeping?* *Rocky Mountain* *Great Big House* *Liza Jane* *I've Been to Harlem* *Scotland's Burning* *Sur le Pont d'Avignon*

Table 10.3 *Continued*

Rhythm/Theory	**Corresponding Concept**	**Rhythm Syllables**	**Songs**
			Without text: *Snail Snail,* *Lucy Lockett without words*
Meter $\frac{2}{4}$, $\frac{3}{4}$. $\frac{4}{4}$.	Pattern of strong and weak beats Bar lines, measures		$\frac{2}{4}$ *Rocky Mountain* $\frac{3}{4}$ *Oh How Lovely Is the evening—canon* $\frac{4}{4}$ *Great Big House*
Half note and half note rest 𝅗𝅥 𝄼	1 sound that lasts for 2 beats No sound on two beats	*ta-a*	*Who's That Tapping at the Window?* *Are You Sleeping?* *Hey Ho Nobody Home* *Long Legged Sailor*
Whole note 𝅝	One sound held for four beats		*I Got a Letter*
Dotted half note 𝅗𝅥.	One sound held for three beats		*Oh How Lovely Is the Evening*
Counting with numbers			
Teaching sixteenth notes ♬♬	Four even sounds on a beat	*ta ka* *di mi*	*Dinah* *Tideo* *Kookaburra* *Who's That Tapping at the Window?*
Sixteenth note combinations made up of one eighth note or two sixteenth notes or two sixteenth note and one eighth note	Three sounds on a beat; the first sound is longer than the last two sounds, long sound followed by two short sounds	*ta di mi*	*Car Song* *John Cukoo* *Koodaburra* *Draw Me a Bucket of Water* *Zum Gali Gali*
♪♬ ♬♪	Three uneven sounds on a beat; the last sound is held longer than the first two sounds, two short sounds followed by a long sound	*ta ka di*	*Jim Along Josie*
Internal upbeats	Internal phrases begin with unstressed beats		*Fed My Horse* *Over the River*
External upbeats	External phrase begin with unstressed beats		*Good Bye Old Pain*
Syncopation ♪ ♩ ♪	Three uneven sounds over two beats, one short, one long and one short	*ta di-di*	*Hill and Gully Rider* *Alabama Gal* *Land of the Silver Birch*
Dotted quarter followed by eighth note ♩. ♪	Two uneven sounds over two beats where the first sound lasts a beat and a half	*ta di*———	*Liza Jane*

continued

Table 10.3 *Continued*

Rhythm/Theory	Corresponding Concept	Rhythm Syllables	Songs
Dotted eighth followed by sixteenth note 	Two uneven sounds on one beat; the first sound is three times longer than the second	*ta-mi*	*Shady Grove*
Sixteenth note followed by a dotted eighth	Two uneven sounds on one beat; the first sound is shorter than the second	*ta ka*	
Eighth note followed by a dotted quarter note	Two uneven sounds over two beats where the first sound lasts half a beat and the second sound lasts a beat and a half	*ta di*——	
Eighth note rest			
6/8 meter with even division 		*ta* *ta ki da* *ta da*	
6/8 meter with uneven divisions  		*ta di da*	
Triplet	Three sounds on one beat in simple meter	*ta ki da*	
Duplet	Two sounds on one beat in compound meter	*ta di*	

Table 10.4 Concepts associated with melodic elements

Element	Concept	Solfege	Songs
Major trichord	Three adjacent picthes	*do-re-mi*	*Great Big House* *Au Clair de la Lune* *Long Legged Sailor* *The Boatman* *Dinah* *Fed My Horse in a Popular Trough*
Bichord and trichord of the pentatonic scale			*Dinah* for s–m *Pizza Pizza* –l–s–m
Pentatonic tetrachord		*do-re-mi-so*	*Dinah*
Pentatonic scale		*do-re-mi-so-la*	*Rocky Mountain* *Hill and Gully Rider*
Begin to work on absolute letter names			

Table 10.4 *Continued*

Element	Concept	Solfege	Songs
Major pentachord hexachord		*do-re-mi-fa-so* *do-re-mi-fa-so-la*	*Old Woman* *Alabama Gal* *When I First Came to This Land* Introduce b-flat
Major extended pentachord, hexachord, and pentatonic scales		*la-so-mi-re-do-la,-so,*	*Dance Josey* *Turn the Glasses Over*
Minor pentachord hexachord scale		*la,-do-re-mi-so*	[New tonal center]
Minor pentatonic scale		*so,-la,-do-re-mi-so-la-do'*	
Minor extended pentatonic scale			
Scales based on permutations of the pentatonic scale		*so pentatonic scale*	
Major Scale	Eight adjacent pitches with a half step between the third and fourth and the seventh and eighth degrees of the scale	*do-re-mi-fa-so-la-ti-do'*	*Alleluia* *Kookaburra* *Viva la Musica*
Minor scale	Eight adjacent pitches with a half step between the second and third and fifth and sixth degrees of the scale	*la,-ti-do-re-mi-fa-so-la'*	*Sweet William* *Drill Ye Tarriers*
Harmonic minor scale		*la,-ti-do-re-mi-fa-si-la'*	*Ah Poor Bird*
Melodic minor scale		*la,-ti,-do-re-mi-fi-si-la'* *la'-so-fa-mi-re-do-ti,-la,*	*Who Can Sail*
Dorian mode	Eight adjacent pitches with a half step between the second and third and the sixth and seventh degrees of the scale	*re-mi-fa-so-la-ti-do'-re'* *or* *la,-ti,-do-re-mi-fi-so-la*	*Drunken Sailor* *Scarborough Fair*
Mixolydian	Eight adjacent pitches with a half step between the third and fourth and the sixth and seventh degrees of the scale	*so,-la,-ti,-do-re-mi-fa-so* *do-re-mi-fa-so-la-ta-do"*	*Old Joe Clark* *Every Night When the Sun Goes Down*
Harmonic functions			
Primary chords			[Inversion]
Dominant seventh chord			

A Sample Integrated Sequence of Melodic and Rhythmic Elements for Teaching Older Beginners

The following is an example of a beginning sequence for older students. Depending on the singing ability of the students, it frequently happens that music instructors can spend more time initially on rhythmic elements while developing the students' singing voices. Once the students have developed their singing voices, then the music instructor can follow the suggested preparation, practice, and presentation sequence in chapter 5.

Beginning Sequence for Older Students

1. In-tune singing
2. Steady beat
3. Rhythm/theory
4. Beat in duple and compound meter
5. Simple duple, triple, and quadruple meter
6. Form
7. Dynamics
8. Rhythm
9. Teaching quarter and eight notes and rests
10. Simple, duple, triple, and quadruple meter
11. Major trichord *do—re—mi*
12. Pentatonic bichord and trichord
13. Pentatonic tetrachord
14. Pentatonic scale
15. Begin to work on absolute letter names
16. Major pentachord scale
17. Major hexachord scale
18. Half note and half note rest
19. Whole note
20. Dotted half note
21. Counting with numbers
22. Teaching sixteenth notes
23. Teaching sixteenth note combinations made up of one eighth note and two sixteenth notes or two sixteenth notes and one eighth note
24. Continue to work on absolute letter names
25. Major extended pentachord, hexachord, and pentatonic scales
26. Syncopation
27. Minor pentachord scale
28. Dotted quarter note followed by an eighth note
29. Minor hexachord scale
30. Minor pentatonic scale
31. Major scale
32. Dotted eighth note followed by a sixteenth note
33. Minor scale
34. Compound meter

Lesson Design

The same types of lesson plans as described in chapter 9 can also be used with older beginners. However, more attention on developing vocal skills needs to occur throughout the lesson. The preparation/practice lesson plan may be modified to permit the instructor to work on developing the students' intonation while working on specific rhythmic concepts and elements.

Framework for Lesson Plan Outline

The lesson plan outline in table 10.5 may be used for teaching older beginners. It is a blend of all other lesson plans used with the beginning music student. Each new musical element taught should be reinforced in each section of the lesson plan. This will enable the students to reinforce each new concept through practice exercises, sight singing, memory work, dictation, and part singing.

Table 10.5 Lesson plan outline

Introduction	1. Vocal warm-up 2. Sing known songs with rhythm and solfège syllables 3. Review
Main section	1. Teaching a new song 2. Continually introduce new songs to students. They may draw phrases, identifying form, and create beat charts as well as sing. With continual repetition students will more readily sing in tune. 3. Preparation and presentation of new musical element 4. Movement 5. Practice of new element with selected skill areas. Select from the following: Development of musical memory Inner hearing Sight-singing Dictation Ensemble singing Improvisation skills Instrumental skills Listening skills
Close	Review of musical materials covered during the class Listening

Preparation and Practice Activities for Rhythm and Melody

Table 10.6 Procedures for preparing rhythmic elements

Echo clapping	Clap the rhythm of a melody or a rhythmic pattern.
Melodic contour and rhythm	Demonstrate the melodic contour of the song while clapping the rhythm
Perform rhythm and beat at the same time	Divide the class into two groups; one group performing the rhythmic pattern, the other keeping the beat. This activity may be practiced in different combinations: 1. teacher/class 2. class/teacher 3. divided class 4. two individual students 5. student keeps the beat with one hand and taps the rhythm with the other hand 6. perform the rhythm and beat at the same time
Conduct	Sing and conduct at the same time
Aural analysis	Identify which beat or beats contain the new rhythmic element
Visual representation	Create a beat chart and write solfège syllables on each beat to indicate the number of sounds within the beat

Table 10.7 Procedures for preparing melodic elements

Melodic contour	Demonstrate the melodic contour of a melody with arm motions. Motions should be natural and appropriate to the text and tempo of the song.
Melodic contour and rhythm	Demonstrate the melodic contour while clapping the rhythm of a melody
Echo singing	Sing melodic patterns sung or played by the teacher
Writing	Write the rhythm of a melody spatially
Aural analysis	Identify which beat or beats contain the new melodic element
Visual representation	Create a representation using solfège syllables written spatially to indicate the position of the new melodic element

Developing ear-training abilities and mastering sight singing normally takes many hours of practice. Practice sessions can be made more efficient by using a variety of practice techniques. Practicing in small groups is valuable for students on many levels. In addition to sharpening their listening skills by evaluating each other's performances, students who practice with their peers are far more secure in their performance when called on in class.

Table 10.8 Procedures for practicing rhythmic elements

Rhythm syllables	Sing a melody with rhythm syllables while tapping the beat
Conducting	Sing with rhythm syllables while conducting
Echo singing	Echo sing rhythm syllables to a rhythm pattern clapped by the instructor
Aural dictation	Identify the meter and rhythm patterns clapped or sung by the instructor
Writing	Change a rhythm pattern from a given pattern into a new rhythm pattern. One person writes a sixteen-beat pattern, then claps a slightly different pattern. The other person must identify where the changes occur.
Improvise rhythm patterns	Select a meter and length for the pattern then determine the rhythmic form (for example, ABA or ABAB) to use
Writing	Students memorize a phrase of a melody and write it from memory
Perform a rhythmic canon	a) Say rhythm syllables while clapping the rhythm b) Think the rhythm syllables and clap the rhythm c) Clap the rhythm in canon with someone else d) Perform the rhythmic canon by yourself. Clap one part with one hand and the other part with the other.

Table 10.9 Procedures for practicing melodic elements

Conducting	Sing song or solfège syllables and conduct
Hand signs	Sing solfège syllables and show hand signs
Rhythm and hand signs	Sing solfège syllables while showing hand signs
Sight singing from hand signs	Sing solfège syllables or show hand signs for a pattern; ask another student to sing it back
Memory	Memorize an exercise and notate it without referring to the book. First analyze the form by looking for repetition and similar patterns. This helps simplify the task.
Error detection	Select a phrase of music. One person plays the selection, deliberately making a melodic mistake. Another person follows the score and locates the error.

Developing Musical Memory

Musical memory plays an important role in singing accurately and being able to recall a pattern for the purposes of dictation. The following techniques can be helpful. Memorizing by ear is more difficult than memorizing from notation, as it involves no visual aid. Melodies used for memorizing by ear should be easier than those used with notation. Extracts should be played on the piano or another instrument and sung a few times. The following procedures may be used for both rhythmic and melodic memorization.

When students have gained experience in unison memory work, they can begin to memorize two-part extracts. Accompaniments may be drawn from a rhythmic pattern, a rhythmic or melodic ostinato, chord roots, a contrapuntal melodic line, or typical cadential idioms in modal or harmonic music.

Table 10.10 Developing musical memory

Memorize from hand signs	1. Show typical melodic patterns and ask the students to sing patterns back. Start with short patterns such as *so–la–so–mi* or *mi–fa–mi–re–mi*. 2. Once melodic patterns can be echoed with ease, progress to singing four and eight beat melodies 3. Show a melody in hand signs. Select pentatonic melodies or rounds. The students sing the melody in canon using solfa or absolute letter names and write the example from memory. 4. Sing a known melody with absolute letter names while using hand signs
Memorize from staff notation	1. Memorize a short fragment of a musical example from a score using hand signs 2. The instructor sings the unknown part of a musical example. Students memorize and sing the motifs. 3. Students write the melody on staff paper. At a more advanced level, the students can write the example in another key using a different clef.
Memorizing by ear	The instructor plays a melody on the keyboard; students: 1. Identify the meter 2. Identify the ending and starting pitches 3. Students sing and conduct 4. Students sing with hand signs 5. Students sing with absolute pitch names and hand signs 6. Students sing with rhythm syllables 7. Students write or play it back on the piano. The example may be transposed.
Memorizing two-part examples	1. Sing the two-part example 2. Memorize one part silently using solfa 3. Sing that part out loud while conducting 4. Practice the other part following steps 1 through 3 5. Sing both parts in a group and then as solos, using both solfège syllables and note names 6. Write both parts of the extract 7. Sing one part and play the other on the piano, or sing one part and show the second part with hand signs
Error detection	Select a phrase of music. One person plays the selection, deliberately making a melodic mistake. Another person follows the score and locates the error.

Sight-Singing

The sight-singing exercises may be memorized and notated.

Table 10.11 Sight-singing exercises

Prior to sight singing	Practice basic rhythmic and melodic patterns from the sight-reading exercise with the students while the students follow the staff notation. Difficult rhythms should be practiced with a suitable rhythmic ostinato or subdivision of the beat. Sing these preparatory exercises in the same key as the reading example. Exercises should be sung in solfège, letter names and neutral syllables.
Sight singing	1. Discuss the meter and key. Determine an appropriate tempo. 2. Determine the form. Look for repeated patterns. 3. Ask students to *think* through the melody. Students may conduct or use hand signs while thinking through the melody. 4. Students sing the exercise while conducting
Memorize	4. Memorize the example and notate it if appropriate
Practice	Read melodic patterns not associated with rhythms; read a serious of notes on the staff or a series of solfège syllables. Teachers should devise a variety of ways to practice a reading exercise. For example: read the melody backwards; read a unison melody while clapping a rhythmic ostinato; sing a melody in canon at the fifth (reading only the first voice).

Dictation

Dictation is closely linked to the development of musical memory, inner hearing, and reading and writing skills. Memory is essential for successful musical dictation. Beginning dictations should be based on patterns that have been memorized by the students. As the student's memory develops, the teacher can begin more formal dictation practice. Initially, the students should sing the melody before attempting to notate it. In this way, the instructor can determine whether the students are hearing the example accurately. Initial dictation material can be based on simple folk music. Later, music of other styles may be added.

The procedures set out in table 10.12 may be used for melodic dictation.

Table 10.12 Procedures for melodic dictation

Prepare the key	Prepare the key with hand signs and staff notation
Sing typical melodic patterns	Sing typical melodic patterns found in the dictation. Students sing using solfège syllables and letter names. During beginning stages of formal dictation the instructor may also give the student a score with the bar lines indicated and certain notes or rhythms filled in to aid students' memory.

continued

Table 10.12 *Continued*

Perform the melody	Perform the melody on the piano or another instrument
Aural analysis	Students determine the final note and the beginning note as well as some or all of the following, as appropriate: mode, melodic cadences, melodic contour, patterns, and meter
Students perform	Students sing the melody using solfège syllables and absolute letter names
Students perform	Students sing the melody using rhythm syllables and hand signs
Students write	Students write the melody from memory
Students perform	Students sing the melody from their score. This melody may be used to practice additional skills; transpose it into other keys or practice the intervals in the melody.

The procedures set out in table 10.13 may be used for rhythm dictation.

Table 10.13 Procedures for rhythm dictation

Prepare the example	The instructor plays a melody on the piano; students determine the meter and the number of bars
Instructor performs	Instructor plays the musical example while students conduct.
Students perform	Students conduct and sing using rhythm syllables
Students write	Students write the dictation with stick or traditional notation
Instructor plays the musical example	Instructor plays the musical example students check their written work

Part-Work

Singing and playing part music are important aspects of musical training. This enables the student to learn to hear several voices simultaneously.

The procedures set out in table 10.14 may be used for developing two-part singing.

Table 10.14 Procedures for developing two-part singing

Perform	Sing folk songs or other exercises while clapping the beat or the rhythm
Perform	Sing folk songs, dividing the singing by phrases in call-and-response style. This enables Group I to hear what Group 2 sings, and vice versa.
Ensemble work	Add a rhythmic ostinato and sing using rhythm syllables
Develop two-part singing	1. Students sing while teacher claps the rhythm 2. Students and teacher exchange parts

Table 10.14 *Continued*

	3. Divide the students into two groups, one group sings and another performs the rhythm 4. Two students perform the work 5. One student may sing one voice while playing the other voice on the piano 6. Students clap a series of rhythmic patterns while singing a known song 7. Sing in two parts from hand signs. This helps students see the intervals spatially. 8. Sing simple pentatonic folk songs in canon 9. Sing a well-known song and at the same time clap various rhythms indicated by the instructor. The students may also read an exercise while the teacher improvises an extended rhythmic ostinato. The students must sing and listen at the same time, then try to recall the rhythmic pattern. Begin with simple, familiar patterns. 10. Sing one part and clap the second part simultaneously
Performing two-part music	1. If the two-part selection is a folk song, teach the song first either by rote or from the music, then teach the second part 2. Divide the class into two groups. Group A sings the top line while group B sings the bottom. Reverse. 3. Group A sing the bottom line and Group B claps the top. Reverse. 4. Perform the work as a group and then with soloists. Individuals may then sing any part while clapping the other or may sing one part and play the other part on the piano.

Discussion Questions

1. What are some of the general considerations in teaching songs to older beginners?
2. How does the choice of songs you use in your classroom affect the teaching sequence of rhythmic and melodic elements for older beginners?
3. We should avoid teaching singing and developing music literacy skills to older beginners. Older beginners need intellectual challenges. Because they have not previously learned basic concepts associated with music theory, the instructor should teach music theory and music appreciation and music history to these students. Discuss.

Ongoing Assignment

1. The principal of your school has just informed you that you will be teaching music to a fifth grade next year. Unfortunately, none of these students have had any previous experience with music. Develop a teaching philosophy and curriculum goals for these students.

2. Develop a repertoire list of songs and games suitable for teaching older students.
3. Develop a lesson plan to teach the quarter and eighth note as well as the quarter note rest and tunefully singing to older students.
4. Develop a lesson plan to teach the *do* pentatonic scale and practice $\frac{2}{4}$ meter using quarter note, eighth note, and half note to older students.

References

Bacon, Denise. *46 Two-Part American Folk Songs for Elementary Grades.* Wellesley, Mass.: Kodály Center of America, 1973.

———. *50 Easy Two-Part Exercises: First Steps in A Cappella Part Singing Using Sol-fa and Staff Notation.* 3rd ed. Clifton, N.J.: European American Music Corporation, 1980. Originally published as *50 Easy Two-Part Pentatonic Exercises,* published by European-American Music Corporation, 1977. Contains exercises written in both solfège and staff notation.

———. *185 Unison Pentatonic Exercises: First Steps in Sight-Singing Using Sol-fa and Staff Notation According to the Kodály Concept.* West Newton: Kodály Center of America, 1978.

Bidner, Sara Baker. "A Folk Song Approach to Music Reading for Upper Elementary Levels Based on the Kodály Method." Ph.D. thesis, Louisiana State University and Agricultural and Mechanical College, 1978.

Choksy, Lois. *The Kodály Method Comprehensive Music Education.* 3rd ed. Upper Saddle River, N.J.: Prentice Hall, 1999.

Eisen, Ann, and Lamar Robertson. *Directions to Literacy.* Lake Charles, La.: Sneaky Snake Publications, 2005.

Herboly-Kocsár, Ildikó. *Teaching of Polyphony, Harmony and Form in Elementary School,* trans. Alexander Farkas, revised by Lilla Gábor. Kecskemét: Zoltán Kodály Pedagogical Institute, 1984.

Houlahan, Mícheál, and Philip Tacka. "Sound Thinking: A Suggested Sequence for Teaching Musical Elements Based on the Philosophy of Zoltán Kodály for a College Music Theory Course." *Journal of Music Theory Pedagogy* 4/1 (1990): 85–110. A discussion of an approach to college-level theory instruction based on teaching melodic and rhythmic patterns in association with musical compositions rather than a subject-logic sequence. Includes philosophical considerations and a discussion of materials.

———. "Sequential Order for the Preparation, Presentation, Practice and Evaluation of Rhythmic and Melodic Concepts." *Journal of Music Theory Pedagogy* 4/2 (1990): 243–268. A detailed sequence of musical concepts and elements extending from two- and three-note melodic and rhythmic groupings through harmonic concepts.

———. *Sound Thinking: Music for Sight Singing and Ear Training.* 2 vols. New York: Boosey & Hawkes, 1991.

———. *Sound Thinking: Developing Musical Literacy.* 2 vols. New York: Boosey & Hawkes, 1995.

Chapter 11

Evaluation and Assessment

> There is an important distinction between evaluation and assessment. The primary function of assessment in music education is to provide feedback to students about the quality of their growing musicianship. Learners need constructive feedback about why, when and how they are or are not meeting musical challenges in relation to musical standards and traditions. Overall, the assessment of students' achievement gathers information that benefits students directly in the form of constructive feedback. Assessment also provides useful data to teachers, parents, and the surrounding educational community. Building on the accumulated results of continuous assessments, evaluation is primarily concerned with grading, ranking, and other summary procedures for purposes of students promotion and curriculum evaluation.
>
> D. J. Elliot, *Praxial Music Education: Reflections and Dialogues*

Key Questions

What is the purpose of student assessment?

What are the components of a student profile chart?

How can we develop scoring rubrics to assess a student's progress in the music classroom?

What is the purpose of teacher assessment?

What should be included in an assessment for the evaluation of an instructor?

The goal of this chapter is to try to develop assessment activities that can evaluate students' and instructors' performance in a Kodály-based program, as well as provide feedback for the music instructor. We are providing instructors with sample ideas regarding assessment. Educators want to make a difference in the lives of the students. We all devote many hours in the consideration of how we deliver our curriculum and then concern ourselves with the implementation of our program of study. Most teachers want to know: How am I doing? Am I making a difference? Are the students benefiting? Will the results of a music assessment of both the teacher and the students help with the growth of my music program? It is clear that evaluation and assessment needs to be ongoing and be built into the music curriculum from the first day. Assessment is stage 3 of the assimilation phase of learning.

Supervisors or principals generally conduct the evaluation of music teachers. Often music teachers do not provide for their administrators the information needed to evaluate their work successfully. We believe that the teaching resource portfolio will be an important tool for principals to use in evaluating the work of the music teacher. Once teachers have communicated to their supervisors what their philosophy and curriculum goals are for their music program, it is much easier to conduct a constructive evaluation that will result in the growth of a music program.

Assessment Tool for Curriculum Planning and the Music Lesson

The following is an assessment tool with a rubric for evaluating an instructor's performance in the classroom. The assessment tool for evaluating music teaching is divided into five sections:

Section 1: Curriculum Planning
Section 2: Evaluation of a Lesson Plan Format
Section 3: Instructor's Musicianship
Section 4: Lesson Evaluation
Section 5: Assessment of Student Learning

Section 1 (curriculum planning) evaluates an instructor's ability to plan for long-term teaching. The use of the teaching resource portfolio, as described in chapter 1, provides a wealth of information for the evaluator to assess.

Section 2 (evaluation of a lesson plan format) evaluates an instructor's ability to plan individual lessons. Lesson plans built on the students' prior knowledge is critical to the design of a well-structured lesson, as well as the various teaching strategies that will be used throughout the lesson. There should be a connection between the instructor's philosophy of music and curriculum goals for each lesson plan.

Section 3 (instructor's musicianship) evaluates the instructor's ability to transform a script of a lesson into practice. This evaluation requires the evaluator to observe the lesson.

Section 4 (lesson evaluation) evaluates the pedagogical decisions that a teacher makes during the lesson to insure maximum student learning. This evaluation takes place during the lesson.

Section 5 (assessment of student learning) evaluates the assessment tools the instructor uses throughout the lesson to evaluate students' knowledge of the objectives for the lesson. It also assesses the students' participation during the lesson.

The following is our Assessment Tool for Evaluating Music Teaching that may be used by teachers or supervisors to assess a music lesson.

Name: School District:

Grade Observed: Supervisor:

Date:

Table 11.1 Assessment tool for evaluating music teaching

	Criteria	Comments
Section 1: Curriculum planning		
4	Curriculum planning fosters appropriate learning goals and active musical behaviors as evidenced by the teaching resource portfolio	
3	Curriculum planning does not always foster appropriate learning goals and active musical behaviors but occasionally detracts from planning behaviors as evidenced by the teaching resource portfolio	
2	Curriculum planning does not always foster appropriate learning goals and active musical behaviors and detracts from planning behaviors as evidenced by the teaching resource portfolio	
1	Curriculum planning does not foster appropriate goals and active musical behaviors	
Section 2: Evaluation of a lesson plan format		
Behavioral/objectives		
4	Behavioral/ objectives describe appropriate active musical behaviors within the lesson	
3	Behavioral/ objectives do not always describe appropriate active musical behaviors within the lesson but occasionally detract from the lesson	
2	Behavioral/ objectives do not always describe appropriate active musical behaviors within the lesson and detract from the lesson	
1	Behavioral /objectives do not describe appropriate active musical behaviors	
Selection of music material		
4	Selection of music material is always appropriate	
3	Selection of music material is not always appropriate and occasionally detracts from the lesson	
2	Selection of music material is not always appropriate and detracts from the lesson	
1	Selection of music material is not appropriate	
Instructor's understanding of students' prior knowledge		
4	There is evidence that Behavioral/objectives are build upon students' prior knowledge	

continued

Table 11.1 *Continued*

	Criteria	Comments
3	It is not always evident that Behavioral/ objectives are build upon students' prior knowledge and this occasionally detracts from the lesson	
2	It is not always evident that Behavioral/ objectives are build upon students' prior knowledge and this detracts from the lesson	
1	Behavioral/ objectives are not build upon students' prior knowledge	
Sequence of teaching strategies		
4	Sequence of teaching strategies is always evident	
3	Sequence of teaching strategies is not always evident and occasionally detracts from the lesson	
2	Sequence of teaching strategies is not always evident and detracts from the lesson	
1	Sequence of teaching strategies is not evident	
Musical transitions between teaching segments		
4	Musical transitions are always evident	
3	Musical transitions are not always evident and occasionally detract from the lesson	
2	Musical transitions are not always evident and detracts from the lesson	
1	Musical transitions are not evident	
Alternating periods of concentration and relaxation		
4	There is a balance between periods of concentration and relaxation skills being taught in the lesson	
3	There is some imbalance between periods of concentration and relaxation skills being taught in the lesson and this occasionally detracts from the lesson	
2	There is an imbalance between periods of concentration and relaxation skills being taught in the lesson and detracts from the lesson	
1	There is an imbalance between periods of concentration and relaxation skills	
Section 3: Instructor's Musicianship		
Musicality		
4	Musicality is evident	
3	Musicality errors occur and occasionally detract from the lesson	

Table 11.1 *Continued*

	Criteria	Comments
2	Musicality errors detract from the lesson	
1	Musicality errors consistently detract from the lesson	
In-tune singing		
4	In-tune singing is evident	
3	In-tune singing is not always evident and occasionally detracts from the lesson	
2	In-tune singing is not always evident and detracts from the lesson	
1	In-tune singing is not evident	
Conducting		
4	Conducting skills are evident	
3	Conducting errors occur that occasionally detract from the lesson	
2	Conducting errors occur that detract from the lesson	
1	Conducting is not evident	
Functional keyboard skills		
4	Functional keyboard skills are evident	
3	Errors in functional keyboard skills occur and occasionally detract from the lesson	
2	Errors in functional keyboard skills detract from the lesson	
1	Functional keyboard skills are not evident	
Instrumental skills		
4	Instrumental skills are evident	
3	Errors in instrumental skills occur and occasionally detract from the lesson	
2	Errors in instrumental skills detract from the lesson	
1	Instrumental skills are not evident	
Section 4: Lesson evaluation		
Appropriate starting pitches for songs		
4	Appropriate starting pitch of songs is evident	
3	Appropriate starting pitch is not always correct but does not detract from the lesson	
2	Appropriate starting pitch is not always correct and detracts from the lesson	
1	Appropriate starting pitch is not correct	

continued

Table 11.1 *Continued*

	Criteria	Comments
Appropriate tempo for songs		
4	Appropriate tempo of songs is evident	
3	Appropriate tempo of songs is not always logical but does not detract from the lesson	
2	Appropriate tempo of songs is not always logical and detracts from the lesson	
1	Appropriate tempo of songs is not logical	
Teaching in-tune singing		
4	Sequenced teaching strategies for teaching in-tune singing are evident	
3	Sequenced teaching strategies for teaching in-tune singing are not always evident but do not detracts from the lesson	
2	Sequenced teaching strategies for teaching in-tune singing are not always evident and detract from the lesson	
1	Sequenced teaching strategies for teaching in-tune singing is not evident	
Development of students' musical skills		
4	There is a balance among the musical skills being taught in the lesson	
3	There is some imbalance among the musical skills being taught in the lesson and occasionally detracts from the lesson	
2	There is an imbalance among the musical skills being taught in the lesson and detracts from the lesson	
1	There is an imbalance among the musical skills	
Flexibility in adaptation of lesson plans		
4	Flexibility and adaptation of lesson plan and is always appropriate	
3	Flexibility and adaptation of lesson plan is not always appropriate sometimes detracts from the lesson	
2	Flexibility and adaptation of lesson plan is not always appropriate and occasionally detracts from the lesson	
1	Flexibility and adaptation of lesson plan is not appropriate	
Appropriate pacing of lesson		
4	Appropriate pacing of lesson is evident	
3	Appropriate pacing of lesson is not always present and occasionally detracts from the lesson	

Table 11.1 *Continued*

	Criteria	Comments
2	Appropriate pacing of lesson is not always present and detracts from the lesson	
1	Appropriate pacing of lesson is not present	
Questioning technique		
4	Questioning technique is always effective	
3	Questioning technique is not always effective and occasionally detracts from the lesson	
2	Questioning technique is not always effective and detracts from the lesson	
1	Questioning technique is not effective	
Error correction of students		
4	Error correction is evident	
3	Error correction is not always evident and occasionally detracts from the lesson	
2	Error correction is not always evident and detracts from the lesson	
1	Error correction is not evident	
Classroom management/discipline		
4	Successful classroom management is evident	
3	Appropriate classroom management is not always evident and occasionally detracts from the lesson	
2	Appropriate classroom management is not always evident and detracts from the lesson	
1	Appropriate classroom management is not evident	
Assessment of student learning		
Assessment of student participation		
4	75% or more of students are participating successfully in observed activities	
3	50 % or more of students are participating successfully in observed activities	
2	25% or more of students are participating successfully in observed activities	
1	Less than 25% of students are participating successfully in observed activities	
Teacher assessment of students		
4	Appropriate student assessment tools are evident	
3	Appropriate student assessment tools are not always evident and occasionally detracts from the assessment of the lesson	

continued

Table 11.1 *Continued*

	Criteria	Comments
2	Appropriate student assessment tools are not always evident and detracts from the assessment of the lesson	
1	Appropriate student assessment are not evident	

Synopsis/summary		
Lesson plan	Commendations	Recommendations

Assessment and Evaluation of Students: Student Profiles

This chapter presents several assessment and evaluation indicators, as well as rubrics to assess music students. The purpose of assessment in the music classroom is to evaluate the students':

Knowledge of music repertoire: Children as cultural stewards
Performance skills: Children as performers
Music literacy skills: Children as critical thinkers
Creative skills: Children as composers and improvisers
Listening skills: Children as listeners

Remember that there are two forms of music assessment: formative and summative assessment. Formative assessment is used during the course of a lesson, while summative assessment is used at the end of semester.

Data Collection: Formative Assessment

Data collection for compiling a student's profile chart based on formative assessment may take several forms. Formative assessment is the informal assessment of the students' work during the class lesson. A student's work is not to be graded or evaluated during formative assessment. A music instructor can assess a student's progress while in the process of teaching. This allows teachers to address their instructional approach to improve classroom instruction. In general, the instructor assesses the performance of the class while observing those students that need more individual attention. The type of teaching we describe in this book provides many opportunities for assessment. During the course of a lesson the instructor may assess the following:

- Repertoire

  During the introduction of the lesson, the instructor can observe the students' knowledge of musical repertoire based on their ability to sing song segments or whole songs independently.

- Performance

  During the core activities segments of the lesson, the instructor can assess the students' performing abilities.

- Creative skills

  During the performance and development of musical skills segments, the instructor can assess the students' ability to improvise or compose music with known rhythmic and melodic elements.

- Critical thinking: Music literacy

  During the performance and preparation of the new musical concept and performance and development of music skills segment of the lesson, the instructor can assess the students' music literacy skills. For example, in the visual awareness stage of preparing a new musical element, the instructor asks the students to create a representation of the target phrase containing that element. These representations can be collected and evaluated.

Ideally, the instructor should write an evaluation of he lesson based upon the information collected in the formative assessments.

Data Collection: Summative Assessment

Summative assessment occurs at the end of teaching a concept. It is a more formal evaluation of the students understanding of the concept. Student profile charts may be used to document student assessment.

Consider developing a profile chart for each class (class profile) and for each student (student profile) in your class where you can record information concerning student achievement. The following is a sample of possible areas of assessment to be included in a student profile chart based on national content standards and the music curriculum presented in this text. We present this as a sample profile chart. It should be modified for individual teaching situations. The following are components of the student profile.

Repertoire

Music instructors may document the students' knowledge of music repertoire. The rubrics for evaluation may be written in a manner that could allow the students to evaluate their own performance or the performance of their peers.

Performance

Music instructors may document the students' singing, movement, and instrumental ability. The rubrics for evaluation may be written in a manner that could allow the students to evaluate their own performance or the performance of their peers. The student's profile can include a recording of individual or group singing or instrumental playing.

Music Literacy

Music instructors assess the students' knowledge of rhythmic and melodic elements through reading and writing activities. Assessments should focus on the rhythmic and melodic elements covered in each grade. Examples of written work should be included and consist of visual representations for melodic and rhythmic elements, examples of written work done in traditional rhythmic notation and staff notation, and examples of work done on the computer.

Creative Skills

An assessment of creative skills would help document the students' ability to improvise and/or compose music. This type of evaluation would require rubrics that assess the students' abilities to use known rhythmic and melodic elements within specific forms. Examples of composition assignments using traditional rhythmic notation, staff notation, or work on computers should be included.

Listening and Describing

An assessment of listening enables the instructor to evaluate the students' aural and visual analysis skills. Instructors may wish to document whether students can sing the principle themes of a musical composition, use a listening map, or identify specific music compositions.

Cross-Curricular Instruction

An evaluation can be made of the students' abilities to identify and understand the connection between music and other subject areas in addition to the repertoire they are performing. Cross-curricular instruction may also include information presented by instructors of related subject areas.

The instructor should create an evaluation tool for all or some of the suggested components of the student profile. For example, the instructor should create rubrics for evaluating reading and writing skills for each grade. The rubrics in table 11.3 are examples from grade one; they may be adapted to any grade. Performance, reading, and writing assessments are included.

Table 11.2 Assessment and evaluation of students

Name
Grade
Term

Outcomes	**Activities**	**Indicators**
Knowledge of music repertoire	Performance	Students can perform all focus repertoire from memory making no mistakes Student perform focus repertoire making few mistakes that occasionally detract from the overall performance Student performs focus repertoire making mistakes that detract from the overall performance Student cannot perform focus repertoire
Performance (National Standard 1,2,7,8,9)	Singing	Student performs making no mistakes Student performs making few mistakes that occasionally detract from the overall performance Student performs making mistakes that detract from the overall performance Student cannot perform
	Ensemble performance Singing in choir	Student performs making no mistakes Student performs making few mistakes that occasionally detract from the overall performance Student performs making mistakes that detract from the overall performance Student cannot perform
	Movement	Student performs making no mistakes Student performs making few mistakes that occasionally detract from the overall performance Student performs making mistakes that detract from the overall performance Student cannot perform
	Instrument performance	Student performs making no mistakes Student performs making few mistakes that occasionally detract from the overall performance Student performs making mistakes that detract from the overall performance Student cannot perform
	Evaluating music performance	Student can evaluate the quality of their performance Student can evaluate the performance but the description lacks some details Student can describe the performance as good or not good but the description lacks details Student cannot describe the quality of their performance

continued

Table 11.2 *Continued*

Outcomes	Activities	Indicators
Music literacy (National Standard 5)	Rhythm	Student performs making no mistakes
		Student performs making few mistakes that occasionally detract from the overall performance
		Student performs making mistakes that detract from the overall performance
		Student cannot perform
	Melody	Student performs making no mistakes
		Student performs making few mistakes that occasionally detract from the overall performance
		Student performs making mistakes that detract from the overall performance
		Student cannot perform
	Reading	Student performs making no mistakes
		Student performs making few mistakes that occasionally detract from the overall performance
		Student performs making mistakes that detract from the overall performance
		Student cannot perform
	Writing	Student performs making no mistakes
		Student performs making few mistakes that occasionally detract from the overall performance
		Student performs making mistakes that detract from the overall performance
		Student cannot perform
	Computer skills	Student write music making no mistakes
		Student write music making that occasionally detract from the overall performance
		Student performs making mistakes that detract from the overall performance
		Student cannot perform
Creative skills (National Standard 3, 4)	Rhythmic improvisation	Student performs making no mistakes
		Student performs making few mistakes that occasionally detract from the overall performance
		Student performs making mistakes that detract from the overall performance
		Student cannot perform

Table 11.2 *Continued*

Outcomes	Activities	Indicators
	Melodic improvisation	Student performs making no mistakes
		Student performs making few mistakes that occasionally detract from the overall performance
		Student performs making mistakes that detract from the overall performance
		Student cannot perform
	Rhythmic composition	Student's composition demonstrates mastery of concepts
		Student's composition demonstrates mastery of concepts but includes a few mistakes that occasionally detract from the overall composition
		Student's composition demonstrates mastery of concepts but includes mistakes that detract from the overall composition
		Student cannot compose
	Melodic composition	Student's composition demonstrates mastery of concepts
		Student's composition demonstrates mastery of concepts but includes a few mistakes that occasionally detract from the overall composition
		Student's composition demonstrates mastery of concepts but includes mistakes that detract from the overall composition
		Student cannot compose
Listening, analyzing, and describing music (National Standard 6)	Aural analysis	Student can aurally analyze making no mistakes
		Student aurally analyze making few mistakes that do not detract from the overall performance.
		Student aurally analyze making mistakes that detract from the overall performance
		Student aurally analyze
	Visual analysis	Student visually analyze making no mistakes
		Student visually analyze making few mistakes that occasionally detract from the overall performance
		Student visually analyze making mistakes that detract from the performance
		Student cannot visually analyze

continued

Table 11.2 *Continued*

Outcomes	Activities	Indicators
	Student is able to sing musical themes	Student performs making no mistakes Student performs making few mistakes that occasionally detract from the overall performance Student performs making mistakes that detract from the overall performance Student cannot perform
	Student is able to follow a listening map or form map	Student is able to follow a listening map making no mistakes Student is able to follow a listening map making errors that occasionally detracts from the activity Student tries to follow a listening map making errors that detract from the activity Student cannot perform

Table 11.3 Rubrics for evaluating reading and writing skills

	Criteria	Comments
Assessment of tuneful singing		
4 = Advanced	Student sings *Snail, Snail* tunefully making no errors	
3 = Proficient	Student sings *Snail, Snail* tunefully making only a few errors in singing that ocassionally detract from the overall performance	
2 = Basic	Student sings *Snail, Snail* making some errors in singing that detract from the overall performance	
1 = Emerging	Student cannot sing *Snail, Snail* tunefully	
Assessment of students' understanding of one and two sounds on a beat		
Performance assessment of rhythm syllables		
4 = Advanced	Student sings rhythm syllables for *See Saw* or *Rain, Rain*, while clapping the rhythm making no errors	
3 = Proficient	Student sings rhythm syllables for *See Saw* or *Rain, Rain*, while clapping the rhythm making only a few errors that ocassionally detract from the overall performance	
2 = Basic	Student sings rhythm syllables for *See Saw* or *Rain, Rain*, while clapping the rhythm making some errors that detract from the overall performance	
1 = Emerging	Student cannot sing and clap the rhythm of *See Saw* or *Rain, Rain* with rhythm syllables	

Table 11.3 *Continued*

	Criteria	**Comments**
Reading assessment		
4 = Advanced	Student reads stick or traditional rhythmic notation of *See Saw* or *Rain, Rain* using rhythm syllables while clapping the rhythm making no errors	
3 = Proficient	Student reads stick or traditional rhythmic notation of *See Saw* or *Rain, Rain* using rhythm syllables while clapping the rhythm making only a few errors that ocassionally detract from the overall performance	
2 = Basic	Student reads stick or traditional rhythmic notation of *See Saw* or *Rain, Rain* using rhythm syllables while clapping the rhythm making some errors that detract from the overall performance	
1 = Emerging	Student cannot read stick or traditional rhythmic notation of *See Saw* or *Rain, Rain* while clapping the rhythm	
Writing assessment		
4 = Advanced	Student writes stick or traditional rhythmic notation of *See Saw* or *Rain, Rain* making no errors	
3 = Proficient	Student writes stick or traditional rhythmic notation of *See Saw* or *Rain, Rain* making only a few errors that ocassionally detract from the overall performance	
2 = Basic	Student writes stick or traditional rhythmic notation of *See Saw* or *Rain, Rain* making some errors that detract from the overall performance	
1 = Emerging	Student cannot write stick or traditional rhythmic notation of *See Saw* or *Rain, Rain*	
Assessment of students' understanding of *s* and *m*		
Performance assessment of solfège syllables		
4 = Advanced	Student sings *See Saw* tunefully using solfège syllables and hand signs making no errors	
3 = Proficient	Student sings *See Saw* tunefully using solfège syllables and hand signs making only a few errors that ocassionally detract from the overall performance	
2 = Basic	Student sings *See Saw* tunefully using solfège syllables and hand signs making some errors that detract from the overall performance	
1 = Emerging	Student cannot sing *See Saw* tunefully using solfège syllables and hand signs	

continued

Table 11.3 *Continued*

	Criteria	Comments
Reading assessment		
4 = Advanced	Student reads staff notation of *See Saw* while singing solfège syllables, and showing hand signs, making no errors	
3 = Proficient	Student reads staff notation of *See Saw* while singing solfège syllables, and showing hand signs, making only a few errors that ocassionally detract from the overall performance	
2 = Basic	Student reads staff notation of *See Saw* while singing solfège syllables, and showing hand signs, making some errors that detract from the overall performance	
1 = Emerging	Student cannot read staff notation of *See Saw* with solfège syllables and hand signs	
Writing assessment		
4 = Advanced	Student writes stick notation and labels with solfège syllables or staff notation for *See Saw* making no errors	
3 = Proficient	Student writes stick notation and labels with solfège syllables or staff notation for *See Saw* making only a few errors that ocassionally detract from the overall performance	
2 = Basic	Student writes stick notation and labels with solfège syllables or staff notation for *See Saw* making some errors that detract from the overall performance	
1 = Emerging	Student cannot write stick notation and label with solfège syllables or staff notation for *See Saw*	

Discussion Questions

1. Discuss the role of assessment in the music class.
2. How do we assess the students' musical knowledge in the music classroom? Provide examples of each kind of assessment.
3. There is no time to assess student learning during two thirty-minute lessons each week. Music is meant to be a fun activity and assessment has no part of a music curriculum. Discuss.

➤ Ongoing Activities

1. For all of your classes that your will be teaching next year, please develop a student profile sheet, formal assessment activities, as well as the accompanying rubrics. Please include the profile sheets and assessment tools in your teaching portfolio.
2. Imagine that your are having a conference with a parent from a third grade class at the end of your next year at your new school. In preparation for that meeting develop a detailed profile for that student. Please explain to the parents how their child is succeeding in your class and what the implications are for their child's learning across the curriculum. Divide the class into parents and teachers and role play a teacher–parent conference.
3. Because of your incredible success in the classroom you have been asked to become the head of the music department during the second semester of next year in your new school. As part of your responsibilities, you must evaluate teachers' resource portfolios, teachers' lesson plans, teachers' musicianship skills, and evaluate a lesson taught by the teachers in your department. How will you prepare for the evaluation of music instructors under your supervision?

References

Black, Paul, Chris Harrison, Clare Lee, Bethan Marshall, and Dylan William. *Assessment for Learning: Putting it into Practice.* Buckingham, UK: Open University Press, 2003.

Boyle, David J., and Rudolf E. Radocy. *The Measurement and Evaluation of Musical Experiences.* New York: Schirmer Books, 1987.

Colwell, Richard. "Preparing Student Teachers in Assessment." *Arts Education Policy Review* 99/4 (1987): 29–36.

Elliot, David J. *Praxial Music Education: Reflections and Dialogues.* New York: Oxford University Press, 2005.

Freed-Garrod, J. "Assessment in the Arts: Elementary-Aged Students as Qualitative Assessors of their Own and Peer's Musical Compositions." *Bulletin of the Council for Research in Music Education* 139 (1999): 50–63.

Harvard University, "Arts in Education Program." http://www.gse.harvard.edu/~aie_web

———. "Harvard Project Zero." http://www.pz.harvard.edu.

Herboly-Kocsár, Ildikó. *Aching of Polyphony, Harmony and Form in Elementary School,* ed. Lilla Gábor, trans. Alexander Farkas. Kecskemét: Zoltán Kodály Pedagogical Institute, 1984.

Herman, Joan L., Pamela R. Aschbacher, and Lynn Winters. *A Practical Guide to Alternative Assessment.* Alexandria, Va.: Association for Supervision and Curriculum Development, 1992.

Hickey, Maude. "Assessment Rubrics for Music Composition." *Music Educators Journal* 85/4 (1999): 26–33.

Kassner, K. "Would Better Questions Enhance Music Learning?" *Music Educators Journal* 84/4 (1998): 29–36.

Lehman, P. "Curriculum and Program Evaluation," in *Handbook of Research on Music Teaching and Learning,* ed. R. Colwell. New York: Schirmer, 1992.

Scott, Sheila J. "The Construction and Preliminary Validation of a Criterion Referenced Music Achievement Test Formulated in Terms of the Goals and Objectives of a Kodály-Based Music Curriculum." *Bulletin of the International Kodály Society* 17/ (1992): 26–32.

———. "Assessing Student Learning Across the National Standards for Music Education." *General Music Today* 13/1 (1999): 3–7.

Smith, J. "Using Portfolio Assessment in General Music." *General Music Today* 9/1 (1995): 8–12.

Winner, Ellen. *Arts Propel: An Introductory Handbook.* Boston: Harvard Project Zero and Educational Testing Service, 1991.

———, Lyle Davidson, and Larry Scripp, eds., *Arts Propel: A Handbook for Music.* Boston: Harvard Project Zero and Educational Testing Service, 1992.

Appendix 1
Curriculum Goals

Grade 1: Curriculum Goals

Repertoire: Children as Stewards of Their Cultural and Musical Heritage

Expand song repertoire to add to students' knowledge of children's songs and games, folk music of the children's culture, art music, and recently composed music.

Performance: Children as Performers

Broaden performance skills to include:

Singing

1. Be familiar with a repertoire of thirty folk songs and singing games, classical music and recently composed music.
2. Know by memory ten to fifteen songs and are able to sing these with solfege and rhythm names.
3. Perform all songs with accurate intonation, clear diction, clear head tone, musical phrasing/breathing, appropriate dynamics, and tempi.

Part-work

1. Sing songs antiphonally.
2. Practice intervals simultaneously with hand signs.
3. Accompany a song with a rhythmic ostinato using quarter and eighth notes and quarter note rests.
4. Accompany a song with a melodic ostinato using *la, so,* or *mi.*
5. Sing simple rhythmic or melodic canons derived from familiar songs.
6. Perform two-part rhythmic exercises based on rhythmic motifs from known songs.

Movement

1. Perform acting-out games with chase element.
2. Perform winding games.
3. Perform simple line games.
4. Perform circle games.
5. Improvise words and movement to known songs.

Instruments

1. Students demonstrate first grade melodic and rhythmic concepts on classroom instruments.
2. Students accompany classroom singing on classroom instruments.
3. Students conduct in duple meter.

Music Literacy: Children as Critical Thinkers and Problem Solvers

Rhythmic Elements

1. Know names and written symbols for quarter, eighth notes, and quarter note rest, accented beat, bar lines. Conduct in $\frac{2}{4}$ meter.
2. Perform ostinati using quarter and eighth notes consciously.
3. Perform two-part rhythmic exercises and canons.
4. Improvise short motives with quarter, eighth notes, and quarter note rest.
5. Recognize tunes from clapped rhythm patterns.
6. Identify a skipping song and marching song.

Melodic Elements

1. Be able to perform solfa and hand signs for child chant patterns (pentatonic bi chords and tri chords):
   so, mi, la, and intervals formed by them
   (*so–mi mi–so so–la la–so mi–la la–mi*)
2. Learn to read melodic patterns that use the notes *so, mi,* and *la* from rhythmic and staff notation.

Reading and Writing

1. Read or write well-known rhythmic or melodic patterns found in students' repertoire, from hand signs, traditional rhythmic notation, and staff notation.
2. Write rhythmic patterns from memory or when dictated by the teacher.
3. Write melodic patterns found in focus songs from memory or when dictated by the teacher using stick or staff notation.

Inner Hearing

1. Silently sing "inside" from the teacher's hand signs.
2. Silently sing known songs with melodic syllables.
3. Silently read either full or partial rhythms or melodies written in stick or staff notation.
4. Sing back short melodic or rhythmic motives from memory using text, rhythm syllables, or solfege syllables.

Form

1. Recognize same, similar, or different phrases in a song either aurally or through music reading.
2. Use letters to describe a form: AABA.
3. Use repeat signs correctly in reading and writing.

Musical Memory

1. Echo four- and eight-beat rhythm patterns clapped by the instructor.
2. Memorize short melodies through hand signs.
3. Memorize phrases of four or eight beats from known songs using stick or staff notation.
4. Echo rhythm patterns clapped by the teacher saying correct rhythm syllables.
5. Memorize rhythm patterns read from stick notation.

Improvisation/Composition: Children as Creative Human Beings

1. Improvise rhythm patterns of four or eight beats using rhythm instruments.
2. Improvise rhythm patterns of four or eight beats by clapping and saying rhythm syllables.
3. Improvise short musical motives (*la–so–mi*) using hand signs, hand staff, or body signs.
4. Improvise pentatonic bi and tri chord (*so–mi–la*) melodies to simple four- to eight-beat rhythms using the voice or a barred instrument.
5. Improvise a new rhythm and melody to one measure or more of a well-known song.
6. Improvise question and answer motives using known rhythm or melodic patterns.

Listening: Children as Listeners

Expand Listening Repertoire and Revisit Kindergarten Musical Concepts

1. Recognize musical features in classroom song repertoire, folk music, and masterworks.

2. Recognize rhythmic features in classroom song repertoire, folk music, and masterworks including quarter notes, eighth notes, and quarter note rests.
3. Develop awareness of expressive controls, that is, dynamics, tempo, timbre, and their distinctive characteristics in masterworks of various historical periods.
4. Recognize phrase forms (same/different) in classroom song repertoire, folk music, and masterworks.

Grade 2: Curriculum Goals

Repertoire: Children as Stewards of Their Cultural and Music Heritage

Expand song repertoire to add to students' knowledge of folk music of the child's culture, as well as related cultures, art music, and recently composed music.

Performance: Children as Performers

Broaden performance skills to include:

Singing

1. Increase repertoire by learning thirty to thirty-five new folk songs, games, canons, and simple two-part song arrangements.
2. Be able to perform fifteen to twenty songs with rhythmic and melodic solmization.
3. Learn five songs through sight-singing.
4. Know and perform three to five canons, partner songs, or easy two-part song arrangements.
5. Perform all songs with accurate intonation, clear diction, clear head tone, musical phrasing/breathing, and appropriate dynamics and tempi.

Part-work

1. Sing a well-known song and clap its rhythm in canon.
2. Perform a simple two-part exercise individually.
3. Sing in two parts from:
   a. staff notation;
   b. stick notation;
   c. hand signs with one part moving at a time.
4. Sing simple two-part song arrangements.

Movement

1. Perform choosing games.
2. Perform chasing games.

3. Perform chasing games with a stationary circle.
4. Perform partner clapping and body percussion games.
5. Improvise words and movement to known songs.
6. Conduct repertoire in duple simple, compound meter and quadruple meter.

Instruments

1. Students demonstrate second grade melodic and rhythmic concepts on classroom instruments.
2. Students accompany classroom singing on classroom instruments.
3. Students accompany classroom singing with simple xylophone accompaniments.

Music Literacy: Children as Critical Thinkers and Problem Solvers

Rhythmic Elements

1. Recognize and perform half note, whole note, half note rest, whole note rest. Read with rhythm syllables as well as counting with numbers.
2. Perform two-part rhythmic exercises and canons.

Melodic Elements

1. Review pentatonic bichords and trichords (*so–mi–la*).
2. Learn solfege syllables and hand signs and written symbols for *major pentatonic scale.*

Reading and Writing

1. Read and write well-known rhythmic or melodic patterns from hand signs, stick notation, or staff notation.
2. Write rhythmic patterns from memory or when dictated by the teacher.
3. Write melodic patterns found in focus songs from memory or when dictated by the teacher using stick or staff notation.
4. Expand reading and writing of rhythmic and melodic patterns from four to eight to sixteen beats.
5. Sight-sing melodic phrases and songs with solfege syllables.

Inner Hearing

1. Sing known songs silently:
   a. while performing the beat or rhythm of the song;
   b. without performing the beat or rhythm of the song.
2. Recognize songs, rhythm patterns, or melodic patterns from stick or staff notation.

Form

1. Recognize same, similar, or different phrases in a song either aurally or through music reading.
2. Use letters to describe a form: AABA.
3. Use of repeat signs 𝄆 𝄇.
4. Learn to read music with first and second endings.
5. Recognize rhythmic and melodic variation.
6. Create simple forms showing phrase variants; for example:
   a a' b a; a a a' a; a b a' c, and so on

Musical Memory

1. Memorize short melodies from the teacher's hand signs.
2. Memorize phrases of four to eight beats from known songs using stick or staff notation.
3. Echo rhythm patterns clapped by the teacher.
4. Echo rhythm patterns clapped by the teacher using rhythm syllables.
5. Memorize rhythm patterns read from stick notation.
6. Memorize simple two-part exercises.

Improvisation/Composition: Children as Creative Human Beings

1. Improvise rhythm patterns of four or eight beats either by clapping, using rhythm instruments, or clapping and saying rhythm syllables.
2. Improvise short musical motives using pentatonic bichords and trichords (*la–so–mi*) using hand signs, hand staff, or body signs.
3. Improvise pentatonic bichords and trichords (*so–m –la*) melodies to simple four- to eight-beat rhythms using the voice or a barred instrument.
4. Improvise a new rhythm and melody to one measure or more of a well-known song.
5. Improvise question and answer motives using known rhythm or melodic patterns.
6. Improvise rhythms in a chain around the classroom.
7. Improvise rhythms to the form of a simple folk song.
8. Improvise rhythmic accompaniments to familiar songs.

Listening: Children as Listeners

Expand listening repertoire as well as reinforcing second grade musical concepts.

1. Recognize musical features in classroom song repertoire, folk music, and masterworks including pentatonic scales.
2. Recognize rhythmic features in classroom song repertoire, folk music, and masterworks, including half note, whole note, half note rest, and whole note rest.

3. Develop awareness of expressive controls, that is, dynamics, tempo, timbre, and their distinctive characteristics in masterworks of various historical periods.
4. Recognize phrase forms in classroom song repertoire, folk music, and masterworks.

Grade 3: Curriculum Goals

Repertoire: Children as Stewards of Their Music Heritage

Expand song repertoire to add to students' knowledge of folk music, art music, and recently composed music.

Performance: Children as Performers

Broaden performance skills to include: (1) tuneful singing in individual and group situations; (2) two-part singing; (3) movement; and (4) use of classroom instruments, such as pitched and unpitched percussion and barred instruments.

Singing

1. Learn thirty to thirty-five new folk songs, canons, games, and two-part song arrangements.
2. Sing fifteen to twenty songs with solfege and hand signs.
3. Learn ten to fifteen songs by sight-reading.
4. Sing individually and in groups in call and response, echo singing, game songs, and verse and refrain.

Part-work

1. Sing songs antiphonally.
2. Practice intervals simultaneously with hand signs.
3. Accompany a song with a rhythmic ostinato using quarter, eighth notes and quarter note rests, an eighth note followed by two sixteenth note and two sixteenth notes followed by an eighth note combination.
4. Accompany a song with a melodic ostinato using *la, so, mi, re, do, low la, low so,* and *high do.*
5. Sing simple rhythmic or melodic canons derived from familiar songs.
6. Perform two-part rhythmic exercises based on rhythms of known songs.

Movement

1. Perform circle games with chase element.
2. Perform circle games with choosing.
3. Perform double circle games in opposing directions.
4. Perform partner games with changing directions, changing partners.
5. Perform circle games containing simple square dance patterns.

6. Perform line dances containing contra dance patterns.
7. Perform games and dances from various cultures.
8. Perform partner clapping and body percussion games.
9. Improvise words and movement to known songs.
10. Practice tug of war and broad jumping games.
11. Conduct duple simple, compound meter and simple quadruple meter.

Instruments

1. Students demonstrate third grade melodic and rhythmic concepts on classroom instruments.
2. Students accompany classroom singing on classroom instruments.
3. Students accompany classroom singing with simple xylophone accompaniments.

Music Literacy: Children as Critical Thinkers and Problem Solvers

Rhythmic Elements

1. Perform the sixteenth note in eighth note followed by two sixteenth notes and two sixteenth notes followed by an eighth note combinations in four- and eight-beat rhythm patterns.
2. Perform in all known meters using song material with internal and external upbeats.

Melodic Elements

1. Review solfege for the major pentatonic scale.
2. Be able to perform solfege and hand signs for patterns using the extended pentatonic scale.
3. Be able to perform solfege and hand signs for the minor pentatonic scale

Reading and Writing

1. Sight-sing in two parts (up to thirty-two beat exercises).
2. Apply absolute letter names to simple melodic exercises on the staff in G-*do,* F-*do,* and C-*do.*
3. Write a simple melody and compose a rhythmic accompaniment or an ostinato.
4. Write known songs using traditional rhythmic and staff notation in G-*do,* F-*do,* and C-*do.*
5. Apply absolute letter names to simple melodic exercises on the staff in G-*do,* F-*do,* and C-*do.*

Inner Hearing

1. Sing songs "inside your head," using solfege syllables or rhythm names.
2. Memorize easy two-part exercises in solfege or rhythm syllables from hand signs, stick, or staff notation.

3. Sing the next correct letter name or solfege syllable after the teacher or another student in a known song without hearing the pitch.

Melodic concepts to include:

1. Low *la*
2. Low *so*
3. High *do*
4. Minor pentatonic scale

Rhythmic concepts to include:

1. Sixteenth notes
2. Sixteenth note combinations
3. Internal and external upbeats
4. $\frac{6}{8}$ meter

Form

1. Recognize simple song forms (ABAC, AABC, AA'BC).
2. Learn to read music with first and second endings.
3. Recognize rhythmic and melodic variation.
4. Create simple forms showing phrase variants; for example, AA'BA, AAA'A, ABA'C, and so on.

Musical Memory

Expand skills in memory to include the memorization of longer passages (8–32 beats), reading and writing memory work, improvisation work, and adding absolute names directly from solfege without the notes written on the staff. Students will be able to:

1. Memorize a rhythmic pattern from notation that is up to thirty-two beats.
2. Write out simple rhythms of melodies from memory that are sixteen beats.
3. Add absolute letter names to a rhythmic exercise.
4. Improvise movements to represent parts of the song, such as form, text, melody, or rhythm.
5. Form a listening exercise, memorize themes from music literature.

Improvisation/Composition: Children as Creative Human Beings

Expand skills in improvisation and composition to include singing, playing instruments, and moving at the third grade level. Students will be able to:

1. Improvise short melodies for poems and rhymes using known musical elements.
2. Improvise melodies using known melodic syllables (*so, la, do-re-mi, so-la,* and high *do*) in simple song form (ABA, AAAB, ABAB).

3. Improvise movements that reflect the form of the song.
4. Write a simple melody and compose a rhythmic accompaniment or an ostinato.

Listening: Children as Listeners

Expand listening repertoire to teach and reinforce third grade musical concepts. Students will be able to:

1. Recognize a variety of instruments, voices, and dynamic levels.
2. Recognize pentatonic scale and tone sets in the context of listening examples and familiar songs.
3. Perform for each other.
4. Listen to performances by others (other students, parents, teacher, and artists).
5. Listen to and perform folk songs, master works, vocal songs, and instrumental works for third grade concept and elements.

Grade 4: Curriculum Goals

Repertoire: Children as Stewards of Their Music Heritage

Expand song repertoire to add to students' knowledge of folk music, art music, and recently composed music.

Performance: Children as Performers

Broaden performance skills to include: (1) tuneful singing in individual and group situations; (2) two-part singing; (3) movement; and (4) use of classroom instruments such as pitched and unpitched percussion, barred instruments, and recorder.

Singing

1. Sing individually and in groups in call and response, verse and refrain, and game songs.
2. Learn twenty to twenty-five new songs, canons, and two- and three-part song arrangements of various cultural origins.
3. Sing ten to fifteen songs with solfege.
4. Learn ten to fifteen songs by sight-reading.
5. Learn five to seven two-part songs.

Part-work

1. Sing songs antiphonally.
2. Practice intervals simultaneously with hand signs.

3. Accompany a song with a rhythmic ostinato using quarter, eighth notes and quarter note rests sixteenth notes in eighth note plus two sixteenth notes and two sixteenth notes followed by an eighth note combinations, syncopated rhythms, dotted quarter followed by and eight note.
4. Accompany a song with a melodic ostinato using *la, so, mi, re, do low la,low so,* and high *do, fa.*
5. Sing simple rhythmic or melodic canons derived from familiar songs.
6. Perform two-part rhythmic exercises based on rhythms of known songs.
7. Sing and read two-part songs.

Movement

1. Perform double circle games.
2. Perform circle games containing square dance patterns.
3. Perform line dances containing contra dance patterns.
4. Perform basic square dance.
5. Perform games and dances from various cultures.
6. Conduct duple simple and compound meter, triple simple meter, as well as simple quadruple meter.

Instruments

1. Demonstrate fourth grade melodic and rhythmic concepts on classroom instruments such as xylophones, glockenspiels, rhythm instruments, and recorder.
2. Accompany classroom singing on classroom instruments.

Music Literacy: Children as Critical Thinkers and Problem Solvers

Broaden literacy skills in reading and writing music.

Rhythmic Elements

1. Know names and written symbols for syncopated rhythms, dotted quarter followed by an eighth note, dotted eighth followed by a sixteenth note.
2. Perform ostinati using the above notes.
3. Perform two-part rhythmic exercises and canons.
4. Recognize tunes from clapped rhythm patterns.
5. Simple triple meter.

Melodic Elements

1. *So* pentatonic
2. *Do* pentachord and hexachord, and major scale
3. Half steps/whole steps
4. B-flat and F-sharp

Reading and Writing

1. Sight-read in two parts (up to thirty-two beat exercises).
2. Apply absolute letter names to simple pentatonic, pentachord, and hexachord melodic exercises on the staff in G-*do,* F-*do,* and C-*do.*
3. Write a simple pentatonic, pentachord, and hexachord melody and compose a rhythmic accompaniment or an ostinato to accompany it.
4. Write known pentatonic, pentachord, and hexachord songs using rhythmic and staff notation in G-*do,* F-*do,* and C-*do.*
5. Apply absolute letter names to simple pentatonic, pentachord, and hexachord melodic exercises on the staff in G-*do,* F-*do,* and C-*do.*

Inner Hearing

1. Sing songs "inside" with melodic syllables or letter names.
2. Memorize easy two-part melodies from hand signs, stick notation, and staff notation without hearing them aloud.
3. Memorize both parts of an easy two-part exercise, and switch between them without hearing them aloud.
4. Sing the correct solfege syllables or letter names of the next note when the teacher stops at random within a song.
5. "Sing" the indicated measures of a song using inner hearing.
6. On a barred instrument, play back a melody that the teacher has sung.
7. Identify a *do* pentachord or a *do* hexachord melody from the teacher humming or playing on an instrument.

Form

Continue recognition of phrase forms.

Musical Memory

1. Memorize rhythmic exercises from notation up to thirty-two beats in length.
2. Write simple rhythms and melodies from memory up to sixteen beats in length.
3. Improvise movements appropriate to some aspect of the music, for example, form, melody, text, or rhythm.
4. Memorize rhythmic or melodic themes from music literature.
5. Memorize two-part songs and exercises.

Improvisation/Composition: Children as Creative Human Beings

Expand skills in improvisation and composition, to include singing, playing instruments, and moving at the fourth grade level.

1. Improvise several phrases of music using given forms.
2. Improvise a melodic chain: begin each phrase with the last syllable of a previous student.
3. Read an exercise and improvise an alternative ending using a given rhythm and containing selected melodic elements:
   a. read an exercise but improvise at two given places;
   b. perform four and eight beat question and answer phrases;
   c. improvise empty measures within a four measure phrase;
   d. improvise/compose to complete a missing section of a song in a given form;
   e. improvise/compose using two-part hand signs;
   f. improvise/compose short rhythmic canons;
   g. question and answer in eight-beat and sixteen-beat patterns;
   h. play a "fill in the empty measures" game.

Listening: Children as Listeners

Expand listening repertoire to teach and reinforce fourth grade musical concepts.

1. Recognize musical features in classroom song repertoire, folk music, and masterworks, including pentatonic, pentachord, and hexachord scales.
2. Recognize rhythmic features in classroom song repertoire, folk music, and masterworks including syncopations, and dotted quarter-eighth note combinations.
3. Develop awareness of expressive controls, that is, dynamics, tempo, timbre, and their distinctive characteristics in masterworks of various historical periods.
4. Recognize phrase forms in classroom song repertoire, folk music, and masterworks.
5. Recognize tonic, dominant, and subdominant functions.

Grade 5: Curriculum Goals

Repertoire: Children as Stewards of Their Music Heritage

Expand song repertoire to add to students' knowledge of folk music, art music, and composed music.

Performance: Children as Performers

Broaden performance skills to include: (1) tuneful singing in individual and group situations; (2) two- and three-part singing; (3) movement; and (4) use of classroom instruments such as pitched and unpitched percussion, barred instruments, and recorder.

Singing

1. Learn twenty to twenty-five new songs, canons, and two- and three-part song arrangements of various cultural origins.

2. Sing ten to fifteen songs with solfege.
3. Learn ten to fifteen songs by sight-reading.
4. Learn five two- and three-part songs.
5. Sing seasonal and holiday songs.
6. Learn fifteen game songs.
7. Learn songs in preparation for sixth grade concepts.

Part-work

1. Practice intervals simultaneously with hand signs.
2. Accompany a song with a rhythmic ostinato using the following note values.
   ♪. 𝅘𝅥𝅯, 𝅘𝅥𝅯 ♪., ♪ ♩. .
3. Accompany a song in compound meter with subdivisions of the beat.
4. Accompany a song with a melodic ostinato using *la, so, mi, re, do low la, low so,* and high *do, fa, ti,* and *si.*
5. Sing simple rhythmic or melodic canons derived from familiar songs.
6. Perform two-part rhythmic exercises based on rhythms of known songs.
7. Sing and read two-part songs.

Movement

1. Perform double circle games.
2. Perform double line games.
3. Perform basic square games.
4. Perform basic square dances.
5. Perform games and dances from various cultures.
6. Conduct duple simple and compound meter, triple simple meter, as well as simple quadruple meter.

Instruments

1. Students demonstrate fifth grade melodic and rhythmic concepts on classroom instruments.
2. Students accompany classroom singing on classroom instruments.

Music Literacy: Children as Critical Thinkers and Problem Solvers

Rhythmic Elements

1. ♪. 𝅘𝅥𝅯, 𝅘𝅥𝅯 ♪., ♪ ♩. .
2. Compound (one, two, three sound on a beat)—$\frac{6}{8}$ meter
3. Uneven subdivisions in compound meter (dotted eighth, sixteenth, eighth)
4. Subdivisions in $\frac{6}{8}$ meter
5. Triplets

Melodic Elements

1. High *ti* (*la-ti-high do'*) (high *do'-ti-la*) and Major scale
2. Natural minor
3. Dorian scale—*fi*
4. Harmonic minor—*si*
5. Melodic minor
6. Mixolydian scale

Reading and Writing

1. Sight-read in two parts (up to thirty-two beat exercises).
2. Apply absolute letter names to simple major, minor and modal exercises on the staff in various key signatures.
3. Write a major, minor, or modal melody and compose a rhythmic accompaniment or an ostinato to accompany it.
4. Write known songs using rhythmic and staff notation in G-*do,* F-*do,* and C-*do.*
5. Apply absolute letter names to simple major, minor, and modal melodic exercises on the staff in selected key areas.

Inner Hearing

1. Sing songs "inside" with melodic syllables or letter names.
2. Memorize easy two-part melodies from hand signs, stick notation, and staff notation without hearing them aloud.
3. Memorize both parts of an easy two-part exercise, and switch between them without hearing them aloud.
4. Sing the correct solfege syllables or letter names of the next note when the teacher stops at random within a song.

Form

Students analyse the form of typical classical forms such as binary, ternary, sonata and rondo forms.

Musical Elements

1. Harmonic functions, Major: I, IV, and V
2. Harmonic functions, Minor: i, V
3. Naming intervals, for example, Major third, Minor third

Improvisation/Composition: Children as Creative Human Beings

Expand skills in improvisation and composition, to include singing, playing instruments, and moving at the fifth grade level.

1. Improvise phrases of music using given forms.
2. Improvise a melodic chain: begin each phrase with the last syllable of a previous melodic turn.
3. Sing simple major melodies in minor tonality.
4. Read an exercise and improvise an alternative ending using a given rhythm and containing selected melodic elements.
5. Read an exercise but improvise at two given places.
6. Four and eight-beat question and answer.
7. Improvise empty measures within a four-measure phrase.

Listening: Children as Listeners

Expand listening repertoire to teach and reinforce fifth grade musical concepts.

1. Recognize musical features in classroom song repertoire, folk music, and masterworks including pentatonic scales, triple meter, and simple compound meter.
2. Develop awareness of expressive controls, that is, dynamics, tempo, timbre, and their distinctive characteristics in masterworks of various historical periods.
3. Recognize forms in classroom song repertoire, folk music, and masterworks, including compound binary, compound ternary, rondo, and sonata allegro.

Appendix 2
Alphabetical Song List

Grade 1 Alphabetical list

Song List
A la Ronda Ronda
A Tisket a Tasket
All Around the Buttercup
Bee Bee Bumble Bee
Bobby Shaftoe
Bounce High Bounce Low
Bow Wow Wow
Button You Must Wander
Bye Baby Bunting
Chini, Mini
Clap Your Hands Together
Cobbler Cobbler
Doggie Doggie
Down Came a Lady
Engine #9
Frog in the Meadow
Fudge Fudge
Good Night
Here Comes a Bluebird
Hot Cross Buns
Hush Baby Hush
I Climbed up the Apple Tree
In and Out
It's Raining It's Pouring
Jack and Jill
Johnny's It

continued

Grade 1 *Continued*

Song List

Johnny's It
Lemonade
Little Sally Water
Lucy Locket
Nanny Goat
Naughty Kitty Cat
No Robbers Out Today
Pala Palita
Pease Porridge Hot
Pica Perica
Pipirigallo
Pipis y Ganas
Queen Queen Caroline
Quien es esa gente?
Rain Rain
Ring Around the Rosie
See Saw
Snail Snail
Starlight, Starbright
Teddy Bear
This Old Man
Tinker Tailor
Two Four Six Eight
We Are Dancing in the Forest

Games to be played in grade 1

A Tisket a Tasket
All Around the Buttercup
Bounce High Bounce Low
Bow Wow Wow
Button You must Wander
Clap Your Hands Together
Doggie Doggie
Down Came a Lady
Frog in the Meadow
Here comes a Bluebird
In and Out

Grade 1 *Continued*

Song List
Johnny's It
Lemonade
Little Sally Water
Lucy Locket
Nanny Goat
Naughty Kitty Cat
No Robbers Out Today
Rain Rain
Ring Around the Rosie
Tinker Tailor
We Are Dancing in the Forest

Grade 2 Alphabetical list

Song Title
A Tisket a Tasket
All Around the Buttercup
Are You Sleeping
Blue
Boatman, The
Bounce High Bounce Low
Bow Wow Wow
Button You Must Wander
Bye Baby Bunting
Bye Bye Baby
Clap Your Hands Together
Closet Key, The
Cobbler Cobbler
Cocky Robin
Cumberland Gap
Dance Josey
Deedle Deedle Dumpling (rhyme)
Dinah
Do, Do Pity
Doggie Doggie
Down Came a Lady
Duerme Nino

continued

Grade 2 *Continued*

Song List

Duerme Pronto
Fed My Horse
Firefly
Frog in the Meadow
Frosty Weather
Fudge Fudge
Grandma Grunts
Great Big House
Here Comes a Bluebird
Hop Old Squirrel
Hot Cross Buns
Hunt the Cows
Hush Baby Hush
Hush Little Minnie
Ida Red
It's Raining It's Pouring
Johnny's It
Juan Pirulero
Kings Land
Knock the Cymbals
Let Us Chase the Squirrel
Little Sally Water
Long Legged Sailor
Lucy Locket
Mama, Buy Me a Chiney Doll
Matarile
Michael Row the Boat
Mother, Mother
Nanny Goat
No Robbers Out Today
Old Aunt Dinah
Old Brass Wagon
Old Woman
Over in the Meadow
Paw Paw Patch
Rain Rain
Ring Around the Rosie

Grade 2 *Continued*

Song List

Rocky Mountain
Sammy Sackett
Sea Shell
See Saw
Shanghai Chicken
Starlight, Starbright
Teddy Bear
Ten in the Bed
This Old Man
Tideo
Two Rubble Tum
Wallflowers
Walter Jumped a Fox
Who's That Tapping

Games to be played in grade 2

All Around the Buttercup
Are You Sleeping
Bow Wow Wow
Button You Must Wander
Closet Key, The
Dance Josey
Do, Do Pity
Doggie Doggie
Down Came a Lady
Frog in the Meadow
Frosty Weather
Fudge Fudge
Great Big House
Here Comes a Bluebird
Hunt the Cows
Hush Little Minnie
Ida Red
Kings Land
Knock the Cymbals
Let Us Chase the Squirrel

continued

Grade 2 *Continued*

Song List
Little Sally Water
Long Legged Sailor
Nanny Goat
No Robbers Out Today
Old Brass Wagon
Old Woman
Over in the Meadow
Paw Paw Patch
Rain Rain
Ring Around the Rosie
Rocky Mountain
Two Rubble Tum
Wallflowers
Who's that Tapping

Grade 3 Alphabetical list

Song Title
Above the Plain
Acitron de un Fandango
A Don Chin Chino
A Madru Senores
Band of Angels
Big Fat Biscuit
Billy Boy
Blow Ye winds
Bought Me a Cat
Bow Wow Wow
Bye, Baby Bunting
C-Line Woman
Cape Cod Girls
Charlie Over the Ocean
Chickalileelo
Circle Round the Zero
Cock Robin
Cotton Eye Joe
Cumberland Gap

Grade 3 *Continued*

Song List
Dance Josey
Deedle Deedle Dumpling
Deer Chase, The
Dinah
Do, Do Pity
Drunken Sailor
El Coyotito
Fed My Horse
Fire in the Mountain
Firefly
Gallows Pole, The
Golden Ring
Grandma Grunts (variant)
Great Big House
Hambone
Head and Shoulders
Here Comes a Bluebird
Hogs in the Cornfield
Hold My Mule
Hop Old Squirrel
How Many Miles to Babylon?
Hush Little Baby
I Lost the Farmer's Dairy Key
Ida Red
I'll Sell My Hat
Iroquois Lullaby
Jim Along Josie
John Kanaka
Johnny Cuckoo
Johnson Boys
Jolly Miller
Kansas Boys
King Kong Kitchie
King's Land
Knock the Cymbals
Land of the Silver Birch

continued

Grade 3 *Continued*

Song List

Las Estatuas de Marfil
La Patita
Liza Jane
Lullaby, Little Papoose
Mama, Buy Me a China Doll
Mister Rabbit
Mush Toodin
Oh, Fly Around
Old Betty Larkin
Old Brass Wagon
Old Gray Mare
Old House
Old Molly Hare
Old Mr. Rabbit
Old Sow, The
Old Texas
Over the River
Paw Paw Patch
Phoebe
Poor Little Kitty Cat
Porquoi
Riding in the Buggy
Riding of a Goat
Rocky Mountain
Rosie, Darling Rosie
Sailing on the Ocean
San Serafin del Monte
Santo Domingo
Scotland's Burning
Shanghai Chicken
Shortnin' Bread
Skin and Bones
Skip to My Lou
Skip to the Barbershop
Skipping Rope Song
Swapping Song
Tideo

Grade 3 *Continued*

Song List

Turn the Glasses Over

Wallflowers

Walter Jumped a Fox

What'll We Do with the Baby-o?

Wildcat

Yangtze Boatman's Chantey

Grade 4 Alphabetical list

Song Title

Above the Plain

Ah! Vous Dirai-Je, Mamam

Alabama Gal

All God's Children

Among the Plants (Entra las Matas)

Are You Sleeping

Around the Green Gravel

At the Gate of Heaven

Auld Lang Syne

Autumn Canon

Big Fat Biscuit

Birch Tree

Blow Ye Winds

Boat Drifts Away (Se Va la Barca)

Bound for the Promised

Canoe Round

Cedar Swamp

Chatter with the Angels

Chicks (Los Pollitos)

Cindy

Circle Round the Zero

Clementine

Cock Robin

Come On (Al Animo)

Come Thru 'Na Hurry

Debka Hora

Doll (La Muneca)

continued

Grade 4 *Continued*

Song List

Dona, Dona, Dona
Donkey Riding
Down in the Valley
Drill Ye Terriers Drill
Drunken Sailor
Gallows Pole, The
Ghost of Tom
Goose Round, The
Greenland Fisheries
Hashivenu
Hey, Ho, Nobody Home
Hill and Gully Rider
Hills of Arraing
Hogs in the Cornfield
Hours (Las Horas)
How My Finger Hurts!
(Ay! Que me duele un dedo, tilin)
Hungarian Canon
Hunt the Cows
Hush a Bye
Hushabye, My Wee One (Arrorro mi nino)
I am the Lamplighter (Yo Soy Farolero)
I Got a Letter
I Lost the Farmer's Dairy Key
I Saw You (Yo te vi)
John Kanaka
Johnson Boys
King Kong Kitchie
Land of the Silver Birch
Let It Rain (Que llueva)
Liza Jane
Long Road of Iron
MammaLama
Matarile Rile Ro
May Day Carol
Obwisanna
Oh How Lovely Is the Evening

Grade 4 ***Continued***

Song List
Oh, Susanna
Old Gray Mare
Old Molly HareOld Texas
Over the River (Charlie)
Paw Paw Patch
Pick a Bale of Cotton
Pourquoi
Pretty Saro
Redbirds and Blackbirds
Riding in the Buggy
Round and Round We Go (Toron Toron Jil)
Sail Away, Ladies
Sailing on the Ocean
A Sardine (La Sardina)
Sea Lion Woman
She'll Be Coming 'Round the Mountain
Shoo My Love
Sioux Indian Lullaby
Skelaton (La Calavera)
Sour Grapes
Sourwood Mountain
Swapping Song, The
The Streets of Laredo
Tideo
Tom Dooley
Turn the Glasses Over
Viva la Musica
Walter Jumped a Fox
Weevily Wheat
What'll We Do with the Baby-O
When I First Came to This Land
Where Are You Going, Vain One? (A'nde va nina coqueta)
Whistle, Daughter, Whistle
Yankee Doodle

continued

Grade 4 *Continued*

Song List

Games to be played in grade 4

Big Fat Bisquit
Cedar Swamp
Circle Round the Zero
Come Thru 'Na Hurry
Hill and Gully Rider
Hogs in the Cornfield
Hunt the Cows
I Lost the Farmer's Dairy Key
John Kanaka
MammaLama
Obwisanna
Over the River
Paw Paw Patch
Tideo
Turn the Glasses Over
Weevily Wheat

Grade 5 Alphabetical list

Song Title

Above the Plain
Ah Poor Bird
Ah! Vous Dirai-Je, Mamam
Alabama Gal
Alleluia
All Night All Day
All God's Children
An Angel Descended (Bajo un Angel del Cielo)
Are You Sleeping
Around the Green Gravel
As I Roved Out
At the Gate of Heaven
Auld Lang Syne
Autumn Canon
Avondale Mine Disaster
Big Fat Biscuit
Birch Tree

Grade 5 *Continued*

Song List

Blow Ye Winds
Blue Tail Fly
Boston Beans
Bound for the Promised
Bow Belinda
Canoe Round
Carrion Crow
Cedar Swamp
Charlie Over the Ocean
Charlotte Town
Chatter with the Angels
Chickama Craney Crow
Cindy
Circle Round the Zero
City of Nowhere (La Cuidad "No Se Donde")
Clementine
Cock Robin
Come Thru 'Na Hurry
Dance to the Tambourine (Baile de Pandero)
Daughter, Will You Marry?
Debka Hora
De Colores
Dona, Dona, Dona
Donkey Riding
Down in the Valley
Drill Ye Terriers Drill
Drunken Sailor
Dying Cowboy
Early to Bed
Erie Canal
Every Night When the Sun Goes Down
Fly Fly Fly
Gallows Pole, The
Ghost of Tom
Git Along Little Doggies
Go Down, Moses
Goose Round, The

continued

Grade 5 *Continued*

Song List

Go to Sleep (Duermete)

Great Big Dog

Greenland Fisheries

Handsome Butcher

HenAy Ma Tov

Hashivenu

Hey, Ho, Nobody Home

Higher the Plan

Hill and Gully Rider

Hills of Arraing

Hogs in the Cornfield

Hungarian Canon

Hunt the Cows

Hush a Bye

Hushabye My Darling (Duermete mi nino)

I Got a Letter

I Lost the Farmer's Dairy Key

I'm Goin' Home On a Cloud

Inez

Jam on Gerry's Rock

John Kanaka

Johnson Boys

Just Born in Bethlehem
(En Belen Acaba de Nacer)

Kings from the East (Los Reyes de Oriente)

King Kong Kitchie

La Bella Hortelana

La Vibora de I Mar

Land of the Silver Birch

Let's Sing, Dance, Learn to Love
(Vamos Cantando, bailando . . .)

Liza Jane

Long Road of Iron

MammaLamma

May Day Carol

Morning Is Come

My Good Old Man

Grade 5 *Continued*

Song List
My Old Hen
Now Kiss the Cup
Obwisanna
Oh How Lovely Is the Evening
Oh, Susanna
Old Gray Mare
Old Joe Clark
Old Molly Hare
Old Texas
One, Two, Three O'Leary
Over the River (Charlie)
Paw Paw Patch
Pick a Bale of Cotton
Pompey
Pourquoi
Pretty Saro
Quant il rossignols
Redbirds and Blackbirds
Riding in the Buggy
Rise Up, O Flame
Rise Up, Shepherds (Vamos, Pastorcitos)
Row, Row, Row Your Boat
Sail Away, Ladies
Sailing on the Ocean
Sally Go Round the Sun
Scarborough Fair
Sea Lion Woman
Shanghai Chicken
She'll Be Coming Round the Mountain
The Ship That Never Returned
Shoo My Love
Sing and Rejoice
Sioux Indian Lullaby
Sir Eglamore
Skating Away
Skin and Bones
Song of Courtship

continued

Grade 5 *Continued*

Song List

Soon (Hasta Pronto)
Sour Grapes
Sourwood Mountain
The Streets of Laredo
The Swapping Song
Sweet Betsy from Pike
Swing Low, Sweet Chariot
Tallis Canon
Three Rogues
This Little Girl (Esta Muchachita)
Tideo
Tom Dooley
Turn the Glasses Over
Underneath the Button (Dejabo un boton)
Viva la Musica
Wake Up Canon
Walk Along John
Walter Jumped a Fox
Weevily Wheat
What'll We Do with the Baby-O
When I First Came to This Land
Whistle, Daughter, Whistle
Who Can Sail
With Laughter and Singing
Wonderous Love
Yankee Doodle
La Zanduga

Games to be played in grade 5

Big Fat Bisquit
Cedar Swamp
Circle Round the Zero
Come Thru 'Na Hurry
Hill and Gully Rider
Hogs in the Cornfield
Hunt the Cows
I Lost the Farmer's Dairy Key
John Kanaka

Grade 5 *Continued*

Song List
MammaLama
Obwisanna
Over the River
PawPaw Patch
Tideo
Turn the Glasses Over
Weevily Wheat

Appendix 3

Pedagogical Song List

An asterisk means that this is the best song to use to teach the new pattern. The numbers that follow refer to the phrase where you can find the rhythmic or melodic motive. A dash between solfège syllables means that the solfège syllables are sung on one beat.

Grade 1 Pedagogical use

Song Title	Focus Song
Heartbeat simple meter	
Bee Bee Bumble Bee	
Bounce High Bounce Low	•
Cobbler Cobbler	
Engine, Engine #9	
Snail Snail	•
Tinker Tailor	
Heartbeat compound meter	
Here We Go Round the Mulberry Bush	
No Robbers Out Today	
Rhythm	
Bounce High Bounce Low	•
I Climbed Up the Apple Tree	
Lucy Locket	
Nanny Goat	
Rain, Rain	•
Starlight, Starbright	
Quarter and eighth notes	
♩ ♩ ♩ ♩	
Bounce High Bounce Low	•
Good Night	
Snail Snail	•

continued

Grade 1 ***Continued***

Song Title	Focus Song
Starlight, Starbright	
Tinker Tailor	
Two Four Six Eight	
♩ ♩ ♫ ♩	
Bee Bee Bumble Bee	
Queen Queen Caroline	
Rain Rain	•
See Saw	
♫ ♫ ♫ ♩	
All Around the Buttercup	
Bee Bee Bumble Bee *2, 3, 4	
Bobby Shaftoe	
Bow Wow Wow *3	•
Cobbler Cobbler	
Doggie Doggie	
Engine, Engine #9	
Good Night *2	
I Climbed Up the Apple Tree	
Johnny's It	
In and Out *2	
Nanny Goat	
Rain, Rain *2	•
See Saw *2	
Snail Snail *2	
Starlight, Starbright *4	
We Are Dancing in the Forest *2, 4	
♫ ♫ ♩ ♩	
Bobby Shaftoe *4	
Bounce High Bounce Low *2	•
Button	
Clap Your Hands Together	
Frog in the Meadow *3	
Here Comes a Bluebird	
Little Sally Water	
Lucy Locket *2, 4	
Ring Around the Rosie	
Shovel Little Shovel (Pala Palita)	
♩ ♫ ♩ ♩	

Grade 1 *Continued*

Song Title	Focus Song
Bye Baby Bunting	
Down Came a Lady	
Frog in the Meadow	
Here Comes a Bluebird	
so–mi	
so mi so mi	
Good Night	
A Nip and a Peck (Pica Perica)	
Pipis y Ganas	
Snail Snail	•
Tinker Tailor	
Who Are These People (Quien es esa Gente?)	
so mi so–so mi	
Rain, Rain	•
See Saw	
Lemonade	
so–so mi–mi so–so mi	
Doggie Doggie	
Good Night	
See Saw *2	
so–mi so so–mi so	
In and Out	
This Old Man	
Rest	
♩ ♩ ♩ 𝄽	
All Around the Buttercup *2, 4	
Bow Wow Wow *4	
Down Came a Lady *2	
Hot Cross Buns	•
Pease Porridge Hot *4	
♩ ♫ ♩ 𝄽	
Frog in the Meadow	
Peas Porridge Hot	
♫ ♫ ♩ 𝄽	
Clap Your Hands Together	

*2nd and 4th motives

continued

Grade 1 *Continued*

Song Title	Focus Song
Naughty Kitty Cat	
Who Are These People (Quien Es esa Gente?)	
la	
so mi–la so mi	
Little Rooster (Pipirigallo)	
so la so mi	
Bounce High Bounce Low	•
Starlight, Starbright	
so–so la–la so mi	
Bobby Shaftoe	
Bounce High Bounce Low *2	•
Lucy Locket *2, 4	
Round and Round (A la Ronda Ronda)	
so–so la–la so–so mi	
Bobby Shaftoe	
Chini, Mini	
Snail Snail *2	•
Starlight, Starbright *4	
We Are Dancing in the Forest *2, 4	
so-so la–la so–so mi–mi	
Lucy Locket	
We Are Dancing in the Forest	
so so–la so mi	
Bye Baby Bunting	
Here Comes a Bluebird	
so–so so–la so mi	
A Tisket a tasket	
Bye Baby Bunting	
Doggie Doggie	
Fudge Fudge	
Here Comes a Bluebird *3	
Hush Baby Hush	
It's Raining It's Pouring	
Johnny's It	
Little Sally Water	
Nanny Goat	
No Robbers Out Today	

Grade 1 *Continued*

Song Title	Focus Song
Rain Rain	•
Ring Around the Rosie	
Two-beat meter	

Grade 2 Pedagogical use

Song Title	Focus Song
Two-beat meter review	
Bounce High Bounce Low	
Button	
Nanny Goat	
See Saw	
Starlight, Starbright	
This Old Man	
Clap Your Hands Together	
Cobbler Cobbler	
Johnny's It	
Lucy Locket	
Teddy Bear	
do	
so mi do	
Old Woman	
Wallflowers	
Mother, Mother	
Bow Wow Wow	•
do mi so	
Dinah	
Knock the Cymbals	•
Michael Row the Boat	
Rocky Mountain	•
so do	
Hunt the Cows	
Juan Pirulero	
Kings Land	
Over in the Meadow (3rd phrase)	
Ring Around the Rosie	
Sleep, Little One (Duerme nino)	

continued

Grade 2 *Continued*

Song Title	Focus Song
Two Rubble Tum	
do so	
Grandma Grunts	
Sea Shell	
Who's That Tapping	
do mi so la	
Michael Row the Boat	
Rocky Mountain	•
Half note	
𝅗𝅥	
Are You Sleeping	
Let Us Chase the Squirrel	
Bye Bye Baby	
Blue	
Here Comes a Bluebird	•
Who's That Tapping	
re	
mi re do	
Frog in the Meadow	
Hop Old Squirrel	
Hot Cross Buns	•
Ten in the Bed	
do re mi	
Boatman, The	
Closet Key, The	
Long Legged Sailor	
so mi re do	
Blue	
Bye Bye Baby	
Frosty Weather	
do re mi so	
Go to Sleep Now (Duerme Pronto)	
Grandma Grunts	
Let Us Chase the Squirrel	
Matarile	
Old Aunt Dinah	
Sammy Sackett	

Grade 2 *Continued*

Song Title	Focus Song
Who's That Tapping	
la so mi re do	
Cocky Robin	
Do, Do Pity	
Great Big House	
Here Comes a Bluebird	
Hush Little Minnie	
Rocky Mountain	•
do re mi so la	
Bow Wow Wow	•
Button You Must Wander	
Juan Pirulero	
Knock the Cymbals	
Sleep, Little One (Duerme Nino)	
6/8 meter	
$\frac{6}{8}$	
Here We Go Round the Mulberry Bush	•
No Robbers Out Today	
Sixteenth notes	
♬♬	
Sixteenth notes on beat one	
Dance Josey	
Deedle Deedle Dumpling (rhyme)	
Dinah	•
Old Brass Wagon	
Tideo	
Sixteenth notes on beat three	
Cumberland Gap	
Paw Paw Patch	•
Sixteenth notes on beat two	
Paw Paw Patch	•
Shanghai Chicken	

continued

Grade 2 *Continued*

Song Title	Focus Song
Sixteenth notes on beats one, two, or three	
Walter Jumped a Fox	
Do pentatonic (For Letter Names)	
Bow Wow Wow	•
Fed My Horse	
Firefly	
Great Big House	

Grade 3 Pedagogical use

Song Title	Focus Song
Do pentatonic	
Rocky Mountain	•
Bow Wow Wow	
Fed My Horse	
Firefly	
Great Big House	
Here Comes a Bluebird	
Ida Red	
Knock the Cymbals	
Mama, Buy Me a Chiney Doll	
Sailing on the Ocean	
Dance Josey	•
Chatter with the Angels	
Turn the Glasses Over	
Eighth note followed by two sixteenth notes	
Eighth note followed by two sixteenth notes on second beat	
Fed My Horse	•
Mama, Buy Me a Chiney Doll	•
Johnny Cuckoo	
Walter Jumped a Fox	
Eighth note followed by two sixteenth notes on first beat	
Chickalileelo	

Grade 3 *Continued*

Song Title	Focus Song
Drunken Sailor	
Fire in the Mountain	
Golden Ring	
How Many Miles to Babylon?	
Hogs in the Cornfield	
Oh, Fly Around	
St. Serafin of the Mount (San Serafin del Monte)	
Wallflowers	
Wildcat	
Eighth note followed by two sixteenth notes on third beat	
Deer Chase, The	
Hush Little Baby	
Skipping Rope Song	
Swapping Song	
Hogs in the Cornfield	
low la	
re do la,	
Grinding Corn	
Phoebe in Her Petticoat	•
Poor Little Kitty Cat	
Skin and Bones	
Walter Jumped a Fox	
Yangtze Boatman's Chantey	
do la, do	
Big Fat Biscuit	
Cock Robin	
Gallows Pole, The	
Hambone	
Jim Along Josie	
Land of the Silver Birch	
Lullaby, Little Papoose	
Mush Toodin	
Old House	
Old Mr. Rabbit	
Rosie, Darling Rosie	
Sioux Indian Lullaby	

continued

Grade 3 ***Continued***

Song Title	Focus Song
Skip to the Barbershop	
re la, do	
C-Line Woman	
Iroquois Lullaby	
***la* pentatonic**	
C-Line Woman	
Cock Robin	
Gallows Pole, The	•
Land of the Silver Birch	
Walter Jumped a Fox	
Two sixteenth notes followed by an eighth note	
♬♪	
Two sixteenth notes followed by an eighth note on third beat	
Do, Do Pity	•
Cumberland Gap	
Grandma Grunts (variant)	
Hop Old Squirrel	
Jim Along Josie	
Two sixteenth notes followed by an eighth note on first beat	
Kansas Boys	
Old Betty Larkin	
Over the River	
Walter Jumped a Fox	
Two sixteenth notes followed by an eighth note on second beat	
Bought Me a Cat	
Hogs in the Cornfield	•
Ida Red	
Old Molly Hare	
Skip to My Lou	
Skipping Rope Song	
low so	
do la, so,	
Dance Josey	•

Grade 3 *Continued*

Song Title	Focus Song
Band of Angels	
Chatter with the Angels	
Cotton Eye Joe	
Head and Shoulders	
Hold My Mule	
King Kong Kitchie	
Old Gray Mare	
Over the River	
Riding of a Goat	
Sailing on the Ocean	
Turn the Glasses Over	
do so,	
Charlie Over the Ocean	
Jolly Miller	
Little Leg (La Patita)	
Mr. Chi-Chinese (A Don Chin Chino)	
Old McDonald	
Old Sow, The	
Old Texas	
Scotland's Burning	
so, do mi	
Ivory Statues (Las Estatuas de Marfil)	
Little Coyote (El Coyotito)	
so, do re mi	
Acitron de un Fandango	
Santo Domingo	
St. Serafin of the Mount (San Serafin del Monte)	
so, la,	
C-Line Woman	
Internal upbeat, single eighth note	

Old Mr. Rabbit	•
Bye, Baby Bunting	
Do, Do Pity	
Fed My Horse	

continued

Grade 3 *Continued*

Song Title	Focus Song
King's Land	
Over the River	
Internal upbeat, quarter note	
♩	
Turn the Glasses Over	•
High *do*	
do' la so	
Hogs in the Cornfield	•
Cape Cod Girls	
John Kanaka	
Porquoi	
Riding in the Buggy	
Shortnin' Bread	
What'll We Do with the Baby-o?	
do' so la	
Circle Round the Zero	
I Lost the Farmer's Dairy Key	
Liza Jane	
Tideo	
External upbeat, quarter note	
♪	
I'll Sell My Hat	•
Blow Ye winds	
External upbeat, two eighth notes	

Grade 4 Pedagogical use

Song Title	Focus Song
Syncopation	
♪ ♩ ♪	
♪♩ ♪♩ ♩	
Come Thru 'Na Hurry	
Canoe Round	•
Tom Dooley	

Grade 4 *Continued*

Song Title	Focus Song
Weevily Wheat	
♪♩ ♪♫♩	
Canoe Round	•
Riding in the Buggy	
Shoo My Love	
♪♩ ♪𝅗𝅥	
All God's Children	
Canoe Round	•
Lil Liza Jane	
Riding in the Buggy	
♪♩ ♪♩ 𝄽	
Hill and Gully Rider	
Riding in the Buggy	
***la* pentatonic**	
C-Line Woman	
Cock Robin	
Gallows Pole, The	•
Land of the Silver Birch	
Walter Jumped a Fox	
Dotted quarter followed by an eighth	
♩. ♪♫♫	
John Kanaka	
Hush-a-Bye	
Other patterns	
Liza Jane	•
Above the Plain	
Big Fat Biscuit	
fa	
so–fa mi	
Ah! Vous Dira-Je, Mamam	
Goose Round	
Hungarian Canon	•
Mamalama	

continued

Grade 4 *Continued*

Song Title	Focus Song
Redbirds and Blackbirds	
Whistle Daughter Whistle	
mi fa so	
Are You Sleeping	
La Calavera (Skelaton)	
Redbirds and Blackbirds	
do re mi fa so	
Ay! Que me duele un dedo, tilin (How My Finger Hurts!)	
Entra las Matas (Among the Plants)	
La Muneca (Doll)	
Matarile Rile Ro	
Que Llueva (Let It Rain)	
Se Va la Barca (Boat Drifts Away)	
Yo Soy Farolero (I Am the Lamplighter)	
Yo te vi (I Saw You)	
do re mi fa so la	
Al Animo (Come On)	
A'nde va nina coqueta (Where Are You Going, Vain One?)	
Arrorro mi nino (Hushabye, My Wee One)	
Los Pollitos (Chicks)	
Toron Toron Jill (Round and Round We Go)	
Other fa Patterns	
Old Molly Hare	
When I First Came to This Land	
3/4 meter	
$\frac{3}{4}$	
Around the Green Gravel	

Grade 5 Pedagogical use

Song Title	Focus Song
low t,	
do ti, do	
At the Gate of Heaven	
When I First Came to This Land	
do ti, la,	

Grade 5 *Continued*

Song Title	Focus Song
Autumn Canon	
Birch Tree	•
Blow Ye Winds	
Bound for the Promised Land	
Debka Hora	
Drill Ye Terriers	
Drunken Sailor	
Greenland Fisheries, The	
Hunt the Cows	
Hush a Bye	
Sour Grapes	
Viva la Musica	
la, ti, do	
Dona, Dona, Dona	
Ghost of Tom	
Hey, Ho, Nobody Home	
Hashivenu	
Swapping Song	
Yankee Doodle	
so, ti, do	
Las Horas (Hours)	
Old Molly Hare	
Paw Paw Patch	
Pick a Bale of Cotton	
Dotted eighth note followed by a sixteenth note	
♪. ♬	
Donkey Riding	•
Circle Round the Zero	
Sail Away Ladies	
Major scale songs—ti	
la, ti, do	
Alleluia	•
An Angel Descended (Bajo un Angel del Cielo)	
Wake Up Canon	
Blue Tail Fly	

continued

Grade 5 ***Continued***

Song Title	Focus Song
Hushabye My Darling (Duermete mi nino)	
Rise Up, O Flame	
Soon (Hasta Pronto)	
Three Rogues	
Let's Sing, Dance, Learn to Love (Vamos Cantando, bailando . . .)	
do ti, la,	
Ship That Never Returned, The	
Handsome Butcher	
Alleluia	•
Wake Up Canon	
Birch Tree, The	
Three Rogues	
ti so	
Sweet Betsy from Pike	
ti, do	
Just Born in Bethlehem (En Belen Acaba de Nacer)	
City of Nowhere (La Cuidad "No Se Donde")	
mi' ti	
Bound for the Promised Land	
My Old Hen	
so ti do	
Go to Sleep (Duermete)	
Rise Up, Shepherds (Vamos, Pastorcitos)	
Do pentatonic	
This Little Girl (Esta Muchachita)	
Underneath the Button (Dejabo un boton)	
Eighth note followed by a dotted quarter	
♪♩.	
Charlotte Town	•
Shanghai Chicken	
All Night All Day	
♪♩. ♩ ♩	
Erie Canal	
♪♩. 𝅗𝅥	
My Good Old Man	
All Night All Day	
Erie Canal	

Grade 5 *Continued*

Song Title	Focus Song
Other patterns	
Erie Canal	
Great Big Dog	
Go Down, Moses	
Swing Low, Sweet Chariot	
Walk Along John	
When I First Came to this Land	
Natural minor	
Autumn Canon	
Hush-a-Bye	•
Boston Beans	
Hashivenu	
Fly, Fly, Fly	
Compound meter	
$\begin{smallmatrix}6\\8\end{smallmatrix}$	
An Angel Descended (Bajo un Angel del Cielo)	
City of Nowhere (La Cuidad "No Se Donde")	
Row, Row, Row Your Boat	•
Charlie Over the Ocean	
Chickama Craney Crow	
One, Two, Three O'Leary	
Pompey	
Skin and Bones	
Skating Away	
De Colores	
Early to Bed	
Henry Ma Tov	
Sing and Rejoice	
Dorian solfège syllable fi	
Scarborough Fair	•
Bow Belinda	
Carrion Crow	
Dance to the Tambourine (Baile de Pandero)	

continued

Grade 5 *Continued*

Song Title	Focus Song
Drunken Sailor	
Kings from the East (Los Reyes de Oriente)	
Song of Courtship	
Wondrous Love	
Uneven subdivision in compound meter	
♪. ♬♪	
Row, Row, Row Your Boat	•
Hashevinu	
Sir Eglamore	
Git Along Little Doggies	
Now Kiss the Cup	
O, How Lovely Is the Evening	
Harmonic minor form *si*	
Ah, Poor Bird	•
Dance to the Tambourine (Baile de Pandero)	
Go Down Moses	
Inez	
Kings from the East (Los Reyes de Oriente)	
La Zanduga	
Compound meter	
Troubadour Song "Quant il Rossignols"	
With Laughter and Singing	
Higher the Plan	
Morning Is Come	
Melodic minor	
Tallis Canon	
Who Can Sail?	
Triplets	
Daughter, Will You Marry?	
Every Night When the Sun Goes Down	
La Bella Hortelana	

Grade 5 *Continued*

Song Title	Focus Song
La Vibora del Mar	
Sally Go Round the Sun	
Mixolydian	
As I Roved Out	
Avondale Mine Disaster	
Dying Cowboy	
Git Along Little Doggies	
I'm Goin' Home on a Cloud	
Jam on Gerry's Rock	
Old Joe Clark	

Appendix 4

Monthly Plans

Grade 1 Monthly plans

Month	Songs	Prepare	Present	Practice	Reading	Writing
September	**Review kindergarden concepts and elements; teach new repertoire.**					
October	Bee Bee Bumblebee Bounce High Bounce Low Cobbler Cobbler Engine Engine #9 Snail Snail					
	$\frac{6}{8}$ material					
	Charlie Over the Ocean Chickama Craney Crow The Farmer in the Dell				Student taps iconic representations of the heartbeat while others perform the beat with: (a) body percussion; (b) instruments	Teacher draws the phrases on the board Student places the heartbeats under the phrases
					Student taps iconic representations of the heartbeat while singing known songs: (a) on board or on worksheets; (b) on instruments	Teacher sings or plays a known song on the piano or recorder and individual students write or place the beats on the board with singing

Improvisation	Ensemble	Memory	Inner Hearing	Form	Listening	Error Detection
			Review: Internalize known songs	Review form of known songs	Develop awareness of expressive elements such as tempo, dynamics, and timbre	
Students improvise movements to the beat	Teacher or student sings known songs while students play the beat on instruments: (a) small groups; (b) individuals		While tapping the heartbeats on the board or worksheets, students sing the song in their heads changing on teacher's cue	Students identify the form of a song and display the form with different shapes Same or different		
Students improvise the beat on different parts of the body to known and unknown songs, other students imitate	Students sing a known song while patting the heartbeat on different parts of their bodies changing on the teacher's cue		Teacher sings songs on loo while students tap the beat on their lap or on instruments and identify the song	Students draw phrases on board and place or write correct number of beats under each phrase to known and unknown songs		
Students take turns improvising on a drum while the other students keep the beat	Students step the beat while singing					
	Student responsorial singing					

continued

Grade 1 *Continued*

Month	Songs	Prepare	Present	Practice	Reading	Writing
October	All Around the Buttercup Bee Bee Bumblebee Bobby Shafto Bounce High Bounce Low Bow Wow Wow Button You Must Wander Cobbler Cobbler Doggie Doggie Engine Engine #9 Good Night I Climbed Up the Apple Tree In and Out Nanny Goat Johnny's It Queen Queen Caroline Rain Rain See Saw Snail Snail Starlight, Starlight Tinker Tailor Two Four Six Eight We Are Dancing in the Forest	Quarter and eighth notes		Tuneful singing		
					Student taps iconic representations of the heartbeat while others perform the beat with: (a) body percussion; (b) instruments	Teacher draws the phrases on the board Student places the heartbeats under the phrases
			Quarter and eighth notes		Student taps iconic representations of the heartbeat while singing known songs: (a) on board or on worksheets; (b) on instruments	Teacher sings or plays a known song on the piano or recorder and individual students write or place the beats on the board

Improvisation	Ensemble	Memory	Inner Hearing	Form	Listening	Error Detection
			Review: internalize known songs	Review form of known songs	Develop awaremess of expressive elements such as tempo, dynamics, and timbre	
Students improvise movements to the beat	Teacher or student sings known songs while students play the beat on instruments: (a) small groups; (b) individuals		While tapping the heartbeats on the board or worksheets, students sing the song in their heads changing from inner hearing to singing on teacher's cue	Students identify the form of a song and display the form with different shapes Same or different		
Students improvise the beat on different parts of the body to known and unknown songs, other students imitate	Students sing a known song while patting the heartbeat on different parts of their body changing on the teacher's cue		Teacher sings songs on loo while students tap the beat on their lap or on instruments and identify the song	Students draw phrases on board and place or write correct number of beats under each phrase to known and unknown songs		
Students take turns improvising on a drum while the other students keep the beat	Students step the beat while singing					
	Students responsorial singing of known songs					

continued

Grade 1 *Continued*

Month	Songs	Prepare	Present	Practice	Reading	Writing
November	Doggie Doggie Good Night In and Out Lemonade Rain Rain See Saw Snail Snail This Old Man Tinker Tailor Patriotic songs Yankee Doodle The Star Spangled Banner God Bless America This Land Is Your Land	*so-mi*		Quarter and paired eighth notes	Read 4-beat rhythm patterns from: (a) flash cards; (b) board: (c) worksheets	Students write 4-beat patterns in stick notation and traditional rhythmic notation with: (a) manipulatives; (b) on the board; (c) on worksheets; (d) from teacher tapping or clapping rhythm (dictation)
			so-mi			Students write the rhythm to known songs in stick notation and traditional rhythmic notation with: (a) manipulatives; (b) on the board; (c) on worksheets; (d) from teacher tapping or clapping rhythm (dictation)

Improvisation	Ensemble	Memory	Inner Hearing	Form	Listening	Error Detection
Students improvise a 4-beat pattern through the use of form	Half of class claps the rhythm, while the other half pats the beat or individual student sings and claps the rhythm of a known song while other student sings and pats the beat	Students memorize the rhythm by studying and analyzing the rhythmic form of a song Students echo clap with rhythm names	Students identify the form of a song from rhythm patterns on the board	Students identify the form of a song from rhythm patterns on the board Students identify same and different Students identify repetition	Teacher sings a song to the class that will be used for a future concept such as *Do Do Pity my Case* Teacher sings a song to the class for enjoyment	Students identify incorrect rhythmic patterns through the use of form
Students echo each other repeating the first 4 beats of the previous rhythm and creating the next 4 beats	Student sings song and: (a) steps or claps or pats the beats; (b) claps or taps the rhythm	Students identify a song from the teacher clapping the rhythm	Students identify the rhythm to known songs from teacher tapping or clapping rhythm (dictation)	Students create different rhythmic patterns to given forms such as ABA		
	Student creates an eight- to sixteen-beat pattern and performs it in canon with another student Responsorial singing of known repertoire	Teacher and student perform a rhythmic canon		Students listen to a performance of Nutcracker and identify the form of one of the following selections: Trepack: • Russian Dance • Chinese Dance • or March		

continued

Grade 1 *Continued*

Month	Songs	Prepare	Present	Practice	Reading	Writing
December	**Review and prepare for winter concert**					
January	**Review and teach new repertoire**					
February	All Around the Buttercup Bow Wow Wow Down Came a Lady Hot Cross Buns Pease Porridge Hot Frog in the Meadow Clap Your Hands Together Naughty Kitty Kat	Quarter rest	Quarter rest	*so-mi*	Students use solfa syllables and hand signs to read *so-mi* patterns from: (a) iconic representations on the board spatially arranged to show melodic contour; (b) stick notation and traditional rhythmic notation labeled with solfa syllables spatially arranged to show melodic contour; (c) staff notation; (d) flash cards in stick and staff notation	Students write the missing solfa under the pictures for a known song
						Teacher plays a known song on the piano or recorder and individual students write the solfa on the board

Improvisation	Ensemble	Memory	Inner Hearing	Form	Listening	Error Detection
Students use form to improvise a *so-mi* melody on a bar instrument. Class sings "a" and student improvises the "b" section Teacher erases measure from the rhythm of known song and students improvise new rhythm pattern	Students sing a known *so-mi* song with solfa while clapping the rhythm as another group performs the beat. Switch roles	Teacher plays *so-mi* patterns from known songs and students identify	Teacher places iconic representation on the board spatially arranged to show the melodic contour of a known song and students identify song by inner hearing	Teacher has different *so-mi* patterns on flashcards displayed on the board. The students come up with different combinations and sequences of the patterns. Discuss the different forms	Teacher sings a song to the class that will be used for future learning. Such as: (a) *Paw Paw Patch;* (b) *Mama, Buy Me a Chiney Doll;* (c) *Skin and Bones;* (d) *Grandma Grunts;* (e) *America the Beautiful*	Students correct pictures that are showing the wrong contour of a known melody on the board
	Half of students step or pat the beat or clap the rhythm as other half: (a) sings *so-mi* patterns with solfège syllables and hand signs; (b) perform *so-mi* patterns on barred instruments	Students memorize a song by using the form		Teacher has different *so-mi* patterns on the board. The students come up with different combinations of the patterns. Discuss the different forms		

continued

Grade 1 *Continued*

Month	Songs	Prepare	Present	Practice	Reading	Writing
					While spatially clapping the rhythm, students read *so-mi* patterns using solfa syllables from: (a) iconic representations on the board spatially arranged to show melodic contour; (b) stick notation; (c) traditional rhythmic notation; (d) staff notation	Students write so-mi patterns and then perform them while spatially clapping the rhythm showing the melodic contour Students write the missing solfa under the words of a known song
March	Bounce High Bounce Low Lucy Locket Rain Rain See Saw Snail Snail Starlight, Starlight	*la*		Quarter rest	Read 4 beat rhythm patterns from: (a) the board; (b) flash cards; (c) worksheets; (d) charts	Write 4-beat patterns on the board in stick notation
			la		Practice intervals simultaneously with hand signs	Students write the rhythm to known songs

Improvisation	Ensemble	Memory	Inner Hearing	Form	Listening	Error Detection
Teacher has different *so-mi* patterns on flashcards displayed on the board. Students improvise different combinations of the patterns	In two groups, students sing two different *so-mi* songs while clapping the rhythm			Students identify the form of *so-mi* songs from the teacher's singing		Students identify where teacher sings incorrectly on *so-mi* pattern
	Students perform a two-part exercise				Leopold Mozart's Toy Symphony, Mozart's Symphony No. 1	
Students improvise a 4-beat pattern through the use of form	Students create a 16-beat pattern and perform it in canon with another student	Students memorize the rhythm by studying the form of a song	Students identify a song from rhythmic patterns on the board	Students identify the form of a song	Mozart's Minuet and Trio K 315 A Beethoven's Symphony No. 7: Allegretto Mozart Variations on a Folk Song "Ah vous divai-je maman"	Students identify incorrect rhythmic patterns through the use of form
Students echo each other where they repeat the first 4 beats of the previous rhythm and create the next 4 beats	Students perform in two groups: (a) different songs of equal duration concurrently with rhythm syllables; (b) beat versus rhythm Use the following ostinatos to accompany a song: - ♩ ♩ - ♩ 𝄽 - ♫ ♩	Teacher and students perform a rhythmic canon		Students develop different rhythmic patterns to create different forms Repeat sign	Teacher sings a song to the class for enjoyment and modeling of good singing skills or a song that will be used in the future Teacher sings a song to the class. Find an Irish Song for St. Patrick's Day	Teacher changes a rhythm in a motive of a known song

continued

Grade 1 *Continued*

Month	Songs	Prepare	Present	Practice	Reading	Writing
April	Bounce High Bounce Low Button You Must Wander Nanny Goat See Saw Starlight, Starlight This Old Man	Two beat meter $\frac{6}{8}$		*la*	Students read various 4- and 8-beat *mi-so-la* patterns in stick and traditional rhythmic notation labeled with solfa syllables, as well as staff notation from: (a) flash cards; (b) teacher hand signs; (c) exercises; (d) board; (e) worksheets; (f) charts	Students write song fragments in: (a) stick and traditional rhythmic notation labeling with solfège syllables; (b) staff notation Students transpose song motives from stick notation to staff
	Clap Your Hands Together Cobbler Cobbler Johnny's It Lucy Locket Teddy Bear $\frac{6}{8}$ material Jack and Jill Skin and Bones Oats, Peas, Beans and Barley Grow		Two beat meter Stepping and skipping songs that move in 2's Repeat sign		Known and unknown *mi-so-la* songs in stick and traditional rhythmic notation labeled with solfa syllables, as well as staff notation from: (a) teacher hand signs; (b) board; (c) worksheets; (d) charts; (e) exercises; (f) flash cards	Students write patterns on staff from teacher: (a) playing on recorder; (b) playing on piano; (c) singing on neutral syllable
	Baby Bunting Little Sally Water Oats, Peas, Beans and Barley Grow					
May/June	**Review and prepare for spring concert; teach new repertoire**					

Improvisation	Ensemble	Memory	Inner Hearing	Form	Listening	Error Detection
Students improvise *so-la-so-mi* patterns on bar instruments: (a) 4 beats; (b) 8 beats	Two-part exercises using *so-la-so-mi* in: (a) stick notation; (b) staff notation	Students memorize a song from the board, one student then turns back to board and conducts in two while singing the song	Students identify and pair different *mi-so-la* song fragments in staff notation to iconic representations of the songs	Students sing a song while patting the beat on the A phrases and clap the rhythm on the B phrases	Teacher hums the theme of a well-known piece of music for children to listen to or maybe memorize Teach families of instruments in the Symphony Orchestra	Students detect incorrect playing from the teacher on recorder
	mi-so-la melodic canons with solfège syllables			Students analyze the forms of different songs		
Questions and answers using *mi-so-la:* (a) 4 beat; (b) 8 beat	In two groups, half of the class sings known songs with solfège syllables while clapping the rhythm as the other group pats or steps the beat One student conducts Switch parts			Students identify, compare, and label: (a) no. of phrases; (b) rhythm in each phrase; (c) solfège of song	Teacher sings song that will be used for future learning: (a) *Who's That;* (b) *Here Comes a Blue Bird;* (c) *Button You Must Wander;* (d) *Knock the Cymbals;* (e) *Wall Flowers*	Students detect incorrect sound from the teacher singing on neutral syllable

Grade 2 Monthly plans

Month	Songs	Prepare	Present	Practice	Reading	Writing
September	**Review first grade concepts and elements; teach new repertoire**					
October	Are You Sleeping Blue *Bow Wow Wow* Bye Bye Baby Dinah Grandma Grunts *Here Comes a Bluebird* Hunt the Cows King's Land Knock the Cymbals Let Us Chase the Squirrel Michael Row the Boat Ashore Mother Mother Old Woman	*do*		$\frac{2}{4}$ meter	Known songs: (a) in stick notation; (b) from teacher's hand signs; (c) from tone ladder; (d) in staff notation	Songs containing *do* fragments in: (a) stick notation; (b) staff notation; (c) transcribe from stick to staff notation
	Over in the Meadow Ring Around the Rosie Rocky Mountain Sea Shell Two Rubble Tum *Wallflowers* Who's That Tapping at the Window Songs for holidays Witch Witch		*do*		Students read known and unknown material in stick notation and staff notation	
	Chicama Craney Crow				Students read and perform a rhythm notated on the board on an instrument Students read patterns with *mi-la* intervals	Teacher plays a melody on the piano and the students identify and write the rhythm. They also identify where the repeats are and write it again using repeat signs
					Unknown songs: (a) in stick notation; (b) from teacher's hand signs; (c) from tone ladder; (d) in staff notation	Unknown songs in: (a) stick notation; (b) staff notation

Improvisation	Ensemble	Memory	Inner Hearing	Form	Listening	Error Detection
Four-beat question and answer Using *do* as final note for answer	Melodic canons with solfège Two part singing from teacher's hand signs	Four-beat melodic echoes with *do*	Four-beat melodic patterns and melodic dictation		Mozart's 1st Symphony, Haydn's Surprise Symphony 2nd movement Teacher sings a song such as *Frog Went a-Courtin'* while showing pictures of the story	Students identify incorrect melody from the teacher on recorder
Students improvise rhythmic and *mi-so-la* patterns on rhythm instruments and barred instruments	Students sing melodic canons in two beat meter from the staff Ostinato: - ♩ 𝄽 ♩ 𝄽 - ♩ ♩ 𝄽 ♩	Echo with solfège and hand signs from teacher singing with neutral syllable	Identify songs from: (a) stick notation; (b) staff notation; (c) teacher's hand signs		Teacher sings a song to the class for Hispanic Heritage Month. September 15–October 15	Teacher writes a 16 beat rhythmic pattern and puts the barlines in the wrong places. Students correct the barlines
Students improvise a rhythm pattern in the middle of two 4-beat rhythm patterns with a repeat sign	Students perform an ostinato which is written on the board while the teacher sings a song. Switch parts	Rhythm canon from teacher to student. One student to class	Students conduct a two beat pattern while thinking a rhythm from the board. They identify the song		Teacher sings a song to the class that will be used in the future or one for enjoyment of music such as: (a) *De Colores-Cinco de Mayo;* (b) *Who's That Tapping at the Window;* (c) *Here Comes a Blue Bird;* (d) *Button You Must Wander;* (e) *Knock the Cymbals;* (f) *Wall Flowers*	Students detect wrong rhythms, solfège, barlines, and repeat signs from: (a) the board; (b) the teacher's playing; (c) teacher's singing on neutral syllables
Students improvise a phrase within a known song	Accompany songs with a *mi, so, la* melodic ostinato		Match song fragments to iconic representations of songs			

continued

Grade 2 *Continued*

Month	Songs	Prepare	Present	Practice	Reading	Writing
October	Are You Sleeping Blue Bye Bye Baby *Here Comes a Blue Bird* Let Us Chase the Squirrel Who's That Tapping at the Window	Half note		*do*	Known songs with previously learned elements and half notes in: (a) stick notation; (b) traditional rhythmic notation; (c) staff notation	Add bar lines to songs containing half notes
					Song fragments with previously learned elements in: (a) stick notation; (b) traditional rhythmic notation; (c) staff notation	Song fragments with previously learned elements in: (a) stick notation; (b) traditional rhythmic notation; (c) staff notation
			Half note		Unknown songs with previously learned elements in: (a) stick notation; (b) traditional rhythmic notation; (c) staff notation	Unknown songs with previously learned elements in: (a) stick notation; (b) traditional rhythmic notation; (c) staff notation

Improvisation	Ensemble	Memory	Inner Hearing	Form	Listening	Error Detection
Eight-beat question and answer phrases with previously learned elements	Four-beat meter ostinati	Four-beat rhythm patterns	Dictation in 8-beat patterns with previously learned rhythmic elements			
	Canons	Eight-beat rhythm echoes with previously learned rhythmic elements				
	Two-part rhythm exercises containing half notes. Divide class into two groups. Students read from teacher's hand signs	Thirty-two-beat rhythm patterns with previously learned rhythmic elements				

continued

Grade 2 *Continued*

Month	Songs	Prepare	Present	Practice	Reading	Writing
November	Bow Wow Wow Hot Cross Buns Rocky Mountain Frog in the Meadow All Around the Buttercup	*re*		Half note	Song fragments: (a) in stick notation; (b) from teacher's hand signs; (c) from tone ladder; (d) in staff notation Including: (a) *mi-re-do* (b) *do-re-mi*	Unknown songs in: (a) stick notation; (b) staff notation
			re		Unknown songs: (a) in stick notation; (b) from T hand signs; (c) from tone ladder; (d) in staff notation	Unknown songs in staff notation
November	Here We Go Round the Mulberry Bush Old Roger The Allee Allee O	$\frac{6}{8}$ meter Subdivision of skipping songs is in three		*re*	Read 4 beat rhythm patterns from: (a) the board; (b) flash cards; (c) worksheets; (d) charts Practice intervals with hand signs	Write 4 beat patterns on the board in stick notation Students write the rhythm to known songs

Improvisation	Ensemble	Memory	Inner Hearing	Form	Listening	Error Detection
	Sing known songs in canons Sing in two parts from teacher's hand signs	Echo with solfège and hand signs from teacher singing with a neutral syllable	Four-beat melodic patterns			
Students improvise a 4-beat pattern according to given forms	Student creates a sixteen beat pattern and perform it in canon with another student	Students memorize the rhythm by studying the form of a song	Students identify a song from rhythmic patterns on the board	Students identify the form of a song		Students identify incorrect rhythmic patterns according to given forms
Students echo each other by repeating the first 4 beats of the previous rhythm and create the next 4 beats	Students perform in 2 groups: (a) different songs of equal duration concurrently with rhythm syllables; (b) beat versus rhythm Use the following ostinatos to accompany a song: - ♩ ♩ - ♩ 𝄽 - ♫ ♩	Teacher and students perform a rhythmic canon		Students improvise different rhythmic patterns to create different forms		Teacher changes a rhythm in a motive of a known song

continued

Grade 2 *Continued*

Month	Songs	Prepare	Present	Practice	Reading	Writing
	Bow Wow Wow Dance Josey Great Big House Ida Red Rocky Mountain Holiday Song: Grinding Corn America	*do* pentatonic		$\frac{6}{8}$ meter Identifying the subdivision of beats in simple, duple and compound meter	Students read melodic patterns on the staff in two beat meter from flashcards Practice intervals simultaneously with hand signs	Students read a known song from the staff without barlines and draw in barlines on staff to the show 2-beat meter
					Students read known and unknown material in stick notation and staff notation	Students draw barlines on: (a) 8 beat songs; (b) 16 beat songs
						Teacher plays a melody with a repeat on the recorder and students identify the rhythm. Students write the rhythm on the board and put repeat signs where necessary
					Students read and perform a rhythm notated on the board on an instrument Students read patterns with *mi-la* intervals	Teacher plays a melody on the piano and the students identify and write the rhythm. They also identify where the repeats are and write it again using repeat signs

Improvisation	Ensemble	Memory	Inner Hearing	Form	Listening	Error Detection
Students improvise *mi-so-la* and *mi-re-do* patterns on rhythm instruments and barred instruments Improvise rhythmic patterns in 6/8	Students sing melodic canons in two beat meter from the staff Ostinato: - ♩ 𝄽 ♩ 𝄽 - ♩ ♩ 𝄽 ♩	Students memorize a song by using the form Students sing it back in solfège and rhythm syllables Echo clap patterns in 6/8	Students identify a song from: (a) staff notation; (b) rhythm notation on the board; (c) from the teacher pointing to the staff	Students identify the form of a new song that uses elements to be learned in the future		Students identify incorrect melody from the teacher on recorder
Students improvise a rhythm pattern in the middle of two 4-beat rhythm patterns with a repeat sign.	Students perform an ostinato which is written on the board while the teacher sings a song. Switch parts	Rhythm canon from teacher to student, then one student to class	Students conduct a two beat pattern while thinking a rhythm from the board. They identify the song			Teacher writes a 16-beat rhythmic pattern and puts the barlines in the wrong places. Students correct the barlines
Students improvise a phrase within a known song	Accompany notes with a *mi, so, la* melodic ostinato	Students read flashcards with rhythm patterns. As soon as they read the first one it is replaced by a new one. They have to say the card that is not shown and memorize the one that is	Students match different melodies in staff notation to correct songs	Teacher has different rhythmic patterns on the board and the students match the patterns with the correct form		Students detect wrong rhythms, solfège, barlines, and repeat signs from: (a) the board; (b) the teacher's playing; (c) the teacher's singing on neutral syllables
Teacher writes a form on the board and the students improvise a rhythm that will fit the form Students improvise a melody to above activity	In two groups, half of the class sings known songs with sollfege syllables while clapping the rhythm as the others pat or step the beat. One student conducts. Switch parts	Students write songs on paper with all known elements from memory				

continued

Grade 2 *Continued*

Month	Songs	Prepare	Present	Practice	Reading	Writing
December	**Review and prepare for winter program**					
January	**Review and teach new repertoire.**					
Feburary	Cumberland Gap Dance Josey Deedle Deedle Dinah Old Brass Wagon *Paw Paw Patch* Shanghai Chicken Tideo Walter Jumped a Fox Fed My Horse Phoebe in Her Petticoat	Sixteenth notes		*do* pentatonic	Absolute pitch (staff notation): (a) B, A, G; (b) A, G, F; (c) E, D, C *do* pentatonic known songs: (a) in stick notation; (b) from teacher's hand signs; (c) from tone ladder; (d) in staff notation	Song fragments with previously learned rhythmic elements and sixteenth notes in 4-beat meter in: (a) stick notation; (b) traditional rhythmic notation; (c) staff notation
					do pentatonic known songs: (a) in stick notation; (b) from teacher's hand signs; (c) from tone ladder; (d) in staff notation	Known songs with previously learned rhythmic elements in 4-beat meter in: (a) stick notation; (b) traditional rhythmic notation; (c) staff notation
			Sixteenth notes		Song fragments: (a) in stick notation; (b) from teacher's hand signs; (c) from tone ladder; (d) in staff notation	Unknown songs with previously learned rhythmic elements in 4-beat meter in: (a) stick notation; (b) traditional rhythmic notation; (c) staff notation

Improvisation	Ensemble	Memory	Inner Hearing	Form	Listening	Error Detection
Question and answer	*do* pentatonic: 2-part exercises	Four-beat rhythm patterns with previously learned rhythmic elements	*do* pentatonic: identify known songs from hand signs		Mozart's Der Vögelfänger and Queen's Aria from the Magic Flute, Mozart's Turkish Rondo, Villa Lobos' Bachianas Brasileiras No. 5, Saint-Säens' Fossils from Carnival of the Animals	
	Four-beat meter ostinati	Eight-beat rhythmic echoes with previously learned rhythmic elements	Dictation in 8-beat patterns with previously learned rhythmic elements		Teacher sings a song to the class such as *Follow the Drinking Gourd*—African American History Month	
	Four-beat meter: 2-part exercises					

continued

Grade 2 *Continued*

Month	Songs	Prepare	Present	Practice	Reading	Writing
					do: unknown songs: (a) in stick notation; (b) from teacher's hand signs; (c) from tone ladder; (d) in staff notation	*do* pentatonic: unknown songs in: (a) stick notation; (b) staff notation
March	All Around the Buttercup *Bow Wow Wow* Down Came a Lady Here Comes a Bluebird *Hot Cross Buns* Knock the Cymbals	Four-beat meter		Six-teenth notes	Song fragments with previously learned elements in 4-beat meter: (a) stick notation; (b) traditional rhythmic notation; (c) staff notation	Song fragments with previously learned rhythmic elements and sixteenth notes in 4-beat meter in: (a) stick notation; (b) traditional rhythmic notation; (c) staff notation
			Four-beat meter		Known songs with previously learned elements in 4-beat meter: (a) stick notation; (b) traditional rhythmic notation; (c) staff notation	Known songs with previously learned rhythmic elements in 4-beat meter: (a) stick notation; (b) traditional rhythmic notation; (c) staff notation
					Unknown songs with previously learned elements in 4-beat meter: (a) stick notation; (b) traditional rhythmic notation; (c) staff notation	Unknown songs with previously learned rhythmic elements in 4-beat meter: (a) stick notation; (b) traditional rhythmic notation; (c) staff notation

Improvisation	Ensemble	Memory	Inner Hearing	Form	Listening	Error Detection
Four-beat question and answer phrases Eight-beat question and answer phrases with previously learned rhythmic elements		Echo clap patterns Four-beat rhythm patterns with previously known elements Eight-beat rhythm echoes with previously learned rhythmic elements				
	Four-beat meter: 2-part exercises Canons containing previously known elements Two-part rhythm exercises containing previously known elements Divide class into two groups. Students read from teacher's hand signs	Sixteen-beat memory exercises Thirty-two-beat rhythm patterns with previously learned rhythmic elements	Dictation in 8-beat patterns with previously learned rhythmic elements			

continued

Grade 2 *Continued*

Month	Songs	Prepare	Present	Practice	Reading	Writing
April	All God's Children Got Shoes Somebody's Knocking Chicka Hanka Alabama Gal Au Clair de la Lune	Whole note Whole rest	Whole note Whole rest	Pentatonic melodies including some in $\frac{4}{4}$ meter	Song fragments with previously learned elements in 4-beat meter: (a) stick notation; (b) traditional rhythmic notation; (c) staff notation	Song fragments with previously learned rhythmic elements as well as whole notes and rests in: (a) stick notation; (b) traditional rhythmic notation; (c) staff notation
					Known songs with previously learned elements in 4-beat meter: (a) stick notation; (b) traditional rhythmic notation; (c) staff notation	Known songs with previously learned rhythmic elements in: (a) stick notation; (b) traditional rhythmic notation; (c) staff notation

Improvisation	Ensemble	Memory	Inner Hearing	Form	Listening	Error Detection
Question and answer Improvise rhythm patterns of 4 or 8 beats either by clapping, using rhythm instruments, or clapping and saying rhythm syllables Improvise short pentatonic musical motives using hand signs, hand staff or body signs	Sing a well-known song and clap its rhythm in canon	Memorize short melodies from teacher's hand signs, staff notation, or two part exercises	Sing known songs silently while performing the beat and rhythm Recognize songs, rhythm patterns, or melodic patterns from staff notation		Mussorgsky's Great Gate of Kiev from Pictures at an Exhibition, Josquin's El Grillo, Verdi's Anvil Chorus Singing songs to prepare for next year's learning: Jim Along Josie Down Came a Lady Canoe Song Skin and Bones Draw a Bucket of Water	
Improvise pentatonic melodies to simple 4- or 8-beat rhythms using the voice or a barred instrument Improvise a new rhythm and melody to one measure or more of a well-known song Improvise question and answer motives using known rhythm or melodic patterns	Singing simple two part song arrangements Singing from teacher's hand signs				Recognize musical features in classroom song repertoire, folk music, and masterworks including pentatonic scales Recognize rhythmic features in classroom song repertoire, folk music, and masterworks including half note, whole note, half note rest, and whole note rest	

continued

Grade 2 *Continued*

Month	Songs	Prepare	Present	Practice	Reading	Writing
					Unknown songs with previously learned elements in 4-beat meter: (a) stick notation; (b) traditional rhythmic notation; (c) staff notation Absolute pitch: G = *do mi-re-do* F = *do mi-re-do* C = *do mi-re-do*	Unknown songs with previously learned rhythmic elements in: (a) stick notation; (b) traditional rhythmic notation; (c) staff notation
May/June	**Review and prepare for spring concert; teach new repertoire**					

Grade 3 Monthly plans

Month	Songs	Prepare	Present	Practice	Reading	Writing
September	**Review second grade concepts and elements; teach new repertoire**					
September	Review second grade songs				Review quarter and eighth note rest (known songs)	Review quarter and eighth note rest
				Review beat and rhythm, quarter and eighth note rests	Review 2- and 4-beat meters Add bar lines	Review 2-beat meter

Improvisation	Ensemble	Memory	Inner Hearing	Form	Listening	Error Detection
Improvise rhythms in a chain around the classroom Improvise rhythms to the form of a simple folk song Improvise rhythmic accompaniments to familiar songs					Develop awareness of expressive controls, i.e. dynamics, tempo, and timbre, and their distinctive characteristics in masterworks of various historical periods Recognize phrase forms in classroom song repertoire, folk music, and masterworks	

Improvisation	Ensemble	Memory	Inner Hearing	Form	Listening	Error Detection
Quarter and eighth note rest, and half notes: 8-beat question and answer	Review 2 groups: beat and rhythm	Identify missing rhythms in a song or exercise	Review: internalize known songs		Instruments of the Orchestra. A Young Person's Guide to the Orchestra-Benjamin Britten	
Fill in empty measure game		Review: quarter, quarter, eighth rest	Review: identify known songs from rhythm clapping		Listening to music based on folk music —Simple Gifts	

continued

Grade 3 *Continued*

Month	Songs	Prepare	Present	Practice	Reading	Writing
				Review half note	Review *do-re-mi* and *so-la*	Review 4-beat meter
					Review half note	Review repeat sign
					Pentatonic scale: *do* = G, *do* = C, *do* = F (a) *do-re-mi* (b) *do-re-mi so* (c) *do-re-mi so-la*	

Improvisation	Ensemble	Memory	Inner Hearing	Form	Listening	Error Detection
Question and answer with *la, so, mi, re, do*		Four-beat rhythm echoes	*do-re-mi so-la:* identify songs from stick notation			
	Review ostinato: quarter, eighth, quarter rest	Eight-beat rhythm echoes	*do-re-mi so-la:* identify songs from staff notation			
		Echo with solfège and hand signs from teacher singing neutral	*do-re-mi so-la:* identify songs from teacher's hand signs			
		Play a melodic echo on a melody instrument				
	Review *la:* melodic canons	Four-beat rhythm echoes				
		Eight-beat rhythm echoes: quarter, quarter, eighth, rest, half note				
		Sixteenth notes: echo-clapping, 4 beats/8 beats				

continued

Grade 3 *Continued*

Month	Songs	Prepare	Present	Practice	Reading	Writing
	Cumberland Gap Dance Josey Deedle Deedle Dinah Old Brass Wagon Paw Paw Patch Shanghai Chicken Tideo Walter Jumped a Fox				Absolute pitch: A, G, E	Quarter, quarter-eighth, rest
					Absolute pitch: E, D, B	Half note
					Absolute pitch: D, C, A	4-beat meter
					Sixteenth notes: read known songs and song fragments	Sixteenth notes: 4- to 8-beat song motives (board, worksheets)
					Four-beat meter	
					Sixteenth notes: 4-beat motives (board, worksheets)	Sixteenth notes: add bar lines to songs in 2-beat and 4-beat meters (board, worksheets)
					Sixteen-beat songs, 32-beat songs	Sixteenth notes: add rhythm to songs (board, worksheets)
October	Chickalileelo Drunken Sailor Fed My Horse Fire in the Mountain Golden Ring Hogs in the Cornfield How Many Miles to Babylon Hush Little Baby Johnny Cuckoo Mama Buy Me a Chiney Doll Oh Fly Around San Serfin del Monte Skipping Rope Song Swapping Song Wallflowers Walter Jumped a Fox Wildcat	Eighth and two sixteenth notes	Eighth and two sixteenth notes	*do* pentatonic	Reading *do* pentatonic motifs in C, F, G *-do* positions *re-so* interval practice Reading with letter names	

Improvisation	Ensemble	Memory	Inner Hearing	Form	Listening	Error Detection
	Four-beat meter ostinati Four-beat meter: 2-part exercises					Saint-Säens' Carnival of the Animals: Fossils Schuman: Knecht Reprecht—Album for the Young
Four-beat question and answer phrases Eight-beat question and answer						
Question and answer with *la, so, mi, re, do*		Eight-beat dictation Echo sing with solfège and hand signs from teacher singing or playing on the piano			Schumann's Knecht Ruprecht (Album of the Young) Bach's Musette, Britten's Young Person's Guide to the Orchestra: Fugue	

continued

Grade 3 *Continued*

Month	Songs	Prepare	Present	Practice	Reading	Writing
					Song fragments with previously learned elements in 4-beat meter: (a) stick notation; (b) traditional rhythmic notation; (c) staff notation	Song fragments with previously learned rhythmic elements in: (a) stick notation; (b) traditional rhythmic notation; (c) staff notation
					Known songs with previously learned elements in 4-beat meter: (a) stick notation; (b) traditional rhythmic notation; (c) staff notation	Known songs with previously learned rhythmic elements and whole notes and rests in: (a) stick notation; (b) traditional rhythmic notation; (c) staff notation

Improvisation	Ensemble	Memory	Inner Hearing	Form	Listening	Error Detection
Question and answer Improvise rhythm patterns of 4 or 8 beats either by clapping, using rhythm instruments, or clapping and saying rhythm syllables Improvise short pentatonic musical motives using hand signs, hand staff, or body signs	Sing a well-known song and clap its rhythm in canon	Memorize short melodies from teacher's hand signs Memorize short melodies from staff notation Memorize simple two part exercises	Sing known songs silently while performing the beat and rhythm Recognize songs, rhythm patterns, or melodic patterns from staff notation		Mussorgsky's Great Gate of Kiev from Pictures at an Exhibition, Josquin's El Grillo, Verdi's Anvil Chorus Singing songs to prepare for next years learning: Jim Along Josie Down Came a Lady Canoe Song Skin and Bones Draw a Bucket of Water	
Improvise pentatonic melodies to simple 4- to 8-beat rhythms using the voice or a barred instrument Improvise a new rhythm and melody to one measure or more of a well-known song Improvise question and answer motives using known rhythm or melodic patterns	Singing simple two-part song arrangements Singing from teacher's hand signs				Recognize musical features in classroom song repertoire, folk music, and masterworks including pentatonic scales Recognize rhythmic features in classroom song repertoire, folk music, and masterworks including half note, whole note, half note rest, and whole note rest	

continued

Grade 3 *Continued*

Month	Songs	Prepare	Present	Practice	Reading	Writing
					Unknown songs with previously learned elements in 4-beat meter: (a) stick notation; (b) traditional rhythmic notation; (c) staff notation	Unknown songs with previously learned rhythmic elements in: (a) stick notation; (b) traditional rhythmic notation; (c) staff notation
November	Big Fat Biscuit C-Line Woman Cock Robin The Gallows Pole Grinding Corn Hambone Iroquois Lullabye Jim Along Josie Land of the Silver Birch Mush Toodin Old House Old Mr. Rabbit Phoebe Poor Little Kitty Cat Rosie Darling Rosie Sea Lion Woman Sioux Indian Lullaby Skin and Bones Skip to the Barbershop Walter Jumped a Fox Yangtze Boatman's Chantey	*low la,*		Eighth and two sixteenth notes	Absolute pitch (staff notation): (a) B, D, E (b) D, C, A (c) A, G, E *do* pentatonic known songs: (a) in stick notation; (b) from T hand signs; (c) from tone ladder; (d) in staff notation	Song fragments with previously learned rhythmic elements and previously known elements in 4-beat meter in: (a) stick notation; (b) traditional rhythmic notation; (c) staff notation

Improvisation	Ensemble	Memory	Inner Hearing	Form	Listening	Error Detection
Improvise rhythms in a chain around the classroom Improvise rhythms to the form of a simple folk song Improvise rhythmic accompaniments to familiar songs.					Develop awareness of expressive controls, i.e. dynamics, tempo, timbre, and their distinctive characteristics in masterworks of various historical periods Recognize phrase formsin classroom song repertoire, folk music, and masterworks	
Question and answer	*do* pentatonic: 2-part exercises	Four-beat rhythm patterns with previously learned rhythmic elements	*do* pentatonic: identify known songs from teacher's hand signs			

continued

Grade 3 *Continued*

Month	Songs	Prepare	Present	Practice	Reading	Writing
			low la,		*do* pentatonic known songs: (a) in stick notation; (b) from teacher's hand signs; (c) from tone ladder; (d) in staff notation	Known songs with previously learned rhythmic elements and sixteenth notes in 4-beat meter in: (a) stick notation; (b) traditional rhythmic notation; (c) staff notation
					Song fragments: (a) in stick notation; (b) from teacher's hand signs; (c) from tone ladder; (d) in staff notation	Unknown songs with previously learned rhythmic elements and eighth and two sixteenth notes in 4-beat meter in: (a) stick notation; (b) traditional rhythmic notation; (c) staff notation

Improvisation	Ensemble	Memory	Inner Hearing	Form	Listening	Error Detection
Question and answer Improvise rhythm patterns of 4 or 8 beats either by clapping, using rhythm instruments, or clapping and saying rhythm syllables Improvise short pentatonic musical motives using hand signs and/or staff	Four-beat meter ostinati	Eight-beat rhythm echoes with previously learned rhythmic elements	Dictation in 8-beat patterns with previously learned rhythmic elements			
Improvise pentatonic melodies to simple 4 to 8 beat rhythms using the voice or a barred instrument Improvise a new rhythm and melody to one measure or more of a well-known song Improvise question and answer motives using known rhythm or melodic patterns	Four-beat meter: 2-part exercises					

continued

Grade 3 *Continued*

Month	Songs	Prepare	Present	Practice	Reading	Writing
					do: unknown songs: (a) in stick notation; (b) from teacher's hand signs; (c) from tone ladder; (d) in staff notation	*do* pentatonic: unknown songs in: (a) stick notation; (b) staff notation
December	Bought Me a Cat Cumberland Gap Do Do Pity My Case Grandma Grunts Hogs in the Cornfield Hop Old Squirrel Ida Red Jim Along Josie Kansas Boys Old Betty Larkin Old Molly Hare Over the River Skip to My Lou Skipping Rope Song Walter Jumped a Fox	Two sixteenth notes and one eighth note		*low la,*	Read known and unknown songs from stick and staff notation	Eighth and two sixteenth notes: combine with sixteenth note and eighth-two sixteenth note songs and other exercises
					Read an unknown song, read exercises with *la, do-re-mi*	Song fragments in different positions on the staff (staff boards, manuscript paper)
					Read exercises with *la, do-re-mi so-la*	Transcribe known songs from stick to staff notation
			Two sixteenth notes and one eighth note		Melody flashcards	*do* pentatonic

Improvisation	Ensemble	Memory	Inner Hearing	Form	Listening	Error Detection
Improvise rhythms in a chain around the classroom Improvise rhythms to the form of a simple folk song Improvise rhythmic accompaniments to familiar songs						
	Known songs with melodic ostinati				Haydn Symphony # 94, second movement, theme B, variation 3	
	Known songs in canon (words, solfège)					
Sixteenth notes: 8-beat question and answer without cards	Partner songs	Memorize melodies from teacher's hand signs				
Eighth and two sixteenth notes 8-beat question and answer with cards	Two-part exercises	Four-beat echoes Eight-beat echoes Sixteen-beat echoes				

continued

Grade 3 *Continued*

Month	Songs	Prepare	Present	Practice	Reading	Writing
						Eighth and two sixteenth notes: combine with one eighth-two sixteenth note songs and other exercises
December	**Review and prepare for winter concert**					
January	**Review and teach new repertoire**					
Febuary	A Don Chin Chino Acitron de un Fandango Band of Angels C-Line Woman Charlie Over the Ocean Chatter with the Angels Cotton Eye Joe Dance Josey El Coyotito Head and Shoulders Hold My Mule Jolly Miller King Kong Kitchie La Patita Las Estatuas de Marfil Old Gray Mare Old MacDonald Old Texas Over the River Riding of a Goat Santo Domingo San Serafin del Monte Sailing on the Ocean Scotland's Burning The Old Sow Turn the Glasses Over	*low so*	*low so*	Two sixteenth notes and one eighth note	Four-beat motives (board, flashcards) combine patterns to notate 16- and 32-beat songs Exercises of progressive length, combination songs Read an unknown song Two sixteenth-one eighth note: 4 beat motives (board, flashcards), combine patterns to notate 16 and 32 beat songs Reading from hand signs: *la, - re* *la, - mi,* *so - re*	Four- to 8-beat motives (board, worksheet) Add bar lines in 2-beat and 4-beat meters Combine with sixteenth note songs and other exercises Four- to 8-beat motives (board, worksheet) Add bar lines in 2- and 4-beat meters

Improvisation	Ensemble	Memory	Inner Hearing	Form	Listening	Error Detection
		4- to 8-beat echo clapping				
					Tchaikovsky Symphony # 2; Finale	
Eight-beat question and answer, body percussion			Identify mystery songs from notation			
Eight-beat question and answer, unpitched percussion	Two-part rhythm exercises (charts, worksheets, exercise books)	Memory game with unknown material	Song match	Identify forms with letter names (ABC, AA')		
Eight-beat question and answer; vocal, conversational	Add rhythmic ostinato to known songs	Sixteen-beat echoes				
Eight-beat question and answer; vocal with solfège and handsigns	Two-part rhythm exercises (charts, worksheets, exercise books)	Four- to 8-beat echo clapping				

continued

Grade 3 *Continued*

Month	Songs	Prepare	Present	Practice	Reading	Writing
	Bye Baby Bunting Do Do Pity Fed My Horse The King's Land Old Mister Rabbit Over the River	Internal upbeat (split eighth note)	Internal upeat (split eighth note)	*so,*	Read known songs and song fragments from stick and staff notation Melodic flashcards Read exercises with *la, do-re-mi* Read exercises with *la, do-re-mi so* Single eighth note: read songs and song fragments (board, worksheets) Read exercises with *l, drm sl* Single quarter note: Identify single ta in unknown songs	Write rhythm for song phrases
March	Circle Round the Zero Hogs in the Cornfield I Lost the Farmer's Dairy Key John Kanaka Liza Jane Pourquoi Riding in the Buggy	*High do*		Internal upbeats	Absolute pitch (staff notation): (a) B, D, E; (b) D, C, A; (c) A, G, E	Song fragments with previously learned rhythmic elements in 4-beat meter in: (a) stick notation; (b) traditional rhythmic notation; (c) staff notation

Improvisation	Ensemble	Memory	Inner Hearing	Form	Listening	Error Detection
Eight-beat question and answer with cards		Eight-beat echo	Identify known songs from pitch ladder and from handsigns		Mozart Sonata in A Major: Rondo Alla Turca Bach: Little Fugue in g-minor, Bach: Musette from Anna Magdalena Notebook, Rachmaninoff: Prelude in g-minor	
Eight-beat question and answer without cards		Erasing game, rhythm grid Sixteen-beat echoes				
		Four- to 8-beat pattern from teacher's hand signs	Four-beat dictation in stick notation			
Eight-beat question and answer on pitched percussion	*do* and *la* pentatonic: 2-part songs	Four- to 8-beat pattern from teacher's hand signs				
Four-beat question and answer phrases with previously learned rhythmic elements	Sixteenth notes: (a) rhythm canons; (b) 2-pt rhy exercises (1) Sing songs antiphonally (2) Practice intervals simultaneously with hand signs	Four-beat rhythm patterns with previously learned rhythmic elements	Dictation in 8-beat patterns with previously learned rhythmic elements		Grofe: Grand Canyon Suite: On the Trail, Mozart: Contredance in A	

continued

Grade 3 *Continued*

Month	Songs	Prepare	Present	Practice	Reading	Writing
			High do		Song fragments with previously learned elements and sixteenth notes in: (a) stick notation; (b) traditional rhythmic notation; (c) staff notation	Known songs with previously learned rhythmic elements and sixteenth notes in 4-beat meter in: (a) stick notation; (b) traditional rhythmic notation; (c) staff notation
					Known songs with previously learned elements in: (a) stick notation; (b) traditional rhythmic notation; (c) staff notation	Unknown songs with previously learned rhythmic elements in 4-beat meter in: (a) stick notation;
					Unknown songs with previously learned elements in: (a) stick notation; (b) traditional rhythmic notation; (c) staff notation	(b) traditional rhythmic notation; (c) staff notation

Improvisation	**Ensemble**	**Memory**	**Inner Hearing**	**Form**	**Listening**	**Error Detection**
Eight-beat question and answer phrases with previously learned rhythmic elements	(3) Accompany a song with a rhythmic ostinato using quarter, eighth notes, and quarter note rests sixteenth note in eight note + two sixteenth notes and two sixteenth notes = eight note	Eight-beat rhythm echoes with previously learned rhythmic elements and sixteenth notes				
	Four-beat meter ostinati					
	Four-beat meter: 2-part exercises	Thirty-two-beat rhythm patterns with previously learned rhythmic elements				
		Four-beat and 8-beat dictation				

continued

Grade 3 *Continued*

Month	Songs	Prepare	Present	Practice	Reading	Writing
	Above the Plain Band of Angels Billy Boy Blow Ye Winds I'll Sell My Hat Jolly Miller	External Upbeats	External Upbeats	High *do*' extended pentatonic	Sight read in two parts (up to 32-beat exercises) Apply absolute letter names to simple melodic exercises on the staff in G-*do*, F-*do*, and C-*do*	Write a simple melody and compose a rhythmic accompaniment or an ostinato Write known songs using traditional rhythmic and staff notation in G-*do*, F-*do*, and C-*do*
April	Row, Row, Row Your Boat	$^6_8$ time signature (identifying 1, 2, and 3 sounds on a beat)		*do* and external upbeats	Sight read in two parts (up to 32-beat exercises) Apply absolute letter names to simple melodic exercises on the staff in G-*do*, F-*do*, and C-*do*	Apply absolute letter names to simple melodic exercises on the staff in G-*do*, F-*do*, and C-*do*
May/June	**Review and prepare for spring concert; teach new repertoire**					

Improvisation	Ensemble	Memory	Inner Hearing	Form	Listening	Error Detection
Improvise short meodies for poems and rhymes using known musical elements Improvise melodies using known melodic syllables (*so, la, do-re-mi so-la,* and *do'*) in simple song form (ABA, AAAB, ABAB)	Accompany a song with a melodic ostinato using *la, so, mi, re, do-la, so,* and *do'* Sing simple rhythmic or melodic canons derived from familiar songs	Memorize a rhythmic pattern from notation that is 32 beats Write out simple rhythms of melodies from memory that are 16 beats	Sing songs "inside your head," using solfège syllables or rhythm names	Recognize simple song form (ABAC, AABC, AA'BC) Learn to read music with first and second endings	Recognize a variety of instruments, voices, and dynamic levels Recognize pentatonic scale and tone sets in the context of listening examples and familiar songs	
Improvise movements that reflect the form of the song Write a simple melody and compose a rhythmic accompaniment or another ostinato	Perform two-part rhythmic exercises based on rhythms of known song	Add absolute letter names to a rhythmic exercise Improvise movements to represent parts of the song, such as form, text, melody, or rhythm Form a listening exercise, memorize themes from music literature	Memorize easy 2-part exercises in solfège or rhythm syllables from hand signs, stick, or staff notation Sing the next correct letter name or solfège syllable after the teacher or another student in a known song without hearing the pitch	Recognize rhythmic and melodic variation Create simple forms showing phrase variants; for example: AA'BA AAA'A, ABA'C, etc.	Students will perform for each other Students will listen to performance by others (other students, parents, teacher, artists) Students will listen to and perform folk songs, master works, vocal songs, and instrumental works for 3rd grade concepts and elements Songs for next year: Come Thru in a Hurry Canoe Song Liza Jane Hill and Gully Alabama Gal Weevily Wheat	

Grade 4 Monthly plans

Month	Songs	Prepare	Present	Practice	Reading	Writing
September	**Review third grade concepts and elements; teach new repertoire**					
September	Review 3rd grade songs				Known songs and exercises: (a) sixteenth notes, eighth-two sixteenth notes, and two sixteenths-eighth note in 2 and 4 meter; (b) single eighth note; (c) *do* pentatonic; (d) extended *do* pentatonic	Review: previously learned rhythm symbols and sixteenth notes, eighth-two sixteenth notes, and two sixteenths-eighth note in 2 and 4 meter in: (a) stick noltation; (b) traditional rhythmic notation; (c) staff notation
					do' on board, flashcards, staff notation	
					Melodic flashcards in staff notation: (a) *do* pentatonic	
					Unknown *do/la,* pentatonic songs in staff notation	

Improvisation	Ensemble	Memory	Inner Hearing	Form	Listening	Error Detection
Review: question and answer (a) sixteenth note patterns; (b) extended *do* pentatonic patterns	Review 2-part rhythm chart with previously learned rhythm symbols concentrating on sixteenth notes, eighth-two sixteenth notes, and two sixteenths-eighth note in 2 and 4 meter in: (a) stick noltation; (b) traditional rhythmic notation; (c) staff notation	Review: fill in missing rhythms - 8 beats	Review: rhythm dictation in 8-beat patterns	(1) Recognize simple song form (ABAC, AABC, AA'BC) (2) Learn to read music with first and second endings		
	so, 2-part exercises		Review: identify known songs from rhythm clapping	(1) Recognize rhythmic and melodic variation		
			do-re-mi so-la: identify songs from stick notation	(2) Create simple forms showing phrase variants; for example: AA'BA AAA'A, ABA'C, etc.		
			do-re-mi so-la: identify songs from staff notation			
			do-re-mi so-la: identify songs from teacher's hand signs			
	2-part songs					

continued

Grade 4 *Continued*

Month	Songs	Prepare	Present	Practice	Reading	Writing
October	Canoe Round Come Thru in a Hurry Tom Dooley Weevily Wheat Shoo My Love All God's Children Canoe Round Lil Liza Jane Riding in the Buggy Hill and Gully Rider	Synco-pation		*do'*	Sight read in two parts (up to 32-beat exercises) Apply absolute letter names to simple melodic exer-cises on the staff in G-*do,* F-*do,* and C-*do*	Apply absolute letter names to simple melodic exer-cises on the staff in G-*do,* F-*do,* and C-*do*
November	C-Line Woman Cock Robin (The) Gallows Pole Land of the Silver Birch Walter Jumped a Fox	*la* penta-tonic		Synco-pation	Read known songs and song frag-ments from stick and staff notation Melodic flashcards Read exercises with known melody notes	

Improvisation	Ensemble	Memory	Inner Hearing	Form	Listening	Error Detection
Improvise movements that reflect the form of the song. Turn left for A, turn Right for B, and walk to the center of the circle for C	Perform 2-part rhythmic exercises based on rhythms of known song	Add absolute letter names to a rhythmic exercise	Memorize easy 2-part exercises in solfège or rhythm syllables from hand signs, stick, or staff notation	Recognize rhythmic and melodic variation	Students will perform for each other	
Write a simple melody and compose a rhythmic accompaniment or ano ostinato		Improvise movements to represent parts of the song, such as form, text, melody, or rhythm	Sing the next correct letter name or solfège syllable after the teacher or another student in a known song without hearing the pitch	Create simple forms showing phrase variants; for example: AA'BA AAA'A, ABA'C, etc.	Students will listen to performance by others (other students, parents, teacher, artists)	
		Form a listening exercise, memorize themes from music literature			Students will listen to and perform folk songs, master works, vocal songs, and instrumental works	
Eight-beat question and answer with cards		Eight-beat echo	Identify known songs from pitch ladder and from handsigns	with known rhythms: AB, ABC	Mozart's Sonata in A Major: Rondo Alla Turca Bach's Little Fugue in g-minor Bach's Musette from Anna Magdalena Notebook Rachmaninoff's Prelude in g-minor	
Eight-beat question and answer without cards		Erasing game, rhythm grid				
Eight-beat question and answer without cards, empty measure game		Sixteen-beat echoes				

continued

Grade 4 *Continued*

Month	Songs	Prepare	Present	Practice	Reading	Writing
			la pentatonic		Read exercises with known melody notes: Single ti: read songs and song fragments (board, worksheets)	Write rhythm for song phrases
					Read exercises with known melody notes: Single ta: identify single *ta* in unknown songs	
November	Above the Plain Big Fat Bisquit Hush a Bye John Kanaka Lil Liza Jane	Two uneven sounds over 2 beats where the first sound lasts a beat and a half		*la* pentatonic	Known songs: (a) in stick notation; (b) from teacher's hand signs; (c) from tone ladder; (d) in staff notation	Song fragments in: (a) stick notation; (b) staff notation; (c) transpose from stick notation to staff notation
					Song fragments: (a) in stick notation; (b) from teacher's hand signs; (c) from tone ladder; (d) in staff notation	Known songs in: (a) stick notation; (b) staff notation

Improvisation	Ensemble	Memory	Inner Hearing	Form	Listening	Error Detection
Empty measure game		4- to 8-beat pattern from teacher's hand signs	4-beat dictation in stick notation			
Eight-beat question and answer on pitched percussion	*do* and *la* pentatonic: 2-part songs	4- to 8-beat pattern from teacher's hand signs	4-beat melodic dictation (with known melody notes)			
Four-beat question and answer Sing two-part songs Switch parts upon a signal Rhythm canons containing known rhythm patterns Two part rhythm exercises: (a) at board; (b) charts; (c) worksheets Improvise several phrases of music using given forms Improvise a melodic chain: begin each phrase with the last syllable of a previous student	Melodic cannon with solfège Create melodic ostinato Sing songs antiphonally Practice intervals simultaneously with hand signs	Four-beat melodic echoes Echo with solfège and hand signs from teacher's singing with neutral syllable	Four-beat melodic patterns and melodic dictation Identify songs from: (a) stick notation; (b) staff notation; (c) teacher's hand signs		Mozart's Eine Kleine Nachtmusik, Bach's D Major Suite: Gigue, Strauss' Death and Transfiguration Recognize musical features in classroom song repertoire, folk music, and masterworks including pentatonic, pentachord, and hexachord scales Recognize musical features in classroom song repertoire, folk music, and masterworks including syncopations, dotted quater-eighth note and combinations and dotted eighth followed by sixteenth	

continued

Grade 4 *Continued*

Month	Songs	Prepare	Present	Practice	Reading	Writing
			Dotted quarter followed by an eighth note		Unknown songs: (a) in stick notation; (b) from teacher's hand signs; (c) from tone ladder; (d) in staff notation	Unknown songs in: (a) stick notation; (b) staff notation
December	**Review and prepare for winter concert**					
January	**Review and teach new repertoire**					
February	Ah! Vous Dirai-Je Mamam Donkey Riding Goose Round Hungarian Canon Mamalama Redbirds and Blackbirds Whistle Daughter Whistle Are You Sleeping? La Calavera (Skeleton) Ay! Que me dele un dedo, tilin Entra las Matas La Muneca Que Llueva Se Va la Barca Yo Soy Farolero, Yo te vi Al Animo A'nde va nina coqueta Arrorro mi nono Los Pollitos Toron Toron Jill Old Molly Hare When I First Came to this Land	*fa*		Dotted quarter followed by an eighth note	Known songs with previously learned elements in: (a) stick notation; (b) traditional rhythmic notation; (c) staff notation	Known songs with previously learned elements in: (a) stick notation; (b) traditional rhythmic notation; (c) staff notation

Improvisation	Ensemble	Memory	Inner Hearing	Form	Listening	Error Detection
		Memorize rhythmic exercieses from notation up to 32 beats in length Write simple rhythms and melodies from memory up to 16 beats in length	Match song fragments to iconic representations of songs Sing songs "inside" with melodic syllables or letter names Memorize easy two-part melodies from hand signs, stick notation, and staff notation without hearing them aloud			
Eight-beat question and answer phrases with previously learned elements Sing two-part songs Switch parts upon a signal Rhythm canons containing known rhythm patterns Two part rhythm exercises: (a) at board; (b) charts; (c) worksheets Improvise several phrases of music using given forms	Four-beat meter ostinato Sing songs antiphonally Practice intervals simultaneously with hand signs	Four-beat rhythm patterns	Dictation in eight-beat patterns with previously learned rhythmic elements Memorize both parts of an easy two-part exercise, and switch between them without hearing them aloud Sing the correct solfège or letter names of the next note when the teacher stops at random within a song		Bartok's Rondo for piano, Pachabel's Canon, Beethoven's Ode to Joy, Mozart's Ah! Vous Dirai-Je, Maman Develop awareness of expressive controls, i.e. dynamics, tempo, timbre, and their distictive characteristics in masterworks of various historical periods	

continued

Grade 4 *Continued*

Month	Songs	Prepare	Present	Practice	Reading	Writing
			fa		Song fragments with previously learned elements in: (a) stick notation; (b) traditional rhythmic notation; (c) staff notation	Song fragments with previously learned elements in: (a) stick notation; (b) traditional rhythmic notation; (c) staff notation
					Unknown songs: (a) stick notation; (b) traditional rhythmic notation; (c) staff notation	Unknown songs: (a) stick notation; (b) traditional rhythmic notation; (c) staff notation
March	Oh How Lovely is the Evening All Things Shall Perish Around the Green Gravel Coffee Dona Nobis Pacem Down in the Valley Evn'ing Still Hills of Arriang La Calavera (Skelaton) Music Alone Shall Live Rise Up O, Flame The Streets of Laredo There is no sorrow	Triple meter		*fa*, B-flat in the key of F	Read songs with B-flat Known songs with previously learned elements in: (a) stick notation; (b) traditional rhythmic notation; (c) staff notation	B-flat, the *do* pentachord in F *do* Known songs with previously learned elements in: (a) stick notation; (b) traditional rhythmic notation; (c) staff notation

Improvisation	**Ensemble**	**Memory**	**Inner Hearing**	**Form**	**Listening**	**Error Detection**
Improvise a melodic chain: begin each phrase with the last syllable of a previous student	Rhythm canons Accompany a song with a rhythmic ostinato using quarter, eighth notes and quarter note rests sixteenth note in eight note plus two sixteenth notes and two sixteenth notes plus eight note, syncopated rhythms, dotted quarter followed by an eighth note, dotten eighth followed by a sixteenth note	Eight-beat rhythm echoes with previously learned rhythmic elements Improvise movements appropriate to some aspect of the music, for example form, melody, text, or rhythm			Recognize phrase forms in classroom song repertoire, folk musi, and masterworks	
	Two-part rhythm excercises Accompany a song with a melodic ostinato using *la, so, mi, re, do-la, so,* and *do'*	Thirty-two-beat rhythm patterns with previously learned rhythmic elements				
Eight-beat question and answer phrases with previously learned elements Sing two-part songs Switch parts upon a signal	Four-beat meter ostinato Sing songs antiphonally Practice intervals simultaneously with hand signs	Four-beat rhythm patterns	Dictation in 8-beat patterns with previously learned rhythmic elements "Sing" the indicated measures of a song using inner hearing On a barred instrument, play back a melody that the teacher has sung		Recognize tonic, dominant, and subdominant functions	

continued

Grade 4 *Continued*

Month	Songs	Prepare	Present	Practice	Reading	Writing
					Song fragments with previously learned elements in: (a) stick notation; (b) traditional rhythmic notation; (c) staff notation	Song fragments with previously learned elements in: (a) stick notation; (b) traditional rhythmic notation; (c) staff notation
					Unknown songs: (a) stick notation; (b) traditional rhythmic notation; (c) staff notation	Unknown songs: (a) stick notation; (b) traditional rhythmic notation; (c) staff notation
			$\frac{3}{4}$ time signature		Read example with B-flat and unknown songs	

Improvisation	Ensemble	Memory	Inner Hearing	Form	Listening	Error Detection
Rhythm canons containing known rhythm patterns Two-part rhythm exercises: (a) at board; (b) charts; (c) worksheets	Rhythm canons Sing simple rhythmic or melodic canons derived from familiar songs	Eight-beat rhythm echoes with previously learned rhythmic elements	Identify a do pentachord or a do hexachord melody from the teacher humming or playing or an instrument			
Read an exercise and improvise an alternative ending using a given rhythm and containing selected melodic elements: (a) read an exercises but improvise at two given places; (b) perform 4- and 8-beat question and answer phrases; (c) improvise empty measures within a 4-measure phrase; (d) improvise/ compose to complete a missing section of a song in a given form; (e) improvise/ compose using two-part hand signs; (f) question and answer 8- beat and 16-beat patterns	Two-part rhythm excercises Perform two-part rhythmic exercises based on rhythms of known melodies Sing and read two-part songs	Thirty-two-beat rhythm patterns with previously learned rhythmic elements Memorize rhythmic or melodic themes from music literature Memorize two-part songs and exercises				

continued

Grade 4 *Continued*

Month	Songs	Prepare	Present	Practice	Reading	Writing
April	Early to Bed	$\frac{6}{8}$ time Uneven division of beat		*fa*, B-flat in the key of F		
May/June	**Review and prepare for spring concert; teach new repertoire**					

Grade 5/6 Unit plans

Unit	Songs	Prepare	Present	Practice	Reading	Writing
	Review fourth grade concepts and elements; teach new repertoire					
1	Birch Tree At the Gate of Heaven When I First Came to This Land Autumn Canon Blow Ye Winds Bound for the Promised Land Debka Hora Drill Ye Terriers Drunken Sailor The Greenland Fisheries Hunt the Cows Hush-A-Bye Sour Grapes Viva la Musica Dona, Dona, Dona Ghost of Tom Hey, Ho, Nobody Home Hashivenu Swapping Song Yankee Doodle Las Horas (Hours) Old Molly Hare Paw Paw Patch Pick a Bale of Cotton	A pitch between do and la that is a half step below *do*		$\frac{3}{4}$ time	Key, F Major read known songs and examples	
2	Donkey Riding Circle Round the Zero Sail Away Ladies	Two uneven sounds on 1 beat		Low *ti*	F Major	

Improvisation	Ensemble	Memory	Inner Hearing	Form	Listening	Error Detection
					Songs for next year: Debka Hora Drill Ye Tarriers Hashivenue Autumn Cannon Fly Fly	

Improvisation	Ensemble	Memory	Inner Hearing	Form	Listening	Error Detection
					Tchaikovsky's Symphony No. 4 Forth Movement—Little Birch Tree	
					Haydn's Cello Concerto in D major. Op 101, movement 3, Allegro (Rondo)	

continued

Grade 5/6 *Continued*

Unit	Songs	Prepare	Present	Practice	Reading	Writing
			Dotted eighth followed by a sixteenth and sixteenth followed by a dotted eighth note	$\frac{2}{4}$ meter	Known songs: (a) in stick notation; (b) from teacher's hand signs; (c) from tone ladder; (d) in staff notation	Song fragments in: (a) stick notation; (b) staff notation; (c) transpose from stick notation to staff notation
					Song fragments: (a) in stick notation; (b) from teacher's hand signs; (c) from tone ladder; (d) in staff notation	Known songs in: (a) stick notation; (b) staff notation
					Unknown songs: (a) in stick notation; (b) from teacher's hand signs; (c) from tone ladder; (d) in staff notation	Unknown songs in: (a) stick notation; (b) staff notation
				Review fourth grade songs		
3	Drunken Sailor My Old Hen The Ship that Never Returned Sweet Betsy From Pike Crocodile Song *Alleluia*	Major scale, *ti'*		Dotted eighth and sixteenth notes	Known songs and exercises: (a) sixteenth notes and two sixteenth and eighth note in 2 and 4 meter; (b) single eighth note (c) *do* pentatonic; (d) extended *do* pentatonic	Review previously learned rhythm symbols in 2 and 4 meter in: (a) stick notation; (b) traditional rhythmic notation; (c) staff notation

Improvisation	Ensemble	Memory	Inner Hearing	Form	Listening	Error Detection
Four-beat question and answer	Melodic cannon with solfège Create melodic ostinato	Four-beat melodic echoes	Four-beat melodic patterns and melodic dictation			
		Echo with solfège and hand signs from teacher's singing with neutral syllable	Identify songs from: (a) stick notation; (b) staff nottaion; (c) teacher's hand signs			
	Add a *do-so,* or *do-fa,-so,* accompaniment to a melody		Dictation in 8-beat patterns with previously learned rhythmic elements Memorize both parts of an easy two-part exercise, and switch between them without hearing them aloud		Bartok's Rondo for Piano, Pachabel's Canon, Beethoven's Ode to Joy, Mozart's Ah! Vous Dirai-Je, Maman	

continued

Grade 5/6 *Continued*

Unit	Songs	Prepare	Present	Practice	Reading	Writing
				$\frac{2}{4}$ meter	Known songs with previously learned elements in: (a) stick notation; (b) traditional rhythmic notation; (c) staff notation	Known songs with previously learned elements in: (a) stick notation; (b) traditional rhythmic notation; (c) staff notation
			Major scale, *ti'*		Song fragments with previously learned elements in: (a) stick notation; (b) traditional rhythmic notation; (c) staff notation	Song fragments with previously learned elements in: (a) stick notation; (b) traditional rhythmic notation; (c) staff notation
					Unknown songs: (a) stick notation; (b) traditional rhythmic notation; (c) staff notation	Unknown songs: (a) stick notation; (b) traditional rhythmic notation; (c) staff notation

Improvisation	Ensemble	Memory	Inner Hearing	Form	Listening	Error Detection
Eight-beat question and answer phrases with previously learned elements Sing two-part songs Switch parts upon a signal	Four-beat meter ostinato Sing songs antiphonally Practice intervals simultaneously with hand signs	Four-beat rhythm patterns	Sing the correct solfège or letter names of the next note when the teacher stops at random within a song		Develop awareness of expressive controls, i.e. dynamics, tempo, timbre, and their distictive characteristics in masterworks of various historical periods	
Rhythm canons containing known rhythm patterns Two part rhythm exercises: (a) at board; (b) charts; (c) worksheets Improvise several phrases of music using given forms Improvise a melodic chain: begin each phrase with the last syllable of a previous student	Rhythm canons Accompany a song with a rhythmic ostinato using quarter, eighth notes, and quarter note rests sixteenth note and eight note plus two sixteenth notes and two sixteenth notes plus eight note, syncopated rhythms, dotted quarter followed by an eighth note, dotted eighth followed by a sixteenth note	Eight-beat rhythm echoes with previously learned rhythmic elements Improvise movements appropriate to some aspect of the music, for example form, melody, text, or rhythm			Recognize phrase forms in classroom song repertoire, folk music, and masterworks	
	Two-part rhythm excercises Accompany a song with a melodic ostinato using *la, so, me, re, do-la, so,* and *d'*	Thirty-two-beat rhythm patterns with previously learned rhythmic elements				

continued

Grade 5/6 *Continued*

Unit	Songs	Prepare	Present	Practice	Reading	Writing
4	Erie Canal Great Big Dog My Good Old Man Shanghai Chicken Go Down Moses Swing Low Sweet Chariot Charlotte Town When I First Came to This Town Erie Canal Go Down Moses	Two uneven sounds over 2 beats where the first sound lasts half a beat and the second sound lasts a beat and a half		Major scale, *high ti*	Melodic flashcards in staff notation: (a) *do* pentatonic; (b) extended *la* pentatonic G = *do* D = *do*	Review known do pentatonic songs in: (a) stick notation; (b) staff notation
					Known songs with previously learned elements in: (a) stick notation; (b) traditional rhythmic notation; (c) staff notation	Known songs with previously learned elements in: (a) stick notation; (b) traditional rhythmic notation; (c) staff notation
			Eighth note followed by a dotted quarter		Song fragments with previously learned elements in: (a) stick notation; (b) traditional rhythmic notation; (c) staff notation	Song fragments with previously learned elements in: (a) stick notation; (b) traditional rhythmic notation; (c) staff notation
					Unknown songs: (a) stick notation; (b) traditional rhythmic notation; (c) staff notation	Unknown songs: (a) stick notation; (b) traditional rhythmic notation; (c) staff notation

Improvisation	Ensemble	Memory	Inner Hearing	Form	Listening	Error Detection
Eight-beat question and answer phrases with previously learned elements Sing two-part songs Switch parts upon a signal Rhythm canons containing known rhythm patterns Two-part rhythm exercises: (a) at board; (b) charts; (c) worksheets Read an exercises and improvise an alternative ending using a given rhythm and containing selected melodic elements: (a) read an exercises but improvise at 2 given places; (b) perform 4- and 8-beat question and answer phrases; (c) improvise empty measures within a 4-measure phrase;	Four-beat meter ostinato Sing songs antiphonally Practice intervals simultaneously with hand signs Rhythm canons Sing simple rhythmic or melodic canons derived from familiar songs Two-part rhythm excercises Perform two-part rhythmic exercises based on rhythms of known melodies Sing and read two-part songs	Four-beat rhythm patterns Eight-beat rhythm echoes with previously learned rhythmic elements Thirty-two-beat rhythm patterns with previously learned rhythmic elements Memorize rhythmic or melodic themes from music literature Memorize two-part songs and exercises	Dictation in 8-beat patterns with previously learned rhythmic elements "Sing" the indicated measures of a song using inner hearing On a barred instrument, play back a melody that the teacher has sung Identify a do pentachord or a do hexachord melody from the teacher humming or playing or an instrument		Recognize tonic, dominant, and subdominant functions	

continued

Grade 5/6 *Continued*

Unit	Songs	Prepare	Present	Practice	Reading	Writing
5	Fly Fly Fly	Minor scale		Eighth and dotted quarter	Known songs with previously learned elements in: (a) stick notation; (b) traditional rhythmic notation; (c) staff notation	Known songs with previously learned elements in: (a) stick notation; (b) traditional rhythmic notation; (c) staff notation
			Minor scale		Song fragments with previously learned elements in: (a) stick notation; (b) traditional rhythmic notation; (c) staff notation	Song fragments with previously learned elements in: (a) stick notation; (b) traditional rhythmic notation; (c) staff notation

Improvisation	Ensemble	Memory	Inner Hearing	Form	Listening	Error Detection
(d) improvise/compose to complete a missing section of a song in a given form; (e) improvise/compose using two-part hand signs; (f) question and answer 8-beat and 16-beat patterns						
Eight-beat question and answer phrases with previously learned elements Improvise phrases of music using given forms Improvise a melodic chain: begin each phrase with the last syllable of a previous melodic turn Sing simple major melodies in minor tonality Read an exercise and improvise an alternative ending using a given rhythm and containing selected melodic elements Read an exercise but improvise at 2 given places	Four-beat meter ostinato Accompany a song with a rhythmic ostinato using dotted eighth followed by sixteenth, sixteenth followed by dotted eighth, eighth followed by dotted quarter Rhythm canons Accompany a song in compound meter with subdivisions of the beat Accompany a song with a melodic ostinato Sing simple rhythmic canons derived from familiar songs	Four-beat rhythm patterns Eight-beat rhythm echoes with previously learned rhythmic elements	Dictation in 8-beat patterns with previously learned rhythmic elements		Recognize musical features in classroom song repertoire, folk music, and masterworks including pentatonic scales, triple meter, and simple compound meter Develop awareness of expressive controls, i.e. dynamics, tempo, timbre, and their distictive characteristics in masterworks of various historical periods Recognize forms in classroom song repertoire, folk music, and masterworks including compound binary, compound ternary, and sontata allergro	

continued

Grade 5/6 *Continued*

Unit	Songs	Prepare	Present	Practice	Reading	Writing
					Unknown songs: (a) stick notation; (b) traditional rhythmic notation; (c) staff notation	Unknown songs: (a) stick notation; (b) traditional rhythmic notation; (c) staff notation
6	Alley-O Oliver Cromwell Skin & Bones	One, two, and three notes on a beat in compound meter		Minor scale	Known songs with previously learned elements in: (a) stick notation; (b) traditional rhythmic notation; (c) staff notation	Known songs with previously learned elements in: (a) stick notation; (b) traditional rhythmic notation; (c) staff notation
			Present simple rhythm in $^6_8$		Song fragments with previously learned elements in: (a) stick notation; (b) traditional rhythmic notation; (c) staff notation	Song fragments with previously learned elements in: (a) stick notation; (b) traditional rhythmic notation; (c) staff notation

Improvisation	Ensemble	Memory	Inner Hearing	Form	Listening	Error Detection
	Two-part rhythm excercises Perform two-part rhythmic exercises based on rhythms of known songs Sing and read two-part songs	Thirty-two-beat rhythm patterns with previously learned rhythmic elements				
Eight-beat question and answer phrases with previously learned elements Improvise phrases of music using given forms Improvise a melodic chain: begin each phrase with the last syllable of a previous melodic turn Sing simple major melodies in minor tonality Read an exercise and improvise an alternative ending using a given rhythm and containing selected melodic elements Read an exercise but improvise at 2 given places	Four-beat meter ostinato Accompany a song with a rhythmic ostinato using dotted eighth followed by sixteenth, sixteenth followed by dotted eighth, eighth followed by dotted quarter Rhythm canons Accompany a song in compound meter with subdivisions of the beat Accompany a song with a melodic ostinato using *la, so, mi, re, do, la,* *so,* and *do',* *fa',* *ti'* and *si'* Sing simple rhythmic canons derived from familiar songs	Four-beat rhythm patterns Eight-beat rhythm echoes with previously learned rhythmic elements	Dictation in 8-beat patterns with previously learned rhythmic elements		Recognize musical features in classroom song repertoire, folk music, and masterworks including pentatonic scales, triple meter, and simple compound meter Develop awareness of expressive controls, i.e. dynamics, tempo, timbre, and their distictive characteristics in masterworks of various historical periods Recognize forms in classroom song repertoire, folk music, and masterworks including compound binary, compound ternary, and sontata allergro	

continued

Grade 5/6 *Continued*

Unit	Songs	Prepare	Present	Practice	Reading	Writing
					Unknown songs: (a) stick notation; (b) traditional rhythmic notation; (c) staff notation	Unknown songs: (a) in stick notation; (b) traditional rhythmic notation; (c) staff notation
7	Scarborough Fair The Ash Grove Drunken Sailor Bow Belinda	Syllable *fi*—a sound that is a half step above *fa*	Solfege syllable *fi* dorian scale	Compound meter $\frac{6}{8}$ time signature simple patterns	Review pentatonic	Known songs with previously learned elements and half notes in: (a) in stick notation; (b) traditional rhythmic notation; (c) staff notation
	Row, Row, Row Your Boat Hashevinu Sir Eglamore Git Along Little Doggies Now Kiss the Cup O, How Lovely Is the Evening	Uneven subdivision in compound meter	Presentation of more patterns in compound meter	Dorian mode		Song fragments with previously learned elements and half notes in: (a) in stick notation; (b) traditional rhythmic notation; (c) staff notation
	Ah, Poor Bird Dance to the Tambourine (Baile de Pandero) Go Down Moses Inez Kings From the East (Los Reyes de Oriente) La Zanduga	*si*		Uneven subdivison patterns in $\frac{6}{8}$		Unknown songs: (a) in stick notation; (b) traditional rhythmic notation; (c) staff notation

Improvisation	Ensemble	Memory	Inner Hearing	Form	Listening	Error Detection
	Two-part rhythm excercises Perform two-part rhythmic exercises based on rhythms of known songs Sing and read two-part songs	Thirty-two-beat rhythm patterns with previously learned rhythmic elements				
Eight-beat question and answer phrases with previously learned elements Improvise phrases of music using given forms	Four-beat meter ostinato	Four-beat rhythm patterns	Dictation in 8-beat patterns with previously learned rhythmic elements		Recognize musical features in classroom song repertoire, folk music, and masterworks including pentatonic scales, triple meter, and simple compound meter	
Improvise a melodic chain: begin each phrase with the last syllable of a previous melodic turn Sing simple major melodies in minor tonality	Rhythm canons	Eight-beat rhythm echoes with previously learned rhythmic elements			Develop awareness of expressive controls, i.e. dynamics, tempo, timbre, and their distictive characteristics in masterworks of various historical periods	
Read an exercise and improvise an alternative ending using a given rhythm and containing selected melodic elements Read an exercise but improvise at 2 given places	Two-part rhythm excercises	Thirty-two-beat rhythm patterns with previously learned rhythmic elements			Recognize forms in classroom song repertoire, folk music, and masterworks including compound binary, compound ternary, and sontata allergro	

continued

Grade 5/6 *Continued*

Unit	Songs	Prepare	Present	Practice	Reading	Writing
8			Harmonic minor		Known songs with previously learned elements and half notes in: (a) in stick notation; (b) traditional rhythmic notation; (c) staff notation	Known songs with previously learned elements and half notes in: (a) in stick notation; (b) traditional rhythmic notation; (c) staff notation
					Song fragments with previously learned elements in: (a) in stick notation; (b) traditional rhythmic notation; (c) staff notation	Song fragments with previously learned elements in: (a) in stick notation; (b) traditional rhythmic notation; (c) staff notation
					Unknown songs: (a) in stick notation; (b) traditional rhythmic notation; (c) staff notation	Unknown songs: (a) in stick notation; (b) traditional rhythmic notation; (c) staff notation
9						Writing scales

Improvisation	Ensemble	Memory	Inner Hearing	Form	Listening	Error Detection
Eight-beat question and answer phrases with previously learned elements	Four-beat meter ostinato	Four-beat rhythm patterns	Dictation in 8-beat patterns with previously learned rhythmic elements			
	Rhythm canons	Eight-beat rhythm echoes with previously learned rhythmic elements				
	Two-part rhythm excercises	Thirty-two-beat rhythm patterns with previously learned rhythmic elements				
Eight-beat question and answer phrases with previously learned elements Improvise phrases of music using given forms Improvise a melodic chain: begin each phrase with the last syllable of a previous melodic turn	Four-beat meter ostinato Accompany a song with a rhythmic ostinato using dotted eighth followed by sixteenth, sixteenth followed by dotted eighth, eighth followed by dotted quarter				Recognize musical features in classroom song repertoire, folk music, and masterworks including pentatonic scales, triple meter, and simple compound meter	

continued

Grade 5/6 *Continued*

Unit	Songs	Prepare	Present	Practice	Reading	Writing
10	Troubadour Song "Quant il Rossignols" With Laughter and Singing	Compound meter	$\frac{6}{8}$ time signature	Minor scale: natural and harmonic	Review *do-re-mi-so-la do'* and *so, la, do-re-mi-so-la* and *do* pentatonic and *la* pentatonic. Practice first and second endings in known songs and in exercises	Review previously learned rhythmic elements with rhythm syllables by inserting bar lines in 3-beat meters

Improvisation	Ensemble	Memory	Inner Hearing	Form	Listening	Error Detection
Sing simple major melodies in minor tonality Read an exercise and improvise an alternative ending using a given rhythm and containing selected melodic elements Read an exercise but improvise at 2 given places	Rhythm canons Accompany a song in compound meter with dubdivisions of the beat Accompany a song with a melodic ostinato using *la, so, mi, re, do, la,* *so,* and *do',* *fa, ti',* and *si'* Sing simple rhythmic canons derived from familiar songs Two-part rhythm excercises Perform two-part rhythmic exercises based on rhythms of known songs Sing and read two-part songs				Develop awareness of expressive controls, i.e. dynamics, tempo, timbre, and their distictive characteristics in masterworks of various historical periods Recognize forms in classroom song repertoire, folk music, and masterworks including compound binary, compound ternary, and sontata allergro	
Eight-beat question and answer phrases with previously learned elements Improvise phrases of music using given forms Improvise a melodic chain: begin each phrase with the last syllable of a previous melodic turn	Four-beat meter ostinato Accompany a song with a rhythmic ostinato using dotted eighth followed by sixteenth, sixteenth followed by dotted eighth, eighth followed by dotted quarter				Recognize musical features in classroom song repertoire, folk music, and masterworks including pentatonic scales, triple meter, and simple compound meter	

continued

Grade 5/6 ***Continued***

Unit	Songs	Prepare	Present	Practice	Reading	Writing
		Melodic Minor scale		Compound Meter		
			Melodic Minor			
	Daughter, Will You Marry? Every Night When the Sun Goes Down La Bella Hortelana La Vibora del Mar Sally Go 'Round the Sun	Triplets	Triplets	Melodic Minor scales		
11	As I Roved Out Avondale Mine Disaster Dying Cowboy Git Along Little Doggies I'm Goin' Home On a Cloud Jam on Gerry's Rock Old Joe Clark	solfège syllable *ta*—a sound that is a half step lower than the seventh degree of a major scale	Mixolydian solfège syllable: *ta*	Triplet	Known songs with previously learned elements in: (a) stick notation; (b) traditional rhythmic notation; (c) staff notation	Known songs with previously learned elements in: (a) stick notation; (b) traditional rhythmic notation; (c) staff notation

Improvisation	Ensemble	Memory	Inner Hearing	Form	Listening	Error Detection
Sing simple major melodies in minor tonality Read an exercise and improvise an alternative ending using a given rhythm and containing selected melodic elements Read an exercise but improvise at 2 given places	Rhythm canons Accompany a song in compound meter with dubdivisions of the beat Accompany a song with a melodic ostinato using *la, so, mi, re, do, la, so,* and *do',* *fa', ti',* and *si'* Sing simple rhythmic canons derived from familiar songs				Develop awareness of expressive controls, i.e. dynamics, tempo, timbre, and their distictive characteristics in masterworks of various historical periods Recognize forms in classroom song repertoire, folk music, and masterworks including compound binary, compound ternary, and sontata allergro	
	Two-part rhythm excercises Perform two-part rhythmic exercises based on rhythms of known songs Sing and read two-part songs					
Eight-beat question and answer phrases with previously learned elements	Four-beat meter ostinato	Four-beat rhythm patterns	Dictation in 8-beat patterns with previously learned rhythmic elements			

continued

Grade 5/6 *Continued*

Unit	Songs	Prepare	Present	Practice	Reading	Writing
					Song fragments with previously learned elements in: (a) stick notation; (b) traditional rhythmic notation; (c) staff notation	Song fragments with previously learned elements in: (a) stick notation; (b) traditional rhythmic notation; (c) staff notation
					Unknown songs: (a) stick notation; (b) traditional rhythmic notation; (c) staff notation	Unknown songs: (a) stick notation; (b) traditional rhythmic notation; (c) staff notation

Improvisation	Ensemble	Memory	Inner Hearing	Form	Listening	Error Detection
	Rhythm canons	Eight-beat rhythm echoes with previously learned rhythmic elements				
	Two-part rhythm excercises	Thirty-two-beat rhythm patterns with previously learned rhythmic elements				

Notes

Introduction

1. Catherine Christian, *The Pendragon* (New York: Warner Books, 1980), 298–299.
2. David J. Elliot, ed., *Praxial Music Education: Reflections and Dialogues* (New York: Oxford University Press, 2005), 12.
3. David J. Elliot, *Music Matters: A New Philosophy of Music Education* (New York: Oxford University Press, 1995), 271.
4. Ibid., 298–299.
5. Lori-Anne Dolloff, "Elementary Music Education: Building Cultures and Practice," in Elliott, *Praxial Music Education: Reflections and Dialogues,* 283.
6. See also Martin Gardiner, Alan Fox, Faith Knowles, and Donna Jeffrey, "Learning Improved by Arts Training." *Nature* 381 (May 23, 1996): 284.
7. Zoltán Kodály, "Bartók The Folklorist," in Ferenc Bónis, ed., *The Selected Writings of Zoltán Kodály,* trans. Lili Halápy and Fred Macnicol (orig. pub. Budapest: Zeneműkiadó Vállalat, 1964; London: Boosey & Hawkes, 1974), 107.
8. Zoltán Kodály, "Ancient Traditions—Today's Musical Life," in Bónis, *The Selected Writings,* 175.
9. Kokas Klára, *Joy through the Magic of Music* (Budapest: Akkord Zenei Kiadó, 1999).

Chapter 2

1. See Micheál Houlahan and Philip Tacka, *Zoltán Kodály: A Guide to Research* (New York: Garland, 1998).
2. László Eősze, Micheál Houlahan, and Philip Tacka, "Zoltán Kodály (1882–1967)," in *The New Grove Dictionary of Music and Musicians,* ed. Stanley Sadie (London: Macmillan; Millennium Edition).
3. Zoltán Kodály, "Bicinia Hungarica—Elöszó" [Bicinia Hungarica—Foreword], in Bónis, *The Selected Writings,* 215.
4. Zoltán Kodály, *333 olvasógyakorlat* [333 Elementary Exercises in Sight Singing] (1943) (Budapest: *Magyar Kórus,* 1948).
5. Zoltán Kodály, "Ötfokú zene" [Pentatonic Music] (Budapest: *Magyar Kórus,* 1945–1948).
6. Zoltán Kodály, "Hungarian Music Education," in Bónis, *The Selected Writings,* 152–155.
7. Zoltán Kodály, "A Hundred Year Plan," in Bónis, *The Selected Writings,* 160.
8. Erzsébet Szönyi, *Musical Reading and Writing,* trans. Lili Halápy (London: Boosey & Hawkes, 1954; English edition, 1974), 22.
9. Zoltan Kodály, "A zenei írás-olvasás módszertana" Elöszó Szönyi's Erzsébet könyvéhez [Preface to Erzsébet Szönyi's *Musical Reading and Writing*], in Bónis, *The Selected Writings,* 201–205.
10. Zoltán Kodály, *Let Us Sing Correctly!* in Bónis, *The Selected Writings,* 216–219.

11. Jenö Ádám, "The Influence of Folk Music on Public Musical Education in Hungary," *Studia Musicologica* 7/1–4 (1965): 11–18.
12. Zoltán Kodály, "On the Anniversary of Beethoven's Death," in Bónis, *The Selected Writings,* 77.
13. Ibid., 122.
14. Zoltán Kodály, "Inauguration of the New Building of the Kecskemét Music Primary School," *Bulletin of the International Kodály Society* 1 (1985): 9.
15. Zoltán Kodály, "Music in the Kindergarten," in Bónis, *The Selected Writings,* 130.
16. Zoltán Kodály, "Children's Choirs," in Bónis, *The Selected Writings,* 121.
17. Kodály, "Music in the Kindergarten," in Bónis, *The Selected Writings,* 130.
18. Zoltán Kodály, introduction to the volume "Musical Education in Hungary" ed. Frigyes Sándor, in Bónis, *The Selected Writings,* 206.
19. Zoltán Kodály, "Fifty-Five Two-Part Exercises," in Bónis, *The Selected Writings,* 225.
20. Kodály, "Children's Choirs," in Bónis, *The Selected Writings,* 124.
21. Ibid., 120.
22. Kodály, "On the Anniversary of Beethoven's Death," in Bónis, *The Selected Writings,* 76.
23. Zoltán Kodály, "Who is a Good Musician," in Bónis, *The Selected Writings,* 199.
24. Zoltán Kodály, "Introduction to *Music Education in Hungary,*" in Bónis, *The Selected Writings,* 206.
25. Ibid., 204.
26. Kodály, "Who is a Good Musician," in Bónis, *The Selected Writings,* 193.
27. Kodály, *Let us Sing Correctly!* in Bónis, *The Selected Writings,* 216.
28. Zoltán Kodály, "After the First Solfege Competition," in Bónis, *The Selected Writings,* 163.
29. Kodály, "Fifty-Five Two-Part Exercises," in Bónis, *The Selected Writings,* 224.
30. Kodály, "Who is a Good Musician," in Bónis, *The Selected Writings,* 196.
31. Ibid., 193.
32. Kodály, "Music in the Kindergarten," in Bónis, *The Selected Writings,* 151.
33. Kodály, "Pentatonic Music," in Bónis, *The Selected Writings,* 221.
34. Zoltán Kodály, "Children's Games," in Bónis, *The Selected Writings,* 46.
35. Kodály, "Bicinia Hungarica," in Bónis, *The Selected Writings,* 215.
36. Janet Mills, *Music in the Primary School* (Cambridge: Cambridge University Press, 1991).
37. Zoltán Kodály "Music in the Kindergarten," in Bónis, *The Selected Writings,* 145.
38. Zoltán Kodály "Children's Choirs," in Bónis, *The Selected Writings,* 120.
39. Ruth Crawford Seeger, *American Folk Songs for Christmas* (Garden City, N.Y.: Doubleday, 1953), 21.
40. Zoltán Kodály, "The Role of the Folksong in Russian and Hungarian Music," in Bónis, *The Selected Writings,* 36.
41. Zoltán Kodály "Children's Choirs," in Bónis, *The Selected Writings* 120.
42. Kodály, "Music in the Kindergarten," in Bónis, *The Selected Writings,* 141.
43. Kodály, "Children's Choirs," in Bónis, *The Selected Writings,* 122.
44. Zoltán Kodály, "The National Importance of the Workers' Chorus," in Bónis, *The Selected Writings,* 156.
45. Kodály, "Bartók the Folklorist," in Bónis, *The Selected Writings,* 106.
46. Kodály, "Who is a Good Musician," in Bónis, *The Selected Writings,* 197.
47. Ibid., 196.
48. Zoltán Kodály, "The Role of Authentic Folksong in Music Education" [lecture at Interlochen, 1966], *Bulletin of the International Kodály Society* 1 (1985): 15.
49. Kodály, "Who is a Good Musician," in Bónis, *The Selected Writings,* 198.
50. Zoltán Kodály, "Preface to *Musical Reading and Writing,*" in Bónis, *The Selected Writings,* 204.
51. Consortium of National Arts Education Associations, *National Standards for Arts Education* (Reston, Va.: Music Educators National Conference, 1994).

Chapter 3

1. Kodály, "Music in the Kindergarten," in Bónis, *The Selected Writings,* 145.
2. Kodály, "Children's Games," in Bónis, *The Selected Writings,* 46–47.
3. Kodály, "The Role of Authentic Folksong in Music Education," 17.
4. Ibid., 18.
5. Ibid.
6. Ibid., 16.
7. Zoltán Kodály, "Ancient Traditions—Today's Musical Life," in Bónis, *The Selected Writings,* 177.
8. Kodály, "The Role of Authentic Folksongs in Music Education," 18.
9. Kodály, "Pentatonic Music," in Bónis, *The Selected Writings,* 221.
10. Zoltán Kodály, "A Hundred Year Plan," in Bónis, *The Selected Writings,* 161.
11. Ibid.
12. This paragraph is based on a presentation given by Jill Trinka at the 18th International Kodaly Symposium, Capital University, Columbus, Ohio 2007, "From Soulful Singing to Music Literacy."
13. Kodály, "Children's Choirs," in Bónis, *The Selected Writings,* 126.
14. Kodály, "Pentatonic Music," in Bónis, *The Selected Writings,* 221.
15. Floice R. Lund, *Research and Retrieval: Music Teacher's Guide to Material Selection and Collection* (Westborough, Mass.: Pro Canto Press, 1981), 4–10.
16. See Mary Epstein and Jonathan C. Rappaport, *The Kodály Teaching Weave,* vol. 2, *Song Analysis Forms and Definitions* (Westborough, Mass.: Pro Canto Press, 2000) for more detailed song analysis definitions as well as sample song analysis.

Chapter 4

1. We recommend the following source for ideas on the teaching of singing: Gordon Pearse, *Sound Singing Ideas for Improving the Quality of Singing in Class & Choir,* ed. Carole Lindsay-Douglas (Bedfordshire, England: Lindsay Music, 2000).
2. Kodály, *Let Us Sing Correctly!* in Bónis, *The Selected Writings,* 216.
3. Kodály, "Children's Choirs," in Bónis, *The Selected Writings,* 123.
4. Kodály, "Fifty-Five Two-Part Exercises," in Bónis, *The Selected Writings,* 224.

Chapter 5

1. Kodály, "Preface to *Musical Reading and Writing,*" in Bónis, *The Selected Writings,* 203. Kodály quotes Émile Artaud's 1878 *Solfège Universel.*
2. Kodály, *Let Us Sing Correctly!* in Bónis, *The Selected Writings,* 217.
3. Richard Hoffman, William Pelto, and John W. White, "Takadimi: A Beat-Oriented System of Rhythm Pedagogy," *Journal of Music Theory Pedagogy* 10 (1996): 7–30. Throughout this text, we cite this approach to teaching rhythm. From our own work with university as well as elementary school students, we are strongly convinced that it is a superior system for rhythmic reading and hearing.
4. See Jonathan C. Rapport, *The Kodály Teaching Weave,* vol. 1, *Concepts, Elements and Skills* (Westborough, Mass.: Pro Canto Press, 2000); and Ann Eisen and Lamar Robertson, *An American Methodology* (Lake Charles, La.: Sneaky Snake Publications, 1997).

Chapter 6

1. Gary E. McPherson and Alf Gabrielsson, "From Sound to Sign," in *The Science and Psychology of Music Performance: Creative Strategies for Teaching and Learning,* ed. Richard Parncutt and Gary E. McPherson (New York: Oxford University Press, 2002), 99–115.

2. Patricia Shehan-Campbell and Carol Scott-Kassner, *Music in Childhood: From Preschool through the Elementary Grades* (New York: Schimrer Books, 1995), 9.

3. Jerome Bruner, *Towards a Theory of Instruction* (Cambridge, Mass.: Harvard University Press, 1966).

4. Edwin Gordon, *Learning Sequences in Music: Skill, Content and Patterns* (Chicago: GIA Publications, 1994).

5. To enable students to read and write music, the instructor should (1) identify song repertoire that contains basic and repeating rhythmic and melodic patterns that are initially four beats in length, and (2) sequence these patterns (target patterns) based on their frequency of occurrence in song material.

6. David Perkins, *The Intelligent Eye: Learning to Think by Looking at Art* (Santa Monica, Ca.: Getty Center for Education in the Arts, 1998).

7. Lois Choksy, *The Kodály Method Comprehensive Music Education,* 3rd ed. (Upper Saddle River, N.J.: Prentice Hall, 1999), 171–173; Micheál Houlahan and Philip Tacka, *Sound Thinking: Developing Musical Literacy,* 2 vols. (New York: Boosey & Hawkes, 1995).

8. Judith Brindle, "Notes from Eva Vendrai's Kodály Course," *British Kodály Academy Newsletter* (Spring 2005): 6–11.

9. Rita Aiello, "The Importance of Metacognition Research in Music," in *Proceedings of the 5th Triennia ESCOM Conference* (Hanover, Germany: Hanover University of Music and Drama, 2003), 656.

10. Jeanne Bamberger, *Developing Musical Intuitions* (New York: Oxford University Press, 2000).

11. W. J. Dowling, "Tonal Structure and Children's Early Learning of Music," in *Generative Processes in Music: The Psychology of Performance, Improvisation, and Composition,* ed. J. A. Sloboda (Oxford: Clarendon Press, 1988), 113–128.

12. We use the word "pattern" to distinguish a particular musical motive. For example, a pattern could be a four-beat phrase of two quarter notes followed by two eighth notes followed by a quarter note. In this "pattern" the "concept" would be the recognition of two sounds on one beat. The musical "element" would be the two eighth notes.

13. It is currently a practice of national, state, and local curriculums to specify the order and presentation of musical elements. For example, for rhythmic elements, the instructor first presents quarter and eighth notes. For melodic elements, the instructor first presents the solfege syllables *so* and *mi,* followed by *la* then *do.* The order of elements is determined by their frequency in song repertoire.

14. By "movement activities" we mean singing games as well as gestures and movements that imitate the text of a song or highlight the melodic contour or rhythmic pattern of a phrase.

15. Ray Levi, "Towards an Expanded View of Musical Literacy," *Contributions to Music Education* 16 (1989): 36.

16. Robert A. Cutietta and Gregory D. Booth, "The Influence of Meter, Mode, Interval Type and Contour in Repeated Melodic Free Recall," *Psychology of Music* 24/2 (1996): 222–236.

17. I. Peretz, "Auditory Agnosia: A Functional Analysis," in *Thinking in Sound,* ed. S. McAdams and E. Bigand (Oxford: Clarendon Press, 1993), 199–230.

18. According to Jukka Louhivuori, there is an intrinsic link between the stability of melodic formulas and the capacity of short-term memory. Therefore, the main role of the instructor should be the solidification of melodic and rhythmic formulas and schemes typical for specific music cultures. "Memory Strategies in Writing Melodies," *Bulletin of the Council for Research in Music Education* 142 (Fall 1999): 81–85.

19. Douglas Bartholomew, "Sounds Before Symbols: What Does Phenomenology Have to Say?" *Philosophy of Music Education Review* 3/1 (1995): 3–9.

20. R. G. Petzold, "The Perception of Music Reading by Normal Children and by Children Gifted Musically," *Journal of Experimental Education* 28 (1960): 271–319.

21. A. T. Hewson, "Music Reading in the Classroom," *Journal of Research in Music Education* 14 (1966): 289–302.

22. Joyce Gromko and A. Poorman, "Developmental Trends and Relationships in Children's Aural Perception and Symbol Use," *Journal of Research in Music Education* 46/1 (1998): 16–23.

23. The *new sound* may also refer to something specific, for example, the number of sounds on specific beats. The instructor might ask, "On which beat did you sing four sounds?"

24. David Perkins, *The Intelligent Eye: Learning to Think by Looking at Art* (Santa Monica, Ca.: Getty Center for Education in the Arts, 1998).

25. Bamberger, *The Mind behind the Musical Ear,* 282.

26. Sharon J. Derry, "Cognitive Schema Theory in the Constructivist Debate," *Educational Psychologist* 31/3–4 (1996): 163–174.

27. *Piano Roll Notation* uses horizontal lines to indicate the pitch and duration of sounds.

28. Lyle Davidson and Larry Scripp, "Surveying the Coordinates of Cognitive Skills in Music," in *Handbook of Research on Music Teaching and Learning,* ed. Richard Colwell (New York: Schirmer Books, 1992), 407.

29. Hand signs offer visual and physical motions, which develop the ability to inner hear.

Relative solmization is discussed in relation to other systems in Bruce E. More's "Sight Singing and Ear Training at the University Level," *Choral Journal* 25/7 (1985): 9–11.

30. B. Colley, "A Comparison of Syllabic Methods for Improving Rhythm Literacy," *Journal of Research in Music Education* 35 (1987): 221–235. See also M. Palmer, "Relative Effectiveness of Two Approaches to Rhythm Reading for Fourth-Grade Students," *Journal of Research in Music Education* 24 (1976): 110–118. P. C. Shehan, "Effects of Rote Versus Note Presentations on Rhythm Learning and Retention," *Journal of Research in Music Education* 35 (1987): 117–126.

31. Lyle Davidson and Larry Scripp, "Surveying the Coordinates of Cognitive Skills in Music," in *Handbook of Research on Music Teaching and Learning,* ed. Richard Colwell (New York: Schirmer Books, 1992), 407. See also J. Brown, "Situated Cognition and the Culture of Learning," *Educational Researcher* (1990): 32–4, and M. Polyanyi, *Personal Knowledge* (Chicago: University of Chicago Press, 1962).

32. Benward has aptly described this sound into notes and notes into sound transference as developing the "seeing ear" and the "hearing eye"; quoted in Michael R. Rogers, *Teaching Approaches in Music Theory* (Carbondale, Illinois: Southern Illinois University Press, 2004).

33. Edwin E. Gordon, *Learning Sequences in Music* (Chicago: G.I.A. Publications, 1980), 25.

34. See Lucy Green, "Meaning, Autonomy and Authenticity in the Music Classroom," lecture, Institute of Education, University of London, 2005.

35. Bamberger, *The Mind Behind the Musical Ear,* 265.

36. See Judith Brindle, "Notes from Eva Vendrei's Kodály Course," *British Kodály Academy Newletter* (Spring 2005): 6–11. See also Lois Choksy, *The Kodály Method: Comprehensive Music Education* (Upper Saddle River, N.J.: Prentice Hall, 1999). Both the article and book provide procedures for the teaching of music elements based on the preparation, presentation, and practice model.

37. Choksy, *The Kodály Method,* 171–172. See also Ann Eisen and Lamar Robertson, *An American Methodology* (Lake Charles, La.: Sneaky Snake Publications, 1997).

38. Joyce E. Gromoko, "Student's Invented Notations as Measures of Music Understanding," *Psychology of Music* 22/2 (1994): 146.

39. See Choksy, *The Kodály Method,* 172.

Chapter 7

1. Kodàly, "Ancient Traditions—Today's Musical Life," in Bónis, *The Selected Writings,* 172.
2. Kodàly, *Let Us Sing Correctly!* in Bónis, *The Selected Writings,* 216.
3. Kodály, "Who is a Good Musician," in Bónis, *The Selected Writings,* 198.
4. Kodàly, Preface to the Volume *Musical Reading and Writing,* in Bónis, *The Selected Writings,* 204.
5. Kodàly, "A Hundred Year Plan," in Bónis, *The Selected Writings,* 160.

6. Zoltán Kodály, "The Role of Authentic Folk Song in Music Education 1966," *Bulletin of the International Kodály Society* 1 (1985): 18. Also found as "Folk Song in Hungarian Music Education," *International Music Educator* 15 (March 1967): 486–490.

7. Kodàly, "Who is a Good Musician," in Bónis, *The Selected Writings,* 198.

8. Kodály, "The Role of Authentic Folk Song in Music Education 1966," 18.

9. The following outline of a teaching strategy was developed at the Texas State University 2003 Kodály Certification Program by students of Level 3, John Gillian and Micheal Houlahan.

Chapter 8

1. Kyle D. Brown, "An Alternative Orientation to Developing Music Literacy Skills in a Transient Society," *Music Educators Journal* 90/2 (November 2003): 46–54.

2. Jonathan Rappaport, "Readers Comments and Author's Response," *Music Educators Journal* 90/4 (March 2004): 9–11.

3. Edward Klonoski, "A Perceptual Learning Hierarchy: An Imperative for Aural Skills Pedagogy," *College Music Symposium* (online) 40 (2000): 1.

4. Ibid., 4.

5. Lyle Davidson, Larry Scripp, and Patricia Welsh, "'Happy Birthday': Evidence for Conflicts of Perceptual Knowledge and Conceptual Understanding," *Journal of Aesthetic Education* 22/1 (1988): 65–74.

Song Index

Index of Teaching Strategies

General Index